PIERRE BONNARD

early and late

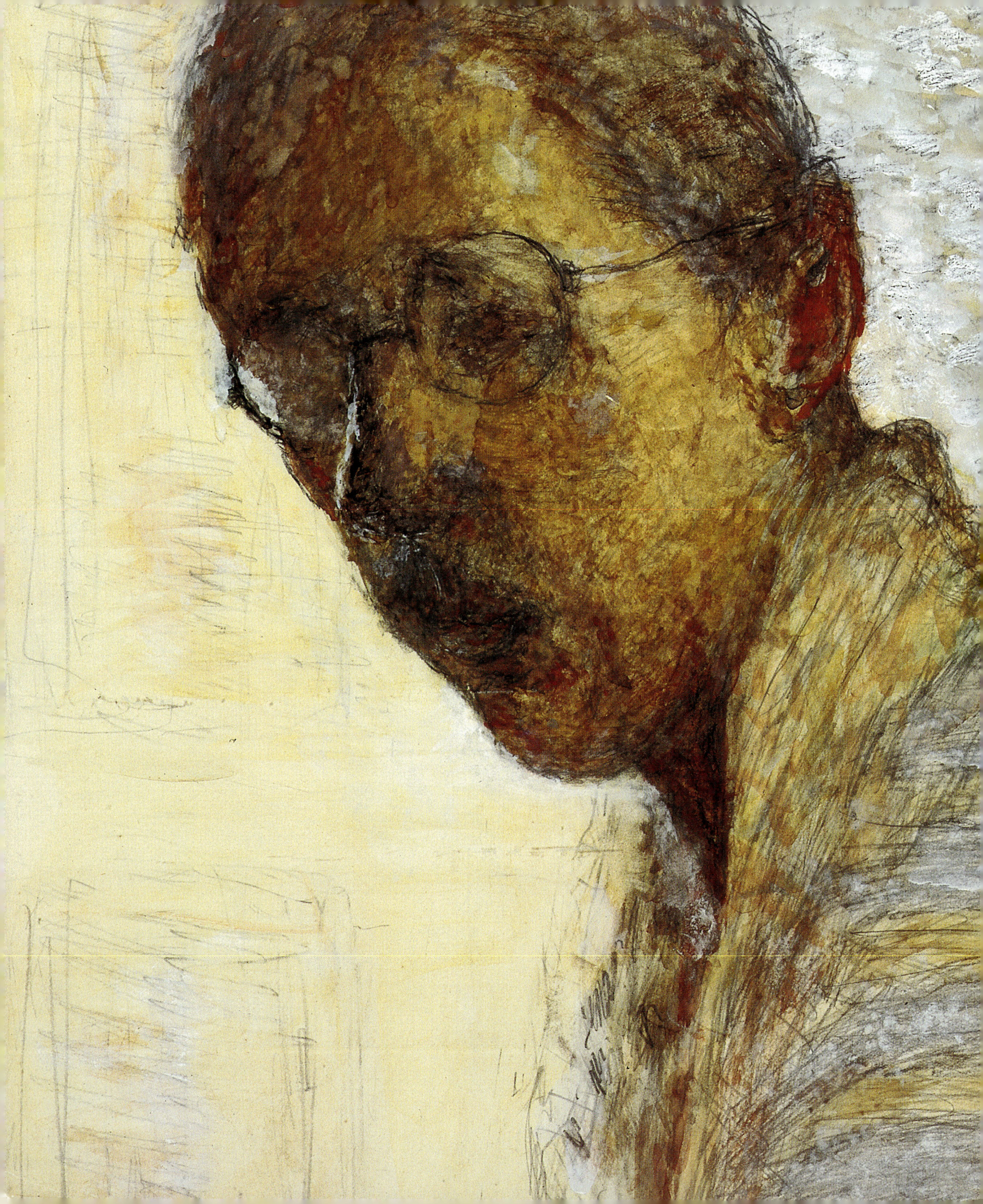

PIERRE BONNARD

early and late

Elizabeth Hutton Turner
with contributions by Nancy Coleman Wolsk,
Ursula Perucchi-Petri,
Elsa M. Smithgall and Lisa Lipinski

Philip Wilson Publishers
in collaboration with
The Phillips Collection,
Washington, D.C.

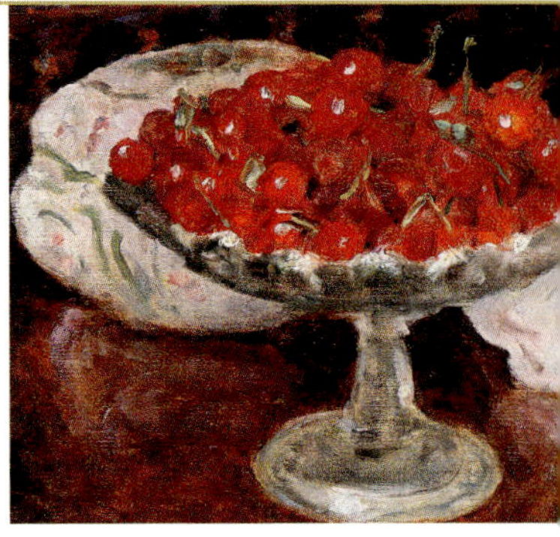

First published in 2002 by Philip Wilson Publishers
7 Deane House, 27 Greenwood Place,
London NW5 1LB

Published on the occasion of the exhibition
Pierre Bonnard: Early and Late.

September 22, 2002–January 19, 2003
The Phillips Collection
Washington, D.C.

March 1, 2003–May 25, 2003
Denver Art Museum
Denver, Colorado

Copyright © 2002 The Phillips Collection
1600 21st Street, NW; Washington, D.C. 20009
The Imaginary Cinema of Pierre Bonnard © 2002 by
Elizabeth Hutton Turner. *Japonisme in Bonnard's Early
and Late Work* © 2002 by Ursula Perucchi-Petri. *From
Thought to Form* © 2002 by Nancy Coleman Wolsk

All rights reserved.
This book may not be reproduced, in whole or in
part, including illustrations, in any form or by any
means, electronic or mechanical, including photocopy,
recording, or any other information storage and retrieval
system (beyond that copyright permitted by Sections 107
and 108 of the U.S. Copyright Law and except by review-
ers for the public press), without written permission from
the publishers.

Edited by Fronia W. Simpson
Designed by Anikst Design
Misha Anikst and James Warner
Printed by Artes Graficas Toledo, Spain

Catalogue of an exhibition held at The Phillips Collection
and the Denver Art Museum. Includes bibliographical
references and index.
ISBN 0 85667 556 3 (clothbound edition)
ISBN 0-943044-29-4 (softcover edition)

Library of Congress cataloging-in-publication data

Turner, Elizabeth Hutton, 1952–*Pierre Bonnard: Early and
Late*/Elizabeth Hutton Turner with contributions by
Nancy Wolsk. . . [et al.].
Published to accompany an exhibition held at the Phillips
Collection, Washington, D.C., Sept 22, 2002–Jan. 19, 2003
and the Denver Art Museum, Denver, Colo., Mar. 1–May
25, 2003.
Includes bibliographical references and index.
ISBN 0943044-29-4 (softcover ed.)
1. Bonnard, Pierre, 1867–1947--Exhibitions. I. Bonnard,
Pierre, 1867–1947. II. Wolsk, Nancy. III. Phillips
Collection. IV. Denver Art Museum. V. Title
N6853.B57 A4 2002
759.4–dc21

Jacket front:
The Palm (detail), 1926, Oil on canvas, 45 × 57⅞ in.
(114.3 × 147 cm), The Phillips Collection, Washington,
D.C.

Title page:
Self-Portrait (detail), 1930, Gouache and pencil,
25⅝ × 19⅝ in. (65 × 50 cm), Private collection.

Top:
Bowl of Cherries (detail), 1920, Oil on canvas, 11⅞ ×
16½ in. (30.2 × 41.9 cm), The Phillips Collection,
Washington, D.C.

Opposite page (left to right):
Landscape with Mountain (detail), 1924, Oil on canvas,
15¾ × 23¼ in. (40 × 59 cm), The Phillips Collection,
Washington, D.C.
The Lesson (detail), 1926, Oil on canvas, 30 × 20 in.
(76 × 51 cm), The Phillips Collection, Washington, D.C.
Nude in Bathroom (detail), 1932, Oil on canvas,
47⅝ × 46½ in. (121 × 118.1 cm), The Museum of Modern
Art, New York, Florene May Schoenborn Bequest, 1996.
Reflecting on the Day (detail), 1924, Oil on canvas,
21 ¼ × 19¹¹⁄₁₆ in. (54 × 50 cm), Private collection; Courtesy
Guggenheim, Asher Associates, Inc., New York.

Contents

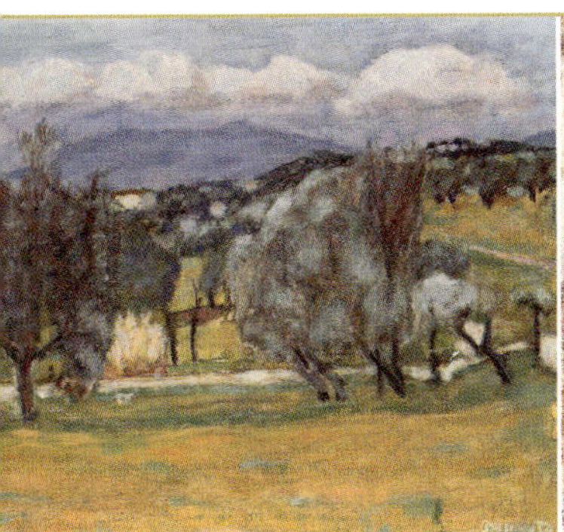 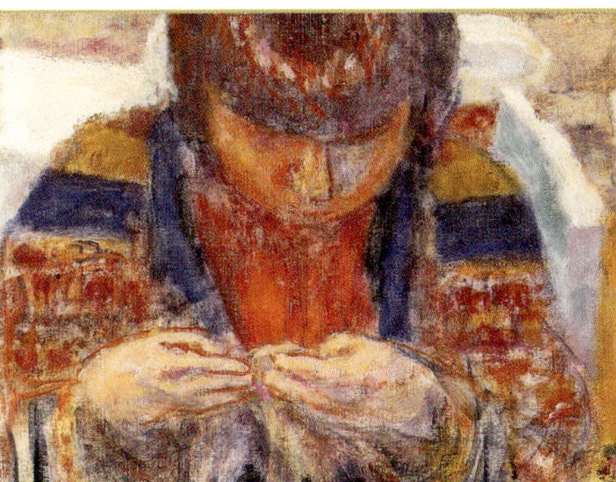 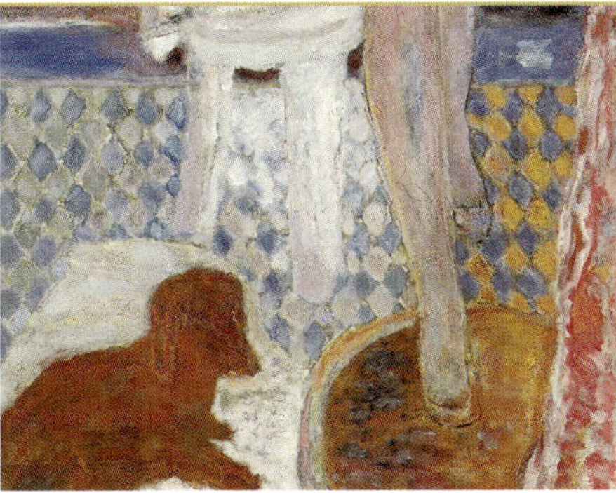 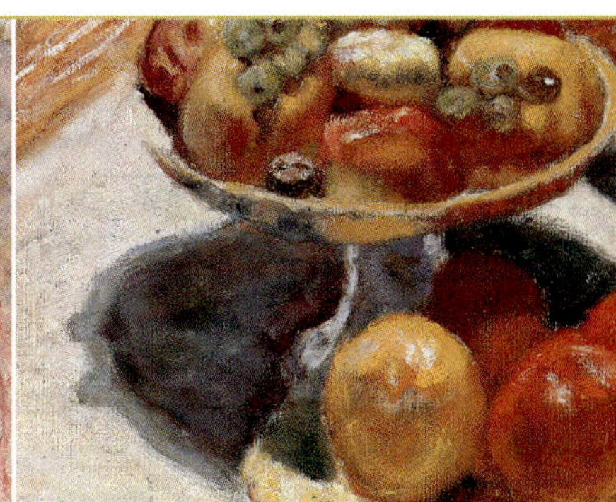

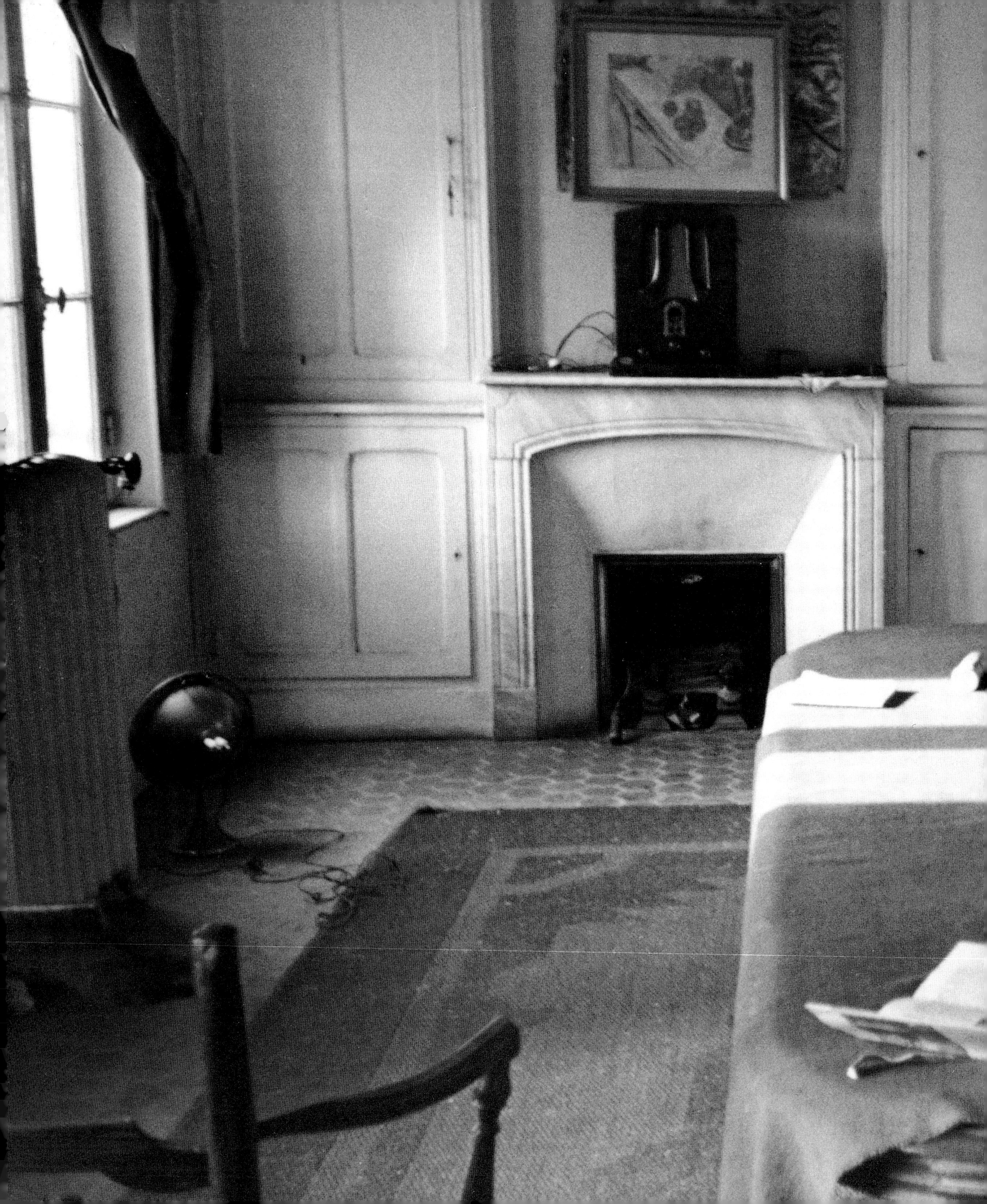

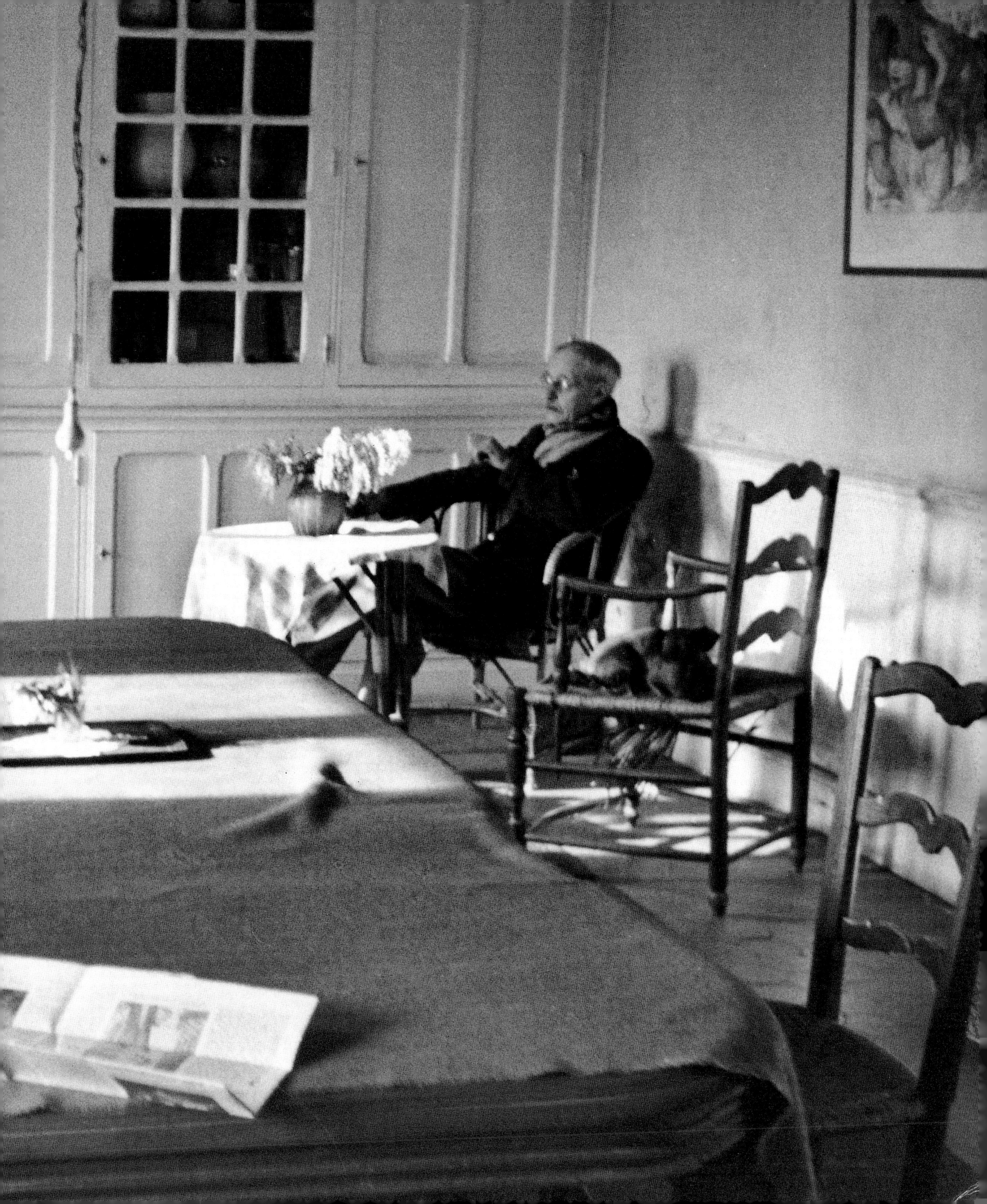

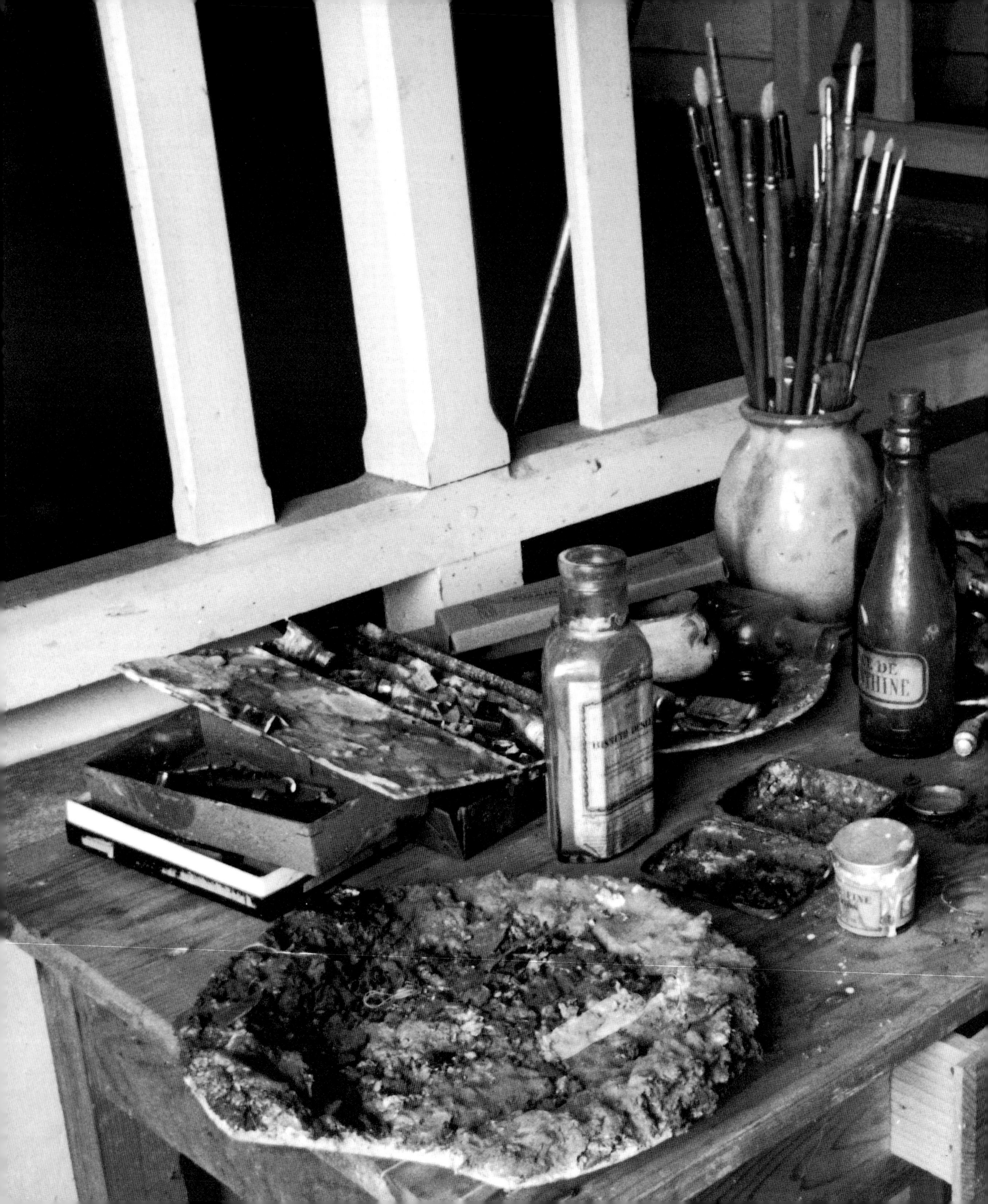

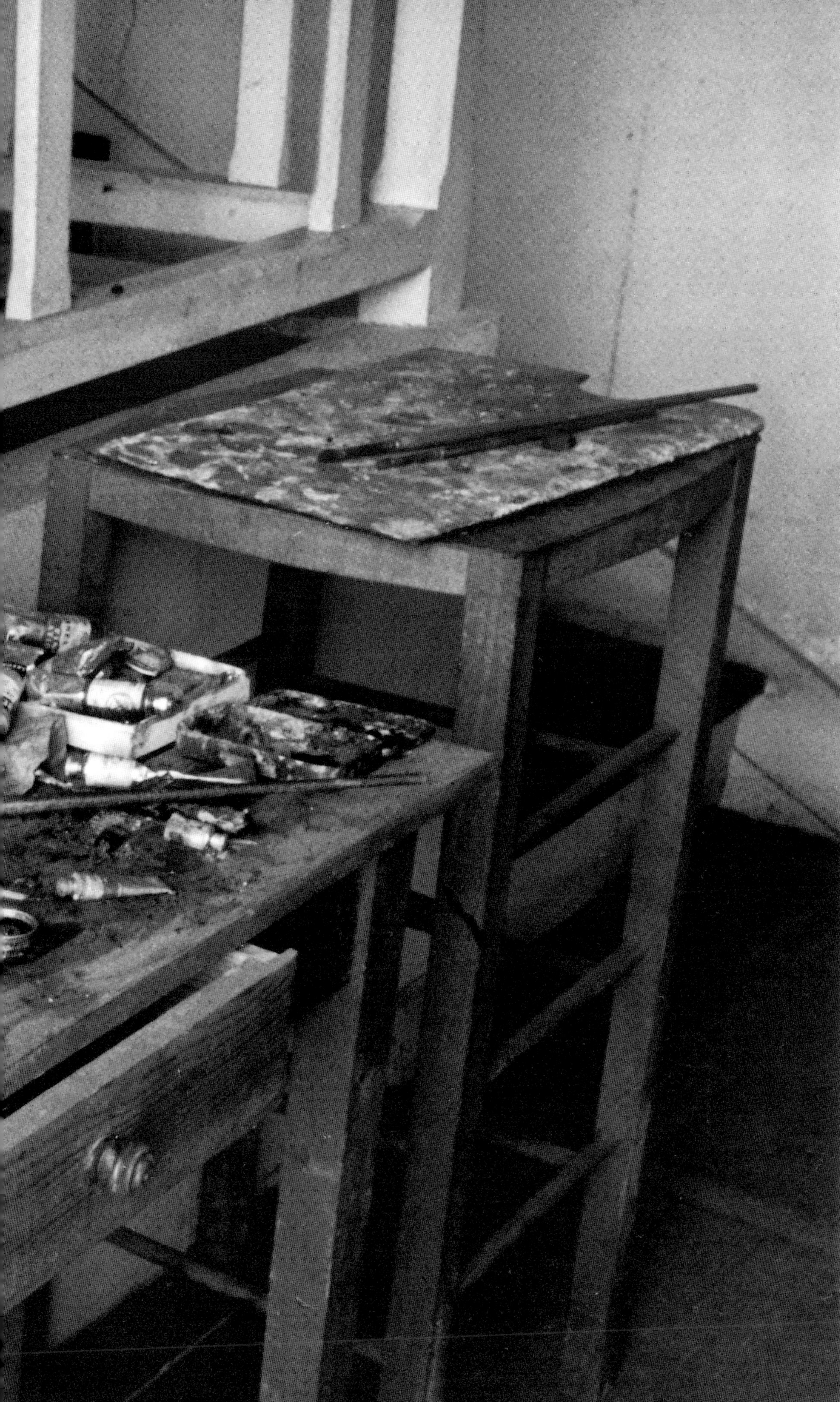

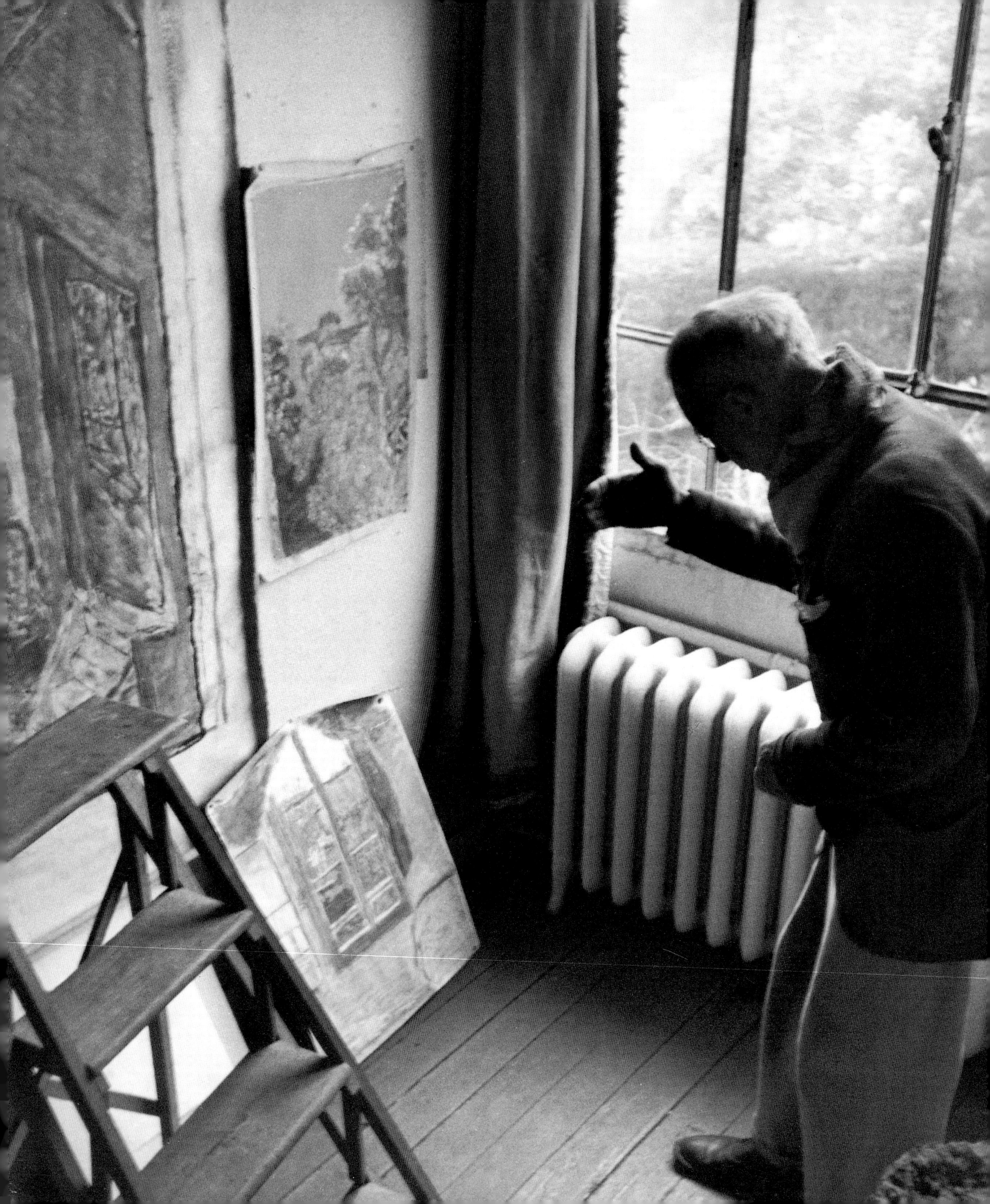

Henri Cartier-Bresson
September 9, 2000

There is in the work of Pierre Bonnard a trembling
and a humility, which have always overwhelmed me.
Certain painters became fully accomplished at the end
of their life. Bonnard blossomed from the beginning
to his last breath. His profound intelligence never
suffocated his sensuality.

Pages 6–7:
Henri Cartier-Bresson, *Bonnard in the
Dining Room at Le Cannet*, 1945,
Photograph.

Pages 8–9:
Henri Cartier-Bresson, *In the Studio at Le
Cannet. The Table with the Plate-Palette*,
1945, Photograph.

Page 10:
Henri Cartier-Bresson, *Bonnard in the
Studio at Le Cannet*, 1945, Photograph.

Should I have the good fortune to go to Washington this fall to see the Bonnard exhibition organized by The Phillips Collection, my first thought will be with Mr. and Mrs. Duncan Phillips. Duncan Phillips and his wife were among the very first to understand and to love Bonnard and also have those around them understand and love him. Certainly Bonnard is famous, but his fame does not even approach the level of his genius. There are several reasons for this, foremost among them his modesty: Bonnard never incited others to speak about him. Then fashion was focused on intellectualism: a black circle on a white background, one white dot. That did not interest Bonnard. Already Cézanne, before Bonnard, was vituperating against "the intellectuals and their abstractions."

At the end of his life, he would say: "that which begins from nothing, that which does not mean anything, a picture just for the sake of a picture, appears to me as a monstrosity." And he added: "Art will never be able to do without nature. When one forgets everything, all that remains is oneself and that is not enough."

Every morning, Bonnard followed a fixed ritual. Whether in the Dauphiné, in Normandy, in Paris, in the Midi, wherever he was, he would set off for his morning walk before breakfast, take a breath of fresh air, look, get his fill of life. He never painted from life. The quasitotality of his work was painted from memory, reflecting on drawings taken from life. He was incessantly active, from before breakfast until after dinner. A number of his works were drawn, if not painted, by artificial light.

I was able to demonstrate in the book I dedicated to the creation of his work that most of his interiors and still lifes were nocturnal visions. Inspiration would come to him from the surprise of happiness, the emotion that all elements of life offered to his gaze, grandiose or humble without hierarchy, the immense sea, the simple poppy, from the ability to discover each day what he saw every day. He seized all subjects. Intimate family scenes, portraits, nudes, landscapes, views of Paris, animals, flowers. The assembled paintings of only one of these genres would suffice to bring him fame.

The representations of himself, his self-portraits, are not vanity or indulgence. They point to a man alone, anxious, prisoner of his creation, portraits all charged with a gravity in contradistinction to the radiant plenitude of his works. The work is reassuring: it seems to have fixed a moment in time. The creation of the work is agonizing, it is a struggle with the moment that slips away. "The work of art, time suspended; one should never torture nature, for it approaches the abstract," wrote Bonnard. The acuity of his eye, the prodigious intelligence of his skill as a painter, his obsession to look, to see, his capacity to wonder, led Bonnard to discover the centering of images, compositions, connections between forms, and connections of colors no one before him saw.

When I saw my great-uncle for the last time, I asked him three questions. About drawing he said: "You must draw continually so as always to have a repertoire of forms at hand." About subject matter: "You must never seek material for its own sake. Every true artist finds the subjects that he needs." About the future of painting. "In the future one will have to know whether one is a painter-decorator or a painter of feeling." The "painter of feeling," he added, is a "rare bird." Bonnard was a rare bird.

Should I have the good fortune to go to Washington, I will think of Duncan Phillips. I will also be thinking of Henri Matisse, who on visiting The Phillips Collection in 1930, had the generosity and the intelligence to tell Duncan Phillips: "Bonnard is the greatest among us."

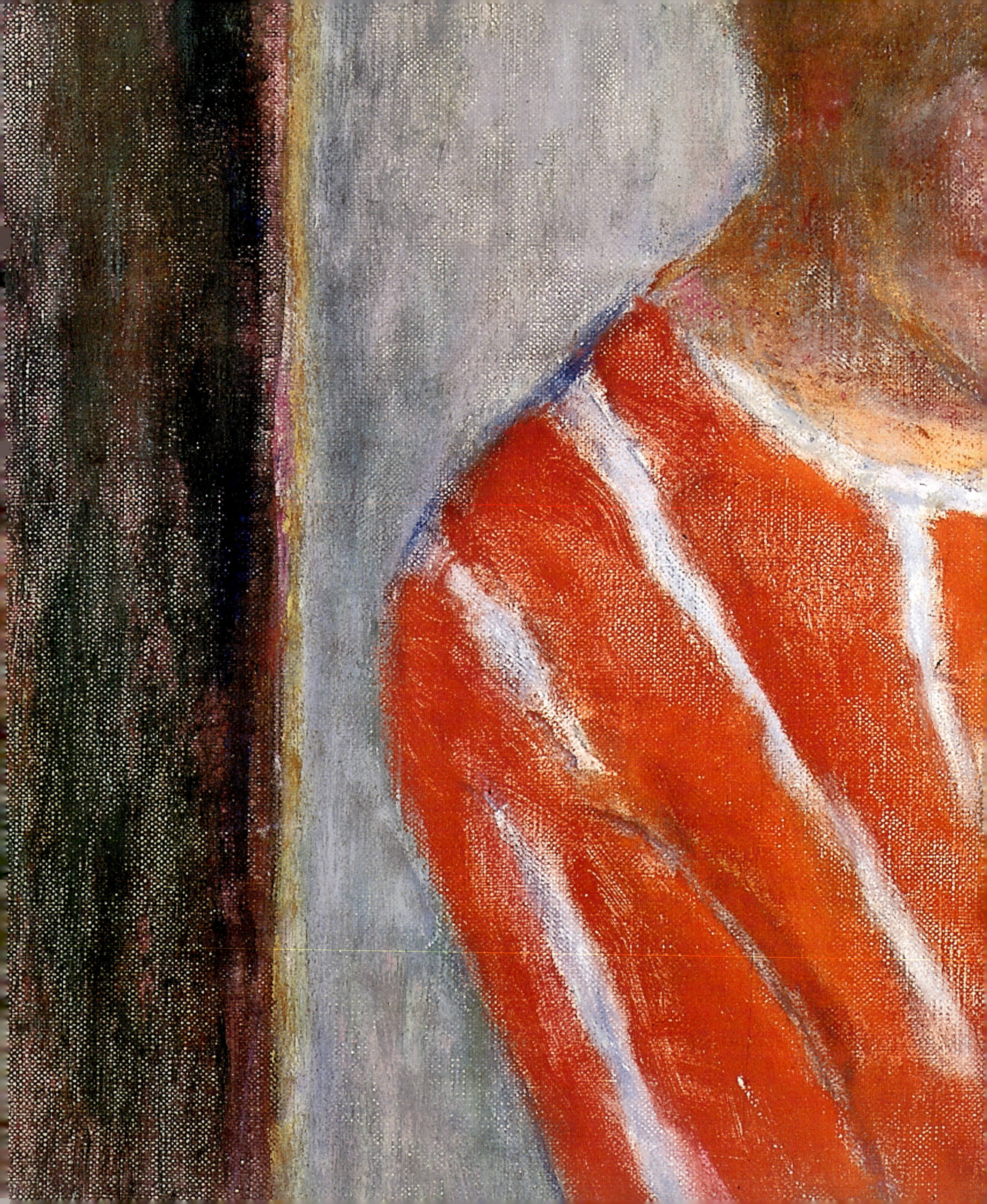

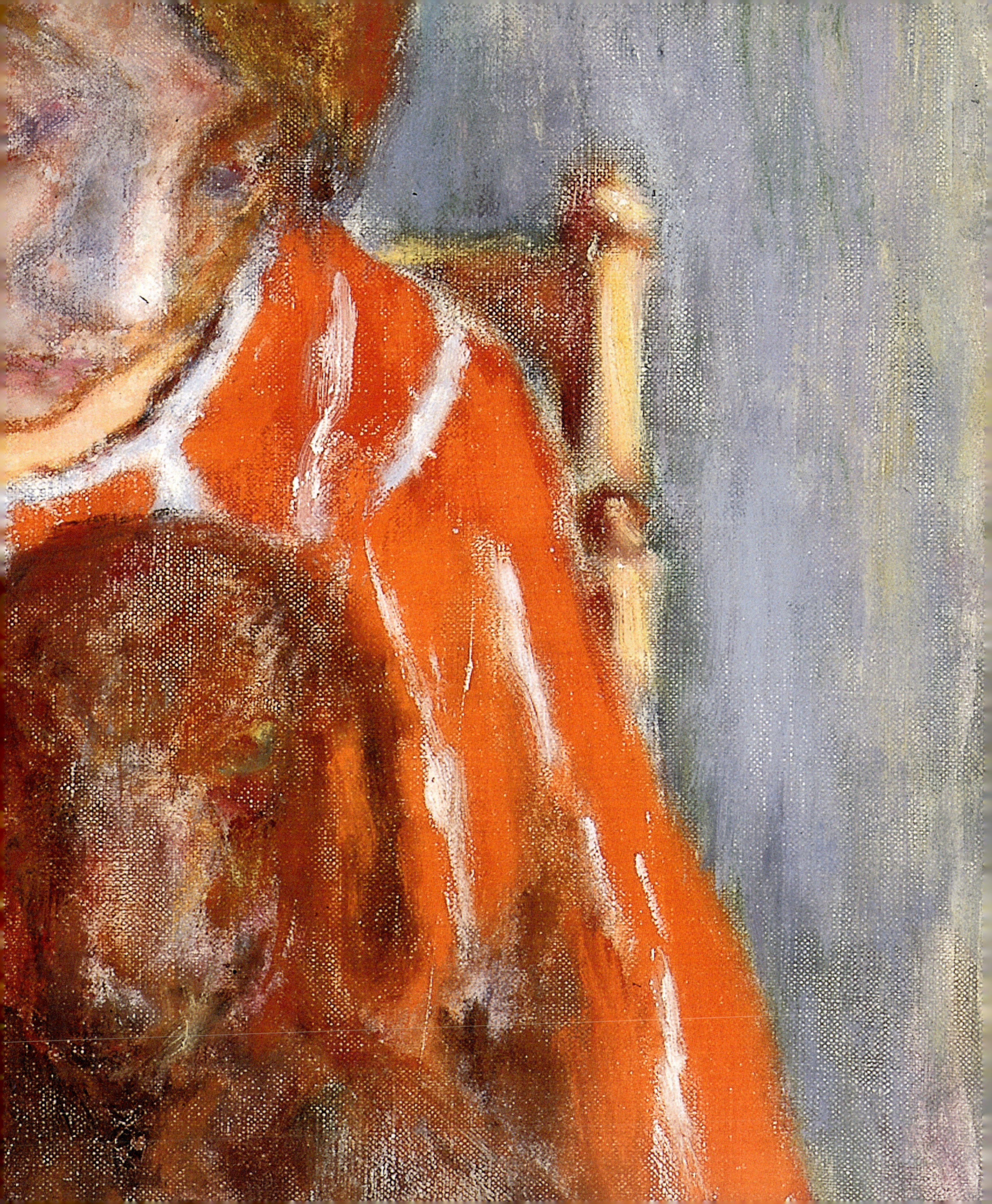

Previous spread:
Woman with Dog
(detail), 1922, Oil on
canvas, 27¼ × 15½ in.
(69.2 × 39.3 cm), The
Phillips Collection,
Washington, D.C.

He's one of those modernist masters who seem to keep slipping in and out of focus,
not unlike some of the objects in his paintings—Robert Hughes, 1998

The vibrant, sometimes volatile, colors of Pierre Bonnard (1867–1947) continue to
surprise new generations of painters—as he once proposed, "with the wings of a butterfly." Yet, a question of timing always has haunted succeeding generations of historians
and critics dealing with the issue of Bonnard's modernity. To be sure, Bonnard broke
new ground. His first poster published in 1891 inspired Henri Toulouse-Lautrec to
begin his own posters. Bonnard, together with Alfred Jarry, created the first artist's
book of the twentieth century entitled *Almanach illustré du Père Ubu* (1901). Yet, in
the 1900s, ignoring the revolution of Cubism, Bonnard adopted the optics of
Impressionism. At the time of Renoir's death in 1919, Bonnard was hailed, not for his
modernism, but for his atavism—his singular devotion to "pure painting." How can
Bonnard's early radicalism be reconciled with his apparent stylistic anachronisms?
Given the sheer range of his explorations—prints, illustrations, screens, theatrical sets,
ceramics, sculpture, and painting—where do we look to distinguish the unity of his
artistic vision over a nearly sixty-year span from the late nineteenth century well into
the middle of the twentieth century?

The Phillips Collection brings to this inquiry a firsthand account of Bonnard.
In 1925 Duncan Phillips was among the first in America to assert the modernity of
Bonnard's work and to create a setting for its appreciation. Between 1925 and 1954
Phillips accumulated the largest and most diverse collection in the United States of

paintings, drawings, and prints by Bonnard. Both artist and collector maintained a correspondence over the course of twenty years. When Bonnard came to America to serve on the jury of the Carnegie International in 1926, he visited The Phillips Memorial Gallery. Marjorie Phillips later recalled finding Bonnard quietly self-assured. Touring the collection, perhaps seeing Duncan Phillips's desire to demonstrate connections between past and present, Bonnard told Phillips that Monet was the artist to whom he owed the most. Bonnard freely offered his hand in friendship, urging Marjorie, as he often urged himself, "to draw more." At one point during the visit, Bonnard asked to borrow Marjorie's paint box to add color to his painting entitled *Early Spring* (1910), which was then hanging in the museum's main gallery.

Phillips recognized in Bonnard a passion for seeing, not unlike his own, that left him open to learn but independent from prevailing trends. Phillips took pride in the idea of having discovered Bonnard at a culminating moment in his career, when his paintings were at the peak of their ecstatic color. Phillips also admired the fact that, as he said in 1949, "Bonnard's art in essence continued to the end very much as it began." Building on this insight, we mount this exhibition of over one hundred works combining prints, posters, screens, books, sculptures, photographs, and paintings in order to explore how Bonnard's unique creative process and adept versatility in different materials belie a remarkably profound philosophical and aesthetic unity.

Without our partnership with the Denver Art Museum, this exhibition would never have been possible. I am immensely grateful to Director Lewis Sharp for his vital support and cooperation. The Phillips Collection and the Denver Art Museum are fortunate in sharing this exhibition that brings together works of exceptional quality from collections all over the world. In addition, we are very grateful for an indemnity from the Federal Council for the Arts and Humanities. The Phillips Collection's Senior Curator and Project Director, Elizabeth Hutton Turner, has been an ever-present guiding force behind the successful realization of this project. We have been inspired by her passion for Pierre Bonnard and her unwavering enthusiasm, expertise and commitment.

The knowledge, experience, and advice of many individuals have contributed a great deal to the project's success. First and foremost we owe a special debt of gratitude to Antoine Terrasse and the late Michel Terrasse for their support since the project's inception. We have benefited considerably from their scholarship and counsel. We are indebted to Henri Cartier-Bresson who shared his reminiscences of Bonnard, and to Laughlin Phillips and Liza Phillips for their guidance and assistance. We also want to extend our warmest gratitude to His Excellency The Ambassador of France and Mrs. Bujon de l'Estang. Special thanks also to Roland Cellette, Cultural Attaché, Embassy of France. We benefited greatly from the thoughtful guidance and assistance of Sarah Whitfield. Marjorie Balge-Crozier, Roger Shattuck, and Merry Foresta have also shared rich insights and provided valuable feedback. Charles Moffett of Sotheby's is due a special word of thanks.

Above all, we are deeply indebted to the individuals, galleries, and institutions willing to lend important works by Pierre Bonnard to this exhibition. Their sacrifice and cooperation have made this exhibition possible. The nearly fifty individuals and institutions willing to share their works of art are to be warmly thanked by name. We are enormously grateful to: Mr. and Mrs. Joe L. Allbritton, Dr. and Mrs. Ira Jackson, Mr. and Mrs. Donald B. Marron, Liza Phillips, in addition to several private collectors who wish to remain anonymous. We likewise extend heartfelt thanks to the following lending institutions and staff: The Art Institute of Chicago: James N. Wood, Director and President, Gloria Groom, Associate Curator, Stephanie D'Allessandro, Assistant Curator, Darrell Green, Assistant Registrar, Nicole G. Finzer, Photographic Rights Assistant; The Baltimore Museum of Art: Doreen Bolger, Director, Katy Rothkopf, Curator of Painting and Sculpture, Melanie Harwood, Senior Registrar, Sarah Jeschke Harman, Associate Registrar, Nancy Press, Director of Rights and Reproductions, Robin Churchill and Beth Ryan, Rights and Reproductions; Bibliothèque Nationale de France: M. Jean-Pierre Angremy, President, Mme Jacqueline Sanson, Deputy General and Director, Director of Collections, Sylviane Dailleau, Conservator, Mme Laure Beaumont-Maillet, Director Department of Photography, Cyril Chazal, Outside Exhibitions Correspondent; Carnegie Museum of Art: Richard Armstrong, The Henry J. Heinz II Director, Louise Lippincott, Curator, Monika Tomko, Registrar, Heather G. Domencic, Coordinator of Rights and Reproductions; Centre Georges Pompidou. Musée National d'Art Moderne/ Centre de Création Industrielle: Philippe Bidaine, Deputy Director, Christina Agostinelli, In charge of Research and Cultural Projects, Alfred Pacquement, Director, Nathalie Leleu, Conservator, Darrell Di Fiore, Registrar of Collections; Flint Institue of Arts: John Bittenry, Director, Melissa Miller Farr, Registrar, Regina Schreck, Assistant Curator of Collections; Galerie Cazeau-Béraudière: Philippe Cazeau, President, Jacques de la Béraudière, President; Galerie Felix Vercel: Alain Vercel, Director, Nicole Simonart, Registrar; Galerie Jan Krugier, Ditesheim & Cie, Geneva: Jan Krugier, Director, Tzila Krugier, Evelyne Ferlay; Hirshhorn Museum and Sculpture Garden: Ned Rifkin, Director, Phyllis Rosenzweig, Curator of Works on Paper, Valerie Fletcher, Curator of Sculpture and Loan Coordinator, Brian G. Kavanagh, Registrar, Margaret Dong, Assistant Registrar for Loans, Amy Densford, Photography Coordinator; Kunsthaus Zurich: Dr. Christoph Becker, Director, Dr. Felix Baumann, Former Director, Karin Martin, Registrar, Cécile Brunner, Image Resources and Copyright Management; Kunstmuseum Winterthur: Dr. Dieter Schwartz, Director, Erica Rüegger, Registrar; Library of Congress: Daniel De Simone, Curator of the Rosenwald Collection, Rare Books and Special Collections, Katherine Blood, Assistant Curator of Fine Prints, Sara W. Duke, Assistant Curator Popular & Applied Graphic Art, Prints and Photographs Division, Raymond White, Music Specialist, Department of Music, Margaret Brown, Exhibition Registrar, Maricia Battle, Exhibition Liaison, Dr. Carol Armbruster, French/Italian Area Specialist, Rosemary Hanes and Madeline Matz, Reference Librarians, Motion Picture and Television Reading Room; The Metropolitan Museum of Art: Philippe de Montebello, Director, William S. Lieberman, Curator of Paintings, Colta Ives, Curator, Minora

Collins, Senior Associate Loans Coordinator, Ida Balboul, Research Associate, Exhibitions Office, Deanna Cross, Photograph Library; The Minneapolis Institute of Arts: Evan M. Maurer, Director and President, Patrick Noon, Curator of Paintings, Erika Holmquist-Wall, Department of Paintings, Tanya Morrison, Associate Registrar, DeAnn M. Dankowski, Permissions Assistant; Musée de Grenoble: Gwunaul Rimaud, Director, Isabelle Varloteaux, Registrar, Pascal Boissin, Copyright Coordinator, Photographic Archives; Musée Départemental Maurice Denis, Saint-Germain-en-Laye: Agnés Delannoy, Director, Frédéric Bigo, Registrar; Musée des Beaux-Arts, Lyon: Vincent Pomarède, Conservator and Director, Muriel Le Payen, In Charge of Photography; Musée d'Orsay: Serge Lemoine, Director, Dominique Viéville, Interim Director, Claire Frèches-Thory, Curator, Caroline Mathieu, Curator, Françoise Heilbrun, Curator, Henri Loyrette, Former Director, Isabelle Cahn, Curator, Geneviève Lacambre, Curator; Musée d'Unterlinden: Ms. Sylvie Lecoq-Ramond, Director, Jean Lorentz, President of the Society Schongauer; Museum of Fine Arts, Boston: Malcolm Rogers, Director, Cliffard Ackley, Ruth and Carl Shapiro, Curator of Prints and Drawings, Sue Reed, Associate Curator, Department of Prints and Drawings, Kim Pashko, Associate Registrar, Chris Atkins, Coordinator of External Media Licensing, Department of Rights & Licensing; The Museum of Modern Art: Glenn Lowry, Director, John Elderfield, Deputy Director Curatorial Affairs & Chief Curator at Large, Cora Rosevear, Associate Curator, Fereshteh Daftari, Assistant Curator, Avril Peck, Registrar, Mikki Carpenter, Director Department of Imaging Services; The National Gallery of Art: Earl A. Powell III, Director, Philip Conisbee, Curator of Paintings, Judith Brodie, Associate Curator, Department of Prints and Drawings, Alicia Thomas, Loan Officer, Barbara C.G. Wood, Photographic Rights/Reproductions, Color Imagery, Ted Dalziel, Interlibrary Loans; Öffentliche Kunstammlung Basel, Kunstmuseum: Dr. Katharina Schmidt, Director, Charlotte Gutzwiller, Rights and Reproductions; Philadelphia Museum of Art: Anne d'Harnoncourt, Director and CEO, Ann Tempkin, Curator of Twentieth Century Paintings, Michael Taylor, Assistant Curator, Nancy Wulbrecht, Registrar, Sarah Powers, Departmental Assistant of Modern and Contemporary Art , Stacy Bomento, Rights and Reproductions/ Photography; Riggs National Corporation; Joe L. Allbritton, Vice-Chairman; Southampton City Art Gallery: Stephen Snoddy, Director, Godfrey Worsdale, Art Gallery Manager, Tim Craven, Collection Manager, Vicky Isley, Registrar; Städelscher Museums-Verein e.V., Frankfurt am Main: Alfred Mauritz, Head of Städelscher Museums, Prof. Dr. Herbert Beck, Director, Sabine Schulze, Curator of 19th and 20th Century Paintings, Ute Wenzel-Förster, Exhibitions Office, Elisabeth Heinemann, Department of Photographs; Sterling and Francine Clark Art Institute: Michael Conforti, Director, Richard Rand, Curator of Paintings, Mattie Kelley, Registrar, Kris Walton, Assistant Registrar; Tate: Nicolas Serota, Director, Susan Liddell, Senior Curator, Catherine Clement, Senior Loans Registrar, Jon Astbury, Loans Registrar, Alison Miles, Picture Library; and The Toledo Museum of Art: Roger M. Berkowitz,

Director, Lawrence W. Nichols, Curator of European Painting and Sculpture, Patricia J. Whitesides, Registrar.

In addition, colleagues in museums, galleries and auction houses also provided important assistance in locating key works and contacting lenders. They include: Christie's: Sarah Scharf, Twentieth Century Art Department; Fine Art Society: Andrew McIntosh Patrick, Managing Director; The Fondation Beyeler: Ernst Beyeler, Director, Oliver Wick, Exhibition Office; Fondation Maeght: Jean-Louis Prat, Director; Galerie Schmit: Manuel Schmit, Director; Richard L. Feigen & Co., New York: Richard L. Feigen, President, Frances F. L. Beatty, Senior Vice President; Jeff Bailey, Former Assistant to the Director; Diana Kunkel, Private Curator; Sotheby's: Charles S. Moffett, Executive Vice President, Co-Chairman of Impressionist and Modern Art Worldwide, Kate Garmeson, Archivist, Harriet Warden, Elizabeth Gorayeb, Researcher, Stephane Cosman Connery, Senior Vice President, Jacqueline Lawrence, Researcher, Christian Anderson, Eva Avloniti; Abigail Asher, Partner, Guggenheim Asher Associates; and Wildenstein and Co.: Guy Wildenstein, President, Ay-Whang Hsia, Vice President.

The exhibition has also benefited from the expertise and enthusiasm of talented consultants. We express our warmest gratitude for the insightful essays of Ursula Perucchi-Petri, Curator, Museum of Villa Flora Winterthur (Switzerland), and Nancy Coleman Wolsk, Associate Professor, Transylvania University, (Lehigh, Ky.). For her exhibition research as well as her contributions to the catalogue bibliography, exhibition histories, and chronology, we thank independent scholar Lisa Lipinski. Shalaka Karbhari, curatorial assistant, Department of Prints and Drawings, Jane Voorhees Zimmerli Art Museum, and Andràs Goldinger also assisted with our research. For her advice and help with our numerous loan requests we are grateful to Ruth Rattenbury. Janet Lloyd of Masterpiece International has provided tremendous assistance in coordinating transport of the exhibition. For his creative solutions to the installation of this exhibition we are indebted to the very talented Val Lewton. We thank David Rhodes of Arnold & Porter for sound legal counsel. For their valuable assistance with research and reproduction rights we especially want to mention Jessica David of Art Resource and Madeleine Gonçalves of Gallimard Publications. An enormous debt of gratitude is owed to the copy editor, Fronia W. Simpson, and to the translator, Maria Alexandra Razi, who provided invaluable assistance in preparing the manuscript for the publisher. Our collaboration with Philip Wilson Publishers has been especially productive, and we want to acknowledge Philip Wilson, Anne Jackson, Cangy Venables, Norman Turpin, Misha Anikst, and James Warner.

A project of this scope necessarily requires the commitment of a museum team. We would like to extend our gratitude to the Denver Art Museum staff: Gwen Chanzit, Curator, Modern & Contemporary Art, Timothy Standring, Curator Painting and Sculpture, Adam J. Lerner, Master Teacher of Modern & Contemporary Art, Lori Iliff, Registrar, and David Kennedy, Exhibition Management. The entire staff of The Phillips Collection also deserves credit for adopting this exhibition with such enthusiasm: Eliza

Rathbone, Chief Curator, Mary Hannah Byers, Curatorial Assistant, Stephen Bennett Phillips, Associate Curator, Susan Behrends Frank, Assistant Curator, Joseph Holbach, Chief Registrar, Chris Ketcham, Assistant Registrar for Rights and Reproductions, Barbara Benney, Director of Human Resources, Chris Leahy, Director of Finance, Richard Rutledge, Chief Operating Officer, Laura Atchison, Executive Assistant to the Director, Ruth Perlin, Special Assistant to the Director for Education and Technology, Thora Colot, former Director of Marketing & Business Activities, Johanna Halford-MacLeod, Director of Programming and Publications, Amy Mannarino, Public Relations Assistant, Lynn Rossotti, Director of Public Relations, Nathan Martin, Research Coordinator, Jennifer Juzaitis, Development Coordinator, Mark Mills, Membership Manager, Kelly Gotthardt, Museum Shop Manager, Franck Cordes, Assistant Shop Manager, Darci Vanderhoff, Chief of Information Systems, Faith Flanagan, Director of Graphic Communications, Mary Alice Nay, Events Coordinator, Dan Datlow, Director of Operations and his staff, Suzanne Wright, Director of Education, Joanna Rothman, Education Assistant and Tour Coordinator, Shellie Marker, Museum Educator.

We would especially like to acknowledge the key people who have devoted most of the past year to the realization of this exhibition. We are greatly indebted to Assistant Curator Elsa M. Smithgall, for assisting with the management of the overall project. Her keen intellect, steadfast assistance, and scrupulous attention to every phase of this exhibition and publication have been invaluable. Elizabeth Steele, Paintings Conservator at The Phillips Collection, who has assumed the responsibility of the condition of all the loans to the exhibition, has enjoyed the collaboration and support of her colleagues, Sylvia Albro, Independent Conservator, and Holly Fiedler, Assistant Conservator. Associate Registrar Linda Clous has assumed responsibility for the registering of the loans and arranging details of shipping, couriers, insurance, and indemnity. Bill Koberg and his staff, Shelly Wischhusen-Burke, Chief Preparator, Alec MacKaye, Preparator, Rachel Waldron, Preparatory Assistant, have assumed responsibility for the unprecedented installation plan to fill Duncan Phillips's building with this exhibition. Carolien van den Akker, Curatorial Assistant, obtained virtually all the illustrations for this book, and coordinated numerous important aspects involved in this catalogue and exhibition. Librarian Karen Schneider has contributed greatly to the research for this exhibition and catalogue handling myriad requests. This project has also profited from the contributions of numerous interns and volunteers: Holly Bennett, Amanda Blumburg, Alexia DePottere Smith, Lucy Dinsmore, Ricardo Harris Fuentes, Nicole Laurent, and Sabrina Paige. A special word of thanks is due to Evelyn Braithwaite, Nichole Westerweel, and Afaf Zurayk, for their invaluable assistance and tireless devotion.

Jay Gates
Director, The Phillips Collection

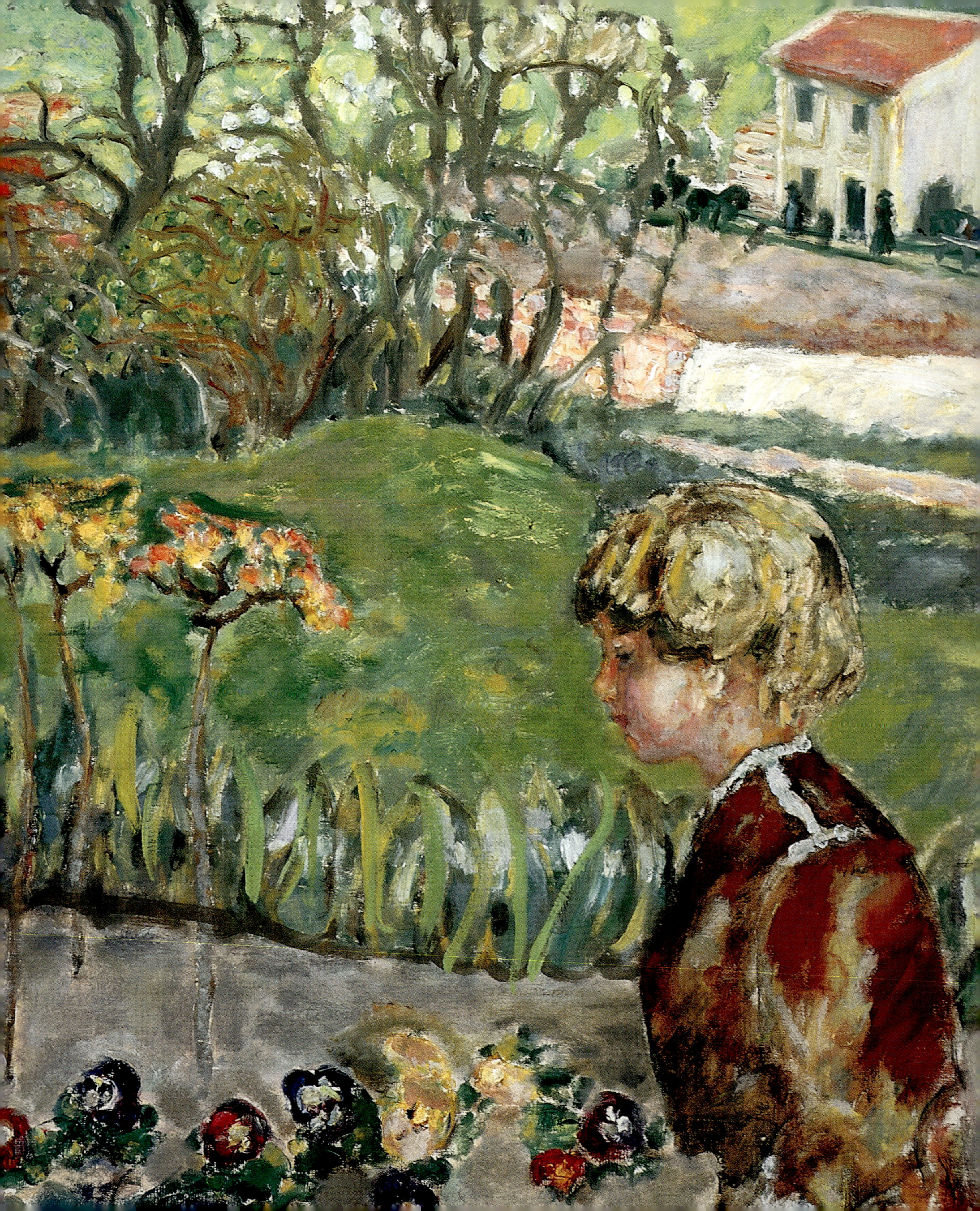

Lenders to the Exhibition

Mr. and Mrs. Joe L. Allbritton

Art Gallery of New South Wales, Sydney

The Art Institute of Chicago

The Baltimore Museum of Art

Bibliothèque Nationale de France, Paris

Carnegie Museum of Art, Pittsburgh

Centre Georges Pompidou. Musée National d'Art Moderne/ Centre de Création Industrielle, Paris

Flint Institute of Arts

Galerie Félix Vercel, Paris

Galerie Jan Krugier, Ditesheim & Cie, Geneva

Hirshhorn Museum and Sculpture Garden, Smithsonian Institution, Washington, D.C.

Virginia and Ira Jackson Collection

Kunsthaus Zurich

Kunstmuseum Winterthur

Library of Congress, Washington, D. C.

Mr. and Mrs. Donald B. Marron

The Metropolitan Museum of Art, New York

The Minneapolis Institute of Arts

Musée de Grenoble

Musée Départemental Maurice Denis,

Saint-Germain-en-Laye

Musée des Beaux-Arts, Lyon

Musée d'Orsay, Paris

Musée d'Unterlinden, Colmar

Museum of Fine Arts, Boston

The Museum of Modern Art, New York

National Gallery of Art, Washington, D. C.

Öffentliche Kunstammlung Basel, Kunstmuseum

Philadelphia Museum of Art

The Phillips Collection, Washington, D. C.

Ms. Liza Phillips

Riggs National Corporation

Southampton City Art Gallery, Hampshire, England

Städelscher Museums-Verein e.V., Frankfurt

Sterling and Francine Clark Art Institute, Williamstown

Tate, London

Toledo Museum of Art

Fifteen Anonymous Lenders

Opposite page:
Early Spring (detail), 1910, Oil on canvas, 34¼ × 52 in. (86.9 × 132 cm), The Phillips Collection, Washington, D.C.

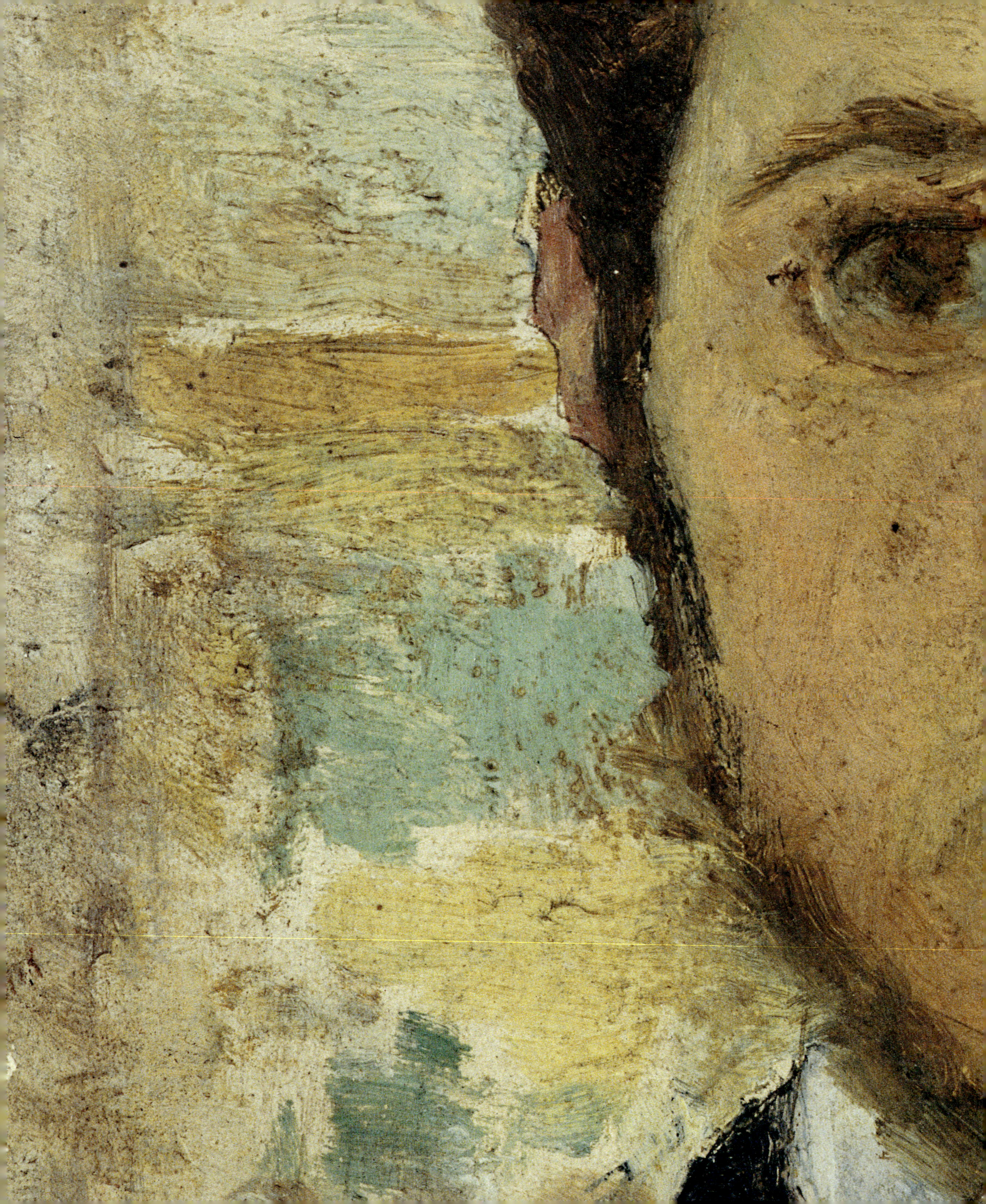

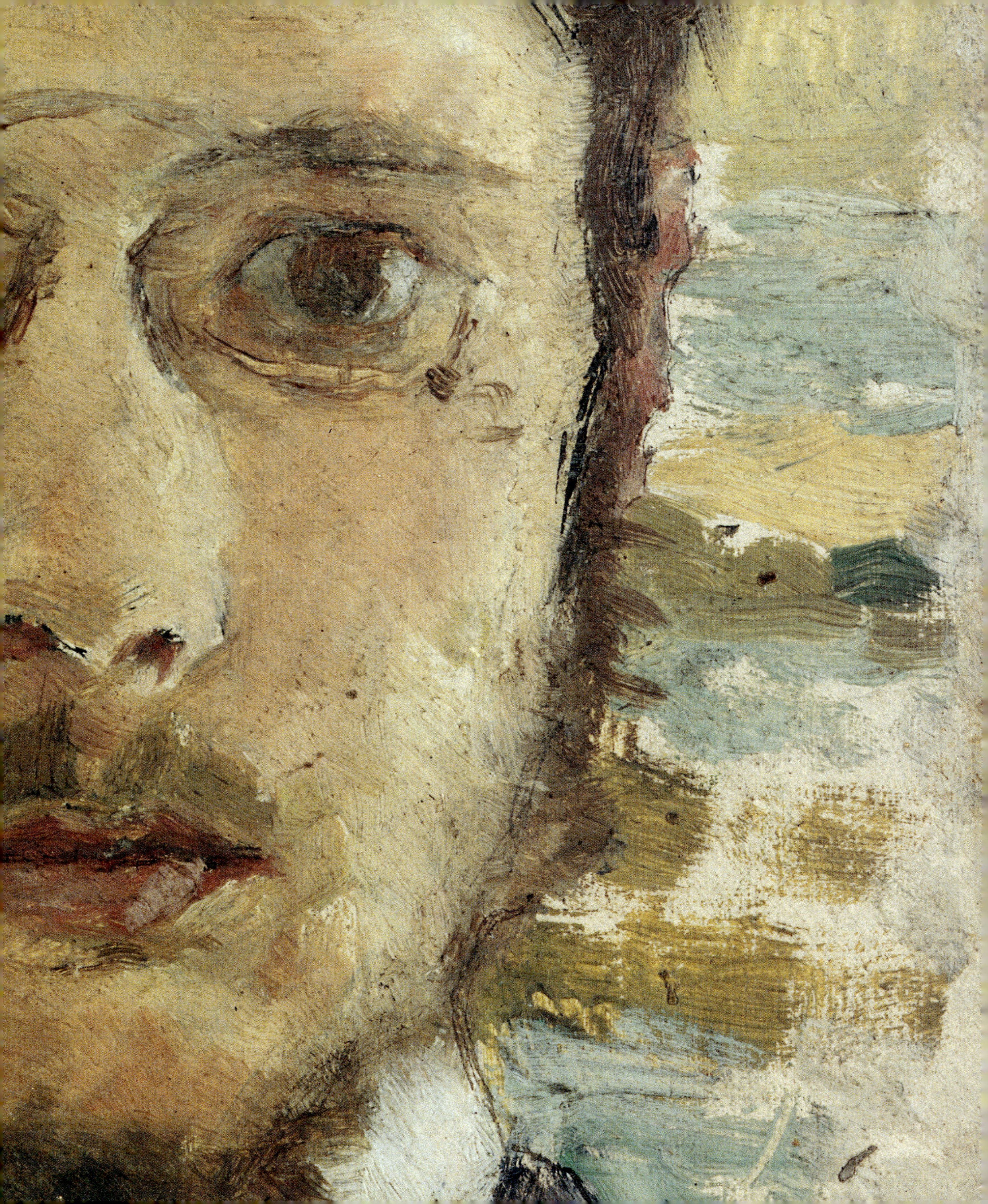

Chronology

Elsa M. Smithgall with a
contribution by Lisa Lipinski.

I don't know that the word vocation is exactly
appropriate to me. I wasn't all that aware that I
wanted to become a painter. What attracted me, at
that time, was less art itself than the artist's life and
all that it meant for me: the idea of creativity and
freedom of expression and action. I had been
attracted to painting and drawing for a long time,
but it was not an irresistible passion; what I wanted,
at all costs, was to escape the monotony of life.[1]

1867

3 October: Pierre Bonnard is born to Elizabeth
(Mertzdorff) of Alsace and Eugène Bonnard of the
Dauphiné at Fontenay-aux-Roses, a village a few
miles south of Paris. His father is employed as the
bureau chief of the war ministry. He is the middle
child of three, with an older brother, Charles
(b. 1864), and younger sister, Andrée (b. 1872).

Spends his childhood primarily in Fontenay
and Paris with summer gatherings of the family at
their country house in Le Grand-Lemps, situated
near La Côte-Saint-André (Isère region), in the
Dauphiné (figs. 1, 2).[2] Named Le Clos (The
Orchard), the house, which originally belonged to
his grandfather, Michel, a farmer and grain mer-
chant, is enlarged over the years and includes a
large garden and ten acres of woods.[3]

1875

Begins his elementary studies at a boarding school
in the town of Vanves.[4]

1881

Begins high-school studies at the prestigious Lycée
Charlemagne in Paris.[5]

1884

1 January: Transfers from the Lycée Charlemagne
to the Lycée Louis-le-Grand, where he studies in
the rhetoric and philosophy sections through the
end of June.[6] During this time, lives at 94, boulevard d'Enfert, Paris.[7] Shows a keen interest in
drawing and color. Likes philosophy, Latin, and
Greek, as well as modern literature. Reads and
memorizes fables of the seventeenth-century
French writer Jean de Lâ Fontaine, with whom
he shares a similar sense of humor and love of
animals. As Charles Terrasse later recounts,
"Bonnard always had an eye for the ways in
which animals . . . express themselves."[8] Toward
the end of the decade, he makes 121 marginal
illustrations in a copy of an 1867 edition of La
Fontaine's *Fables.*[9]

1885

Receives his baccalauréat.

Has his first drawing published, a pencil sketch
of a seated man entitled *Portrait of M. Dolbeau.*[10]

Following his father's wishes, enrolls in law
school. Renounces the idea of becoming an artist
full-time while maintaining a strong interest in
painting as a pastime. As he writes to his father in
early November, "Now that I have given up the
idea of earning a living from painting, it strikes
me as the most wonderful thing. I am going to
devote all my spare time to working at it seriously,

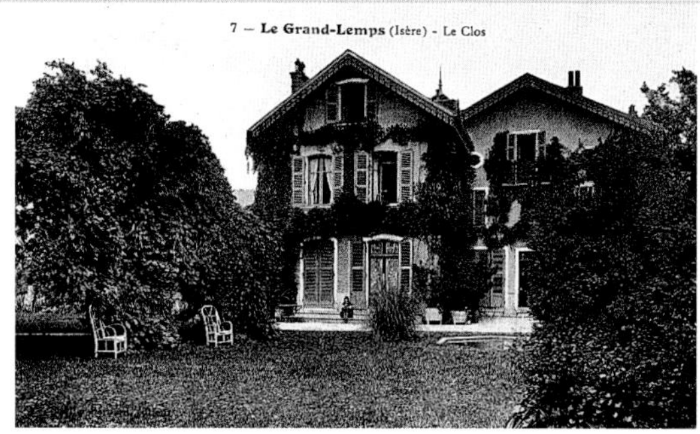

Previous spread:
Self-Portrait (detail),
1889, Oil on board,
7⅞ × 6⅛ in.
(20 × 15.5 cm),
Private collection.

1. *The Home of the
Bonnard Family at Le
Grand-Lemps*, 1890,
Photograph, Private
collection.

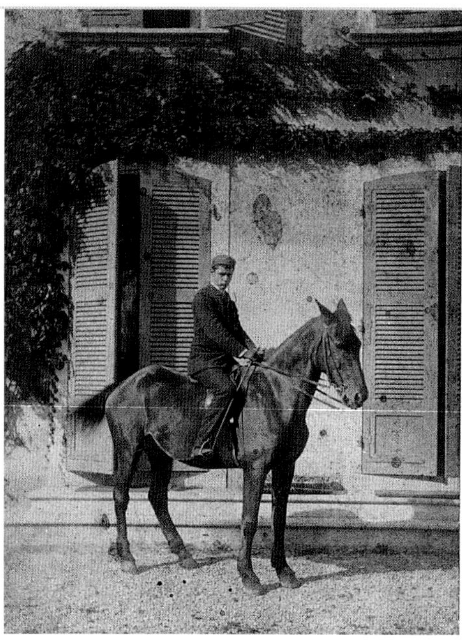

2. *Bonnard on the
Grounds of Le
Grand-Lemps*, ca.
1885, Photograph,
Private collection.

even copying from the Antique, but I shall only do as much of that as I choose, and not more than is useful to me."[11]

Studies briefly at the Ecole des Arts Décoratifs.

1886

While living with his maternal grandmother at 8, rue de Parme, near rue de Clichy, expresses an interest in painting outdoors in the suburbs of Chatou and Bougival.

1887

Registers at the Académie Julian, where he meets Paul Sérusier (1863–1927), Henri-Gabriel Ibels (1867–1936), Paul Ranson (1864–1909), and Maurice Denis (1870–1943), the latter of whom recalled how Bonnard "painted gray and copied the model scrupulously."[12]

11 March: While continuing to study law, pursues painting by gaining admission to painting section of the Ecole des Beaux-Arts, where he will study intermittently.[13]

1888

February: Works part-time for the treasurer of the records office of Courbevoie, a suburb of Paris.

20 July: Receives his law degree. While spending a vacation at Le Grand-Lemps, continues to devote his spare time to painting. As Bonnard writes to his mother, "Do not imagine I am coming to [Grand-] Lemps just to sit around and observe. I am going to bring a load of canvases and pigments and I plan to paint from morning til night."[14] Has his first studio there, from which he produces several small landscape paintings. Returns for visits every autumn and sometimes also in winter through about 1925, with the house and property serving as the setting for later paintings and photographs.[15] Accompanied at times by friends Edouard Vuillard (1868–1940) (fig. 3), Thadée Natanson (1868–1951), Alfred Jarry (see fig. 45) (1873–1907) and frequently by the film pioneers and autochrome inventors, Auguste and Louis Lumière, whose first film, *Arrivée d'un train en gare de la Ciotat*, shows in Paris in 1895 (see fig. 51).[16]

October: Sérusier shows him and Denis, Ibels, and Ranson a small abstract landscape (later called The Talisman) which he had painted on a cigar-box lid under Paul Gauguin's (1848–1903) supervision at Pont-Aven, Brittany. With these young artists, founds a group called the Nabis (the Hebrew word for prophets).

1889

Competes unsuccessfully for the Prix de Rome.[17]

Wins first prize in a competition for a poster advertising a popular brand of champagne, earning him one hundred francs, his first monetary compensation for artistic work (plate 5). "I was proud to have it in my pocket,"[18] he writes his mother.

Fails the civil service examination. Gives up law to pursue a career as a painter.[19] "My father, a civil servant, did not take at all well to my becoming an artist," he later confesses.[20]

Meets Ker-Xavier Roussel (1867–1944) and Edouard Vuillard (1868–1940), with whom he will

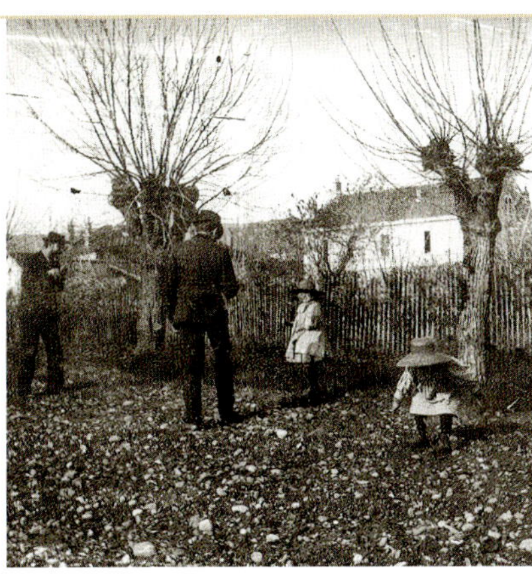

3. Edouard Vuillard, *Le Grand-Lemps. Bonnard Photographing Renée; Ker-Xavier Roussel Seen from the Back and Another Little Girl*, ca. 1900, Photograph, Paris, Musée d'Orsay.

develop a close personal and artistic kinship. "Bonnard and Vuillard studied the masters, visited museums and ended up being particularly interested in the art of China and the art of Japan. The Orientals brought to them 'liberation,'" Charles Terrasse later recalls.[21]

Rents his first of more than seven studios in Paris, on 14, rue Le Chapelais, off the avenue de Clichy, in the Batignolles district.[22]

End of December: With his friend and future brother-in-law Claude Terrasse, plans to visit the resort town of Arcachon, where he is eager to paint. As he writes to Andrée: "I'm bringing my box of pigments; waves of green, blue, and yellow will flow, each in turn. Arcachon: four patches of color—the dark green of the fir trees, the light green of the sea, the yellow of the sand, and the blue of the sky. One has only to change the sizes of the patches to create twenty different views of Arcachon. This is how I imagine that enchanting land."[23] Returns to Arcachon for brief periods from 1920 through 1933.

1890

Continues to balance a public government career with a private life as an artist (fig. 4). Works for the Paris courts as public prosecutor of the Seine. While working, enjoys making sketches of the lawyers, judges, and other staff.[24]

Rents a studio at 28, rue Pigalle, which he shares with Vuillard, the actor Aurélien Lugné-Poë, a classmate from secondary school, and Denis, who later expresses his indebtedness to "the fantasist of research, line and colour . . . what spirit he gave me!"[25]

Of Bonnard's working process at this time, Léon-Paul Fargue, a poet and close friend of Alfred Jarry, keenly observes, "He paints slowly, with this obvious yet secretly feverish indifference that we have always known in him."[26]

His important patrons Thadée and Alexandre Natanson become publishers with the young critic and political radical Félix Fénéon as managing editor of *Le Revue blanche* (founded in 1889) when it moves its offices from Liège to Paris. His work will later appear in the bimonthly avant-garde literary magazine.

Meets André Antoine, founder of the Théâtre Libre, for which he later designs programs, and Paul Fort, founder of the Théâtre d'Art.

8 April–24 May: Serves in the 52nd infantry regiment in Bourgoin as a soldier second class.

May: After completing his military service, returns to the Ecole des Beaux-Arts, where he sees the most extensive survey of Japanese prints to date in France, including 725 ukiyo-e woodcuts and 421 illustrated books, organized by the art dealer and promoter of Japanese art and culture Siegfried Bing, who becomes an important mentor and patron. Inspired by the example of Japanese art, Bonnard purchases *crépons*, a type of inexpensive, popular Japanese print, at a local department store; these purchases evolve into a small collection of ukiyo-e woodcuts. His encounters with Japanese art prove decisive for his work, as he explains much later, "[In a department store,] for one or two pennies, I found *crépons* or crumpled rice papers in astonishing colors. I covered the walls of my room with this naïve and gaudy art. Gauguin and Sérusier alluded to the past. But what I had in front of me was something

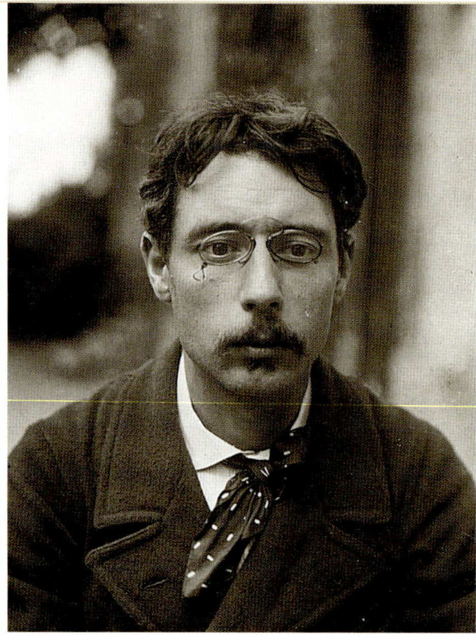

4. Alfred Natanson, *Bonnard*, ca. 1890, Photograph, Private collection.

tremendously alive and extremely clever. . . . I realized after contact with these rough common images that color could express everything with no need for relief or texture. I understood that it was possible to translate light, shapes and character by color alone, without the need for values."[27]

25 September: At Le Grand-Lemps, his sister Andrée marries the young composer Claude Terrasse, with whom he will collaborate on illustrations for musical albums, beginning with *Le Petit Solfège illustré* the following year.

1891

Participates in the first group exhibition of the Nabis, *Peintres impressionistes et symbolistes*, organized by Louis-Léon Le Barc de Boutteville at his gallery at 47, rue Le Peletier.

13 April: While working on illustrations for Terrasse's *Petit Solfège illustré* (plates 14a–b), "look[s] for encouragement to the artists of the past who illustrated missals and to the Japanese, who put art in encyclopedias."[28]

20 March–27 April: Participates for the first time in the exhibition of the Salon des Indépendants, where he shows five paintings and four decorative panels, entitled *Women in the Garden*. Exhibits with the Indépendants through 1947.

March: The prize-winning poster *France-Champagne* (plate 5) is met with critical acclaim when it is distributed in Paris at the end of the month. Fénéon contends that it is "superior to those of Appel and Levy. . . . Bonnard likes to develop his composition behind an arabesque motif which partly conceals it."[29] Of its design Paul Signac (1863–1935) will later observe an affinity with ukiyo-e woodcuts, noting, "if one were to trace its outlines, one would get the contours of an Utamaro."[30] The poster also attracts the attention of Henri de Toulouse-Lautrec (1864–1901), who will design posters after being introduced to Bonnard's printer Edward Ancourt.

Summer: Submits a design for a large sideboard for a contest sponsored by the Union Centrale des Arts Décoratifs. Motifs from the design also appear in his painting *Two Poodles* (plate 7), from the same year.[31]

11 December: With Ibels, designs the set for the production of *Geste du roy Fierabras* at the Théâtre Moderne.

28 December: In his first public statement published in *L'Echo de Paris*, renounces his early traditional academic training in favor of an overriding interest in decoration, exclaiming, "I do not belong to any school. I am only trying to do something personal, and I am trying to unlearn, at this moment, what I worked so hard to learn during the four years at the Ecole des Beaux-Arts."[32] Bonnard further declares, "Painting must above all be decorative," echoing Denis's celebrated statement of the previous year in *Art et critique*, "Remember that a picture, before being a battle horse, a naked woman, or some sort of narrative, is basically a flat surface covered with paints put together in a certain order."[33]

1892

Paints a portrait of his cousin Berthe Schaedlin, whom he had photographed in 1890 or 1891 (fig. 7), his first known photograph. His marriage proposal to her is turned down about this time.

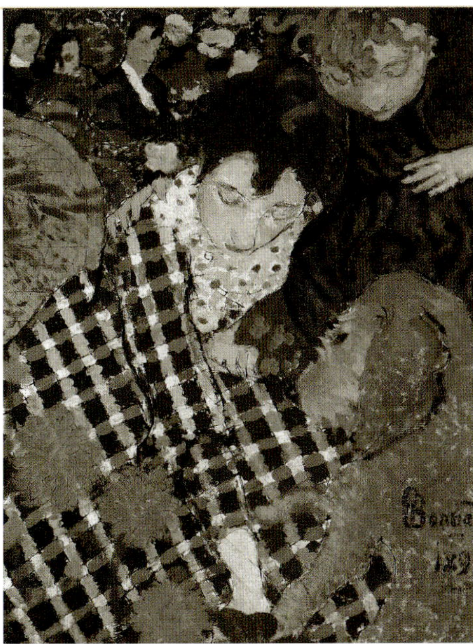

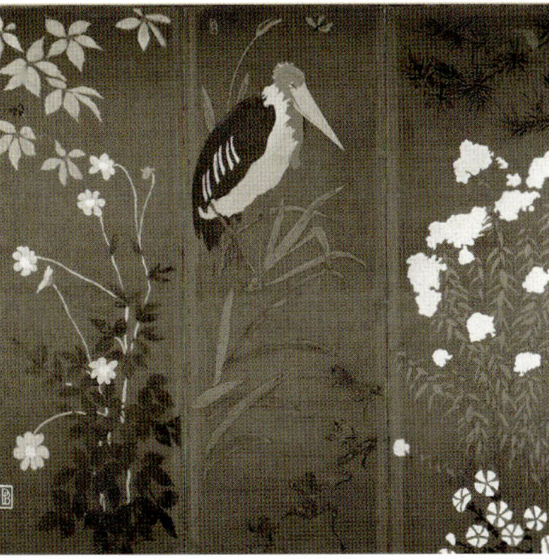

5. Pierre Bonnard, *Women with Dog* 1891, Oil on canvas, 16 × 12¾ in. (40.6 × 32.4 cm), Sterling and Francine Clark Art Institute, Williamstown, Massachusetts.

6. Pierre Bonnard, *Marabout (Stork) and Four Frogs*, ca. 1889, Distemper on fine canvas (three-paneled screen), each panel, 62¾ × 21½ in. (159.5 × 54.5 cm), Private collection.

Makes his first lithographs, about which he writes to his parents: "I did some printmaking this week and I learned many things. . . . I really hope to make the most of them."[34]

19 March–27 April: Exhibits seven paintings at the Salon des Indépendants—among them *Checked Blouse; Portrait of Mme Claude Terrasse, the Artist's Sister* (plate 3) and his first multifigure composition, *Croquet Game* (Musée d'Orsay). Receives high praise from the critics, who underscore both the Japanese underpinnings of his aesthetic. "Un Nabis Japonard," writes Fénéon, coining what becomes Bonnard's long-held nickname.[35] "A delightful ornamentalist, clever and ingenious like a Japanese,"[36] says G. Albert Aurier.

September: While continuing to work with illustrations, prints, and the decorative arts, increasingly devotes himself to painting, writing to Vuillard: "Painting, especially in oils, has kept me very busy, it's going slowly, very hesitantly, but I believe I am on the right track."[37]

November: Has work included in the third *Exposition des peintres impressionistes et symbolistes* at Le Barc de Boutteville's gallery, from which the academic painters Albert Besnard (1849–1934) and Henri Lerolle (1848–1929) each buy one of his decorative panels. Geffroy sees in Bonnard and Vuillard kindred spirits: "The eye can only rejoice in noticing the affinities between these two artists, Mr Pierre Bonnard and Mr Edouard Vuillard, who certainly possess the gift of nuance and a play on symmetrical and opposing lines."[38]

1893

His twenty lithographs illustrating Claude Terrasse's album of music *Petites Scènes familières* (plate 15) are published after much deliberation with the printer: "I'm again turning my hair white in trying to obtain the impossible from the printer," Bonnard writes.[39]

Meets Maria Boursin (1869–1942) who goes by the name Marthe de Méligny; she becomes his life companion, and they marry in 1925.

Through Denis, meets Ambroise Vollard (1865–1939), art collector, dealer, and publisher, from whom he will receive numerous commissions for book illustration projects. "He helped us very much. The editions he made will remain and few men will have the courage to make such masterpieces," he will later say of this important patron.[40]

11 February: Begins preparations for a new illustration project, an album for children entitled *Alphabet sentimental*, as he explains to his mother, "For each letter there will be a word beginning with that letter and representing an emotion or a mood, which I will render by little everyday scenes. . . . The idea is to make things and beings speak."[41]

March–April: Exhibits four paintings at the ninth Salon des Indépendants. Praising his work, the critic Claude Roger-Marx writes that Bonnard "catches fleeting poses, steals unconscious gestures, crystallizes the most transient expressions."[42]

April: Thadée Natanson marries Misia (Marie) Godebska (fig. 8), of whom Bonnard will later paint several portraits.

December: Contributes *Parisiennes*, his first black-and-white lithograph, to *La Revue blanche* (plate 18).

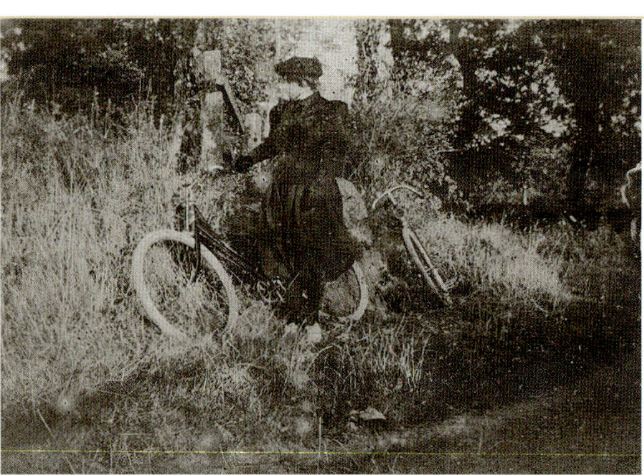

7. Pierre Bonnard, *Berthe Schaedlin during a Bicycle Ride*, ca. 1891, Photograph, Paris, Musée d'Orsay.

1894

Designs poster for *La Revue blanche* (plate 23), which is shown the following year at the annual poster exhibition in Brussels.

Completes a screen, *Nannies' Promenade, Frieze of Carriages*, using a distemper technique he had learned from the theater.[43]

March–April: Attends exhibition at Galerie Durand-Ruel of Odilon Redon (1840–1916), about whose work he later says, "What strikes me most about his work is the union of two virtually opposing elements: pure material substance and an expressive sense of mystery."[44]

May–end of June: Participates in the Nabis exhibition in the Toulouse offices of the newspaper *La Dépêche de Toulouse*, which includes his work *Two Poodles* (plate 7).

1895

Has a creative breakthrough, which he later relates to Raymond Cogniat: "It was during a vacation in the Dauphiné, at a house belonging to my family. The year was around 1895. One day, the words and theories that were the foundation of our conversations—color, harmony, the relation between line and tone, balance—lost their abstract significance and became very concrete. I had understood what I was seeking and how I would try to obtain it. What came after? The point of departure had been given to me; the rest was just daily life."[45]

Bonnard's stained-glass window design *Maternité* (private collection), commissioned the previous year by Siegfried Bing and manufactured by the American designer Louis Comfort Tiffany,

is exhibited in the Salon de la nationale, Paris, together with designs by Toulouse-Lautrec, Roussel, Vuillard, Ibels, Sérusier, and Denis.[46]

Summer: Stays with a group of artists and writers from the circle of *La Revue blanche* at La Grangette, the summer house of Misia and Thadée Natanson in the village of Valvins near Fontainebleau, "just a few steps" from the summer cottage on the Seine of Stéphane Mallarmé. Among "those chosen by [Misia's] heart," participates in the "utopian community" there, together with Vuillard and Toulouse-Lautrec.[47]

22 November: His father dies.

1896

Rents another studio in the Batignolles district.

Makes first color lithographs, including one in four colors based on his *Nannies' Promenade, Frieze of Carriages* (plate 24). His five-color lithograph *The Little Laundry Girl* (plate 27) is published in Vollard's first *Album d'estampes originales*. Later Bonnard acknowledges how the methods of color lithography imparted lessons for his painting: "When one must study the relationship among tones while playing with only four or five colors which one either superimposes or puts side by side, one discovers many things."[48]

January: Receives first one-man exhibition at Galerie Durand-Ruel, featuring fifty-six works. Invoking the opinion of his colleagues Pierre Puvis de Chavannes (1824–1898), Edgar Degas (1834–1917), Pierre-Auguste Renoir (1841–1919), and Claude Monet (1840–1926), Camille Pissarro (1830–1903) denounces the work of "the Symbolist named Bonnard" as "hideous."[49] The conservative

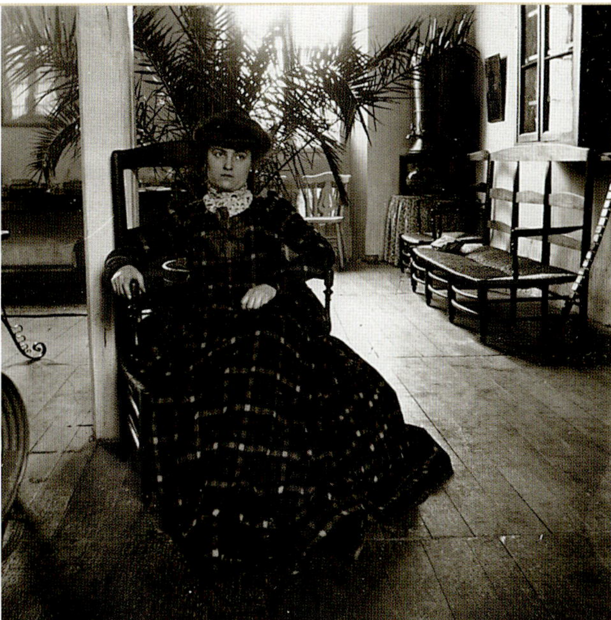

8. Edouard Vuillard, *Misia Natanson at Her House in Villeneuve-sur-Yonne*, 1898, Photograph, Private collection.

art critic Camille Mauclair further argues that Bonnard made the "mistake of mixing up the principles of decoration with those of painting, which are totally different."[50]

April: Designs the program for Maxime Gray's play *La Dernière Croisade* presented at the Théâtre de L'Oeuvre founded by Lugné-Poë in 1893.

10 December: Chief designer for the first performance of the Théâtre de l'Oeuvre's production of Alfred Jarry's absurdist, obscene play *Ubu roi* at the Salle du Nouveau Théâtre, 15, rue Blanche, with music by Claude Terrasse. Collaborates with Sérusier, Toulouse-Lautrec, Vuillard, Ranson, and Jarry on sets and masks. Will produce more than one hundred pen drawings on the Ubu theme over the next five years.[51]

December: The Nabis exhibition organized by Le Barc de Boutteville gallery was the last at this venue, owing to de Boutteville's death.

1897

Designs the cover of the second *Album d'estampes originales* (plate 29) issued by the Galerie Vollard and a poster for the review *L'Estampe et l'affiche*, edited by Clément Janin and André Mellerio.

May–June: His illustrations for *Marie*, a novel by the Danish writer Peter Nansen, which is published the following year, appear in four issues of *La Revue blanche* (plate 20). Renoir calls them "most exquisite," adding, "They are really yours; keep this art."[52]

1898

Draws cover and title page for *La Lithographie en couleurs*, a book by André Mellerio.

His first suite of color lithographs, *Quelques Aspects de la vie de Paris (Some Scenes of Parisian Life)*, is published by Vollard (plates 30, 33, 36).

January: Designs puppets for the Théâtre des Pantins, founded by Jarry, Franc-Nohain, and Claude Terrasse and set up in Terrasse's apartment at 6, rue Ballu. On 20 January they present a new production of Jarry's play *Ubu roi* adapted for marionettes.

Takes candid snapshots of his grandmother, Madame Mertzdorff, and the Terrasse children at the vacation home rented by the Terrasse family at Noisy-le-Grand, outside Paris, and at Le Clos at Le Grand-Lemps, and again on return visits through 1905 (figs. 9, 10, 14; plates 12, 13, 44).

10 September: Attends the funeral of Mallarmé.

1899

Jarry's *Petit Almanach du père Ubu* with illustrations by Bonnard is published. Travels to Venice and Milan with Vuillard and Roussel (figs. 11–13).

March: Ten works by Bonnard are featured in *L'Ecole moderne*, an exhibition of contemporary art organized by Signac in homage to Redon at the Galerie Durand-Ruel.

April: At Galerie Vollard, participates in "a most remarkable exhibition of modern prints in black and white, and in color, by [Henri] Fantin-Latour, Maurice Denis, O. Redon, Vuillard, Bonnard, Roussel. It is one of the most interesting exhibitions at the present time—and there is no shortage of them."

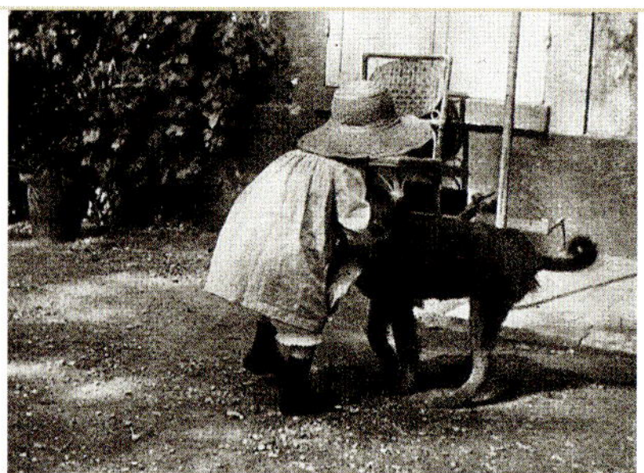

9. Pierre Bonnard, *Noisy-le-Grand. Family Scene: Renée Embracing a Dog*, 1903, Photograph, Paris, Musée d'Orsay.

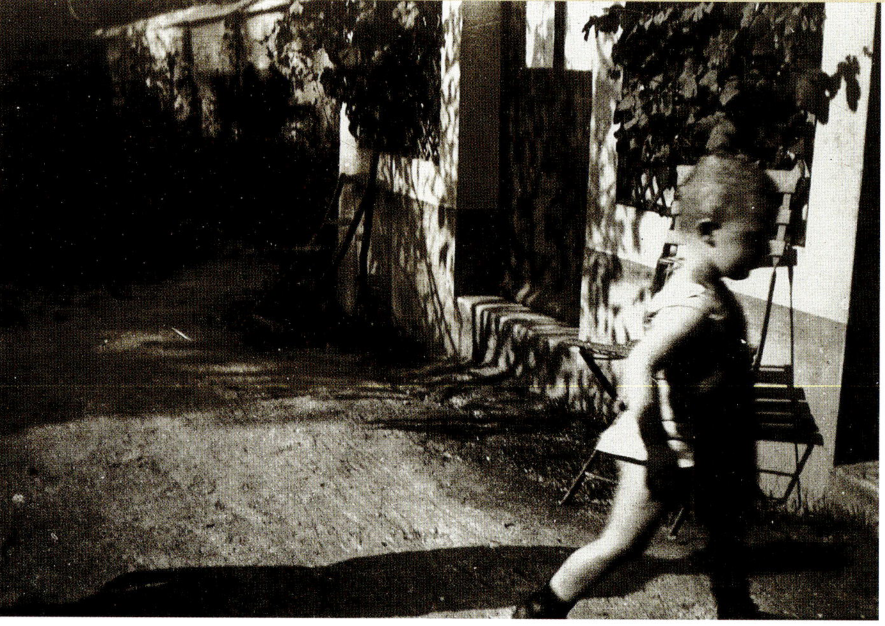

10. Pierre Bonnard, *Noisy-le-Grand. Family Scene: Profile of View of Robert Walking*, 1898, Photograph, Paris, Musée d'Orsay.

Autumn: Rents a studio and apartment at 65, rue de Douai, near the place Pigalle (fig. 15), with "a wonderful view from the studio over the convent garden and toward Montmartre." Charles Terrasse later recalls of it: "There were canvases, easels all around, and in an angle a small table where one would have lunch. The balcony was a place that was particularly attractive. From there one could see so many things. A whole world. The street below was bustling . . . agitated like a sea."[54] Takes a series of nude photographs of his companion, Marthe, posed on a bed in a corner of his apartment, several of which will serve as studies for his book illustration projects, prints, and paintings (fig. 18).[55]

1900

About this time, rents a small house outside Paris at 5, rue de la Montagne, in Montval, near Marly-le-Roi, to which he retreats each April.[56] Takes a series of nude photographs of Marthe in the garden of the house (plates 45, 47–54).[57]

Is included in the Nabis group portrait painted by Denis, *Hommage à Cézanne*, but in a marginal position at the far right of the canvas. Although Denis acknowledges Bonnard for his Nabis roots, Denis later celebrates Bonnard for his fiercely independent vision: "His system consists in having no system; he easily escapes analysis. . . . It is owing to the circumstances of the times and to his own mischievous mind that he became a painter of modern life."[58]

His large group portrait, *The Bourgeois Afternoon* (Musée d'Orsay), is purchased by the Galerie Bernheim-Jeune, the gallery's first purchase of his work. Founded in 1899 by the brothers Joseph ("Josse") and Gaston Bernheim, the gallery subsequently becomes his dealer.

2–22 April: Is included in a group exhibition at Galerie Bernheim-Jeune. In Bonnard's exhibited work, the critic Fontainas discovers significant developments: "Mr. Bonnard no longer likes capricious deformation where his sarcastic verve long ago exerted itself so cleverly. He reverts back to calmer and reflective observation, and his work gains in depth and solidity what it might have lost in vivacity."[59]

September: Four years after the death of the poet Paul Verlaine, Vollard publishes his last major collection of verse, a book of erotic poems entitled *Parallèlement* (plate 43), with 109 lithographs by Bonnard. The lithographs, based on photographs Bonnard took of Marthe in the nude, are reproduced in rose-sanguine, "because it allowed . . . [him] to convey more of the poetic atmosphere of Verlaine."[60] Oversees the process, working directly on the proofs from the publisher.[61] Despite the lack of success of *Parallèlement*, receives an even larger commision from Vollard to illustrate Longus's fourth or fifth century A.D. Greek pastoral of *Daphnis and Chloë*, which is published in November 1902.

1901

Visits Spain with Vuillard and the Romanian princes Antoine and Emmanuel Bibesco.

January: Has seventy-nine lithographic illustrations published in Jarry's *Almanach illustré du père Ubu* (plates 41, 42), in collaboration with Claude Terrasse, Fagus, and Vollard.

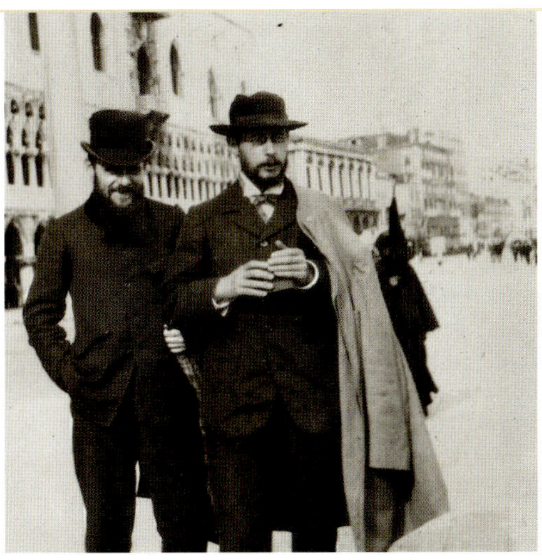

11. Edouard Vuillard, *Bonnard and Roussel in Venice*, 1899, Photograph, Paris, Musée d'Orsay.

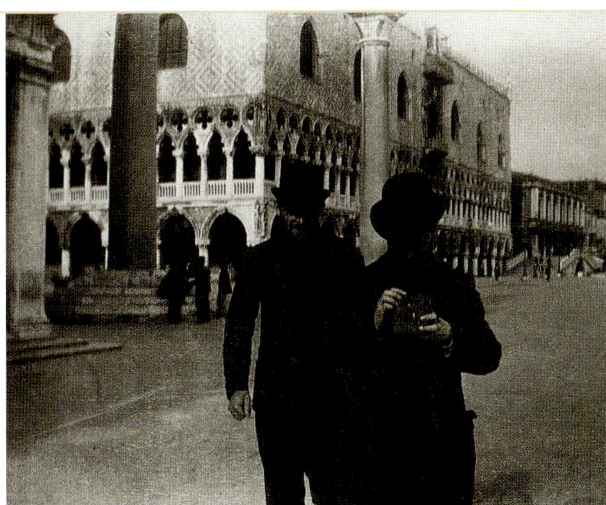

12. Pierre Bonnard, *Roussel Standing beside Vuillard Who Is Photographing Bonnard, in Front of the Ducal Palace, Venice*, 1899, Photograph, Paris, Musée d'Orsay.

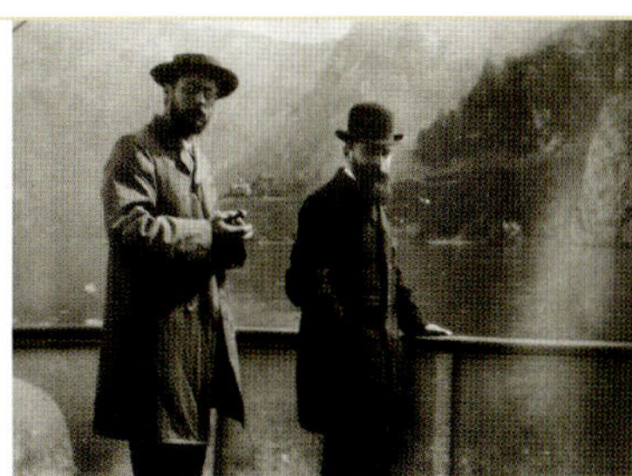

13. Ker-Xavier Roussel, *Bonnard and Vuillard on a Boat on Lake Como, Italy*, 1899, Photograph, Paris, Musée d'Orsay.

1901–1905

20 April–21 May: Exhibits nine paintings in the seventeenth exhibition of the Salon des Indépendants. His work attests to "his gift as a composer," writes Thadée Natanson.[62]

1902

By this time, has completed more than 250 lithographs.[63]

November: Vollard publishes *Daphnis and Chloë* with 156 lithographs by Bonnard, several of which are related to his earlier nude photographs of Marthe in the garden at Montval (plates 45, 47–54). Writing for *La Revue blanche*, Jarry says of his lithographs, "With an admirable lightness, [Bonnard] tumbled softly on the candid sheets of these pages."[64]

1903

Exhibits at the Vienna Secession.

31 October–6 December: Exhibits in the first Salon d'Automne. Of the three works presented, *Bourgeois Afternoon* draws critical notice: "Bonnard painted with a light touch, with drawing slightly paradoxical, and with a delightful gray tone."[65] Exhibits regularly at the Salon d'Automne through 1930.

15 April: *La Revue blanche* ceases publication.

1904

With Vuillard, takes first trip to the South of France, staying in St.-Tropez, where he visits Roussel and meets Paul Signac (1863–1935) and Louis Valtat (1869–1952) for the first time.

Jules Renard's *Histoires naturelles* is published with sixty-seven drawings by Bonnard (plates 60, 62a, 64).

25 February–9 March: Participates in a major impressionist exhibition at the Salon de la Libre Esthétique in Brussels, and again in March–April 1909.

1905

Travels to Berlin to paint the portrait of Sophie Herrmann, wife of the painter Curt Herrmann (1854–1929).

Though Marthe serves as his most frequent model for photographs and paintings, also begins using professional models, a practice that he continues intermittently through the end of his life (fig. 21).

June–July: With the artist and writer Pierre Laprade and the composer Maurice Ravel, takes first of two trips to Belgium and Holland on the yacht of the owner of the *Le Matin* newspaper, Alfred Edwards and his wife, Misia (former wife of Thadée Natanson), from whom he will receive in 1906 a commision for four large decorative panels, *Landscape with Bathers, After the Flood, Pleasure,* and *Fountains* or *The Voyage.*

18 October–25 November: Included in third exhibition of the Salon d'Automne. Addressing those who are still not receptive to Bonnard's work, the critic André Gide writes: "More than spirit, or even mischievousness, reason makes the composition of each one something bizarrely new and exciting. . . . Whether he paints an omnibus, a dog, a cat, a stool, his touch is naughty, totally independent of the subject."[66]

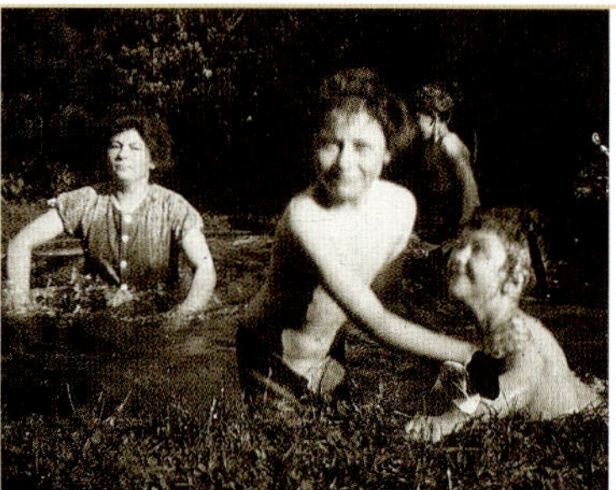

14. Pierre Bonnard, *Le Grand-Lemps, Family Scene. Bathing: Vivette (on the Right) in the Pool with a Nursemaid and Other Children,* 1903, Photograph, Paris, Musée d'Orsay.

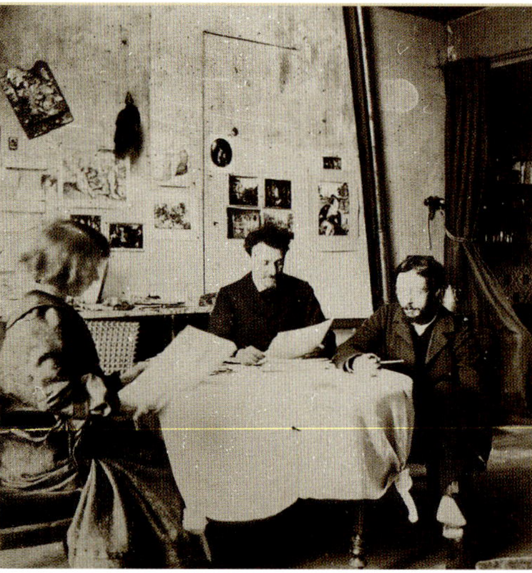

15. *Bonnard in His Studio, 65, rue de Douai, with Marthe and a Friend,* ca. 1903, Photograph, Private collection.

December: Rents two large rooms at 60, rue de Douai (fig. 16) (a former convent he could see from his old studio): "I shall have sunshine, and a view on the boulevard and the gardens."[67]

1906

February: Travels to the South of France, staying briefly in Banyuls with the sculptor Aristide Maillol (1861–1944), to whom he will later pay homage in a painting of 1917 (plate 81).

3–15 April: His one-man show at Vollard's gallery features a table centerpiece in bronze, a medium Bonnard had begun to explore at the beginning of the century at Vollard's urging: "One day, I saw Bonnard molding breadcrumbs. Gradually, with his fingers, he shaped them into a little dog. . . . I say Bonnard, you are doing a sculpture. . . . Why don't you make statuettes?"[68] Admires sculpture of his contemporaries, including that of the Nabi Georges Lacombe (1868–1916) and Maillol; he integrates Maillol's statuettes into his paintings (plate 81).[69] His treatment of the standing nude reflects this close study of sculpture (plate 57).

9–20 November: Receives first one-person exhibition at Galerie Bernheim-Jeune's new location, 25, boulevard de la Madeleine, featuring forty-one paintings.

1907

Moves his studio to 60, rue de Douai, where he had been living since December 1905. By 1909, the critic George Besson will visit Bonnard there, later recalling, "One morning in May I arrived at his studio, a cell in a former convent on rue de Douai [in Paris]. He sat me in an old easy chair by a yellow door, rubbed his hands together energetically (a characteristic gesture), and began to paint my portrait. As he painted he smoked a pipe and munched pralines from a tiny paper bag on a little, round, rusty stove."[70]

1908

Travels to London with Vuillard.

Moves to an apartment at 49, rue Lepic, but maintains his studio at 60, rue de Douai.

Octave Mirbeau's travel book about a car journey through Belgium and the Netherlands, titled *La 628-E8* after Mirbeau's license plate number, is published with illustrations by Bonnard. "I drew a whole sequence in the margins. I enjoyed it very much because I like Mirbeau's humor immensely," Bonnard later said of his old friend and fellow anarchist from the circle of *La Revue blanche*.[71] Mirbeau expresses similar adoration for Bonnard's work, noting, "The purpose, which is manifest in the slightest of his strokes and in his seemingly most delicate color-notes, makes even the tiniest sketch of his a thing complete in itself with a life of its own. There is not here among his works a single piece—no matter how limited in dimensions—of which he has failed to make a perfect composition, vigorously drawn."[72]

Explores the subject of the female nude at her toilette in a series of paintings that often use Marthe as his model (fig. 17; plates 66, 73, 107); the subject becomes a central theme in his later work.

February: Travels to Algeria and Tunisia.

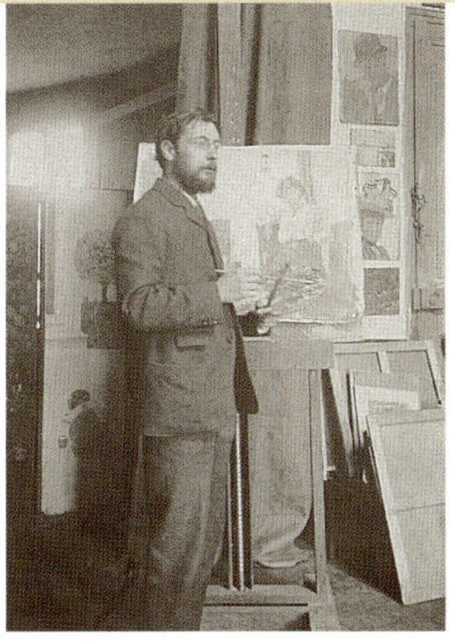

16. *Bonnard in His Studio on rue de Douai*, ca. 1905, Photograph, Private collection.

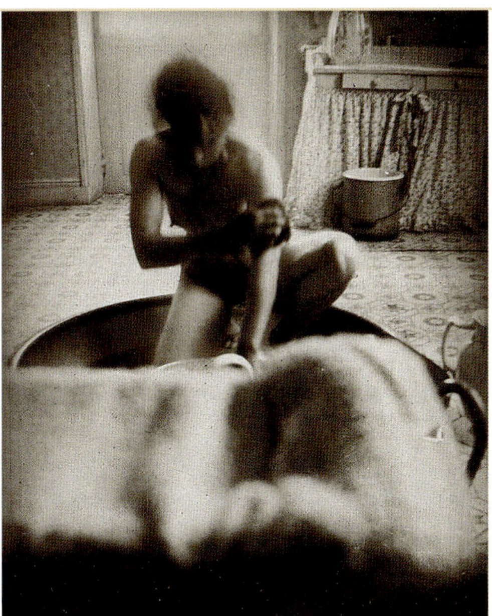

17. Pierre Bonnard, *Marthe in the Tub*, 1907, Photograph, Paris, Musée d'Orsay.

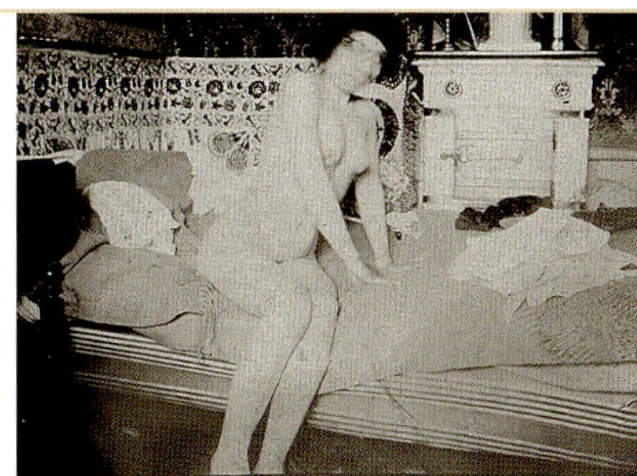

18. Pierre Bonnard, *Marthe Leaning Forward*, 1899–1900, Photograph, Paris, Musée d'Orsay.

12–13 June: Nineteen paintings by Bonnard are among those on sale from the collection of Thadée Natanson at the Hôtel Drouot.

1909

June: Like Signac, Matisse, and the Fauves before him, makes first extended visit to the South of France, staying with the artist Henri Manguin (1874–1949) in St.-Tropez, about which he writes to his mother, "It struck me like the *Thousand and One Nights* . . . the sea, yellow walls, reflections as bright as lights. . . . After a fragrant midday meal we went to call on some neighbors and I had a vision of a very dark girl in a pink dress down to her feet with an enormous parakeet, uncaged, against the yellow, red and green background. . . . I think I shall soon be longing for the green grass and the clouds."[73]

Returns each year to the South of France, renting villas at St.-Tropez, Grasse, Antibes, and Le Cannet (fig. 19), until buying a house at Le Cannet in 1926.

1910

Moves his studio to 21, quai Voltaire.

February: Acquires a drawing by Auguste Rodin (1840–1917).

1911

Rents a studio at 22, rue Tourlaque, near his apartment in the rue Lepic.

Buys his first car, an 11CV Renault (fig. 20), which he has painted a pale yellow.[74] Charles Terrasse later recalled: "From now on Bonnard hardly travels any other way. . . . For him, a car is the ideal dispenser of the new sights for which he yearns. He drives slowly, fascinated to see in succession changing aspects of the open country and towns. That queen of highways—Route 7—going from Paris to Antibes and Nice, delighted him. . . . He drives scarcely more than thirty miles a day, sometimes less, stopping here and there, . . . ever interested in the daily life of the region where he happens to be, observing the people with that scrutinizing look which might well embarrass them were it not tempered with good nature."[75]

Makes three trips to St.-Tropez, including one in July with Signac.

1912

Bonnard is offered the Légion d'Honneur, which he declines, as do his colleagues Vuillard, Roussel, and Félix Vallotton (1865–1925).

One year after Henri Matisse's (1869–1954) purchase of his *Soirée in the Salon,* buys Matisse's *Open Window, Collioure* from Galerie Bernheim-Jeune, a painting with which he never parts and which he hangs next to Paul Cézanne's (1839–1906) *Bather with Outstretched Arms.*[76] Later conveys his admiration for Matisse's ability to realize his artistic vision on the first try: "He knows what he is doing and he manages to do it the first time around. Whereas I leave, I touch up, and I never know where it will take me."[77]

Rents a house in St.-Germain-en-Laye at 40, rue Voltaire.

1908–1912

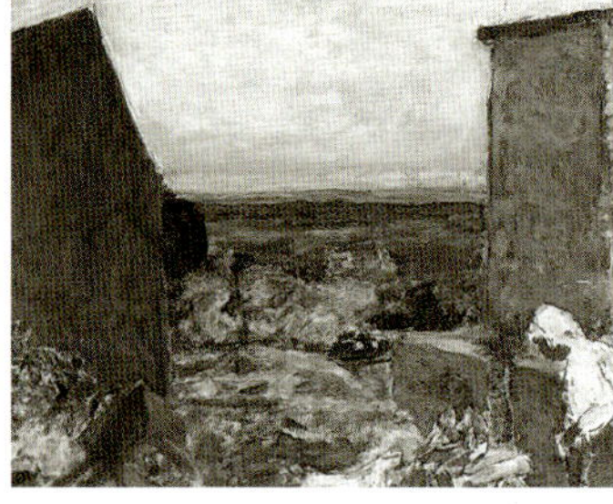

19. Pierre Bonnard, *Pays du Midi, Soleil Couchant (Le Cannet),* ca. 1910, Oil on canvas, 17⁵⁄₁₆ × 20⁷⁄₁₆ in. (44 × 52 cm), Private collection.

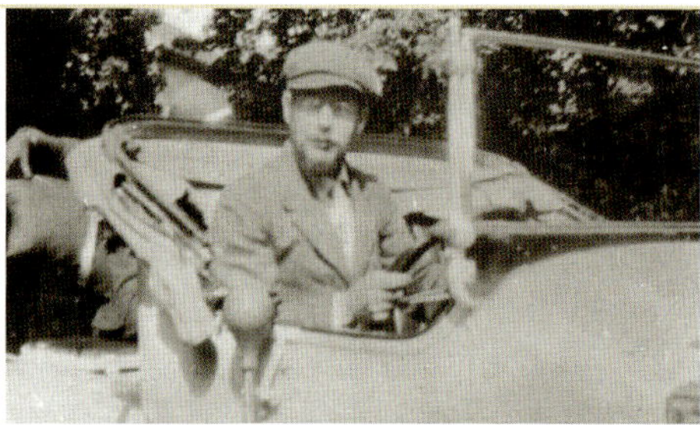

20. *Bonnard Driving His 11CV Renault,* 1912, Photograph, Private collection.

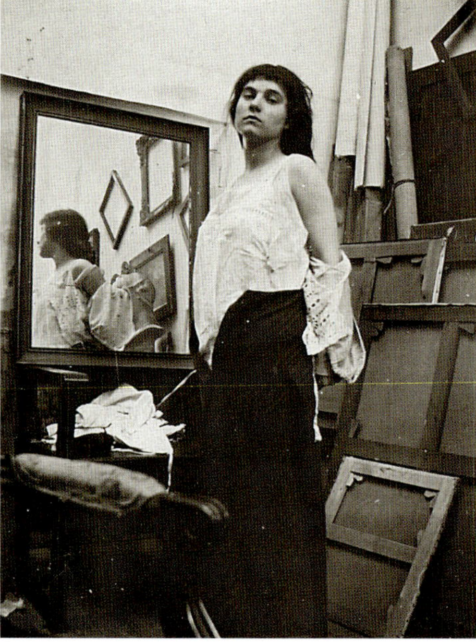

21. Pierre Bonnard, *Model Removing Her Blouse in the Artist's Studio,* ca. 1916, Photograph, Paris, Musée d'Orsay.

15 June: First major profile of his work written by Thadée Natanson is published in *La Vie*.

August: Buys a small house at Vernonnet, near Vernon in the Eure Valley (fig. 23), which is close to Monet's home at Giverny, where he will visit (fig. 24). Alternates between his residence here and in Paris. Calls it Ma Roulotte (My Caravan). Charles Terrasse wrote of it: "It stood between the river and the road that led from the village of Vernonnet to Pressagny, like a hyphen between road and river. . . . [Bonnard] described the view from his window, or from the top of the neighboring hill: the pale green and golden fields of early summer; the riverbanks lined with poplars, elms, ash trees, and the silvery patches of willows; the majestic river itself, alive with boats, and blue in the sunshine or lead-gray in the rain."[78]

20 December: Important critical study of his work by Lucie Cousturier is published in *L'Art décoratif*.

1913

His discovery of the shimmering light and colors of the southern French landscape provoked a concerted shift toward drawing and composition in his work, as he later explains to his nephew Charles Terrasse: "I have gone back to school. . . . I wanted to forget all that I knew. I am trying to learn what I do not know. I am redoing my studies from the principles, from the a, b, c's. I mistrust myself and all that I had been passionate about: this color which drives one wild. Certainly color had carried me away. I sacrificed form to it almost unconsciously. But it is true that form exists. . . . It is therefore drawing that I must study."[79]

May–June: Travels with Vuillard to Hamburg, at the invitation of the mayor Alfred Lichtwerk.

15 November–5 January 1914: Exhibits *The Dining Room in the Country* (fig. 26, plate 78) at the Salon d'Automne.

Has one work included in the Armory Show in New York.

1914

May: Designs a poster for the Ballets Russes.

15 June: "Bonnard," a text by his friend Pierre Laprade and illustrated by the artist's four ink drawings and Gauguin's caricature of him as the frontispiece, is published in the French literary periodical *Les Marges*. Explaining the choice of Bonnard as his subject, Laprade states outright, "I believe that Bonnard has a unique place in modern painting."[80]

1915

Stays at St.-Germain-en-Laye and Vernon for most of the year.

Submits a drawing for the Comité de la Fraternité des Artistes' publication, *Album national de la guerre*, which also includes work by Degas, Monet, Renoir, Signac, and Vuillard.

1916

Works on four panels commissioned by the Bernheim-Jeune family, including *Earthly Paradise* (fig. 28, plate 80).

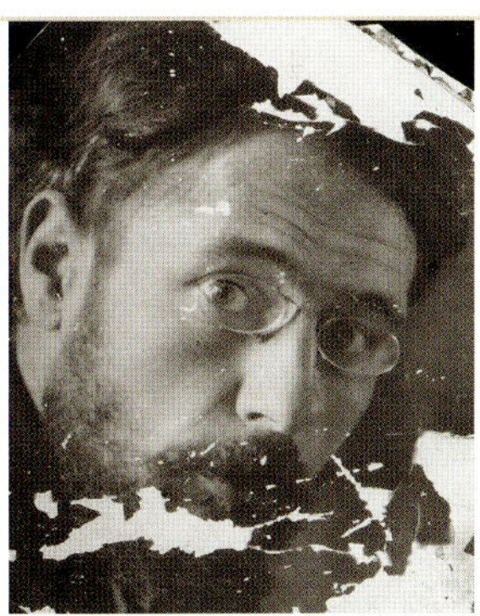

22. *Bonnard*, ca. 1920, Photograph, Private collection.

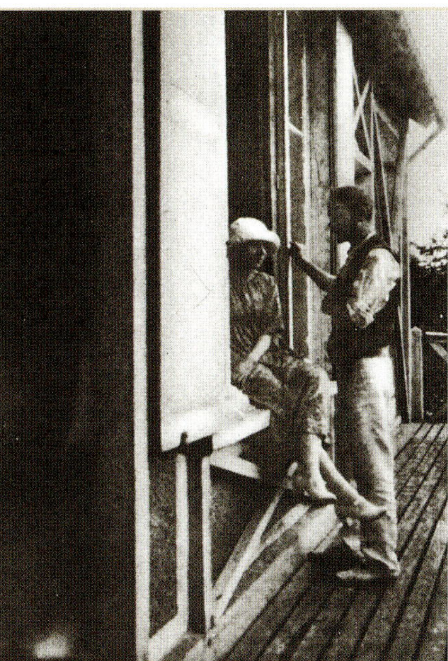

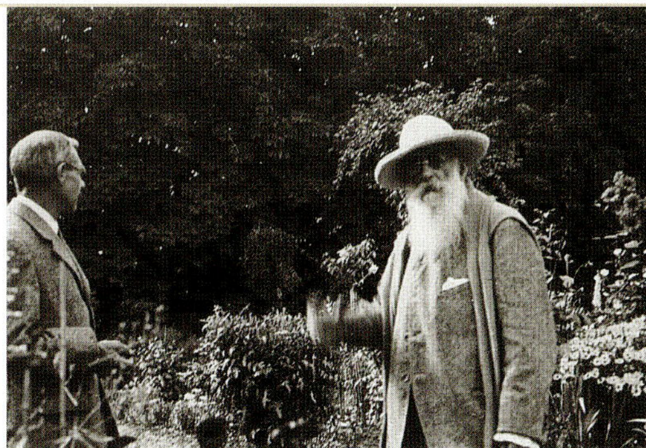

23. *Bonnard and Marthe on the Balcony of Ma Roulotte*, 1920, Photograph, Private collection.

24. Jacques Salomon, *Bonnard and Claude Monet in Monet's Garden at Giverny*, ca. 1925, Photograph, Private collection.

1916–1921

Makes an etching of Renoir, his only engraved portrait of an artist (plate 84a).[81]

October: Moves to rue Molitor, in the suburb of Auteuil, where his brother-in-law had moved with his family.[82]

October–November: Is featured in an exhibition of French painting at Winterthur, which he visits as the guest of the Swiss collectors Dr. Arthur Hahnloser and his wife, the painter-designer Hédy Hahnloser-Bühler.

The following year the Hahnlosers will commission a large decorative painting, *Summer* (Fondation Maeght), for their house. Bonnard misjudges the dimensions. He explains, "On seeing the piece of canvas, I noticed that it was . . . more than double the size I had in mind at the outset—and therefore I have had to look for subjects that are more decorative than expressive."[83] He will eventually exchange the painting for a smaller one, *The Fauns*, 1905. Hédy Hahnloser's cousin, Richard Bühler, also commissions a number of paintings to decorate his paneled dining room in Winterthur.

1918

Completes *The Terrace* (plate 86), the first of three large-scale panoramic landscapes based on the view from the terrace of Ma Roulotte, which is exhibited at the Salon d'Automne the following year. Subsequently paints *The Terrace at Vernonnet*, 1920/39 (plate 88) and *Terrace at Vernon*, 1928.

Le Groupement de la Jeune Peintre Française chooses Bonnard and Renoir as honorary presidents.

December: Travels to Antibes, where Matisse visits him.

1919

First two monographs on him are published: François Fosca, *Bonnard* (Geneva) and Léon Werth, *Bonnard* (Paris).

16 March: His mother dies.

1920

Contributes to the purchase by the Musée du Louvre of Gustave Courbet's (1819–1877) *The Painter's Studio*.

Abandons photography about this time (fig. 22).[84]

August: André Gide's *Promethée mal enchaîné* is published with thirty of Bonnard's illustrations.

September: Is the subject of an article in *Art et décoration* by the art critic François Fosca, who explains Bonnard's position within the history of French art: "An obedience as scrupulous to nature is newer than one would think. The impressionists, themselves, aside from Degas, hadn't dared go there."[85]

October: Designs large stage sets for the Swedish Ballet Company's production of *Jeux*.

1921

March: Stays in Rome for two weeks with his lover, Renée Monchaty, an aspiring artist in her early twenties whom he met in 1918 and hired as his model.

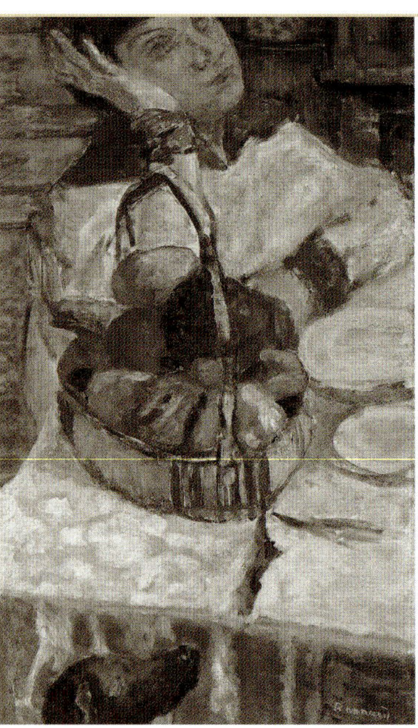

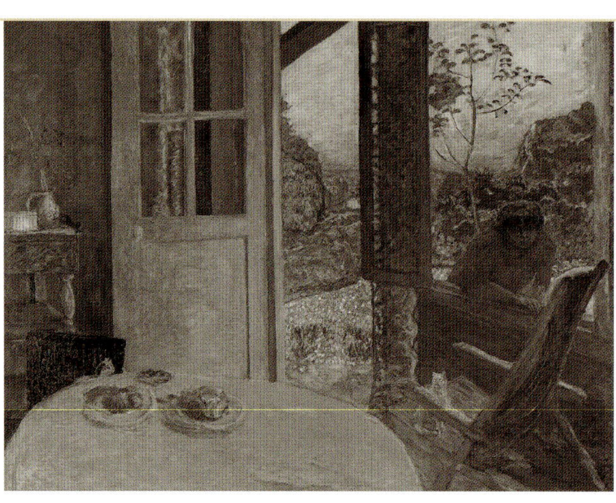

25. Pierre Bonnard, *Woman with Basket of Fruit*, 1915–1918, Oil on canvas, 27¼ × 15¾ in. (69.2 × 40 cm), The Baltimore Museum of Art: The Cone Collection, formed by Dr. Claribel Cone and Miss Etta Cone of Baltimore, Maryland BMA1950.190

26. Pierre Bonnard, *The Dining Room in the Country*, 1913, Oil on canvas, 64¾ × 81 in. (164.5 × 205.7 cm), The Minneapolis Institute of Arts, The John R. Van Derlip Fund 54.15.

1922

Represented at the Venice Biennale.

Catches pneumonia.

October: Claude Anet's *Notes sur l'amour* is published with fourteen ink drawings by Bonnard engraved on wood by Yvonne Maillez. Monchaty served as model for the drawings.[86]

1923

Works at Vernon and at Le Cannet, where he paints *The Riviera* (plate 114).

Receives third prize and $500 at Carnegie International Exhibition, Pittsburgh.

30 June: His brother-in-law, Claude Terrasse, dies, followed three months later by his sister, Andrée.

1924

Vollard publishes another book by Octave Mirbeau, *Dingo*, with fifty-five etchings by Bonnard.

Returns to the place Clichy neighborhood in Paris, moving to 48, boulevard des Batignolles, but works primarily at Le Cannet and Vernon.

Is the subject of a small monograph by Claude Roger-Marx, which posits that "While the impressionists, to which he is hardly indebted, even from the beginning, see everywhere only appearances, in his eyes, to the contrary, all is reality, everything lives and is equally assertive, everything breathes and participates in the charming disorder which the human being creates around himself." Roger-Marx further remarks on the slow nature of Bonnard's creative process: "A painting is rarely finished right away; he repeatedly goes over it for several weeks, sometimes over a period of several years, working on three or four works simultaneously, waiting for the unforeseen analogy which allows him finally to give a sincere response to a particular problem that seemed unresolved. . . . Bonnard works slowly and produces little."[87]

7–18 April: First retrospective exhibition (1891–1922), organized by the Galerie E. Druet. *Circus Rider*, 1894 (plate 22), is among the sixty-eight paintings shown, which the critic Jacques Trapenard distinguishes from "the sharp almost cruel analysis of a Toulouse-Lautrec." Trapenard further identifies the defining qualities of Bonnard's talent, notably, "a spiritual disdain of academic formulas (if they were of the Academy Julian) . . . and the most personal imagination."[88] For the critic André Lhote, Bonnard's use of line and space conjures up an association with Cubism. As Lhote explains, "For me who has never been a fanatic of 'conceptual' cubism, I enjoy, facing a painting of Bonnard, seeing the surface of the canvas divided in such an ingenious way."[89]

December: Goes to Villa Le Rêve at Le Cannet; stays through most of 1926.

1925

13 August: Without informing any family members, marries Marthe in a civil ceremony in Paris. Only two witnesses, Louisa Poilard, their concierge, and her husband, Joseph Tanson, are present.

9 September: Monchaty, Bonnard's lover and presumed model for *The Open Window* (plate 93), commits suicide.

Duncan Phillips purchases two paintings from

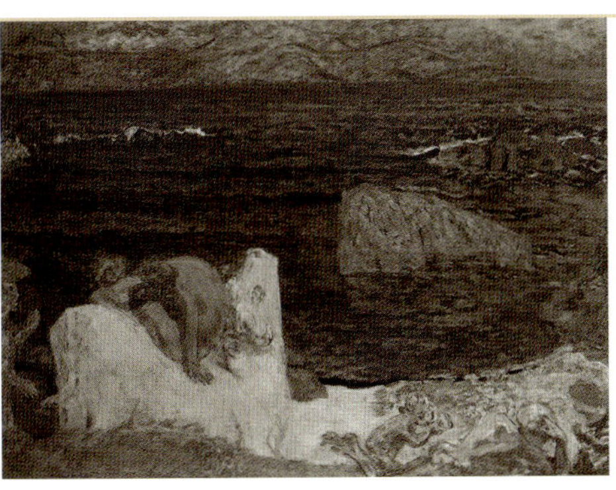

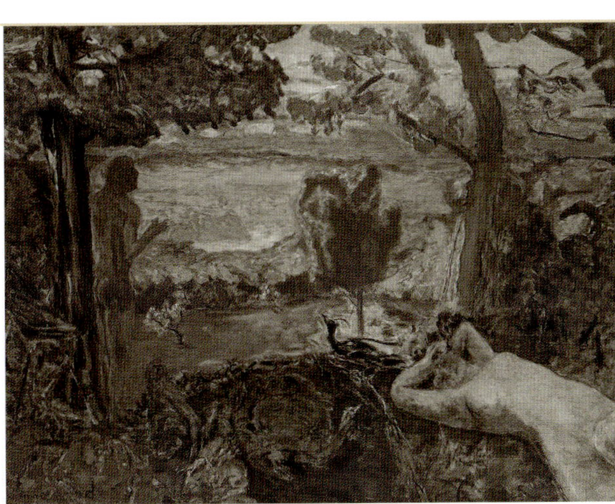

27. Pierre Bonnard, *The Abduction of Europa*, 1919, Oil on canvas, 46¼ × 60¼ in. (117.5 × 153 cm), Toledo Museum of Art; Purchased with funds from the Libbey Endowment, Gift of Edward Drummond Libbey.

28. Pierre Bonnard, *Earthly Paradise*, 1916–1920, Oil on canvas, 51½ × 63 in. (130 × 160 cm), The Art Institute of Chicago, Estate of Joanne Toor Cummings; Bette and Neison Harris and Searle Family Trust endowments; through prior gifts of Mrs. Henry C. Woods.

Bernheim-Jeune that had been in Carnegie International exhibitions: *Early Spring*, 1910 (plate 68) and *Woman with Dog*, 1922 (plate 96). From now until 1952, Phillips, who becomes his most important American patron to promote Bonnard's work, builds a collection of seventeen oils, five drawings, and nine prints by the artist, the largest and most diverse collection of his work in the United States. Later Phillips writes: "our very personal collection of [Bonnard's] work is in itself a recognized memorial to his genius. . . . With us Bonnard is at home."[90]

1926

February: Buys a small hillside villa, which he calls Le Bosquet (The Grove), at Le Cannet, a village in the hills above the seaside resort of Cannes, near Renoir's house in Cagnes, which he will visit. Le Bosquet, which he will renovate, becomes his primary residence in the South of France after 1931 and the primary setting for his mature paintings.[91]

September: As a member of the Carnegie International Jury, travels to the United States. Visits Pittsburgh, Philadelphia, Chicago, New York, and Washington, D.C., where he goes to the Phillips Memorial Gallery, meeting Duncan and Marjorie Phillips for the first time.

1927

Claude Anet's *Les Histoires du petit Renaud* is published with illustrations by Bonnard.

One of his nephews, Charles Terrasse, writes a long monograph published by Floury, based on reminiscences Bonnard shares with him about his painting, among them his thoughts about "the painter's eye": "our vision is above all empirical and conventional. . . . This conventional reflection of the outside world that drawing gives us is incomparably more true than the dry process of photography. . . . The eye of the painter gives a human value to objects. . . . And this vision is *mobile*. And this vision is *variable*."[92]

In assessing the development of Bonnard's art, Terrasse recognizes an underlying continuity, arguing against the separation of his work into two creative periods. As Terrasse writes, "There is not a first or second period in Bonnard's work. There is only one, which is and which was perpetually changing and diverse. His art evolves constantly, and is an incessant state of 'becoming.'"[93]

Begins to record the weather, draw, and make brief notes and observations about painting in a small daybook that he carries on daily walks (fig. 29), a practice he continues through 1946.

February-March: Is included in the Phillips Memorial Gallery's *Tri-Unit Exhibition of Paintings and Sculpture* alongside paintings by John Marin (1870–1953), Augustus Vincent Tack (1870–1949), John Twachtman (1853–1902), Maurice Prendergast (1858–1924), Cézanne, Georges Seurat (1859–1891), and an 18th-Dynasty Egyptian stone head. In the accompanying catalogue, Phillips explains his rationale for uniting these works: "Our exquisite . . . portrait in stone . . . is not out of place in the midst of modern paintings, no less marked by sensibility and simplification. . . . It was a challenge in its day to the Academies of Egypt just as these paintings are a challenge to our arbiters of art. . . ." In a separate essay in the catalogue, Phillips shares further insight into Bonnard's

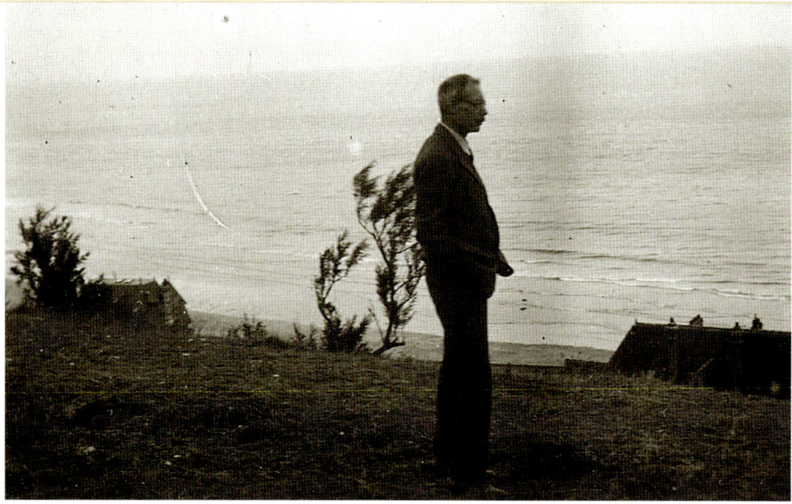

29. Thadée Natanson, *Bonnard in Trouville*, 1927, Photograph, Private collection.

approach and contribution to the history of art: "Nature is never too sacred for Bonnard to rearrange, but ever a source-book for this playboy of pictorial design. . . . As with [Redon and Matisse], so with Bonnard, the color is often Persian in clarity and tonic dissonance. It is tempting also to see in Bonnard an affinity to the magical [Claude] Debussy. These two masters of nuance are corresponding links between the old and the new in music and painting. Neither of them laid firm foundations for the future, but both helped to break down barriers of resistance to freedom of invention."[94]

May: Purchases a piece of land with an almond tree adjacent to his house in Le Cannet, enabling him to enlarge his garden.[95]

1928

February: Has two simultaneous exhibitions at the Contemporary Art Society and the Salon des Indépendants. Seeing Bonnard's methods as the pictorial counterpart to the sensibility of Marcel Proust, the critic Roger Fry contends, "Both these create a shifting, shimmering texture. . . . Proust plays tricks with time which remind one of Bonnard's tricks with pictorial space."[96]

6–28 April: Receives his first solo exhibition outside France, at the De Hauke Gallery in New York, to which the Phillips Memorial Gallery lends several works. Claude Anet, writing in the preface to the catalogue, proclaims, "The miracle of Pierre Bonnard is that his sensibility instead of becoming blunt has remained young and fresh. He has acquired through so many years of work, a technique marvellously supple, audacious, clever,

subtle, and varied. But this technique belongs to a man who has retained the power to be stirred as if he saw the light to-day for the first time. From this inexhaustible source of emotion springs the secret life . . . which animates the canvases of Pierre Bonnard."[97]

Critics continue to debate his rank within modern art, associating him with the retrograde tradition of the impressionists while distinguishing him from the latest developments of the cubists. Margaret Breuning notes: "Pierre Bonnard is so much himself that he continues to be an impressionist in the moment when this form of art is not the mode. He is not of the first generation of impressionists yet he stems from them, perhaps most from Renoir."[98]

26 November–14 December: Given one-man show at Galerie Bernheim-Jeune, about which the art critic André Lhote writes, "One could thus measure the extent of his conquest in the realm of composition as well as color. Disdaining more and more the impressionistic division of objects, Bonnard tries to integrate them into the architectural forms that normally surround them."[99]

1929

October: Attends the exhibition of works by Jean-Siméon Chardin (1699–1779) at the Galerie du Théâtre Pigalle.

7 November–10 December: Included in *Exhibition of French Art since Eighteen Hundred* organized by The Cleveland Museum of Art.

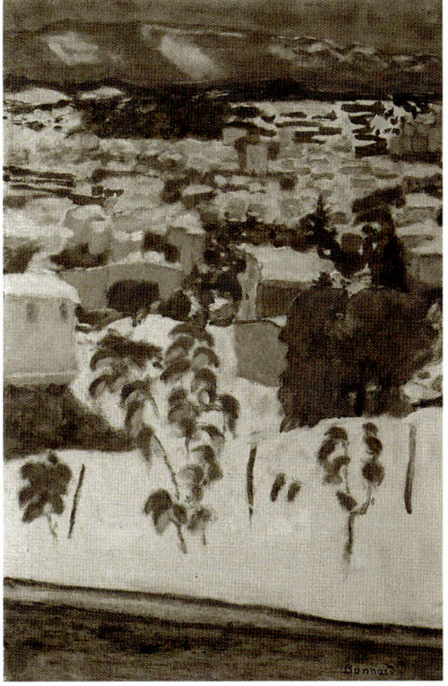

30. Pierre Bonnard, *Effect of Snow* or *Le Cannet under the Snow*, 1927, Oil on canvas, 29⅛ × 19⁵⁄₁₆ in. (74 × 49 cm), Kunstmuseum Winterthur, Inv. No. 1531. Gift of Dr. Herbert and Charlotte Wolfer-de Armas, 1973.

1930

His nephew Jean Terrasse dies.

While recovering in a clinic from an outbreak of boils and unable to paint on a large scale, explores watercolor and gouache for the first time in thirty years (plate 134).[100]

Vollard's *Sainte Monique* is published with 29 transfer lithographs, 17 original etchings, and 178 woodblocks by Bonnard. Still attracting critical notice three years later, they prompt Waldemar George to write, "The drawings he did for *Ste-Monique*, text by Ambroise Vollard, restore to us, in a pleasant form and stripped of all vain solemnity, a world which moulded our sensitivity. The 20th century painter thus rejoins the anonymous sculptors of the Gallo-Roman steles, those first craftsman [*sic*] with a national artistic vision."[101]

19 January–16 February: Seven paintings included in exhibition *Painting in Paris from American Collections* held at the Museum of Modern Art in New York, among them *Woman with Dog*, 1922, *The Riviera*, ca. 1923, and *The Palm*, 1926 (plates 96, 110, 114).

5 October–25 January 1931: Receives first one-person museum exhibition in the United States at the Phillips Memorial Gallery. The following year, writes expressing gratitude for Phillips's support: "I am touched by the interest you take in my painting despite its great flaws—I am always striving to improve my style, and I am not indifferent to the fact that the like-minded support my efforts."[102]

March–June: Is included in the Phillips Memorial Gallery's exhibition *Modern Art and Its Sources*. Writing in the accompanying catalogue, Phillips addresses the ongoing critical debate about the currency and significance of Bonnard's work to modern art: "What matters it to us if Bonnard, like Cézanne, belongs to the ages?* The New York dealers, repeating propaganda from Parisian dealers, pronounce that he is not of the hour. . . . If, however, a living painter is by turn of mind or by habit of vision imbued with even the best qualities of the generation which preceded his own, then he is what we revolted against. . . . (*Meier-Graefe, Eli Faure, Roger Fry, Clive Bell, Felix Feneon, Leon Werth, and many others, have declared that Bonnard is one of the two or three finest living artists. I am told that Matisse is of the same opinion.)."[103]

October: Is included in group exhibition with Vuillard and Roussel at Jacques Seligmann and Co. in New York, the first of many group exhibitions, beginning in the 1930s, in which his work is seen alongside that of his fellow former Nabis artist Vuillard.

November: Stays at the Villa Castellamare in the Ville d'Hiver at Arcachon for six months, during which time he paints *The Breakfast Room* (fig. 31, plate 118).

1931

Is included in the historical survey *Modern French Painting* by Adolphe Basler and Charles Kunstler, who write, "Vuillard and Bonnard, friends of Toulouse-Lautrec, evolved from impressionism a decorative style of painting, full of intimacy, nuance and charm, a style very soon approved by the advanced public. . . . An astonishing vitality supports Bonnard on the descent to old age. Far from growing old, he renews his youth ceaselessly,

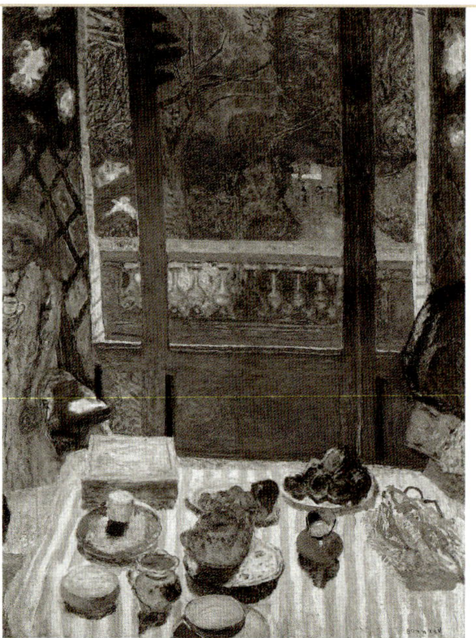

31. Pierre Bonnard, *The Breakfast Room*, ca. 1930–1931, Oil on canvas, 62⅞ × 44⅞ in. (159.6 × 113.8 cm), The Museum of Modern Art, New York. Given anonymously, 1941.

and his work flows on joyfully like an inexhaustible fountain bathed in the softest light."[104]

April: Shows six paintings in the exhibition *Van Gogh, Toulouse-Lautrec, Bonnard et son époque* organized by George Besson at the Galerie Braun, Paris.

Winter: At Le Cannet, immerses self in painting, fulfilling his long-professed desire to "escape the monotony of life,"[105] as he writes his nephew Charles Terrasse, "I am working hard, buried deeper and deeper in that old-fashioned passion for painting. Perhaps I am, with a few others, one of its last survivors. The main thing is that I am not bored."[106]

June: Moves to an apartment at 16 bis, rue Caulincourt, Paris, to which he returns intermittently for brief stays, as he explains to Pierre Courthion: "I only spend two months of the year in Paris. I come back in order to keep in touch, to compare my paintings with other paintings; in Paris, I am a critic. I cannot work there: too much noise, too many distractions. . . . I usually spend six months in the Midi and four in Normandy, in my Vernon house, where I am going to return."[107]

Looking back on his earliest painting from the age of sixteen, which he shows to Courthion, Bonnard considers how his own approach to art has changed over fifty years later: "I believe that when one is young, it is the object, the outside world that carries you away: that fills you with enthusiasm. Later, it is the interior realm, the need to express an emotion, which pushes the painter to choose this or that point of departure, this or that form."[108]

June: His exhibition at Galerie Bernheim-Jeune features twenty-six recent works (fig. 34). After seeing the exhibition, Signac writes him enthusiastically: "Prodigious. The unexpected, the rare, the new. I swear to you, dear Bonnard, that since 1880, when I 'discovered' Claude Monet, I have never had such a deep feeling. . . . What a lesson; what an encouragement. You give me renewed strength."[109]

Critics acclaim his accomplishments:

André Lhote: "Without thinking about it, Bonnard became the most abstract painter of our time."[110]

Claude Roger-Marx: "A permanent transposition, whether by line or color, the gift of forgetting the particular shade of objects, as well as the usual appearance of shapes, the art of considering each painting as a world with its own requirements— that is what moves us so greatly in those landscapes, those nudes, those still-lifes in which everything seems false from the point of view of logic and knowledge, but everything becomes right through yielding to pictorial needs."[111]

Germain Bazin: "Bonnard made his way through the art of our time as a loner. . . . [T]his great painter had for a long time a position set slightly apart. Today a great tide of opinion is becoming apparent in favor of Bonnard, and it seems . . . that many are close to considering him as the greatest master of our time. Though it took time, he exercises even now an influence on the young of which the effects are noticeable time and again in exhibits."[112]

October–December: Travels to the town of La Baule on the northern coast of France, staying at

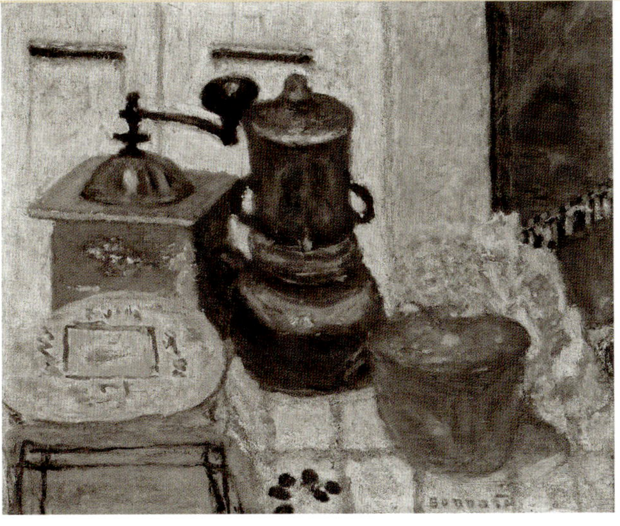

32. Pierre Bonnard, *The Coffee Grinder*, 1930, Oil on canvas, 18⅞ × 22½ in. (48 × 57 cm), Kunstmuseum Winterthur, Inv. no. 1528. Gift of Dr. Herbert and Charlotte Wolfer-de Armas, 1973.

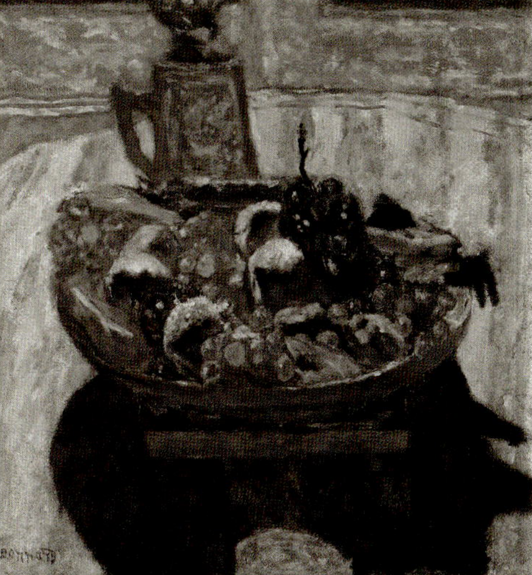

33. Pierre Bonnard, *Still Life with a Bowl of Fruit*, 1933, Oil on canvas, 22¹³⁄₁₆ × 20⅞ in. (57.9 × 53 cm), Philadelphia Museum of Art: Bequest of Lisa Norris Elkins, 1950.

the Villa Nirvana through April of the following year, his first of several lengthy stays at the seaside and resorts along the English Channel.[113]

1934

26 February–17 March: Forty-four works are represented in his solo exhibition at Wildenstein Gallery, New York, including *Nude in Bathroom* (plate 126).

Critics embrace his work:

Margaret Breuning: "Bonnard's design and his color are indivisible. His designs often suggest Persian art, for they are not organized in the solidity of structure that modern artists strive for, but are often laid delicately on the canvas as a cobweb might be so that a single inadvertent touch would seem to mar them. Or they spread out with a rhythmic beat over the canvas much as Persian miniature paintings do, yet reach an astounding soundness of balanced design."[114]

Mary Morsell: "The fullness of his vision, the delicate unfolding of the everyday world in all its luminous variety of unexpected and thrilling hues, seems only to have come at an age when most artists are vainly struggling to preserve their visual innocence."[115]

Henry McBride: "For Pierre Bonnard is an extremely fashionable Parisian painter who has never had much luck in New York. . . . This was the rough, tumultuous advent of the abstract painters, Picasso, Braque and Léger, flanked by the suave but also tumultuous Henri Matisse. They got all the headlines, they got the attention of the more daring dealers, and they ended by giving the 'tone' to the period."[116]

March: Discussed in the article "L'Epoque du symbolisme," by Denis, as "The example of a painter who remained faithful to the aesthetics of his beginnings. . . . One praises the persistent youthfulness of his most recent works."[117]

May–August: Lives in the rented Villa Grand-Liouville in Bénerville-Blonville on the Normandy coast. Thereafter stays primarily in Normandy, particularly Deauville, with brief stays in Paris and Le Cannet, until 1938. "It was Boudin who told me about Deauville. He maintained that no other place in France was so beautiful and varied, and I must say he was right."[118]

1935

1 February: In Le Cannet, exchanges thoughts with Matisse about the importance of color, writing: "I agree with you that the painter's only solid ground is the palette and colors, but as soon as the colors achieve an illusion, they are no longer judged, and the stupidities begin. For the moment I go walking in the countryside and try to see it the way a peasant does."[119]

This same month, has work featured in the *Artistes de Paris* exhibition at the Palais des Beaux-Arts, Brussels.

May: Featured in group exhibition at the Reid & Lefevre Gallery, London, which he sees on a brief visit 20–21 May.

1936

Renews his early interest in the subject of the nude with the first of three major paintings on the theme, *Nude in the Bath* (Musée d'Art Moderne de la Ville de Paris), after which follow *The Large Bath, Nude*, 1937–39 and *Nude in Bathtub*, 1941–46 (fig. 37, plates 123, 127).

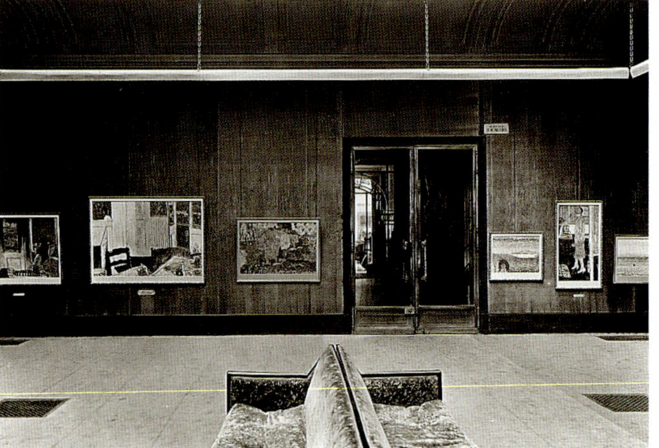

34. *Galerie Bernheim-Jeune. Installation View during the 1933 Bonnard Exhibition,* 1933, Photograph, Private collection.

Participates in the thirty-seventh exhibition of the Salon des Indépendants, from which the French state will buy his painting *Le Coin de table.*

Included in the retrospective exhibition *Peintres de La Revue blanche* in Paris organized by Bolette Natanson, daughter of Thadée and Misia.

Waldemar George professes: "Bonnard and Vuillard are therefore the last survivors of a paradise that must be reconquered. They are in our opinion like the supreme witnesses of a golden age."[120]

Begins work on *The Circus Horse*, his last major painting, which he completes in 1946.

27 April–2 September: Featured in the Museum of Modern Art's exhibition *Modern Painters and Sculptors as Illustrators.*

July: Elected an associate member of the Royal Academy of Belgium.

October: Wins second prize in the Carnegie International Exhibition in Pittsburgh.

4–30 November: Is among twelve painters exhibited by Galerie Paul Rosenberg, which shows him alongside Georges Braque (1882–1963), André Derain (1880–1954), Marie Laurencin (1885–1956), Fernand Léger (1881–1955), André Masson (1896–1987), Matisse, Pablo Picasso (1881–1973), Georges Rouault (1871–1958), Albert Marie André Dunoyer De Ségonzac (1884–1974), Maurice Utrillo (1883–1955), and Vuillard.

1937

Receives his first two solo exhibitions of drawings at the Phillips Memorial Gallery: *Drawings by Pierre Bonnard Illustrating "Histoires Naturelles" by Jules Renard,* 15–30 April and *Drawings by Pierre Bonnard*, 10 October–12 November.

Summer: In his interview at Deauville with the Swedish journalist Ingrid Rydbeck, accompanied by the photographer Rogi André, provides telling insights into his creative process and aesthetic philosophy, including his ongoing indebtedness to Japanese art. Interview is published in *Kontrevy.* While showing Rydbeck his work in progress tacked on a wall flanked by Japanese prints and set against flowered wallpaper, he says, "It's amusing to look at the pattern of this wallpaper with its shadows and relief effects, and to contrast a Western decorative concept with an Oriental one, characterized by plain, blank decorative surfaces."[121]

Later, when addressing the gouache landscapes on the opposite wall, he acknowledges his tendency to work on paintings at great length and simultaneously, keeping many in an incomplete state for some time, "These are not gouaches as one ordinarily thinks of them. . . . They are watercolors with a lot of white [paint] added in. . . . I work so slowly that I must use paints that can be revised or added to continually."[122]

June–October: Shows thirty-three paintings in *Les Maîtres de l'art indépendant, 1895–1937,* at the Musée du Petit Palais, Paris.

1938

Sells Ma Roulotte at Vernonnet.

Summer: Designs special cover for *Verve,* an arts magazine founded the previous year by Efstratios Eleftheriades Tériade, with whom he collaborates on his 1944 publication, *Correspondances.*

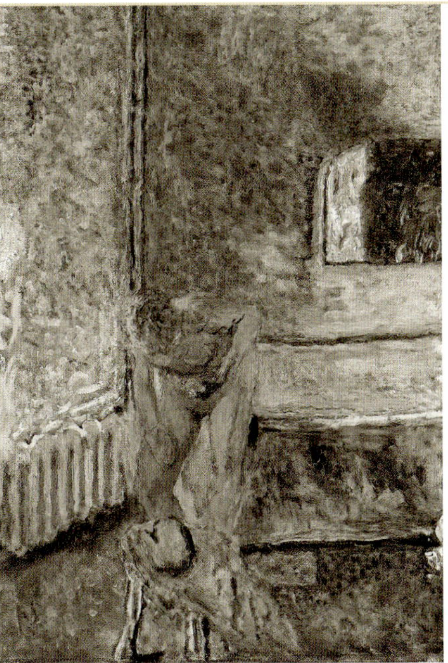

35. Pierre Bonnard, *Nude in an Interior,* ca. 1935, Oil on canvas, 28¾ × 19¾ in. (73 × 50.2 cm), The Phillips Collection, Washington, D.C.

15 December–15 January 1939: Featured in joint exhibition with Vuillard of paintings and prints at the Art Institute of Chicago, including five paintings lent by The Phillips Collection: *The Terrace*, 1918; *The Open Window*, 1921; *Woman with Dog*, 1922; *The Riviera*, ca. 1923, and *The Palm*, 1926 (plates 86, 93, 96, 110, 114). Touting him as "the only living affinity of Renoir," the critic Julius Meier-Graefe argues, "this painter par excellence still belongs to the 1890s, the period when he began to work with a group of young men who had renounced the easel in order to produce decorative objects. . . . The propensity for decoration remained with Bonnard, in great contrast to Renoir."[123]

1939

Works on *Studio with Mimosas*, his last major painting of an interior scene, which he completes in 1946 (fig. 38, plate 131).

24 March: While back in Paris from Le Cannet, moves to 2, place de la Porte-des-Ternes, his last apartment in Paris.

March: Receives a fifty-one painting retrospective at Svensk-Franska Konstgalleriet in Stockholm; the Swedish Royal Academy of Fine Arts elects him a foreign member in April.

May: Participates in Galerie Durand-Ruel's group exhibition, where he is put forward by Albert Charpentier as "the impressionist one hundred per cent: the painter of the moment which slips away."[124]

July–August: Makes his last visits to Normandy, staying at Trouville.

10 September: Travels to Le Cannet from Paris, to which he will not return until the end of World War II

1940

Ceases to travel between northern and southern France, settling in Le Bosquet, in Le Cannet, where he remains and paints until the end of his life. Six of his paintings are sold with Félix Fénéon's collection.

January: Receives visit from Matisse, who finds his work "surer than ever." Bonnard responds, "When I think of you, I think of a mind cleansed of every old aesthetic convention, and it is that alone that permits a direct view of nature, the greatest joy that can befall a painter."[125]

4 February: Anticipating his visit with Matisse in Nice, writes, "I very much need to see another kind of painting besides my own."[126]

April: Through Augustus John's (1878–1961) nomination, elected Honorary Academician by the Royal Academy of Arts, London.

21 June: Vuillard dies at La Baule.

1 September: Reflects on his symbolist origins and his long-deceased friend, writing in his diary: "Mallarmé. Searching for the absolute."[127]

1941

His portrait is painted by Kostia Terechkovitch (1902–1978), who later publishes an account of their sittings at Le Bosquet.[128]

End of February: Facing food shortages because of the war, writes Matisse, "As for moving to some palatial hotel for a little material comfort, I would lose what constitutes the basis of my existence and my kind of work: the constant contact with nature."[129]

March: His brother Charles dies in Algeria.

1938–1941

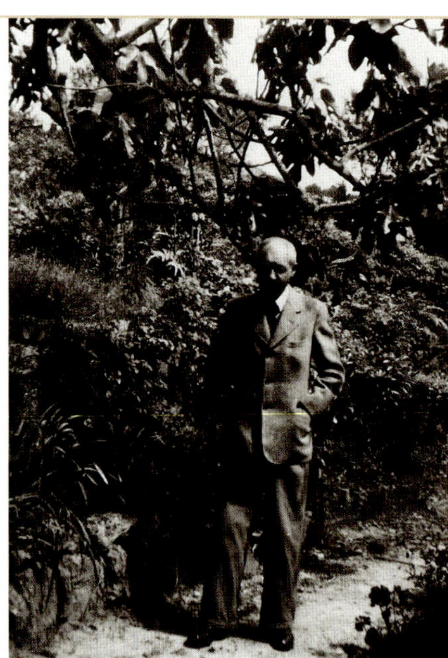

36. *Bonnard in the Garden of Le Bosquet*, 1942, Photograph, Private collection.

18 October: His "Souvenirs sur Renoir" are published in *Comœdia*.

As part of a project commissioned by Parisian gallery owner and publisher Louis Carré, begins a series of eleven gouaches from which Jacques Villon makes transfer lithographs. Working closely with Villon over the next four years, oversees the entire process.[130]

26 January: His wife, Marthe, dies. Isolated from family members due to the war, finds the loss "unbearable. . . . After all, it's impossible to paint all the time, and around five o'clock in the evening I start wandering aimlessly opening empty cupboards, going upstairs only to come down. The time passes endlessly."[131] "You can imagine my grief and my solitude, filled with bitterness and worry about the life I may be leading from now on," he writes Matisse (fig. 36).[132]

3–31 March: Has exhibition of drawings, watercolors, and engravings at the Weyhe Gallery in New York, from which Phillips buys the drawings *Ants*, 1904 (plate 64), *Grasshoppers*, 1904 (plate 63), *Canaries*, 1904. (plate 62), *The Woodchopper*, 1904, and *Cows Under a Tree*, n.d.

December: Suffering from severe fatigue, spends most of the month in a clinic in Cannes, where he is placed on a special diet.[133]

Admitted to the hospital owing to congestion of the lungs.

Jean and Henry Dauberville begin to compile a catalogue raisonné of the artist's oil paintings, which is published in 1965.

January: The magazine *Le Point* devotes a special issue to his work, examining the development of his career, with articles by Maurice Denis, René Marie (Francis Jourdain), George Besson, and Charles Terrasse.

His old classmate from the Académie Julian, Denis, writes, "his painting remains young and faithful to the youthful spirit of his first works. . . . He is the most modern and advanced of today's painters."[134]

Noting his elusiveness as an artist who "speaks little, explains little, and does not write," George Besson, art critic and longtime friend of Bonnard since 1909, notes how Bonnard takes his studio with him wherever he goes, with daily life serving as his point of departure: "Bonnard has had a studio in Montmartre nearly forever. He uses empty barns and warehouses. But his true studio is anywhere and everywhere: in furnished villas and hotel rooms with indescribable decor—often a cheap light fixture in the ceiling, always that flowered wallpaper, which the paintings covered over, little by little."[135]

23 January: Interviewed by Marguette Bouvier for her article "Pierre Bonnard, revient à la lithographie" in *Comœdia*, who declares the seventy-five-year-old, "at the age when Renoir and Cézanne won their most beautiful victories," adding, "his slenderness, his ivory skin, his little rounded head, makes one think of a Japanese."[136]

15 May: André Giverny's conversation with the artist is published in *La France libre*, providing an account of the modest and spare conditions and daily rituals under which Bonnard produced such grand paintings. "There are only two large Renoir

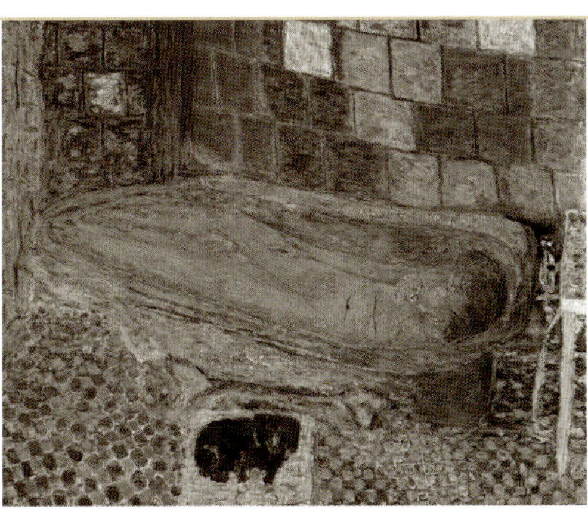

37. Pierre Bonnard, *Nude in Bathtub*, 1941–1946, Oil on canvas, 48 × 59½ in. (121.9 × 151.1 cm), Carnegie Museum of Art, Pittsburgh. Acquired through the generosity of the Sarah Mellon Scaife Family, 1970.

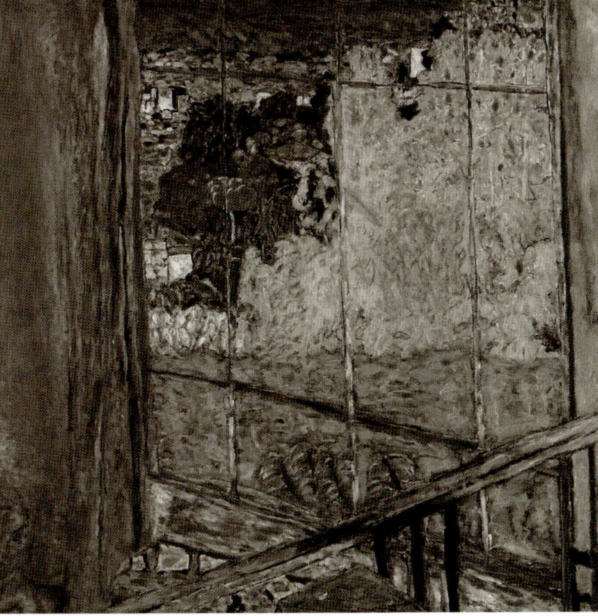

38. Pierre Bonnard, *Studio with Mimosas*, 1939–October 1946, Oil on canvas, 50 × 50 in. (127.5 × 127.5 cm), Centre Georges Pompidou, Paris. Musée National d'Art Moderne/Centre de Création Industrielle.

lithographs on the wall," Giverny observes on entering Bonnard's house through the dining room. Later viewing his studio, he notes, "In this very limited space, big canvases pinned up on the wall are in the process of being completed." Bonnard recounts to him his typical day at Le Cannet: "I go for a walk very early in the morning, I go behind Le Cannet, it's still untamed, and I reflect, then around 10, I return and I work."[137]

10 July: During a visit from Gaston Diehl at Le Cannet, reveals major philosophical underpinnings of his art, which Diehl publishes in "Pierre Bonnard: dans son univers enchanté" in *Comœdia*. "All art is in the composition; it is the key to everything. The power of invention resides more in the composition and the sense of proportions," Bonnard is quoted as saying.[138]

November: Maurice Denis dies.

1944

Correspondances, a book recording childhood memories through fictionalized letters exchanged with his family, is published by Tériade (fig. 39). Also includes twenty-eight pencil and pen drawings purportedly from his youth but made at this time. Bonnard confides his concern about the book's reception: "I am simultaneously looking forward to and fearing the publication of my little manuscript. I wonder if it will be greeted with a lack of interest."[139]

Five articles in *Formes et couleurs* are devoted to his work, written by Jean René Bazaine, Stanislas Fumet, Jacques Laprade, Charles Terrasse, and André Lhote. In his article "Gravures, illustrations, dessins de Pierre Bonnard," Laprade looks back to the artistic climate of the 1890s in which Bonnard launched his career, reflecting, "He escapes from a neglected door. The one of posters, illustrations, lithographs. . . . The illustrator prevails so well . . . over the painter. . . . I believe that the practice of lithography taught Bonnard the science of choosing rare tones and reducing their numbers to the extreme."[140]

Assessing Bonnard's work within the current political and artistic climate of nonfigurative art, Lhote addresses the modernity of Bonnard's painterly vision, noting, "his works turn to abstraction, that is to say, give prominence to . . . the purest values of painting."[141]

June: Ker-Xavier Roussel dies.

24 September: Aristide Maillol dies.

5–20 December: His graphic work exhibited at Pierre Berès's gallery presents *Correspondances* for the first time. Although exhibited apart, his graphic work conjures up an immediate association with his paintings, according to the critic Louis Parrot, who writes, "the graphic artist and the illustrator equal the painter *chez* Bonnard."[142]

1945

July: After the end of the war in France in May, makes first trip to Paris since 1939. Visits the contemporary French paintings exhibition at the Château Fontainebleau organized by Charles Terrasse, the museum's curator; the show includes ten of his paintings alongside works by Braque, Matisse, and Kees van Dongen (1877–1968)—from private collections and the Galerie Bernheim-Jeune, which had stored them during the war at the château. Returns later that year to Le Cannet with

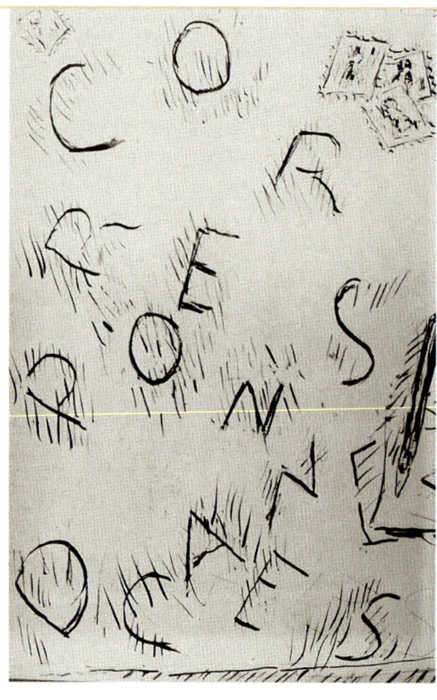

39. Pierre Bonnard, Cover for *Correspondances*, 1944, Heliogravure after ink drawing, 12 × 8⅝ in. (30.5 × 21.9 cm), The Phillips Collection Archives, Washington, D.C.

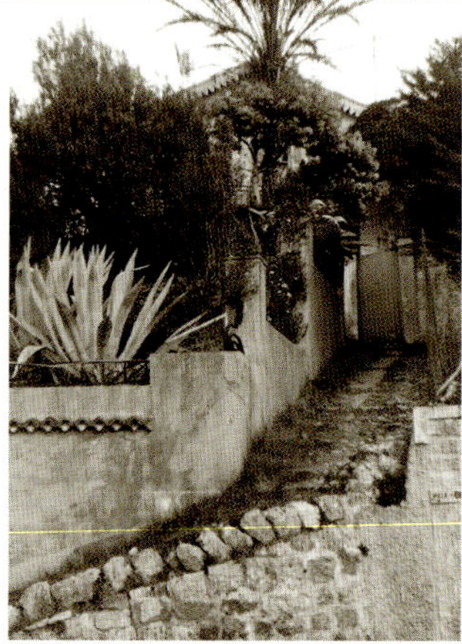

40. Henri Cartier-Bresson, *Path to Villa Le Bosquet at Le Cannet*, 1945, Photograph.

his niece, Renée Terrasse, who settles nearby.[143]

His home and studio at Le Cannet are photographed by Henri Cartier-Bresson (see pp. 6–10, figs. 40, 41, 42).

1946

Spring: Begins what will be his last painting, *Blossoming Almond Tree* (plate 132), based on the view of the tree from his bedroom window, a subject that, according to Charles Terrasse, "entranced and delighted him. . . . almost every year he would paint his almond tree in blossom. Possibly never had the tree been clad in a more sumptuous array of blossoms than it was that spring, as if it wanted to promise the painter pleasant and gentle days. Bonnard painted it one more time with passion and enthusiasm. . . . he had never painted as freely or as spontaneously before."[144]

June–July: Returns to Paris to see his large exhibition at Galerie Bernheim-Jeune, its first postwar show, which Jean and Henry Dauberville (Josse Bernheim-Jeune's sons) have devoted entirely to his works, covering the period 1898–1945. Attends the first major exhibition of nonfigurative art in France at the Salon des Réalités Nouvelles. Visits Louis Carré's gallery, where he meets his early critic André Lhote and the artists Jean Bazaine (1904–2001), Marc Chagall (1887–1985), and Jacques Villon. Visits the Musée du Louvre at the invitation of its director, Georges Salles, accompanied by the curator Jean Leymarie, where he admires the view of the riverside quays in the evening light. "The most beautiful things in museums are the windows," he tells Leymarie.[145]

August: Receives a visit from Brassaï at Le Cannet, who photographs his studio, including the wall on which Bonnard has tacked images ranging from a small painting by Renoir to reproductions of antique sculpture and paintings by Jan Vermeer (1632–1675), Monet, Gauguin, Seurat, and Picasso to Japanese woodcuts (fig. 43).

Agrees to a large retrospective in 1947 to be organized by the Museum of Modern Art, New York, in celebration of his eightieth birthday. The retrospective takes place in Cleveland and New York between March 1947 and September 1948.

October: Travels to Paris, staying a few days at Fontainebleau, where he finishes two major paintings, *Studio with Mimosas* (fig. 38, plate 131) and *The Circus Horse*.

December: Takes part in the exhibition *Le Noir est une couleur* at Aimé Maeght's.

1947

January: Still dissastisfied with the lower portion of his painting *Blossoming Almond Tree* (plate 132), instructs Charles Terrasse to change the green there to yellow. "The green of that bit of ground on the bottom on the left is not as it should be. It needs yellow."[146]

23 January: Dies at Le Cannet.

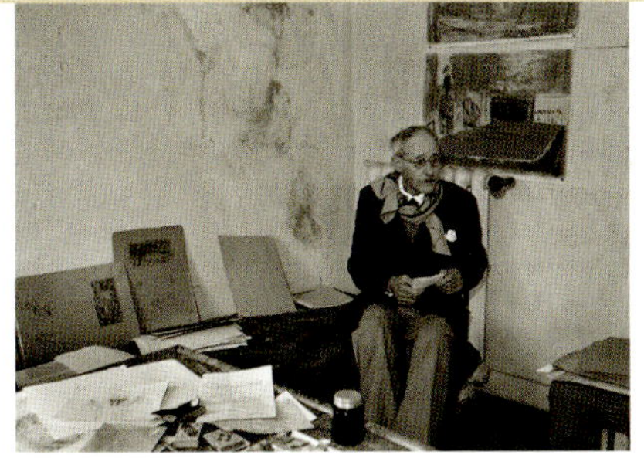

41. Henri Cartier-Bresson, *Bonnard Seated, Sketching at Le Cannet*, 1945, Photograph.

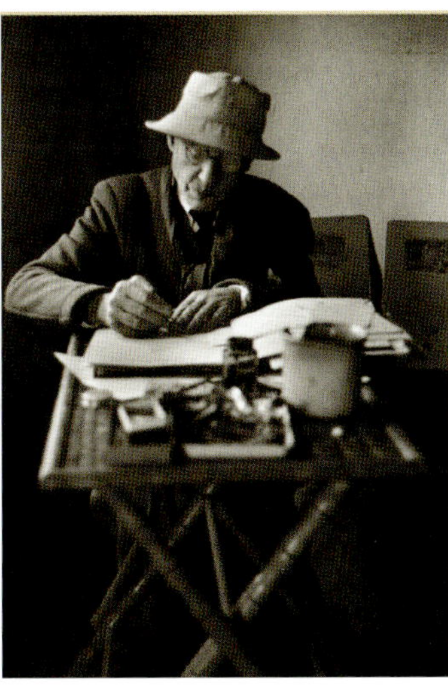

42. Henri Cartier-Bresson, *Bonnard Seated, Drawing*, 1946, Photograph.

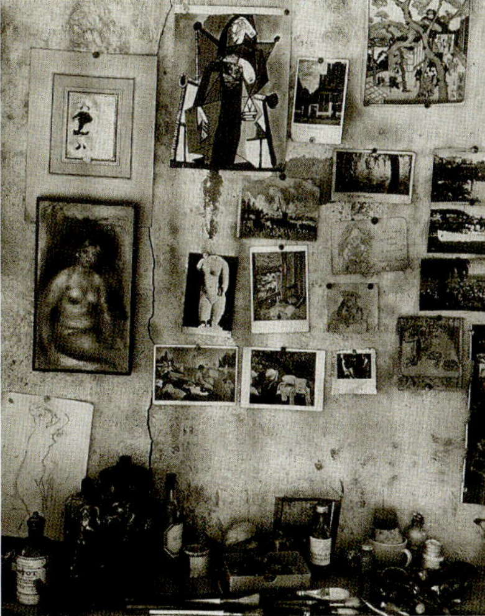

43. Gilberte Brassaï, *Bonnard's Studio Wall at Le Cannet*, 1946, Private collection.

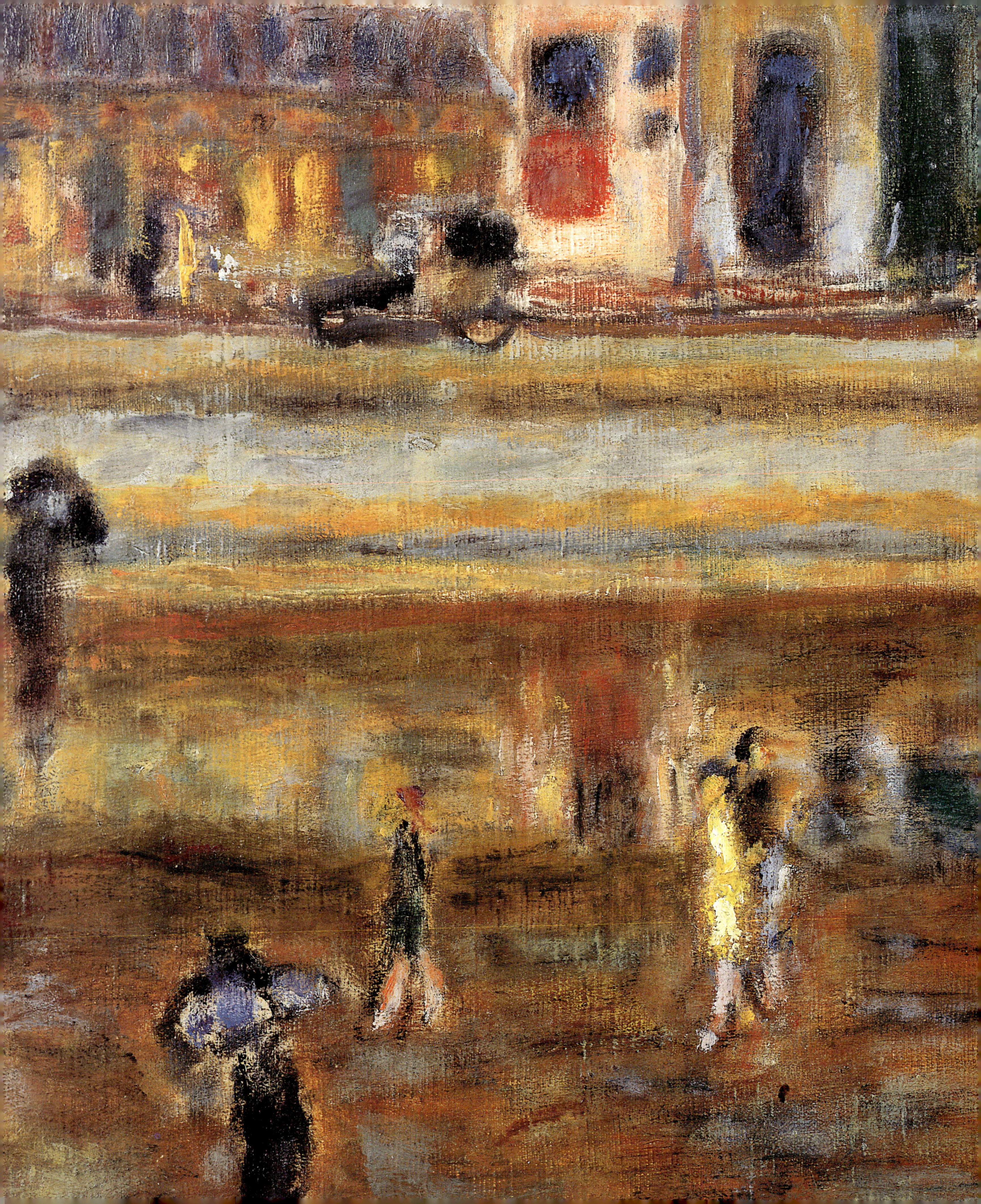

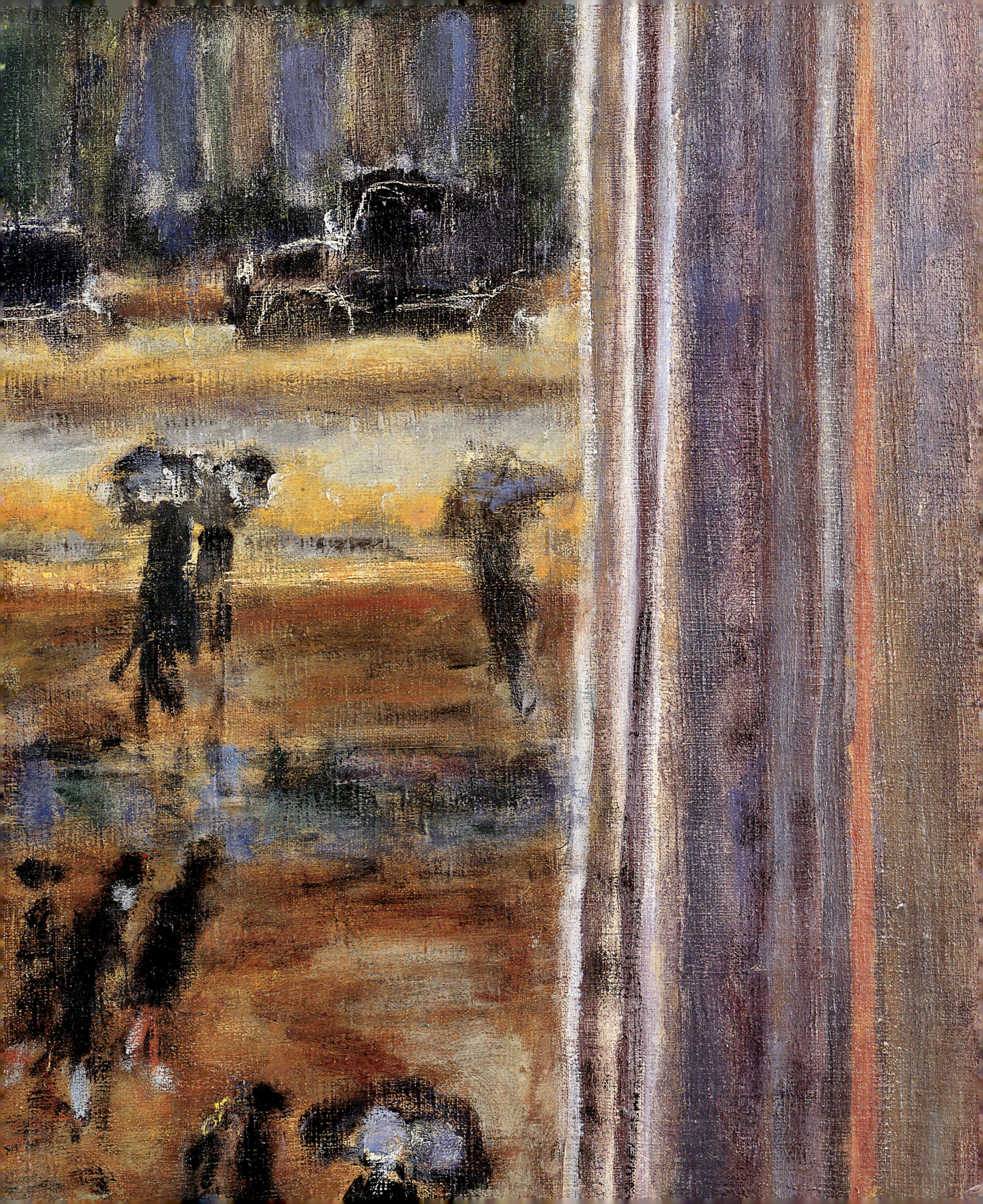

The Imaginary Cinema of Pierre Bonnard

Elizabeth Hutton Turner

Previous spread:
*Boulevard des
Batignolles* (detail),
1926, Oil on canvas,
24¾ × 25⅝ in.
(62.9 × 65.1 cm),
Private collection,
Washington, D.C.

I do not belong to any school. I am only trying to do something personal, and I
am trying to unlearn, at this moment, what I worked so hard to learn during the
four years at the Ecole de Beaux-Arts. Pierre Bonnard, 1891[1]

Pierre Bonnard's diverse art—his prints, his book illustrations, and his paintings
are explorations of a single question: How do we see?[2] Like Edgar Degas before
him, Bonnard brought new ways of seeing and novel procedures to painting, a new
awareness of time and space registered in new color and composition. For most
viewers, Bonnard has assumed preeminence as a master of color. Many have seen
and named his colors; many have savored the intimate psychology of his spaces.
Few, however, have explored the importance of his periodic bouts of questioning
and relearning. What Bonnard chose to forget and how he retaught himself to
paint constitute the profile of a radical artist who for the most part drops out of
the avant-garde after the advent of Cubism. This is the Bonnard who traveled
incognito in the twentieth century once he adopted the light ground and brighter
colors of Impressionism. This is the Bonnard who forged a union between external
and internal reality. This is the Bonnard who built a bridge between Claude
Monet's Impressionism and Stéphane Mallarmé's Symbolism. Anointed as the
defender of painting by his friends in the School of Paris, this is nevertheless the
Bonnard whose canvases created a playground for the eye and mind with tools
worthy of the dadaists and surrealists: namely a fantasy of painting with light.

A Riddle of Seeing

Bonnard discussed his thinking about painting only late in his career. In 1927 Bonnard's first published statement about his experience of vision combines a vivid analogy to the camera's lens with a disavowal of the value of static photography:

> The lens records unnecessary lights and shadows, but the artist's eyes add human values to objects and reproduce them as seen through human eyes. Moreover, this visual image is mobile. Moreover, this visual image is variable. I am standing in a corner of the room near a table bathed in sunlight. Distant masses look almost linear, without volume or depth. Close objects, however, rise up toward my eyes. The sides run straight. This vanishing is sometimes linear (in the distance) and sometimes curved (in the foreground). The distance looks flat. It is the foreground that gives us our concept of the world as seen through human eyes, of a world of undulations, or of convexities and concavities.[3]

Embedded in this observation is the acknowledgment of the reflexive distortions that come with transforming visual reality into a picture—a process of holding a mirror to the light known since the earliest camera. Bonnard's roving eye slips in and out of focus much like the objects in his description of the room as they are received from one source and projected onto another. Bonnard required the same roving freedom to explore light-filled spaces in paint. What did he say about the desired effect? "A painting is a series of marks that join together to form an object or work, the unit over which one's eye wanders without obstruction."[4] How did Bonnard's photographic eye, his internal camera, affirm the painter's touch? Did each apparation coming from the light in some way share the same essence?[5]

The unexpected and untraditional properties of mechanical vision, like the snap of the shutter of the lens, made their way into Bonnard's thinking accompanied by an obsession to return to the root of perception, what he much later called "finding again the first sensation."[6] To import this experience into his art, Bonnard knew that he needed to operate outside the confines of the way he had been taught to paint. In 1891 he declared his independence: "I do not belong to any school. I am only trying to do something personal, and I am trying to unlearn, at this moment, what I worked so hard to learn during the four years at the Ecole de Beaux-Arts."[7] In fact, Bonnard had spent the four years since graduation from the *lycée* in law school. Painting, as taught at the Ecole, was resistible, something he told his father, that he could pick up and put down at will in the evenings and in the summer. What liberated and empowered Bonnard, along with his compatriots Maurice Denis, Ker-Xavier Roussel, and Edouard Vuillard, to dispose of the Ecole and to devise their own paths came in the form of a story.

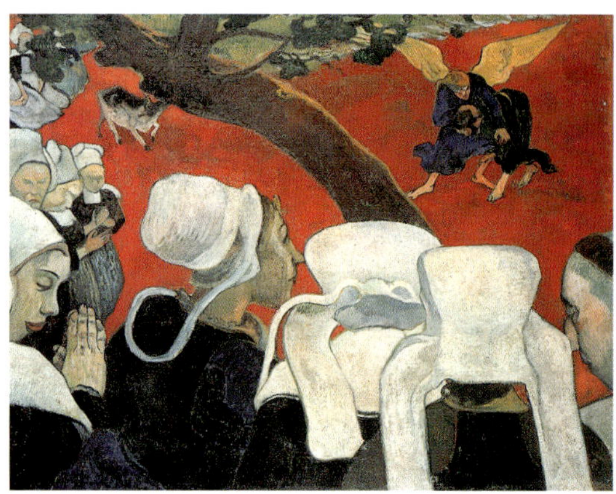

44. Paul Gauguin, *The Vision after the Sermon*, 1888, Oil on canvas, 28¾ × 36¼ in. (73 × 92 cm), National Gallery of Scotland.

Paul Sérusier, prefect at the Académie Julian, came back from his summer in Pont-Aven in Brittany in October 1888 with a small painting composed of small dabs of color to signify his initiation into the way of a new master. Sérusier explained how Paul Gauguin had set him down in the landscape and asked him, "What colour do you see that tree? is it green? then use green, the finest green on your palette. And that shadow? It's blue, if anything? don't be afraid to paint it as blue as you possibly can."[8] The story, meant to engage the imagination in a kind of time travel back to the root of perception and its relationship to the origins of language, called on ancient wisdom as known through the teachings of Kakki from the Song dynasty in fifth-century China. "The wise teacher set him down before rock and clouds, and asked what he saw." The question, meant to make the student accountable only to his own perception, left the mind free to build up its own subtle affinities with things.[9] Like Gauguin, Bonnard adopted Eastern aesthetics. The flat color and strong lines in Gauguin's *The Vision after the Sermon* (fig. 44) are indebted to Hokusai's figure sketches called *Manga* in much the same way one might, as Paul Signac said, "trace the outline" in Bonnard's *France-Champagne* poster and find the posture of a geisha by Utamaro.[10]

Looking back on this early period, Bonnard found it very important to see ukiyo-e, their shared source of inspiration, as operating in the present tense.[11]

> In the department store, for one or two pennies, I found *crépons* or crumpled rice papers in astonishing colors. I filled the walls of my room with this naïve and gaudy art. In fact, Gauguin and Sérusier have mentioned this in the past. But these things that I had there in front of me were extremely skillful and lively. I understood immediately from those crude images that color could express all things without needing modeling or relief. It seemed to me then that it was possible to translate light, form, and character with nothing more than color.[12]

Bonnard's attraction to *ukiyo-e*, the Japanese depictions of everyday life, was commensurate with his desire to discover nonhabitual ways of seeing.[13] Japanese systems of depiction fused the momentary view with decorative arrangement.[14] Its forms and patterns acknowledged the flux of visual experience.[15] The forms do not define, they contrast (see fig. 92). Their relationships are not fixed, as Clive Bell once noted, "not built up masonry wise" as in Western painting, but remain equivocal, fluid, like the new stream of visual contingencies in contemporary life.[16]

This "alive," "unprivileged" conception of ukiyo-e, a popular as opposed to academic conception, put Bonnard on the street or across the room or at the table with patterns to capture "the casual and the chaotic."[17] In his paintings, a black undulation of dogs tumble on a green rug (plate 7); the tall, serpentine figure of his sister Andrée at table picks up her fork and puts it down, accompanied by the mimicking motion of the cat's paw (plate 3); the checkered array of his cousin Berthe Schaedlin out for a stroll bends forward to pat an errant dog (plate 6). Beyond or partially behind Bonnard's obvious decorative configurations resides his own reality play. As Félix Fénéon observed, " Bonnard likes to develop his composition behind an arabesque motif which partly conceals it."[18] Bonnard understood, as perhaps no other artist except Degas, that the pictorial spaces of ukiyo-e did not contain the form but literally enacted the artist's observation of it. Form and process then became inextricably linked to the content of his vision.

Bonnard made his practice of "intimism," what he called "a taste for everyday spectacles" and "the ability to draw emotion from the most modest acts of life,"[19] dependent on his ability to foreshorten the space and to frame the encounter. Finding the angle or creating an oblique line of vision permitted him to choose whether to place himself inside or outside the frame.[20] He chose whether to be seen or not to be seen. He chose whether or not to be obscured.[21] Varying the viewing distance suited his nervous reticence—what Thadée Natanson described as Bonnard's proclivity "to walk fast" or "to flee" or "to find the bottom of a chair."[22] At the point where "method nourished instinct," Bonnard's ability to create a living ukiyo-e, like street photography, became possible.

Given his appreciation of the Japanese print, it is not surprising to find that Bonnard made his early breakthroughs in printmaking, not painting. There was a moment in 1891 when everyone was asking for his *France-Champagne* poster.[23] At one point in 1893, Bonnard could envision supporting himself by making and selling special-edition prints, as he told his family, "for the foreseeable future."[24] Printmaking was the open road, untrammeled by convention with all the necessary accommodations along the way. Many of the printers, publishers, and dealers, including most notably Edouard Ancourt, Thadée Natanson, and Ambroise Vollard, would make their mark on his résumé. Bonnard engaged in every genre of printed image available to the progressive artist: posters, music sheet covers, multiartist albums, book covers, and text illustrations. He rode the wave of rapidly evolving machine-made graphic languages, including new color printing as well as the photo processes. Watching "the transfer from the fixed matrix of one surface to another" trained him to think of the entire composition in terms of fewer colors and their equivalents.[25] Restricting the number of his colors to four, as in color printing, led to his close study of relationships among hues, as he said, "either superimposed or set side by side."[26] He appreciated the new and often surprising transformations achieved by the machine intercessor. In many ways Bonnard's artistic development can be gauged by his appropriation of new discoveries in lithography.

In printing there was something to engage the imagination of the child.

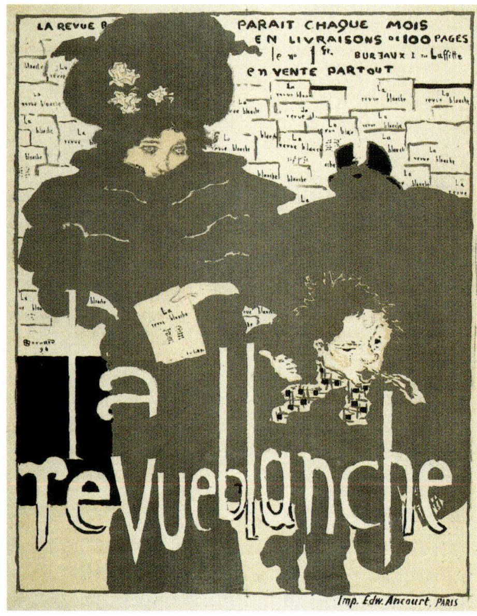

45. Pierre Bonnard, Poster for *La Revue blanche*, 1894, Lithograph printed in four colors, 31⁵⁄₁₆ × 24 ⁷⁄₁₆ in. (79.5 × 62 cm), Museum of Fine Arts, Boston. Bequest of W. G. Russell Allen, 1960 60.65.

46. Pierre Bonnard, *Nannies' Promenade, Frieze of Carriages*, 1895; published 1899, Lithograph printed in five colors, mounted on four-fold screen, each panel approximately 59⅞ × 19⅞ in. (151.8 × 50.5 cm), Museum of Fine Arts, Boston. Ernest W. Longfellow Fund, 1976 1976.605.

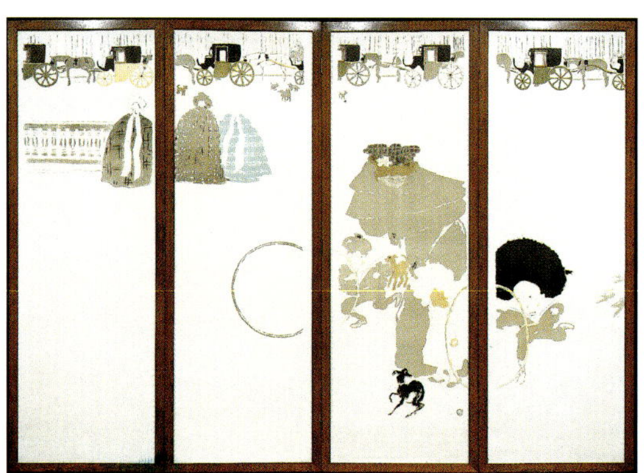

Accompanying the lessons of the *Petit Solfège illustré* (1893), a music book collaboration with his brother-in-law, the composer Claude Terrasse, amalgams of dabs, dots, and dashes, even shadows unfold faces and figures of teachers and students, audiences, and performances in, around, and through the margins (plates 14a–b). They conflate the sights and symbols with the rhythms of music. The openly seductive patterns of Bonnard's advertising posters similarly liberated the adult imagination. In the poster for *France-Champagne* the waitress topples forward, proffering her glass as if about to be carried into the street on crenellated foam (plate 5). Remarking on Bonnard's "cruel and serpentine eroticism," Fénéon jokingly speculated about the possibilities if Bonnard should ever be asked to advertise the circus or the Moulin Rouge.[27]

In 1894, when Thadée Natanson commissioned a poster for *La Revue blanche* (1894), Bonnard provided yet another visual installment for the adventurous passerby and, in so doing, answered Fénéon (fig. 45, plate 23).[28] Bonnard's advertisement provocatively displayed the chance encounter of an approaching woman, a street urchin, and a departing flâneur as they pass a newsstand selling *La Revue blanche.* What was being advertised? Out of the mélange of letters, capes, top hat, and umbrella reiterating the words *La Revue blanche* comes the seduction of a flashing glance from the woman who holds her own copy of the review. Her staring eyes, incised features, still as a photograph, are not unlike the symbolist portraits of his contemporary from Brussels, Fernand Khnopff (fig. 47).[29] Perhaps, at that moment Bonnard associated the instantaneity of photography with Bergson's "sudden intuition" and the arresting of time and memory. The unforgettable face of the woman with *La Revue blanche* captures the attention and provokes or implies a scenario. Ultimately, she advertises no more than her suggestion.[30] Bonnard would later expand on the psychology of the gaze. His 1926 painting entitled *The Palm*, for example, advertises his picture postcard view from his new home in the Midi with the "come hither" gaze of a violet lady holding out an apple standing against the pink-ochre of the shaded garden path (fig. 48, plate 110). For the time being in the 1890s, however, Bonnard continued to follow the movement in the street for graphic fluency.

Eighth Wonder of the World

In 1894 Bonnard wrote to his mother, "I'm making a screen for the Champ des Mars [Salon des Indépendants]. In any case it will be for the present time the eighth wonder of the world." Bonnard's screen staged a woman with her clutch of children—two boys running with wheeling hoops and a toddling child crossing the vast, white expanse of the place de la Concorde, as he told his mother, "when it is dusty and resembles a little Sahara."[31] Rendered first in distemper, next transferred to large lithographic stones for an edition of one hundred, to be sure the six-foot-long and five-foot-tall, four-paneled screen was a technical marvel (fig. 46, plate 24). Yet the screen is perhaps most remarkable for the open silences of the empty paper. Only by way of his total mastery of compositional space could the barest rhythms, the strategic placements of stripes and checks, the rippling of a single mark or half a form be seen as a picture.

Divided in four stanzas by way of wooden frames surrounding each of the four panels, the composition reads erratically, as if the scene were lines of an errant and immense zigzag poem jumping frame to frame, only to double back and spill forward. The eye tracks the space as follows: start along the long horizon of repeating carriages and horses facing left; jump down to enter again advancing left through the first and second panels along the balustrade which is extended by the line of the capes of three nursemaids waiting; jump down to second panel a bit lower down to find advancing from the right the half circle of the spinning hoop of the little boy whom we engage at eye level; in the third panel slide down the contours of shuffling leg and feet to the hoop of the second boy in the fourth panel; there a black hat lobs us high and back to the third panel to the black hat of the woman bending down and pointing in an effort to avert the oncoming collision with the little black dog who ironically at the end of the sequence seizes the dramatic focus.

The large lithographic screen, Bonnard's so-called eighth wonder, aspired to occupy the entire visual field of the spectator in real time in much the same way as shadows moving through light-filled gauze played out their parts at the Théâtre des Ombres at Le Chat noir. Embedded in the patterns of Bonnard's prints resides the seemingly simultaneous translation of direct observation and indirect perception of motion. Therein lies the visual kindling of Bonnard's mature artistic signature. What remained was to ignite it with a new graphic translation of light.[32]

Cinematograph: Writing Movement with Light

Bonnard said he formed a concrete realization of his mature approach in the summer of 1895 at Le Grand-Lemps. As he later told Raymond Cogniat, "One day, the words and theories that were the foundation of our conversations—color, harmony, the relation between line and tone, balance—lost their abstract significance and became very concrete. I had understood what I was seeking and how I would try to obtain it."[33]

Bonnard knew about the cinematograph soon after it was invented in 1895. Through his brother-in-law Claude Terrasse, he had met the brothers Auguste and Louis Lumière from Lyon. They spent time in the summers at Bonnard's family home at Le Grand-Lemps.[34] The Lumière camera, which unfolded into three parts, had three functions: it took the picture; it processed the picture; and it projected the picture with remarkable fluency, from 16 up to 18 frames per second, far surpassing the staccato flicker of Thomas Edison's kinetscope.[35]

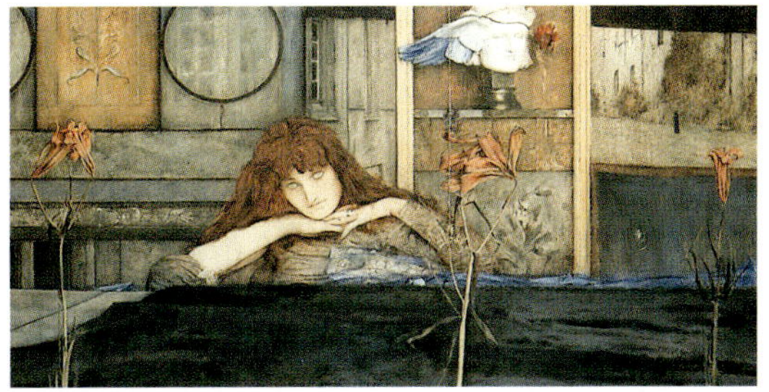

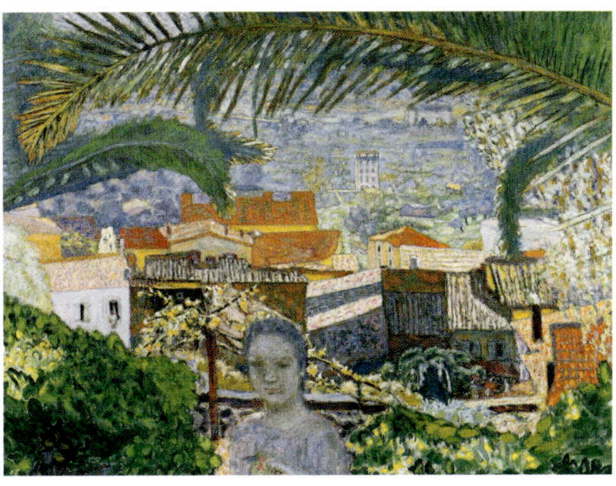

47. Fernand Khnopff, *I Lock the Door upon Myself*, 1891, Oil on canvas, 28⁵⁄₁₆ × 55¹⁄₈ in. (72 × 140 cm), Bayerische Staatsgemälde-sammlungen, Neue Pinakothek Munich.

48. Pierre Bonnard, *The Palm*, 1926, Oil on canvas, 45 × 57⁷⁄₈ in. (114.3 × 147 cm), The Phillips Collection, Washington, D.C.

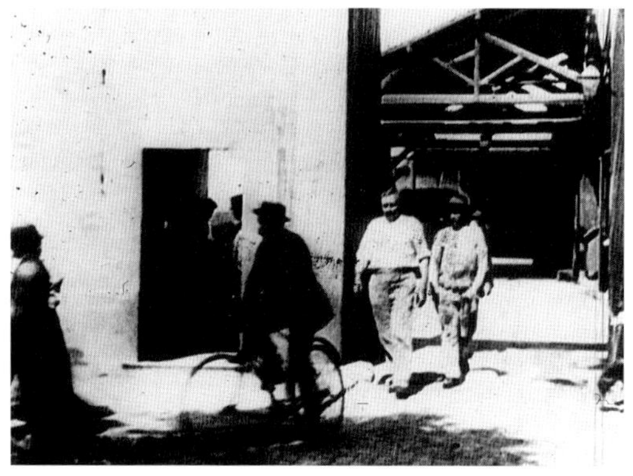 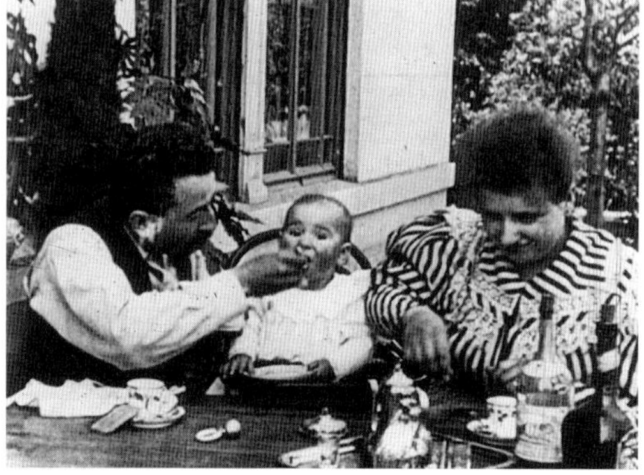 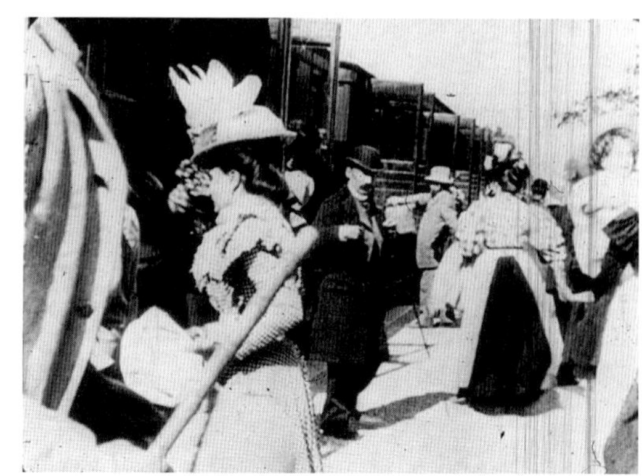

49. Louis Lumière, La Société Lumière, Scene from *La Sortie des usines*, 1895, Frame enlargement, From the Collections of the Motion Picture and Television Reading Room, Library of Congress, Washington, D.C.

50. Louis Lumière, La Société Lumière, Scene from *Le Repas de bébé*, 1895, Frame enlargement, From the Collections of the Motion Picture and Television Reading Room, Library of Congress, Washington, D.C.

51. Louis Lumière, La Société Lumière, Scene from *Arrivée d'un train en gare de la Ciotat*, 1895, Frame enlargement, From the Collections of the Motion Picture and Television Reading Room, Library of Congress, Washington, D.C.

The first film, screened in Lyon in June 1895, shows workers coming out of the gates of the Lumière factory, among them quite surprisingly, a dog, a horse, and a man on a bicycle. The figures walk across the street and out of the frame (fig. 49). Other subjects for films that year included feeding the baby (fig. 50) and the pranks of two men with a garden hose. Another, the demolition of a wall, was mistakenly shown in reverse at the time it was projected and thus depicted the sudden re-gathering of the tumbling wall. A year of explorations culminated on 28 December 1895 with the showing of *Arrivée d'un train en gare de la Ciotat,* which depicted the rush of the approaching train, the doors opening, and hurried travelers on the platform (fig. 51). Together the films constitute a stunning celebration of daily life; the ordinary suddenly becoming extraordinary through the unexpected incident.[36]

Bonnard—the prodigious noticer, the relisher of accident—clearly would have recognized aspects of his own ambitions in the operation of this machine. If his large lithographic screen unfolded space like the Sahara, the cinematograph projected (literally spread) images over time and on a single surface in shimmering white light (fig. 46, plate 24). In January 1896 Gustave Geffroy, on the occasion of Bonnard's one-man show at Galerie Durand-Ruel, named the common denominator: "A curious line in movement, of a monkey-like suppleness, captures these casual gestures of the streets, these fleeting expressions born and vanished in an instant. It is the poetry of a life that is past, the remembrance of things, of animals, of human beings."[37] Given the predisposition evident in his pictures, what did the new reality of moving pictures portend for Bonnard?

Bonnard's course of action presents itself most clearly with a new style of drawing, which, like the cinematograph, would literally write the movement of the light. In Vollard's album, *Some Scenes of Parisian Life,* scribbled textures of lithographic crayon overlaid with varying transparencies of ink and color graphically mete out cycles of day and night and weather in the city. It can be followed best in the light streaking yellow from the shop windows across the scratchy pavement of rain-drenched streets or in the agitated dimness of the milling pedestrians seen from a window overlooking the narrow street (plate 32). Bonnard's new light-ensnaring lines that incise bold shapes and contrasts probe most deeply in *Child with Lamp* (ca. 1897) (plate 28), done probably in preparation for Vollard's unrealized album.[38] The little child's face and forearm are bleached white beneath the green-black arc of the lamp. On the orange tabletop just within reach, she tumbles red and green trucks. Her play on the bright orange stage has no audience. The thin, inky diffusion of tan, green, and orange beyond the stage filters toward the uncertain boundaries of the print perimeter. Visible through the dimness on the wall resides an effervescence of dots and scratches like the memory of childhood's version of Lascaux. Like the child in lamplight, Bonnard toyed with the idea of graphically writing the light. He resisted the opacities of modeled color. He invoked reality with only the simplest residue of shadow and movement. In so doing he pushed himself outside the conventional standards of painting and managed to go beyond what his compatriots could understand. An offended and impatient Camille Pissarro wrote his son, that he and his fellow painters including Puvis de Chavannes, Degas, Pierre-Auguste Renoir, and Monet saw Bonnard's show at Durand-Ruel as "hideous," "a complete fiasco."[39] Just how much further was Bonnard willing to push conventions into the realm of simplicity and shadow?

Illustrator of Ubu

> The *Grand almanach illustré* was composed in the rue Laffitte cellar. Everyone knows that Alfred Jarry wrote the text, Bonnard illustrated it, and Claude Terrasse created the music, while the song is the work of Mr. Ambroise Vollard. Everyone knows this, and yet no one seems to have noticed that the *Grand Almanach illustré* was published without names of authors or publisher.—Apollinaire, 1918.[40]

Unlike painting, the cinematograph disrupted and exceeded Bonnard's vision even while it affirmed his direction. If Bonnard had found the answer to the riddle of his vision in the action of movie light, then he needed to marry his logic with the Lumières' machine. He needed to receive and project the light. His figures needed to body forth and assume unchoreographed aspects of reality. Where was the arena for the gestation of such an absurdly protean idea?

It was in 1898, in the small Théâtre des Pantins in Montmartre, by the place Clichy, on the rue Ballu, at the end of a courtyard, on the second floor, in the home of Claude Terrasse.[41] In this setting before a handful of people, Alfred Jarry revived his epic *Ubu* for a run of several evenings, using some three hundred marionettes made by Bonnard. Bonnard's puppets acted out Jarry's fantasies of the outrageous destructive Ubu roi, who operated in a universe

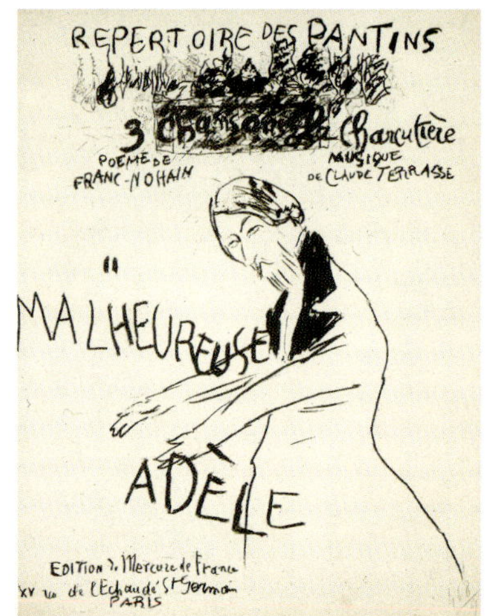

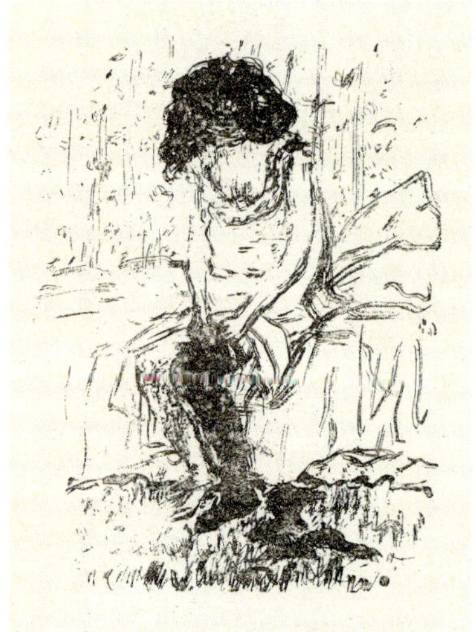

52. Pierre Bonnard, Cover for *Unfortunate Adèle* from *Répertoire des Pantins*, 1898, Lithograph, 12¹³⁄₁₆ × 9¹³⁄₁₆ in. (32.6 × 24.9 cm), Virginia and Ira Jackson Collection. Partial and Promised Gift to the National Gallery of Art, Washington.

53. Pierre Bonnard, *Marie Putting on Her Stockings* in Peter Nansen's *Marie*, 1898, Process print, 7⅜ × 4⅝ in. (18.7 × 11.7 cm), The Metropolitan Museum of Art, The Elisha Whittelsey Collection, The Elisha Whittelsey Fund, 1969 (69.636).

governed by singularities and exceptions and, in the process, inverted all rules of polite society.[42] Therein lay a virtual realm for Bonnard to play with new ideas. Bonnard's scribbled lettering and crude marks accompanied Jarry's transforming puns and caricature in the sheet music published for the Théâtre des Pantins including such titles as *Trois chansons à la charcutière* (Three songs to the Pork Butcher Woman, published in 1898) and the ode to *Unfortunate Adèle*, in which "Mort Adèle" sounds like mortadelle or Bologna sausage (fig. 52, plate 39).[43] The close repartee culminated in 1900 with *Almanach illustré du Père Ubu*, a parody based on the French government censor's confusion between a book on geometry and Verlaine's erotic poem, *Parallèlement*, illlustrated by Bonnard (plates 41– 43). Here, among their portrayals of the alphabet as well as new renditions of folk songs,[44] Jarry's wordplay and Bonnard's visual puns duel for dominance. Most notable is Jarry's salacious *Tatane* (Nookie) illustrated by Bonnard's gyrating black ink blobs.[45] For his help with *Almanach illustré du Père Ubu* (1901), Jarry conferred on Bonnard the Grand Cross of the Order of the Belly.[46] And, as future grist for the mill of the imagination, Jarry dedicated one chapter of his ongoing "neoscientific" novel, *Exploits and Opinions of Doctor Faustroll Pataphysician*, to Bonnard. The chapter, entitled "How One Obtained Canvas," places in the hands of the self-taught Henri Rousseau a painting machine that ejaculates images gyroscopically.[47]

One Morning in Montval

During this period of rapid acceleration into child's play and eroticism, Bonnard picked up a Kodak camera. In 1900, away from the family at Le Grand-Lemps, in a garden across from a rented house in Montval, Bonnard engaged in a photography session with a companion in private.[48] She was Maria Boursin. They had met on the street in Paris in late 1893.[49] Under the assumed name Marthe de Méligny she immediately became a part of his work. Marthe is the young woman in black stockings in *In Private* (1893) (plate 19); she is the woman in front of a wheeling carriage in *The Omnibus* (1895) (plate 26); she is the woman he sees when he illustrates *Marie Putting on Her Stockings* in Peter Nansen's *Marie* (1898) (fig. 53, plate 20) as well as in Verlaine's *Parallèlement* (1900) (plate 43); and she is the woman who languishes in his bed in *L'Indolent* (1899). Though Bonnard never called her by her real name, never met her real family, she maintained a real presence in his life and inhabited the spaces of his work for the rest of her life. Until the day she died, Bonnard's friends and family never knew that they had married. Certainly Bonnard had other lovers. Nevertheless her body and the physical closeness of their relationship engaged the painter as no other subject.[50] All that remains of what happened that day in Montval between Bonnard and Marthe (and this must be the most coherent body of his photographic endeavors) is a series of twenty-two snapshots. They

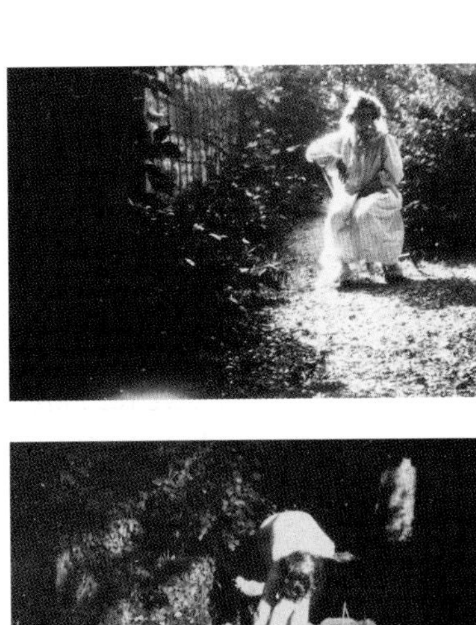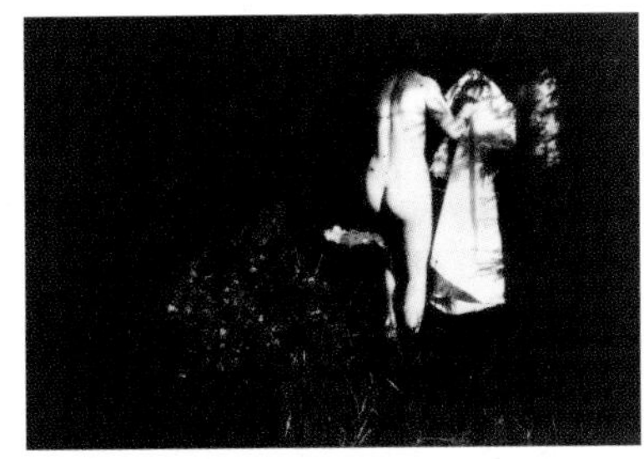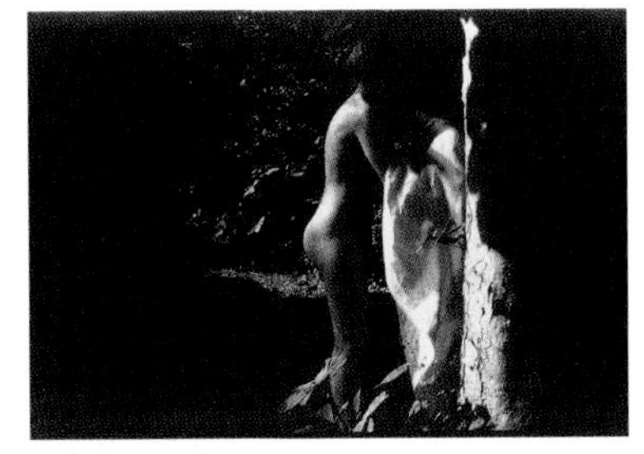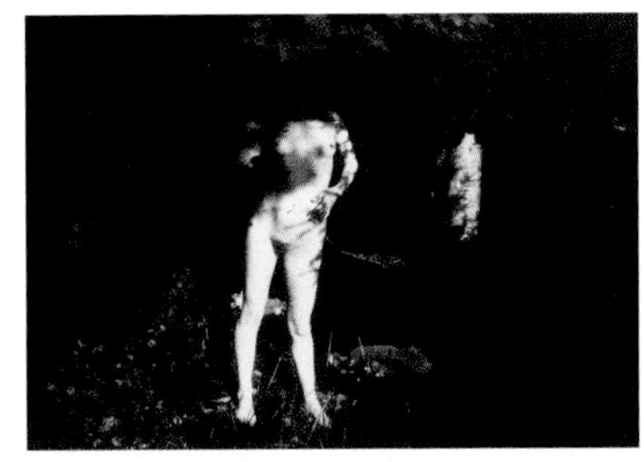
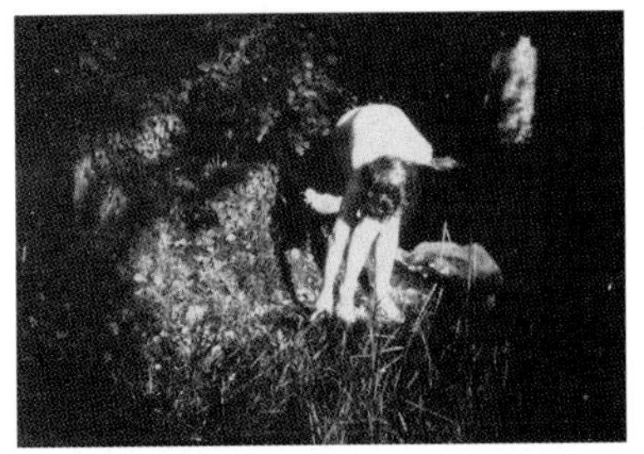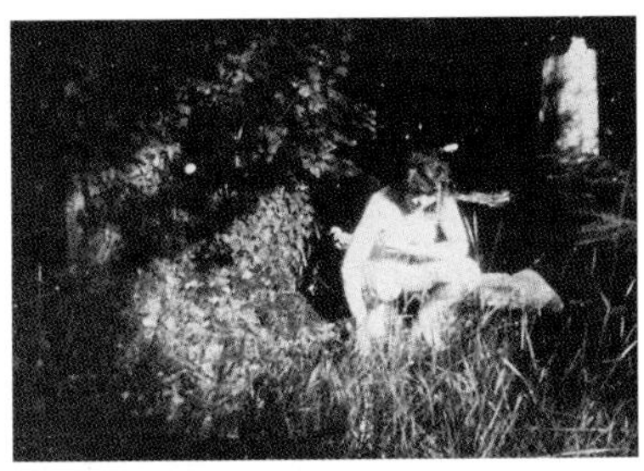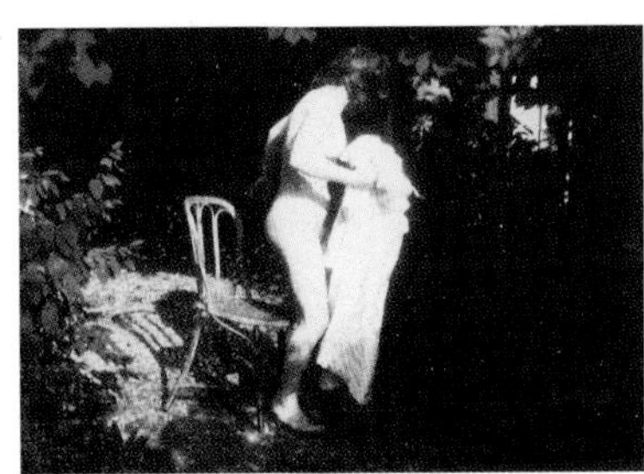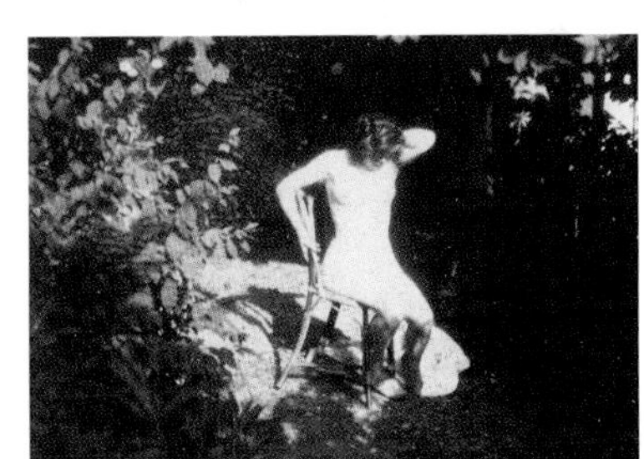
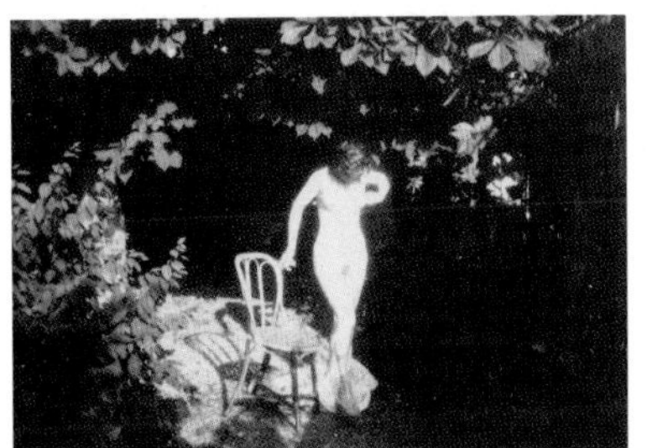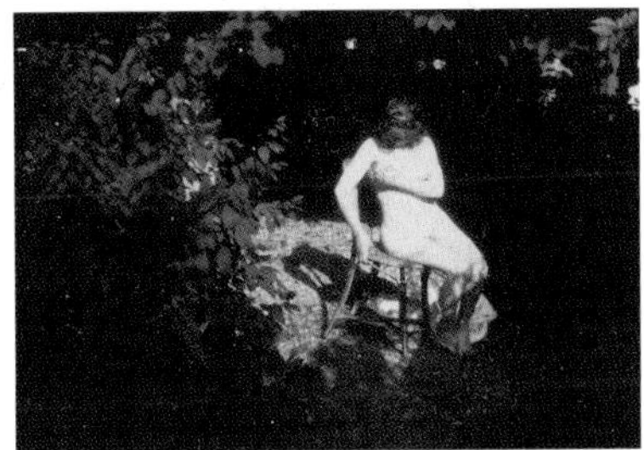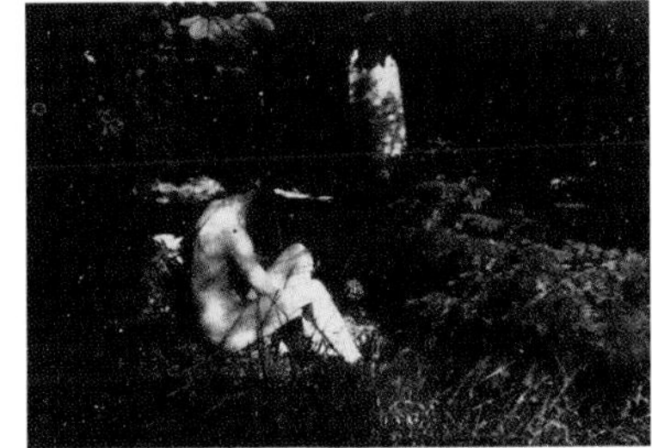

54. Pierre Bonnard, *Marthe Seated in Her Nightdress in the Garden at Montval*, 1900–1901, Contemporary print from original film negative, 7¹⁄₁₆ × 9⁷⁄₁₆ in. (18 × 24 cm), Paris, Musée d'Orsay, donation with a life interest from Charles Terrasse's children, 1987, inv: PHO 1987 27 21.

58. Pierre Bonnard, *Marthe Bending to Touch the Ground in the Garden at Montval*, 1900–1901, Contemporary print from original film negative, 7¹⁄₁₆ × 9⁷⁄₁₆ in. (18 × 24 cm), Paris, Musée d'Orsay, donation with a life interest from Charles Terrasse's children, 1987, inv: PHO 1987 30 35.

62. Pierre Bonnard, *Marthe Standing next to a Chair in the Garden at Montval*, 1900–1901, Contemporary print from original film negative, 7¹⁄₁₆ × 9⁷⁄₁₆ in. (18 × 24 cm), Paris, Musée d'Orsay, donation with a life interest from Charles Terrasse's children, 1987, inv: PHO 1987 30 37.

55. Pierre Bonnard, *Marthe with Her Back to the Camera in the Garden at Montval*, 1900–1901, Contemporary print from original film negative, 7¹⁄₁₆ × 9⁷⁄₁₆ in. (18 × 24 cm), Paris, Musée d'Orsay, donation with a life interest from Charles Terrasse's children, 1987, inv: PHO 1987 27 25.

59. Pierre Bonnard, *Marthe Crouching down in the Garden at Montval*, 1900–1901, Contemporary print from original film negative, 7¹⁄₁₆ × 9⁷⁄₁₆ in. (18 × 24 cm), Paris, Musée d'Orsay, donation with a life interest from Charles Terrasse's children, 1987, inv: PHO 1987 30 36.

63. Pierre Bonnard, *Marthe Seated with Her Hand on Her Right Breast in the Garden at Montval*, 1900–1901, Contemporary print from original film negative, 7¹⁄₁₆ × 9⁷⁄₁₆ in. (18 × 24 cm), Paris, Musée d'Orsay, donation with a life interest from Charles Terrasse's children, 1987, inv: PHO 1987 30 40.

56. Pierre Bonnard, *Marthe Removing Her Nightdress in the Garden at Montval*, 1900–1901, Contemporary print from original film negative, 7¹⁄₁₆ × 9⁷⁄₁₆ in. (18 × 24 cm), Paris, Musée d'Orsay, donation with a life interest from Charles Terrasse's children, 1987, inv: PHO 1987 27 23.

60. Pierre Bonnard, *Marthe Holding Her Nightdress in the Garden at Montval*, 1900–1901, Contemporary print from original film negative, 7¹⁄₁₆ × 9⁷⁄₁₆ in. (18 × 24 cm), Paris, Musée d'Orsay, donation with a life interest from Charles Terrasse's children, 1987, inv: PHO 1987 30 38.

64. Maria Boursin, *Pierre Bonnard Seated in Profile*, 1900–1901, Original contact print on gelatin paper, 1⁷⁄₁₆ × 2³⁄₁₆ in. (3.6 × 5.5 cm), Paris, Musée d'Orsay, donation with a life interest from Charles Terrasse's children, 1987, inv. PHO 1987 31 42.

57. Pierre Bonnard, *Marthe Standing in the Sunlight in the Garden at Montval*, 1900–1901, Contemporary print from original film negative, 7¹⁄₁₆ × 9⁷⁄₁₆ in. (18 × 24 cm), Paris, Musée d'Orsay, donation with a life interest from Charles Terrasse's children, 1987, inv: PHO 1987 27 29.

61. Pierre Bonnard, *Marthe Seated with Her Left Hand behind Her Neck in the Garden at Montval*, 1900–1901, Contemporary print from original film negative, 7¹⁄₁₆ × 9⁷⁄₁₆ in. (18 × 24 cm), Paris, Musée d'Orsay, donation with a life interest from Charles Terrasse's children, 1987, inv: PHO 1987 30 39.

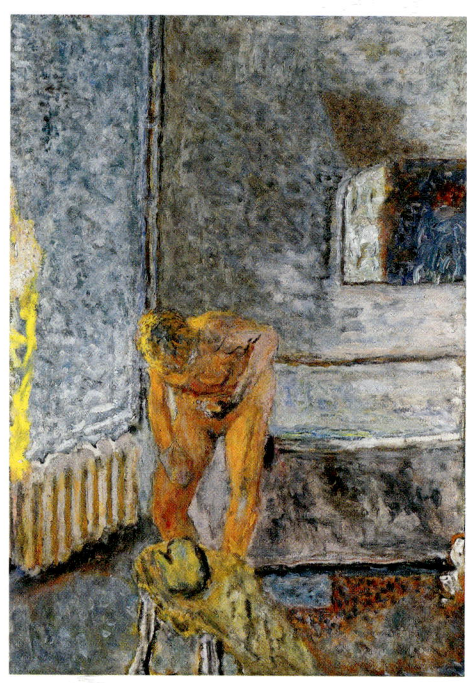

65. Pierre Bonnard, *Nude in an Interior*, ca. 1935, Oil on canvas, 28¾ × 19¾ in. (73 × 50.2 cm), The Phillips Collection, Washington, D.C.

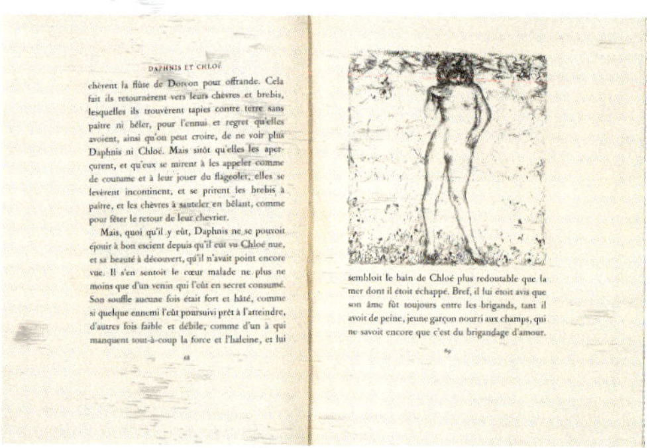

66. Pierre Bonnard, Illustration for Longus's *Les Pastorales* or *Daphnis et Chloé*, 1902, Lithograph in book, 12 × 9⅞ in. (30.5 × 25 cm), Lessing J. Rosenwald Collection, Library of Congress, Washington, D.C.

were treated in the usual way and sent to Kodak for development (the family still has the Kodak envelopes).[51]

The sequence of small negatives on pliable film is something like a movie. It begins with Marthe in her nightgown seated in a closed garden (figs. 54–64, plates 46–55a). At her back, the morning sun comes streaming in, opening out the space. It surrounds her hair and clothing with a white halo and casts deep shadows in the surrounding shrubs. Marthe gazes directly at Bonnard crouching low in front of her. Snap. She stands and reaches for her button to disrobe. Snap. Bonnard is much closer now and his view is partially obscured by a tree; Marthe's nude figure is in profile and the nightgown tumbles down her arms. Snap. Again in profile, Marthe's nude body is half in shadow, half in light. She now looks at Bonnard. Snap. From the other side at a distance, Bonnard finds Marthe with her back turned, standing in full sun holding up the gown; the contours of her body are cut in deep shadows. Snap. Marthe turns to Bonnard and touches her abdomen and hip; light from the left. Snap. Now in shadow she reaches into a stream of sunlight. Snap. Marthe touches her breast with her right hand and reaches around to her back with her left and turns to Bonnard crouching low in the shadows at a distance. Snap. She bends down to pick up a watering can. Snap. Camera even lower, the sun at her back lights only the limbs that are in motion. Snap. Marthe, as if bathing, in profile, raises her left leg to dry her foot. Snap. Bonnard now with the direction of the sun finds Marthe head down-turned but body otherwise spotlit, surrounded by deep shadows. She touches the front of her body. Snap. She bends over, now only her back and legs are revealed in the light. Snap. She squats with her left hand touching her right breast. Snap. Touching her left breast she stands beside the chair. Snap. Holding her nightgown she sits down, with shoes half on, half off. Snap. Now seated, nightgown and shoes at her feet, she basks in full sun. Snap. At this point Bonnard hands the camera to Marthe. Bonnard stands nude in profile, much as Marthe had done. Snap. He also bends over, thereby reducing his figure to the contours of his arms and legs in the light. Snap. He sits on the ground with his back to the sun, gazing on the light-filled gauze of the nightgown hanging in the distance. Snap. Where does this lead?

These photographs are studies in movement like those of Degas or Eadweard Muybridge or Thomas Eakins. Yet the movements in Bonnard's photographs serve a different purpose. Bonnard is moving as he is making the pictures and directing the action like a cinematographer. The photographs unfold as a story like Bonnard's private version of Pygmalion. Marthe is his erotic muse, aglow like a living marble moving in and out of the light in the leafy undergrowth. The scenario enjoys the full participation of its author who is both the observed (in the light) and the observer (in the shadows). The automatic Kodak, the great enabler, made the act of taking the picture synonymous with the instant of seeing. As Emile Zola stated unequivocally, "In my opinion, you cannot say you have thoroughly seen anything until you have got a photograph of it revealing a lot of points which otherwise would be unnoticed and which in most cases could not be distinguished."[52] Bonnard's Kodak sequences proposed an expression so fluid and so graphic as to make vision and desire synonymous with the moment.

The experience of the Montval morning propelled Bonnard into something beyond the small Kodak strips. Looking ahead, one feels the same proximity to the radiance of Marthe bending toward the camera conveyed in his 1935 painting of a woman bending forward performing her ablutions in the steamy light-filled bathroom (fig. 65, plate 125). Bonnard's 1943 instruction to his model Dina Vierny, "to live in front of him and try to forget him," recalls the choreography of his morning with Marthe disrobing.[53] In 1902 one finds the same figures and same poses emerging from the thatch of lines he used to illustrate the tale of *Les Pastorales* or *Daphnis et Chloé* by Longus published by Vollard (fig. 66, plate 56). One glimpses the action of light of the Montval snapshots reenacted movie-like on a silver screen entitled *Screen with Rabbits* (ca. 1902–1906) and in the corresponding sculpture entitled *Daphnis and Chloé* with its thumbprinted contours articulating the reflective surfaces of his bronze castings of nudes and nymphs surrounding a mirrored pool (fig. 67, plate 59; fig. 68, plate 58). Squeezing the shutter of his Kodak was not a viable option. Professional photography, what Bonnard called "the cut and dry method of photography,"[54] had yet to combine eroticism and narrative except in the voyeurism parading as allegory among the pages of *L'Etude académique* where, for example, a reclining nude with legs splayed was entitled *La Culture physique* (fig. 69).[55] Bonnard's own painted *études* seem strangely static and naïve, almost hieratic—the deliberate unmaking of his earlier fluidity, strangely simulating the sculptural presence of *L'Etude académique* (fig. 70). Represented by the Galerie Bernheim-Jeune via its director Fénéon, Bonnard was known as a promising painter of nudes and portraits.

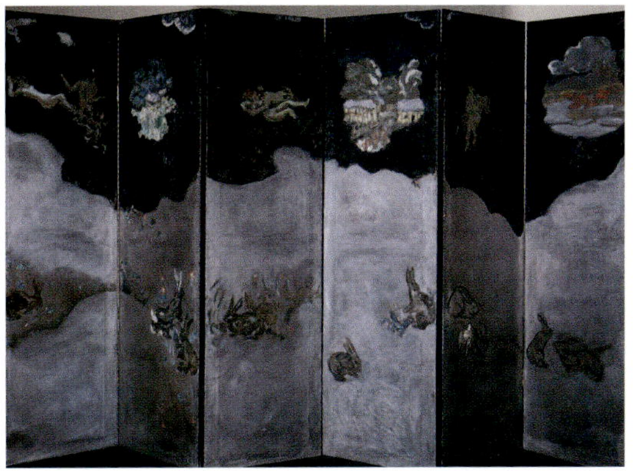

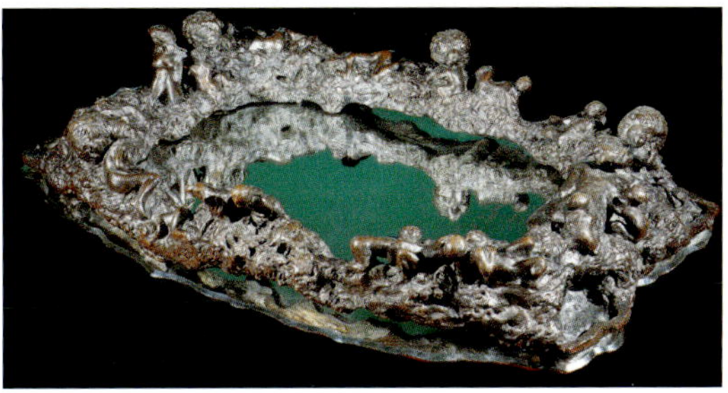

67. Pierre Bonnard, *Screen with Rabbits*, ca. 1902–1906, Oil on paper mounted on canvas, each panel, 63⅜ × 17¾ in. (161 × 45 cm), Musée Départemental Maurice Denis, Saint-Germain-en-Laye.

68. Pierre Bonnard, *Daphnis and Chloé*, 1904–1905, Bronze and glass, 5¹⁵⁄₁₆ × 32 ¹¹⁄₁₆ × 9¹¹⁄₁₆ in. (15 × 83 × 50 cm), Paris, Musée d'Orsay.

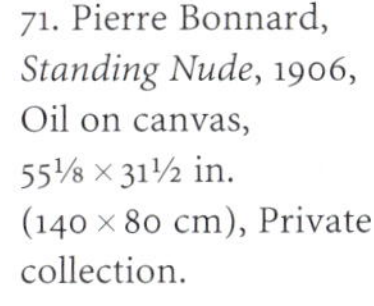

71. Pierre Bonnard, *Standing Nude*, 1906, Oil on canvas, 55⅛ × 31½ in. (140 × 80 cm), Private collection.

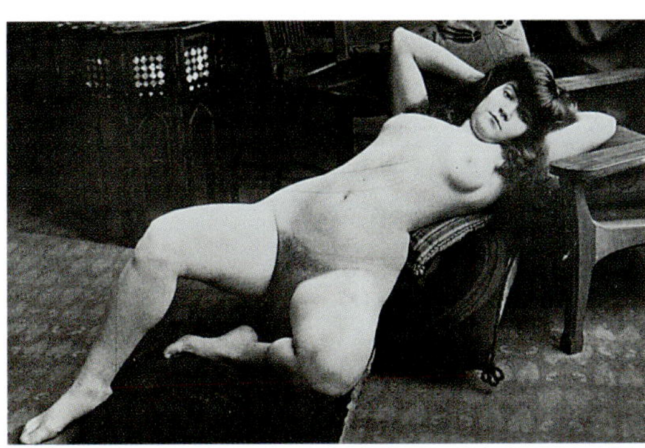

69. *La Culture physique, action d'étendre* from *L'Etude académique*, 15 March 1906, Photograph.

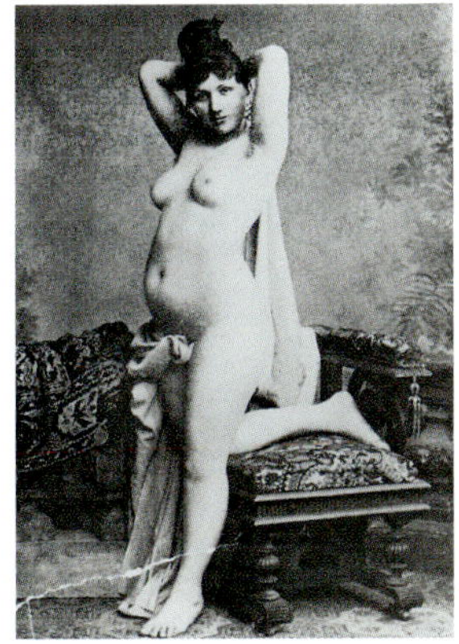

70. *Indulgence* from *L'Etude académique*, 15 November 1906, Photograph.

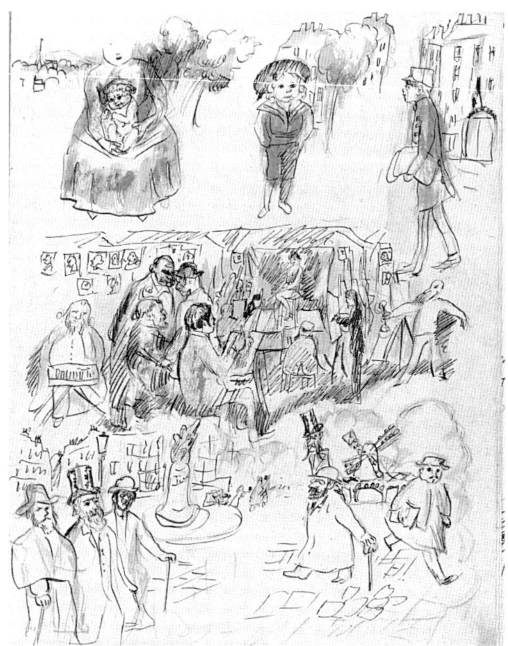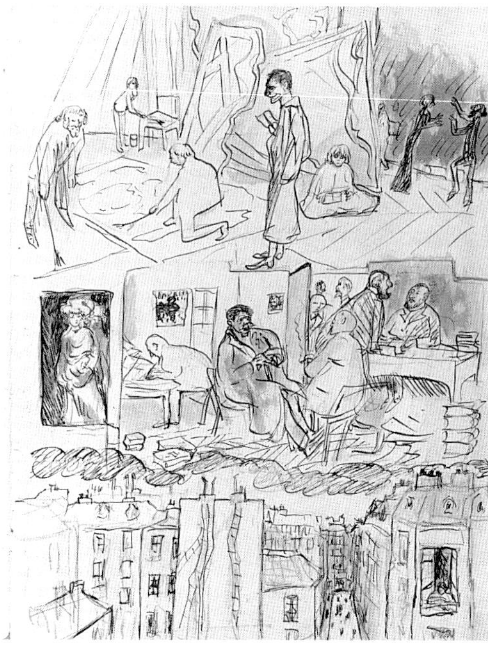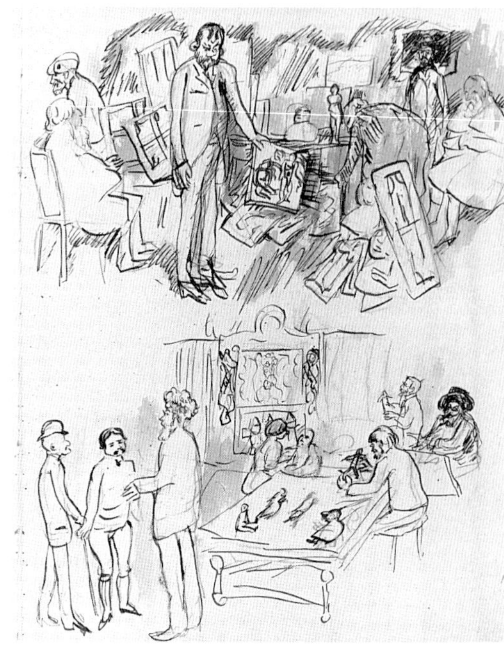

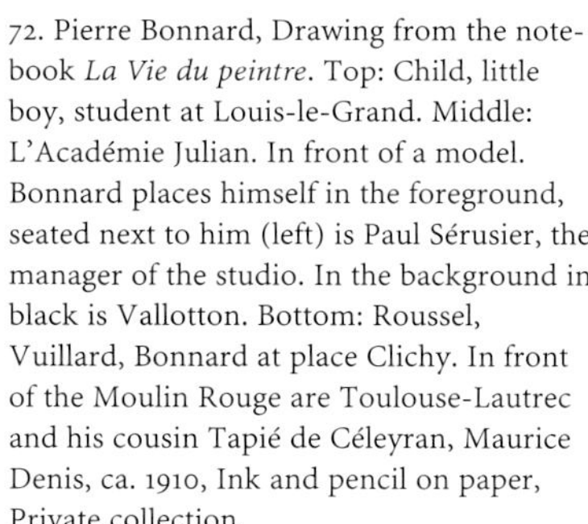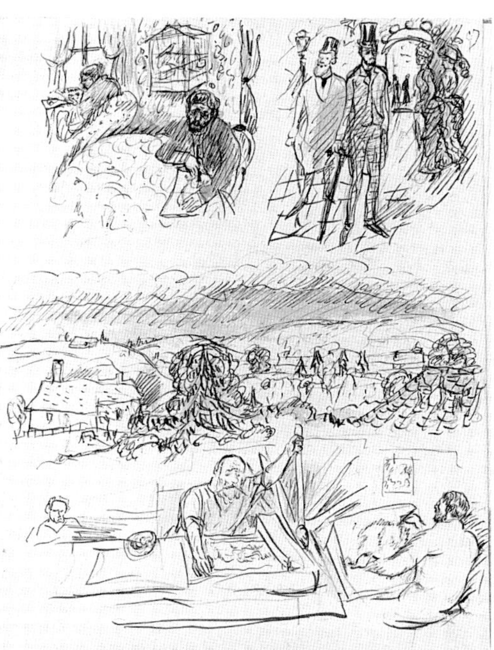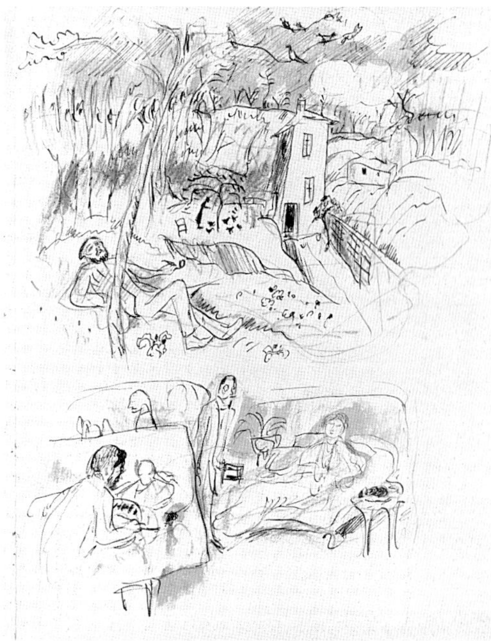

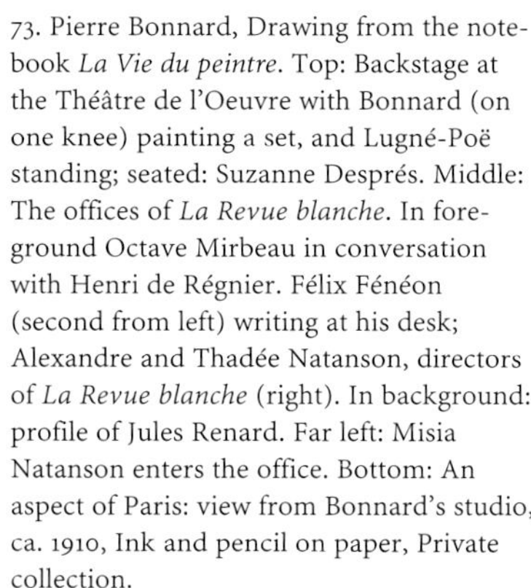

72. Pierre Bonnard, Drawing from the notebook *La Vie du peintre*. Top: Child, little boy, student at Louis-le-Grand. Middle: L'Académie Julian. In front of a model. Bonnard places himself in the foreground, seated next to him (left) is Paul Sérusier, the manager of the studio. In the background in black is Vallotton. Bottom: Roussel, Vuillard, Bonnard at place Clichy. In front of the Moulin Rouge are Toulouse-Lautrec and his cousin Tapié de Céleyran, Maurice Denis, ca. 1910, Ink and pencil on paper, Private collection.

73. Pierre Bonnard, Drawing from the notebook *La Vie du peintre*. Top: Backstage at the Théâtre de l'Oeuvre with Bonnard (on one knee) painting a set, and Lugné-Poë standing; seated: Suzanne Després. Middle: The offices of *La Revue blanche*. In foreground Octave Mirbeau in conversation with Henri de Régnier. Félix Fénéon (second from left) writing at his desk; Alexandre and Thadée Natanson, directors of *La Revue blanche* (right). In background: profile of Jules Renard. Far left: Misia Natanson enters the office. Bottom: An aspect of Paris: view from Bonnard's studio, ca. 1910, Ink and pencil on paper, Private collection.

74. Pierre Bonnard, Drawing from the notebook *La Vie du peintre*. Top: The Vollard gallery, 6, rue Laffitte. In the foreground, Vollard, standing. To the left, seated, Pissarro and, behind him, Renoir. To the

right, seated, Degas. Standing, Bonnard. Bottom: The Théâtre des Pantins, 6, rue Ballu. In the foreground, Claude Terrasse (with beard and full head of hair) in deep conversation with Alfred Jarry (dressed like a cyclist) and their colleague Franc-Nohain. Bonnard is seated at right, making marionettes. Far right: Charles Bonnard and Ferdinand Hérold. Scenery by Vuillard and Bonnard in the background, ca. 1910, Ink and pencil on paper, Private collection.

75. Pierre Bonnard, Drawing from the notebook *La Vie du peintre*. Top: Bonnard and his grandmother Mertzdorff in Paris;

Bonnard and a friend. Middle: Landscape in Dauphiné. Bottom: Printmaker Clot working at his press; to his right, Bonnard working on a lithographic stone, ca. 1910, Ink and pencil on paper, Private collection.

76. Pierre Bonnard, Drawing from the notebook *La Vie du peintre*. Top: Bonnard in l'Etang-la-Ville. Bottom: Has Bonnard become a fashionable painter, ca. 1910, Ink and pencil on paper, Private collection.

In 1906 the American newcomers to Paris and aspiring modernists Gertrude and
Leo Stein hung Bonnard's sepia-modeled *Siesta* (1900) with a Rose Period
Picasso *Young Girl with Bouquet of Flowers* (1905) (fig. 77). The shared audience
of Picasso and Bonnard soon changed.

The meteoric advent of Fauvism and Cubism along with the advance of
Matisse and Picasso brought a profound shift that apparently left Bonnard out
of step. Bonnard saw it that way. The arrival of Cubism left Bonnard, as he said,
"hanging in midair."[56] In 1910 he looked back as if to make his own mocking
assessment in a series of hasty sketches entitled *Life of the Painter* (figs. 72–76).
As in storyboards for a film, Bonnard depicted himself walking to school, listening to Sérusier's sermonizing at the Académie Julian, watching Jarry giving stage
directions while he was making puppets for the Théâtre des Pantins, and standing in the dim recesses of Vollard's cellar listening to Degas. For the last two
scenes, where he juxtaposes himself at work painting a society portrait and at
play feigning retirement in front of a little house in the countryside, the caption
asks, "Has Bonnard become a fashionable painter?" The avant-garde replied:
Yes. Indeed. In 1910 Roger Fry's exhibition of Post-Impressionism in London
excluded him. This was to be expected. Sometime around 1910 Bonnard adopted
the white ground, the broken brushstroke, the rainbow of spectrum colors after
Apollinaire had decried the "ignorance and frenzy" of Impressionism.[57] Bonnard
held fast to fleeting sensations of light when Matisse, among his first published
statement in 1908, distinguished himself from the impressionists by claiming he
would "risk losing charm in order to gain greater stability."[58] Impressionism was
Bonnard's deliberate anachronism. Jarry's stage direction for Ubu roi "to fire a
revolver in the year 1000"[59] taught Bonnard the arresting power of cross-refer-
encing time. Pursuing what he called "the color program of the Impressionists"[60]
seemingly pulled Bonnard out of the rapid pace of the avant-garde. It left him
where he always had been most comfortable, free to destabilize things on the
periphery. Quietly enacting his own drama, Bonnard would be learning and
unlearning. As he told his nephew Charles Terrasse, "I want to forget all I know.
I am trying to learn what I do not know."[61] Always experimenting, he would not
repeat the past, but intuitively would follow the methods of Impressionism as it
informed investigations and inventions of film. In so doing Bonnard taught
himself new ways to see.

The Last Impressionist and the First Autochrome

Out of his experiences leading to Cubism, given his desire to break free from
academicism, given his love of graphic arts, given his propensities for appropriation,
Bonnard's belated leap into the brightness and chaos of Impressionism had no logic
except the logic of the Lumières' camera shedding its shimmering effects.
Coincident with Bonnard's brightening palette and changing methods,

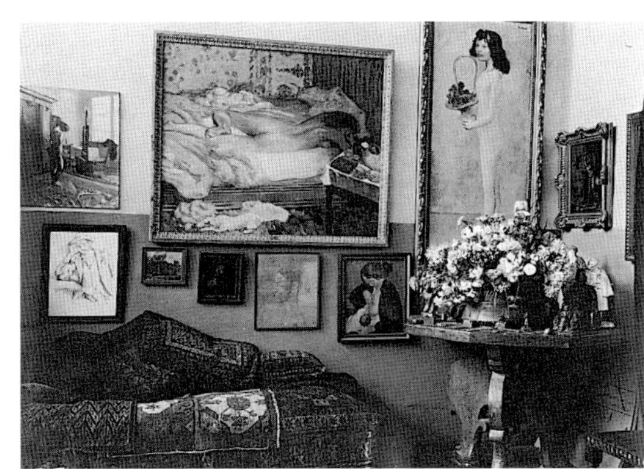

77. *Studio of Leo and
Gertrude Stein, 27, rue
de Fleurus, Paris*, not
dated, Photograph,
Dr. Claribel Cone and
Miss Etta Cone
Papers, The Baltimore
Museum of Art.

coincident with the eclipse of the blunt strokes and bold colors of Matisse's *Blue Nude* and fractured forms of Picasso's *Demoiselles* entered Louis Lumière with his invention of the autochrome that could hardly have escaped notice.

Giant projections of color slides followed the screening of the Lumières' films at the World Exposition of 1900. By 1904 Louis Lumière presented his findings about color film to the National Academy of Science and secured his patent. The newspaper *L'Illustration* published an account of the lecture he delivered to an audience of six hundred on 10 June 1907.[62] Mass production followed. Immediately, with sale of color film to the general public, color photography was within everyone's reach. "From now on, everyone can assume the name of painter with a machine."[63] For the second time since the invention of photography, critics decreed "the end of the art of painting."[64] Looking back, André Derain saw the nascence of Fauvism in the context of this discussion: "It was an era of photography that may have influenced us and contributed to our reaction against anything that resembled a photographic plate taken from life. We treated colours like sticks of dynamite, exploding them to produce light."[65] Unlike the fauves whose reaction was in essence to defend painting by embracing the opacity of pure, flat color and the powerful vibrations of complementary red and green, Bonnard chose to embrace the translucency of color film. Denis recalled that to tease Sérusier, Bonnard adopted the claim that color photography would be the doom of painting.[66] Much as he had done in 1889 with color lithography, instead of fighting the idea of the mechanized transfer of images, Bonnard became its student and, in so doing, adopted divisionist color, adopted the various schema of the impressionists but, as he said, "wanted to go further than the naturalistic impressions of color."[67] Lumière's color film, however static, also contained the most potent elements of Michel-Eugène Chevreul's color wheel. Pressed between a glass plate and photographic emulsion lay grains of potato starch dyed green, violet, and orange. This mosaic pattern generated its own color. Lumière's process was "its own color factory and its turbines ran on light (figs. 78a–b)."[68] At the so-called end of painting, in the shimmer of Lumière's autochrome, Bonnard found another beginning.

Under the guise of Impressionism, Bonnard reconstituted the earlier patterns of his ukiyo-e inspired compositions. The screen, the checkered fabrics, the open window, the doorway ajar, as well as many of the same characters, the nursemaid, the seductress, the pedestrians now come forward as figures rounded in the light—pressed into being through exaggerations of tone and ocular effects. Out of the gray haze of an interior that unfolds like a screen, a table opens across a room in which a woman glides from the kitchen door to the dining room window (plate 65). In *Early Spring* from 1910 the promenade of the nursemaid (complete with runaway children) is surprisingly captured waist-up like a snapshot taken of a roadside event from a car traveling through the

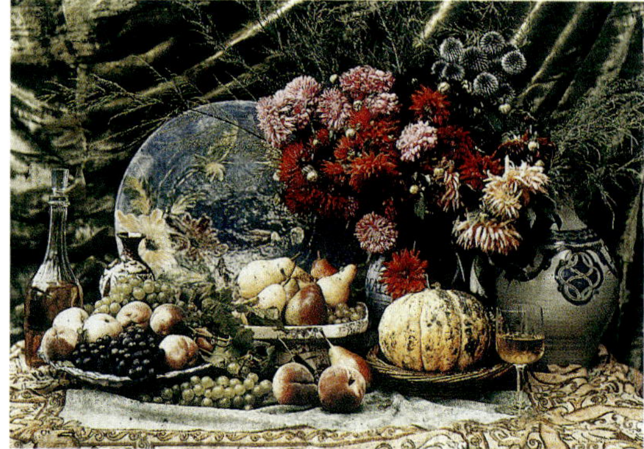

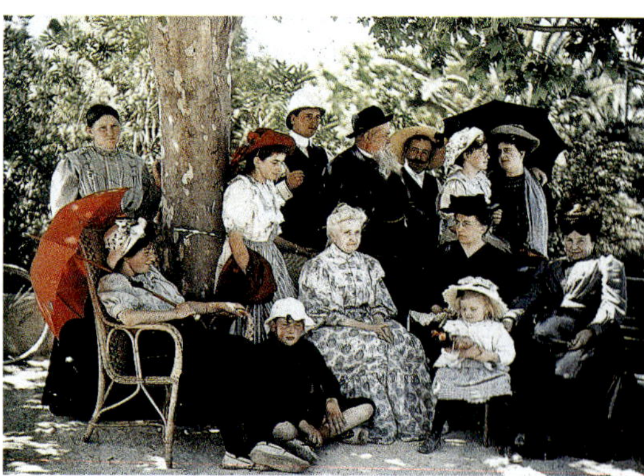

78a. Attributed to Louis Lumière, *Still Life*, 1910, Autochrome, 7¹/₁₆ × 9⁷/₁₆ in. (18 × 24 cm), Musée Autochrome Lumière.

78b. Attributed to Louis Lumière, *Auguste with Family at La Ciotat*, 1910, Autochrome, 5⅛ × 7¹/₁₆ in. (13 × 18 cm), Musée Autochrome Lumière.

yellow-green countryside (plate 68). Absent Andrée and her cat, the checkered cloth is reborn center stage on a round tabletop around which nearby objects, as Bonnard said, "rise up" in a blur, while the woman doting on her admiring pet seated just across from them is distinct (plate 71). These paintings do not evoke a reality as a time of day or condition of weather might trigger the recollection of a poem or a song. Rather, Bonnard's scenarios evoke a process of seeing whose conclusion is neither fixed nor inevitable. It is as if each composition poses a riddle for Bonnard—a question that can only be answered by prolonging the act of painting. How? As early as 1912 Lucie Cousturier observed, "When he has found the expressive gesture, he stretches it out, balances it, sharpens it, with little touches that establish it in the light, completes it with elements which propogate its rhythm, designate it, externalize it by the astuteness of the composition, the spatting of color, persuasive quality of the values and tone."[69]

Judging Color

> With four thumb-tacks he [Bonnard] had pinned a canvas, lightly tinted with ocher, to the dining-room wall. During the first few days he would glance from time to time, as he painted, at a sketch on a piece of paper twice the size of one's hand, on which he had made notes in oil, pencil, and ink of the dominant colors of each little section of the motif. At first I [Félix Fénéon] could not identify the subject. Did I have before me a landscape or a seascape? On the eighth day (until then I had no doubt failed to inspect the canvas), I was astonished to be able to recognize a landscape in which a house appeared in the distance and a young woman on a path, with a child and two dogs beside her. From that time on Bonnard no longer referred to the sketch. He would step back to judge the effect of the juxtaposed tones; occasionally he would place a dab of color with his finger, then another next to the first. On about the fifteenth day I asked him how long he thought it would take him to finish his landscape. Bonnard replied: "I finished it this morning."[70]

By prolonging the act of painting, Bonnard's mature process developed an open and measureless disposition.[71] To that end he seemingly was prepared to abandon any limits of convention, especially the idea of preset or fixed compositional proportions. About 1911, after purchasing a car, Bonnard adopted a pattern of working away from his Paris studio. Traveling south to north seasonally from sunny Cannes to cloudy Vernon, he abandoned the easel, worked only on great sheets of unstretched canvas tacked to a wall (any wall, not just his studio but in his hotel room—anywhere). His relentless play with the viscosity of paint—the marking and unmarking—the building up of certain areas and the thinning down and wiping away of others held open the door to the completion of a composition. In mining the ends of the spectrum, in applying

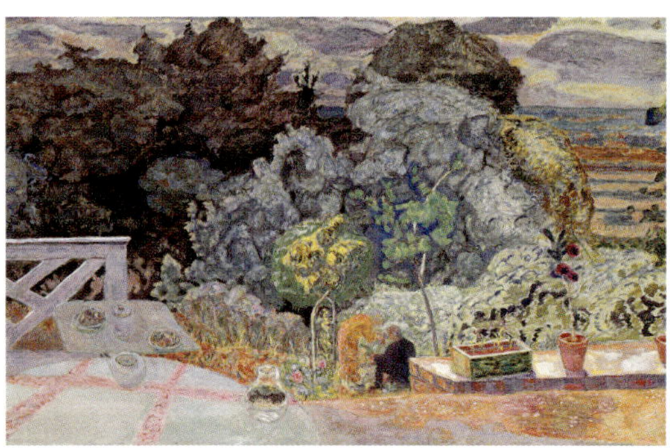

79. Pierre Bonnard, *The Terrace*, 1918, Oil on canvas, 62¾ × 98¼ in. (159.4 × 249.5 cm), The Phillips Collection, Washington, D.C.

highly volatile combinations, it is as if at a certain point Bonnard further ceded control to color. Bonnard once told Matisse that "a painter's only solid ground is the palette and colors but as soon as the colors achieve an illusion, they are no longer judged."[72] Why? The judging of color drained away the last confining taint of illusionism from his eyes—battled the last preconceptions of the picturesque and restored the integrity of his own seeing. It was, as he said, "not a matter of painting life, but of bringing life to painting."[73]

Lively carnavalesque color invaded his work, dappling green against a roaring orange composition. The *Woman Bathing* (1912), seen from above and behind, squats in the round copper tub (plate 73). *The Dining Room in the Country* (1913) puts into play a similar motion while orchestrating the contrasting effects of summer daylight inside and outside through the architectural cadences of window and door frames (plate 78). The range from pink-violet reflections vibrating in the deep heat of yellow-orange to the turquoise and yellow-greens peppered with white-pink gives new meaning to the photographer Alfred Stieglitz's 1907 prediction that "soon the world will be color mad, and Lumière will be responsible."[74] As if to recant, Bonnard later said, "I was carried away by colour."[75] In much the same way that ukioyo-e prints had taught him the expressive value of pure color and made him an apprentice of composition, Bonnard's teasing enthusiasm for filmic color sent him back to drawing. As he said, "I want to forget all I know. . . . I draw all the time."[76] Bonnard sought to make his drawing more automatically attuned to his senses.[77] As he said, "Drawing represents feeling."[78] Michel Terrasse has observed that over the years Bonnard made drawing into a type of "personal stenography," in which "shadings, hatching, little dots, points, smears, and blurs ranging from delicate gray to

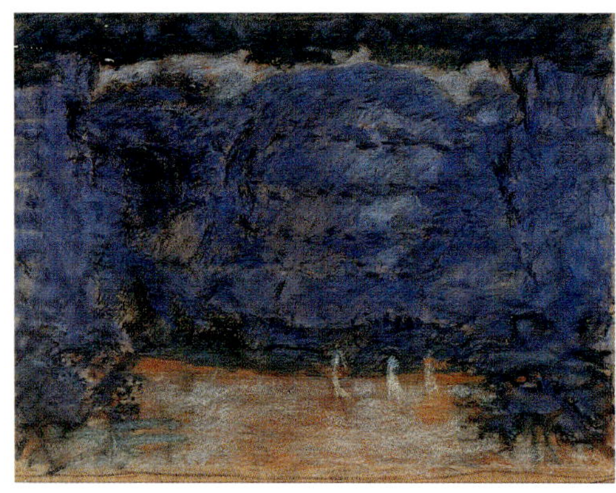

80. Pierre Bonnard, Preliminary décor Design for *Jeux*, 1920, Pastel, 20¹⁄₁₆ × 25⁹⁄₁₆ in. (51 × 65 cm), Courtesy of Stockholm's Dance Museum Archives.

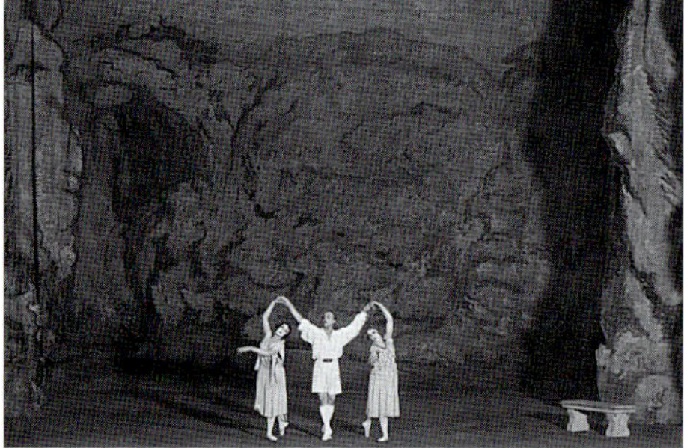

81. Scene from *Jeux*, Danced poem by Claude Debussy, Scenery by Pierre Bonnard, 1920, Photograph, Courtesy of Stockholm's Dance Museum Archives.

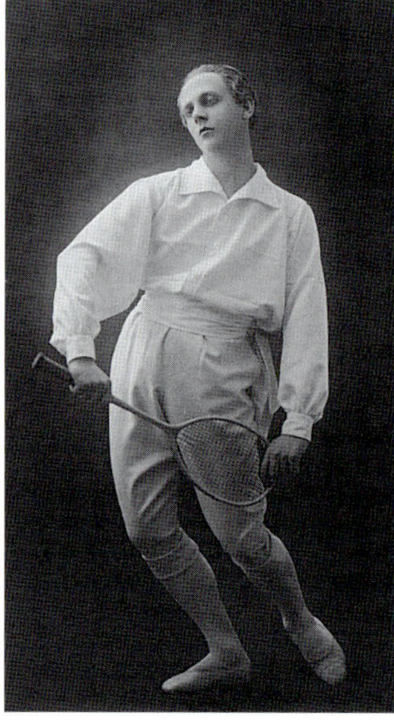

82. Jean Börlin in *Jeux*, 1920, Photograph, Courtesy of Stockholm's Dance Museum Archives.

the darkest black" transcribe the setting.[79] Beyond the preliminary sketch, one finds graphite contours on top of the paint. Bonnard once was found drawing on a photograph of one of his paintings.[80]

Imaginary Cinema

Light—that is to say, Bonnard's ability to generate light through broken impressionistic color—increasingly animated the subjects of his paintings. In *The Terrace*, Bonnard's landscape panorama from 1918, a vast array of marks— from dense jabs of yellow and purple to the long wavy green lines lean with medium—vibrate, variously balancing aspects of the light on a summer after- noon with the rhythm and movement of his strokes (fig. 79, plate 86). From sunny terrace and closed garden to dark thickets and river beyond it, Bonnard used, as he said, the "harmony of lines for the directions and proportions of large spaces."[81] Reality and fantasy combine along the proscenium of his terrace at Vernon. In the distance a man and a woman bend together much like the intertwined vines on the nearby trellis. Sunlight pours like fiery pink-orange syrup across the terrace. Shadows secrete their transparent color on the table in dabbing strokes of pink-white over blue underpaint much like iridescence occurs in mother-of-pearl and soap bubbles. This palette is unmistakably repeated in Bonnard's set for *Jeux*, the 1920 production of the Ballet Suédois, where feathery modulations of blue-green lighted with yellow-pink-orange con- stitute a gigantic amorphous backdrop for the amorous dalliance between the three tennis players (figs. 80–82).[82]

In Bonnard's *The Terrace at Vernonnet*, begun in 1920 and completed much later in 1939, the vibrating ebb and flow of blue-violet-green against pink- orange-ocher unfold the space of the terrace like the zigzag of one of his earlier screens (fig. 83, plate 88). One can read this screen left to right as if following the sequence of a dream. From the conversing orange couple in the upper left one advances to the violet tree trunk on the left that divides the space from the opalescent table. A statuesque woman presiding over the table in the center of the terrace glows in her orange dress like the fruit she holds in her hand. To her right the blue outlines of a pinkish orange bench slide diagonally down and out the lower right corner of the composition. Along the upper right a young woman enters swinging a tennis racket. This unexpected action partially glimpsed from the periphery ricochets the viewer back into the composition.

Iridescent and vibrant color commingle with the real-life drama that occurred when a young artist named Renée Monchaty became his model.[83] Their liaison launches the mature phase of his painting in the 1920s—a trade- mark glow emanating from the volatile interaction of color marks that cannot be mistaken for those of any other painter. Renée is the woman in his illustrations for Claude Anet's *Notes sur l'amour*.[84] Her gaze arrests the eye, it is her face that

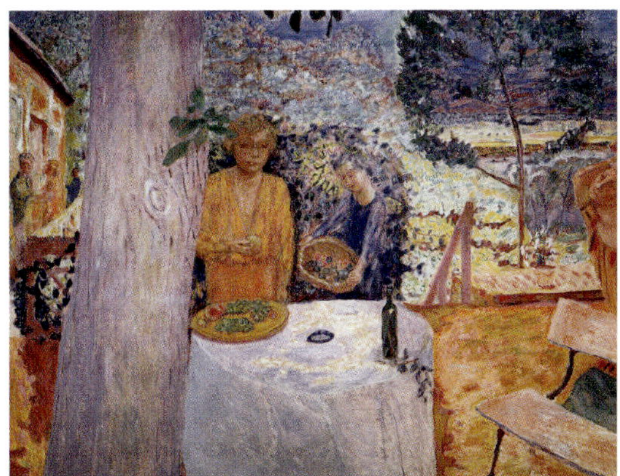

83. Pierre Bonnard, *The Terrace at Vernonnet*, 1920/1939, Oil on canvas, 58¼ × 76¾ in. (148 × 194.9 cm), The Metropolitan Museum of Art, Gift of Mrs. Frank Jay Gould 1968 (68.1).

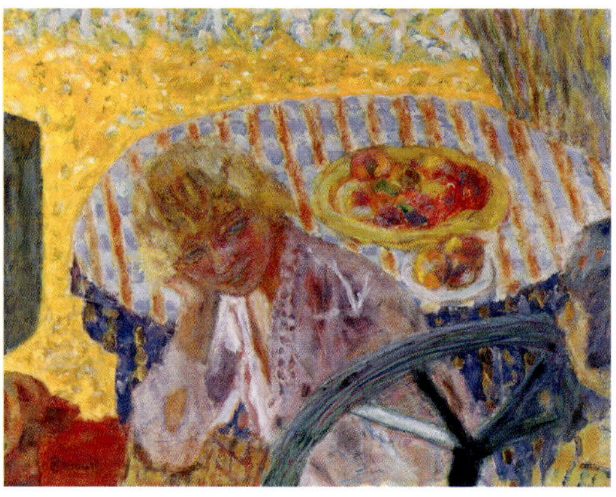

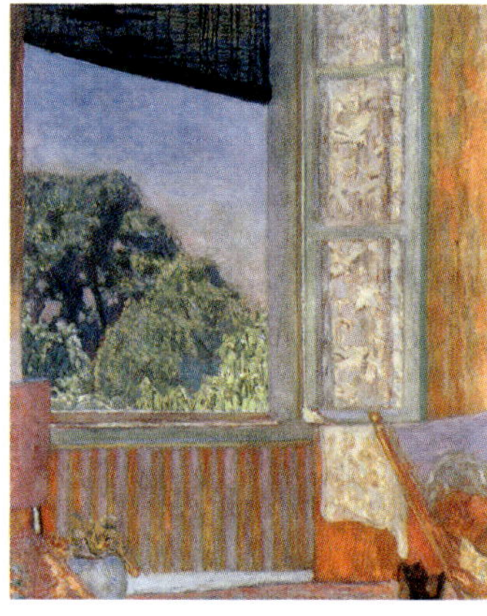

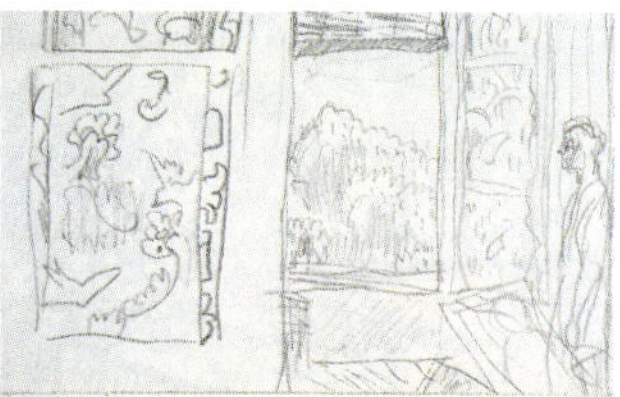

84. Pierre Bonnard, *Young Women in the Garden (Renée Monchaty and Marthe Bonnard)*, ca. 1921–1923, 1945–1946, Oil on canvas, 23¹³⁄₁₆ × 30⁵⁄₁₆ in. (60.5 × 77 cm), Private collection.

85. Pierre Bonnard, *The Open Window*, 1921, Oil on canvas, 46½ × 37¾ in. (118 × 96 cm), The Phillips Collection, Washington, D.C.

86. Pierre Bonnard, Study for *The Open Window*, ca. 1920–1921, Graphite on paper, 4¾ × 8¹⁄₁₆ in. (12 × 20.5 cm), Private collection.

shines like the sun against the striped round table in *Young Women in the Garden* (ca. 1921–1923, 1946–1947) (fig. 84, plate 90). She is the reclining woman toying with the jumping cat in the orange and violet somnolent interior overlooking the greenery in *The Open Window* (1921) (fig. 85, plate 93). In each case, she is accompanied by the abiding shadowy chaperone Marthe. Marthe stands in the sunlit garden to Renée's right as a dark, hovering profile. Marthe stands over Renée in the preparatory sketch for *The Open Window* (fig. 86, plate 92). One senses Marthe hovering still in the ominous blue black window shade whose diagonal directs us to Renée even while it threatens to cut off the view. The imaginary film rolls even as Marthe, ravaged by jealousy, orders that all trace of Renée be expunged from his painting. On 13 August 1925 Bonnard marries his longtime companion Marthe. On 9 September 1925 Renée Monchaty commits suicide.[85] Bonnard's conflicting emotions of love, loyalty, and guilt bind the identities of the two women in his imagination and his painting.[86]

In 1925 Bonnard inaugurates the theme of the nude immersed in the bath that he continues until 1946. Who is depicted in these "Bath nudes"?[87] Is it the youthful Marthe or is it Renée? All writers on the subject agree that there is deep meaning in subject and the form of this compositional structure. Various narrative literary associations have been used to discuss these paintings—from Nicholas Watkins invoking the Gospel of St. John to describe the transfiguring power of their light to John Berger describing the crystallization of love, quoting Stendhal's *De l'amour*.[88] Should we look closer to Bonnard's symbolist roots as a source for an implied narrative? Is the nude immersed related to the image of Ophelia transformed in Georges Rodenbach's *Bruges-la-Morte* (1892), a novel about a widower's grief and obsession in which reflective surfaces distort and conflate the identities of his dead wife and his lover?[89] Or do we see the immersion of the abiding Marthe after the tragic death of Renée as the visualization of a suppressed, disguised, or forbidden memory?[90]

What coalesces in Bonnard's "fantasy of immersion"[91] is the culminating theme and structure of his cinematic gaze. By finding the nude within the oval of the tub and, in turn, framing the oval of the tub within the rectangular picture plane, Bonnard creates a compositional space that is synonymous with the foreground of his vision. As he said, "It is the foreground that gives one a concept of the world as seen through human eyes, of a world which gives the idea of the cosmos as the human eye sees it, of a universe that is rolling, or convex or concave."[92] All that has ever excited Bonnard about vision presents itself here—the culmination of a lifetime of unlearning and relearning. Picture Bonnard as he was photographed in his rented house in Deauville in 1937. Tacked against the flowered wallpaper in the dining room is a canvas with the initial rendering of a nude in the tub with outlines of the tub and tiles, of the walls and floors thinly sketched in. Still teasing the boundaries of East and West, still defining through contrast, Bonnard has tacked two Japanese prints to the opposite wall.[93] Perhaps it amused Bonnard to think that rhythmic pattern on pattern, touch over touch of ecstatic color would soon wash over the tiles like a wave collecting itself in contours or corners, creating reserves of white in others. A dense constellation of shapes would be built up to revolve around the thin washes within the oval tub. Seen from above, the woman's body would soon be covered, caressed, and changed by following the action of the light through the water—a thinly painted ocher bleeding into pinks and blues (plate 123). If, as the critic John Berger observed, water seals off the woman from Bonnard—if, as Berger says, "she is lost in the near,"[94]—then it also serves to displace and project the artist's arousal. Vacillating between transparency and opacity yet somehow fixed within the sanctuary of the tub, the features of the most private aspect of his beloved always remain visible.

Self-Portraits
In 1930 a self-portrait of Bonnard quixotically staring over his shoulder into a mirror inaugurated a period of contemplation and explanations (plate 134). Since 1927 (when his nephew Charles Terrasse first published a monograph on him), he had been keeping daybooks and writing in a journal notes about painting. On the occasion of his large one-person show at Bernheim-Jeune in 1933, he began opening his calendar to critics and reporters publishing interviews. By the end of the decade he had painted four self-portraits. Not since 1890, when he started his life as an artist, had he chosen to make definitive statements or paint a series of self-portraits.

Now Bonnard's position in the art world, something he was never concerned about, became a topic of much discussion. In 1930, when he served on the jury of the Carnegie International in Pittsburgh, Matisse went to the Phillips Memorial Gallery in Washington, then the proud possessor of the best collection of contemporary art from the School of Paris in America. There, in the

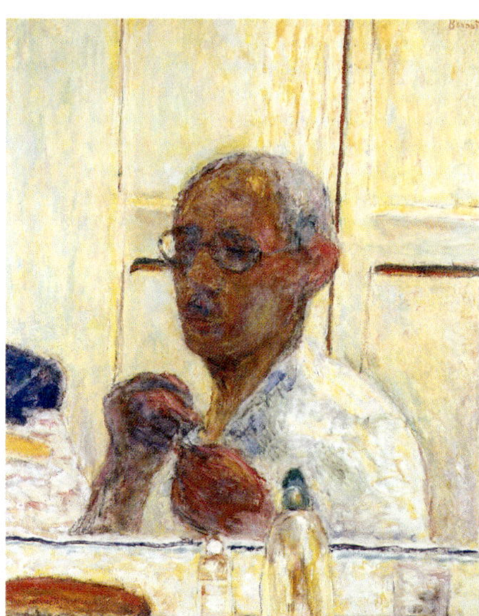

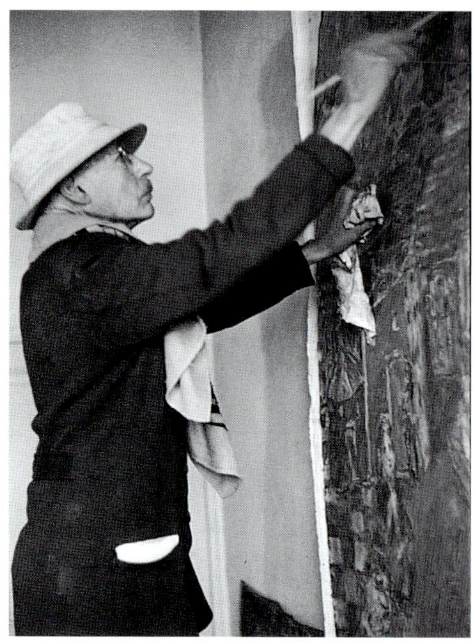

87. Pierre Bonnard, *Self-Portrait*, ca. 1938–1940, Oil on canvas, 30 × 24 in. (76.2 × 61 cm), Art Gallery of New South Wales, Sydney. Purchased 1972.

88. Henri Cartier-Bresson, *Bonnard in the Studio at Le Cannet at Work on "Saint François de Sales,"* 1945, Photograph.

museum, which contained multiple Bonnards and a single Matisse, the artist proclaimed Bonnard "the greatest [painter] of us all."[95]

Bonnard's late self-portraits appear to tell another story. Consider the balding myopic man engulfed in the wide frame of the mirror, raising his fists as if trapped and battling within its golden light (fig. 87, plate 135). Is this the powerful defender of painting? Who could fail to see the irony? To most viewers this genius wore a cloak of invisibility, disguising him as a perpetual student. In August 1931 Bonnard wrote to Duncan Phillips, "I am touched by the interest you take in my painting despite its great flaws—I am always striving to improve my style, and I am not indifferent to the fact that the like-minded support my efforts."[96] Bonnard was quick to point out his flaws. In 1937 when journalist Ingrid Rydbeck interviewed him, Bonnard gave her an astounding list of his so-called deficiencies. Among his remarks offered that day were: "To tell the truth I have trouble with painting"; "I work so slowly that I must use paints that can be revised or added to continually"; "It would bother me if my canvases were stretched onto a frame. I never know in advance what dimensions I am going to choose (fig. 88)."[97]

In light of Bonnard's self-doubts of 1937, consider now a question asked by Christian Zervos, friend of Picasso, "Is there reason to overlook Bonnard's tranquility and detachment?"[98] No. To ignore the deliberate anachronisms of Bonnard's execution and enactment of painting within the twentieth century is to overlook the most elusive and potent force of his genius. Bonnard's so-called flaws, his hesitations and contingencies, are in fact his greatest strengths. The ascetic, aging man in the self-portrait begun in 1940 might be compared to the posture of a great Zen priest from the Song dynasty. Stubbornly holding onto the freedom of his inquiry, open to visual phenomenon from any and all sources, he never wants completely to answer the question, How do I see? He creates from intuition rather than from logic, capturing an experience too fluid, too complex for reason. In the end painting with the light, he stands resolute in his stubborn purpose to change the aspect of both life and art.

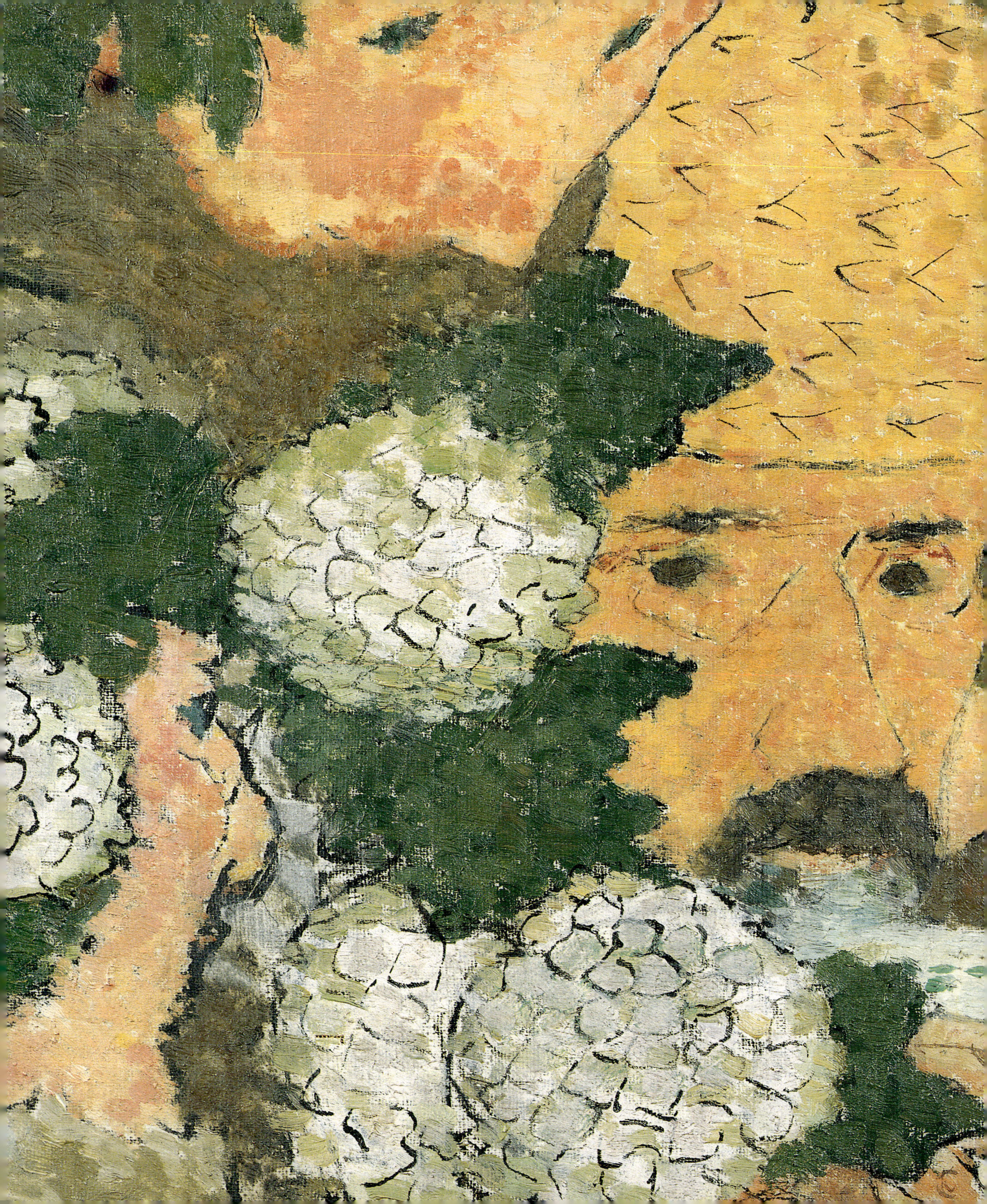

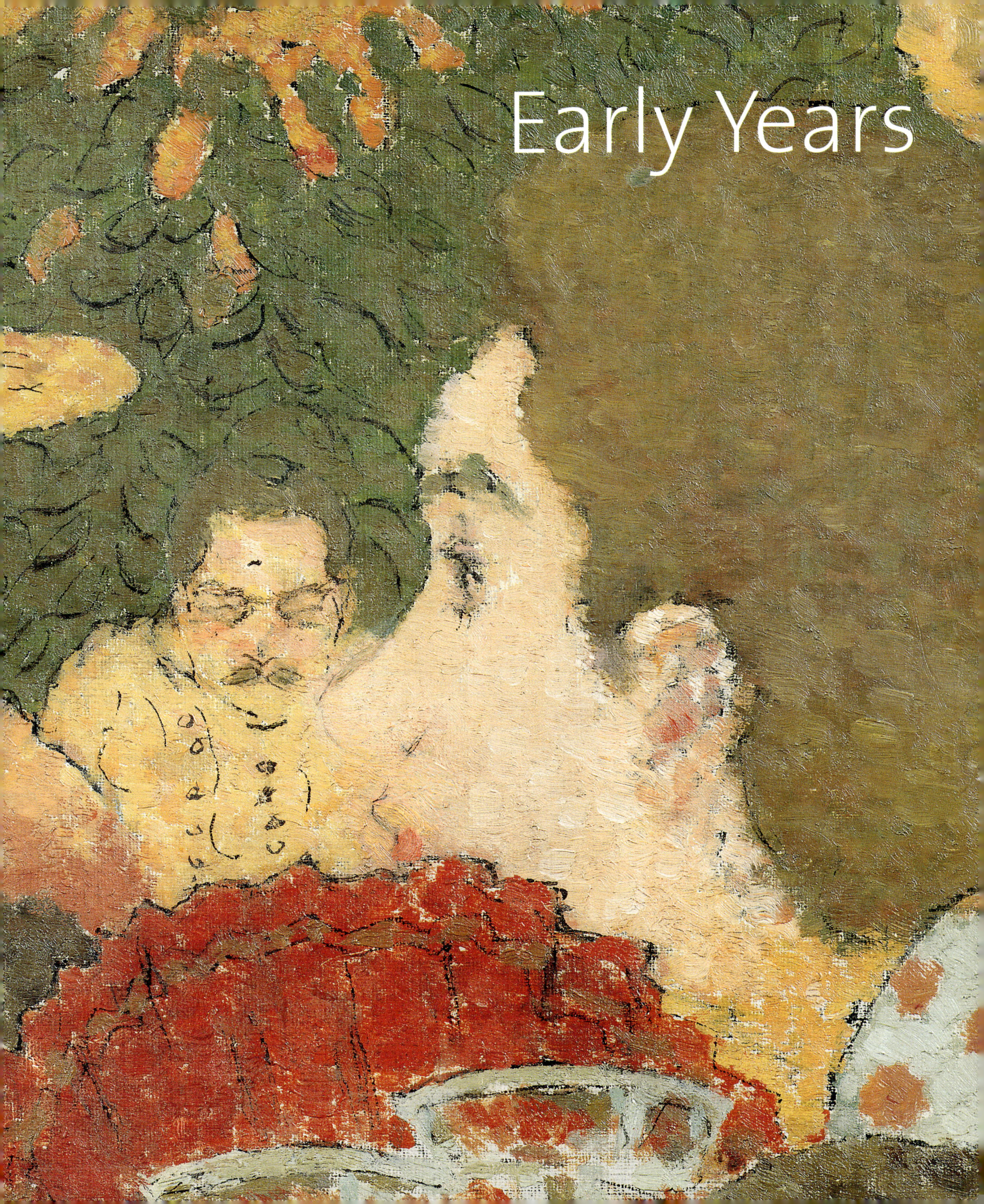
Early Years

Early Years

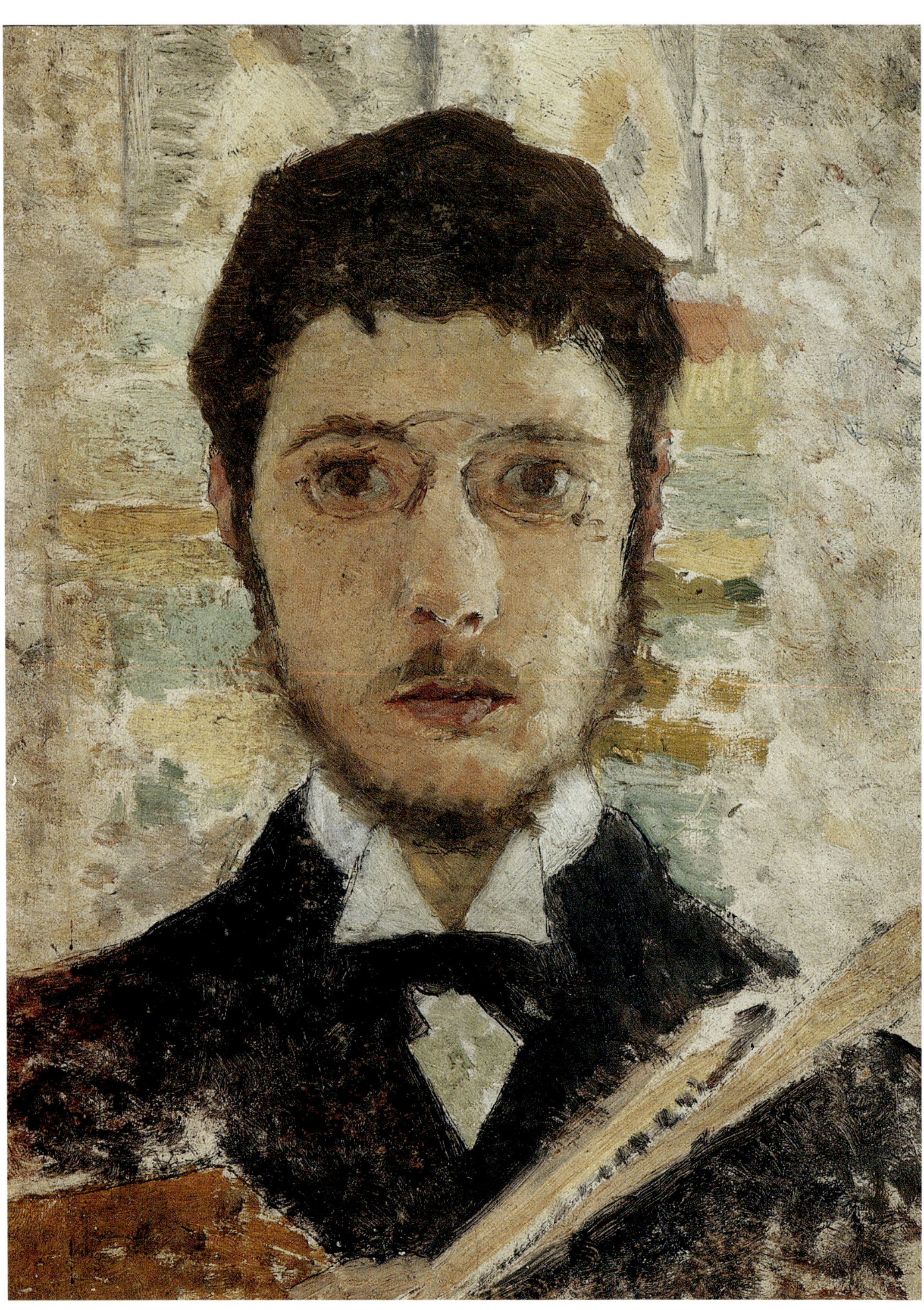

Previous spread:
Afternoon in the Garden
(detail), 1891, Oil and pen and black ink
over pencil on canvas, 14¾ × 17¾ in.
(37.5 × 45.1 cm), Private collection.

1

Self-Portrait
1889, Oil on board, 7⅞ × 6⅛ in.
(20 × 15.5 cm), Private collection.

2

Marabout (Stork) and Four Frogs
ca. 1889, Distemper on fine canvas
(three-paneled screen), each panel,
62¾ × 21½ in. (159.5 × 54.5 cm), Private
collection.

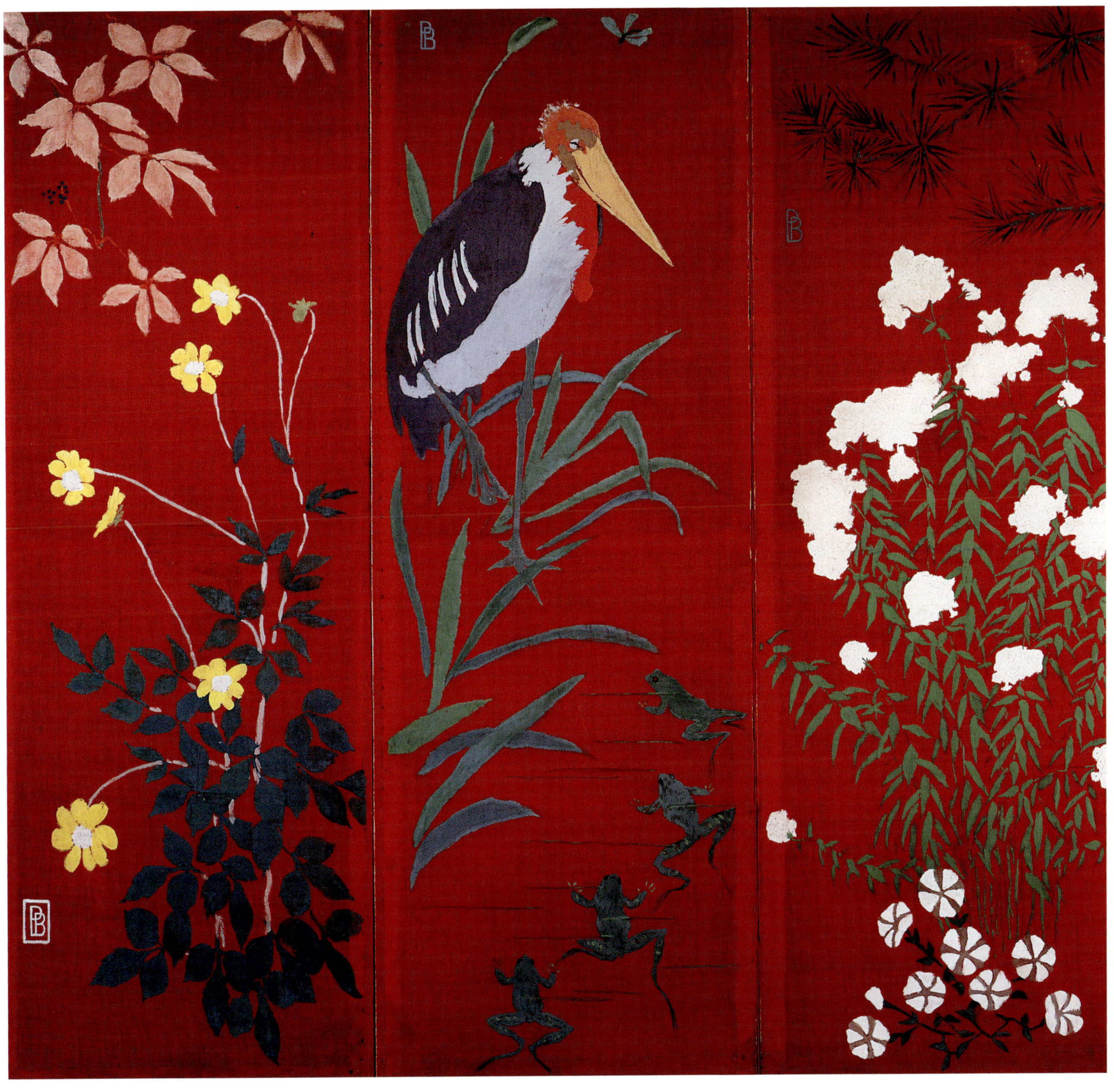

3

**Checked Blouse; Portrait of Mme Claude
Terrasse, the Artist's Sister**
1892, Oil on canvas, 23⅝ × 13 in. (60 × 33 cm),
Private collection, courtesy Galerie Cazeau-
Béraudière, Paris.

Opposite page:
**Checked Blouse; Portrait of Mme Claude
Terrasse, the Artist's Sister** (detail).

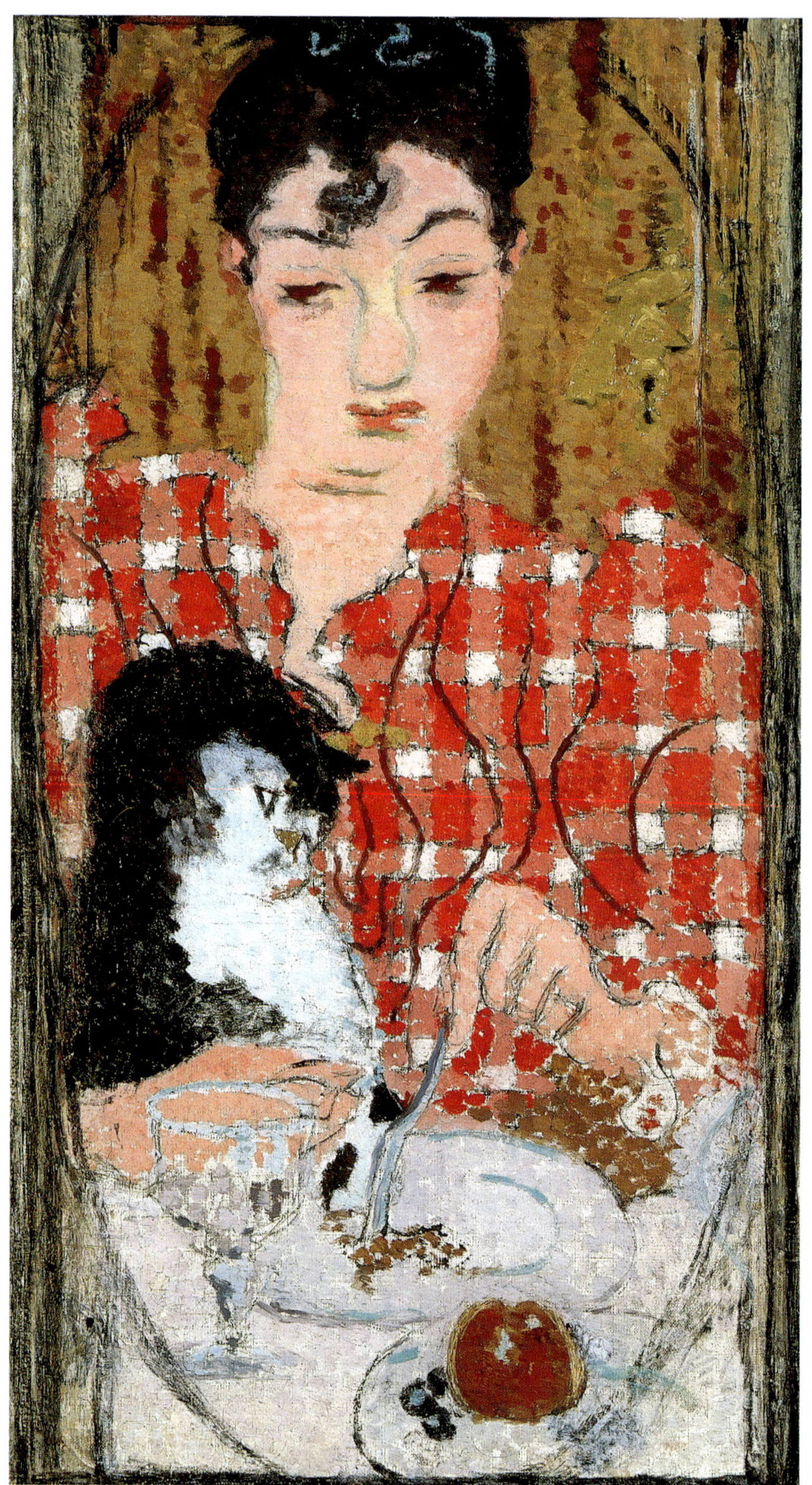

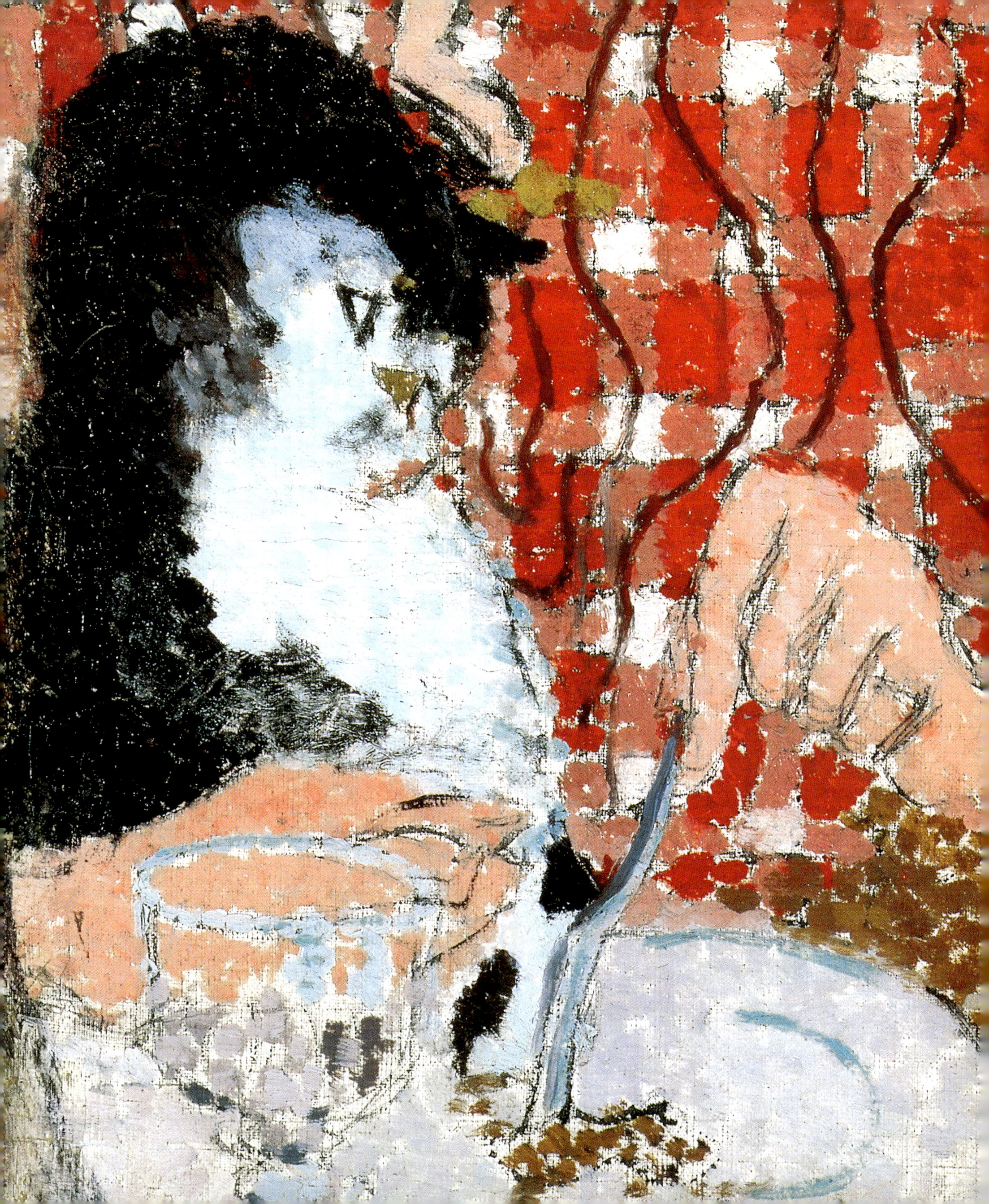

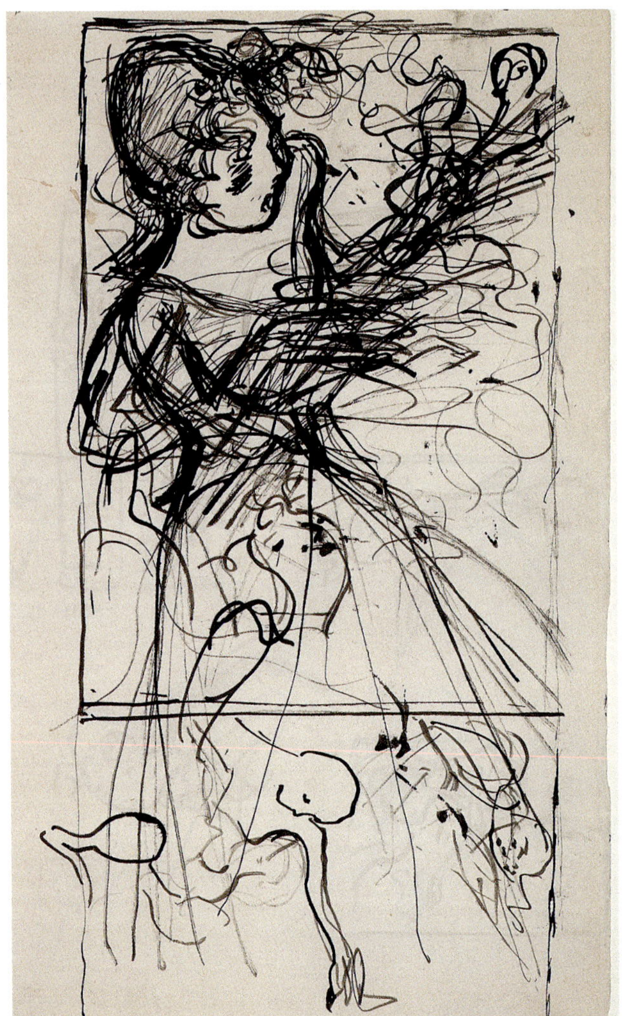

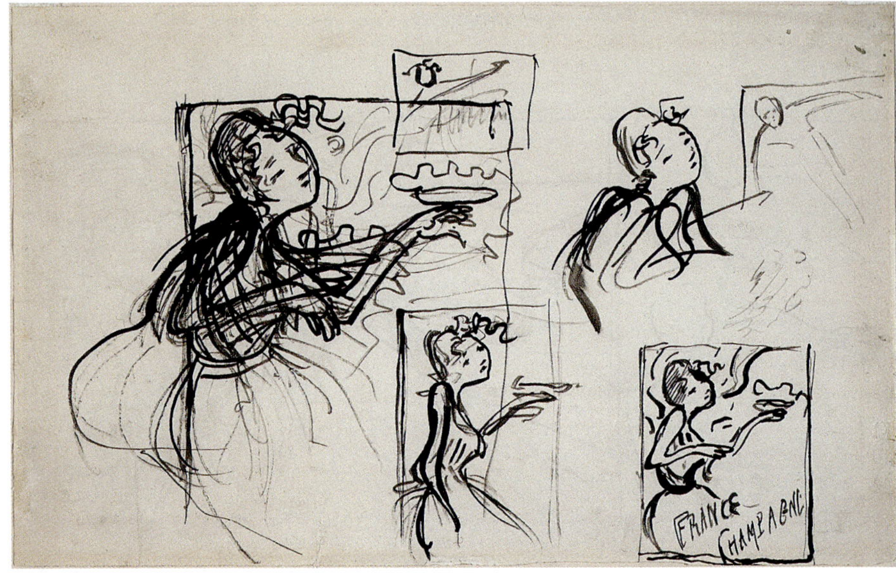

4 a–b

Studies for "France-Champagne"
ca. 1889, Pencil and ink on wove paper
(recto), 12³⁄₁₆ × 7¹³⁄₁₆ in. (30.9 × 19.9 cm),
Pencil and ink on wove paper (verso),
7 ¹³⁄₁₆ × 12³⁄₁₆ in. (19.9 × 30.9 cm), Virginia and
Ira Jackson Collection. Partial and Promised
Gift to the National Gallery of Art,
Washington.

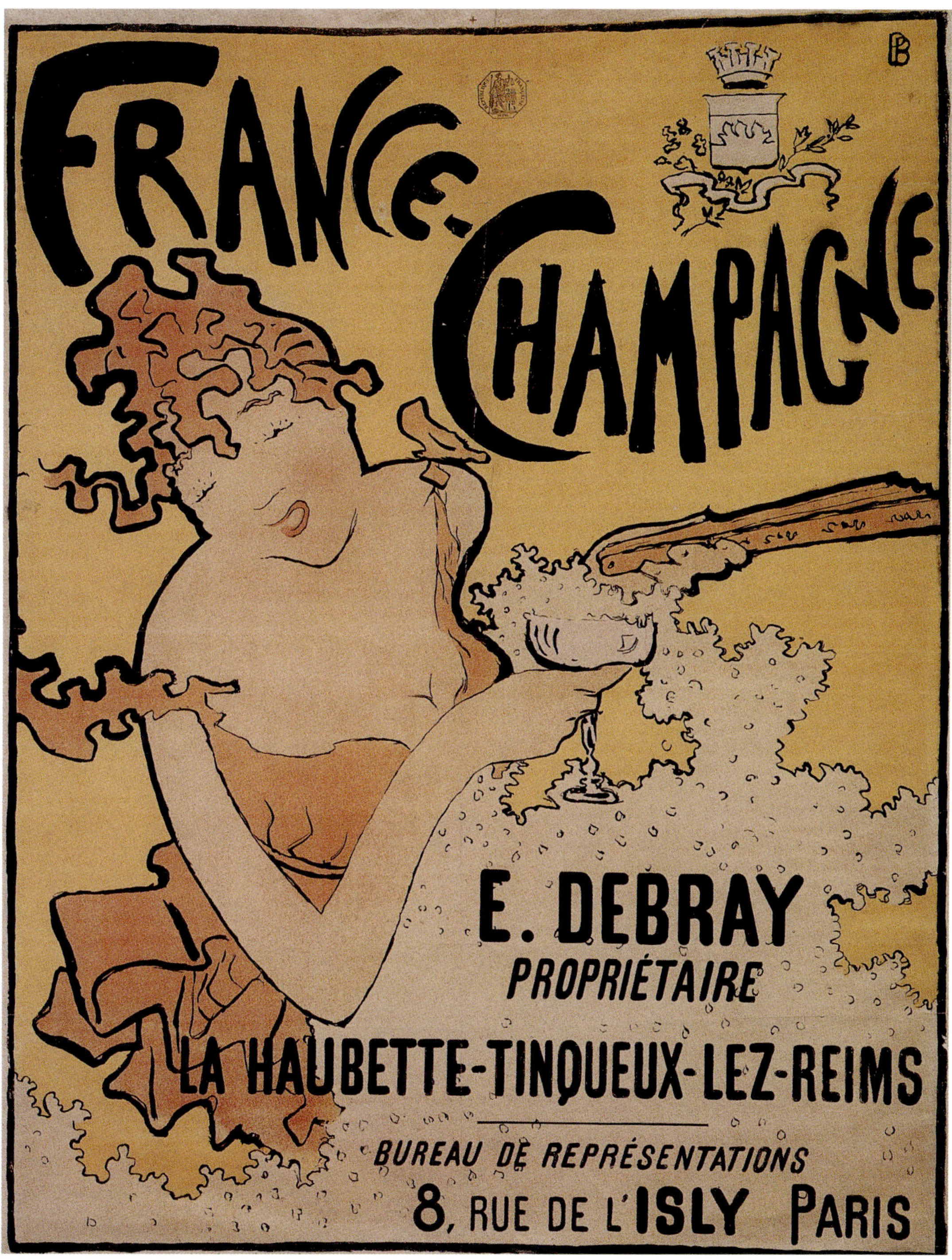

5

Poster for "France-Champagne"
1891, Color lithograph, 31⁷⁄₁₆ × 23¾ in.
(79.8 × 60.3 cm), Virginia and Ira Jackson
Collection. Partial and Promised Gift to the
National Gallery of Art, Washington.

Next spread: **Poster for "France-Champagne"** (detail).

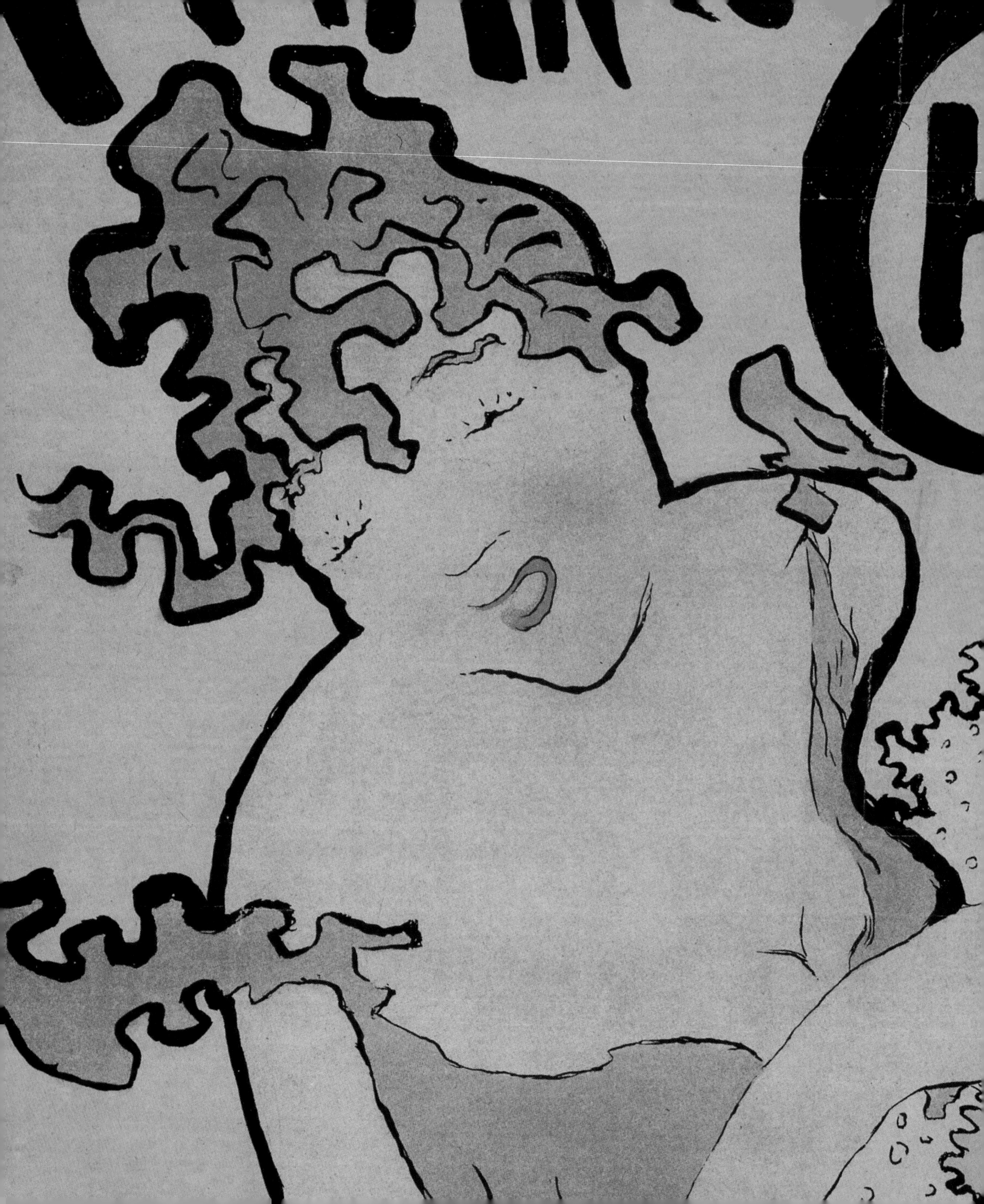

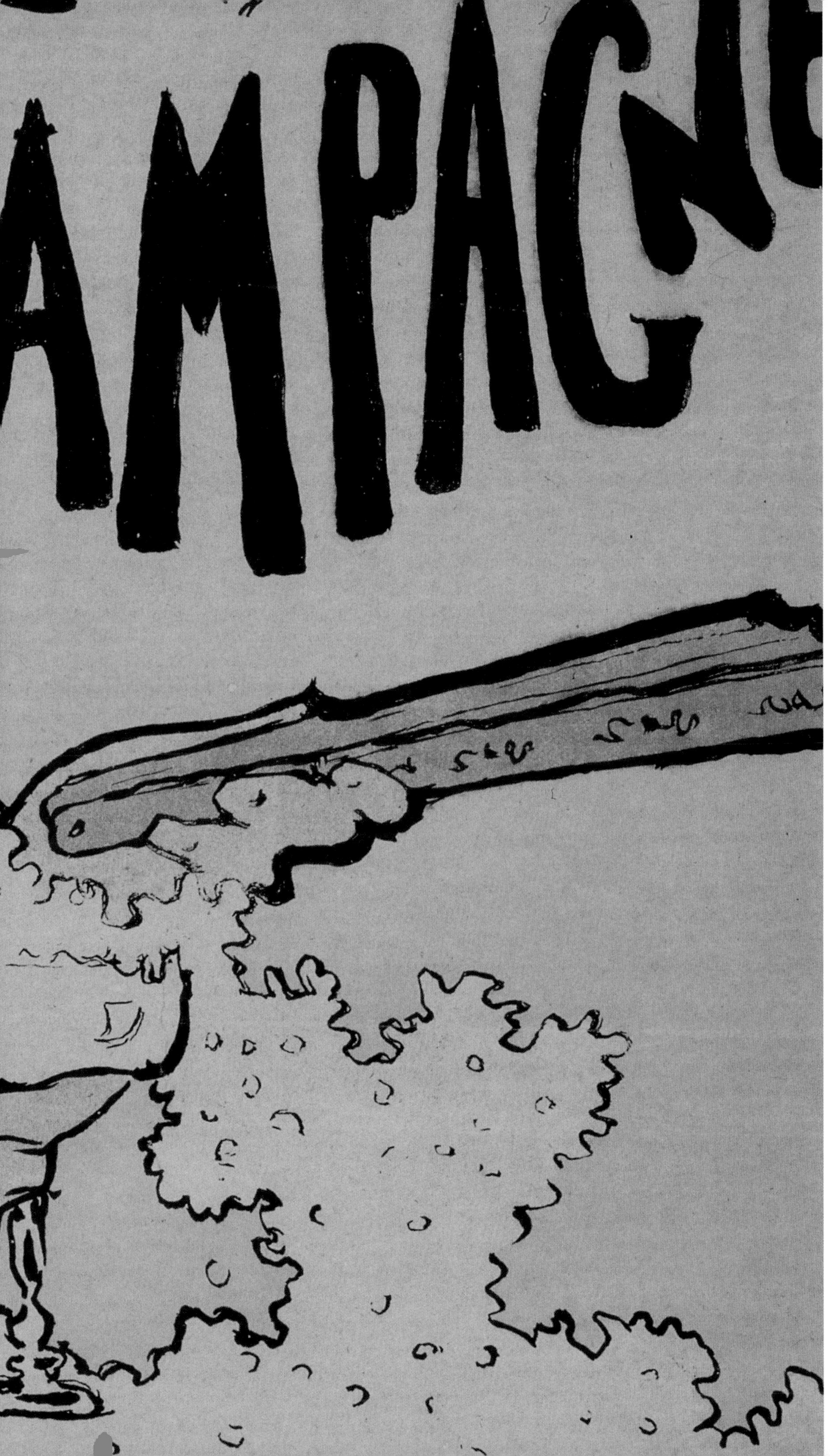

AMPAG

6

Women with Dog
1891, Oil on canvas, 16 × 12¾ in.
(40.6 × 32.4 cm), Sterling and Francine Clark
Art Institute, Williamstown, Massachusetts.

Opposite page: **Women with Dog** (detail).

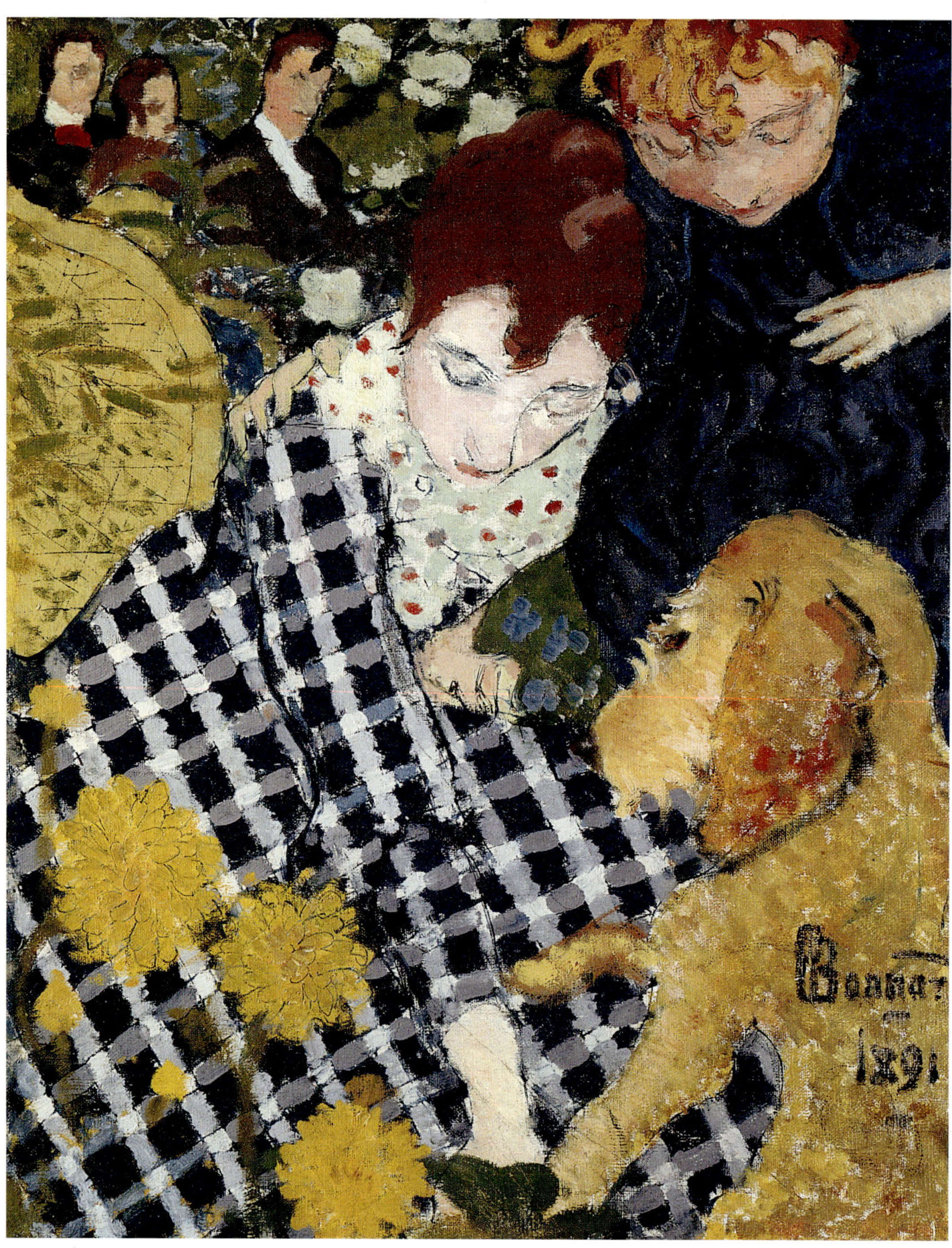

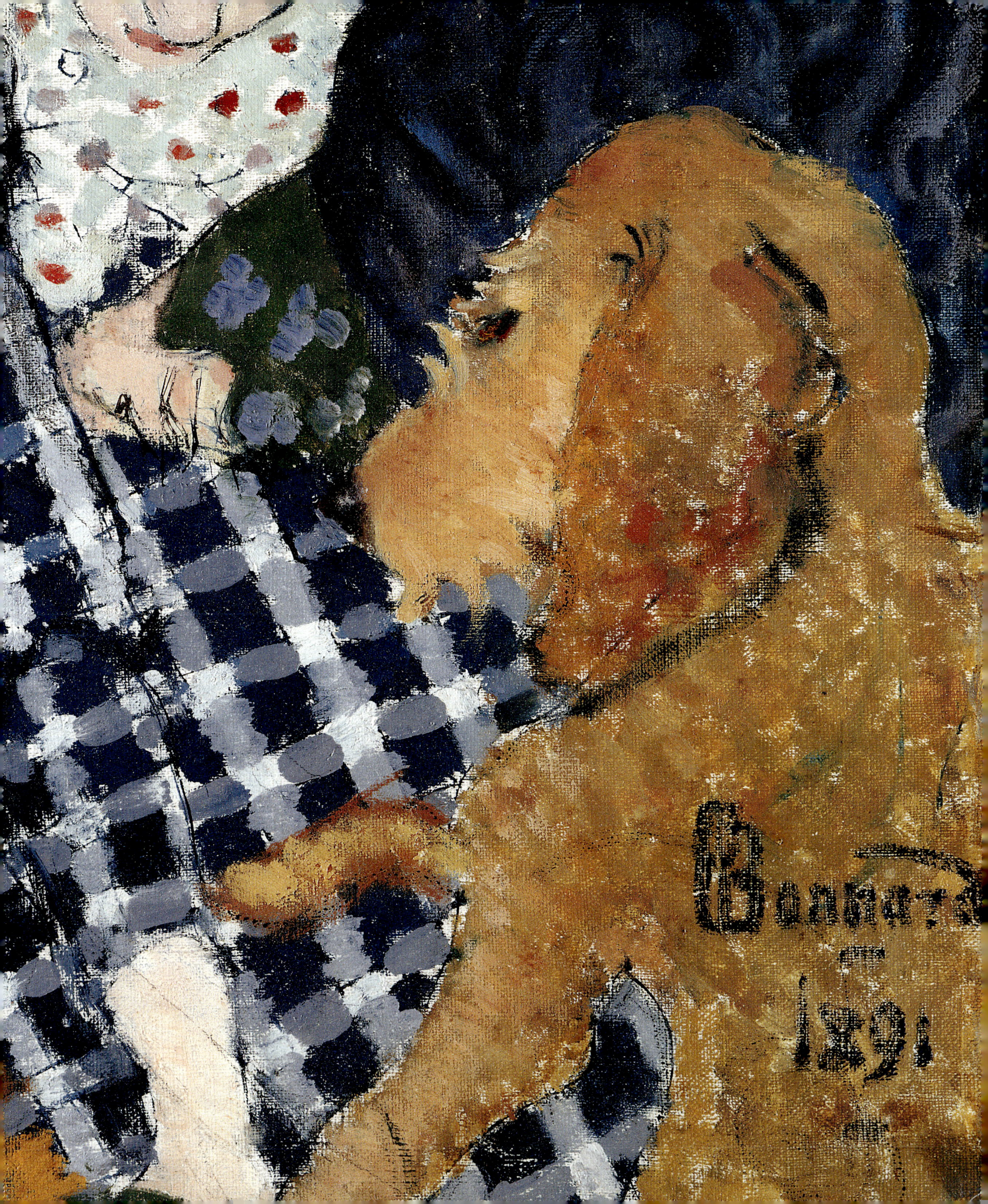

Bonnard
1891

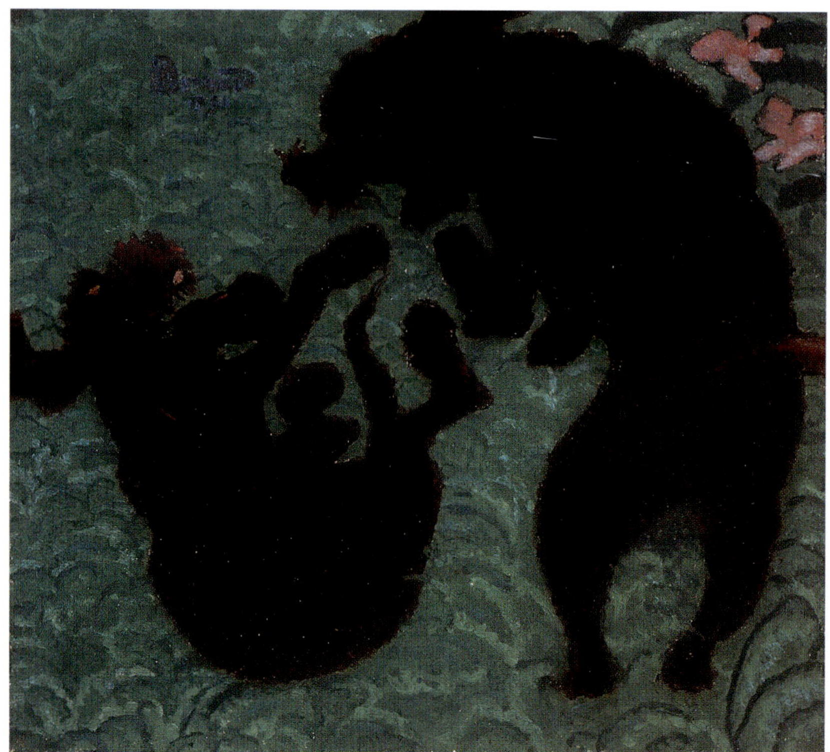

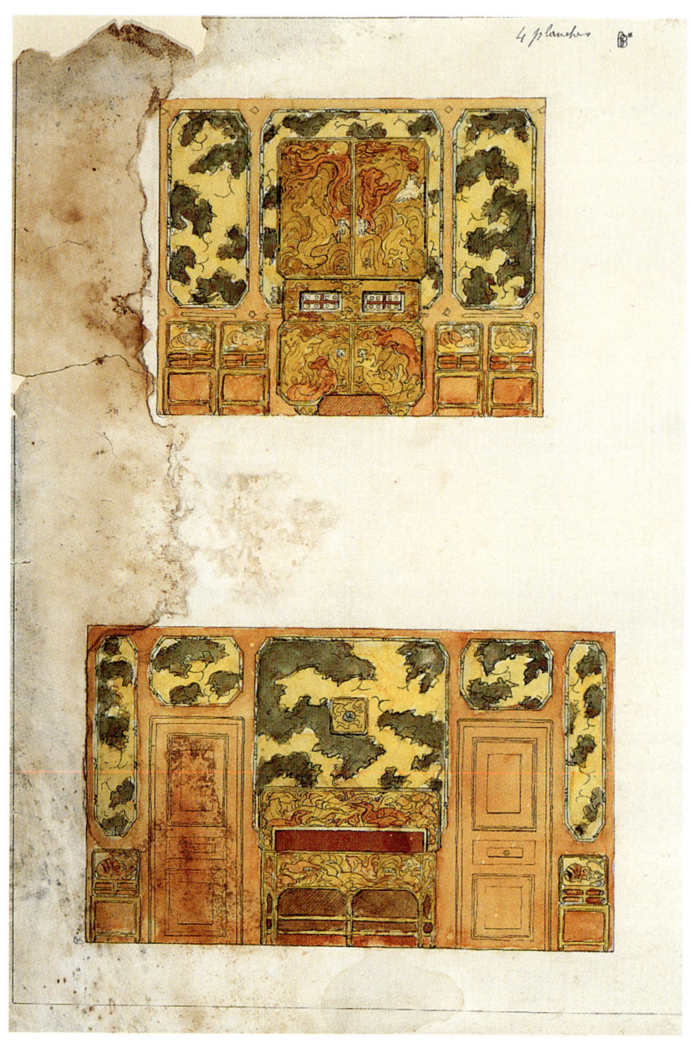

7

Two Poodles
1891, Oil on canvas, 14⁹⁄₁₆ × 15⅝ in.
(37 × 39.7 cm), Southampton City Art Gallery.

8

Decorative Design for a Dining Room
1891, Watercolor over pen and ink,
19⅞ × 14¹⁄₁₆ in. (50.5 × 35.8 cm), Paris, Musée
d'Orsay.

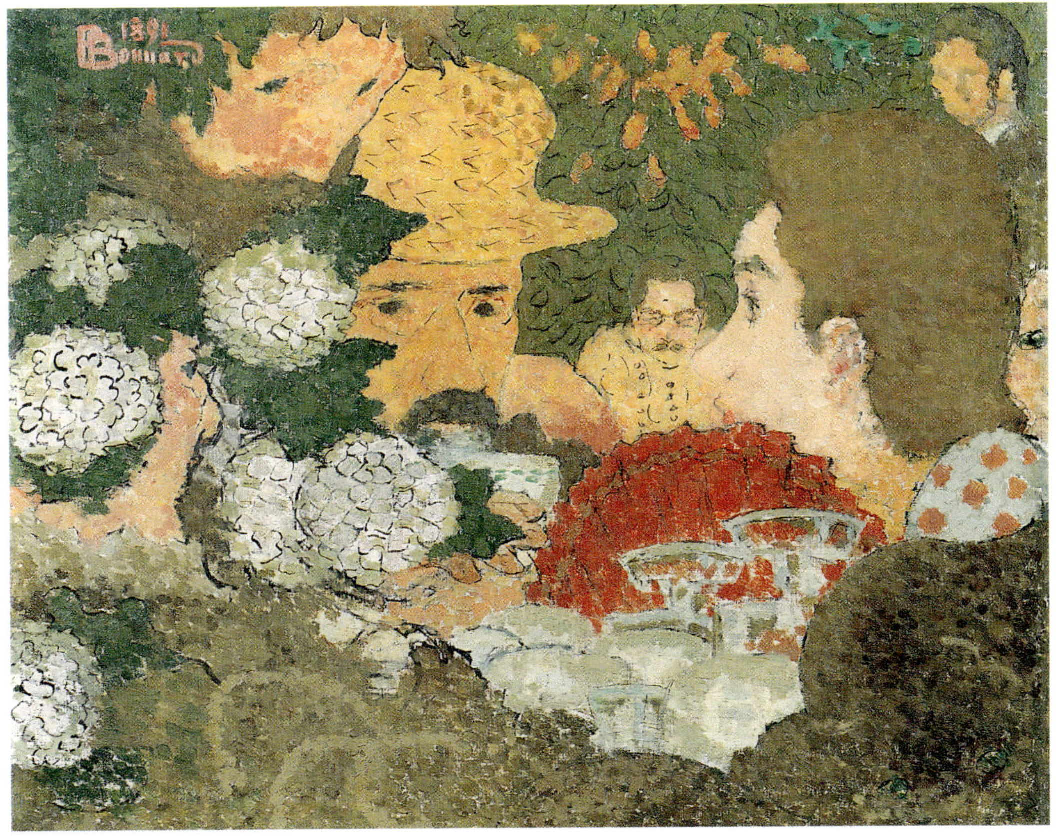

9

Afternoon in the Garden
1891, Oil and pen and black ink over
pencil on canvas, 14¾ × 17¾ in.
(37.5 × 45.1 cm), Private collection.

10

Three Panels of a Screen
1894–1895, Oil on brown twill lined with
canvas, each panel, 65¾ × 20 in. (167 × 50.8
cm), The Museum of Modern Art, New York,
Gift of Mr. and Mrs. Allan D. Emil, 1955.

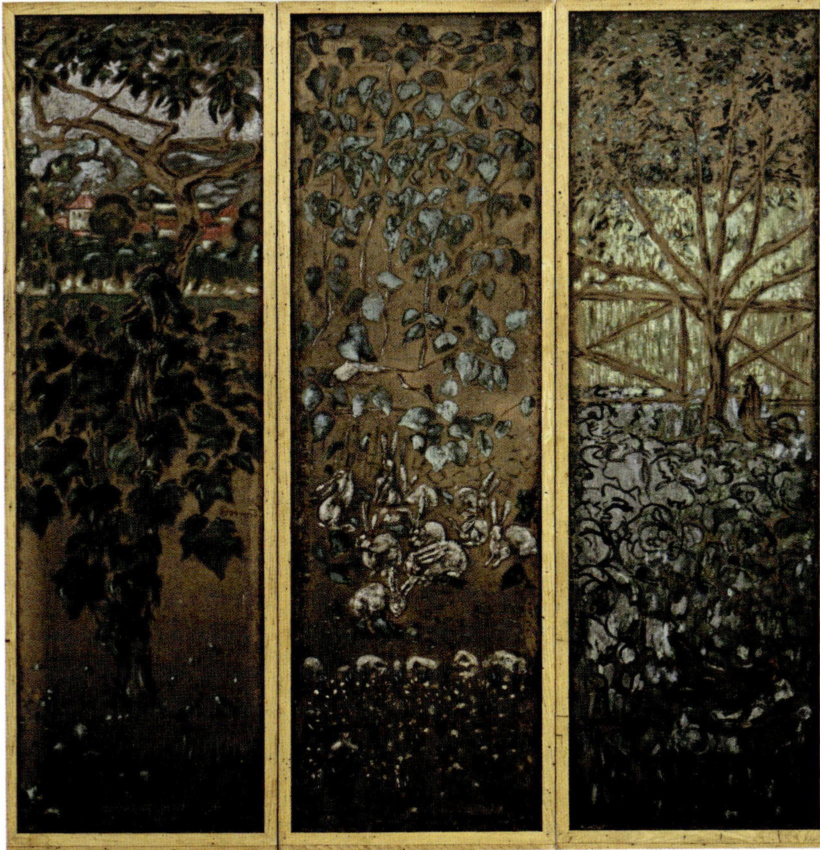

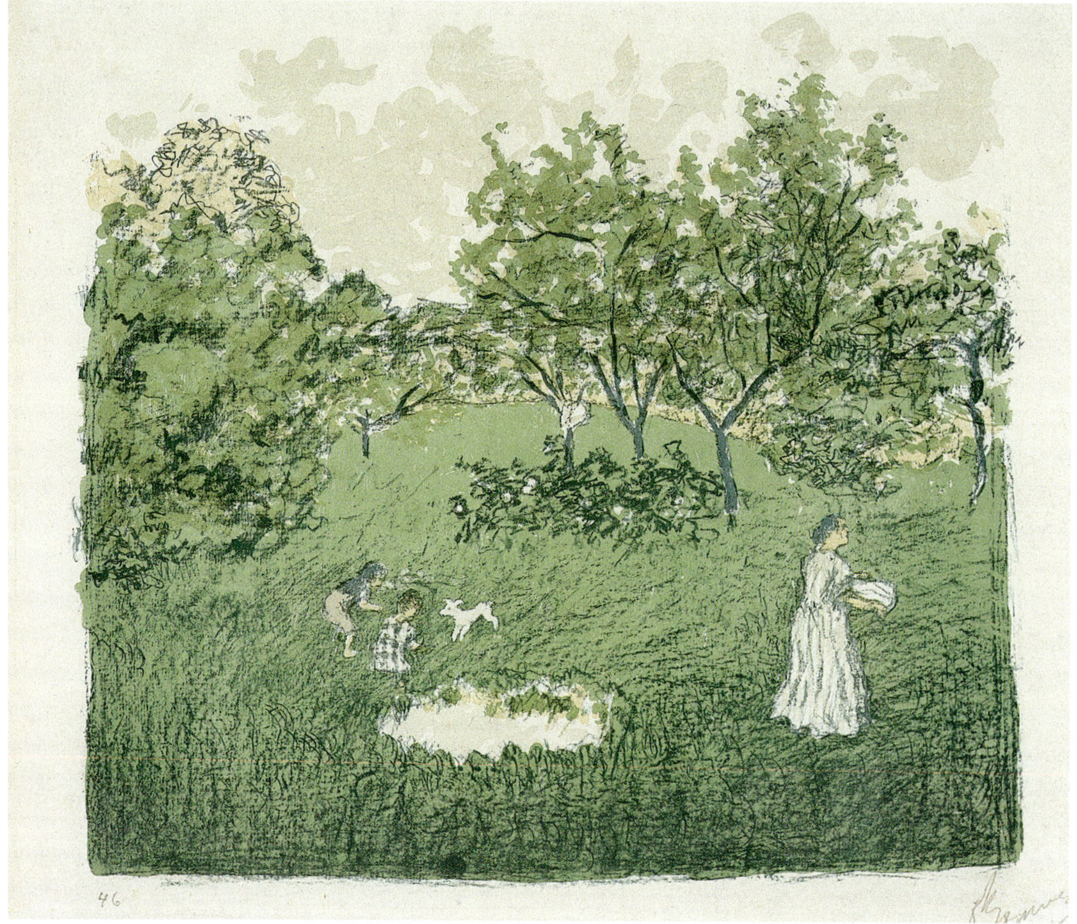

11

The Orchard
1899, Color lithograph on China paper,
15¼ × 19½ in. (38.7 × 49.5 cm), The Phillips
Collection, Washington, D.C.

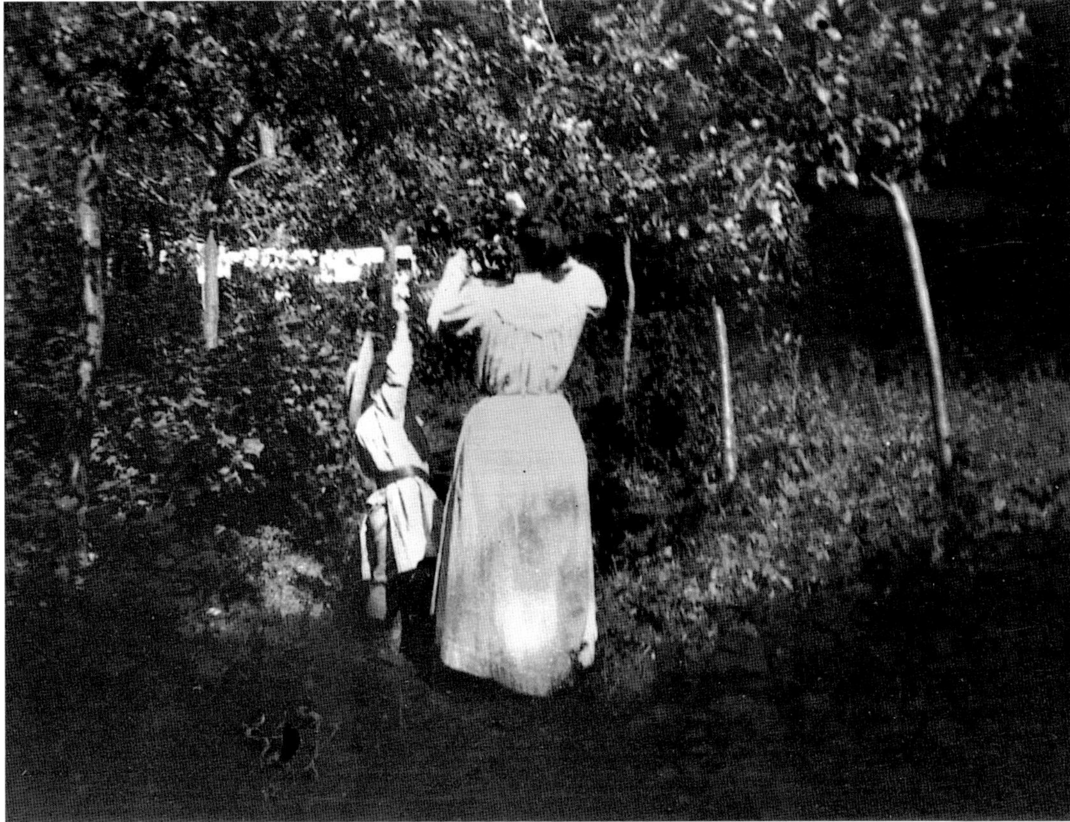

Le Grand-Lemps. The Gathering of Fruit, Andrée Terrasse and Renée
1899–1900, Contemporary print from original film negative, 11¹³⁄₁₆ × 15³⁄₈ in. (30 × 39 cm), Paris, Musée d'Orsay, donation with a life interest from Charles Terrasse's children, 1987, inv: PHO 1987 30 26.

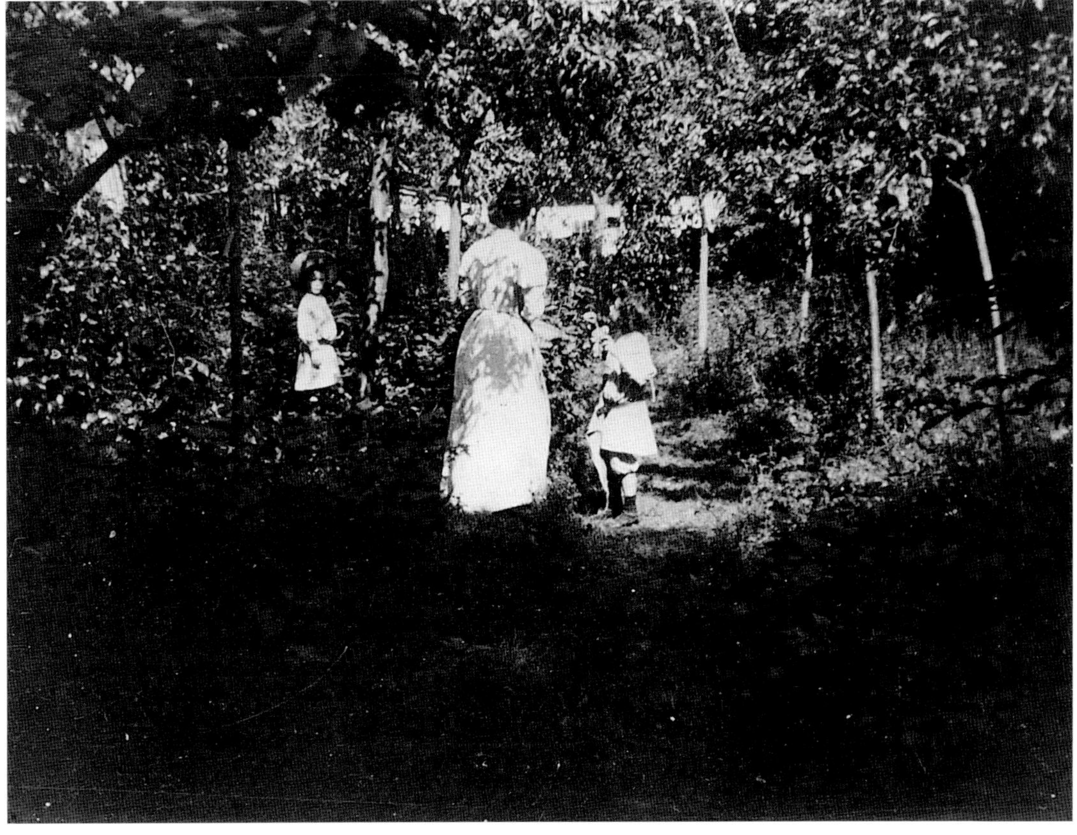

Le Grand-Lemps. The Gathering of Fruit, Andrée Terrasse, an Unknown Child and in the Background, Renée
1899–1900, Contemporary print from original film negative, 11¹³⁄₁₆ × 15³⁄₈ in. (30 × 39 cm), Paris, Musée d'Orsay, donation with a life interest from Charles Terrasse's children, 1987, inv: PHO 1987 30 25.

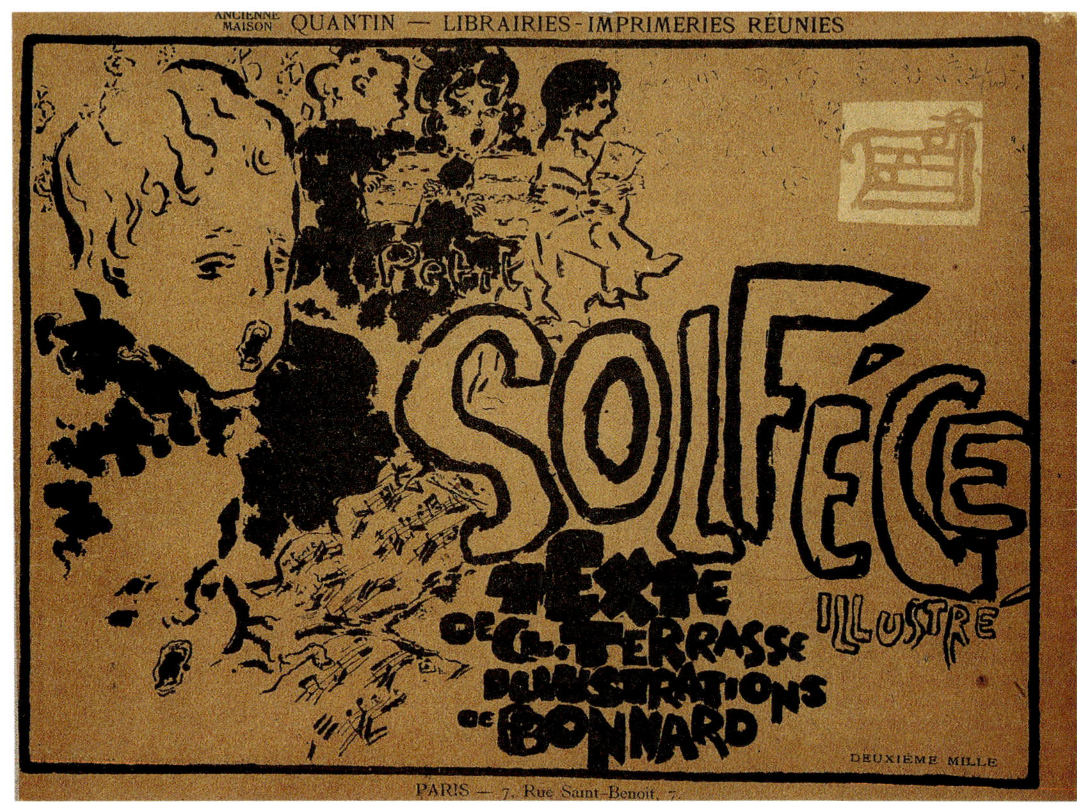

14 a–b

**Cover for Claude Terrasse's
"Petit Solfège illustré"**
1893, Lithograph, 8⅜ × 11¼ in. (21.3 × 28.3 cm),
Heineman Foundation Collection in Honor
of Edward N. Waters, Music Division,
Library of Congress, Washington, D.C.

**"Leçon sur les mesures composées" in
Claude Terrasse's "Petit Solfège illustré"**
1893, Lithograph in book, 8⅜ × 11¼ in.
(21.3 × 28.3 cm), Heineman Foundation
Collection in Honor of Edward N. Waters,
Music Division, Library of Congress,
Washington, D.C.

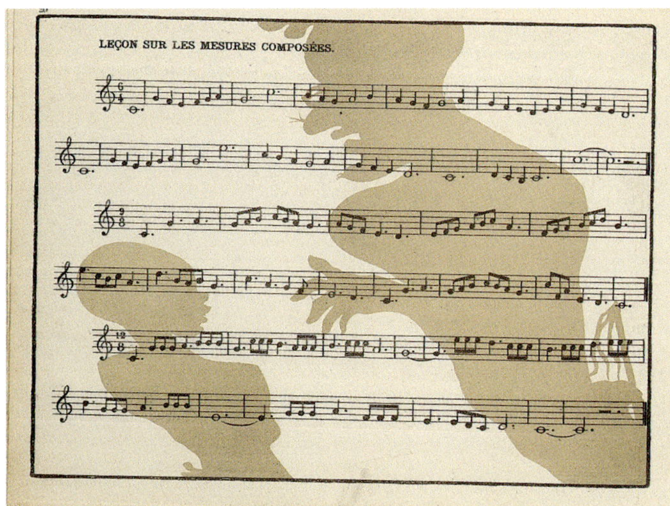

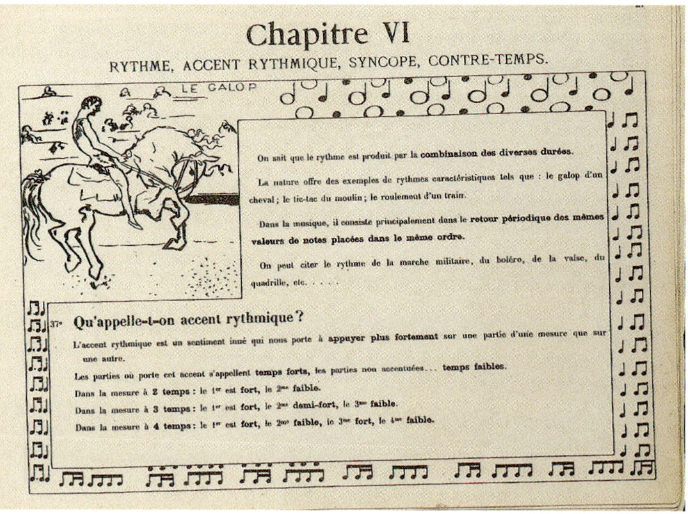

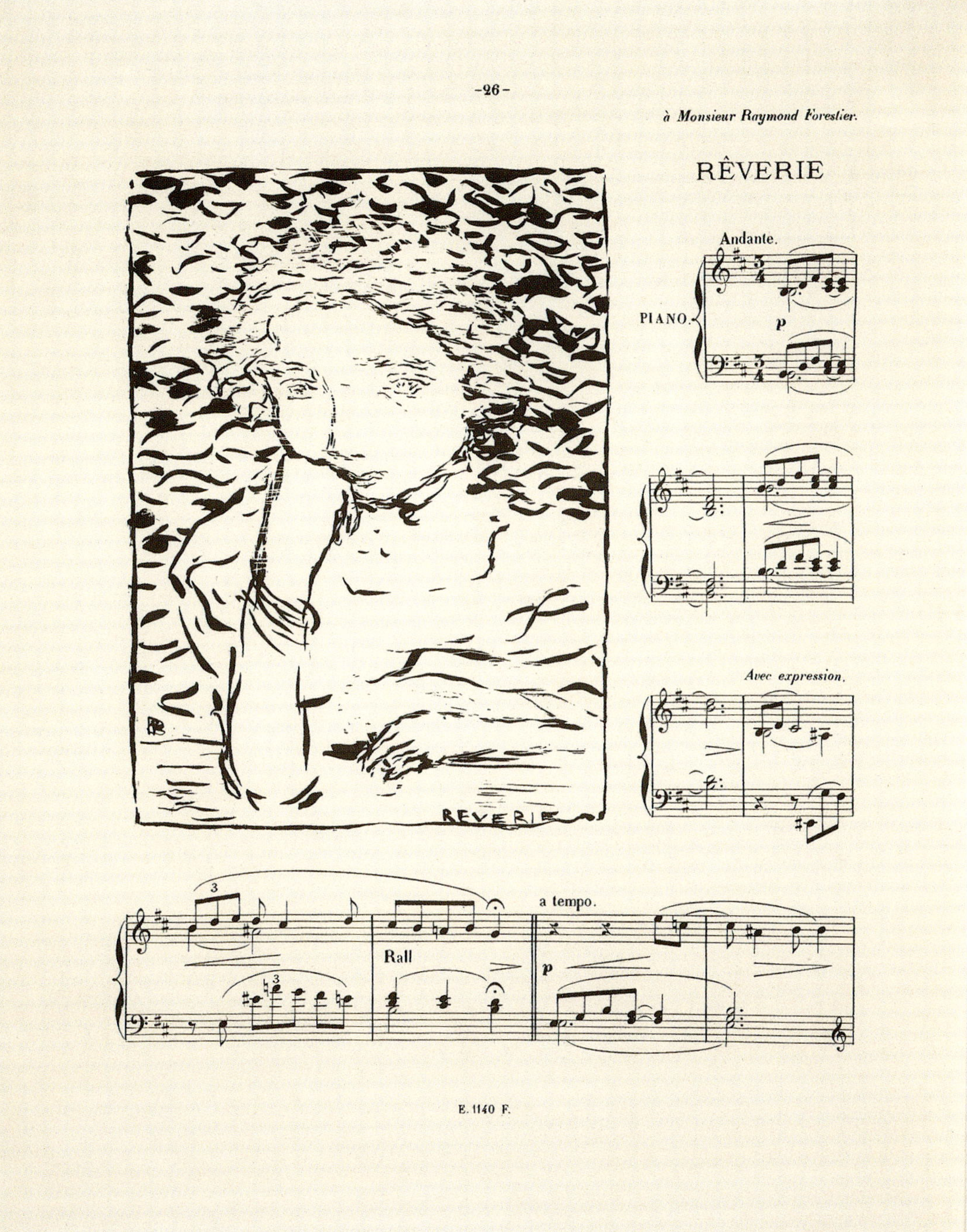

15

**"Rêverie" in Claude Terrasse's
"Petites Scènes familières"**
1893, Lithograph, 13⅞ × 10¾ in. (35.2 × 27 cm),
Museum of Fine Arts, Boston. Bequest of
W. G. Russell Allen, 1963 63.723.

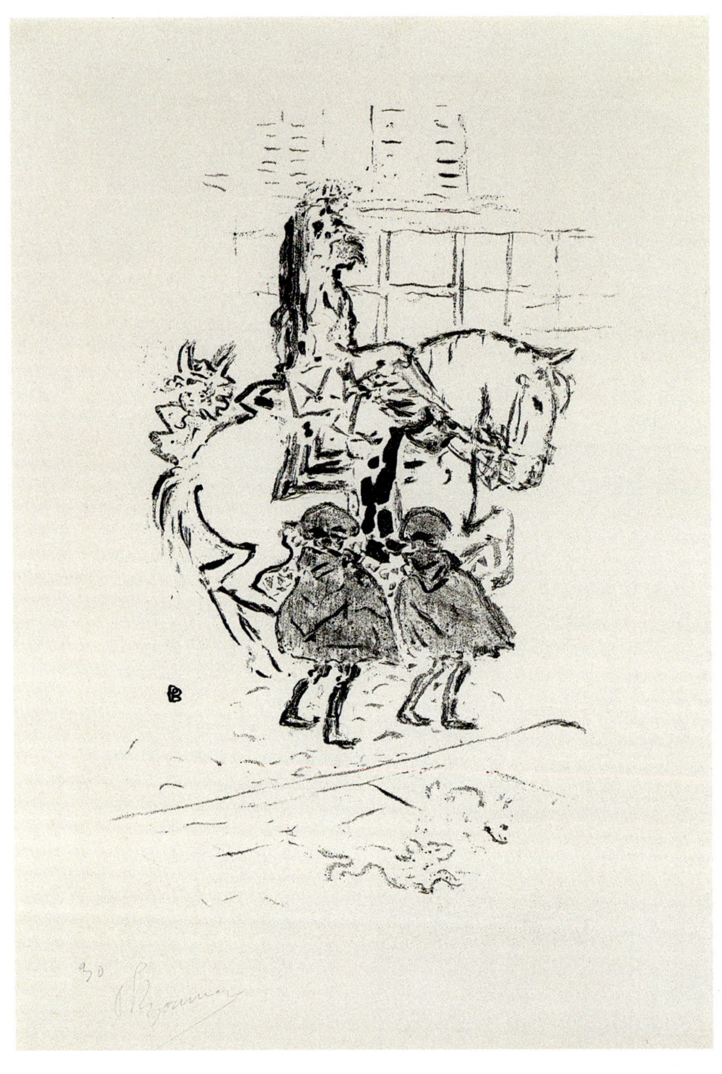

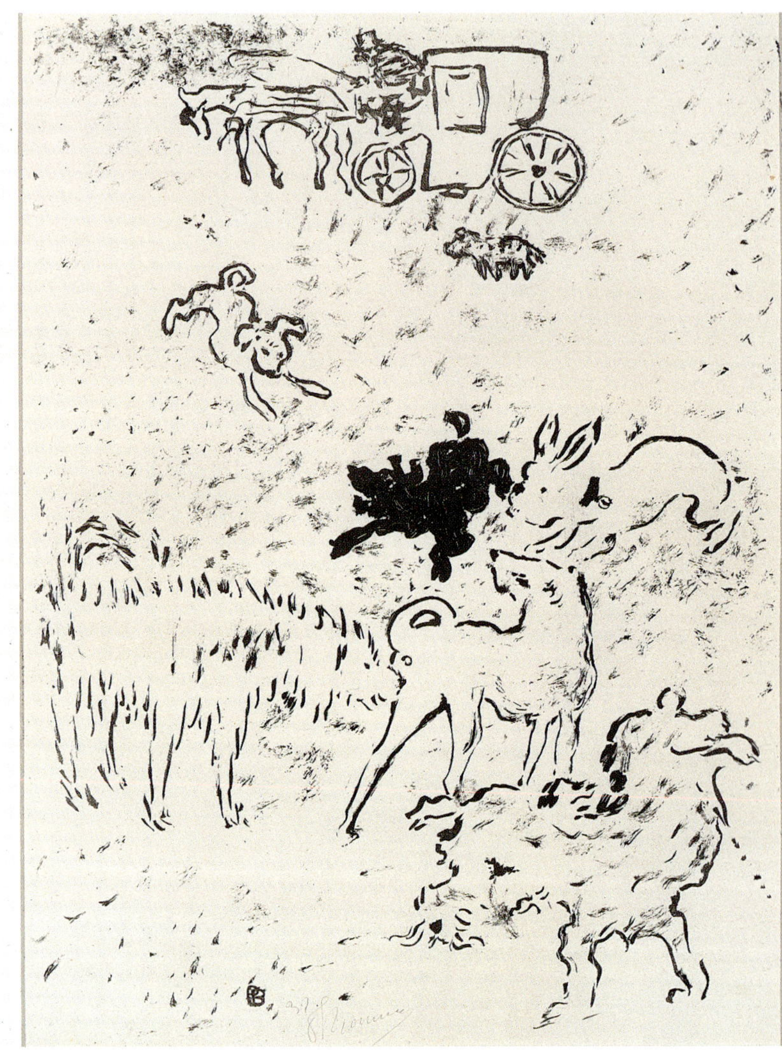

16

Municipal Guard
1893, Lithograph on cream wove paper,
15 × 11 ⅛ in. (38.1 × 28.2 cm), The Phillips
Collection, Washington, D.C.

17

Dogs
1893, Lithograph on cream wove paper,
15 × 11 in. (38.1 × 27.8 cm), The Phillips
Collection, Washington, D.C.

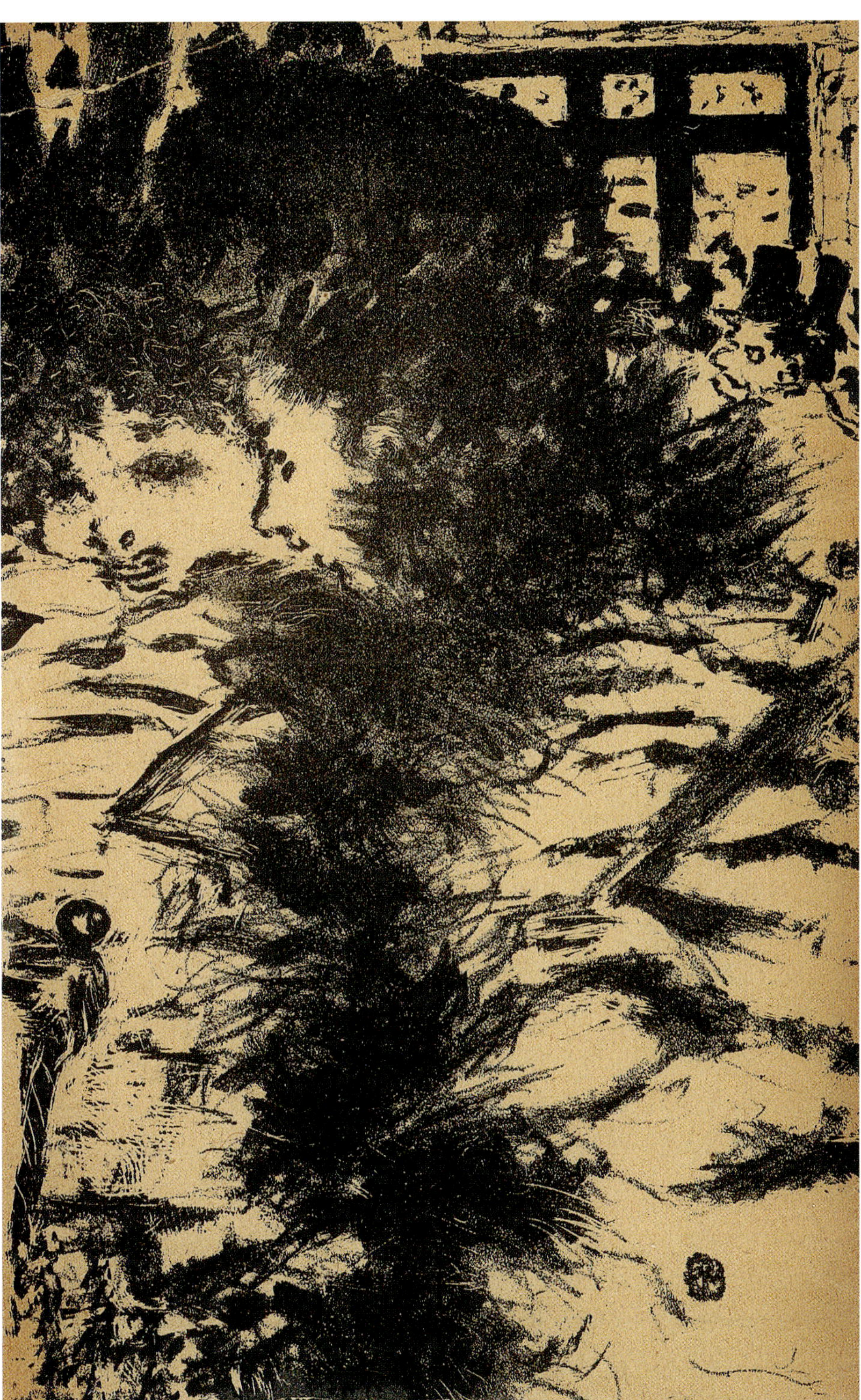

18

The Parisians
1893, Lithograph, 8⅜ × 5 in. (21.3 × 12.7 cm),
Prints and Photographs Division, Library of
Congress, Washington, D.C., Reproduction
numbers: LC-USZC4-10009, LC-USZ62-
130235.

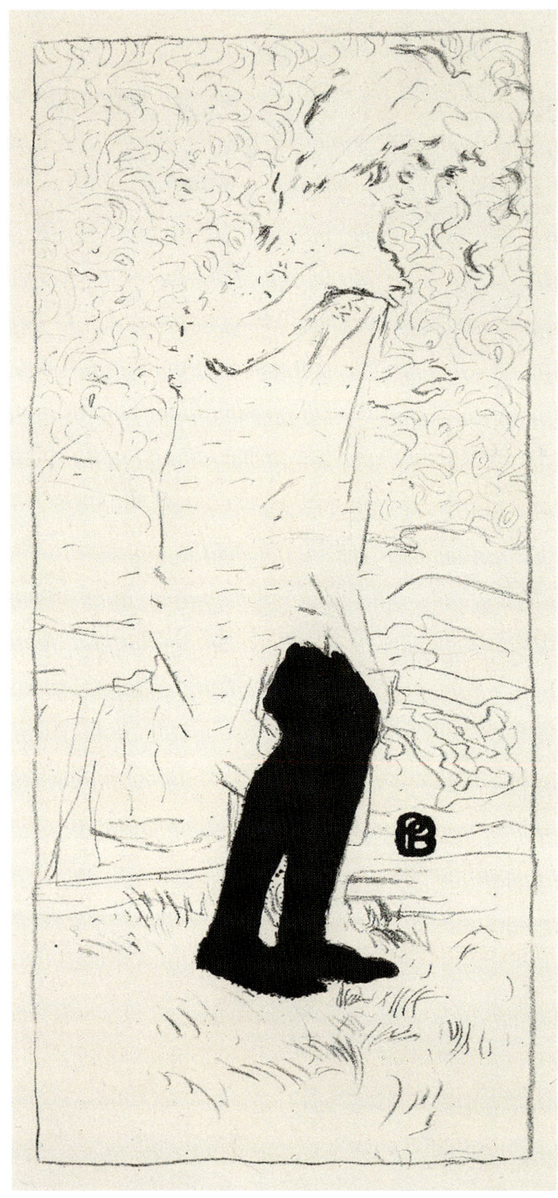

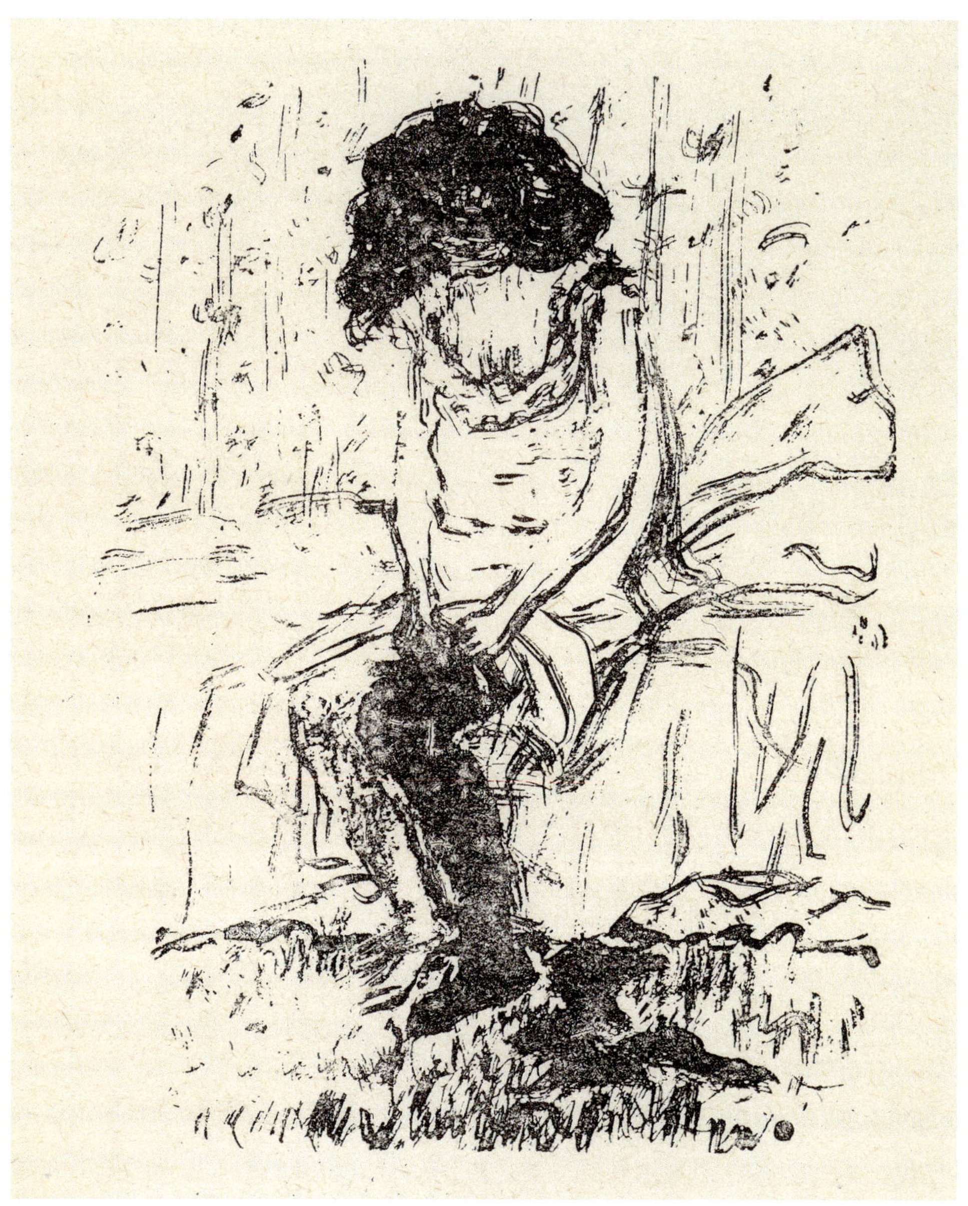

19

**In Private. Young Woman in
Black Stockings**
1893, Lithograph on cream wove paper,
11¼ × 5 in. (28.6 × 12.7 cm), The Phillips
Collection, Washington, D.C.

20

**"Marie Putting on Her Stockings" in Peter
Nansen's "Marie"**
1898, Process print, 7⅜ × 4⅝ in. (18.7 × 11.7 cm),
The Metropolitan Museum of Art, The Elisha
Whittelsey Collection, The Elisha Whittelsey
Fund, 1969 (69.636).

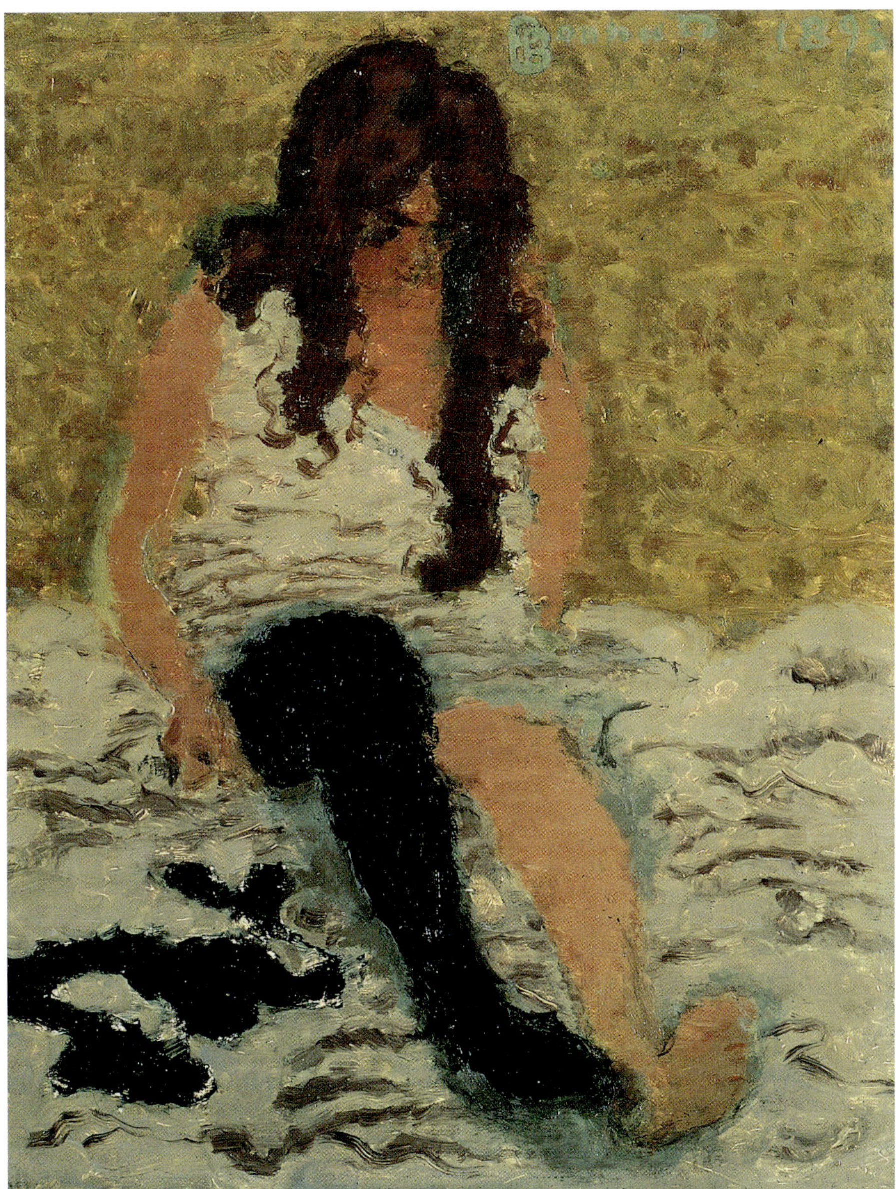

21

Woman Pulling on Her Stockings
1893, Oil on board, 13⅞ × 10⅝ in. (35.2 × 27 cm),
Private collection. Courtesy The Fine Art
Society plc.

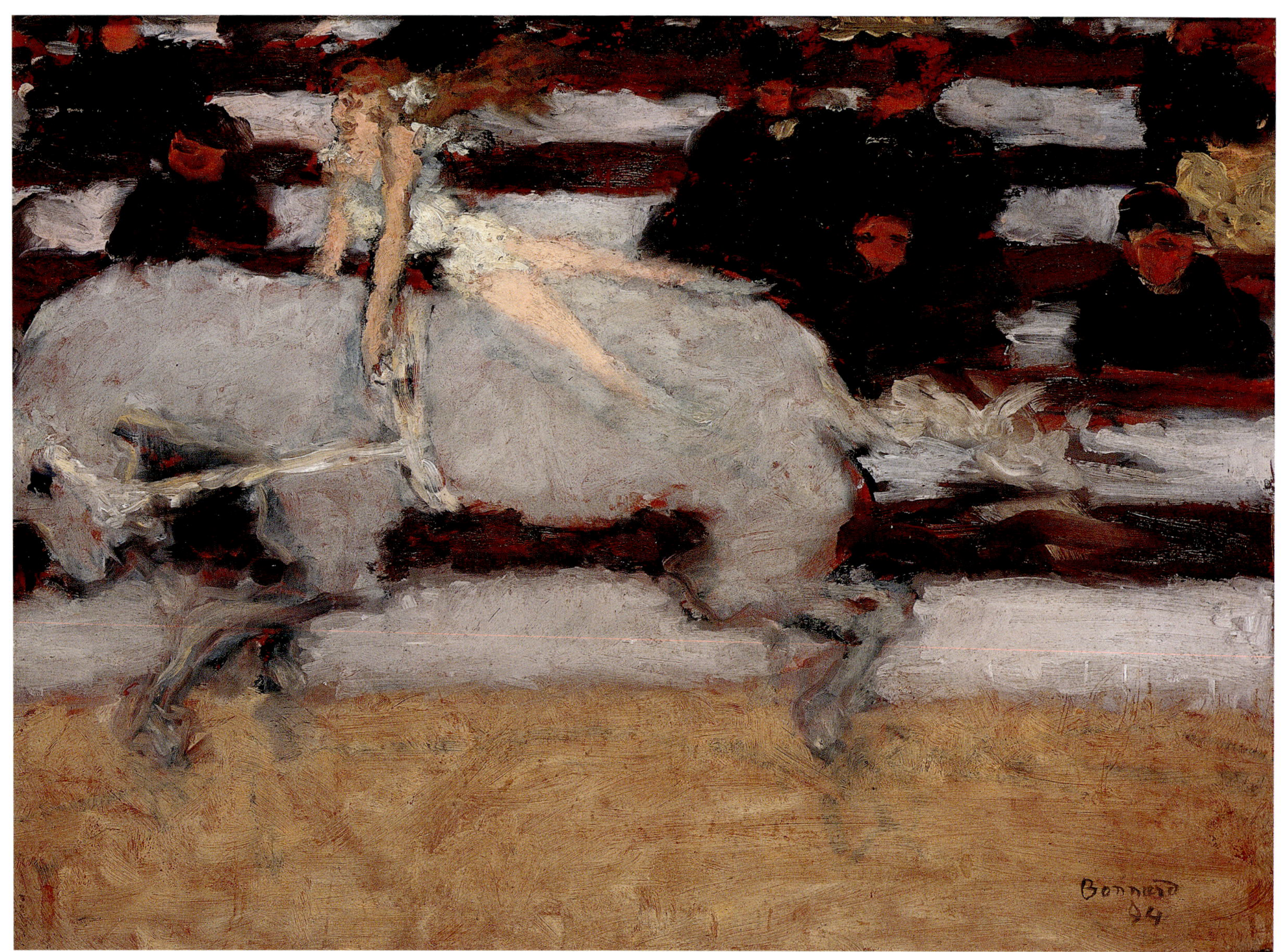

22

Circus Rider
1894, Oil on cardboard, 10⅝ × 13¾ in.
(27 × 34.9 cm), The Phillips Collection,
Washington, D.C.

Opposite page: **Circus Rider** (detail).

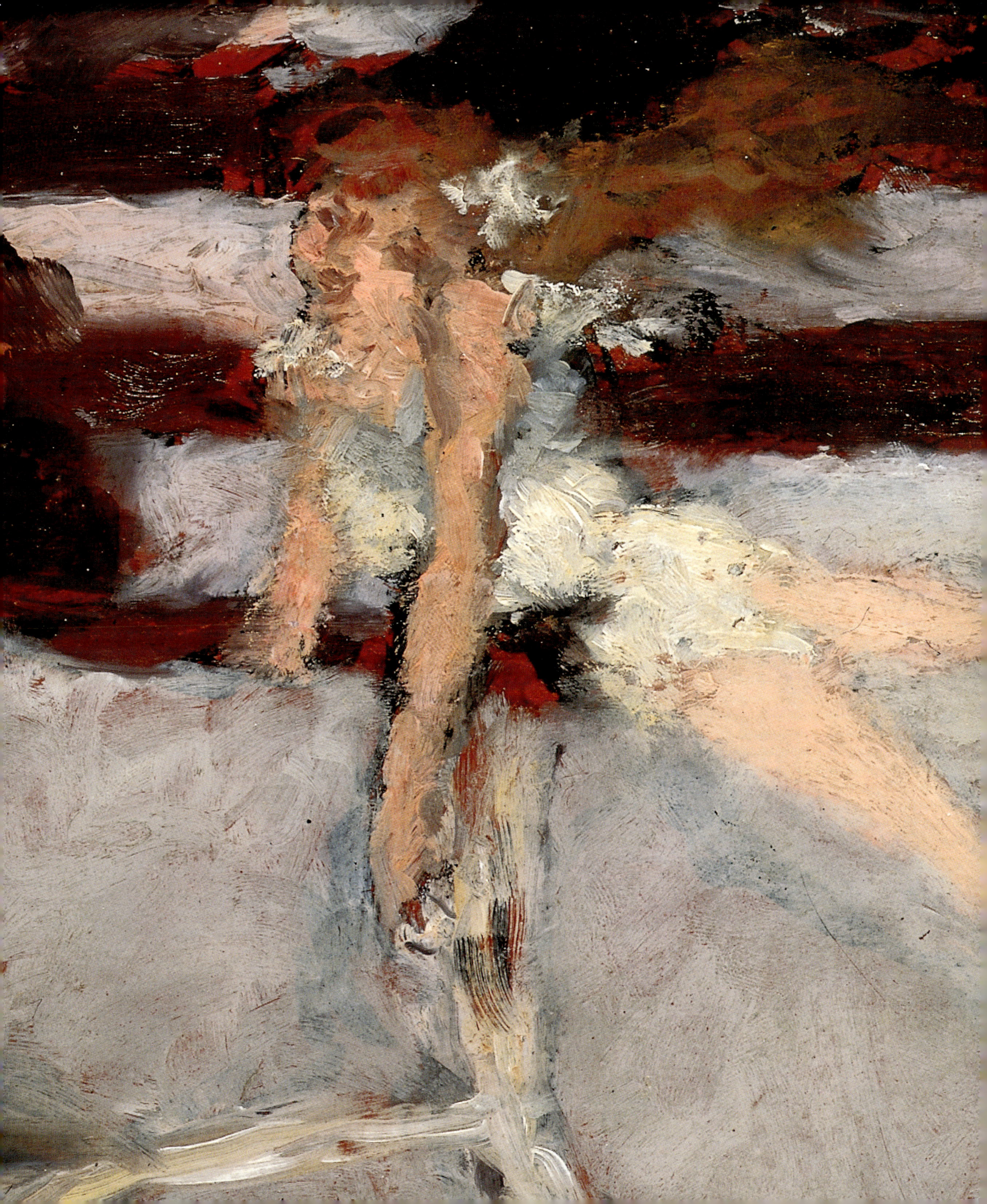

LA REVUE B...
PARAIT CHAQUE MOIS
EN LIVRAISONS DE 100 PAGES
le no 1 fr.   BUREAUX 1 rue Laffitte
en VENTE PARTOUT
Bonnard 94
La revue blanche
Imp. Edw. Ancourt, PARIS

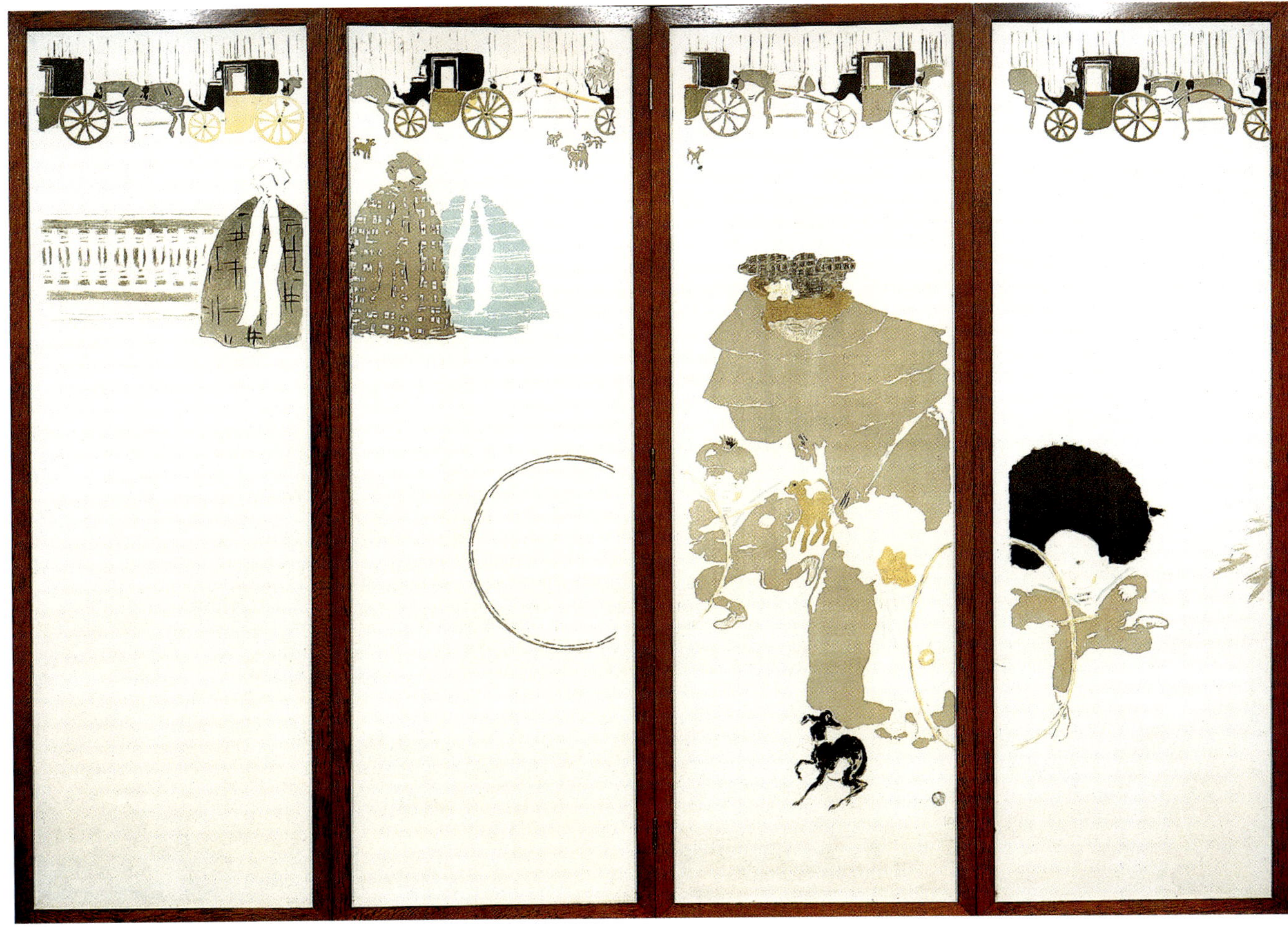

23

Poster for "La Revue blanche"
1894, Lithograph printed in four colors,
31⁵⁄₁₆ × 24⁷⁄₁₆ in. (79.5 × 62 cm), Museum of
Fine Arts, Boston. Bequest of W. G. Russell
Allen, 1960 60.65.

24

Nannies' Promenade, Frieze of Carriages
1895; published 1899, Lithograph printed in
five colors, mounted on four-fold screen,
each panel approximately 59⅝ × 19⅞ in.
(151.8 × 50.5 cm), Museum of Fine Arts,
Boston. Ernest W. Longfellow Fund, 1976
1976.605.

Nannies' Promenade, Frieze of Carriages
1895; published 1899, Lithograph printed in
five colors, mounted on four-fold screen,
Panel one: 58¹³⁄₁₆ × 20⁵⁄₁₆ in. (149.1 × 51.5 cm),
Panel two: 59⁵⁄₁₆ × 19¹⁄₁₆ in. (150.4 × 48.4 cm),
Panel three: 58⅞ × 20⁷⁄₁₆ in. (149.3 × 51.8 cm),
Panel four: 60¹⁄₁₆ × 18¾ in. (152.1 × 47.6 cm),
Property of Mr. and Mrs. Donald B. Marron.

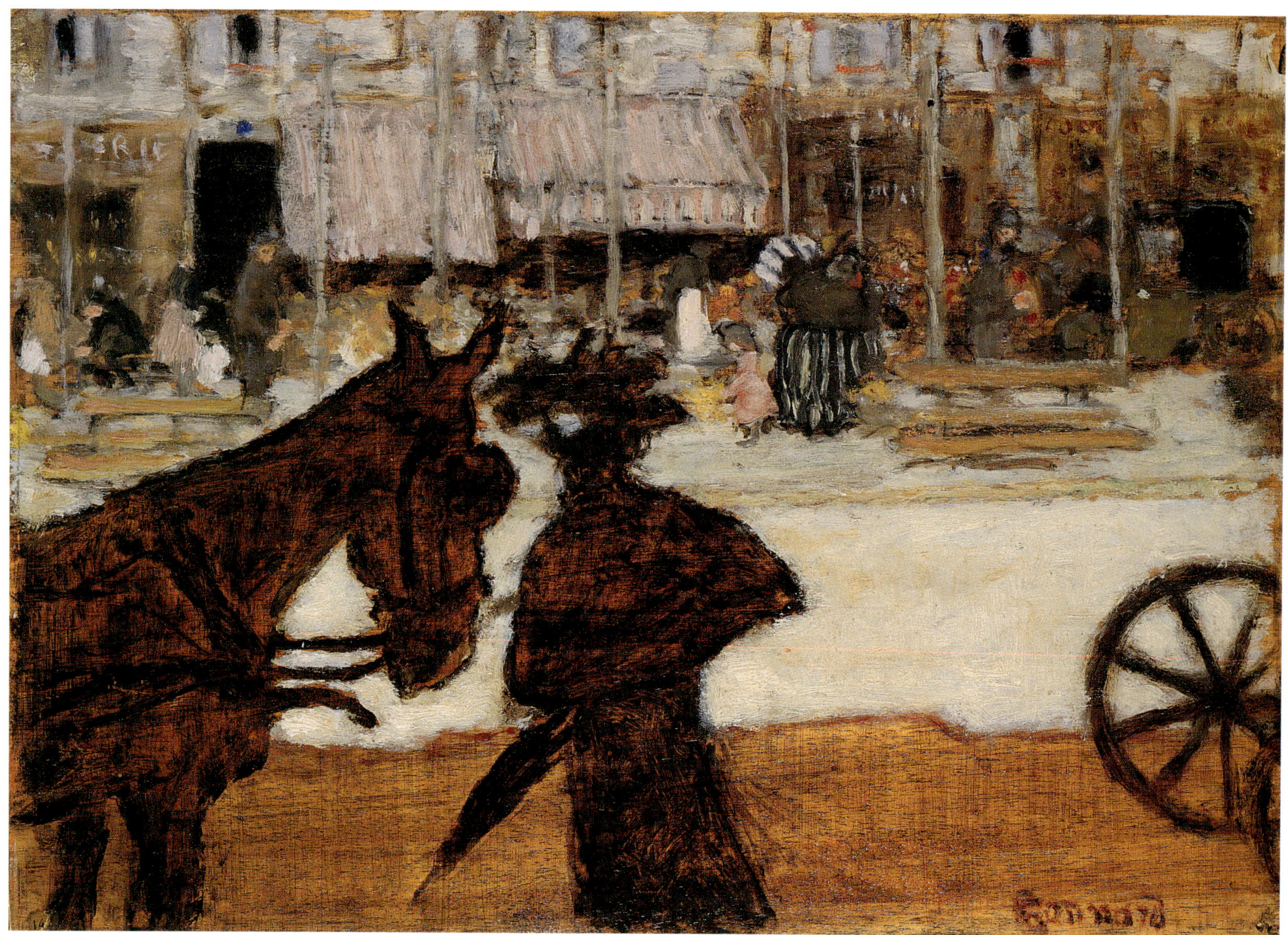

25

The Cab Horse
ca. 1895, Oil on wood, 11¾ × 15¾ in.
(29.7 × 40 cm), National Gallery of Art,
Washington, Ailsa Mellon Bruce Collection
1970.17.4.

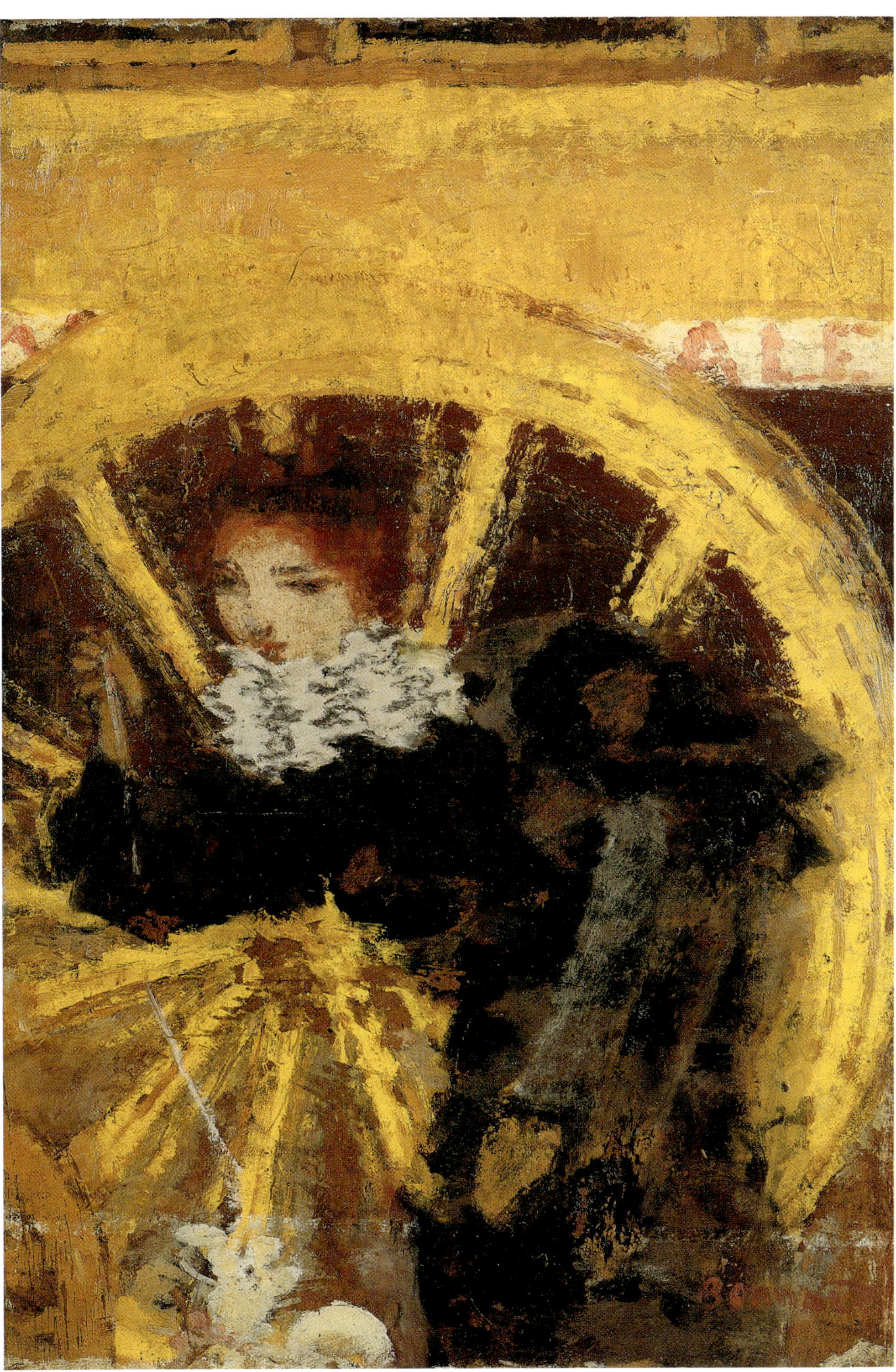

26

The Omnibus
1895, Oil on canvas, 23¼ × 16⅛ in. (59 × 41 cm),
Courtesy Galerie Félix Vercel.

27

The Little Laundry Girl
1896, Color lithograph, 21⅛ × 15⅜ in.
(53.7 × 39.5 cm), Prints and Photographs
Division, Library of Congress, Washington,
D.C., Reproduction numbers: LC-USZC4-
10048, LC-USZ62-72223.

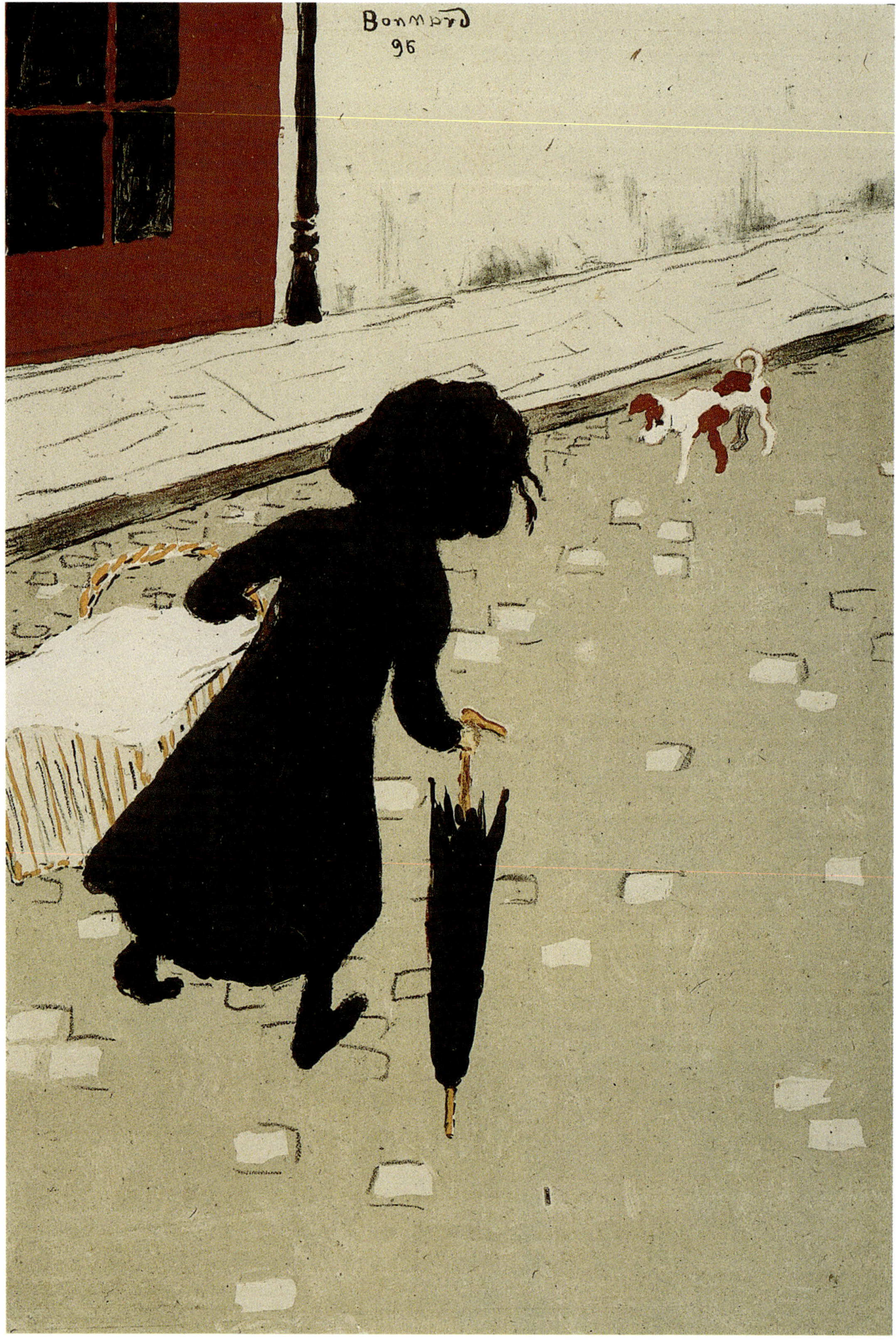

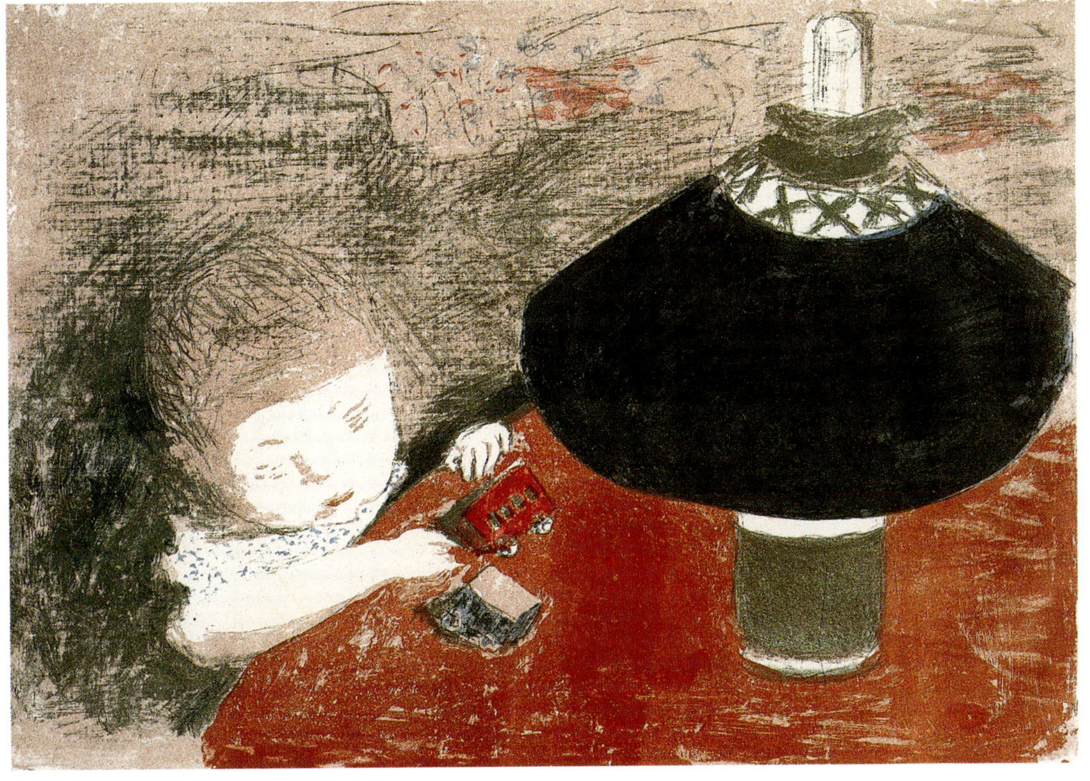

28

Child with Lamp

ca. 1897, Lithograph printed in five colors, 17⅛ × 22¹¹⁄₁₆ in. (43.5 × 57.7 cm), Museum of Fine Arts, Boston. Bequest of W. G. Russell Allen, 1960 60.67.

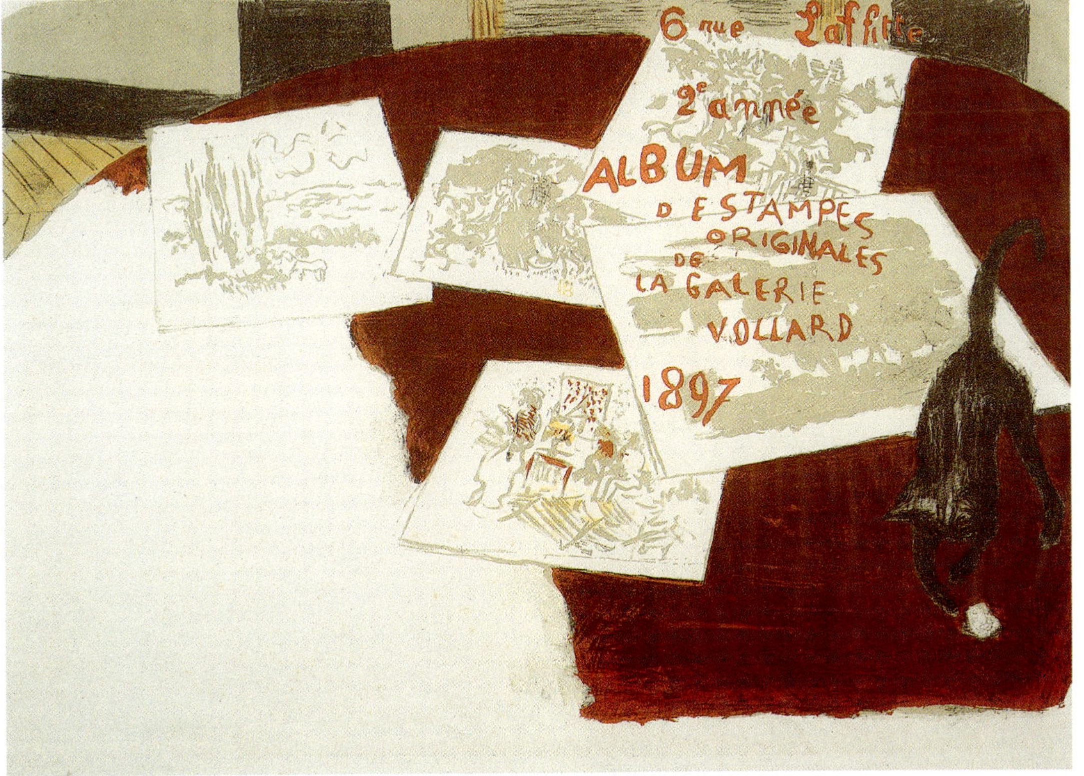

29

Cover for the Second "Album d'estampes originales"

1897, Lithograph printed in four colors, 27¹⁵⁄₁₆ × 36⁷⁄₁₆ in. (71 × 92.5 cm), Museum of Fine Arts, Boston. Frederick Brown Fund, 1955 55.943.

30

Cover for the album "Some Scenes of Parisian Life"
1895, Lithograph printed in two colors,
21 1/16 × 15 7/8 in. (53.5 × 40.4 cm), Museum of
Fine Arts, Boston. Bequest of W. G. Russell
Allen, 1960 60.52.

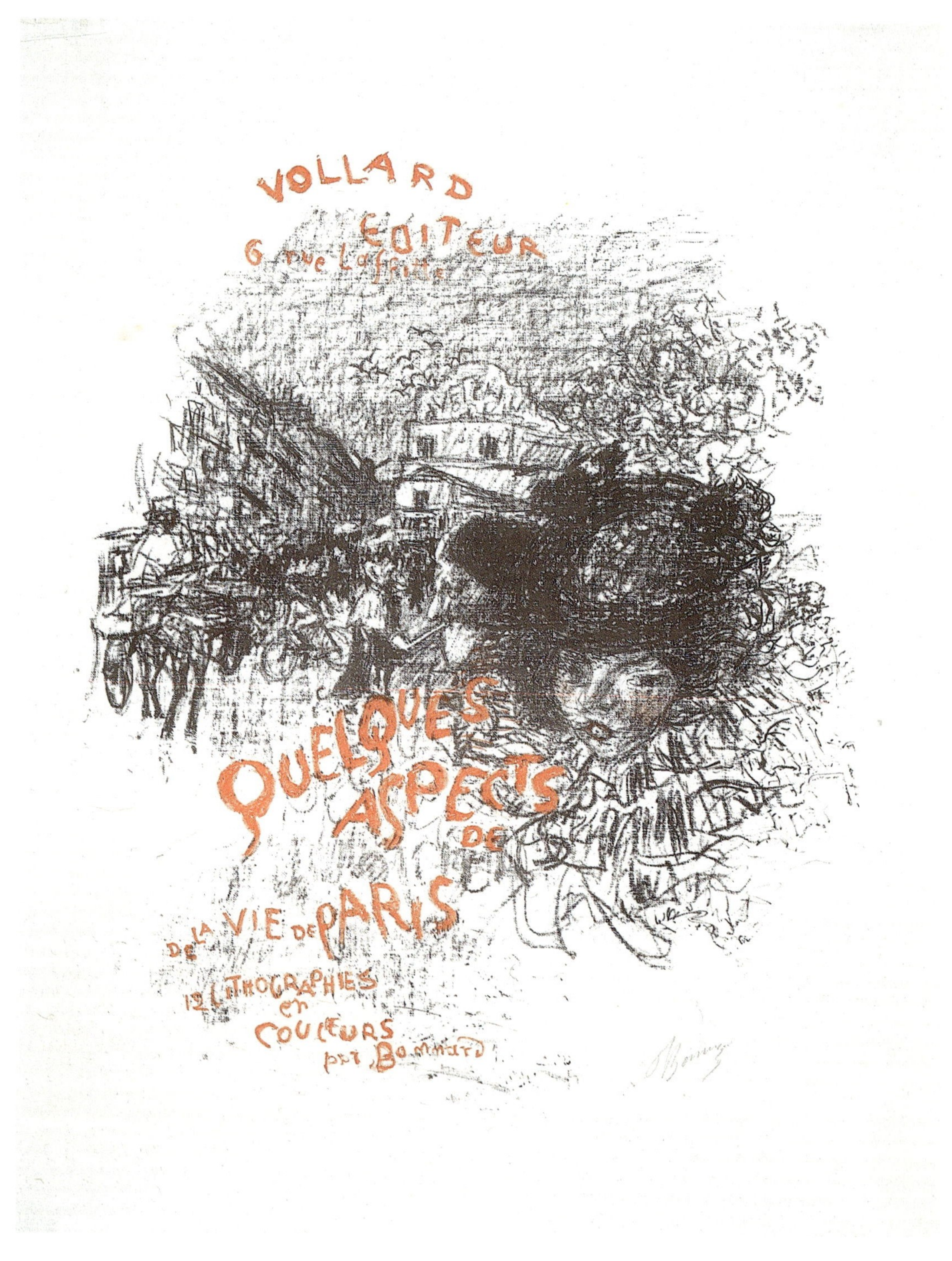

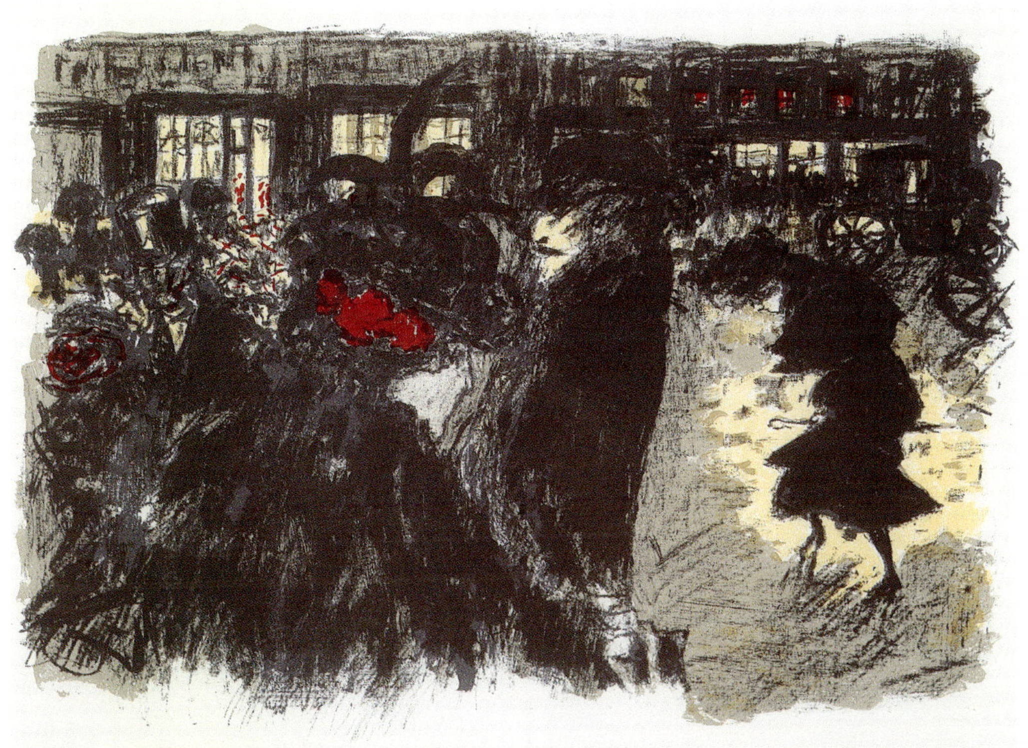

31

The Square at Evening
1899, Color lithograph on cream wove paper,
16 × 21 in. (40.6 × 53.3 cm), The Phillips
Collection, Washington, D.C.

32

Boulevard
1899, Color lithograph on cream wove paper,
16⅛ × 20¾ in. (40.9 × 52.7 cm), The Phillips
Collection, Washington, D.C.

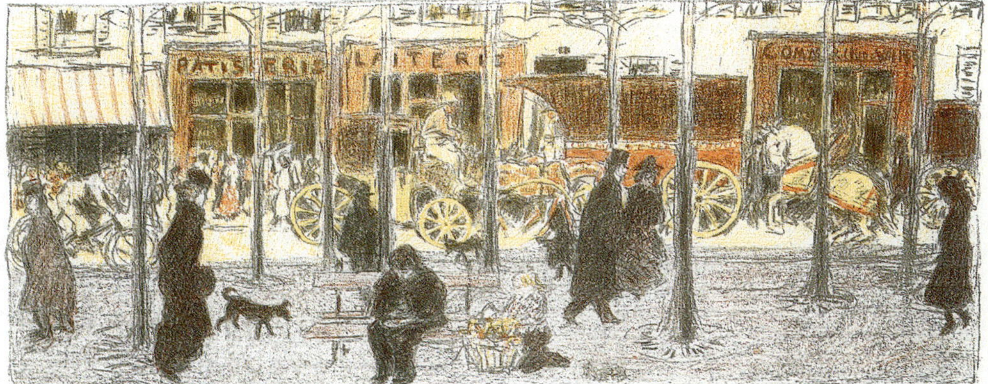

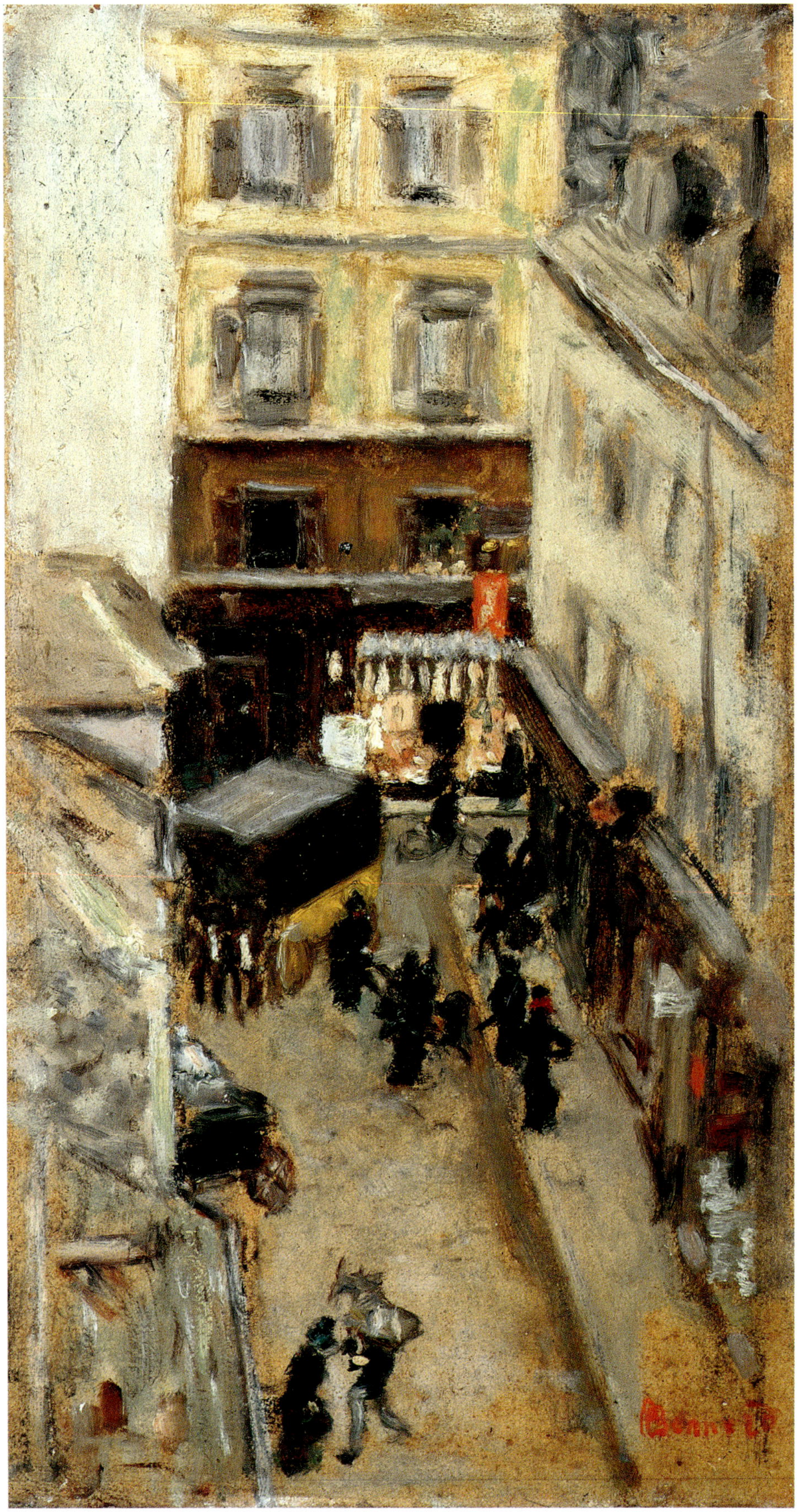

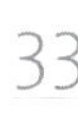
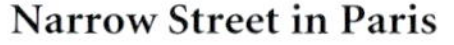

33

Narrow Street in Paris
ca. 1897, Oil on cardboard set into wood
panel, 14⅝ × 7¾ in. (37.1 × 19.6 cm), The
Phillips Collection, Washington, D.C.

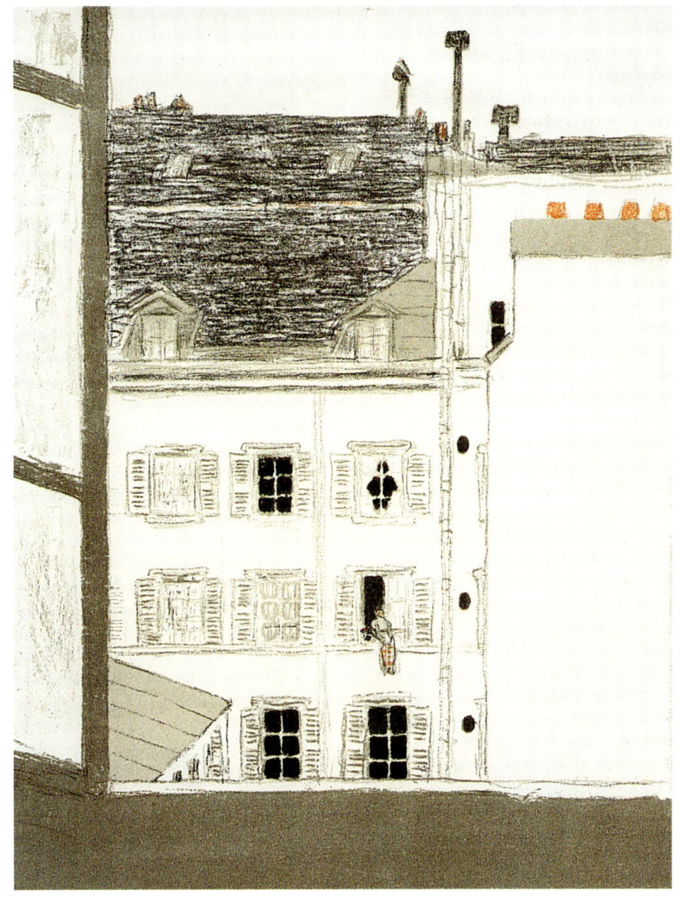

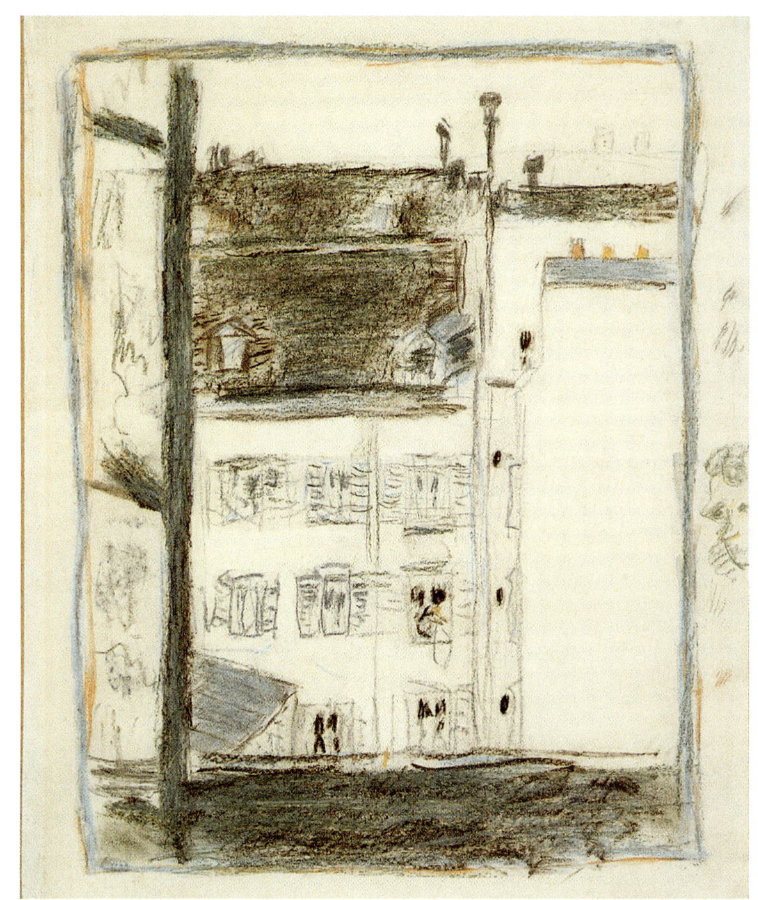

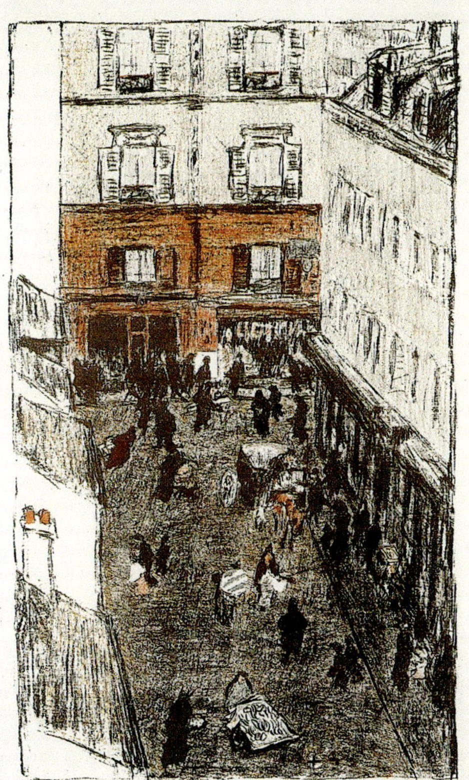

34

Houses in the Courtyard
1895–1896; published 1899, Lithograph printed
in four colors, 21¹⁄₁₆ × 16 in. (53.5 × 40.7 cm),
Museum of Fine Arts, Boston. Bequest of
W. G. Russell Allen, 1960 60.55.

35

Houses in the Courtyard
1895–1896, Pastel on wove paper, 15⅝ × 12¼
in. (39.7 × 31.1 cm), Museum of Fine Arts,
Boston. Gift of Jessie H. Wilkinson. Jessie
H. Wilkinson Fund, 1979.2.

36

Street Corner Seen from Above
1896–1897; published 1899, Lithograph
printed in four colors, 20⅞ × 16⅛ in. (53 × 41
cm), Museum of Fine Arts, Boston. Bequest
of W. G. Russell Allen, 1960 60.64.

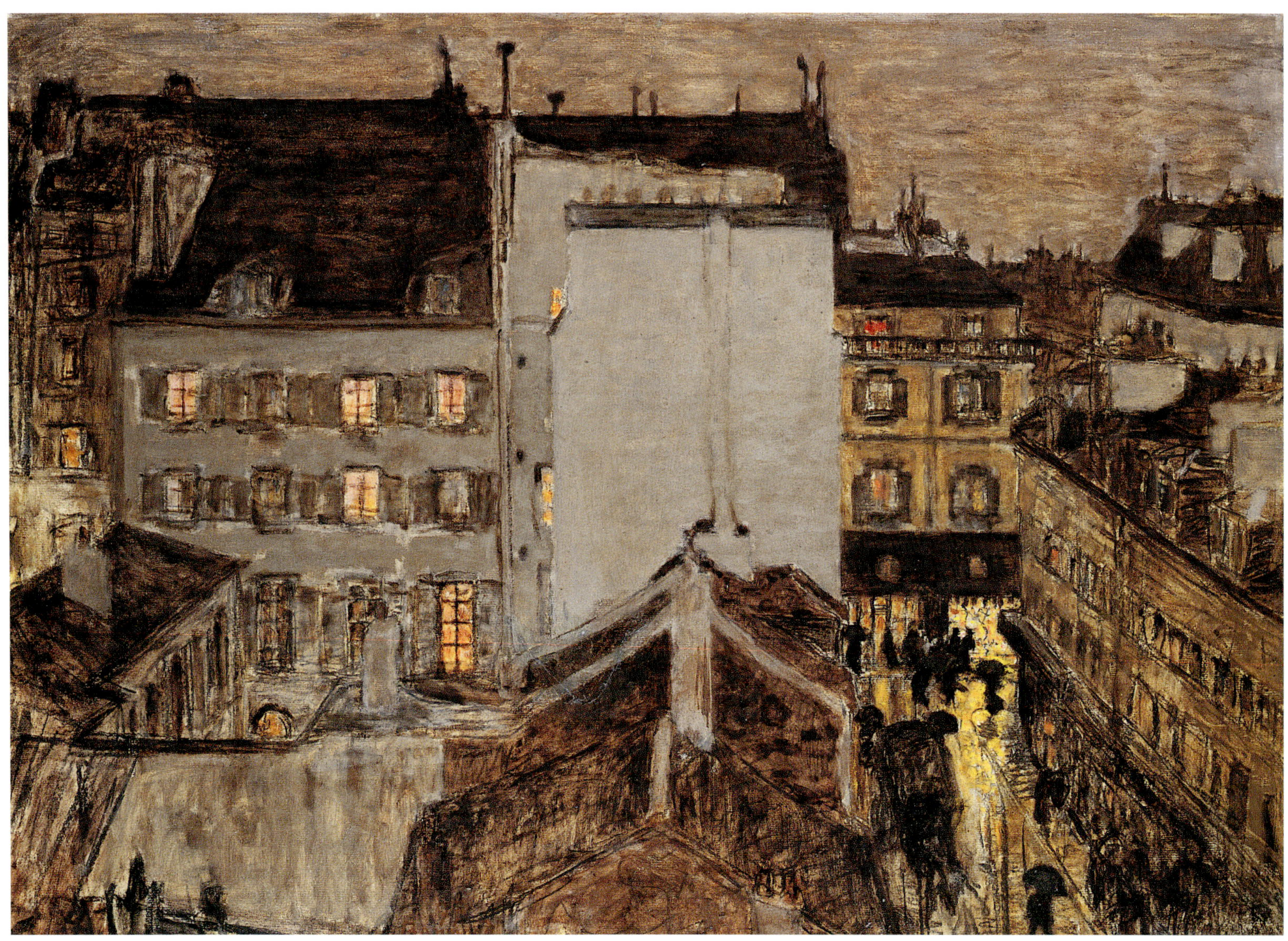

37

Montmartre in the Rain or **Rue Tholozé**
ca. 1897, Oil on paper, laid down on panel,
27⁹⁄₁₆ × 37⅜ in. (70 × 95 cm), Galerie Jan
Krugier, Ditesheim & Cie, Geneva.

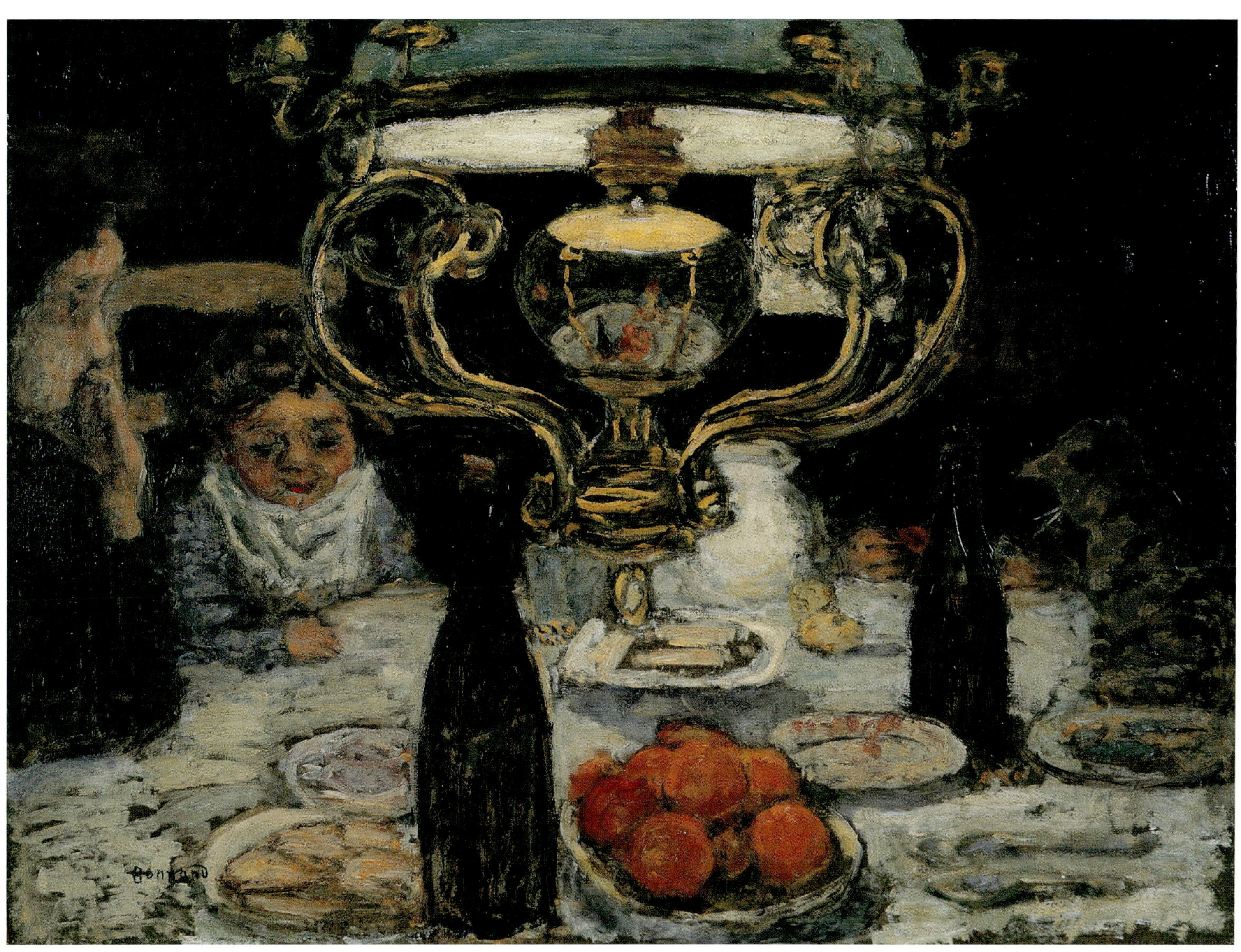

38

The Lamp
ca. 1899, Oil on academy board mounted on
panel, 22¼ × 27½ in. (56.5 × 69.9 cm),
Collection of the Flint Institute of Arts, Gift
of The Whiting Foundation and Mr. and
Mrs. Donald E. Johnson, 1977.25.

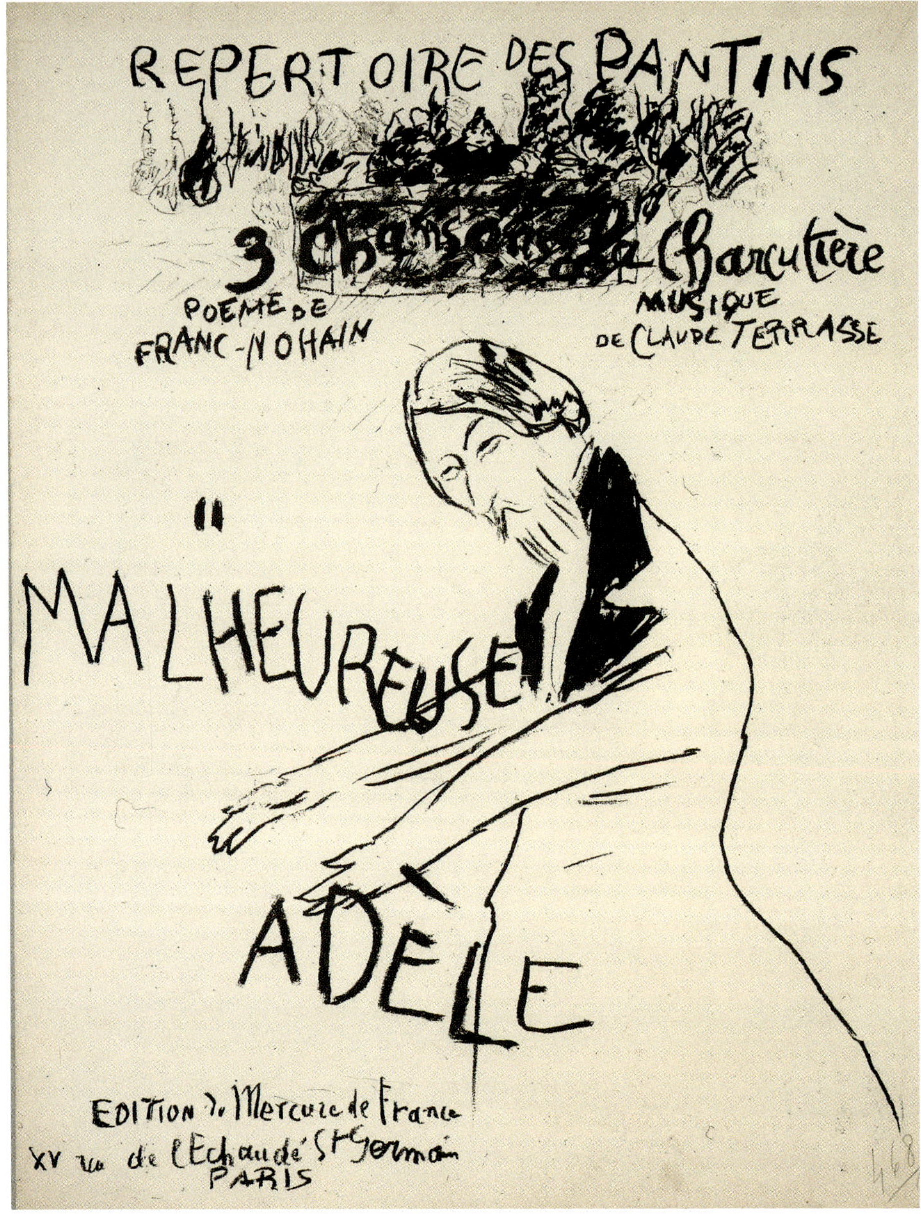

39

Cover for "Unfortunate Adèle" from "Répertoire des Pantins"
1898, Lithograph, 12¹³⁄₁₆ × 9¹³⁄₁₆ in. (32.6 × 24.9 cm), Virginia and Ira Jackson Collection. Partial and Promised Gift to the National Gallery of Art, Washington.

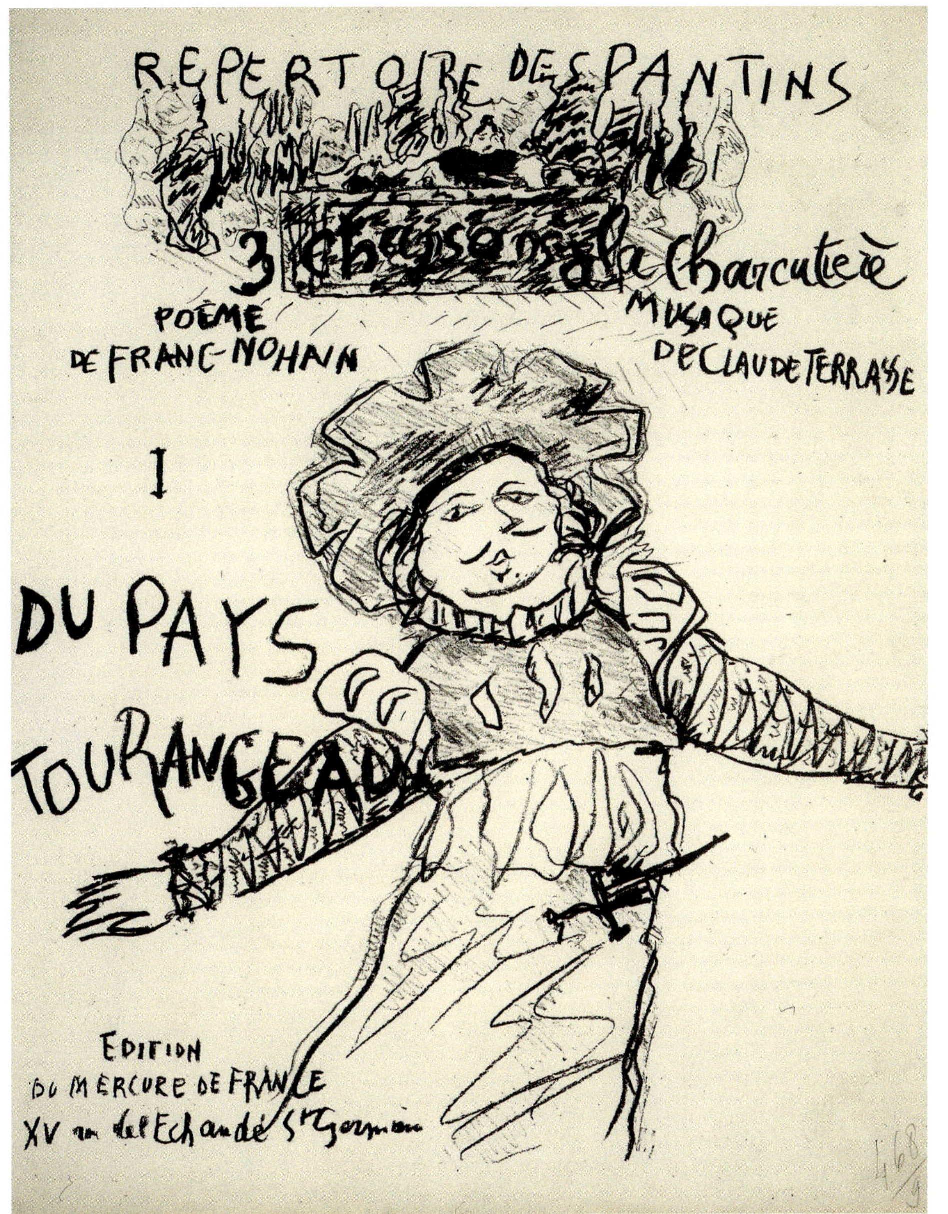

40

**Cover for "From the Land of Touraine"
from "Répertoire des Pantins"**
1898, Lithograph, 12¹³⁄₁₆ × 19¹³⁄₁₆ in.
(32.6 × 24.9 cm), Virginia and Ira Jackson
Collection. Partial and Promised Gift to the
National Gallery of Art, Washington.

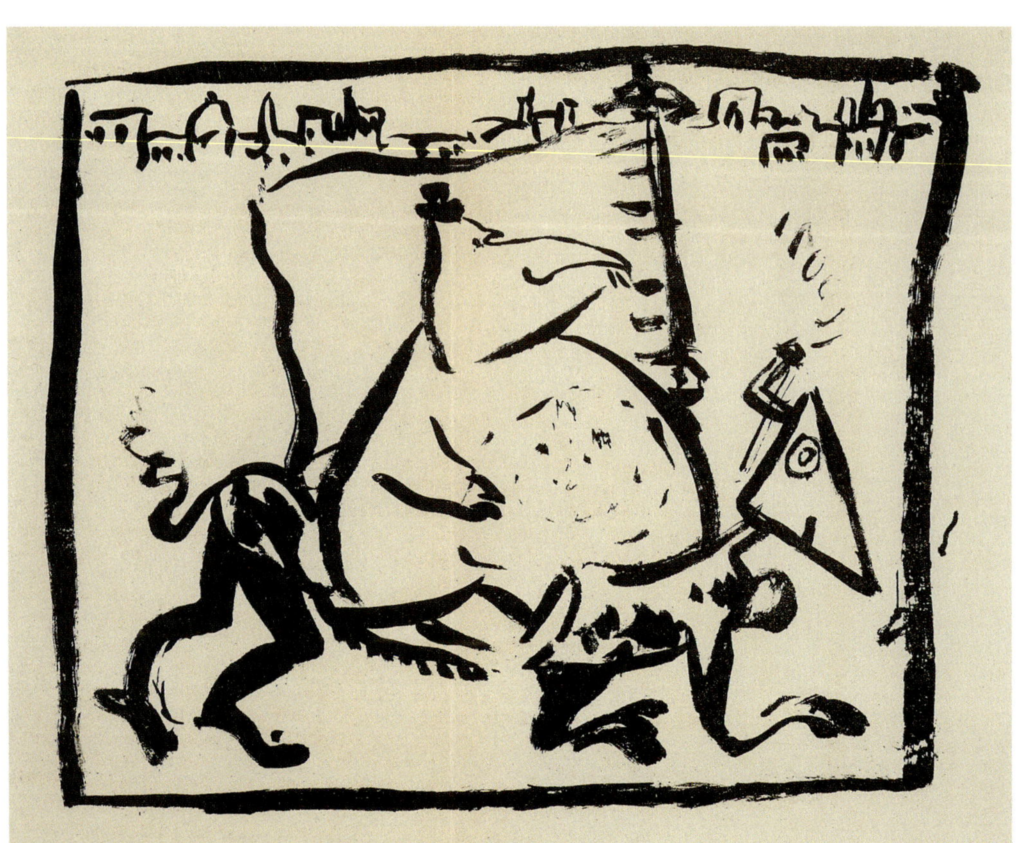

"Ubu à Paris" in Alfred Jarry's "Almanach illustré du Père Ubu"
1901, Lithograph, 11⁵⁄₁₆ × 16 in. (28.7 × 40.6 cm), Virginia and Ira Jackson Collection. Partial and Promised Gift to the National Gallery of Art, Washington.

"Alphabet du Père Ubu" in Alfred Jarry's "Almanach illustré du Père Ubu"
1901, Lithograph, each image, 11⁵⁄₁₆ × 8 in. (28.7 × 20.3 cm), Virginia and Ira Jackson Collection. Partial and Promised Gift to the National Gallery of Art, Washington.

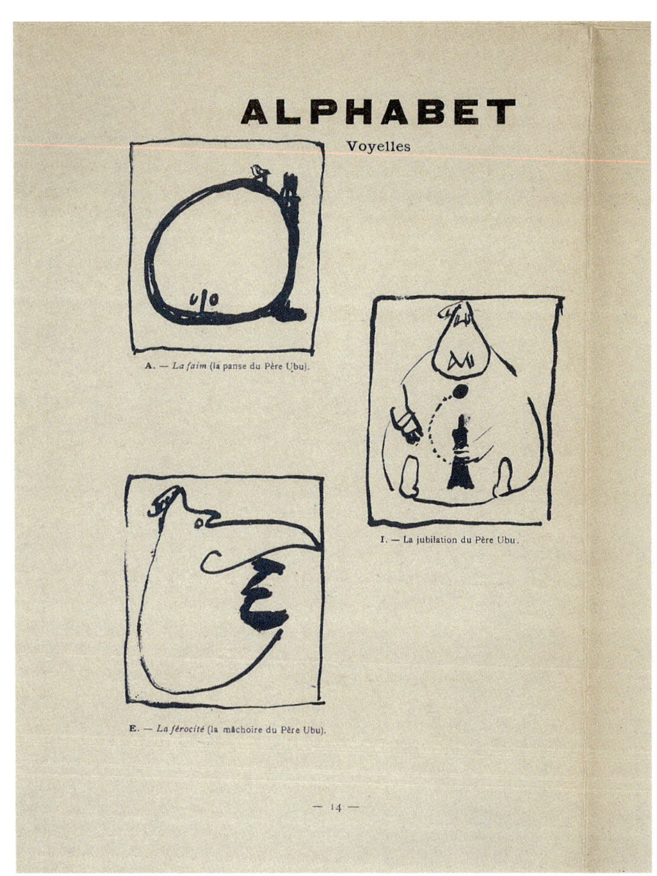

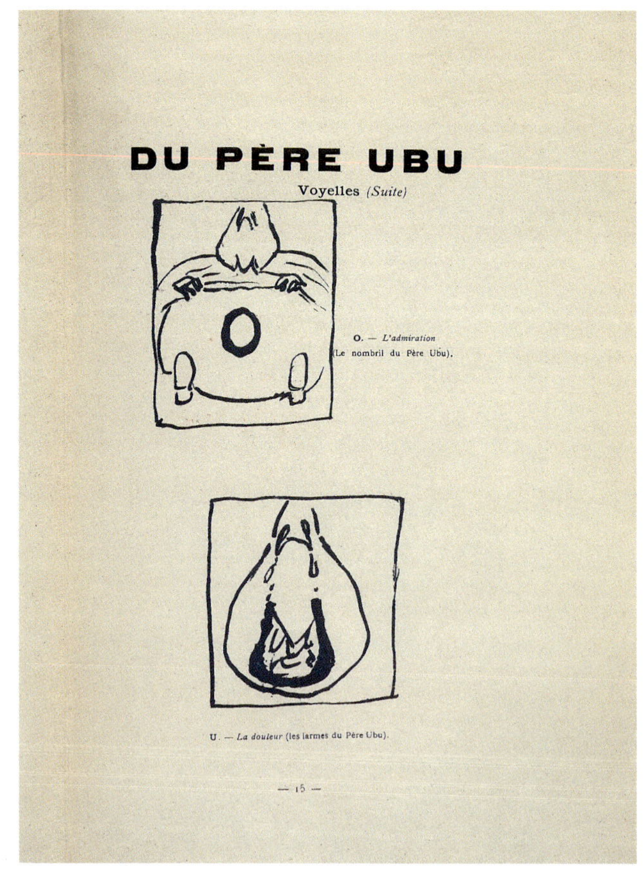

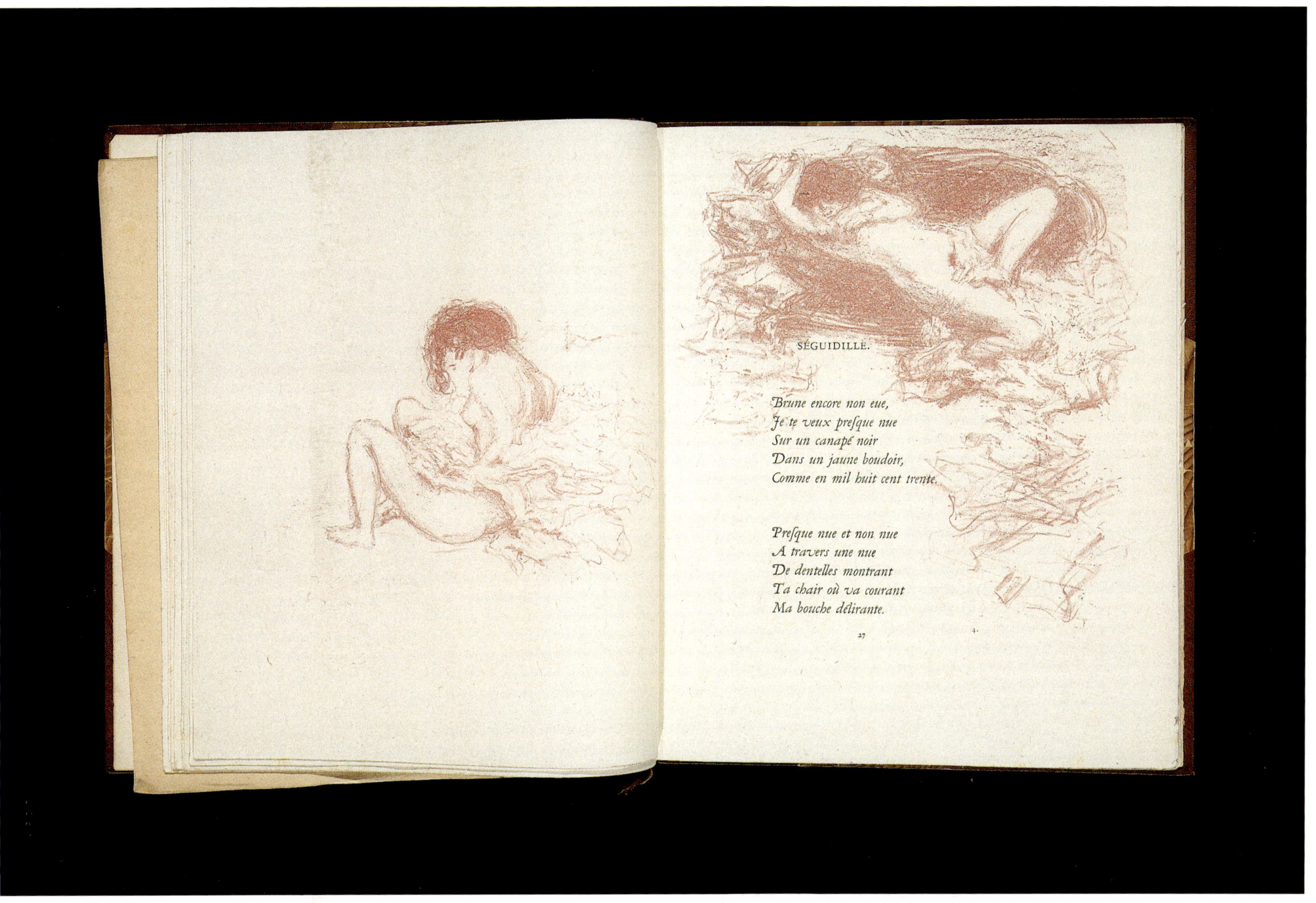

43

"Séguidille" in Paul Verlaine's
"Parallèlement"
1900, Lithograph in book, 12 × 9⅞ in.
(30.5 × 25 cm), Lessing J. Rosenwald
Collection, Library of Congress,
Washington, D.C.

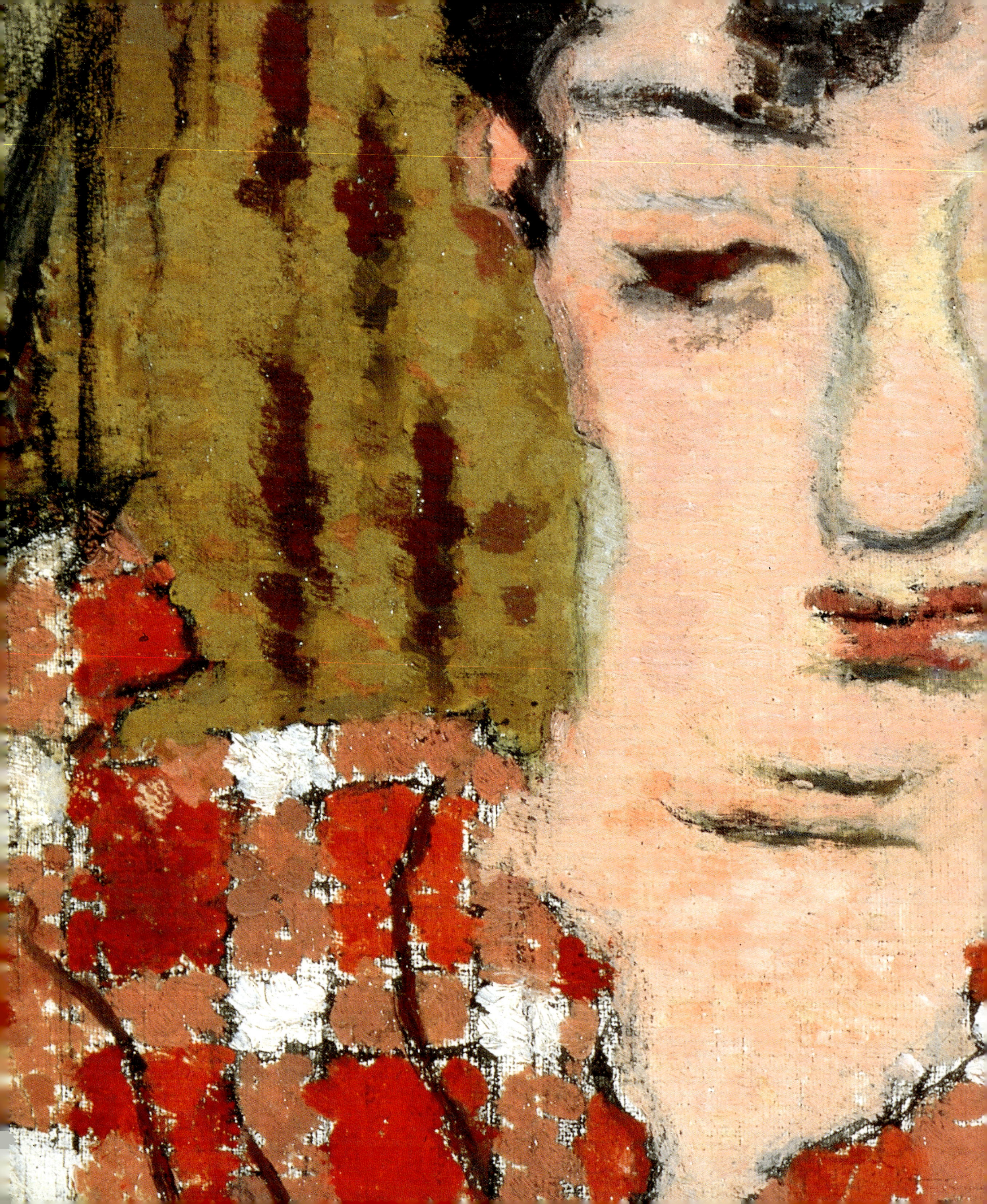

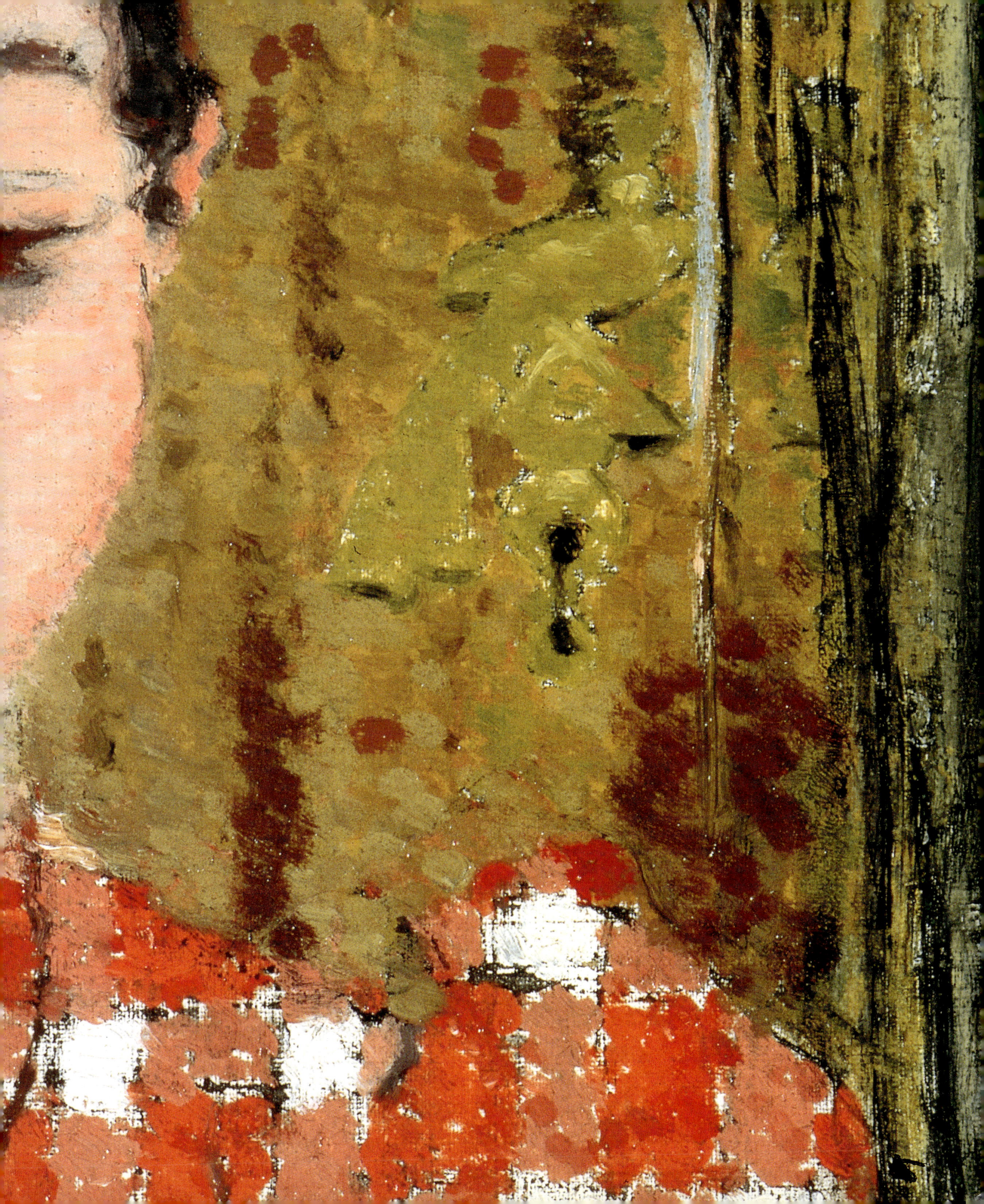

From Thought to Form

Nancy Coleman Wolsk

Previous spread:
Checked Blouse; Portrait of Mme Claude Terrasse, the Artist's Sister (detail), 1892, Oil on canvas, 23⅝ × 13 in. (60 × 33 cm), Private collection, courtesy Galerie Cazeau-Béraudière, Paris.

On 5 August 1884 Eugène Bonnard, a prominent public official and upwardly mobile member of the *grande bourgeoisie*, presented his seventeen-year-old son Pierre to the examiners for the first of two *baccalauréat* examinations. The grueling written and oral *bac* was the keystone of France's *lycée* education, the elite system of secondary schooling that perpetuated the intellectual culture of the nation and qualified youth for a solid position in its social order. The first series of the exams, which tested the boy's knowledge and the quality of his reasoning in literature and history, came after *rhétorique*, the second-to-last year of the *lycée*; if he survived this test, he would go on to *philosophie*, the crowning year of the highly ordered curriculum.

Up to this point, the adolescent had attended three of the nation's best secondary schools—first, the *lycée* in Vanves for the earlier grades, and then the ancient and revered Lycées Charlemagne and Louis-le-Grand in Paris for the upper-division classes. Pierre had been carefully groomed for the examination by years of training in French, Latin, and Greek literature and history; nonetheless, he and his father knew that a little more than half of those who sat for the *bac* would survive and complete their schooling.[1]

Carefully bound volumes in France's national archives preserve the records of these examinations.[2] They tell us that on that summer day in 1884, Pierre Bonnard wrote essays on French literature and history, a translation from a Latin text, and a short essay in a modern language (probably German). The record shows that his essays earned high marks and that he qualified for the final oral section, where he not only analyzed passages from the fables of La Fontaine and selections from Latin and Greek literature but answered *interrogations* on the principal literary ideas of La Fontaine, on history, and on a "living" foreign language. In 1884 just three percent of the students who sat for the exam earned a *bien*; Bonnard was one of them.[3]

The next summer, now eighteen, Bonnard faced his examiners again, this time for the second series of the *bac* where, as with the first, only half of the students who took the exam would pass. Although his showing was a little less glorious in this round, he nonetheless survived, earning an honest *passable*.[4] In all, the *lycée* had provided him with the rich benefits of a rigorous, coherent system of education. By proving himself on its culminating tests, Bonnard showed that he was suited for membership in the exclusive club of men who had been shaped by this exacting system.

After the *baccalauréat* exam, Bonnard's professional training followed two simultaneous courses: on the one hand, he studied law, received his degree in 1888, and became a licensed attorney in 1889; on the other, he flirted with art by enrolling in studio classes at the noted Académie Julian. In March 1887, sponsored by two of his teachers at the academy, he was accepted by the competitive Ecole des Beaux-Arts as a regular student.[5] Although the *lycée* had trained him well for the intellectual rigor of the law, he found that the literary and philosophical studies that had dominated his secondary schooling seemed less suited to the anti-intellectual nature of Julian's academy.[6] Indeed, along with a circle of *lycée*-educated friends that included Paul Sérusier, Maurice Denis, Ker-Xavier Roussel, and Edouard Vuillard, Bonnard chafed at the restrictive lessons of the academy, which unimaginatively directed him to copy nature and to render with near-photographic precision the male and female nude alike.

Despite these strictures, in the end Bonnard chose to become an artist. His decision probably came when he failed the civil service examination (sometime at the end of 1889 or early in 1890) that would have launched him, like his father, into the French bureaucracy. In those years, Bonnard made another major decision: he abandoned the academy.[7] Excited by the possibilities of a revolutionary kind of painting—in particular the painting of Paul Gauguin—he began to absorb lessons from a new breed of painters. Sérusier had introduced the painting style of the renegade artist to his friends at the Académie Julian by means of a little landscape—later called *The Talisman*—that he had painted when he met Gauguin at Pont-Aven in Brittany in October 1888.[8] Though the group never absorbed the older artist's theories, they did learn an expressive language of line and color from him.[9] Thus, with an intellect clearly formed by his schooling and a new system of art that countered the realism of the academy, Bonnard, with his friends, entered the heady ranks of the capital's avant-garde.

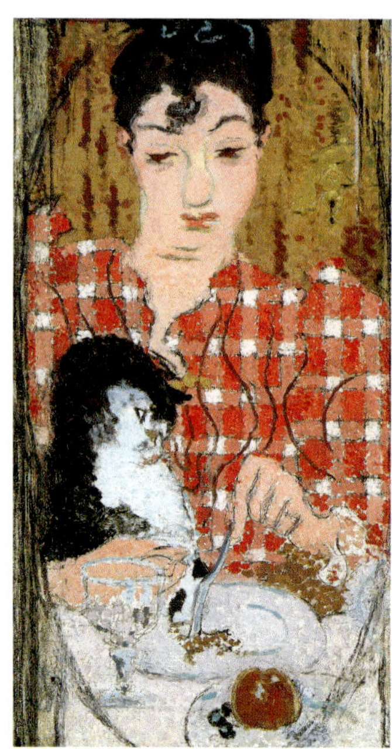

89. Pierre Bonnard, *Checked Blouse; Portrait of Mme Claude Terrasse, the Artist's Sister*, 1892, Oil on canvas, 23⅝ × 13 in. (60 × 33 cm), Private collection, courtesy Galerie Cazeau-Béraudière, Paris.

At the very beginning of their careers, the young critic G. Albert Aurier singled out Bonnard and his group from the countless artists who were then attempting to make their way in Paris as champions of the symbolist movement, and he praised their "poetic" works as part of a "new aesthetic order." He noted that, together, they formed a remarkable presence whose work was "the visible signification of thought," and he added that "all objects were only, in sum, a signified idea."[10] Later, Denis amended Aurier's assessment of the group by emphasizing that for them Symbolism was really less "metaphysical" than the critic would have it.[11] Indeed, Denis and his friends actually valued reality, especially the reality of their personal worlds. What they wished to avoid were the limitations of reality; painting, they all agreed, must reflect sensation and reason as well.[12]

In the same year that Aurier soberly recognized the works of the Nabis as "visible significations of thought," Bonnard painted *Checked Blouse; Portrait of Mme Claude Terrasse, The Artist's Sister* (1892), a small, caricatured—and not altogether kind—representation of his sister Andrée, who, seated behind a table, pokes at her food with a fork in one hand while she holds her pet cat with the other (fig. 89; plate 3). At first glance, the lighthearted work seems hardly more than an innocent moment in the life of the family. In fact, the scene resonates with cleverly controlled sensation and wit. In a series of visual puns, the artist identifies woman with animal and food in an interlocking triad. Restrained by Andrée as it sits on the table, the cat dangles a forepaw down toward the plate; in a parallel gesture, Andrée's forefinger descends along the length of the fork and echoes the shape of the paw. Also linking his sister and the cat, Bonnard restates the crowning arc of Andrée's black hair as a dark crescent of fur on the animal. Further, the flat red-and-white plaid of Andrée's dress comically reads like a tablecloth pattern. And finally, the repeated black curves of the edge of a carafe in the lower right, the contour of the cat's head, the fold lines in the dress, and the contours of Andrée's face and brow tie the whole scene together. Drawn from Bonnard's immediate, intimate world, the scene evokes the senses, as taste and touch play out in the forms of food, cat, and woman. Carefully structured, the whole is controlled by the ordering eye of the artist.[13]

Later in his career Bonnard continued to capture scenes from his intimate world. Now featuring his permanent companion Marthe de Méligny, these images successively called up sensation and mood, each harmonized by a reasoning mind. Thirty years after he painted *Checked Blouse*, Bonnard, at fifty-five, appeared to revive the subject in *Woman with Dog* (fig. 90, plate 96). In this later painting, Marthe holds the couple's pet dachshund on her lap as she sits behind a table covered with plates of food. Bisecting the foreground and cut off by the lower edge of the canvas, a bottle of wine projects upward toward the woman and dog.

In many ways the late work differs from the early scene. Whereas Andrée and the cat remain flat, Marthe and the dog occupy space. The work of 1892 gently sways with *japoniste* curves; in the later, more static composition, Bonnard has fixed the woman, dog, and bottle of wine along a vertical axis that, in turn, squares with the horizontal edge of the table. Both works convey Bonnard's love of color, but the painting of 1922 reveals the subtle fusions of hue and tone that he learned from Claude Monet and Pierre-Auguste Renoir. The most profound difference, however, lies in feeling and mood. The earlier playful scene has given way to reverie: Andrée, active, expands out of the frame; Marthe, small and isolated, quietly withdraws in "infinite sadness."[14]

Even so, Bonnard perpetuates the layered sensations and rational order of the earlier work. Here, food, animal, and woman connect in a clear sequence of forms: the bottle mirrors the dachshund's head and together these shapes repeat the light mass of Marthe's chestnut helmet of hair. In tying the three together, Bonnard calls up different levels of sensation; at the same time, descriptive color both evokes feeling and orders the work. Knitting together the table in front and the wall behind, soft strokes of subdued complementary blues and oranges blend with one another. Further ordering the work, regular, vertical brushmarks define the wall as similarly formed horizontals regulate the table in front. At the same time as it brings reason to bear on the work, the soft unsaturated color creates an elegiac mood that contrasts with the dissonant red of Marthe's blouse.

In both paintings, Bonnard understood line and color as language and, as he matured, he expanded that language to express deeper, more complex levels of meaning. In the course of developing a personal voice, the artist appropriated elements from the works of other artists. He absorbed the lessons of Japanese prints; with his friend Vuillard, he haunted the Louvre, drawing inspiration from Greek sculpture and the Renaissance masters. He borrowed as well from his contemporaries, notably from Monet, Renoir, and Henri Matisse. Indeed, Bonnard owed a debt to Andō Hiroshige and Utagawa, to Gauguin and Sérusier, and to French traditions in art; to popular posters, to Greek sculpture, to Impressionism—and the list could go on. These sources, however, do not explain why the artist did what he did and why he thought as he thought. To find the answer to both these questions, we must turn to his education.

A Habit of Mind

The most important, long-term, formative experience for Bonnard, at twenty-two, had, in fact, been his schooling.[15] The *lycée* classes had taught him methods of teasing layered meanings out of the fables of La Fontaine, the plays of Molière and Sophocles, and the varied works of Cicero. He learned to value literary form through the intricacies of sophisticated textual analysis, and he learned the expressive value of language through exhausting hours of *explication du texte*.

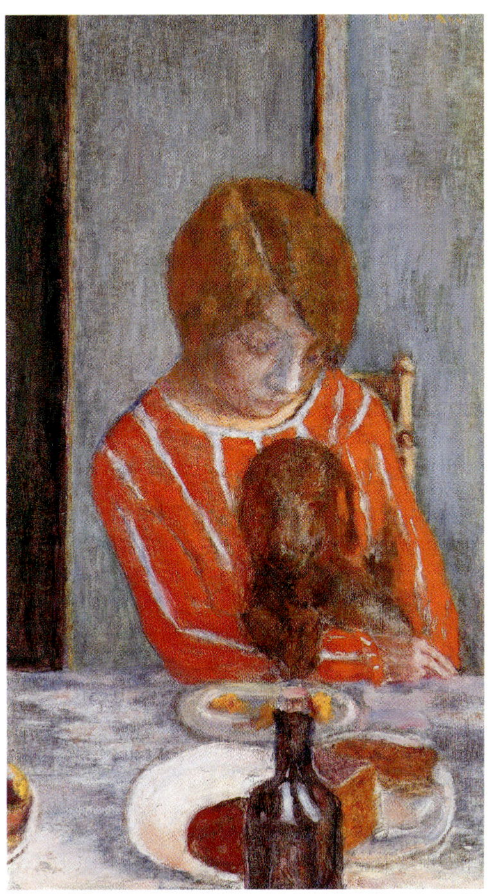

90. Pierre Bonnard, *Woman with Dog*, 1922, Oil on canvas, 27¼ × 15½ in. (69.2 × 39.3 cm), The Phillips Collection, Washington, D.C.

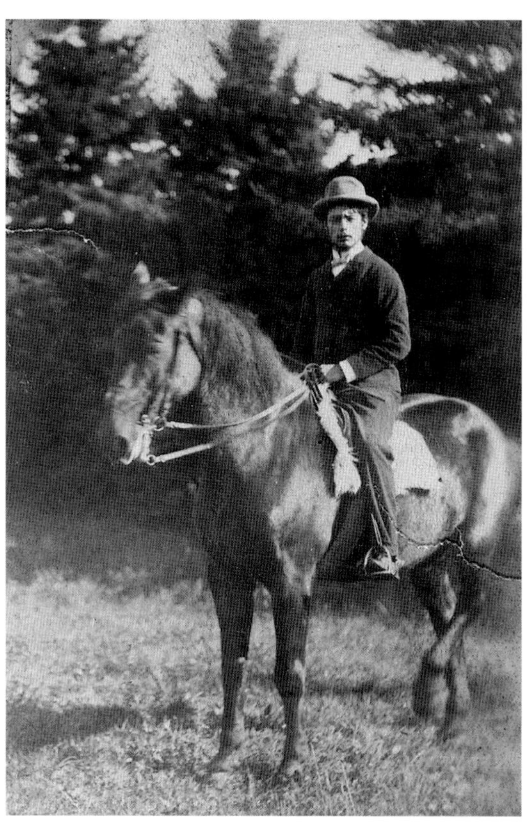

91. *Bonnard on the Grounds of Le Grand-Lemps*, ca. 1885, Photograph, Private collection.

Not least, he learned in philosophy how to give voice to his intellect and, together, history and philosophy taught him to understand the debt that he owed to his cultural past. The synergistic effect of the *lycée*'s carefully ordered, integrated, and graduated programs of study in literature, history, and philosophy—*formation*, as the French call it—inculcated in Bonnard durable and identifiable patterns of thought that later became the blueprints of practice.[16] Indeed, more important than the actual information imparted by curricular programs, textbooks, lectures, study guides, and examinations were the larger, organizing principles of secondary schooling; it was these that established Bonnard's habits of mind.[17]

Actually, one might question whether Bonnard was temperamentally disposed to absorb the lessons of school, because we find that he disliked theory and ridiculed earnest philosophical discussions. Indeed, in many ways, he conducted a rebellion against his social background and schooling: he lived with the uneducated, working-class Marthe for thirty-two years (he finally married her in 1925); he often kept company with mavericks (though they were similarly educated) like the painter Henri de Toulouse-Lautrec and the writer Alfred Jarry; and he often undermined the Nabis' serious round-table discussions on art and art theory with quips and subversive remarks.[18] He especially disliked complicated theories of painting.

Other evidence, however, shows us a different Bonnard, one who was not only a compliant member of his family but also a willing student who absorbed his lessons well. He devotedly wrote letters to his mother and spent frequent and prolonged visits with the family at both their house in Le Grand-Lemps in the Dauphiné (fig. 91) and their permanent residence in Paris's southeastern suburb of Fontenay-les-Roses. He sought male colleagues and companions from his own milieu. Indeed, his friends and fellow painters were identically educated: Denis, Roussel, Sérusier, and Vuillard were all alumni of the Lycée Condorcet in Paris. Most of all, his success on the *baccalauréat* testifies that he willingly learned his lessons well.

As it happened, he went to school at a time of remarkable change. Had Bonnard been a student in an earlier generation, he would have, without doubt, entered adulthood with very different habits of mind. Earlier in the century, *lycée* education tended to be fragmented, one subject having little to do with the next; further, within individual disciplines subjects splintered into unrelated parts; and, not least, students often learned lessons as abstract formulas without much foundation in practice, a process that perpetuated a Cartesian split between the world of objects and the world of ideas.[19] Until 1872 and 1873 Latin dominated the curriculum: children wrote essays in Latin, they memorized pages of Latin grammar—often unanchored to literature—and they learned their own language through the rhetoric of Latin. French, the living language of home and the street, took second place to the dead language of Rome.[20]

In the years following the Franco-Prussian War of 1870–1871, France had to face the consequences of its profound humiliation by Germany, including payment of a heavy reparations bill. To build a new republic out of the ashes of the Second Empire and remain a power in Europe, the nation needed to take an active role in an industrialized world. Along with other institutions that had been shown to be outmoded, the elite secondary schools, training ground of intellectuals and captains of industry alike, came under fire. In 1872 and 1873, charged with the task of modernizing *lycée* education, Jules Simon, minister of education in the new government, began by integrating the curriculum. Not quite a decade later, in 1880, then minister Jules Ferry sponsored a second series of reforms, continuing the programs of his predecessor. Together, Simon and Ferry engineered a holistic curriculum in which each subject followed a carefully orchestrated pattern moving from simple facts to complex philosophical and psychological thought.[21] In the new plans and programs of study, French, Latin, and Greek literature complemented one another, with history forming the foundation for each and for philosophy as well. Supporting this integration was the intent to create a "taste for exactitude, reflection, and self-discovery" and to develop, as well, the "spirit of analysis."[22]

Most important in creating a chasm between matter and reason in *lycée* studies before the Simon and Ferry reforms was the detachment of languages, literature, history, and philosophy from immediate, observable reality. In the course of moving schools toward direct involvement with the real world, Simon himself visited a number of *lycée* classes. Perhaps the most remarkable symptom of the curriculum's detachment from tangible reality lay in the *lycée* geography courses, in which students discussed people and places without the benefit of maps. In a crystallizing—and appalling—moment, Simon listened while a sixteen-year-old boy confidently announced that the Zuider Zee was an island; "not one other student," wrote the minister in disgust, "even blinked."[23] Following this experience, Simon wrote to the headmasters of the *lycées* that children needed to *read* maps, in particular, the map of France. Thus professors should "begin with walks" conducted with maps of the area in hand.[24] The noted historian of Bonnard's Lycée Louis-le-Grand, Gustav Dupont-Ferrier, confirmed Simon's findings when he wrote that the school did not own one atlas in 1873. "But what school did?" he asked.[25]

In commenting on the overall need for reform, Simon noted that "up to now, one gives to children the unknown" and then "moves toward the specific and familiar." With missionary zeal, he set out to reverse that order. Taken together, the major changes under Simon and Ferry created a new system of instruction that rooted French, Latin, and Greek literature, history, and philosophy in the students' own world; from the concrete, students learned to think upward through connecting levels of increasing abstraction that began with feeling and ended with reason. The result was to shift children away from the view that matter and ideas belonged to separate spheres.

The reforms, however, enjoyed only partial success. By anchoring ideas in the students' personal experience, the curriculum succeeded in creating a unified way of thinking that began with things observed and ended with rational thought. However, this structure did not, as hoped, turn students outward into the contemporaneous public world of politics and commerce; instead, it persistently reinforced a retreat into the private world of home and family. In consequence, over the course of his schooling, Bonnard analyzed language and literature in light of what he, as a child, personally knew. In this new curriculum, his relationships with his parents and siblings became the foundation for understanding the relationships between a king and his son, and his love of home and friends formed the basis for understanding the patriotic feelings of heroes.

The reforms did not measurably change what was read in literature, though, in fact, children read more of French and less of Latin. In the first two decades of the Third Republic, children read the classic French literature of the sixteenth and seventeenth centuries; Latin included the works of Cicero, Tacitus, Virgil, Livy, Horace, and Terence; and Greek, selections from Homer, Plato, Xenophon, and Plutarch along with the plays of Euripides, Sophocles, and Aeschylus.[26] The key change that opened the way for students to identify with what they read came, not through new texts, but through a new emphasis on a history of literature that featured the private life and character of the author. Thus, when Bonnard studied the fables of his beloved La Fontaine, for the first time through the classes of his middle-school years and then again in the upper division, he could understand the meanings of the fabulist through the twin filters of his own experience and class discussion of the personality of the author.[27] Indeed, the new, personalized approach to literary analysis is confirmed both in a text by Emile Faguet, a professor of literature at the Lycée Condorcet in Paris, and by a study guide for the *baccalauréat* examination compiled by Edouard de Colonne, a professor of literature at the Lycée Louis-le-Grand.[28]

Just as literature began with the tangible, the history curriculum began with what was known. Reviewing the Ferry reforms, Desiré Blanchet, professor of history at Bonnard's Lycée Charlemagne, confirmed that learning history, like learning language, started off with actual experience and direct observation. Students learned, he said, "from the everyday world," and that French schools had not lost anything by "opening" the minds of students "onto the world that surrounds us." Indeed, "isn't the feeling for the real," he asked, "the nature of a truly modern education?"[29] More specifically, Gustav Jalliffier, who taught at the Lycée Condorcet, defined history as a love of personal place. In a lecture in 1884 to fellow educators, he drew a parallel between ancient Greece and the French present by stating that patriotic feelings for the "Athenian in the time of Sophocles" would be evoked by the "dry plain with its simple ornamentation of olive trees." Similarly, history in the present grew from "a name of a place . . . a

patch of earth connected by a thousand strands to the origins of your family . . .
a narrow, quiet street. . . a garden . . . a stream . . . the family table around which
old parents forget their age."[30]

Though the *lycée*'s insistence on personal experience and objective reality
did not actually shift the focus of history from kings to commoners, it did, particularly after 1880, shift the emphasis of study from public to private life. Small
symptoms of the change occurred even in the general headings of texts. For
example, in a history textbook for *rhétorique* written by Victor Duruy, a subtitle
in the 1879 edition appeared as the "Government of Louis XIV"; in post-1880
editions, it became the "Personal Government of Louis XIV."[31] A somewhat
more profound sign of change lay in the fact that in the 1879 edition, Duruy
drew heavily on impersonal, official political documents to make his points; in
the later edition, he described circumstances through quotations from memoirs
and letters.[32] Examination of study guides for the *bac* also confirms the new
focus. In particular, accounts dwelled on personal relationships and took on
intimate tones. For example, one response given in a *baccalauréat* study guide
tells the tale of Philip II of Spain, successor to his father the Holy Roman
Emperor Charles V. The author directed candidates for the *bac* to focus on the
personalities of the two figures, their intimate correspondence, and the paternal
feelings of Charles for Philip.[33]

Following the structure that began with the familiar and known, philosophy,
occupying eight class hours per week in the final *lycée* year, created "independent and critical thought" and gave final polish to the earlier studies in literature
and history.[34] The course was supported by a weighty text and depended, as
well, on elegant lectures. In Paris, the "crown" of the curriculum was taught by
leading members of the educational establishment. In 1879, anticipating the
reforms, the noted educator and philosopher Paul Janet, once a professor at the
Lycée Louis-le-Grand, published what was to become a classic of philosophy
manuals—the *Traité élémentaire de philosophie à l'usage des classes.* This new
version of the philosophy course devoted a full third of its contents to psychology that was, in turn, firmly rooted in the facts of physiology.[35] Janet's plan set
curricular standards for the forthcoming decade; indeed, Bonnard used Janet's
text, or one similar to it, in 1884 and 1885.

In the psychology section of his *Traité*, beginning with the optic nerve and
other sensory organs, Janet constructed a systematic analysis of the inner per-
son—feelings and intellect—that presented physiology as the foundation for the
thinking man. Here, students moved from the senses to unconscious thought—
dreams, sleepwalking, madness, and hallucination—and then to higher levels of
feeling and finally to intelligence and reason.[36] Intellection, wrote Janet, "does
not depend immediately on the body but on a sequence of intermediary levels."
To "understand evidence, to aspire to virtuous acts, to love someone for his

goodness and nobility of heart" are not in themselves physical acts but are linked to them.[37]

Was the curriculum as presented in Janet's text actually practiced in the classroom? Notes taken in 1890 at the Lycée Henri IV in Paris by two students who attended the philosophy classes of the illustrious Henri Bergson confirm that it was. Though very different in appearance—one set neatly written by a sober future physician named Roques; the other, enhanced by loops, curls, and blobs of ink, by Alfred Jarry, Bonnard's later friend and collaborator and the rambunctious author of the play *Ubu roi*—the two appear identical in content.[38] In each case, Bergson presented a topic—"sentiment," for example—defined it, showed how it connected to other elements in psychology, and finally gave examples of the phenomenon that were situated in the ordinary, everyday world. Here, classroom practice in philosophy repeatedly articulated how reality served as the basis for idea, thereby giving students the means to understand and explain integrated patterns of thought.

Models

Along with the integration of the concrete and abstract, the reformed curriculum that had educated Bonnard established two important models for analyzing and understanding literature. These too not only shaped the boy's ideas on art but provided a methodology for his painting as well. The first, that very French version of literary analysis, *explication du texte,* was introduced into the French literature curriculum only in 1880, when it began to teach students to analyze the actual forms of words and phrases as signifiers of meaning.[39] The second, a new emphasis from 1880 on the history of literature, showed how authors, through individual temperament and imagination, transposed themes and styles from the past into original works of the present.[40] These components of the curriculum would become mainstays of Bonnard's practice of art.

In following the patterns of *explication*, students examined individual words and phrases from a poem or a play in an effort to tease out the secrets of the entire text. Thus Bonnard, in the French literature classes of his last year of middle school and the first three years of the *lycée*'s upper division, was spared the long, deadening lectures that characterized earlier instruction, and through the new demands of *explication* he actively and imaginatively assessed literature in light of its form.[41] To support the practice of *explication*, a standard text written by Auguste Gazier, professor of literature at the Lycées Rollin and St. Louis in Paris, gave explicit instructions on the process.[42] The text showed how form rather than formula conveyed meaning, as it discussed how each author viewed the world through an individualized sensibility and how, as an artist, he developed a personal means of expression based on the elements of written language.

The first chapter of Gazier's manual, "The Author's Style," sounded a death knell for Latin rhetoric; style was not, wrote Gazier, a matter of rhetorical rules but was the imaginative construction of phrases, figures of speech, and individual words. Not only did language carry significance in itself, but words and phrases constructed the meanings of the text as a whole.[43] Gazier enjoined his readers to understand literature in a profound, personal way by researching "what the author is to have said and how he has said it."[44] In a succession of clear, lively chapters, he showed by example rather than by rule how to understand and savor language as it constituted the meaning of poems and plays. Most important, he introduced students to the harmony of words as he demonstrated the aesthetic vibrations of their sounds and expanded their meanings into metaphors.[45]

After they had practiced *explication* in French literature, philosophy taught students to understand language as signs of feeling and intellect. Important here were laws that governed the "contiguity" of words, images, and ideas. Indeed, it was through "association" and resemblance that one drew connections between an object and its meanings.[46] Following the patterns laid down in previous years, the philosopher led his adolescent readers through a series of steps that began with objects and, through memory and imagination, proceeded upward to feelings and sensations. At the highest level, said Janet, associations connected ideas—he referred to this as an operation of pure intelligence.[47] The phenomenon of "association," according to Janet, depended on a human need to abstract from objects and to think in terms of symbols and signs. Students were taught that words in themselves, through "resemblance" and "contiguity," were abstractions thick with feelings, thoughts, and ideas. In turn, as the building blocks of literature, words created layers of meaning in the lines of plays and in the stanzas of poetry; they resonated with suggestion in human exchange. Words formed images and made up metaphors; language, wrote Janet, was an "ensemble of signs."[48]

Also conditioning Bonnard's ideas on art, the history of literature emphasized that the past informed the present through the migration of style and forms from one author to another. Faguet, who taught *lycée* literature, repeatedly showed in his works on French literature that authors absorbed influences from a variety of sources in the process of creating an original work. As an example of the way that Faguet discussed the varied sources for an author's form and style, we turn to what he wrote about La Fontaine. The French fabulist had not actually invented any of his tales; instead, he had borrowed liberally both from nature and from the ancients—from Indian legends, Aesop, Phèdre (a first-century fabulist), and some French storytellers. But while adapting his fables from earlier models, the author had embellished the prototypes—he had "stretched them" and "increased their size." Most important, La Fontaine, through imagination, transformed the original into comedy and created new characters that were well studied and precisely drawn.[49] No matter how concrete the details in La Fontaine might be, Faguet reminded the reader, the stories were always the "occasion" for feeling and reflection.[50]

Réalisation

Certainly, it must be said that Bonnard left little writing on his art, though, at the very end of his life, he did assemble some scattered notes from a sequence of pocket diaries that he kept between 1927 and 1946. The art and literary journal *Verve* was planning to devote a special issue to Bonnard's work, and as a text for the project, the artist transcribed his observations from the diaries into—appropriately enough—a little school notebook. The title page of the collection reads simply, "Observations on Painting."[51] The thoughts on art that Bonnard had jotted next to daily notes on the weather and sketches made on-site reveal that his way of thinking about art in old age was still conditioned by his *lycée* training. Though written over a span of almost twenty years, the notes gathered by the artist into a single document reveal the core of his thinking on art. For Bonnard at seventy-nine, just as it had been in the school curriculum of more than sixty years earlier, sensation and idea were rooted in the personal present; together, nature, feeling, and reason created the total work of art. These notes represent a distillation of his education.

Bonnard spoke of his debt to the objective world when he wrote such entries as, "When one distorts nature, it still remains underneath, unlike [the case in] purely imaginative works," and "It is always necessary to have a subject, however minimal, in order to keep one foot on the ground."[52] In addition, just as *lycée* literature and philosophy connected feelings and ideas to nature, Bonnard insisted that though his images had "one foot on the ground," they must also resonate on other planes, as when he wrote, "execution: the inner model combines with imitation of the material model: one is warned by the first lines and the first applications of paint to a given surface."[53] Here the material—both paint and model—combines with memory and other internal visions on the way to forming the complete work.

Furthermore, the inner model was always shaped by feeling and controlled by reason. In several instances in the "Observations," the artist noted how good painting must surpass imitation, insisting that his images express "feelings through painting and drawing," and in one particular instance, he writes that "a sentimental vision . . . holds the wall together."[54] In a number of entries, Bonnard focuses on color as the language of expressive content: "Sensation leads you to color tones. Tones, in return, bring about the revelation of sensation," and in another, color imposes order on the composition as he calls for "Planes through color. Rough out with color contrasts."[55] In point of fact, of course, Bonnard never intended for his work to express unbridled feelings; the whole must be controlled by the intellect, a point he made when he wrote, "One can take all possible liberties of line, form, proportions, colors, to make feeling intelligible and clearly visible." Indeed, his need for intelligibility is emphasized as he called for "coherence" and reminded himself to "reason while working. Judge without reasoning."[56]

From the very beginning of his career, Bonnard turned to a variety of sources for his images. Just as La Fontaine turned to "Indian tales," Aesop, and Phèdre, Bonnard looked to Japanese woodblock prints and classical sculpture. The works, of course, offer themselves as testaments to this practice, and the notes reveal his conscious search for models. Bonnard's notes also recall the lessons of literature that taught him to value words as signs and to look to the works of others for forms and ideas. Indeed, in the spring of 1929, Bonnard alluded to art as a language and he defined the collaboration between his own vision and the vision of others when he wrote: "Rhetoric in the realization of the work: Calling up one's mental reserves of beautiful shapes and colors, the outcome of personal observation, and observations of the masters, conjured up before one's eyes at each brushstroke."[57]

In many ways, of course, we see that the early works differ from the later pieces. As one pages through this catalogue or walks through the exhibition, flat planes of color drawn from *japoniste* models give way to subtle, soft-layered tones appropriated from Renoir and Monet. The rococo play of bubbles and bosom in the 1891 *Poster for France-Champagne* (plate 5) yields to classical calm in *Marthe in the Dining Room* of 1933 (plate 129), and the lighthearted touch lending impudent form to Jarry's *Ubu* of 1901 (plates 41, 42) plays no part in the mature drawings and paintings. In fact, shortly after Jarry's text of 1901, the somber, reflective mood that sets the early and late works apart appears in paintings like *Portrait of Ambroise Vollard,* dating to sometime about 1906 (plate 67) and *Early Spring*, of 1910 (plate 68). But even if these factors seem to distance the early Bonnard from the late, connecting themes and recurring forms reveal that the ordering mentality of the artist stayed the same.

Returning to *Checked Blouse* (fig. 89, plate 3) and *Woman with Dog* (fig. 90, plate 96), one now sees the role of Bonnard's schooling in shaping both the early and the later images. Using the discussion of these two works as a guide, one can follow the effect of the schooling through the continuing themes that traverse the exhibition—the self-portraits, the scenes viewed through a window or door, and the intimate scenes of Marthe from *Woman Pulling on Her Stockings* of 1893 (plate 21) to *Nude in Bathtub* of 1941–1946 (plate 127)—to see that these connections hold true throughout his career. From what he did in his youth through what he did in his old age, Bonnard's whole body of work depends on the patterns of thought that were fixed by the *lycée.* The repeated lessons of school that related abstractions to personal experience gave the artist a way in which he could always express feelings and ideas. The continuing practice of *explication* taught him to understand form as a language of signs, and the study of history gave him the means to fuse personal vision with the ideas of the past. These together give a coherent voice to Bonnard.

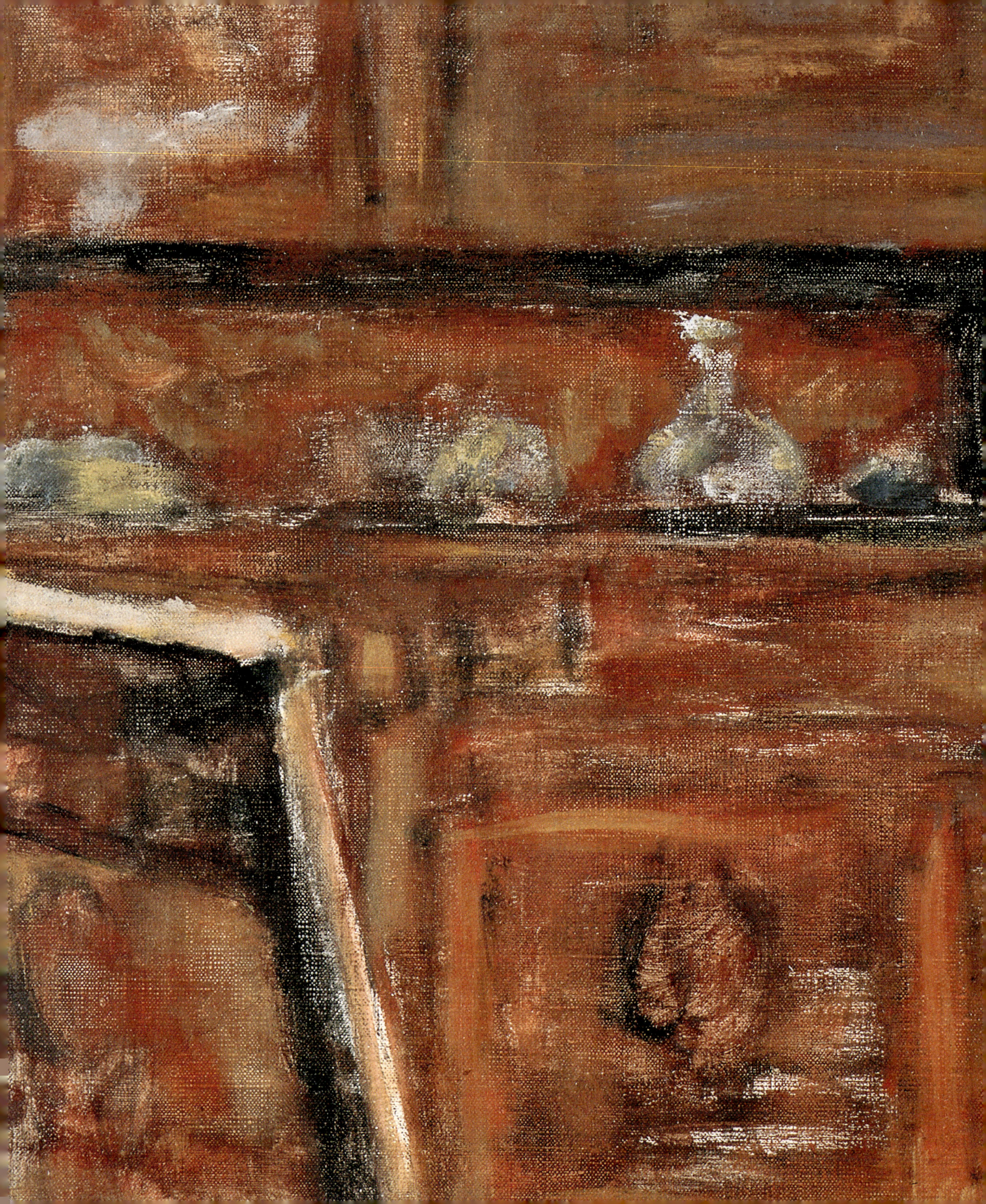

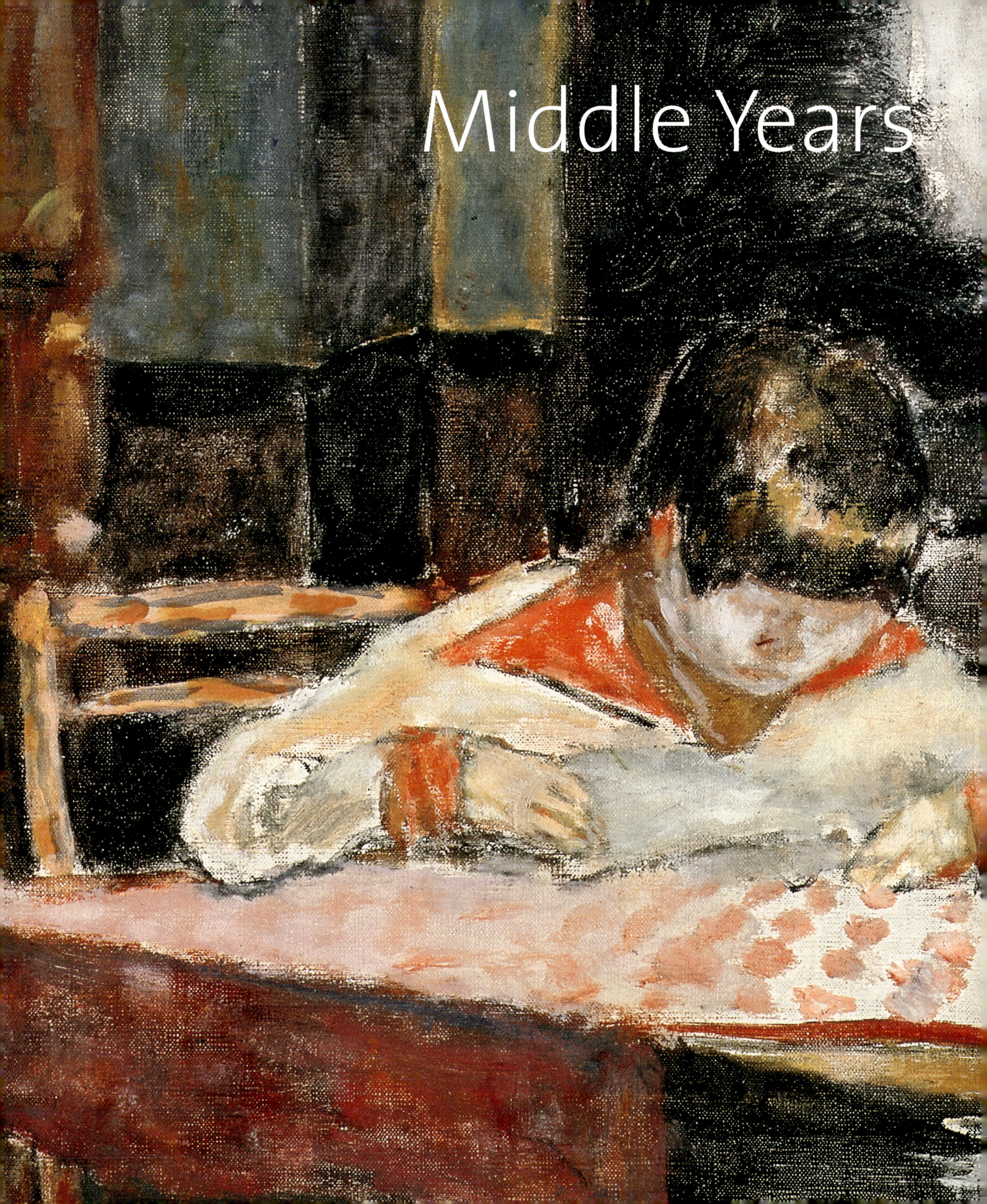
Middle Years

Middle Years

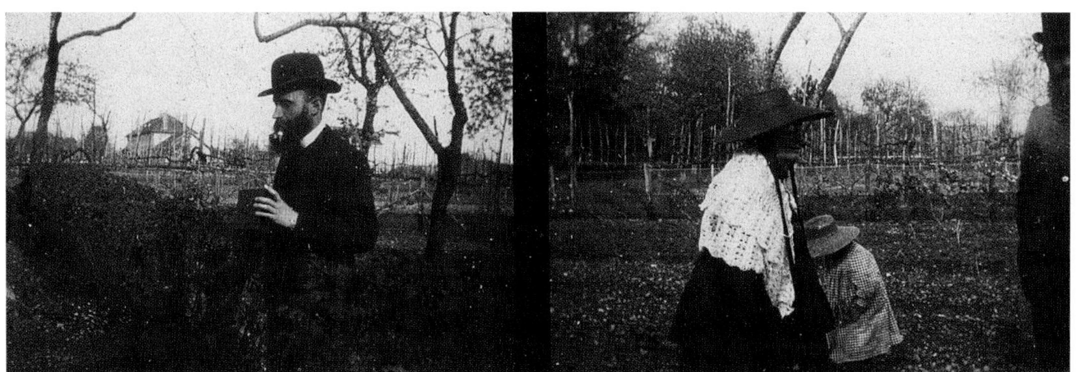

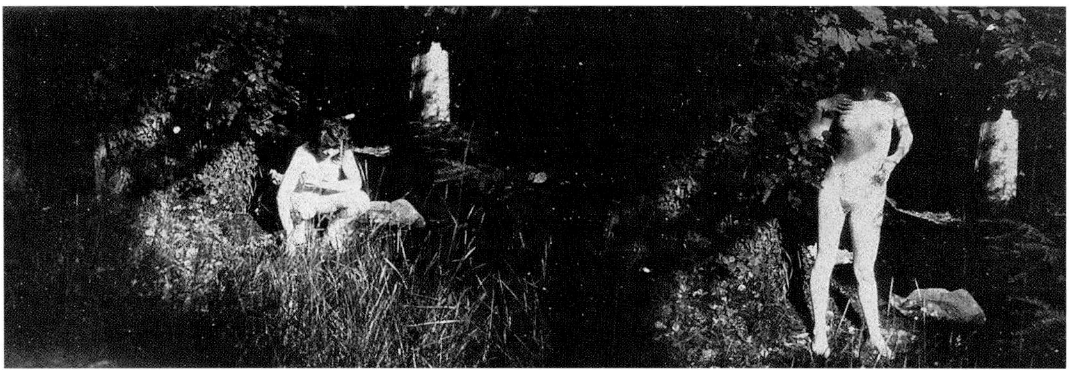

Previous spread:
Interior with Boy (detail)
1910, Oil on canvas, 16 × 25 in. (41 × 63.5 cm),
The Phillips Collection, Washington, D.C.

44

**Edouard Vuillard Holding His Kodak and
Madame Mertzdorff, Renée, and Ker-Xavier
Roussel**
1900, Original contact print on gelatin paper,
1½ × 2³⁄₁₆ in. (3.8 × 5.5 cm) and 1½ × 2 in.
(3.8 × 5.1 cm), Paris, Musée d'Orsay, donation
with a life interest from Charles Terrasse's
children, 1987, inv: PHO 1987 31 18 and PHO
1987 31 19.

45

**Marthe Crouching down in the Garden at
Montval and Marthe Standing in the
Sunlight in the Garden at Montval**
1900–1901, Original contact print on gelatin
paper, 1⁷⁄₁₆ × 2¹⁄₁₆ in. (3.7 × 5.2 cm) and
1½ × 1⁵⁄₁₆ in. (3.8 × 5 cm), Paris, Musée
d'Orsay, donation with a life interest from
Charles Terrasse's children, 1987, inv: PHO
1987 31 36 and PHO 1987 31 34.

46

Maria Boursin
**Pierre Bonnard Seated
in Profile and Pierre Bonnard Viewed
from the Back**
1900–1901, Original contact print on gelatin
paper, 1⁷⁄₁₆ × 2³⁄₁₆ in. (3.6 × 5.5 cm) and
1 ⁷⁄₁₆ × 2¹⁄₁₆ in. (3.6 × 5.3 cm), Paris, Musée
d'Orsay, donation with a life interest from
Charles Terrasse's children, 1987, inv. PHO
1987 31 42 and PHO 1987 31 43.

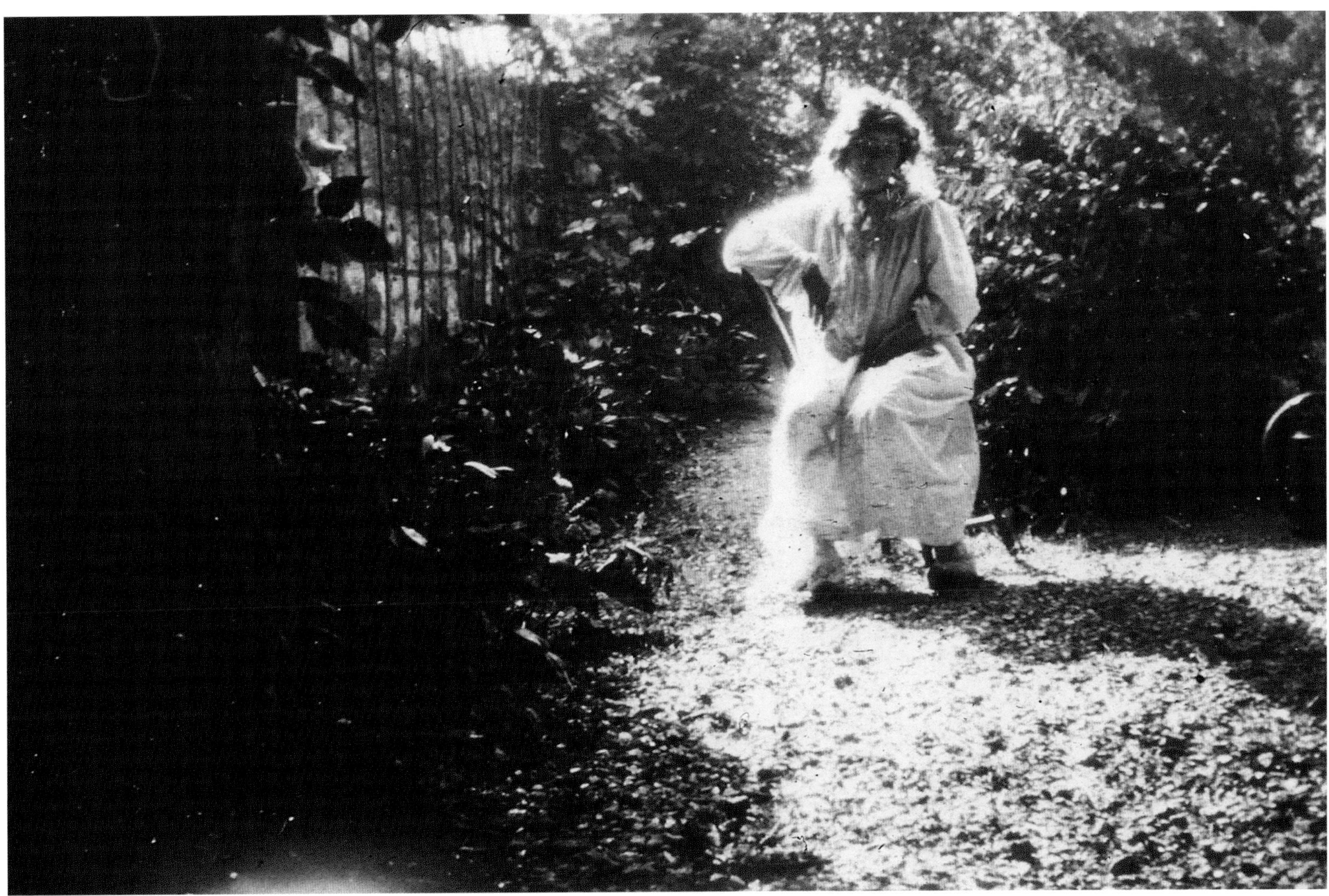

47

**Marthe Seated in Her Nightdress in the
Garden at Montval**
1900–1901, Contemporary print from
original film negative, 9⁹⁄₁₆ × 12³⁄₁₆ in.
(23 × 31 cm), Paris, Musée d'Orsay, donation
with a life interest from Charles Terrasse's
children, 1987, inv: PHO 1987 27 21.

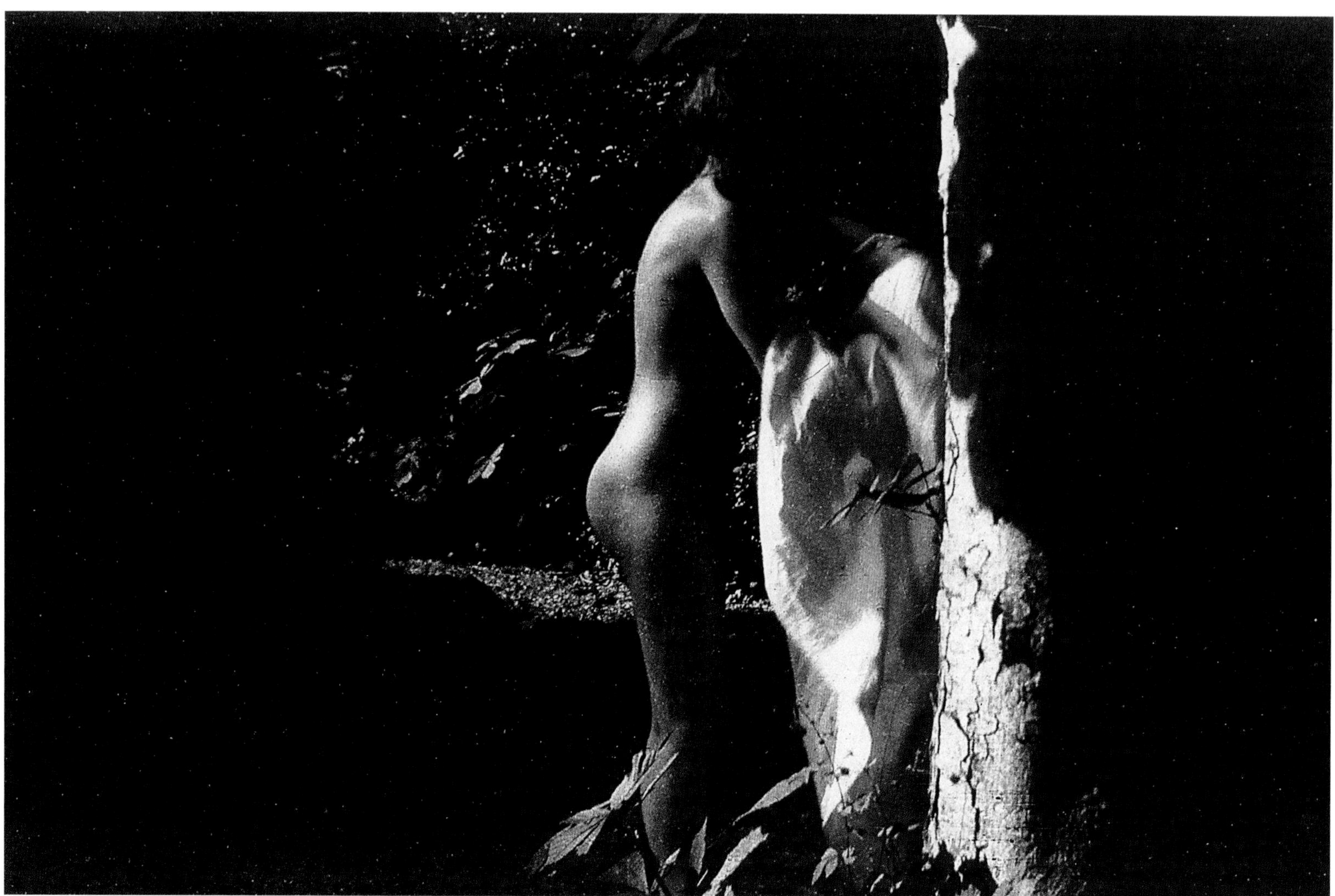

48

**Marthe Removing Her Nightdress in the
Garden at Montval**
1900–1901, Contemporary print from
original film negative, 9⁹⁄₁₆ × 12³⁄₁₆ in.
(23 × 31 cm), Paris, Musée d'Orsay, donation
with a life interest from Charles Terrasse's
children, 1987, inv: PHO 1987 27 23.

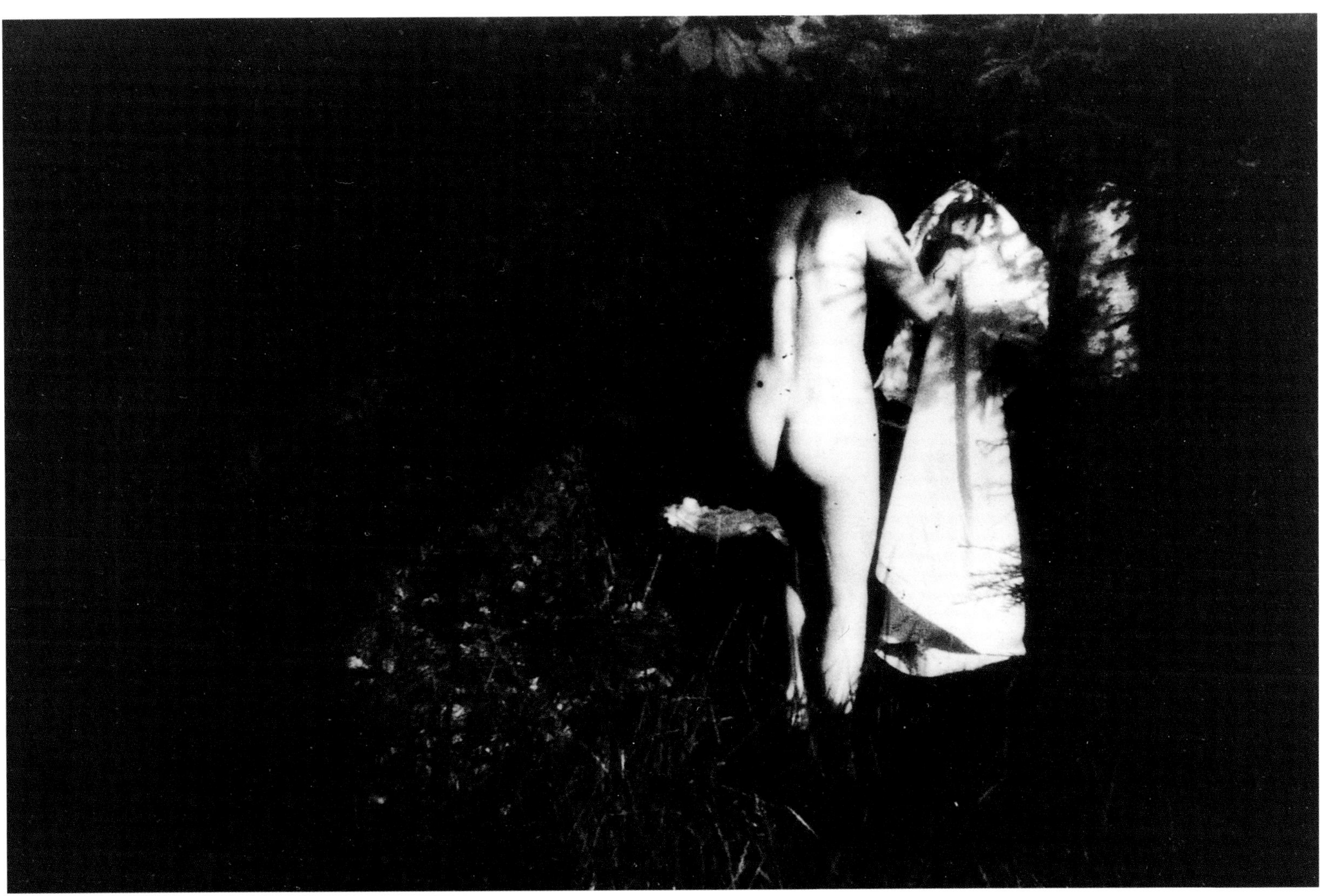

49

**Marthe with Her Back to the Camera in the
Garden at Montval**
1900-1901, Contemporary print from original
film negative, 9⁹⁄₁₆ × 12³⁄₁₆ in. (23 × 31 cm),
Paris, Musée d'Orsay, donation with a life
interest from Charles Terrasse's children,
1987, inv: PHO 1987 27 25.

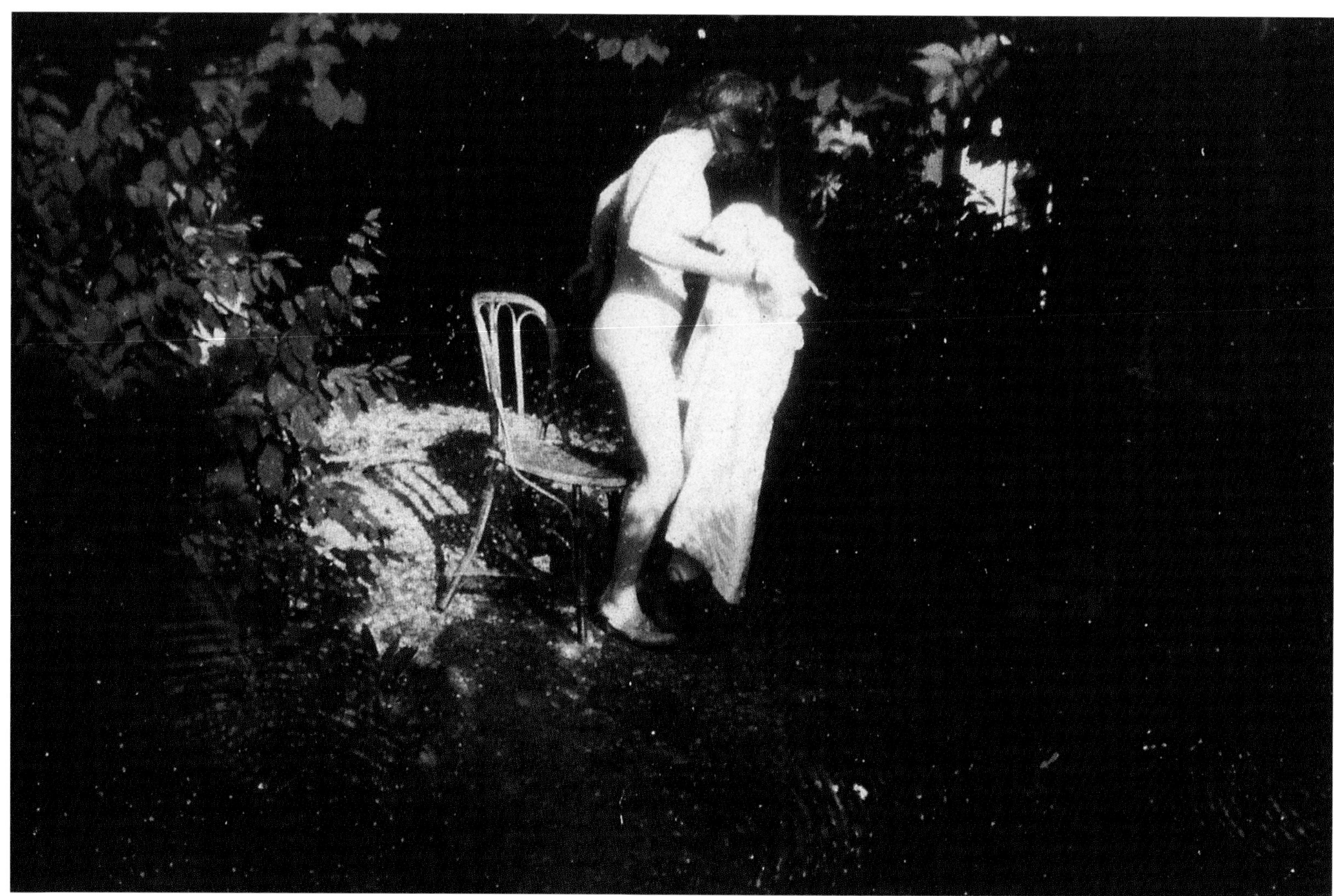

50

**Marthe Holding Her Nightdress in the
Garden at Montval**
1900-1901, Contemporary print from original
film negative, 9⁹⁄₁₆ × 12³⁄₁₆ in. (23 × 31 cm),
Paris, Musée d'Orsay, donation with a life
interest from Charles Terrasse's children,
1987, inv: PHO 1987 30 38.

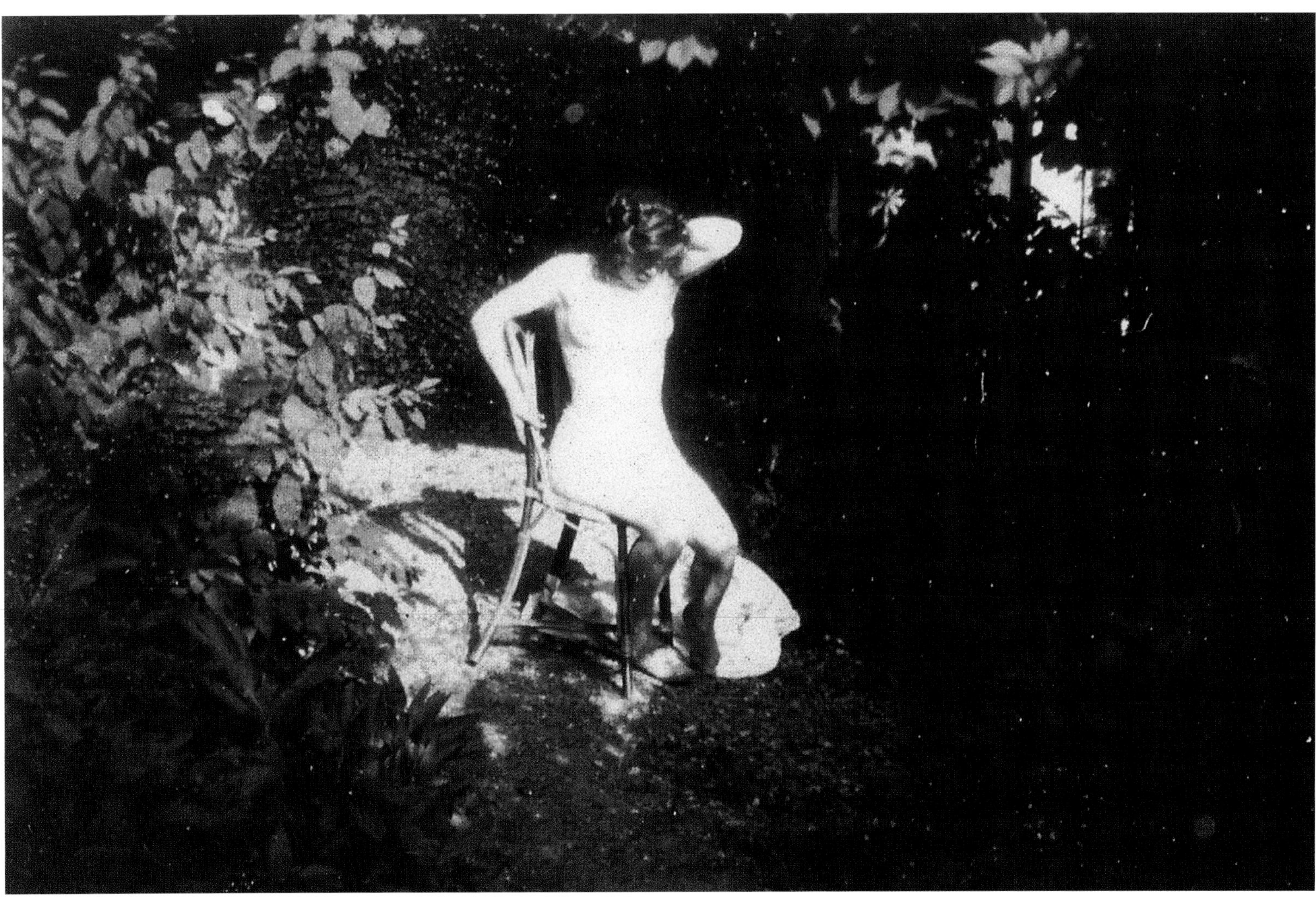

51

**Marthe Seated with Her Left Hand behind
Her Neck in the Garden at Montval**
1900–1901, Contemporary print from
original film negative, 9⁹⁄₁₆ × 12³⁄₁₆ in.
(23 × 31 cm), Paris, Musée d'Orsay, donation
with a life interest from Charles Terrasse's
children, 1987, inv: PHO 1987 30 39.

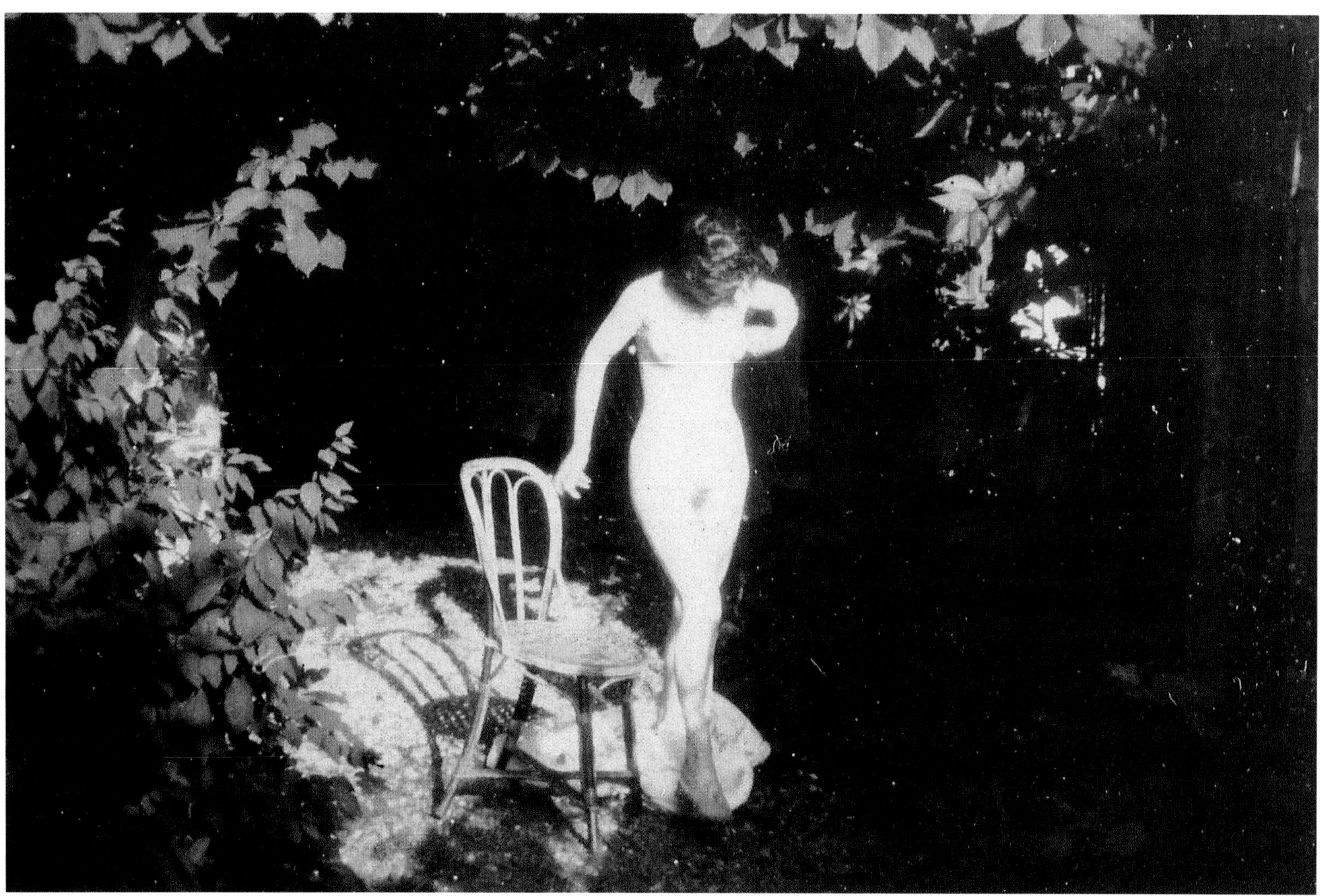

52

**Marthe Standing next to a Chair in the
Garden at Montval**
1900–1901, Contemporary print from
original film negative, 9⁹⁄₁₆ × 12³⁄₁₆ in.
(23 × 31 cm), Paris, Musée d'Orsay, donation
with a life interest from Charles Terrasse's
children, 1987, inv: PHO 1987 30 37.

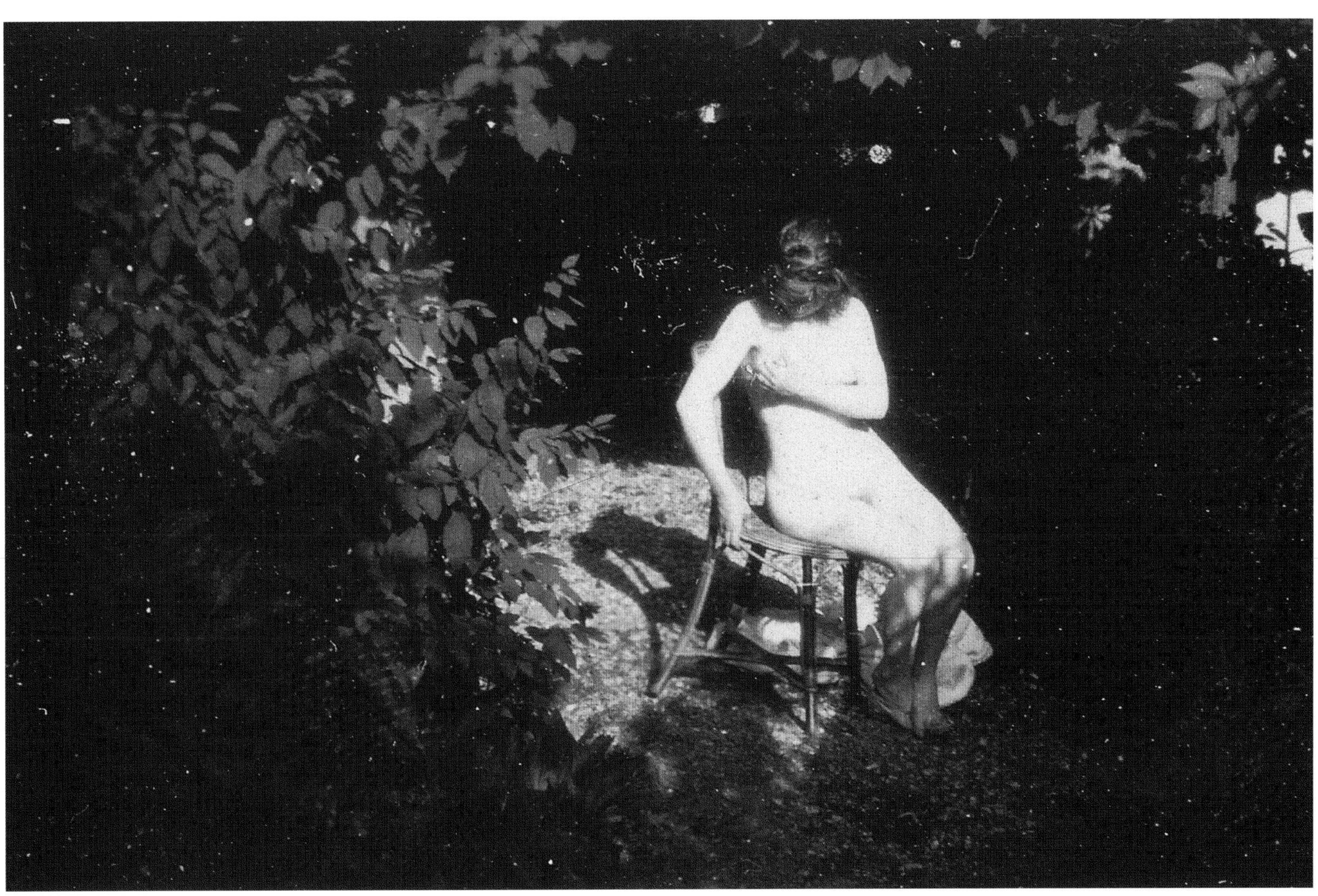

53

**Marthe Seated with Her Hand on Her Right
Breast in the Garden at Montval**
1900–1901, Contemporary print from
original film negative, 9⁹⁄₁₆ × 12³⁄₁₆ in.
(23 × 31 cm), Paris, Musée d'Orsay, donation
with a life interest from Charles Terrasse's
children, 1987, inv: PHO 1987 30 40.

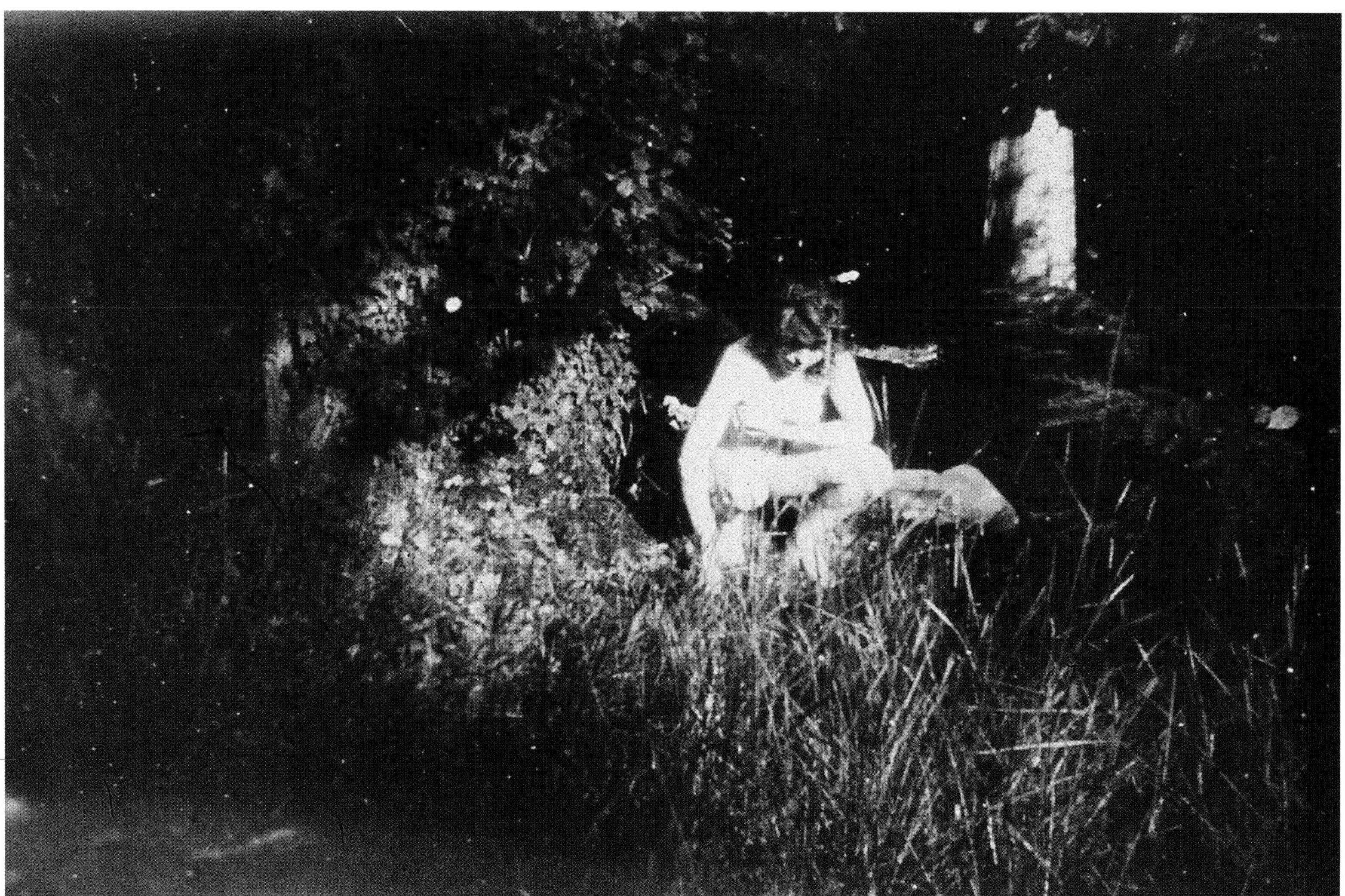

54

**Marthe Crouching down in the Garden
at Montval**
1900–1901, Contemporary print from
original film negative, 9⁹⁄₁₆ × 12³⁄₁₆ in.
(23 × 31 cm), Paris, Musée d'Orsay, donation
with a life interest from Charles Terrasse's
children, 1987, inv: PHO 1987 30 36.

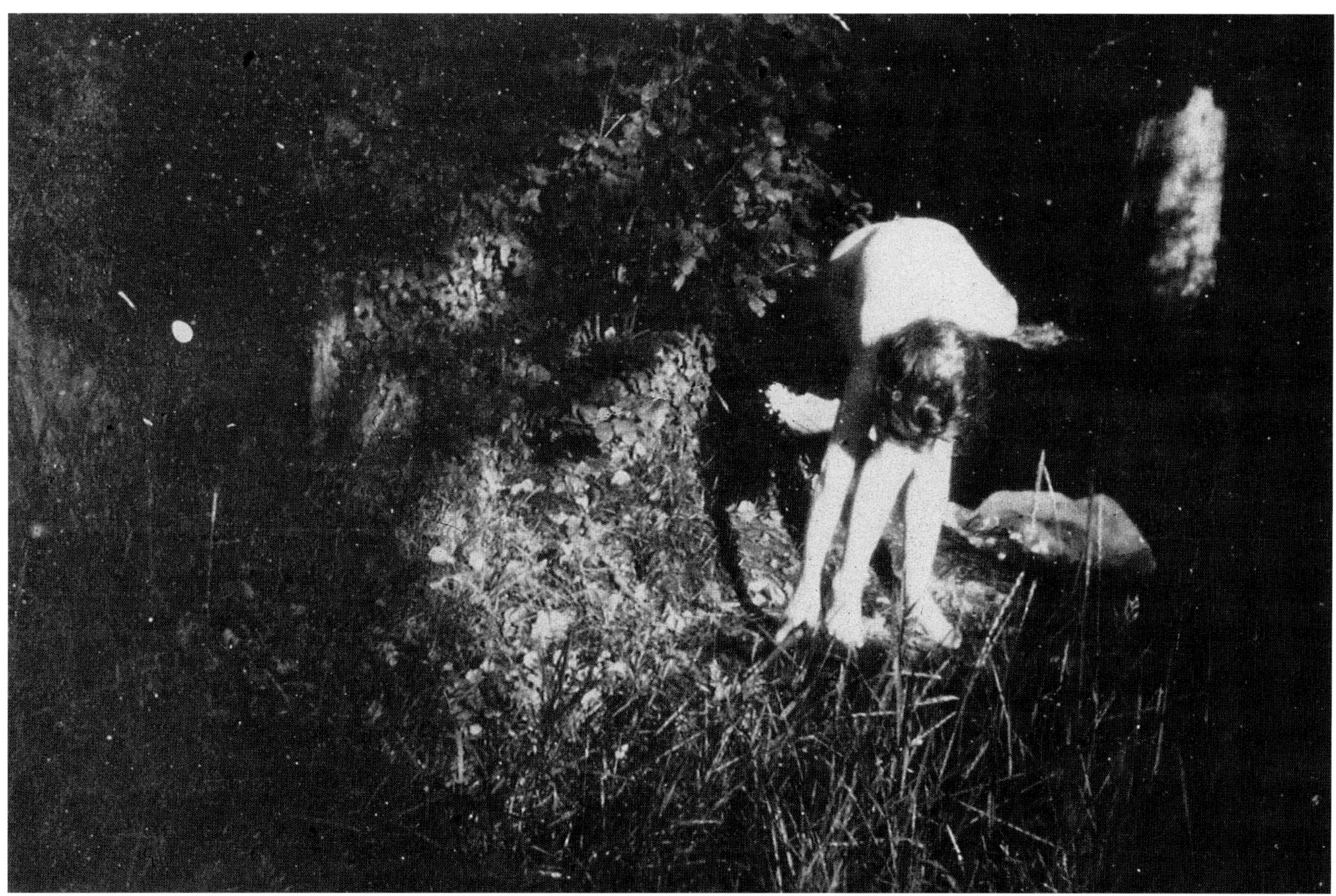

55

**Marthe Bending to Touch the Ground in the
Garden at Montval**
1900–1901, Contemporary print from
original film negative, 9⁹⁄₁₆ × 12³⁄₁₆ in.
(23 × 31 cm), Paris, Musée d'Orsay, donation
with a life interest from Charles Terrasse's
children, 1987, inv: PHO 1987 30 35.

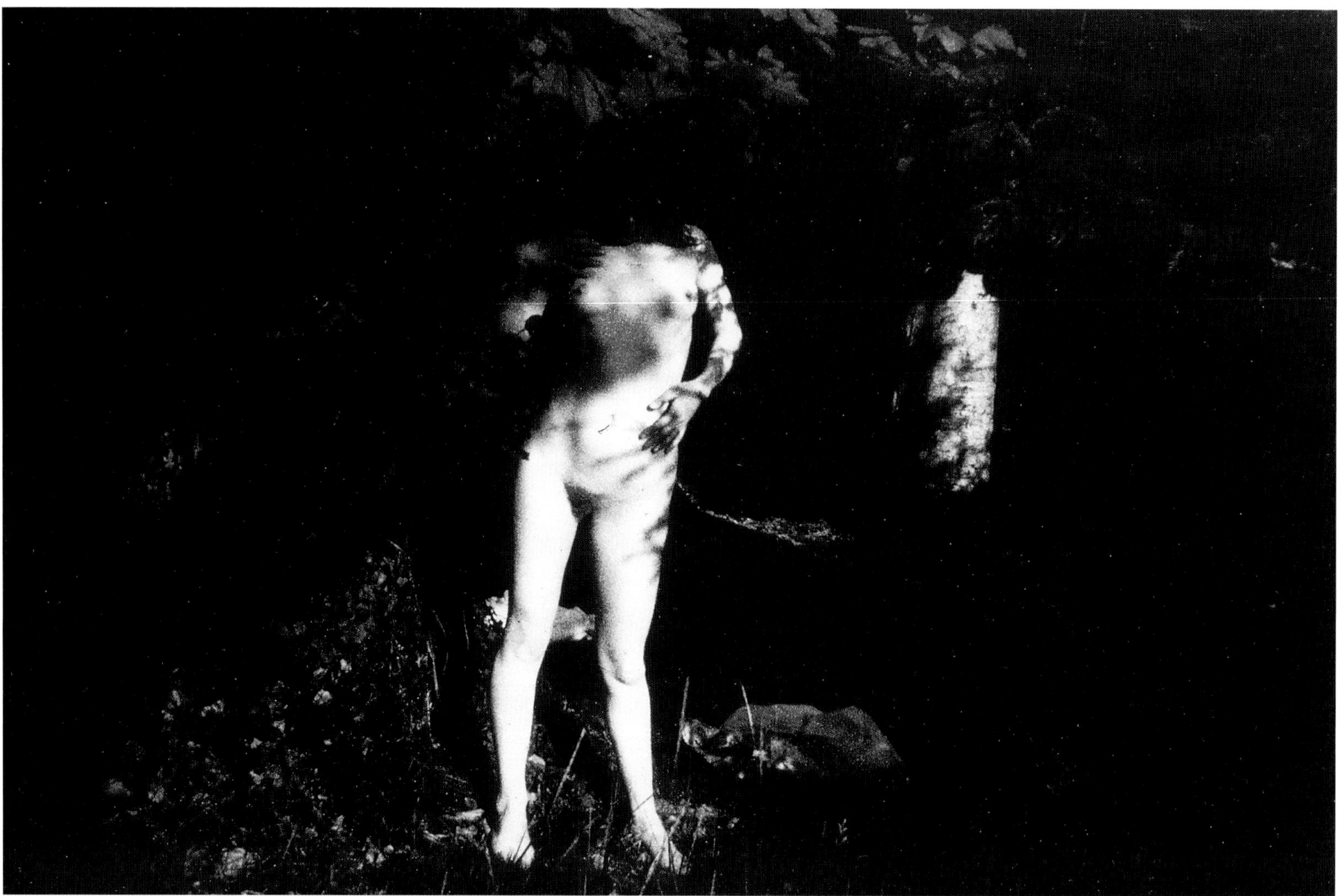

55a

Marthe Standing in the Sunlight in the Garden at Montval
1900–1901, Contemporary print from original film negative, $9\frac{9}{16} \times 12\frac{3}{16}$ in. (23 × 31 cm), Paris, Musée d'Orsay, donation with a life interest from Charles Terrasse's children, 1987, inv: PHO 1987 27 29.

chèrent la flûte de Dorcon pour offrande. Cela fait ils retournèrent vers leurs chèvres et brebis, lesquelles ils trouvèrent tapies contre terre sans paître ni bêler, pour l'ennui et regret qu'elles avoient, ainsi qu'on peut croire, de ne voir plus Daphnis ni Chloé. Mais sitôt qu'elles les aperçurent, et qu'eux se mirent à les appeler comme de coutume et à leur jouer du flageolet, elles se levèrent incontinent, et se prirent les brebis à paître, et les chèvres à sauteler en bêlant, comme pour fêter le retour de leur chevrier.

Mais, quoi qu'il y eût, Daphnis ne se pouvoit éjouir à bon escient depuis qu'il eut vu Chloé nue, et sa beauté à découvert, qu'il n'avait point encore vue. Il s'en sentoit le cœur malade ne plus ne moins que d'un venin qui l'eût en secret consumé. Son souffle aucune fois était fort et hâté, comme si quelque ennemi l'eût poursuivi prêt à l'atteindre, d'autres fois faible et débile, comme d'un à qui manquent tout-à-coup la force et l'haleine, et lui

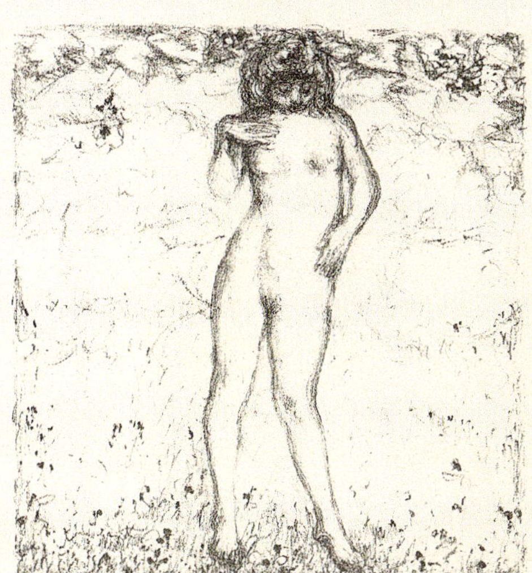

sembloit le bain de Chloé plus redoutable que la mer dont il étoit échappé. Bref, il lui étoit avis que son âme fût toujours entre les brigands, tant il avoit de peine, jeune garçon nourri aux champs, qui ne savoit encore que c'est du brigandage d'amour.

56

Illustration for Longus's "Les Pastorales" or "Daphnis et Chloé"
1902, Lithograph in book, 12 × 9⅞ in. (30.5 × 25 cm), Lessing J. Rosenwald Collection, Library of Congress, Washington, D.C.

57

Woman Bathing
ca. 1900–1906, Bronze, 10¾ × 5 × 4¼ in.
(27.3 × 12.7 × 10.8 cm), Hirshhorn Museum
and Sculpture Garden, Smithsonian
Institution. Gift of Joseph H. Hirshhorn,
1966.

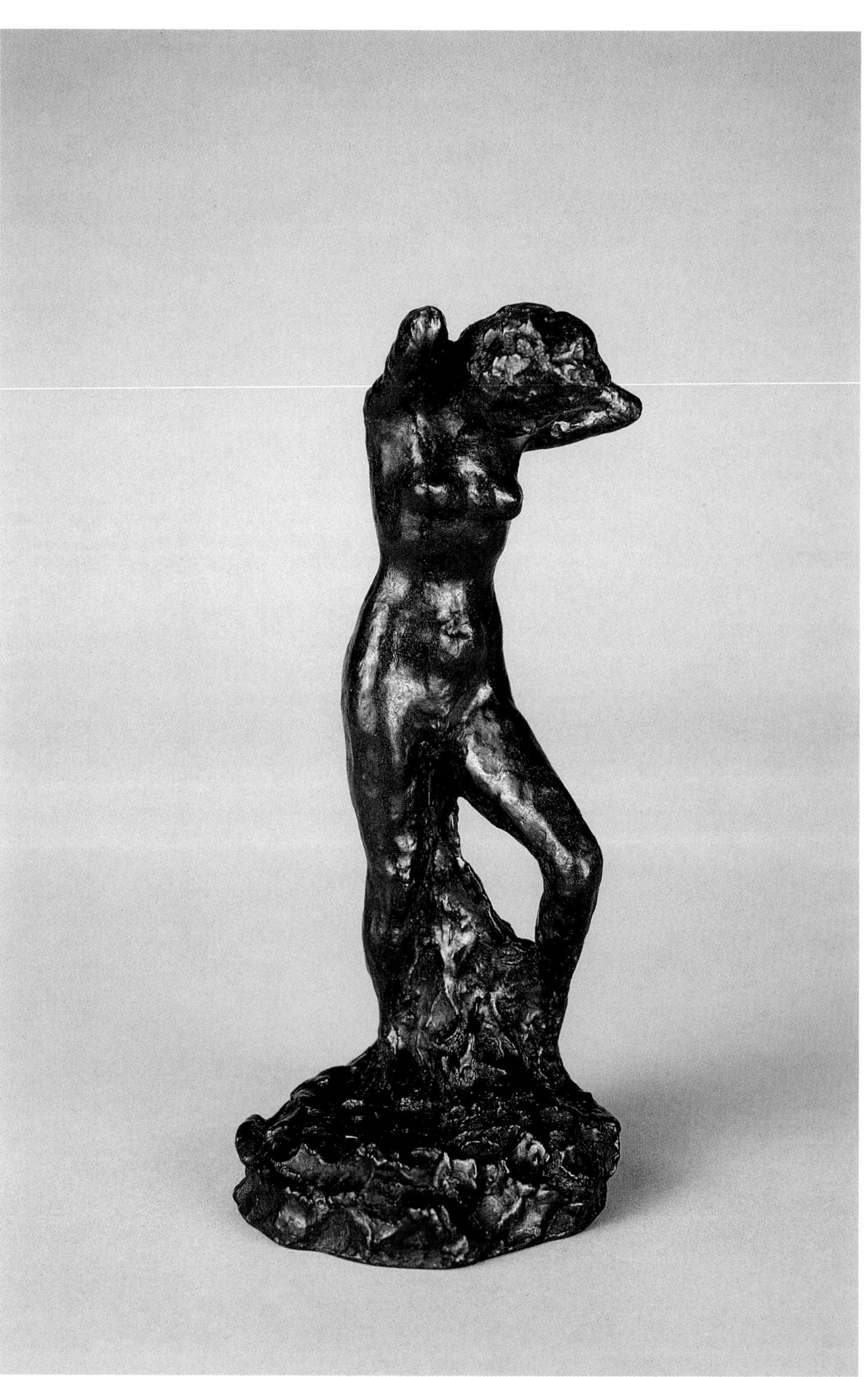

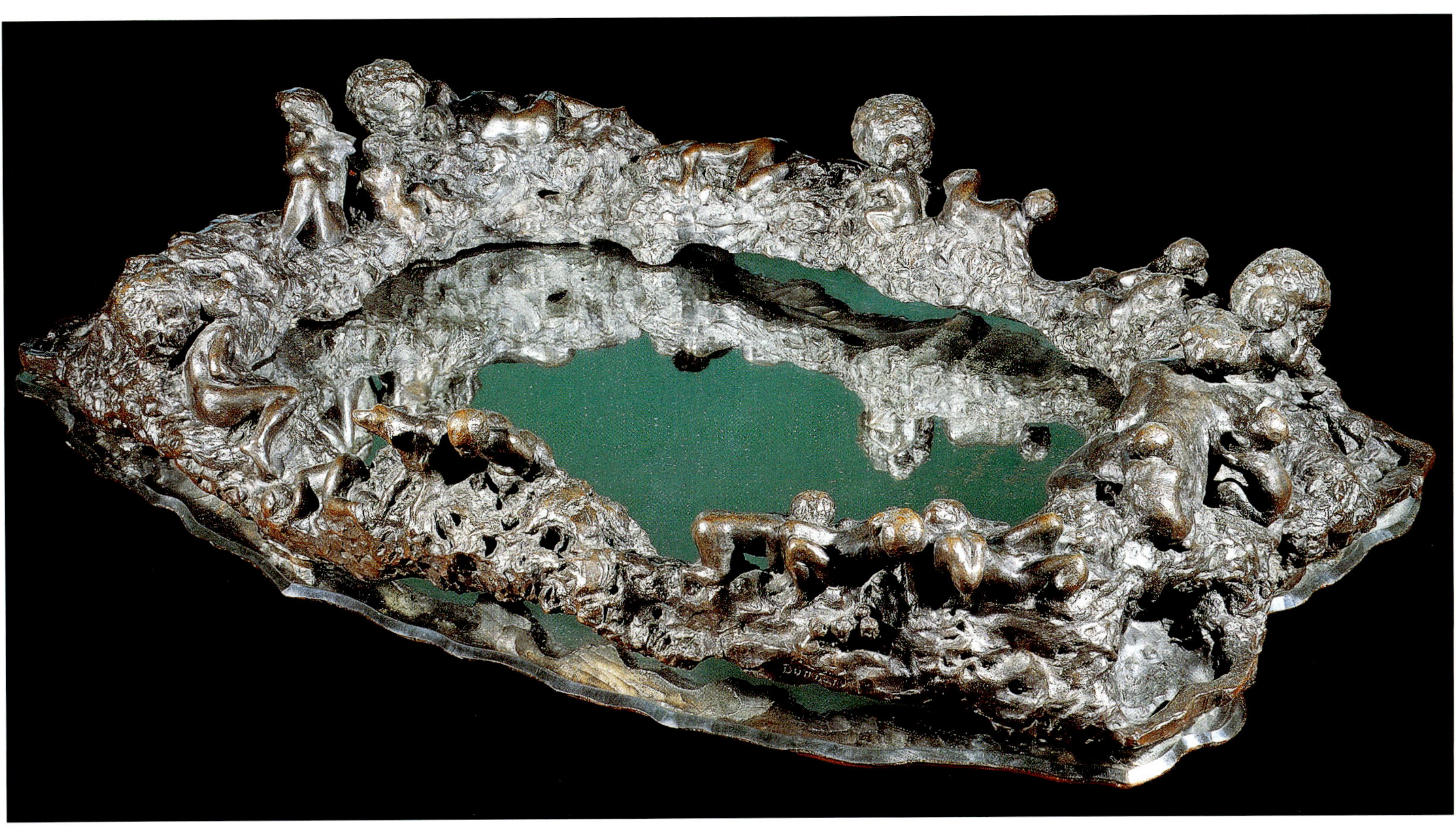

58

Daphnis and Chloe
1904–1905, Bronze and glass, $5^{15}/_{16} \times$
32 $^{11}/_{16} \times 19^{11}/_{16}$ in. (15 × 83 × 50 cm), Paris,
Musée d'Orsay.

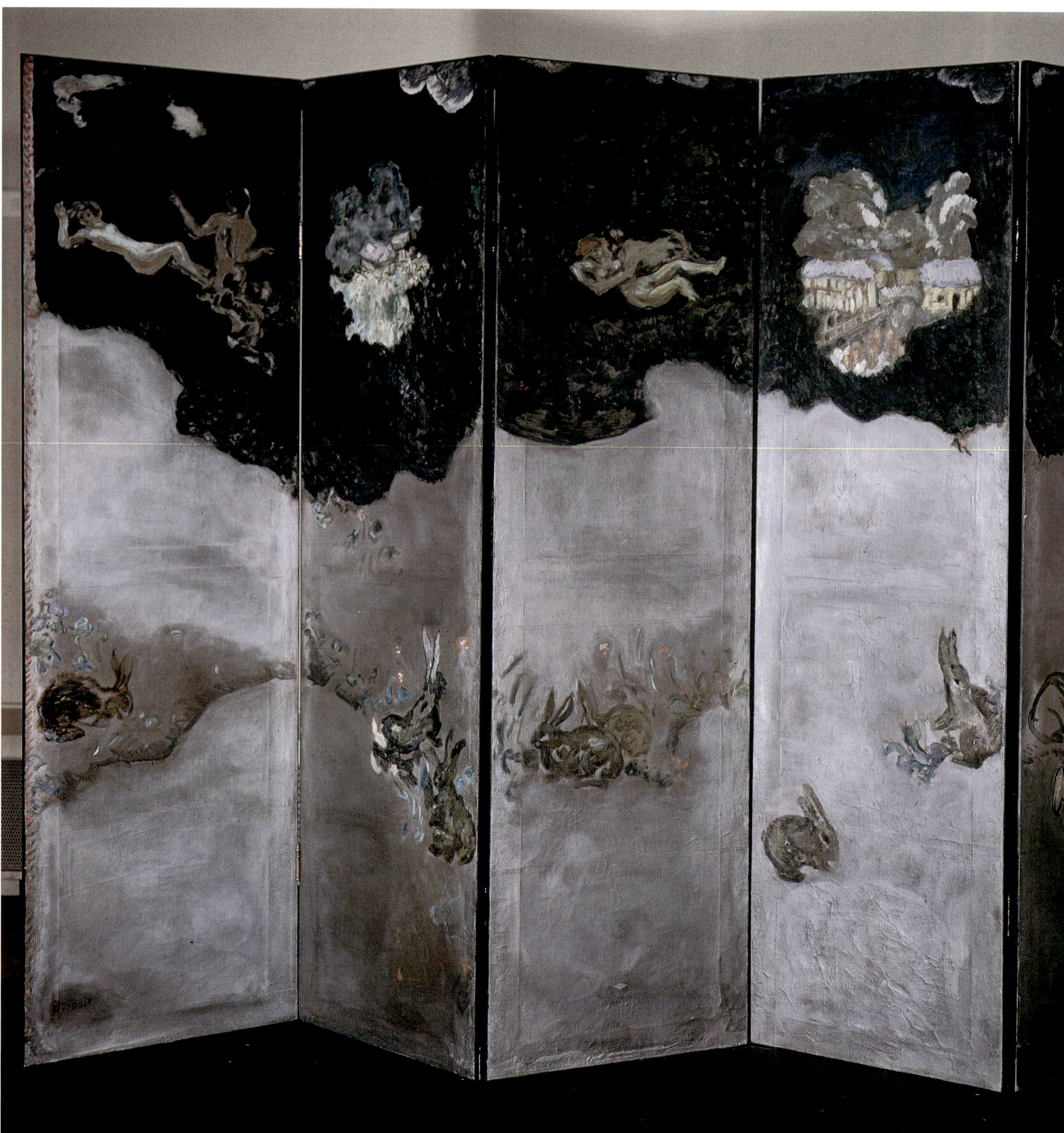

59

Screen with Rabbits
ca. 1902–1906, Oil on paper mounted on
canvas, each panel, 63⅜ × 17¾ in.
(161 × 45 cm), Musée Départemental Maurice
Denis, Saint-Germain-en-Laye.

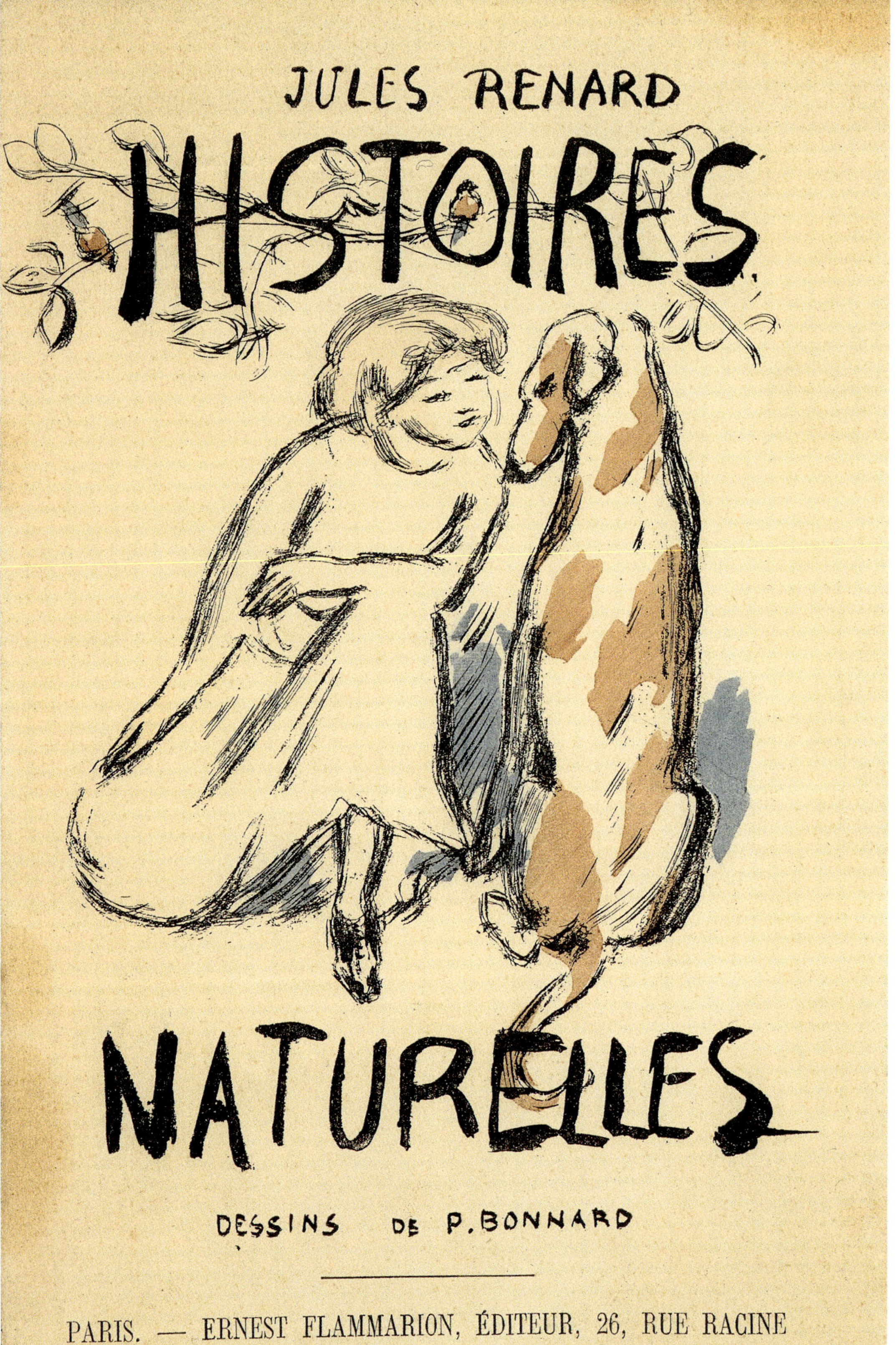

Cover for Jules Renard's "Histoires naturelles"
1904, Lithograph, 7¹¹⁄₁₆ × 4¹⁵⁄₁₆ in. (19.5 × 12.5 cm), Lessing J. Rosenwald Collection, Library of Congress, Washington, D.C.

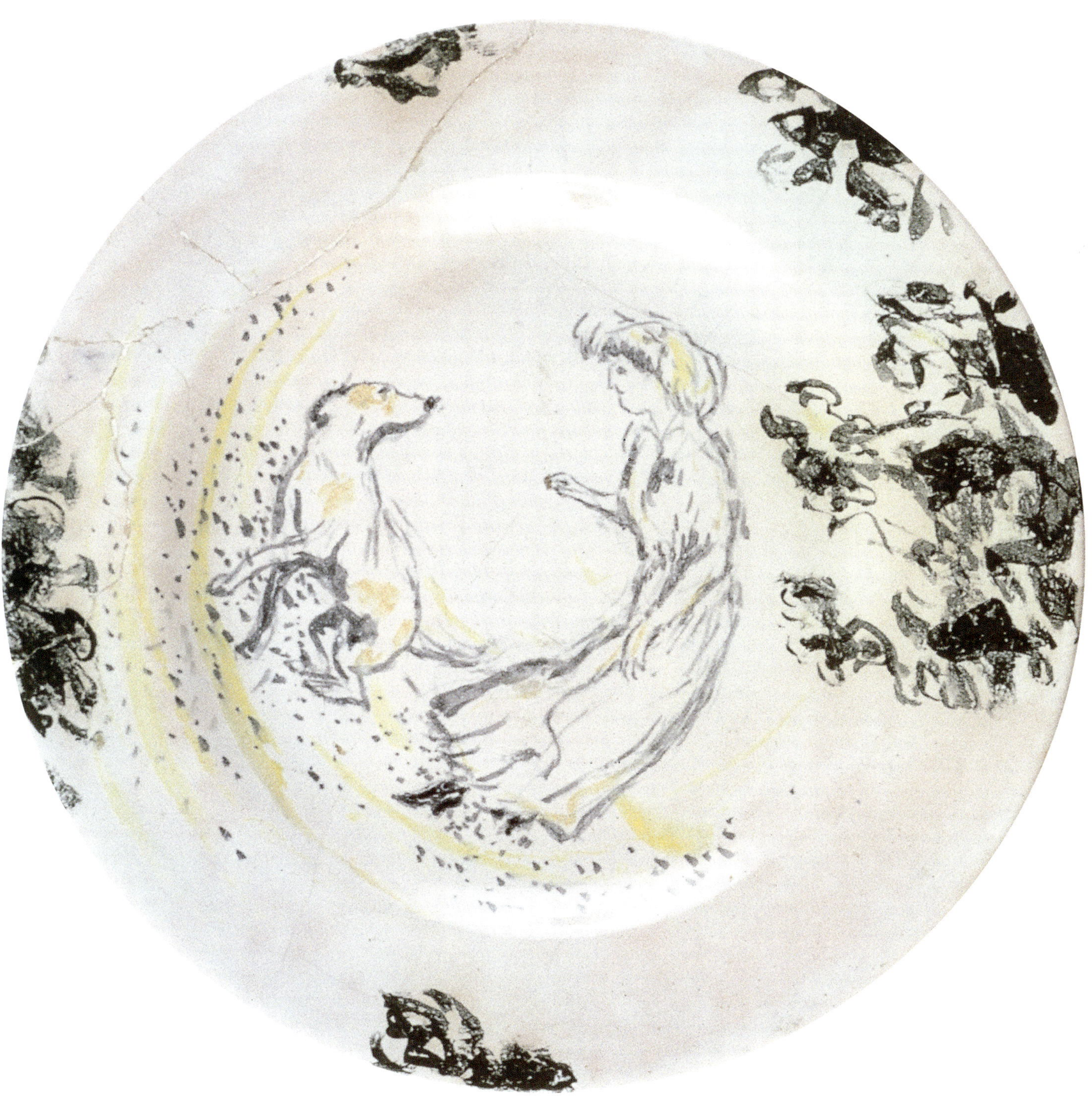

61

Decorated Plate
ca. 1905, Glazed ceramic, diam. 9¼ in.
(23.5 cm), Private collection.

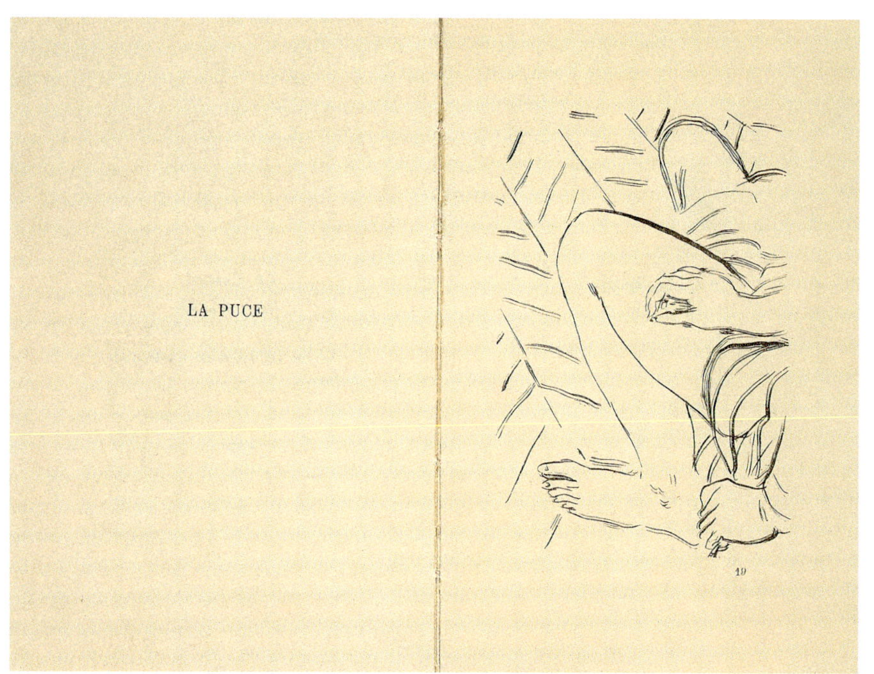

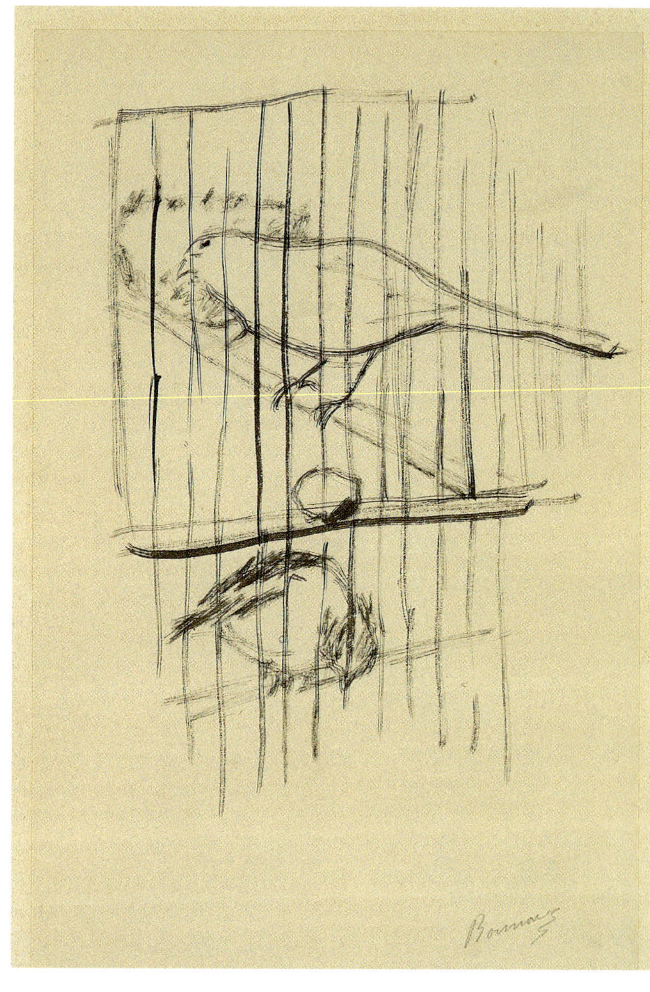

60b

"The Flea" in Jules Renard's "Histoires naturelles"
1904, Lithograph in book, 7¹¹⁄₁₆ × 4¹⁵⁄₁₆ in.
(19.5 × 12.5 cm), Lessing J. Rosenwald
Collection, Library of Congress,
Washington, D.C.

62

Canaries
1904, Ink on *chine collé*, 11⅞ × 7½ in.
(30.3 × 19 cm), The Phillips Collection,
Washington, D.C.

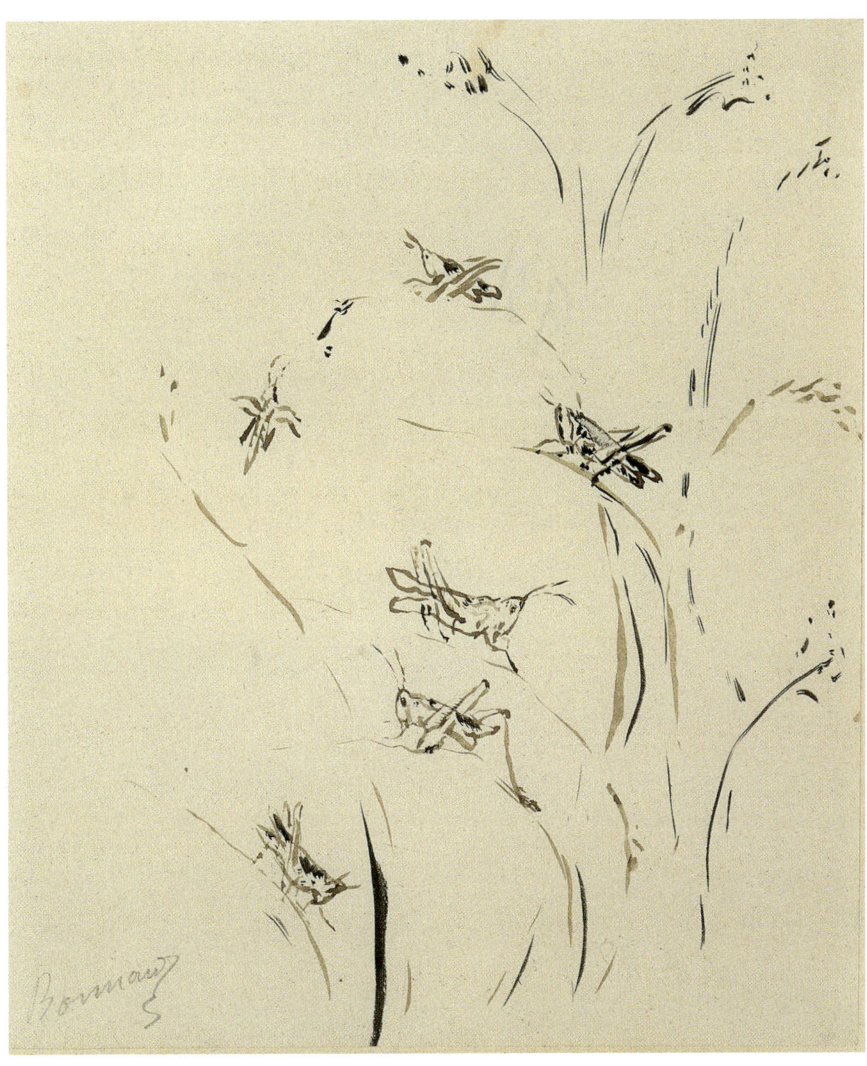

63

Grasshoppers
1904, Ink on *chine collé*, 7½ × 6⅛ in.
(19.1 × 15.6 cm), The Phillips Collection,
Washington, D.C.

64

Ants
1904, Ink on *chine collé*, 2¾ × 7¾ in. (7 × 19.7 cm),
The Phillips Collection, Washington, D.C.

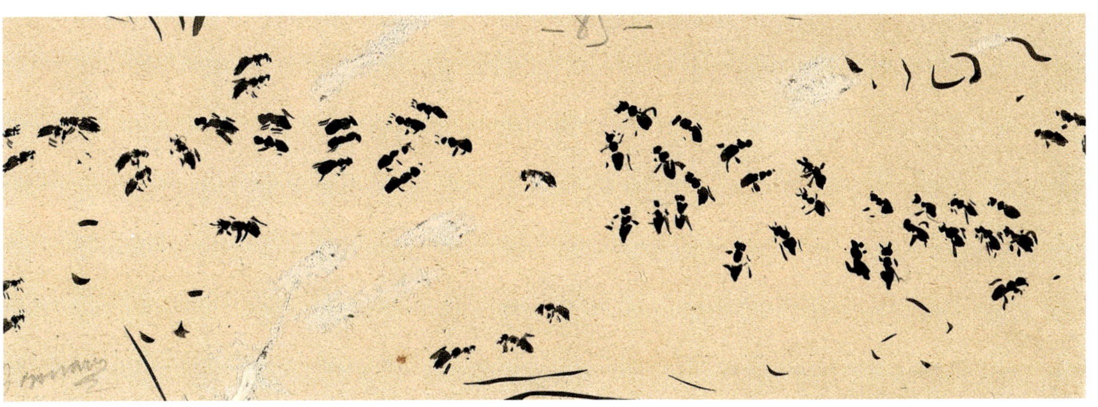

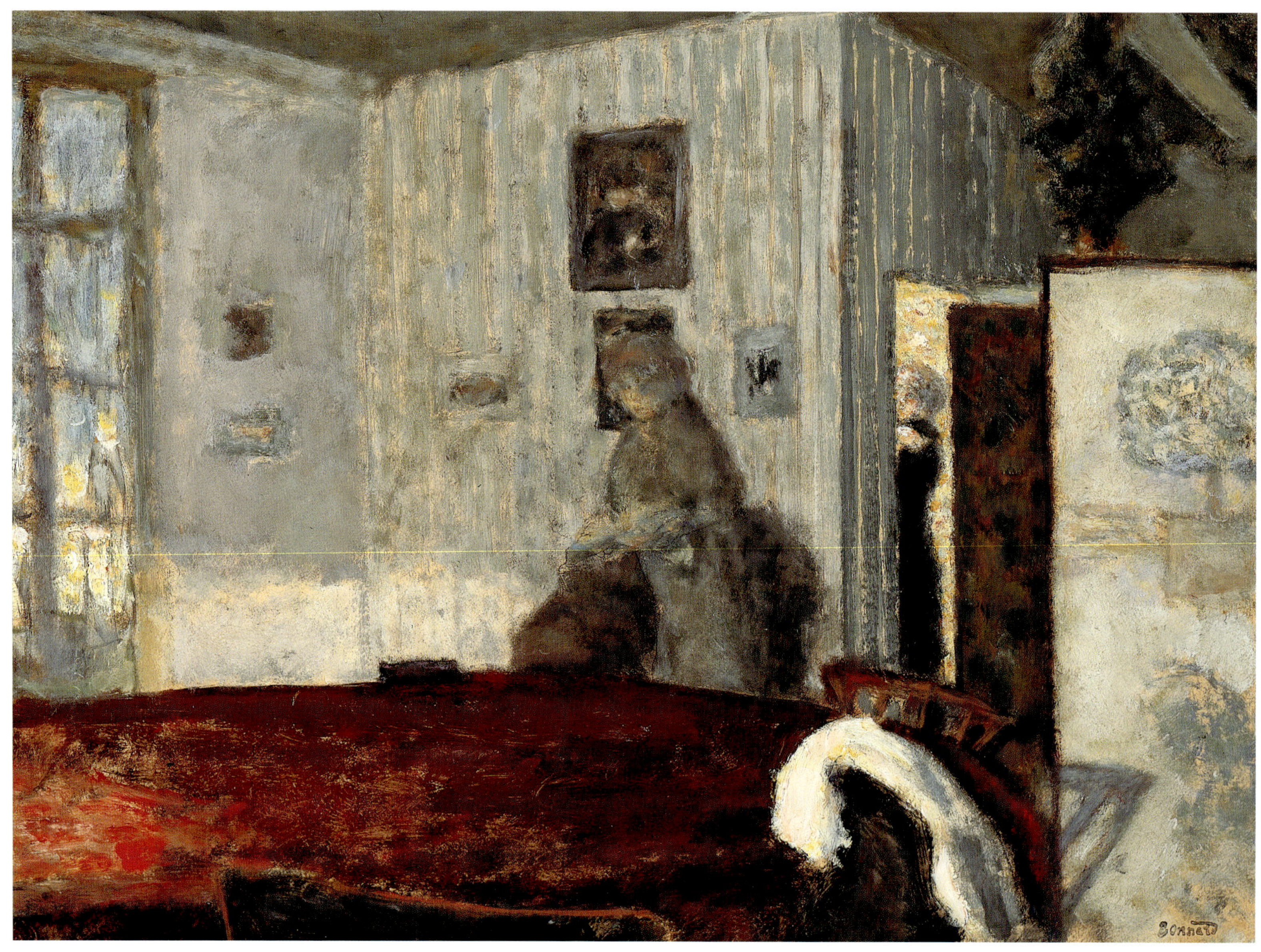

65

Interior with Screen
ca. 1906, Oil on paper laid down on canvas,
18¾ × 24¾ in. (47.8 × 62.9 cm),
Private collection.

66

The Dressing Table
1908, Oil on canvas, 20½ × 17¹¹⁄₁₆ in. (52 × 45 cm),
Paris, Musée d'Orsay, Bequest of Mr. and Mrs.
Frédéric I. Ling, 1961.

Next spread: **The Dressing Table** (detail).

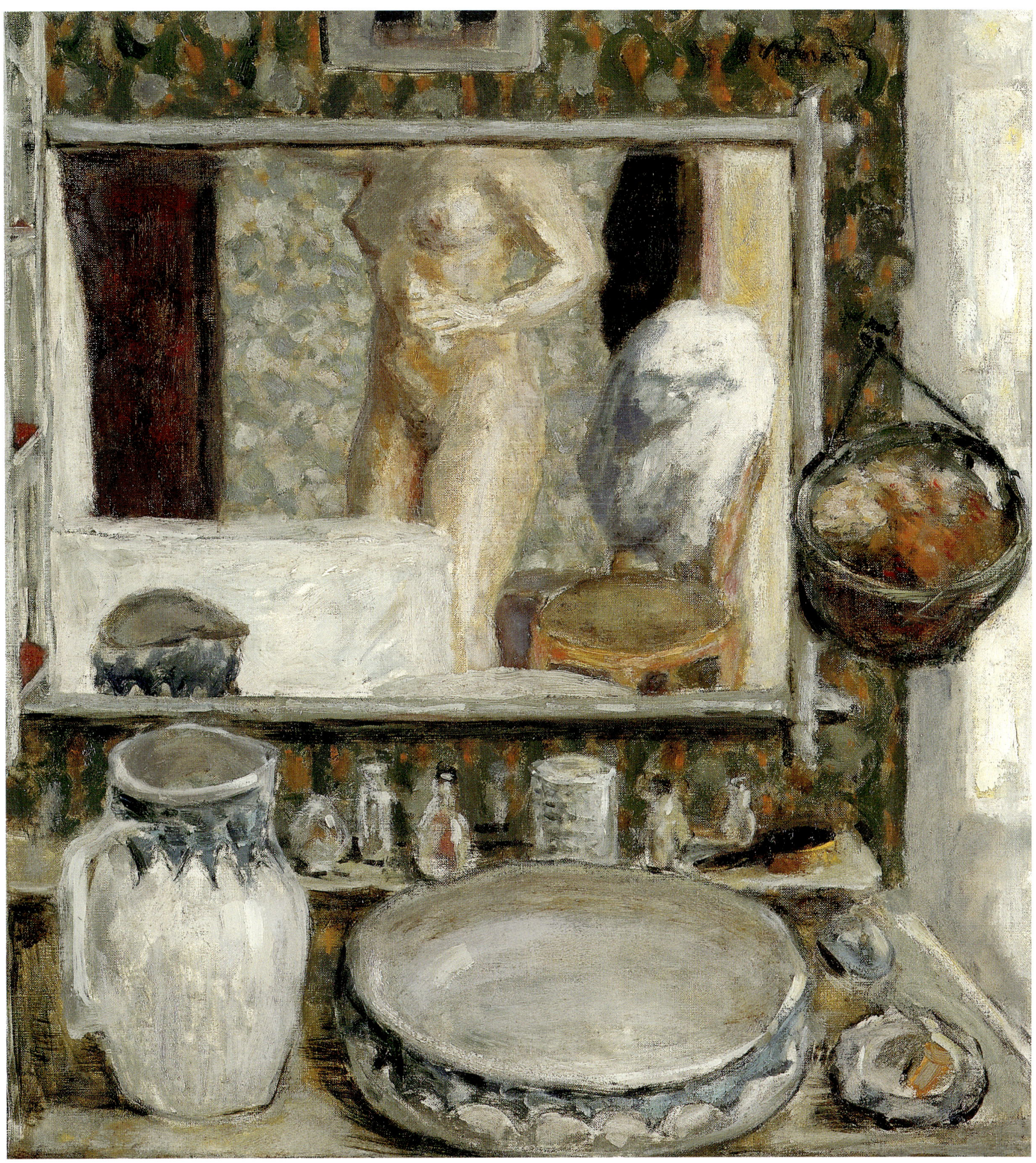

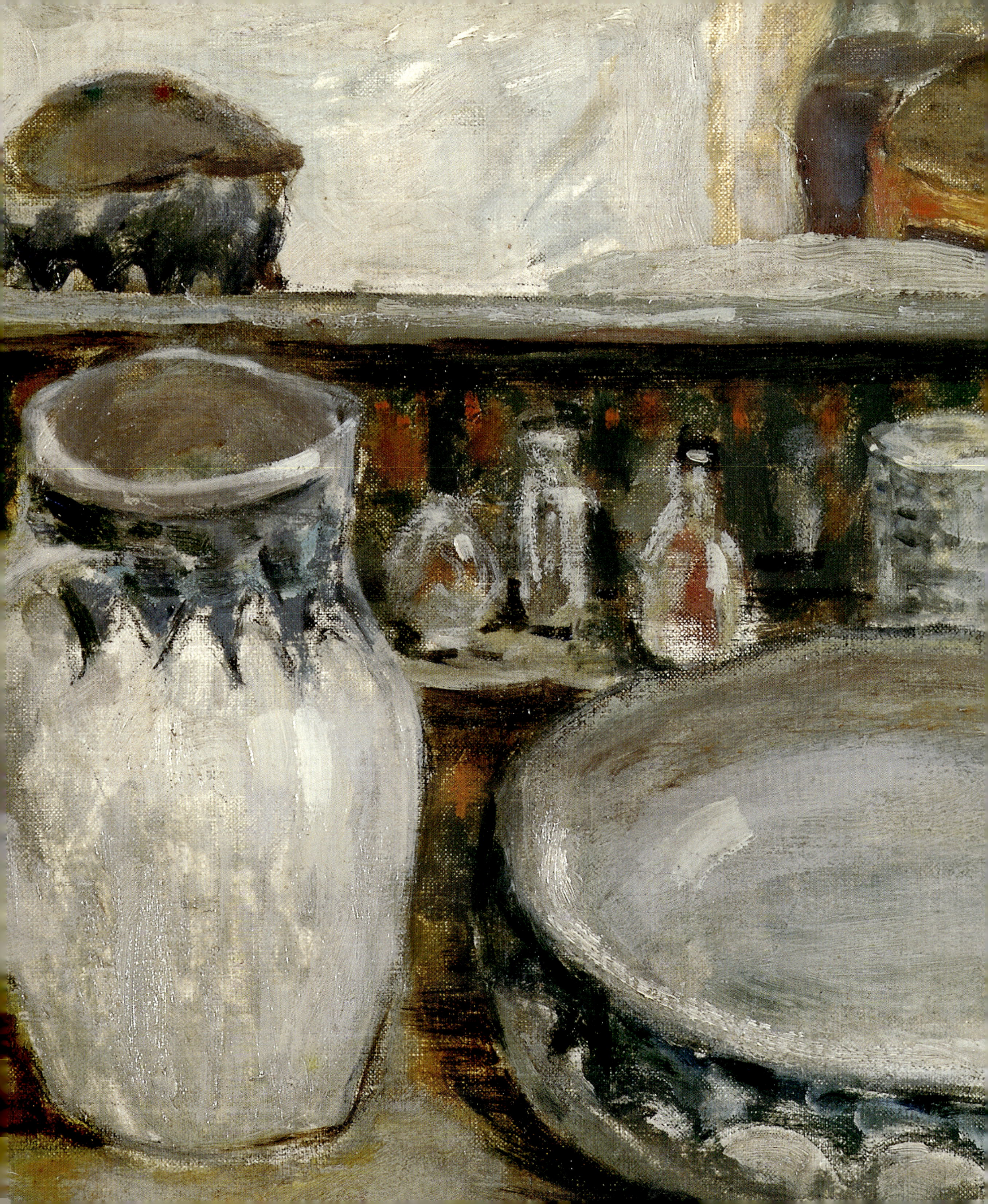

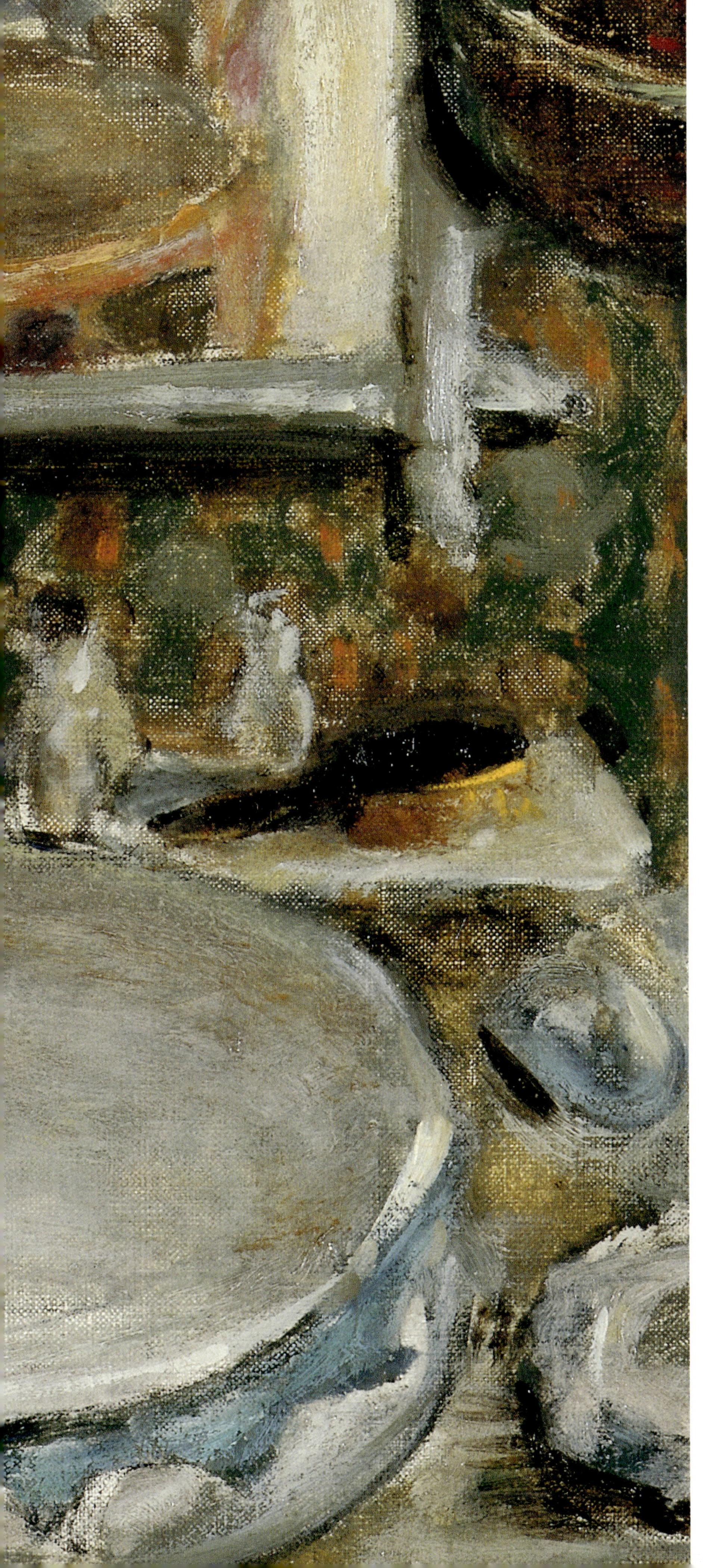

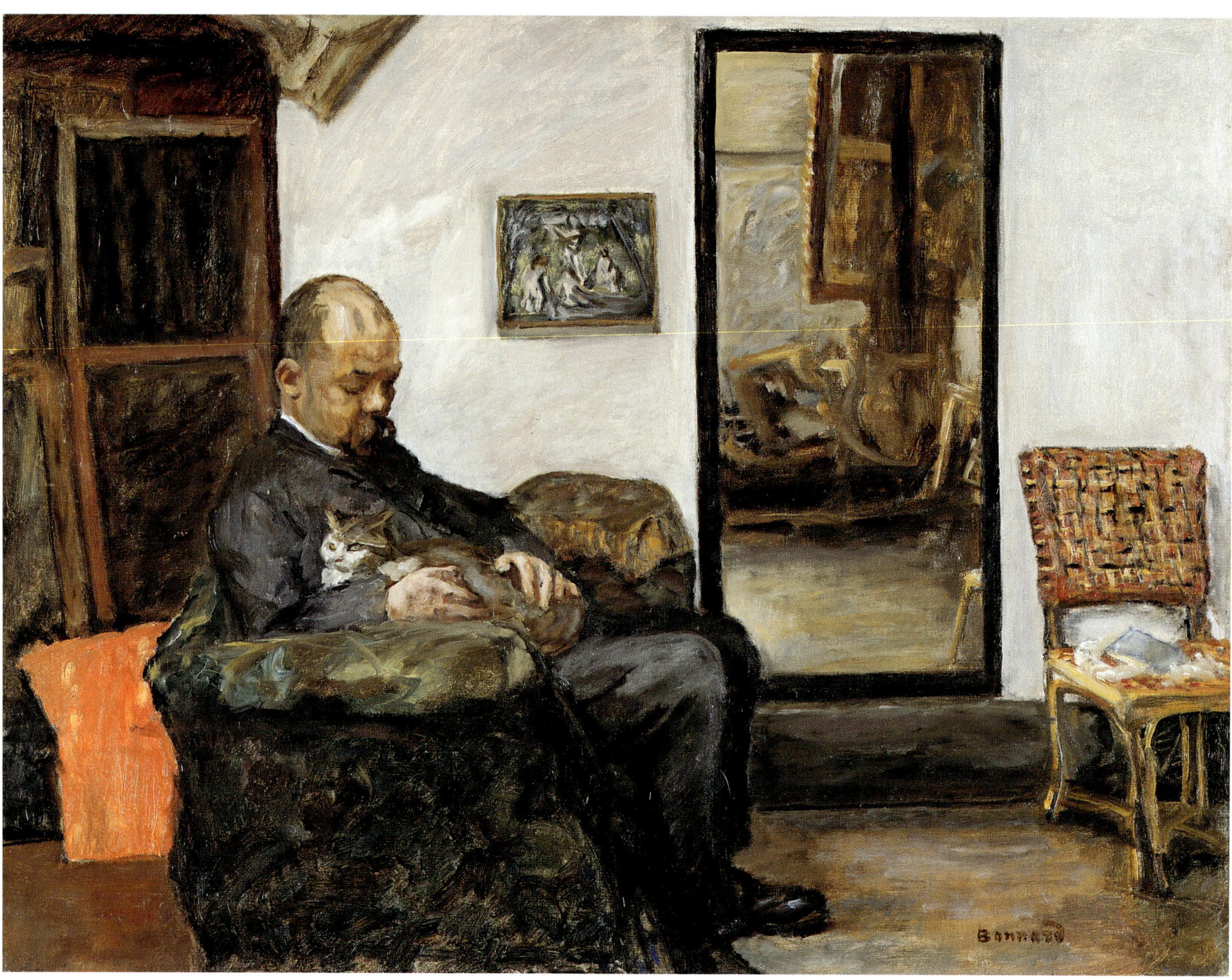

67

Portrait of Ambroise Vollard
ca. 1906, Oil on canvas, 29⅛ × 36⅜ in.
(74 × 92.5 cm), Kunsthaus Zurich.

Opposite page: **Portrait of Ambroise Vollard**
(detail).

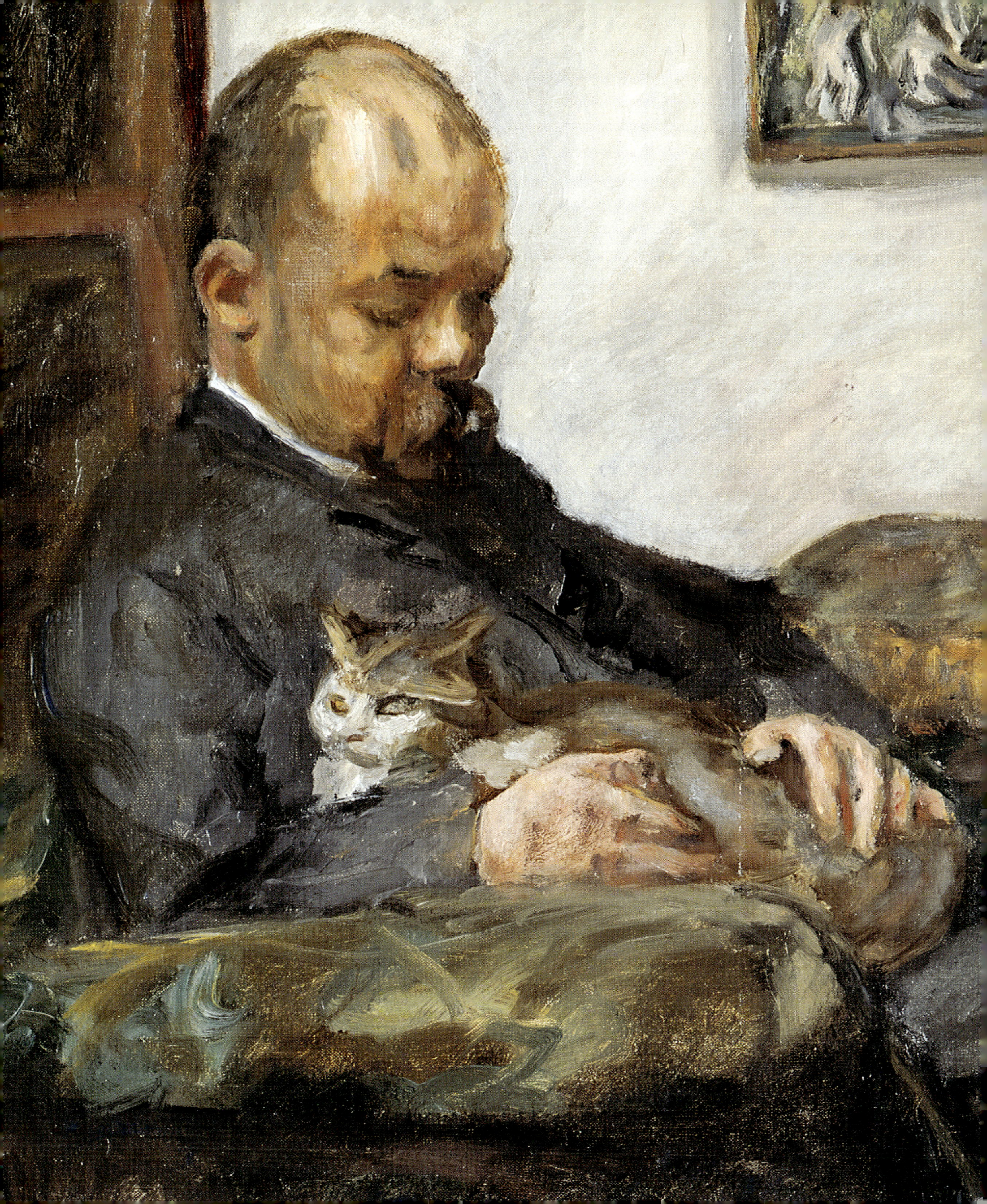

68

Early Spring
1910, Oil on canvas, 34¼ × 52 in. (86.9 × 132 cm),
The Phillips Collection, Washington, D.C.

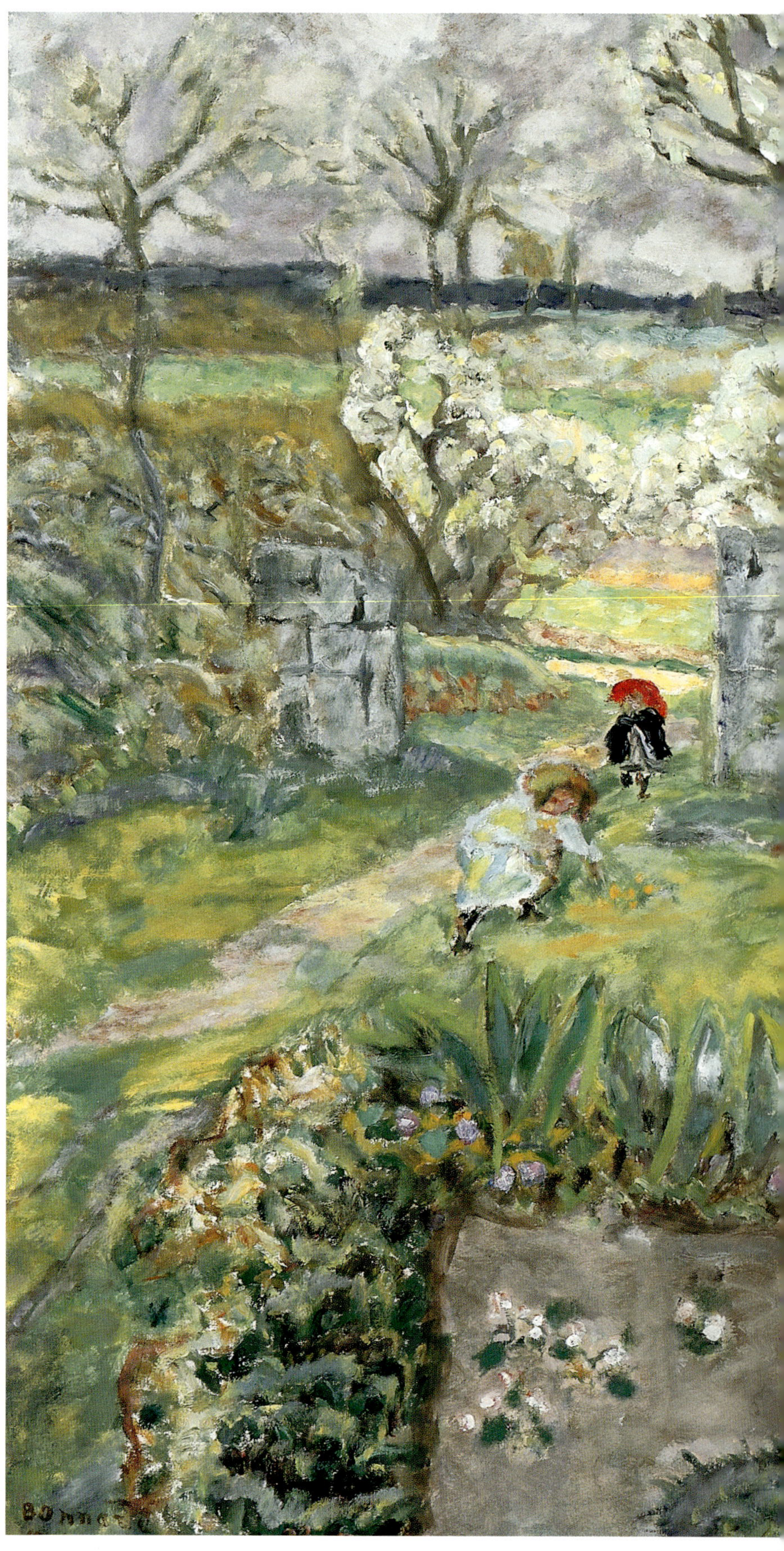

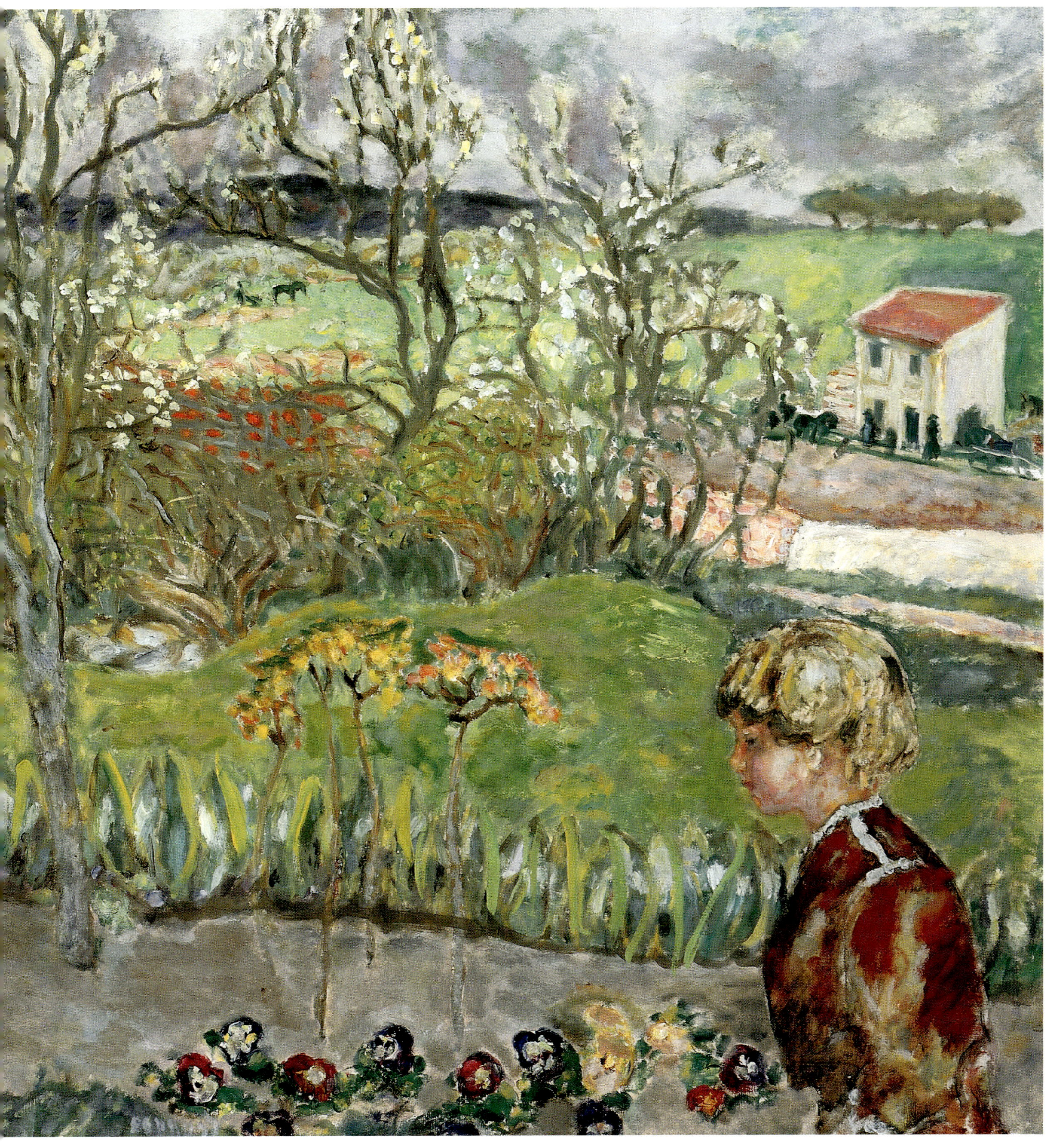

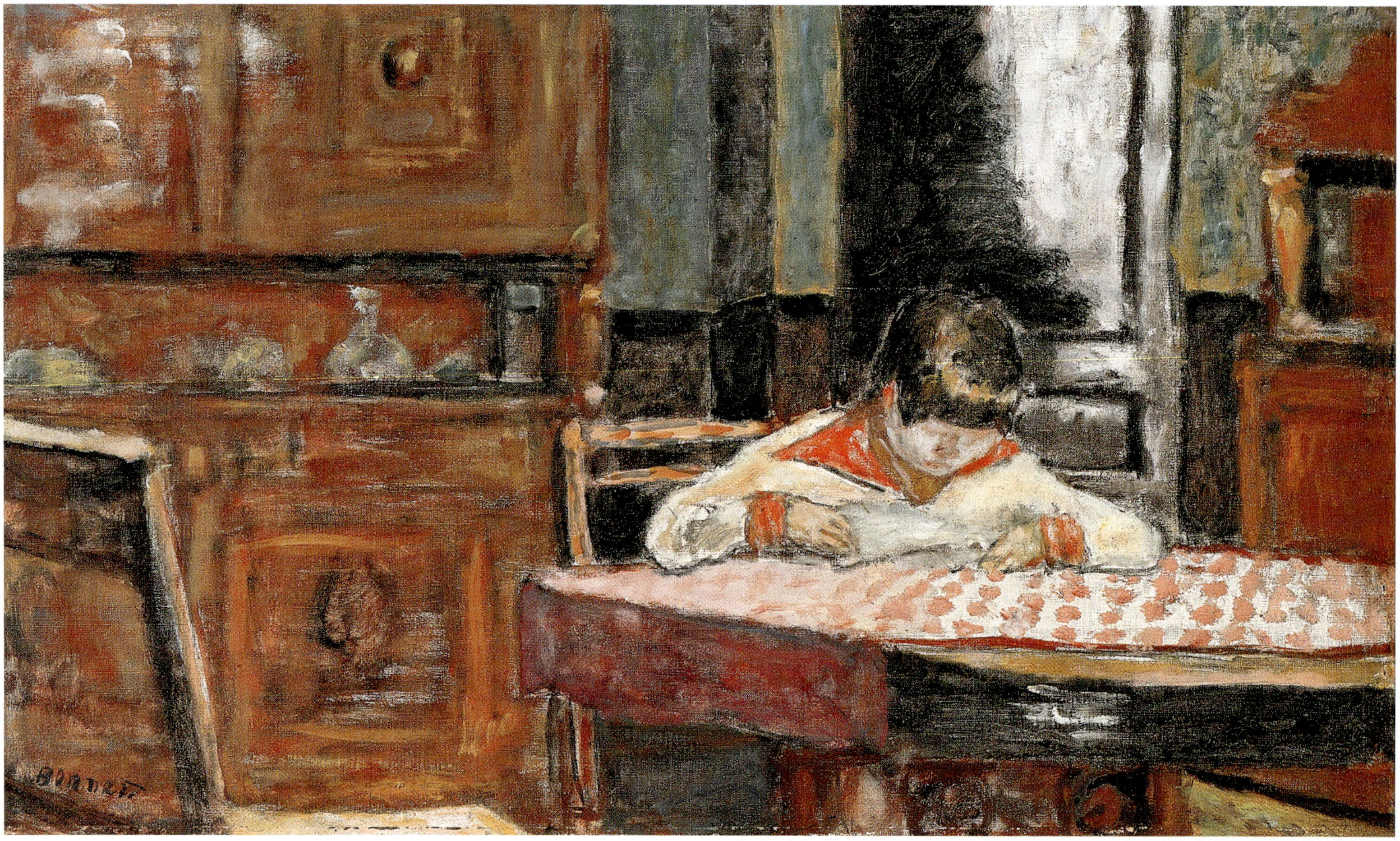

69

Interior with Boy
1910, Oil on canvas, 16 × 25 in. (41 × 63.5 cm),
The Phillips Collection, Washington, D.C.

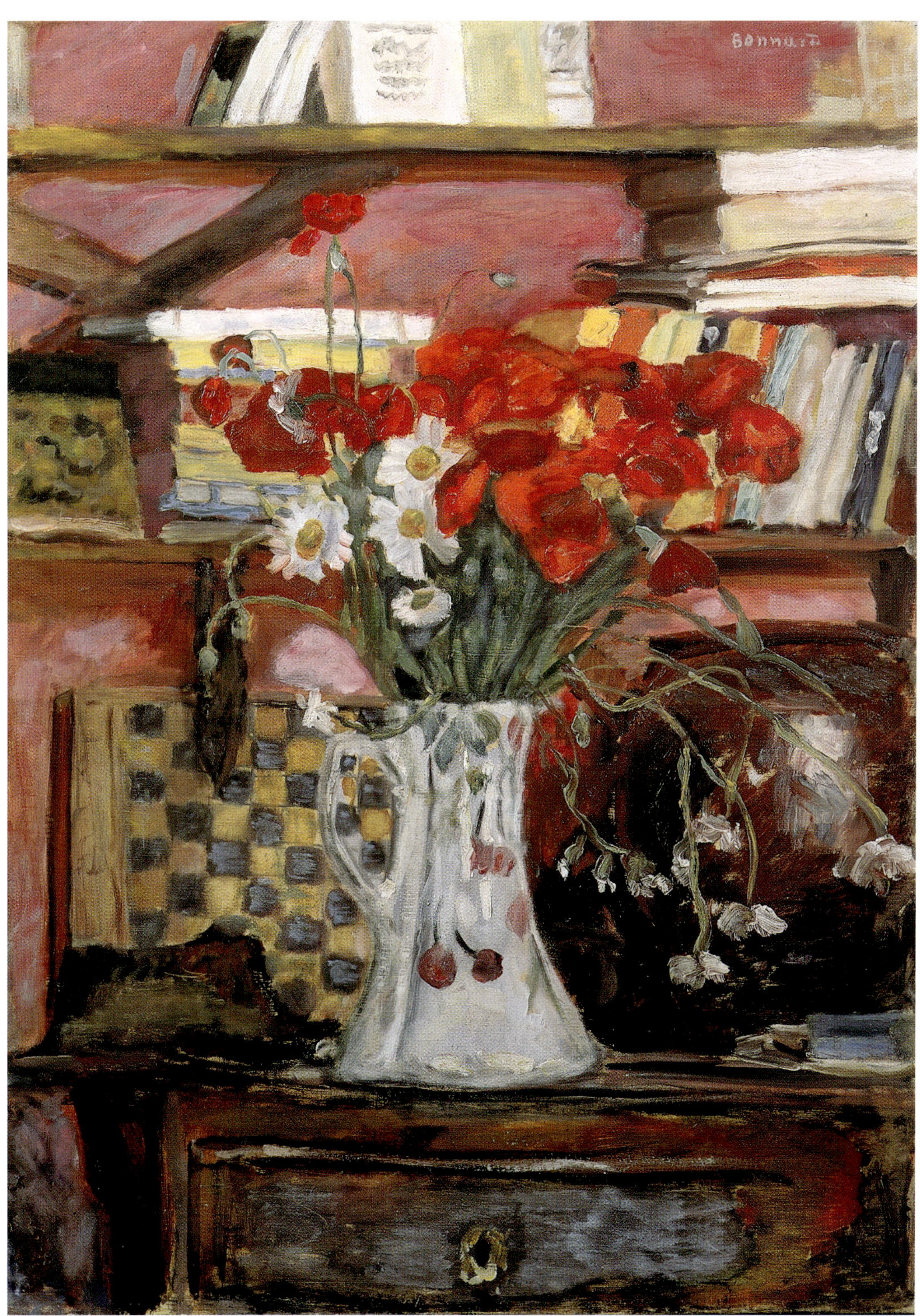

70

Vase of Flowers and Checkers
1912, Oil on canvas, 31⅛ × 22½ in. (79.5 × 57 cm),
Mr. and Mrs. Joe L. Allbritton.

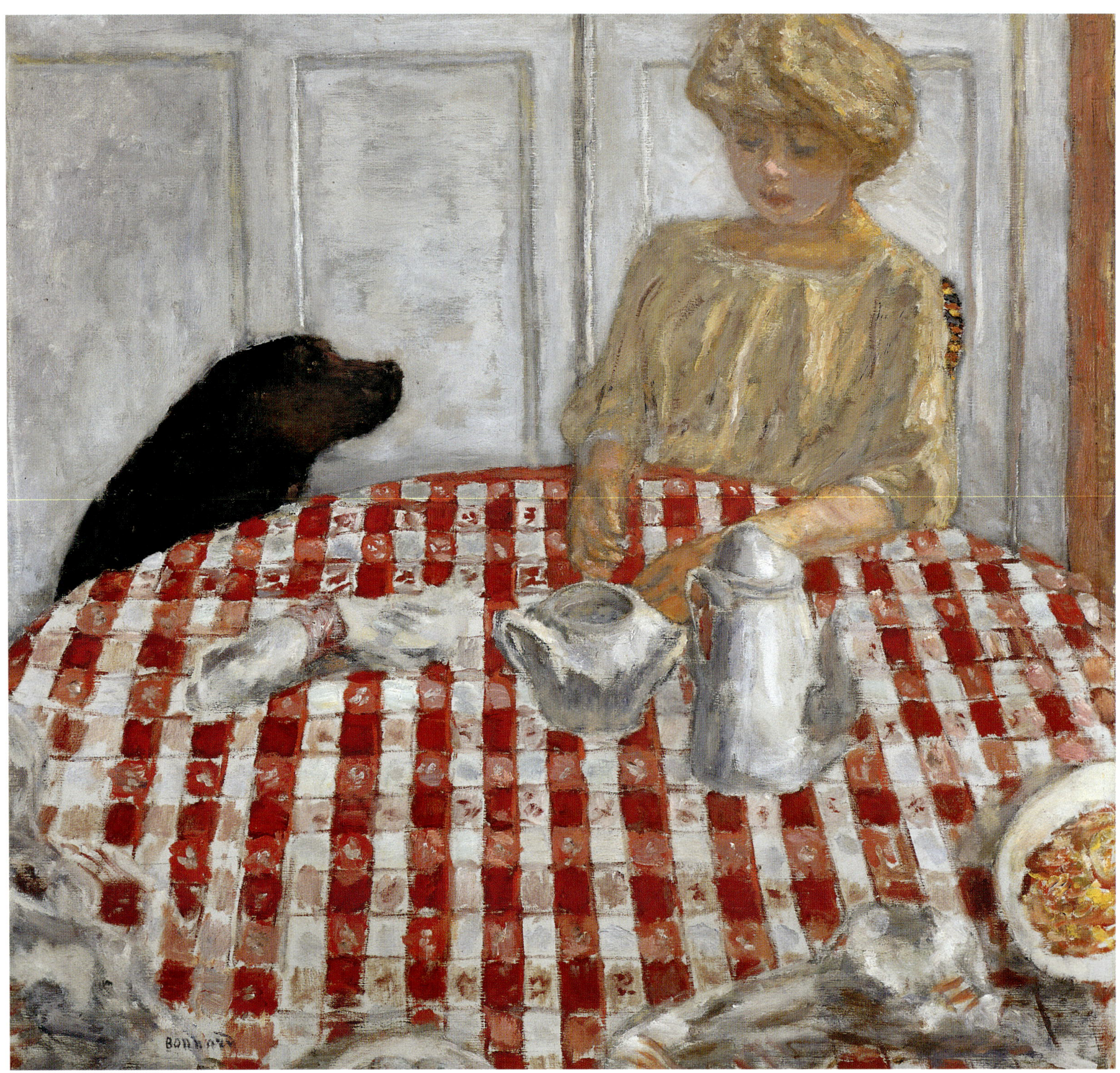

71

The Red Checkered Tablecloth or
The Dog's Lunch
1910, Oil on canvas, 32¹¹⁄₁₆ × 33½ in.
(83 × 85 cm), Private collection.

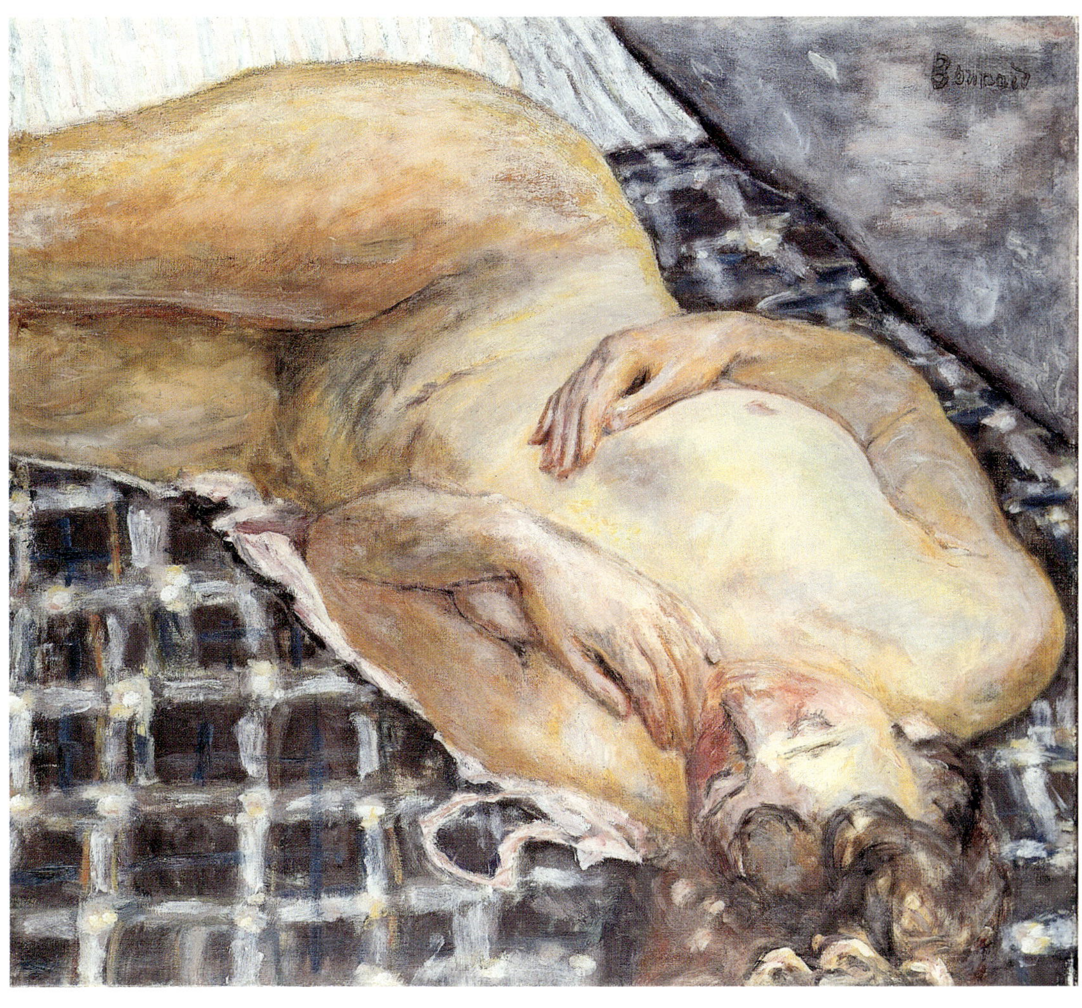

Reclining Nude
ca. 1909, Oil on canvas, 23⅝ × 25⁹⁄₁₆ in.
(60 × 65 cm), Städelscher Museums-Verein
e.V., Frankfurt am Main.

Woman Bathing
1912, Oil on canvas, 26 × 17¾ in. (66 × 45.1 cm),
Private collection courtesy Sotheby's New York.

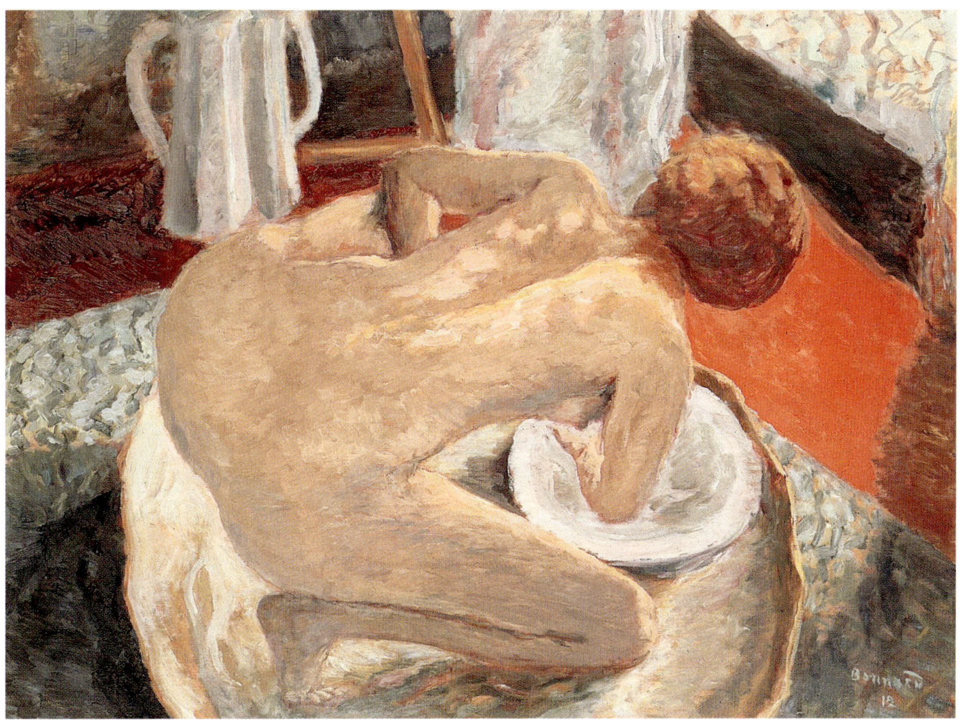

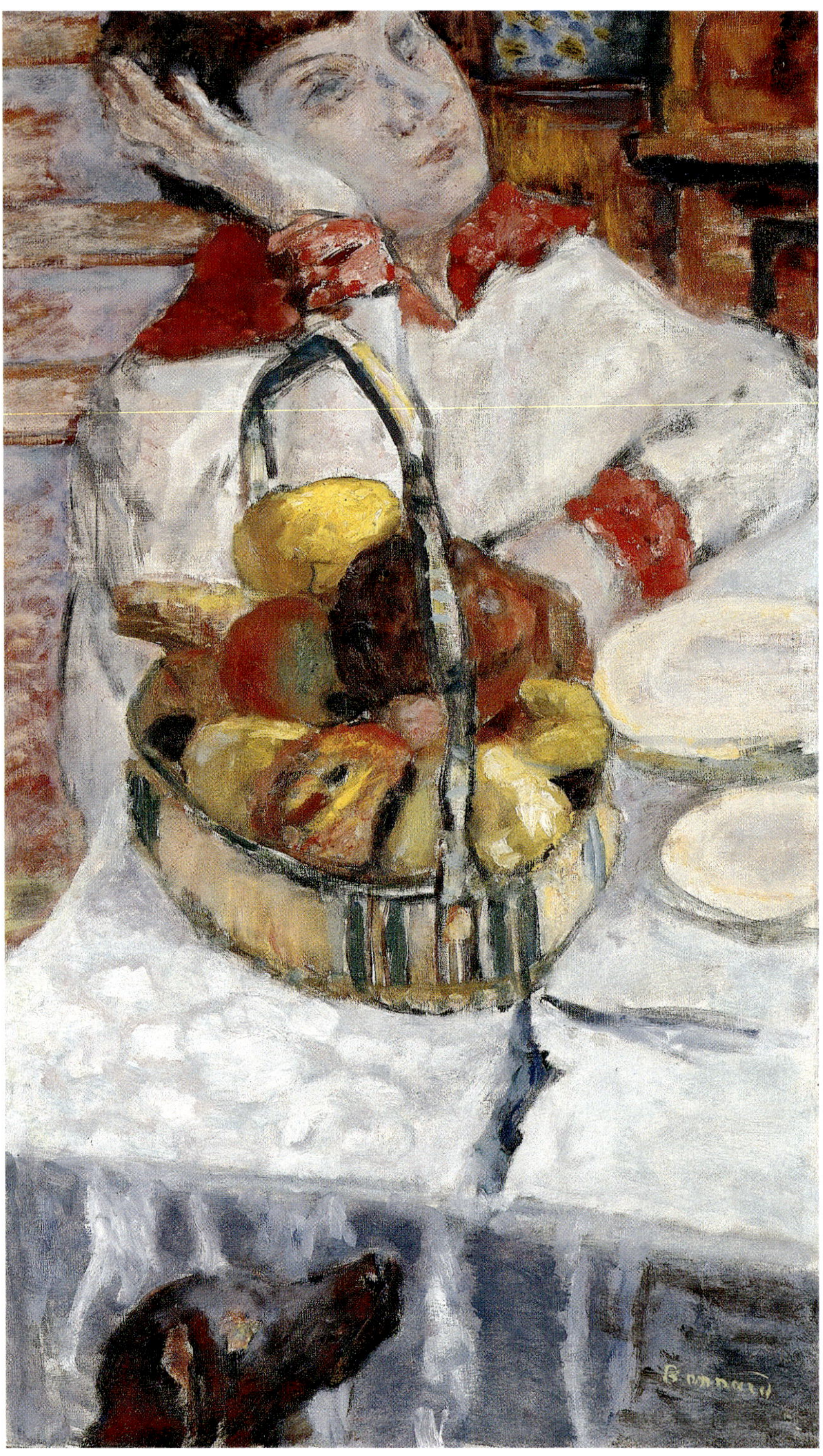

74

Woman with Basket of Fruit
1915-1918, Oil on canvas, 27¼ × 15¾ in.
(69.2 × 40 cm), The Baltimore Museum of
Art: The Cone Collection, formed by Dr.
Claribel Cone and Miss Etta Cone of
Baltimore, Maryland: BMA 1950.190.

Opposite page: **Woman with Basket of Fruit**
(detail).

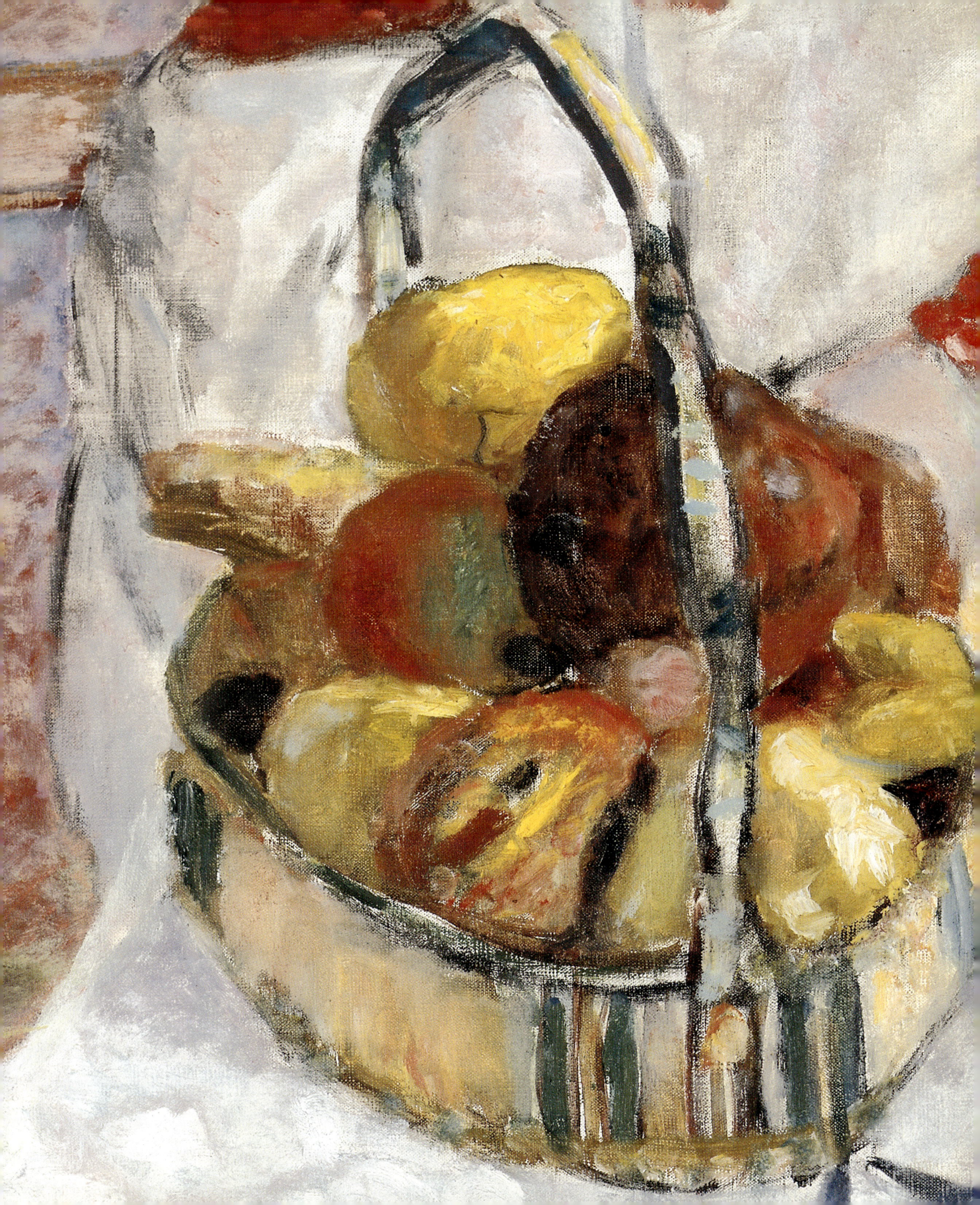

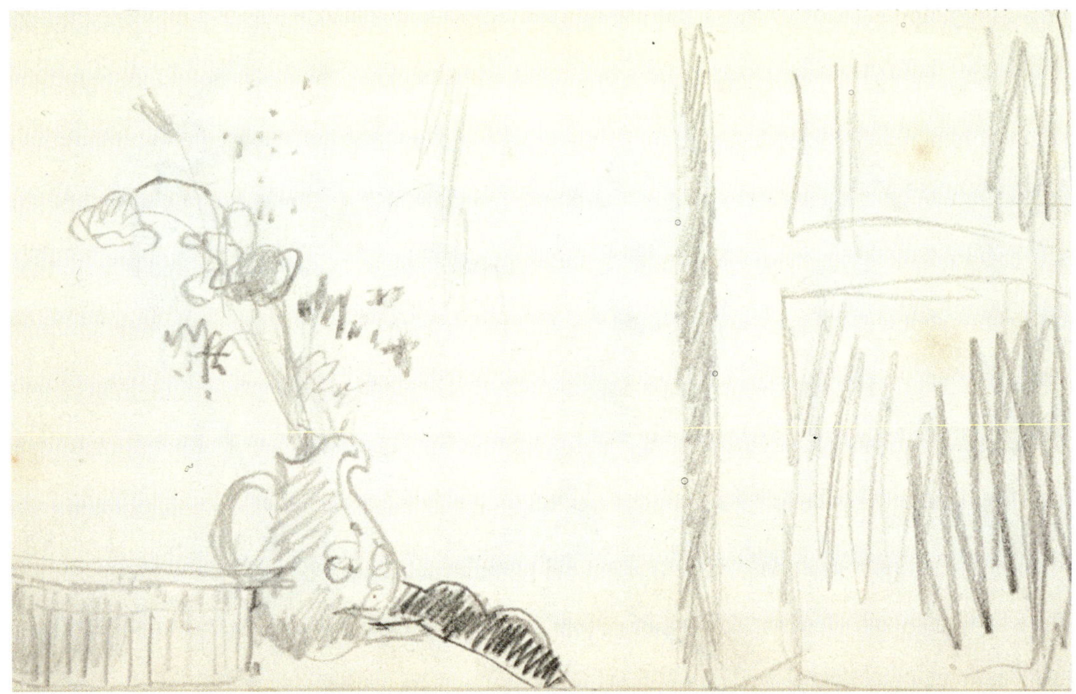

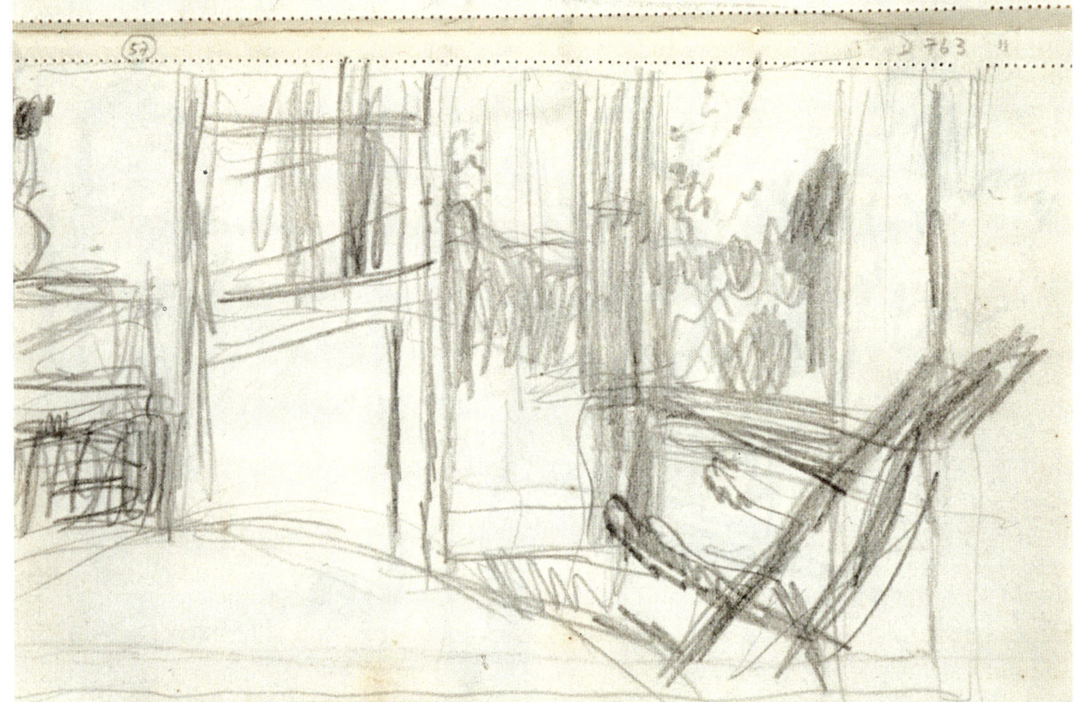

75

Study for "The Dining Room in the Country"
1913, Graphite on paper, 4¹⁵⁄₁₆ × 8¼ in. (12.5 × 21 cm), Private collection.

76

Study for "The Dining Room in the Country"
1913, Graphite on paper, 4¹⁵⁄₁₆ × 8¼ in. (12.5 × 21 cm), Private collection.

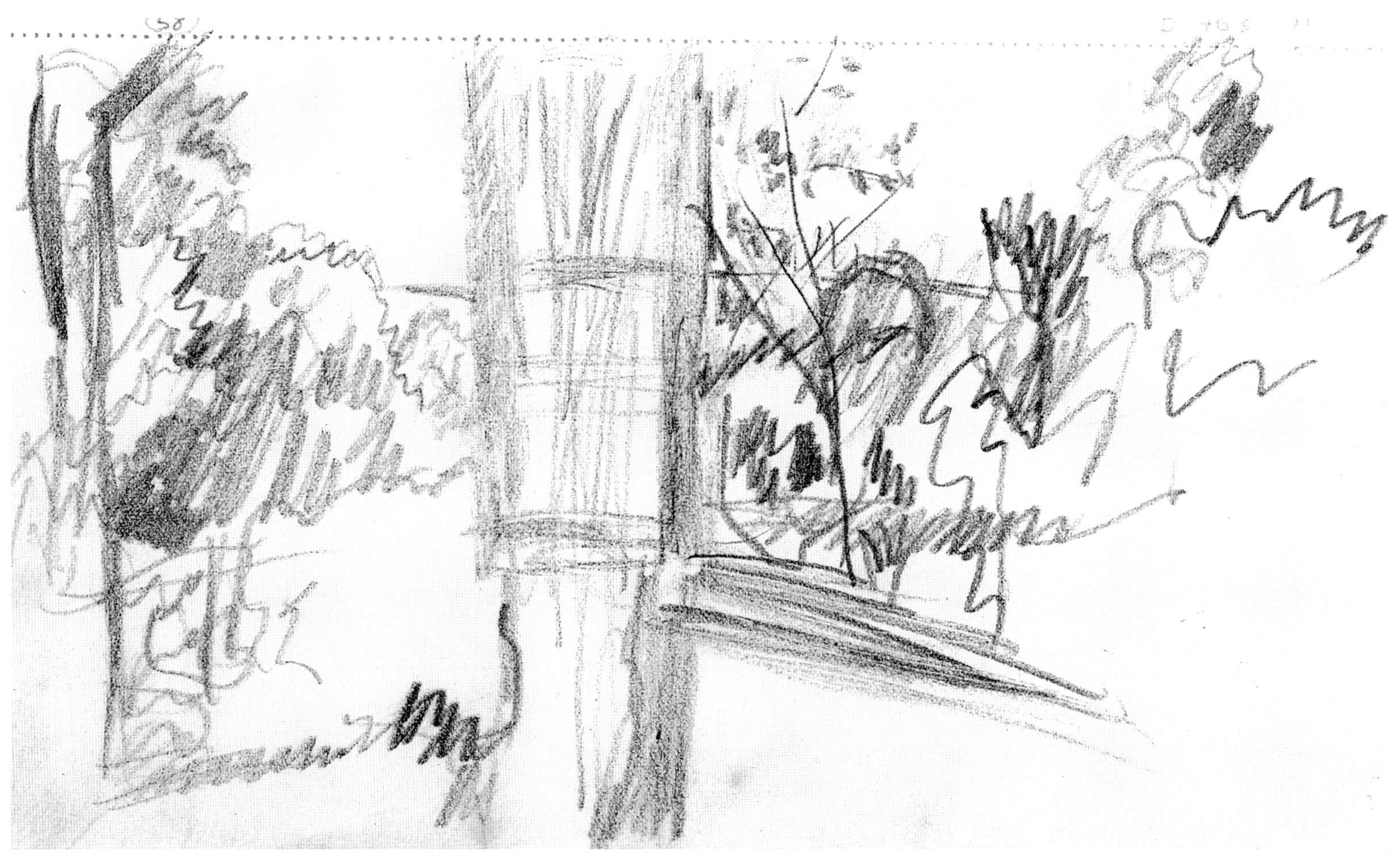

77

Study for "The Dining Room in the Country"
1913, Graphite on paper, 4¹⁵⁄₁₆ × 8¼ in.
(12.5 × 21 cm), Private collection.

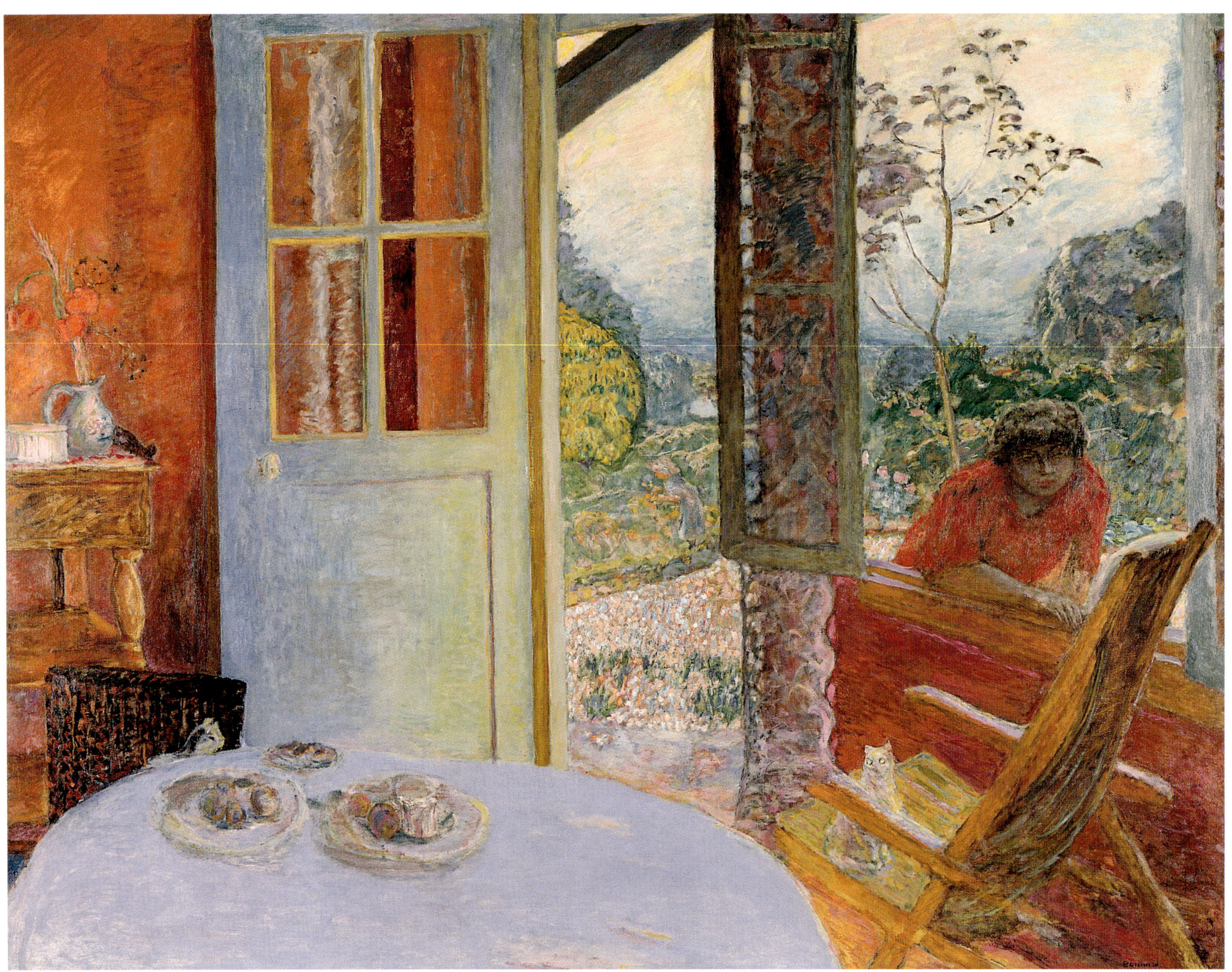

78

The Dining Room in the Country
1913, Oil on canvas, 64¾ × 81 in. (164.5 × 205.7 cm),
The Minneapolis Institute of Arts, The John R.
Van Derlip Fund 54.15.

Opposite page: **The Dining Room in the Country**
(detail).

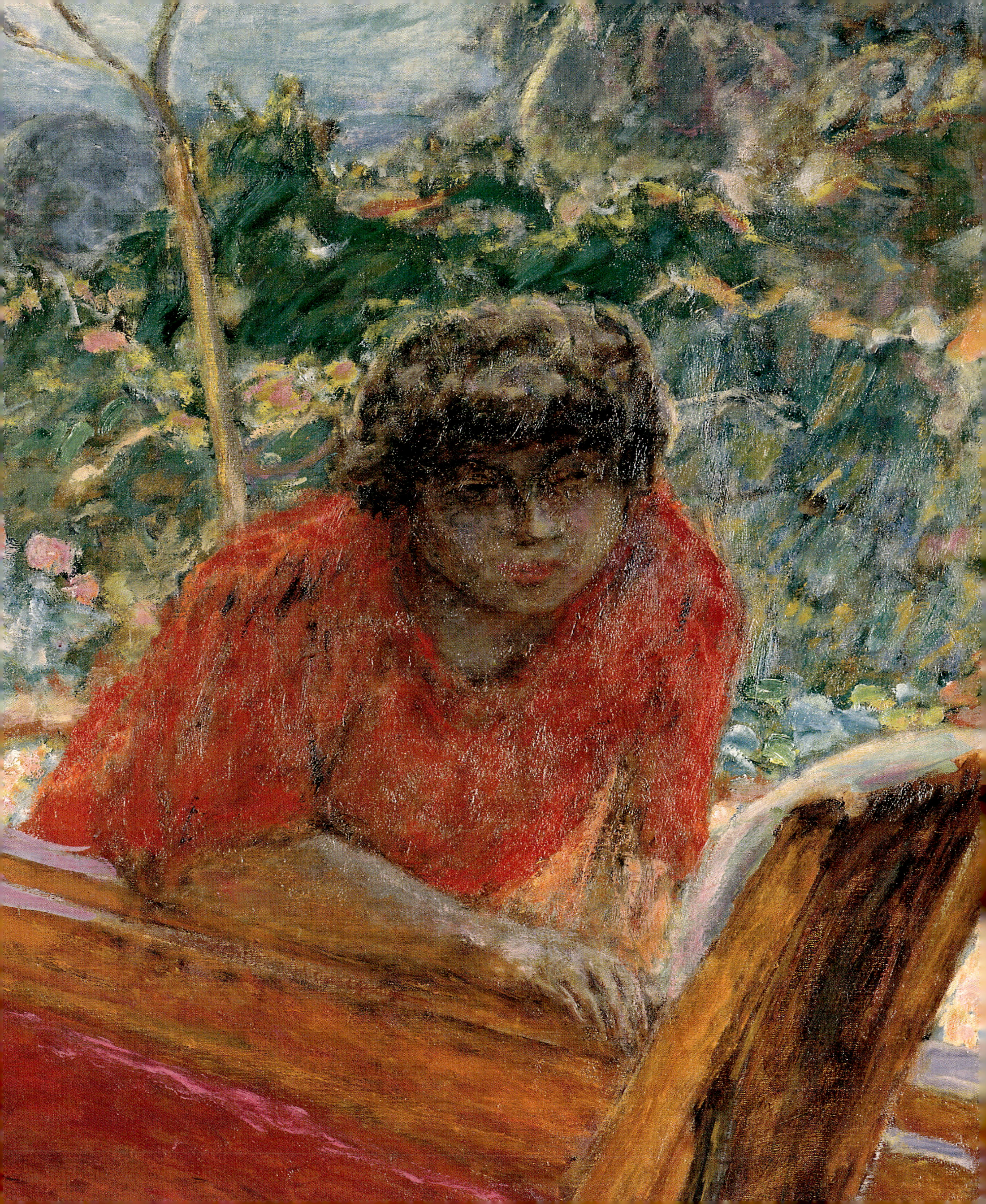

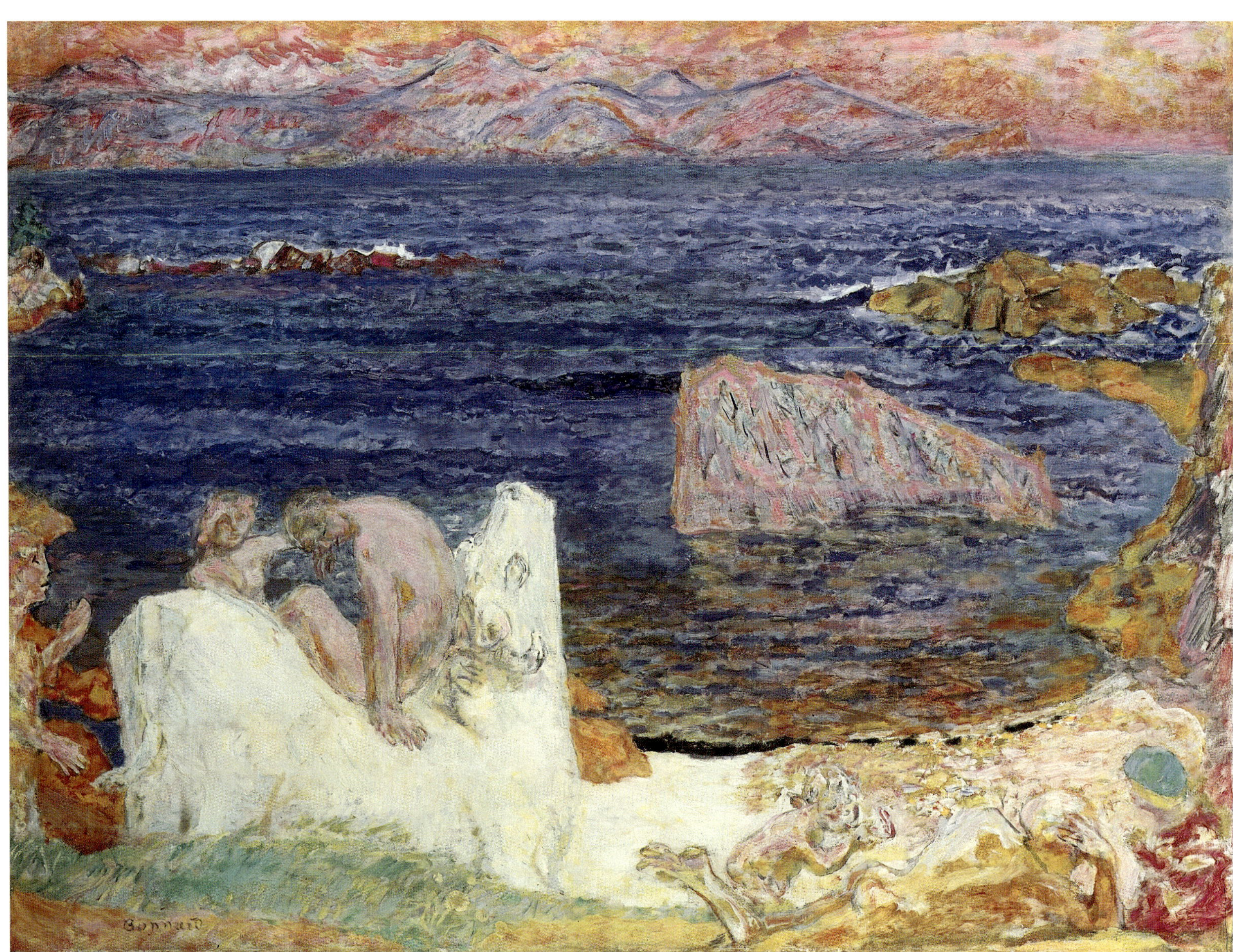

79

The Abduction of Europa
1919, Oil on canvas, 46¼ × 60¼ in. (117.5 × 153 cm),
Toledo Museum of Art; Purchased with funds
from the Libbey Endowment, Gift of Edward
Drummond Libbey.

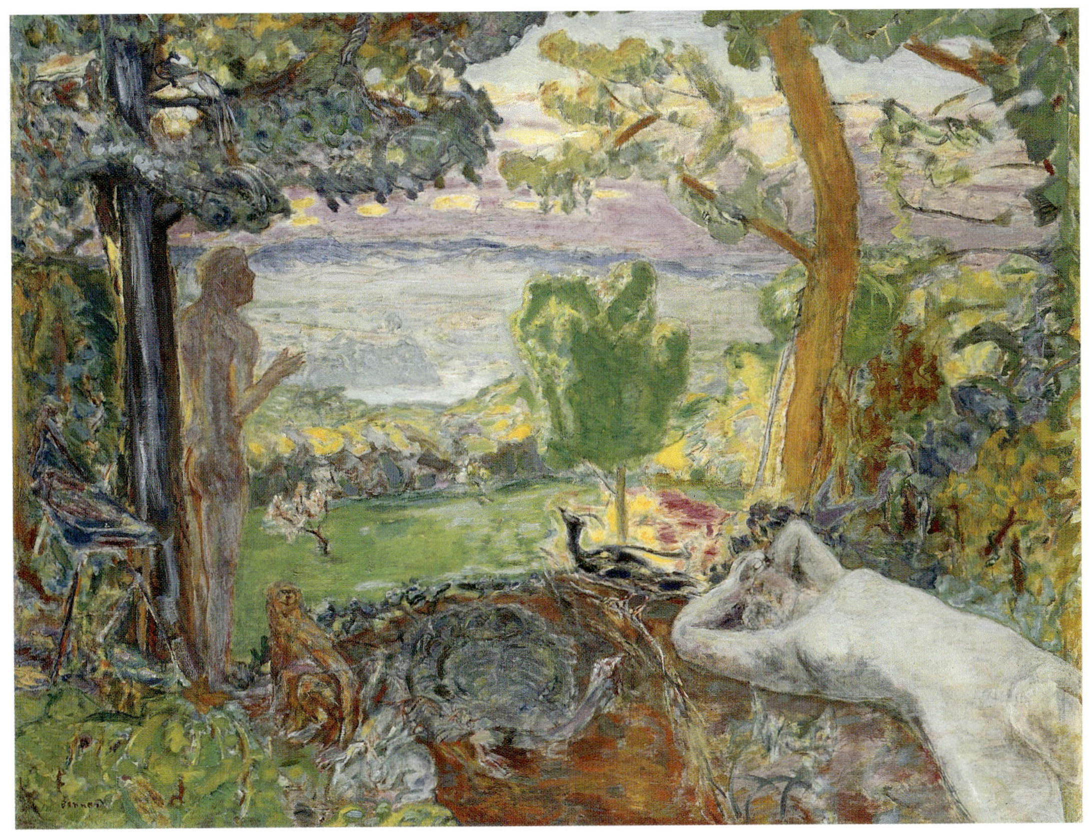

80

Earthly Paradise
1916–1920, Oil on canvas, 51½ × 63 in.
(130 × 160 cm), The Art Institute of Chicago,
Estate of Joanne Toor Cummings; Bette and
Neison Harris and Searle Family Trust
endowments; through prior gifts of Mrs.
Henry C. Woods.

Next page: **Earthly Paradise** (detail).

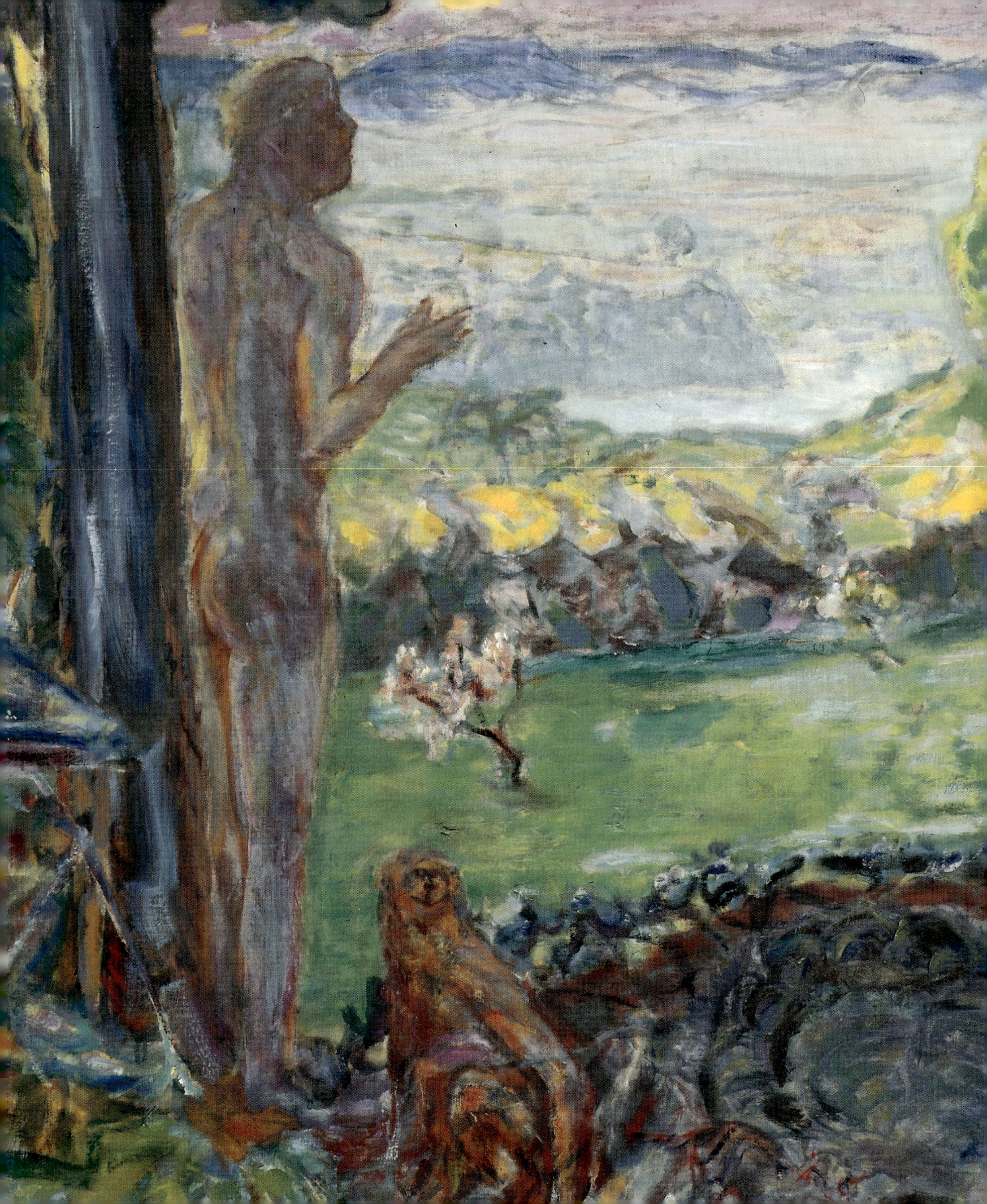

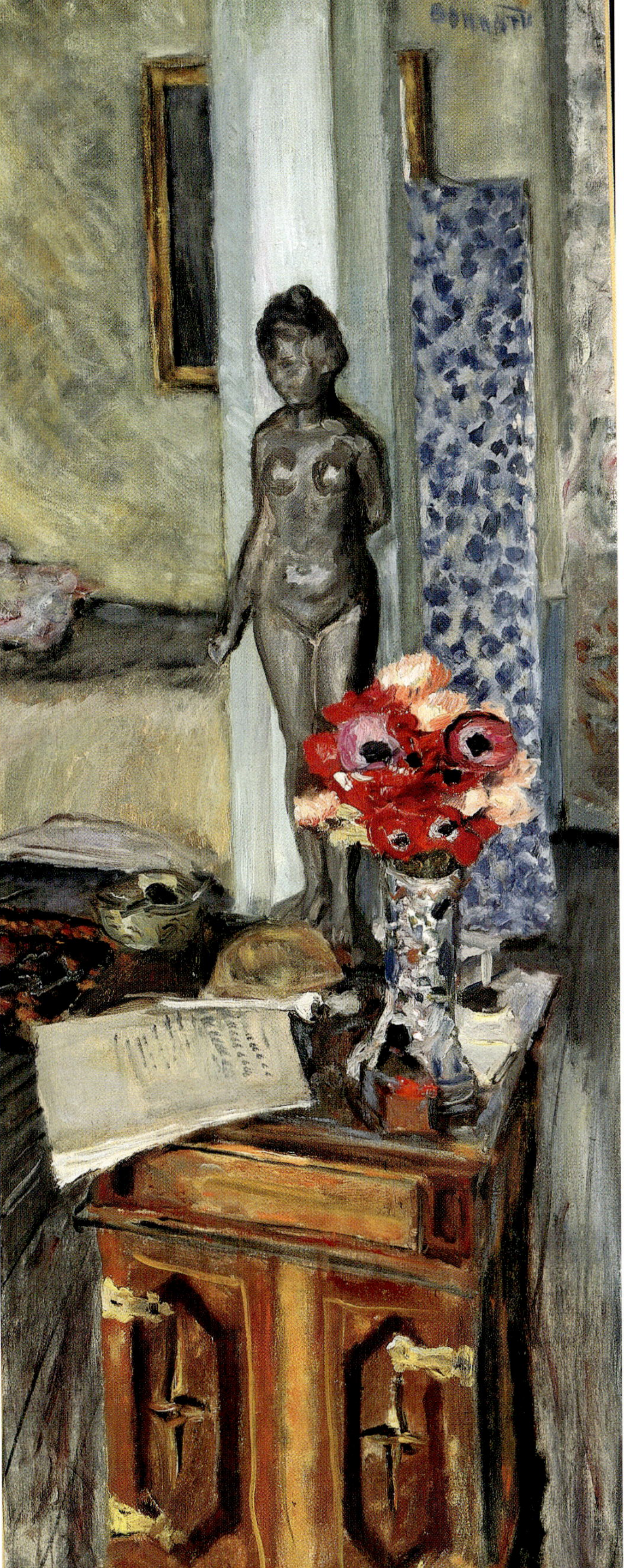

Hommage to Maillol
1917, Oil on canvas, 48 × 18½ in.
(121.9 × 47 cm), Philadelphia Museum of Art,
Louis E. Stern Collection, 1963.

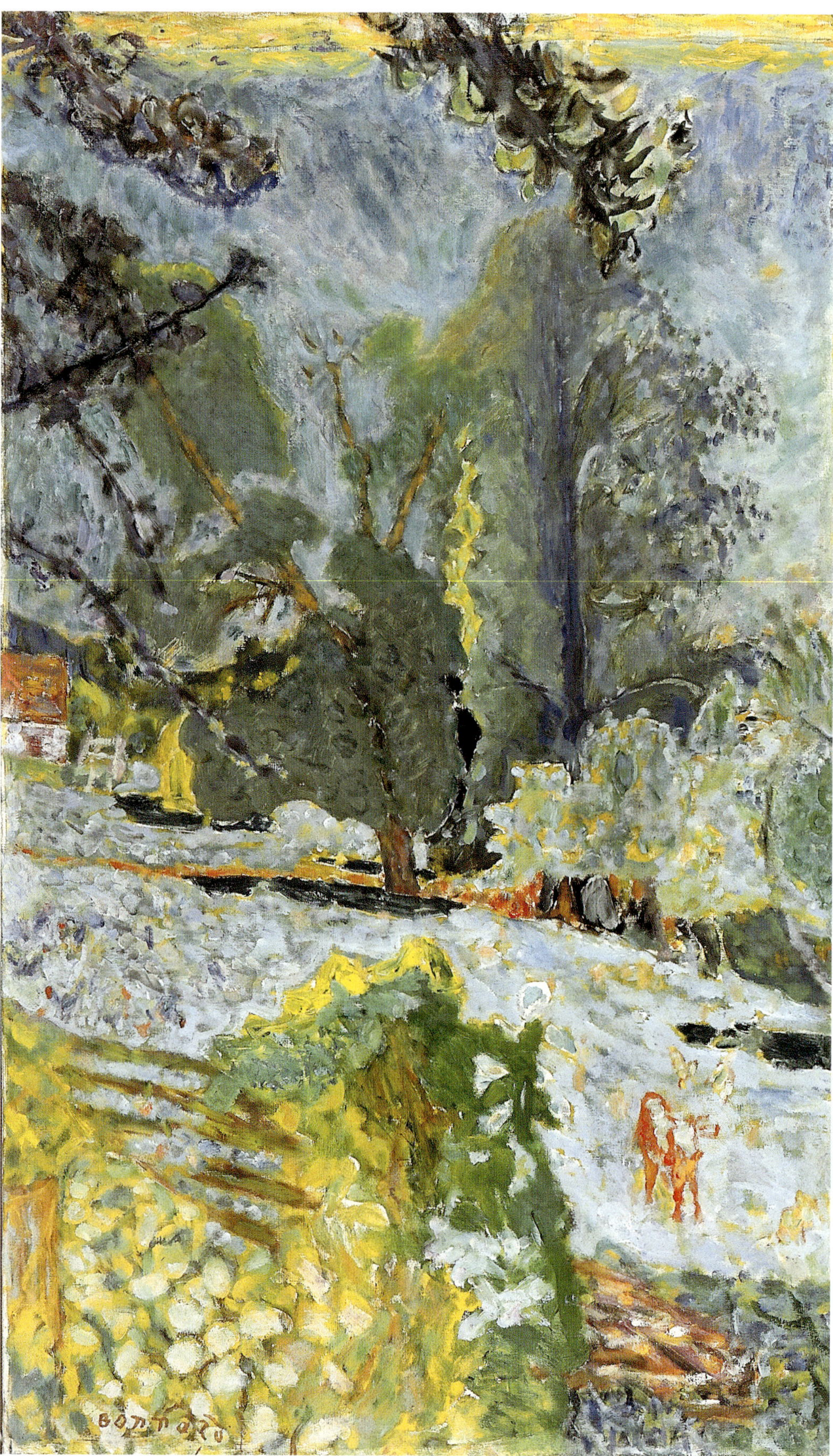

82

Normandy Landscape
1920, Oil on canvas, 41⅜ × 22¾ in. (105 × 57.9 cm),
Musée d'Unterlinden, Colmar.

83

Strawberries
1920, Oil on canvas, 10⅝ × 9⅞ in. (27 × 25.1 cm),
Private collection on loan to The Phillips
Collection, Washington, D.C.

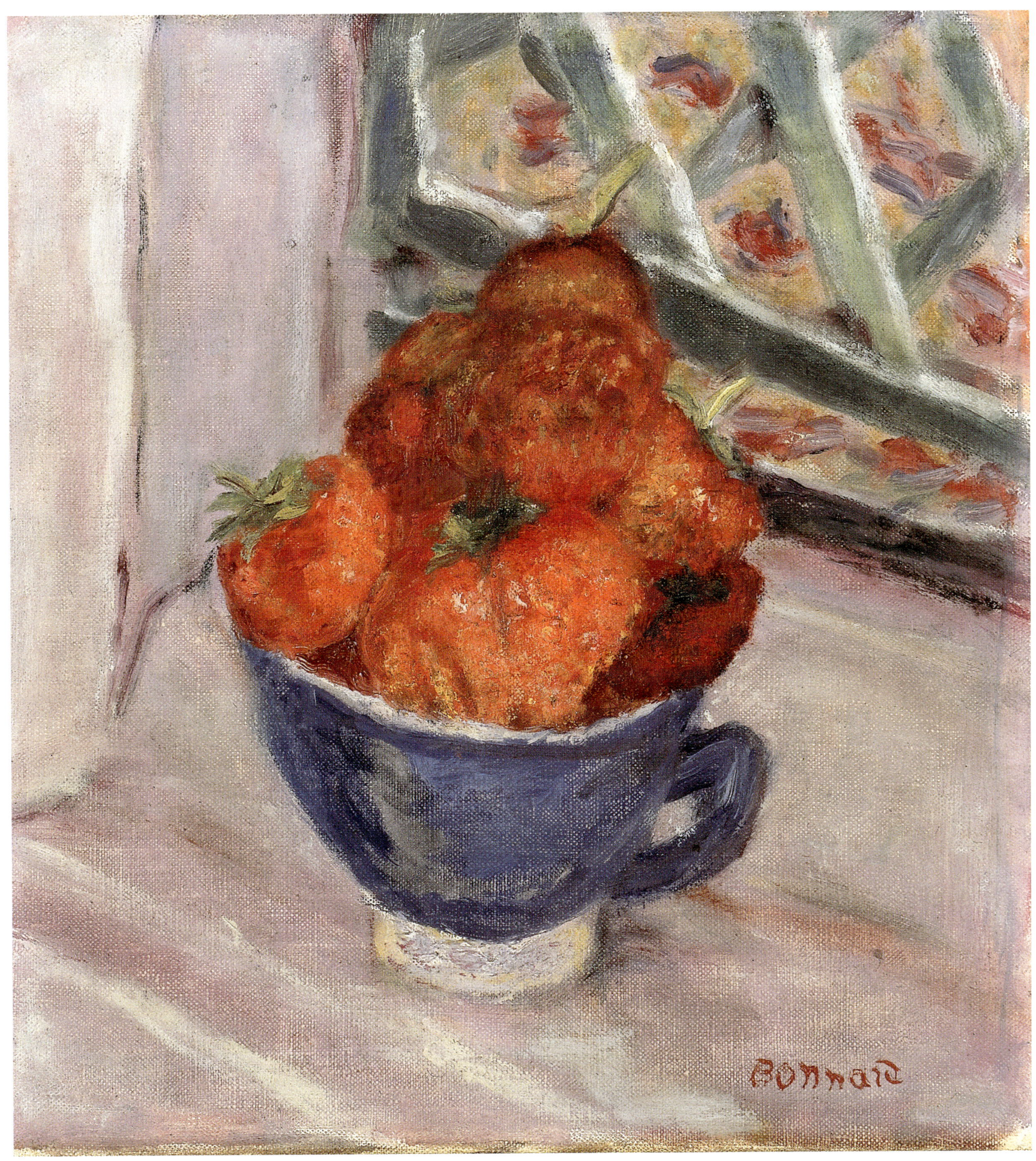
Bonnard

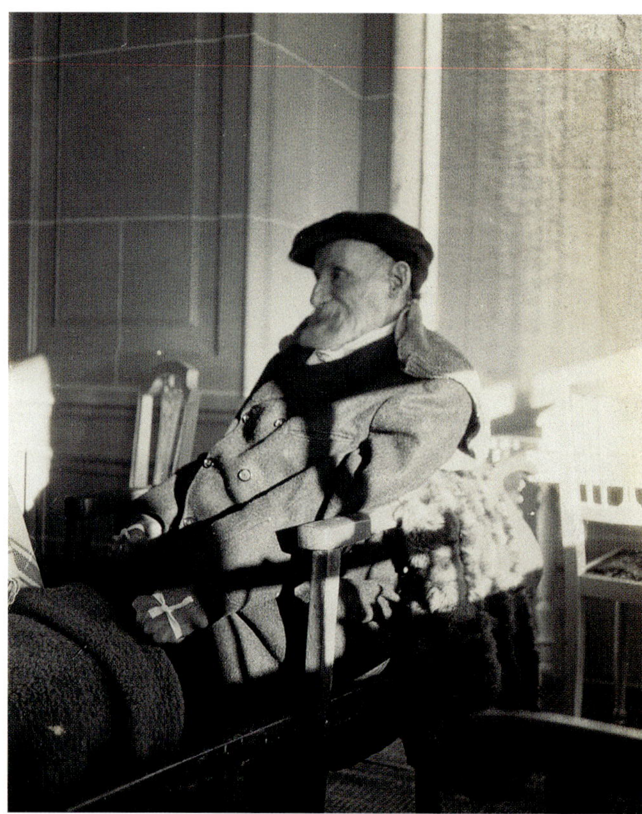

84

Attributed to Pierre Bonnard
Pierre-Auguste Renoir
ca. 1916, Photograph, Paris, Musée d'Orsay.

84a

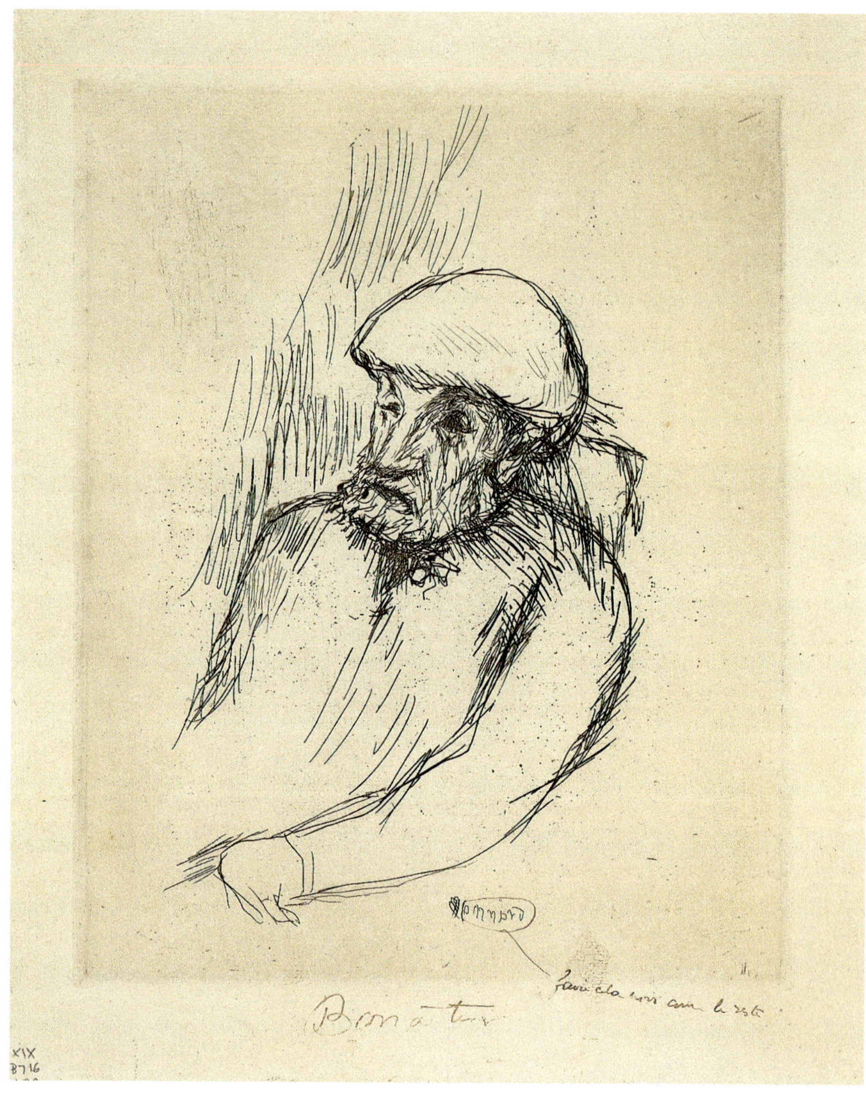

Portrait of Renoir
ca. 1916, Etching, 12¼ × 9⅞ in. (31.1 × 25.1 cm),
Prints and Photographs Division, Library of
Congress, Washington, D.C., Reproduction
numbers: LC-USZC4-10007, LC-USZ62-
130236.

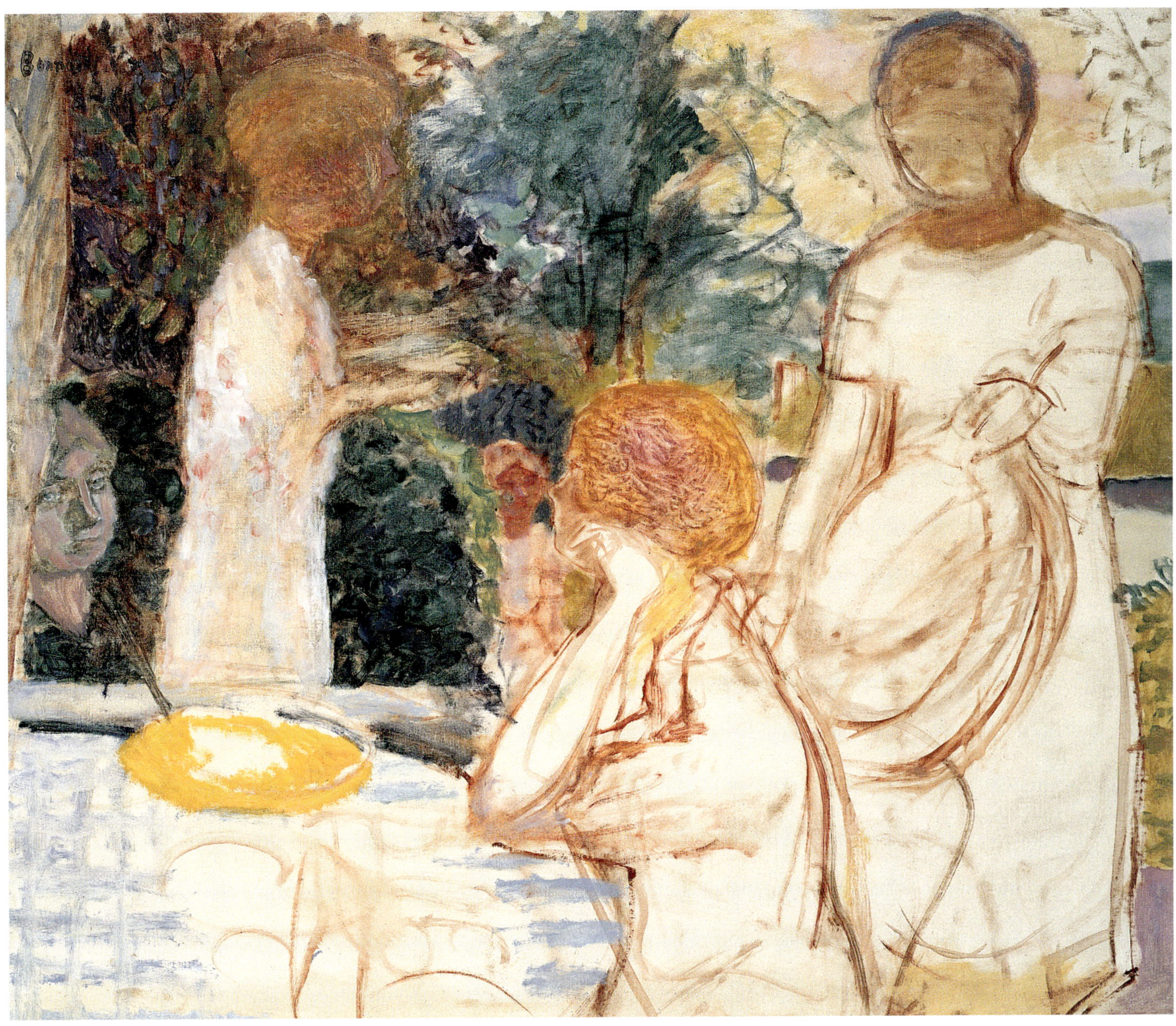

85

Young Women in the Garden
1918, Oil on canvas, 36¼ × 40½ in. (92 × 103 cm),
Galerie Jan Krugier, Ditesheim & Cie, Geneva.

Next spread: **Young Women in the Garden**
(detail).

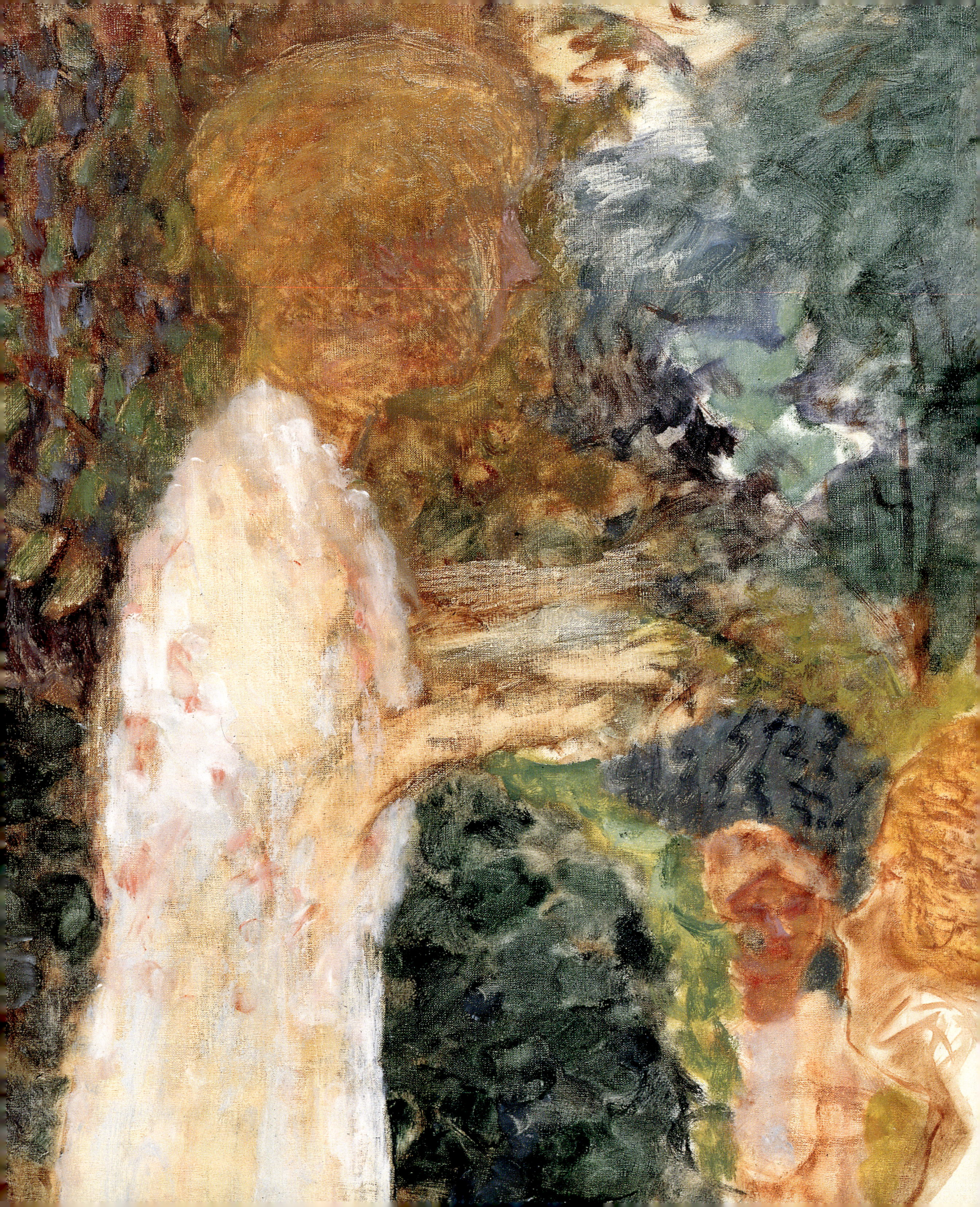

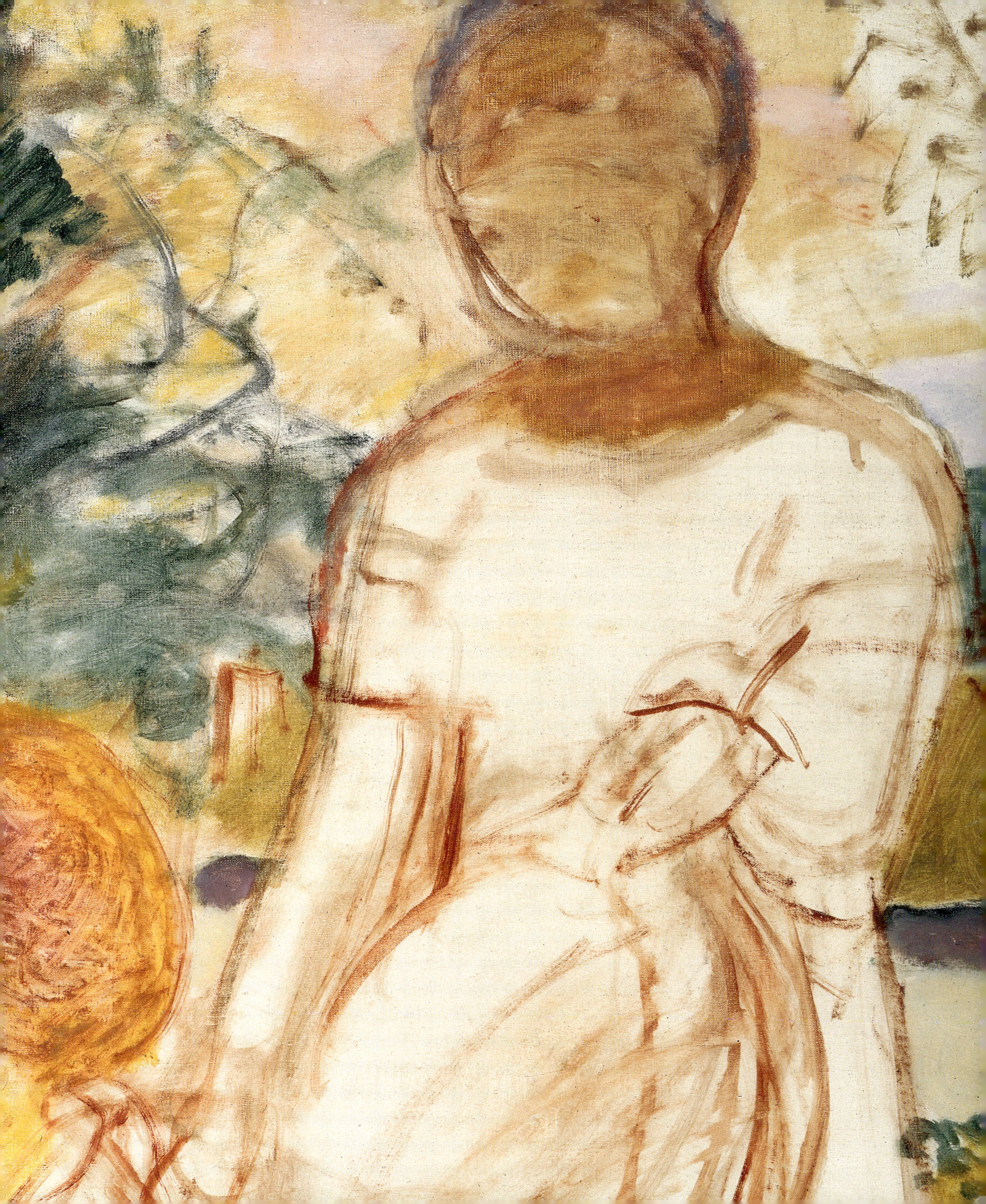

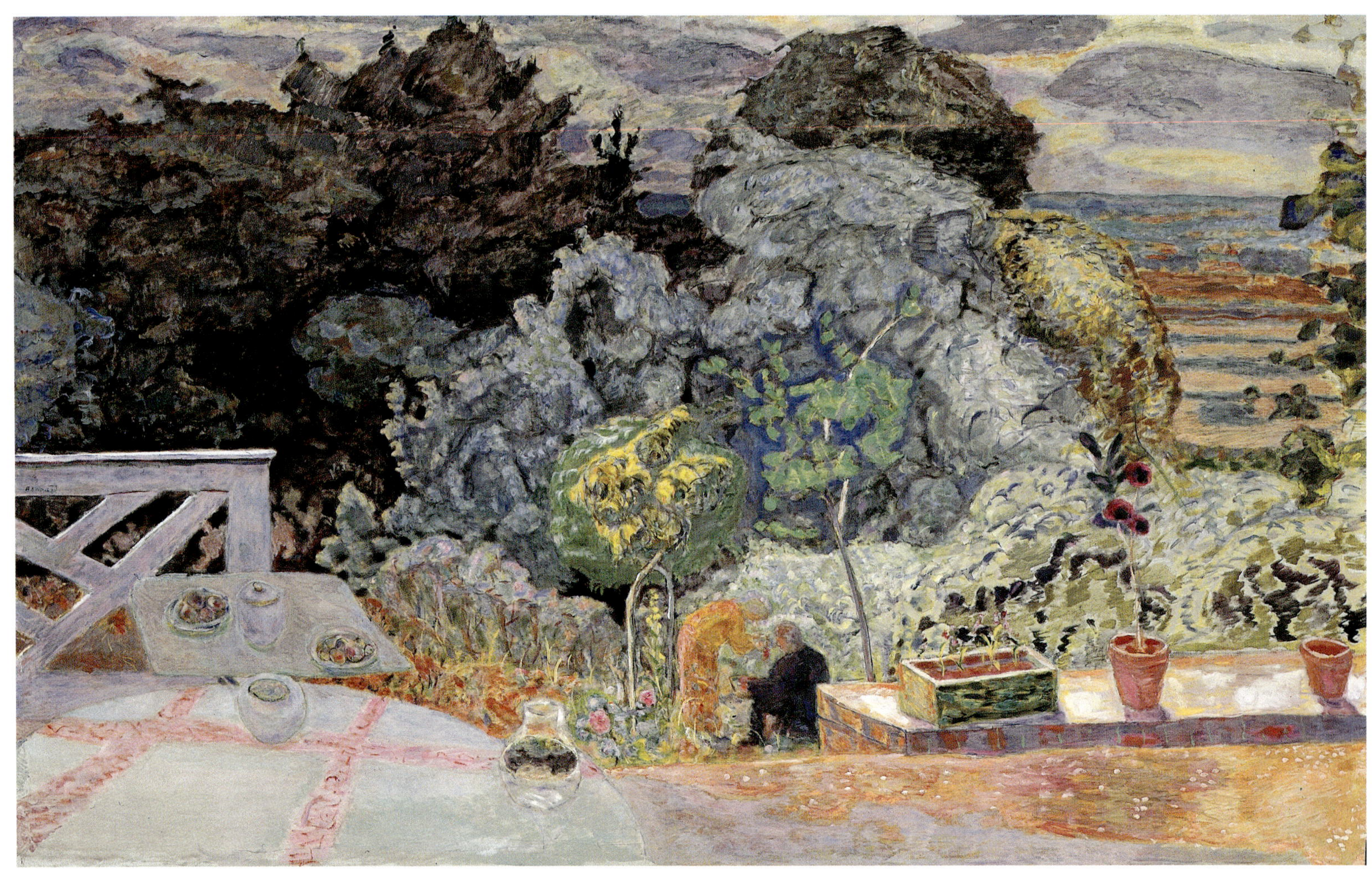

86

The Terrace
1918, Oil on canvas, 62¾ × 98¼ in.
(159.4 × 249.5 cm), The Phillips Collection,
Washington, D.C.

87

Interior with Flowers
1919, Oil on canvas, 45¾ × 35⅛ in.
(116.2 × 89.2 cm), Riggs National
Corporation.

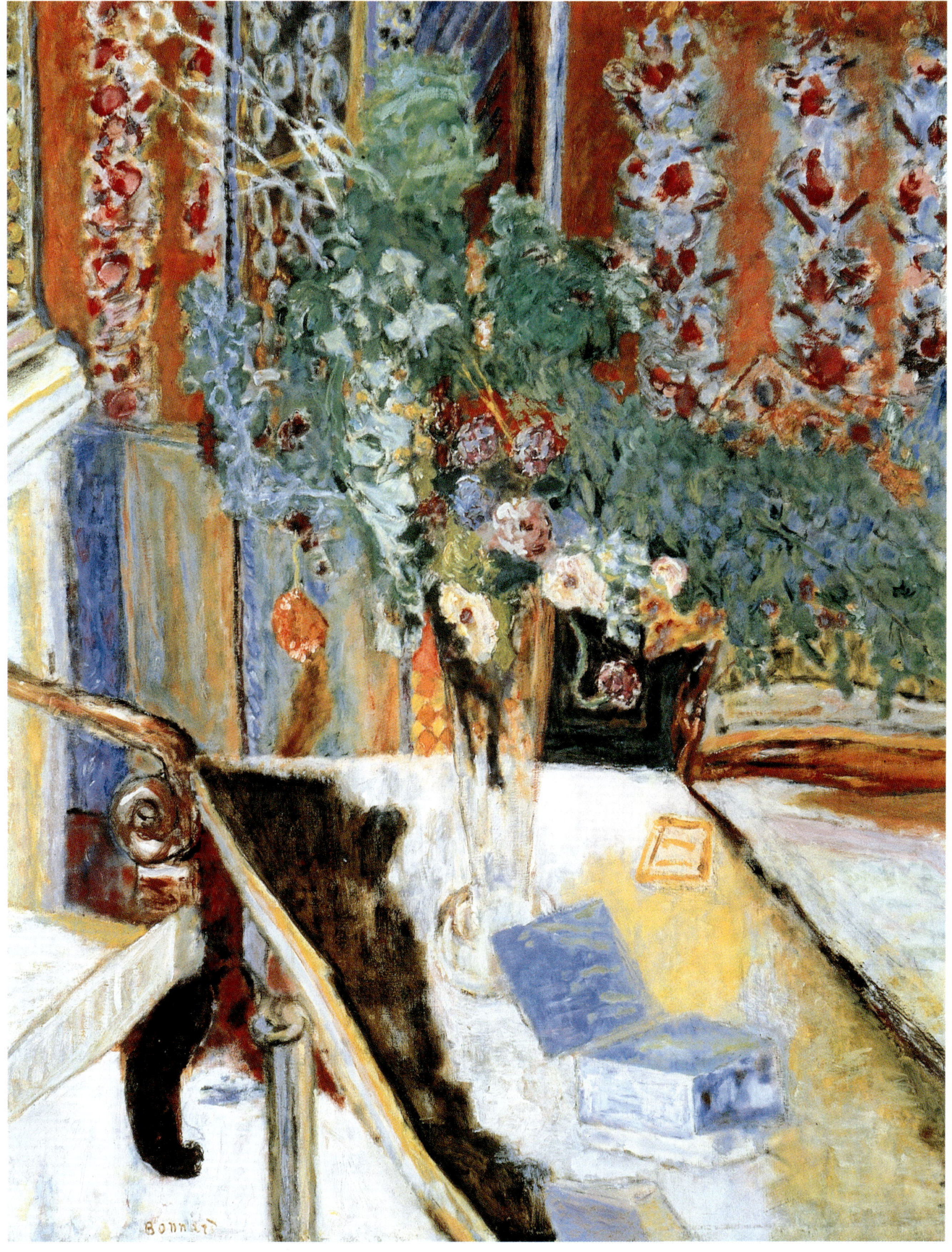

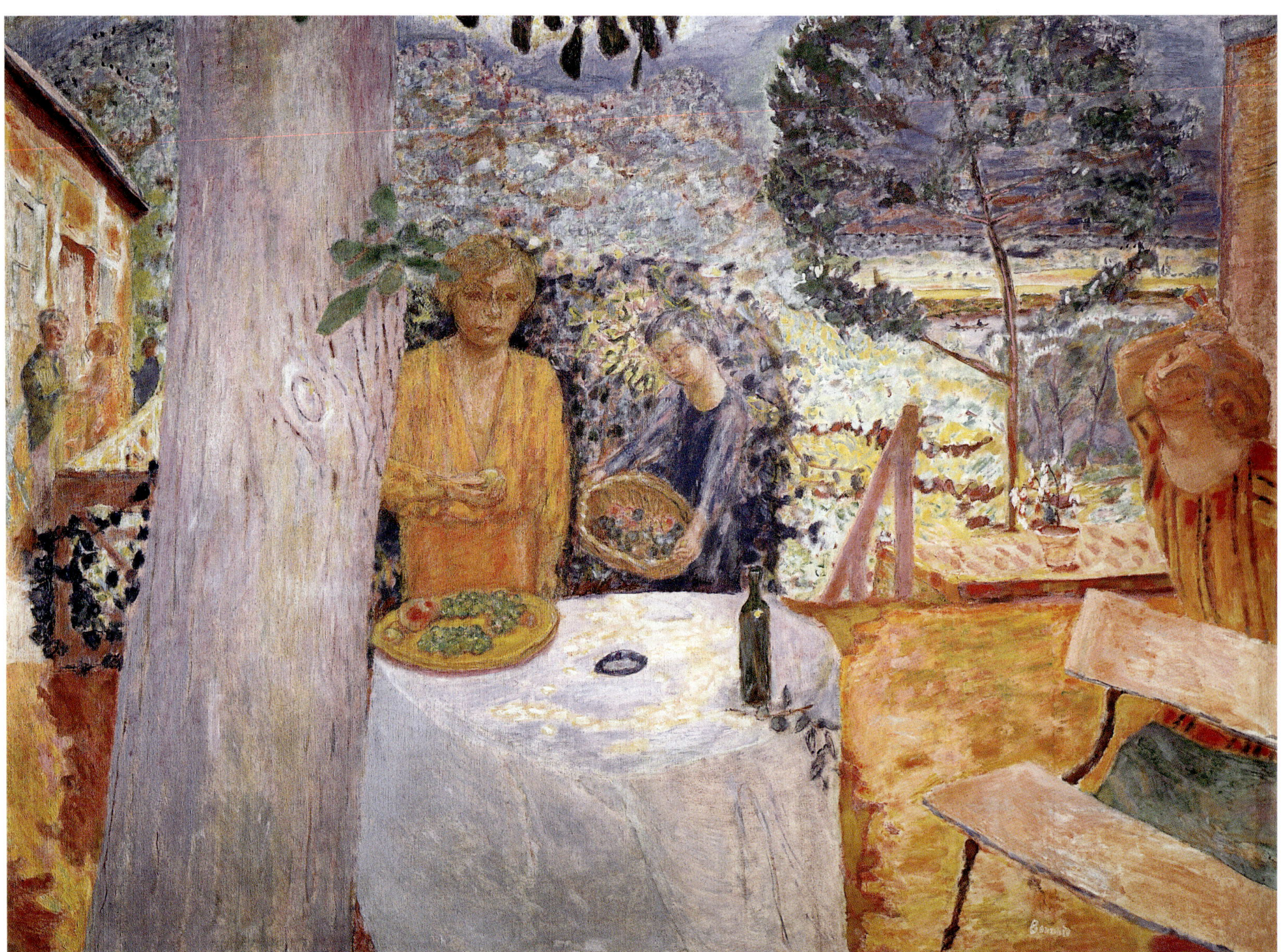

88

The Terrace at Vernonnet
1920/1939, Oil on canvas, 58¼ × 76¾ in.
(148 × 194.9 cm), The Metropolitan Museum
of Art, Gift of Mrs. Frank Jay Gould 1968
(68.1).

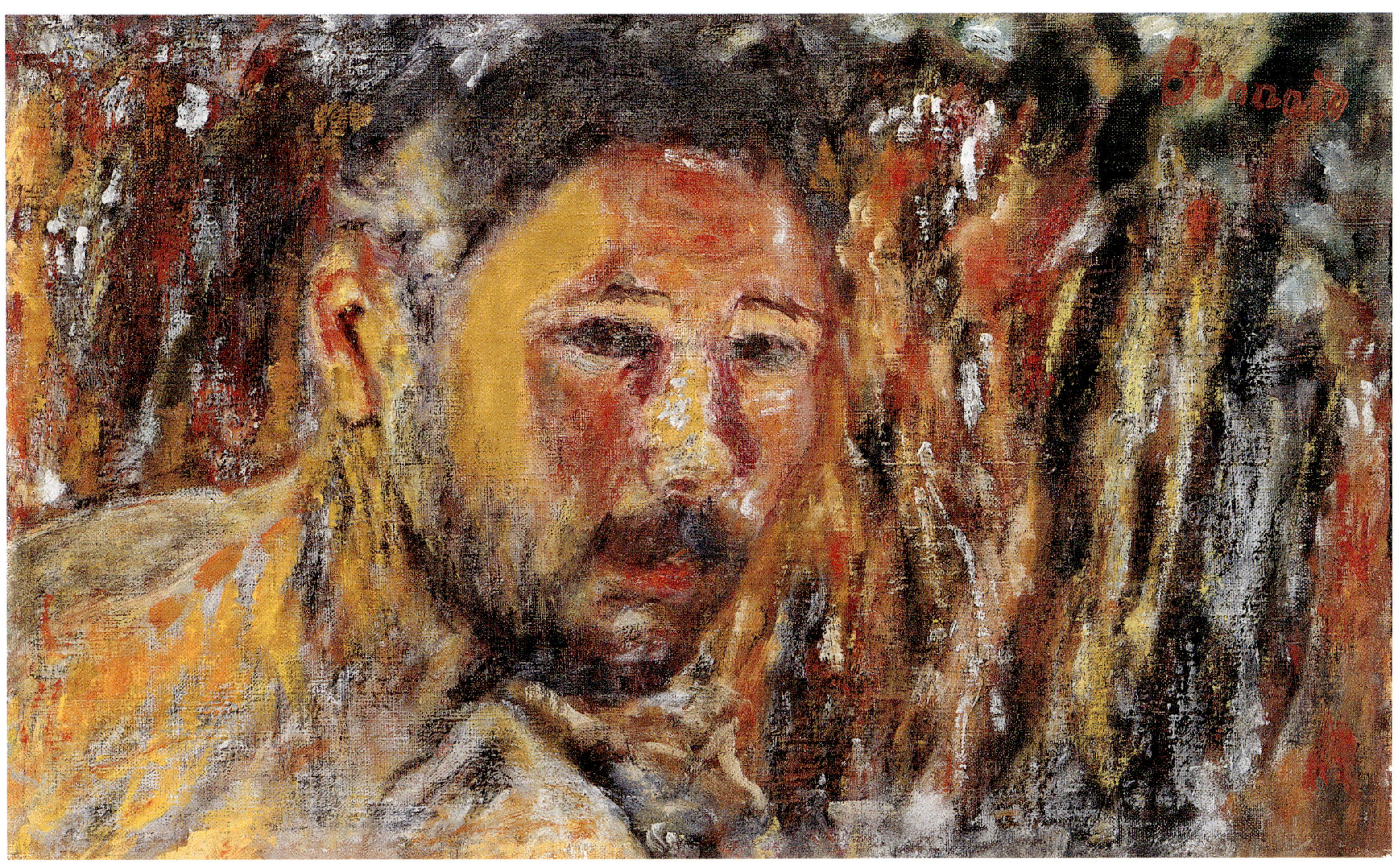

89

Self-Portrait with Beard
ca. 1920, Oil on canvas mounted on panel,
11⅝ × 18 in. (29.5 × 45.7 cm), Private collection.

Next pages: **Self-Portrait with Beard** (detail).

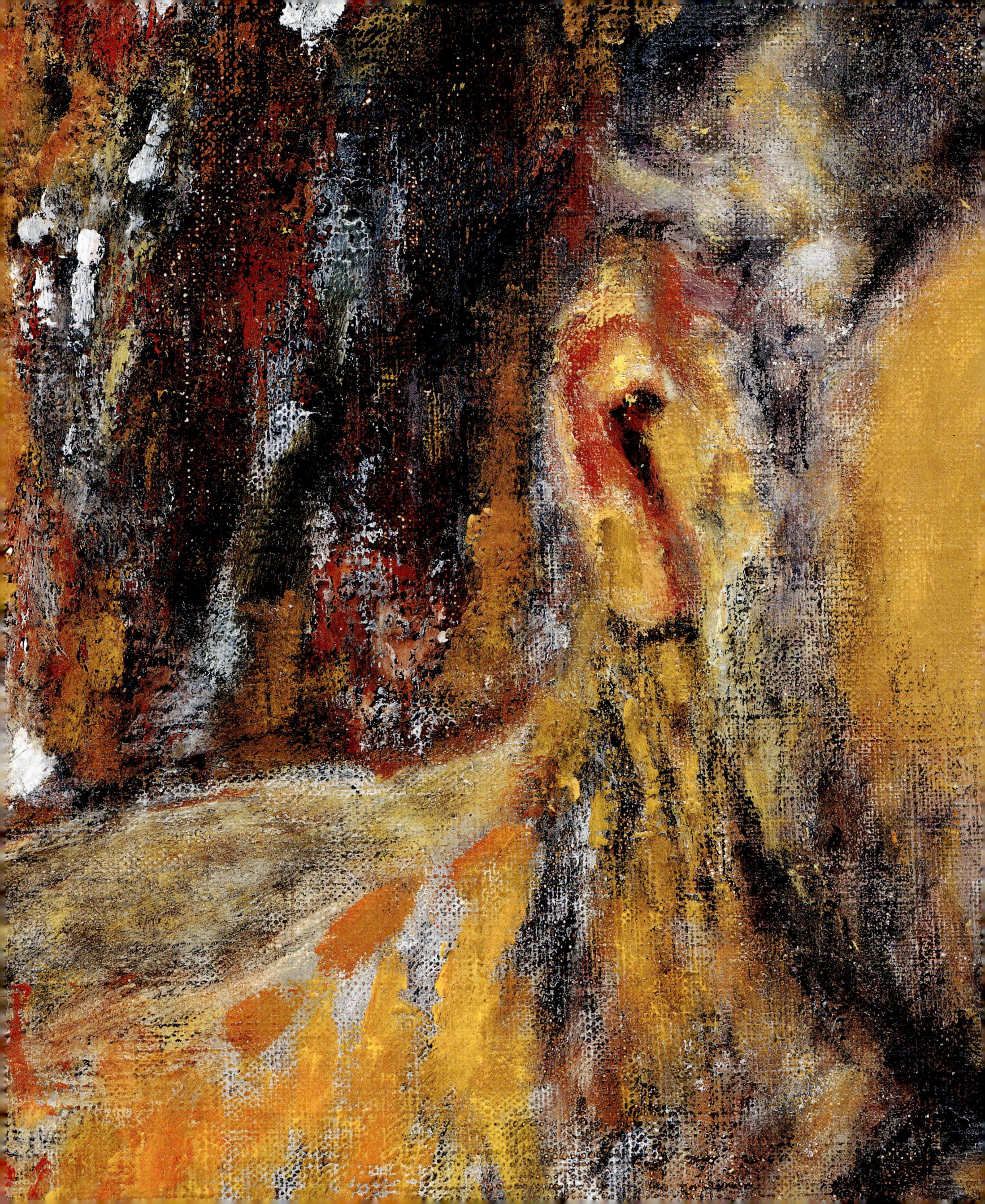

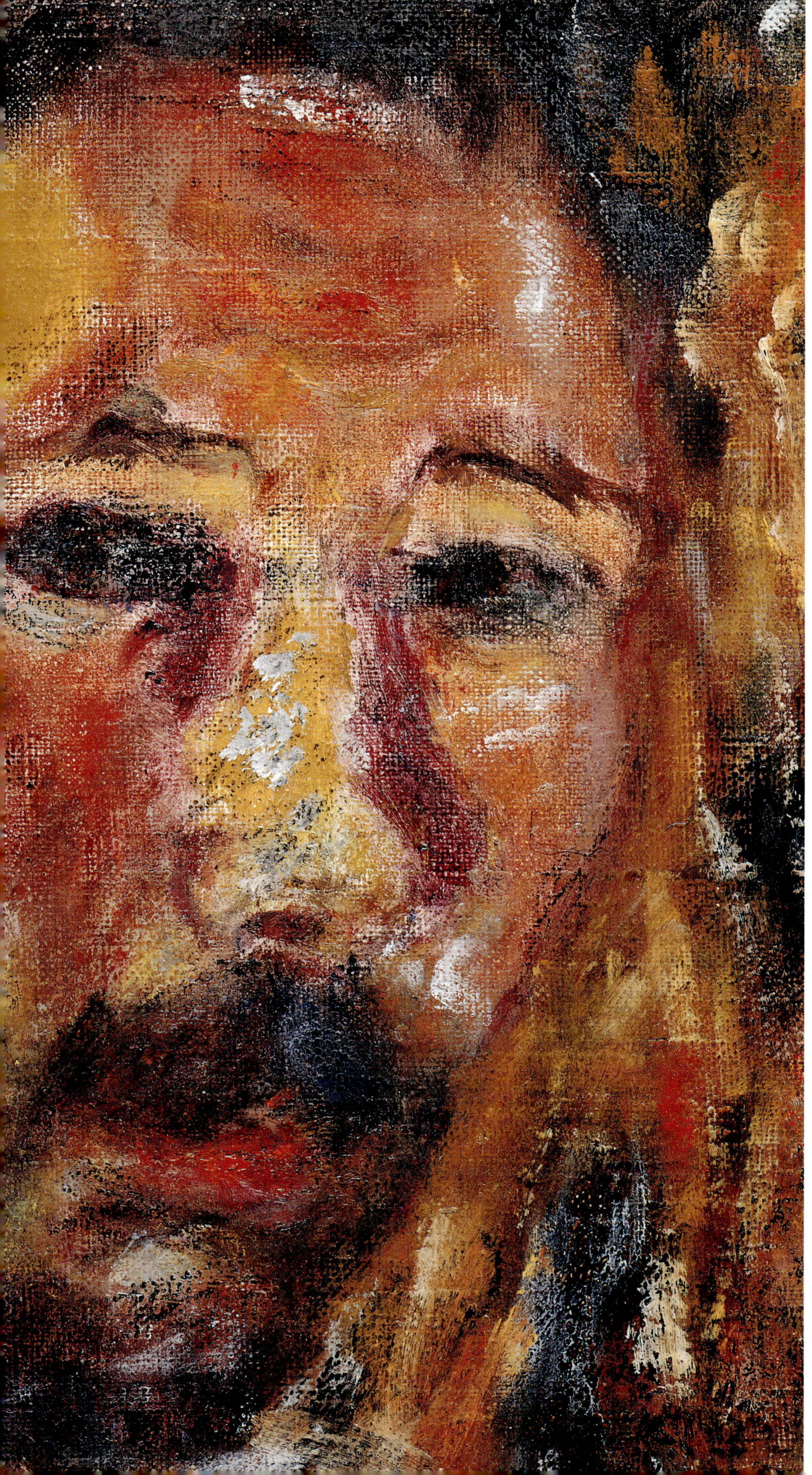

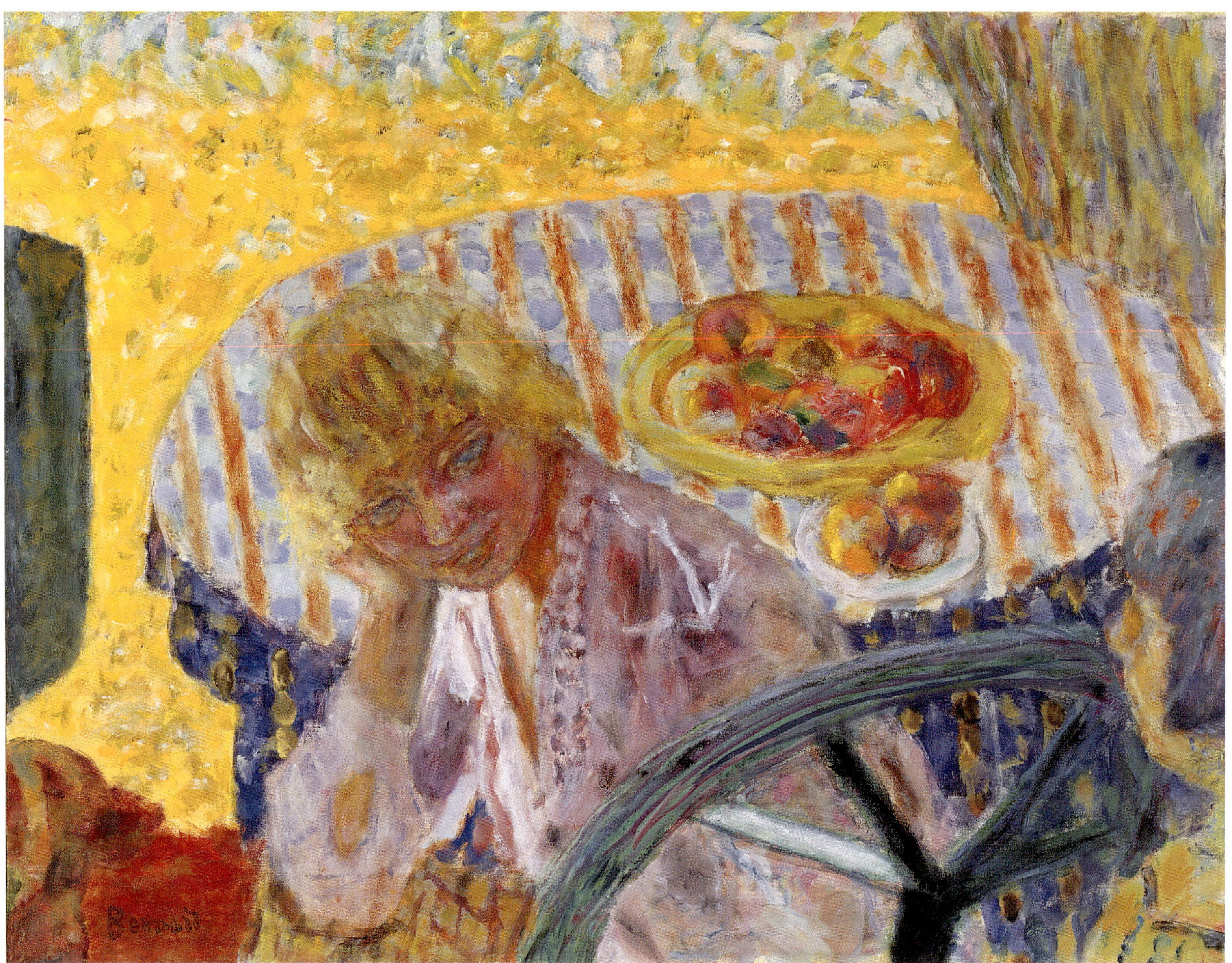

90

Young Women in the Garden (Renée Monchaty and Marthe Bonnard)
ca. 1921–1923, 1945–1946, Oil on canvas,
23¹³⁄₁₆ × 30⁵⁄₁₆ in. (60.5 × 77 cm),
Private collection.

Opposite page: **Young Women in the Garden (Renée Monchaty and Marthe Bonnard)** (detail).

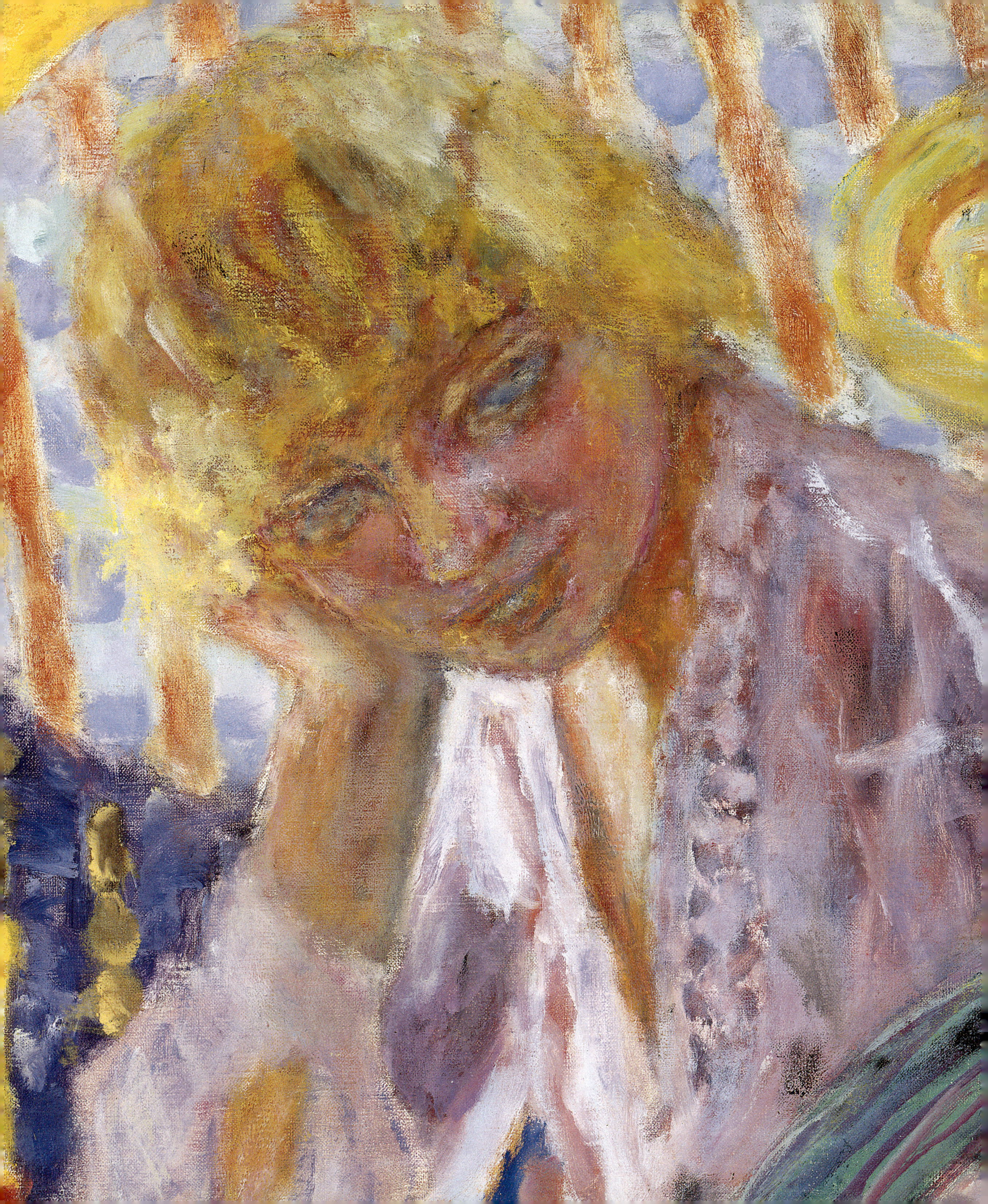

91

Study for "The Open Window"
ca. 1920–1921, Graphite on paper, 4¾ × 8¹⁄₁₆ in.
(12 × 20.5 cm), Private collection.

92

Study for "The Open Window"
ca. 1920–1921, Graphite on paper, 4¾ × 8¹⁄₁₆ in.
(12 × 20.5 cm), Private collection.

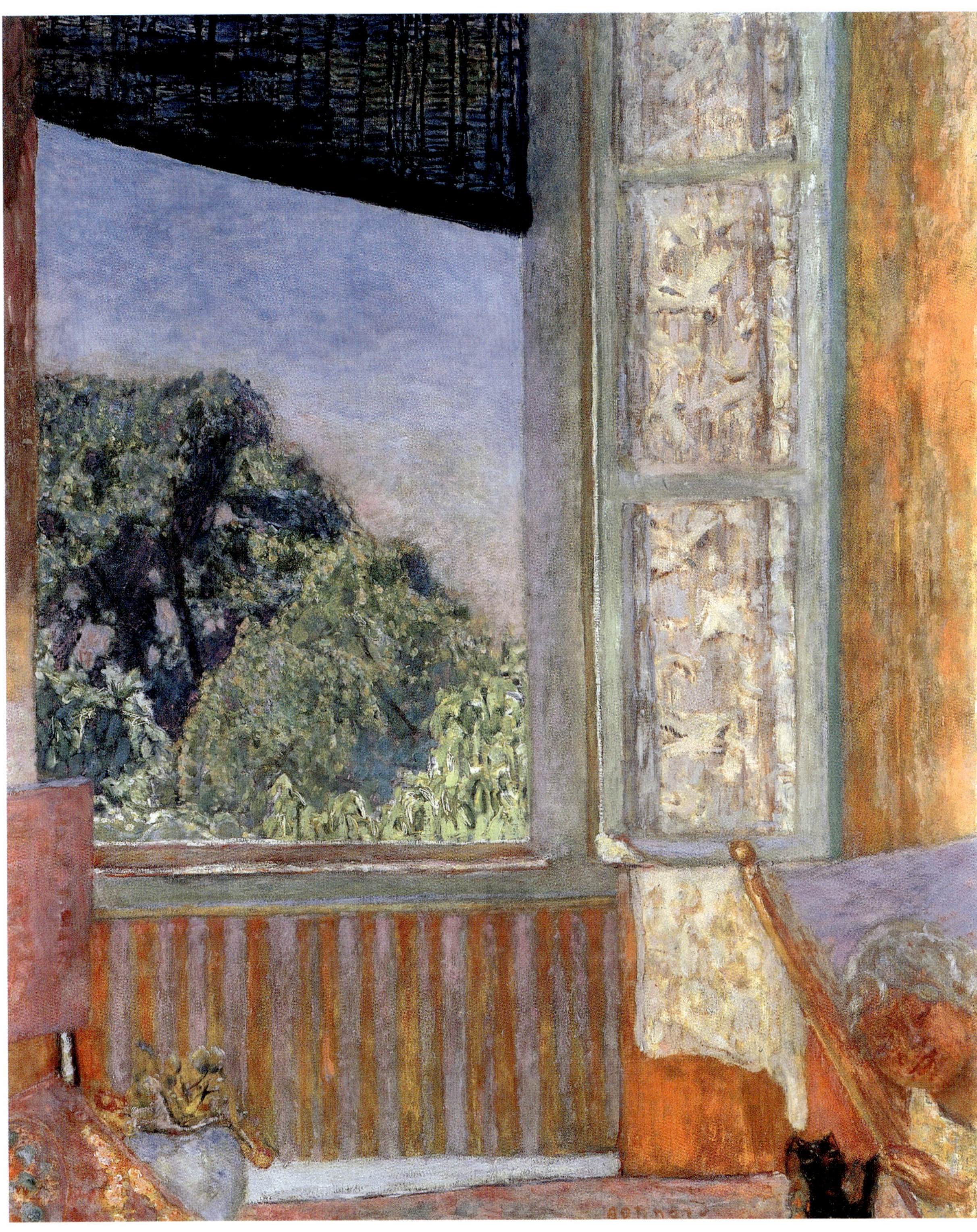

93

The Open Window
1921, Oil on canvas, 46½ × 37¾ in. (118 × 96 cm),
The Phillips Collection, Washington, D.C.

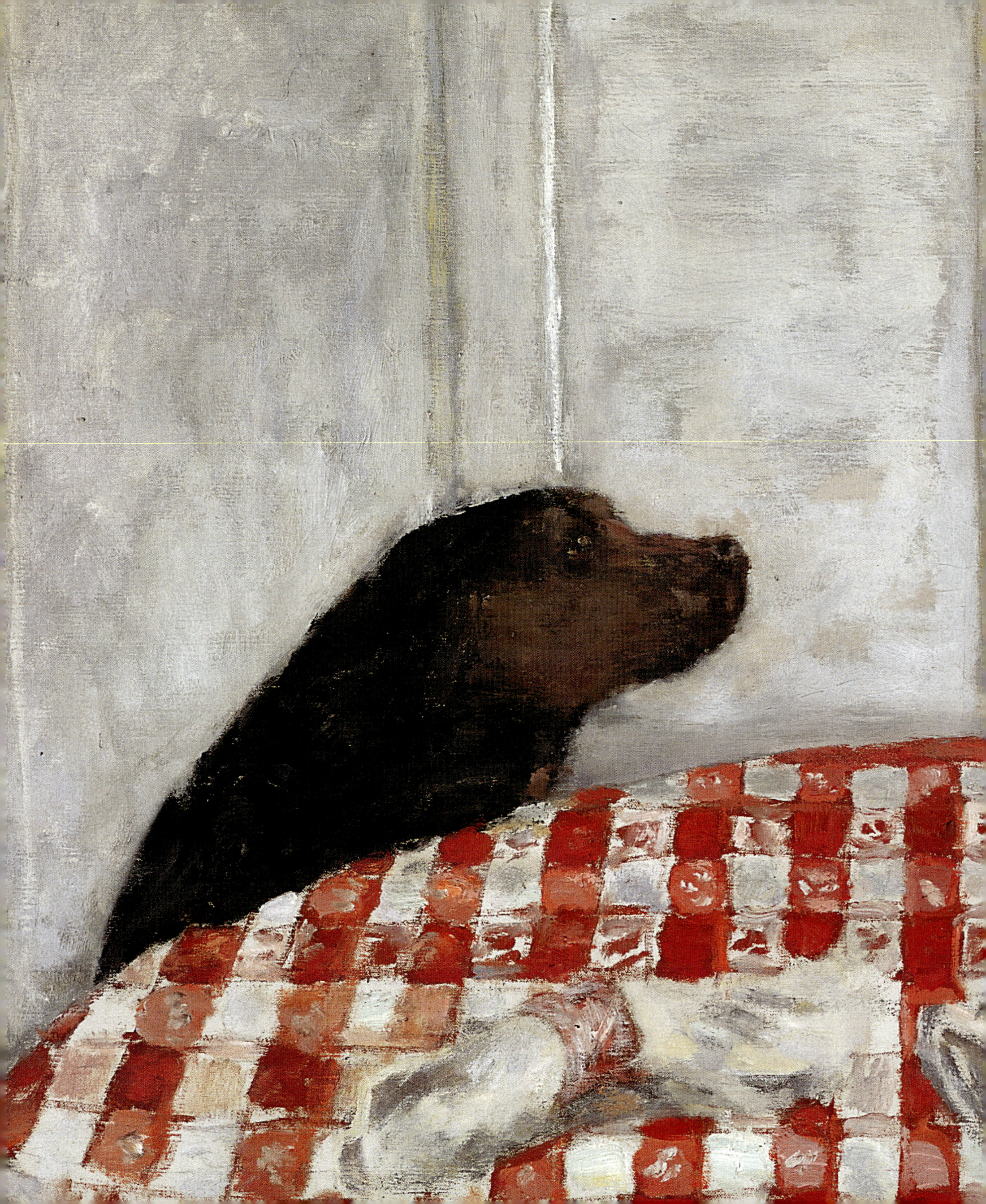

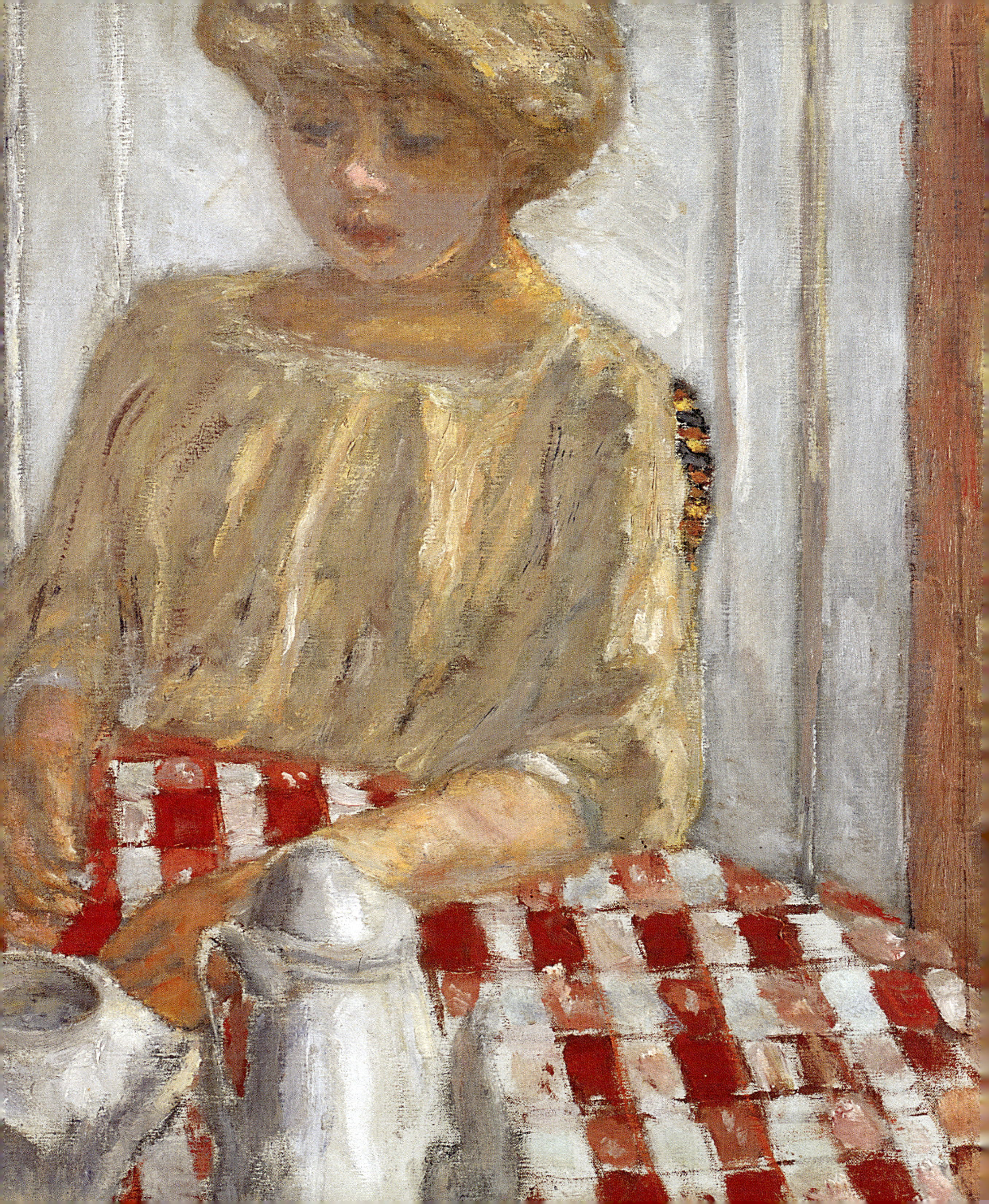

Japonisme in Bonnard's Early and Late Work

Ursula Perucchi-Petri

Previous spread:
The Red Checkered Tablecloth or
The Dog's Lunch
1910, Oil on canvas,
32 ¹¹⁄₁₆ × 33½ in.
(83 × 85 cm),
Private collection.

Every painter must find in his "elements" of work, resources, reminders from which to draw from. He only needs to look until he finds those which are true to his expression, to his usual needs, but there again the role of the unexpected is great. Tout peintre doit trouver dans ses éléments de travail des ressources, des rappels, parmis lesquels il peut puiser. Il n'a qu'à chercher jusqu'à ce qu'il trouve ceux qui sont conformes à son expression, à ses besoins habituels. Mais là encore la part de l'inattendu est grande—Pierre Bonnard

Bonnard was known by his friends as "le nabi très japonard." The epithet, first coined by Félix Fénéon, was nothing if not apt, given the important role that East Asian art played in the development of Bonnard's new aesthetic language. Indeed, when Siegfried Bing presented a sweeping survey of the history of the Japanese woodblock print at the Ecole des Beaux-Arts from 25 April to 22 May 1890, featuring more than seven hundred prints from private collections in Paris, it made an enormous impression on Bonnard. He would trawl the department stores of Paris in search of Japanese prints: "There, for the price of just one or two pennies, I found *crépons* and rice papers in astonishing colors. I covered the walls of my room with these naïve and gaudy pictures."[1] For the most part, he tended to acquire works by nineteenth-century Japanese artists such as Utagawa Toyokuni I (1769–1825), Utagawa Kunisada (1786–1864; fig. 92), Utagawa Kuniyoshi (1792–1861; fig. 93), Yoshimura (fig. 94), and Andō

Hiroshige (1797–1858): "It was not until much later that I became aware of the beauty of the great Japanese masters, more subdued by far, yet less elucidating in terms of pure colour."[2] In photographs of Bonnard's studio, right up to the late period, we can see Japanese woodblock prints on the walls—indicating that he not only collected them but also lived and worked with them. He appreciated their vitality as a source of inspiration toward a truly realistic and positive interpretation of his own era: "[Paul] Gauguin and [Paul] Sérusier allude to the past. But what I had before me was something truly alive and extremely wise."[3] Like his Nabis friends, Bonnard rejected conventional academic tradition and the mimesis propagated by the academies of the day with their illusionistic and naturalistic approach. Instead, even in his days at the Académie Julian, he sought a renewal of art. The quest for visual planarity meant finding a new way of portraying three-dimensional reality in place of the illusionist modeling of form and traditional perspectival space and the laws of proportion and movement that had prevailed since the Renaissance.

The complex and varied inspirations of East Asian art are reflected in a preference for such techniques as cropping, decentralizing, fragmentation, and silhouetting, and in the use of views from above, close-ups, or extreme vertical and horizontal formats. As it would be impossible to address all aspects of Japonisme and its significance for Bonnard within the scope of this essay, I shall concentrate in the following on a number of key issues and, given the focus of the exhibition, I shall attempt to shed some light on the connection between his early work and his later work.

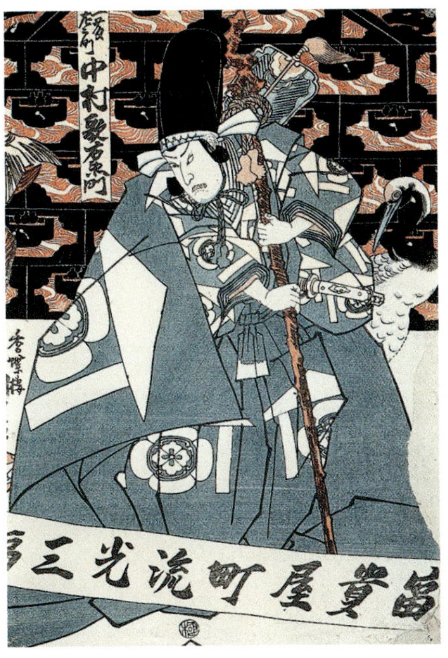

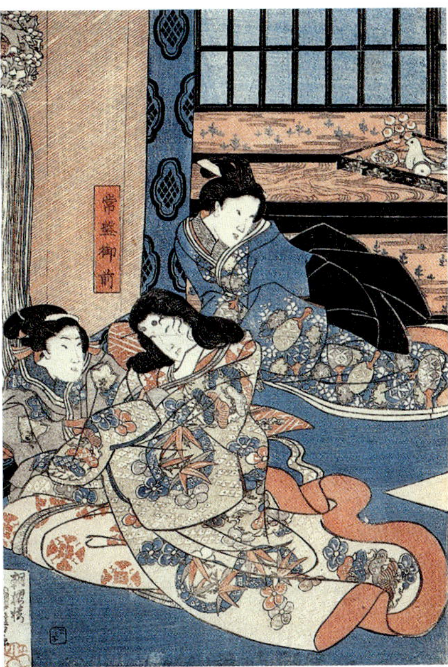

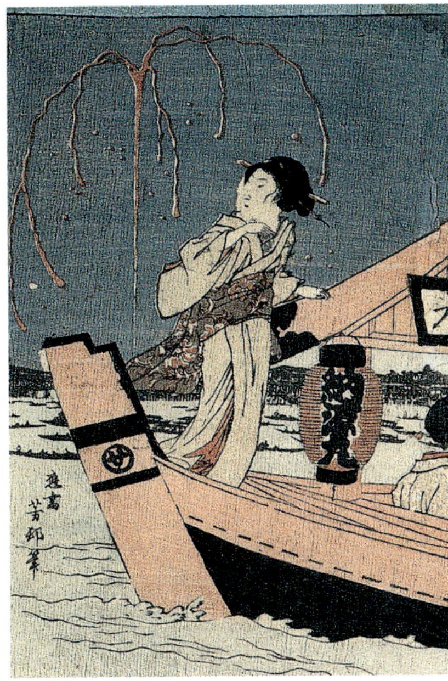

92. Utagawa Kunisada, *Nakamura Utaemon in a Kabuki Scene*, Japanese woodblock print, Private collection. Former collection of Pierre Bonnard.

93. Utagawa Kuniyoshi, *Historical Scene. Tokiwa Gozen, Lover of Minamoto no Yoshibune*, Japanese woodblock print, Private collection. Former collection of Pierre Bonnard.

94. Yoshimura, *Young Woman in a Boat*, Japanese *crépon*, Private collection. Former collection of Pierre Bonnard.

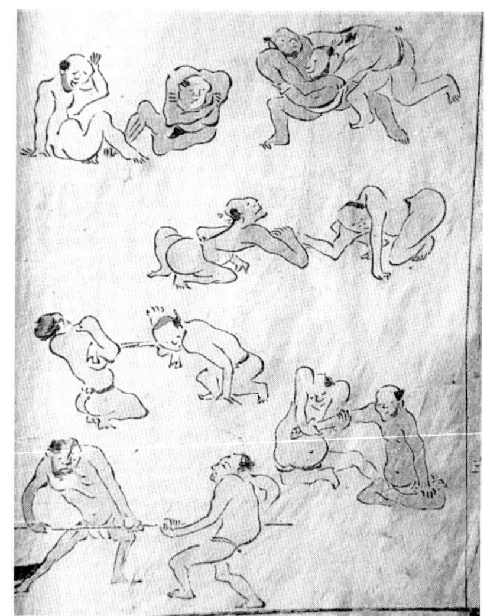

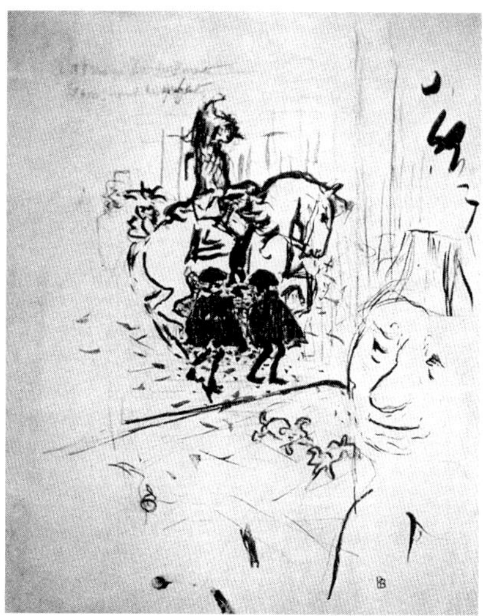

95. Kitao Masayoshi, *Seated Figures.* Excerpt from the *Ryakuga-shiki* sketchbook, 1795, Private collection. Former collection of Edouard Vuillard.

96. Pierre Bonnard, Study for *Municipal Guard*, 1893, Chinese ink, charcoal, and wash, 15¾ × 11¹³⁄₁₆ in. (40 × 30 cm), Private collection.

The Human Figure: A New Approach

The first major work in which Bonnard applied his new formal syntax is the 1889–1891 *Poster for France-Champagne* (plate 5), featuring an arabesque outline as an innovative way of rendering corporeality in the plane. This linear syntax is derived from the East Asian approach (see, for example, the *Ryakuga-shiki* sketchbook of 1795 by Kitao Masayoshi (fig. 95) owned by Edouard Vuillard). Eschewing all illusionist modeling, Bonnard, like the Japanese artists he so admired, succeeds in evoking the sculptural plasticity and movement of an exuberant female figure by means of undulating lines that ebb and flow. It is an approach that emphasizes the value of the line as a means of expression in its own right. By using similarly decorative and stylized forms to render the champagne bubbles, the hair, and the fluttering shoulder straps of the dress, Bonnard creates an analogy between the erotic appeal of the woman and the seductive power of champagne. As Walter Benjamin was later to remark so lucidly, "Modern advertising proves how easily the appeal of women and wares can be blended."[4]

A New Image of Children

From 1893 onward, the "linear" style of Bonnard's early Nabis paintings gradually gave way to a much more "painterly" visual approach. This development can be traced in the drawings and prints that were the focus of his work during this period. The figures are no longer brought to life by the waving line. Instead, their contours have become permeable and sketchy, radiating out into the surrounding area. The broken and fragmented silhouette has become the vehicle by which Bonnard now lends expression in a very different way to the corporeality and movement of his figures.

This is particularly evident in the figures of children—a favorite subject for Bonnard since becoming uncle to the children of his sister Andrée and her husband, the composer Claude Terrasse. His drawings vividly capture their movement and body language, as in the way they trot along on spindly legs that peep out from beneath wide and bulky clothes. Consider, for example, the children running alongside the municipal guard in the 1893 lithograph *Municipal Guard* (fig. 96, plate 16), or the little laundry girl carrying a heavy basket across the street in his 1896 *The Little Laundry Girl* (plate 27). With a keenly observant eye, he realized that little children tend to walk with knees bent and feet wide apart, usually placing their full weight on the supporting leg so that they have a slightly rolling gait. Bonnard's humorous approach to the portrayal of movement owes much to Katsushika Hokusai and Hiroshige, who also like to show people on the move and explore their ever-changing poses. These are not idealized figures, but real-life people in real-life situations. One important visual source for Bonnard and his friends was Hokusai's fifteen-volume *Manga,* in which, in addition to his pictures of plants, animals, and landscape, the Japanese artist presented scenes of everyday life and studies in movement that often depict people in unwittingly comical or even grotesque poses. In Bonnard's day, the sketchbooks of Hokusai were regarded as examples of a new aesthetic that offered to the jaded European eye a more free and spontaneous form of expression. "You were ever young, and we are prematurely old," Ary Renan wrote of Hokusai in *Le Japon artistique* (fig. 97) in 1888.[5] "Japanese artists love movement . . . their extremely simplified means of expression are admirably suited to rendering the momentary movement, the fleeting gesture. And, being such excellent observers, they fragment movement into its component parts; they are aware of rhythms and beats that are unknown to us."[6]

Bonnard's pictures of children involve sequences of movement comparable to some of the prints in Hokusai's *Manga* (fig. 98). Both show children with knees bent and feet turned outward. The fact that the leg and the foot seem almost at right angles lends the child's gait a curiously unstable effect. In the case of Bonnard, this effect is further heightened by the contrast between the thin, little legs and the bulky, hooded cape. The work of Hokusai and Hiroshige also taught Bonnard that the angle of the body axis is crucial to the expression of movement. He, too, uses a forward-leaning stance to suggest the pitter-patter of children scurrying home from school (fig. 99). This is taken to an extreme in the image of the little laundress, whose childlike awkwardness as she strains under her heavy load is heightened by the diagonal silhouette, while a touch of humor is added by the oversize umbrella.

By liberating the portrayal of movement from the fetters of academic convention and exaggerating it at times to the point of the grotesque, Bonnard created a new image of children that is entirely different from earlier nineteenth-

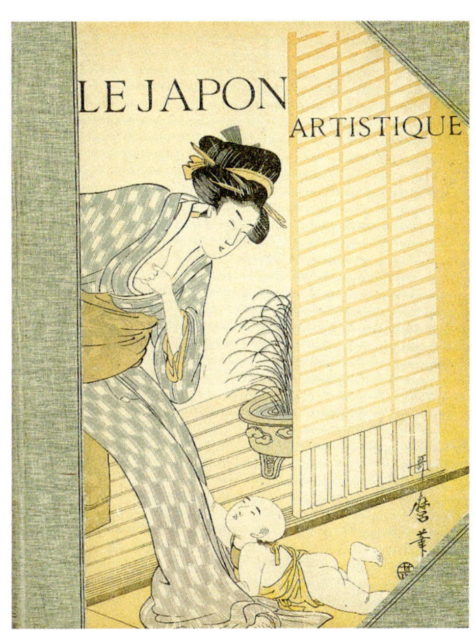

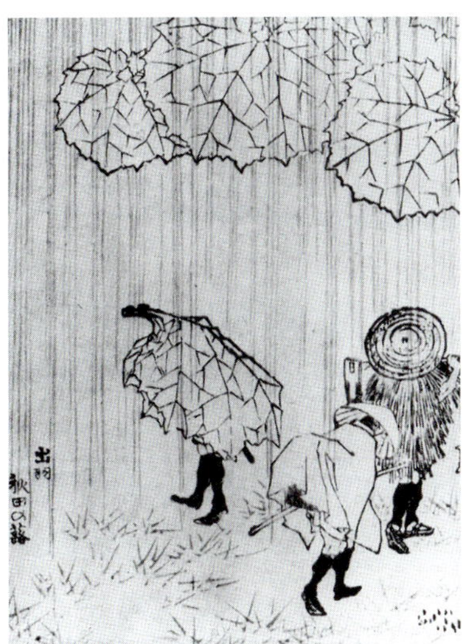

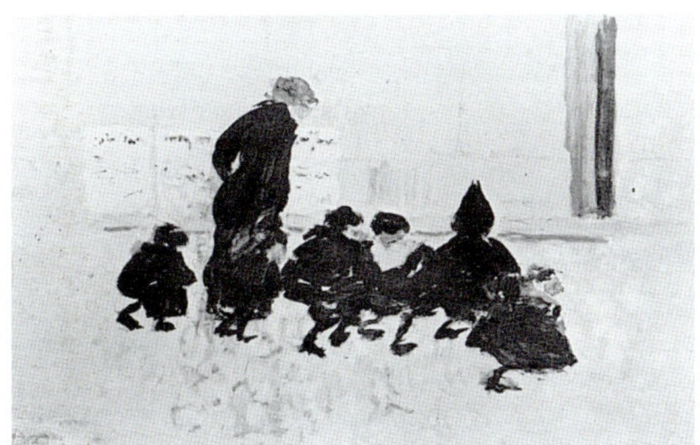

98. Katsushika Hokusai, *Rainy Day in the Countryside*, from *Manga*, ca. 1818.

99. Pierre Bonnard, *Children Leaving School*, ca. 1895, Cardboard on wood, 11⅜ × 17⅜ in. (28.9 × 44 cm), National Gallery of Art, Washington, Ailsa Mellon Bruce Collection.

97. Cover for *Le Japon artistique* 111, (May 1890–April 1891), 13 × 10 in. (33 × 25.4 cm), The Phillips Collection Archives, Washington, D.C.

century portrayals. It is an image informed by contemporary notions of genuine and unspoiled nature. Charles Baudelaire, who played an important role for the Nabis, wrote in *The Painter of Modern Life*, "The child sees everything in a state of newness; he is always *drunk*. Nothing more resembles what we call inspiration than the delight with which a child absorbs form and colour. . . . Genius is nothing more nor less than *childhood* recovered at will."[7] The German philosopher Arthur Schopenhauer, whose *The World as Will and Representation* was published in French in 1888 and eagerly read and debated by the Nabis, described childhood in his chapter "On Genius" as "The time of innocence and happiness, the paradise of life, the lost Eden, to which, throughout the remainder of our lives, we look back in yearning."[8] These yearnings for the primitive and for harmony between man and nature harbor within them an awareness of profound loss as the price we pay for the scientific and technical progress, urbanization and industrialization that have made us strangers to ourselves.

Such notions fitted well with the prevailing wish for simplicity, for the naïve and the archaic, which artists sought to find in the aesthetics of those bygone eras idealized in the late nineteenth century as illustrious examples of an intact and unbroken concept of art. Apart from Byzantine mosaics, medieval stained-glass windows, Egyptian art, and early Italian painting, this included East Asian art, which was long misconstrued as primitive and unsophisticated because of its decorative planarity devoid of the spatial depth and corporeal plasticity fashioned by light and shadow in the European mode. Bonnard himself also misunderstood the Japanese woodblock print: "In my youth I was enthralled by the magnificent mix of colors in the Japanese *crépons*, a kind of paper material in the style of folk art."[9] According to Maurice Denis, "Whenever we mentioned 'primitive art,' he (Bonnard) immediately thought of Japanese prints."[10]

For Bonnard, the "revelation" lay in the compositional principles, so new and unfamiliar to the European eye, still evident in the late flowering of Japanese art that had been the first to arrive in Europe. It was not until the World's Fair of 1900, to which Japan contributed early Buddhist sculptures, brush and ink paintings as well as treasures from the imperial collection and Buddhist temples, that a broader European public became aware of the cultural tradition behind the woodblock prints. Having jettisoned the conventions of academic tradition and in his search for new means of expression, Bonnard found in the Japanese woodblock print an art that satisfied his desire for the original and unspoiled, and tallied with his notion of a nonmimetic means of portrayal. Looking back on this period in 1909, Denis wrote, "Critics accused us at the time of inarticulately babbling like children. Actually, what we did was a return to childhood, playing the fool, and it was without a doubt the most intelligent thing to do. Ours was the art of savages, of primitives."[11]

The Figure in Motion

Like the children in Bonnard's pictures, the women, too, are portrayed in unusual, humorous, and almost caricature-like movement. Their sometimes grotesquely exaggerated poses drew attention even in Bonnard's day. Contemporary art critics, among them Gustave Geffroy and Roger Marx, searched for words to describe them: "cocasse" (comical), "preste" (nimble), "désinvolture" (offhand), "gamin" (cheeky), "malice d'observation" (capriciously observed). The strange contortions of Bonnard's figures are inspired by the Japanese masters of the later period, such as Kunisada and Kuniyoshi, whose works he was able to study in the collections of his friends Vuillard and Denis (fig. 100). As in the Japanese artists' renderings of women, Bonnard expresses movement by a bend of the knee and the hip, and by turning the upper and lower body in different directions. This technique can be seen particularly clearly in the figure of the woman on the right in the 1899 screen *Nannies' Promenade, Frieze of Carriages* (plate 24). Similar figures in motion are to be found in the 1894 poster *La Revue blanche* (plate 23) and in *The Omnibus* of about 1895 (plate 26).

No longer conforming to the classical principle of contrapposto, the figure is heightened to a veritable code of motion. In the figure on the right in *The Square at Evening* lithograph (plate 31) from the series *Some Scenes of Parisian Life* of 1899, the hurried gait is rendered by a zigzag rhythm of opposing forms within the angular silhouette. The hastily stumbling-forward movement is expressed by the exaggerated tilt of the upper body. Bonnard structures the figure within the overall composition so that it appears as part of the vibrant movement of modern city life, illustrating the pulsating rhythm of the metropolis. In the artistic concept of the Nabis, distortion was a legitimate *équivalent plastique*. In his *Théories*, Denis writes of the "clumsiness of execution and almost caricature-like simplification of form" as a new compositional technique, explaining, "*Gaucherie* [clumsiness] is the word I would use to describe this kind of awkward expression through which the personal emotion of an artist is revealed beyond all conventional formulae."[12]

Some recent publications have pointed out that the Nabis were inspired not only by Japanese art but also by the proliferation of popular prints and caricatures.[13] With the relaxation of official censorship in 1881, countless illustrated magazines and satirical periodicals began to appear, among them *Le Chat noir, La Caricature, L'Escarmouche,* and *Le Courrier français,* employing a veritable army of draftsmen and caricaturists. Some of them were artists close to the Nabis, such as Adolphe Willette, Jules Chéret, Hermann-Paul, Henri Rivière, and Théophile-Alexandre Steinlen, and some even exhibited alongside the Nabis at the gallery Le Barc de Boutteville. Their input undoubtedly contributed toward an emancipation from academic traditions and fueled the quest for a formal syntax of greater simplicity and freedom, capable of capturing the

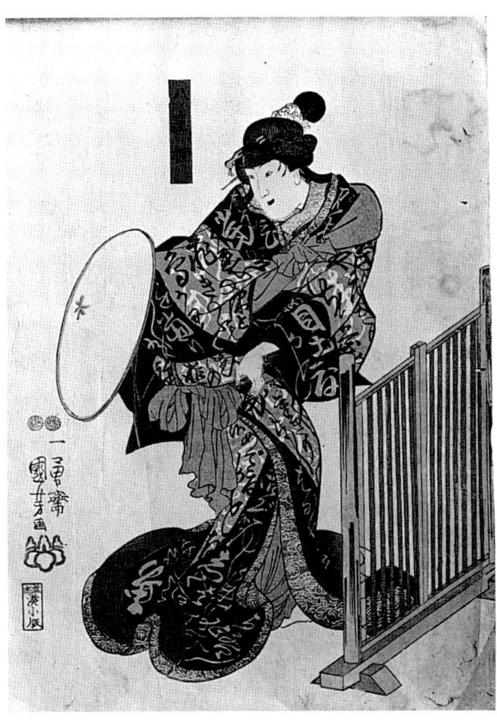

100. Utagawa Kuniyoshi, Japanese woodblock print, Private collection. Former collection of Maurice Denis.

101. Pierre Bonnard, Cover for *Unfortunate Adèle* from *Répertoire des Pantins*, 1898, Lithograph, 12¹³⁄₁₆ × 9¹³⁄₁₆ in. (32.6 × 24.9 cm), Virginia and Ira Jackson Collection. Partial and Promised Gift to the National Gallery of Art, Washington.

102. Pierre Bonnard, Cover for *From the Land of Touraine* from *Répertoire des Pantins*, 1898, Lithograph, 12¹³⁄₁₆ × 19¹³⁄₁₆ in. (32.6 × 24.9 cm), Virginia and Ira Jackson Collection. Partial and Promised Gift to the National Gallery of Art, Washington.

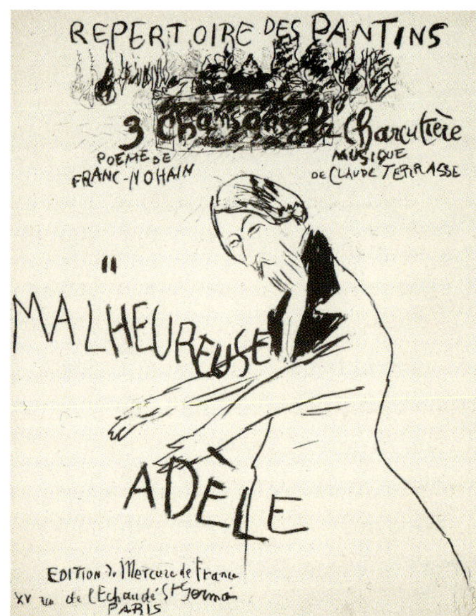

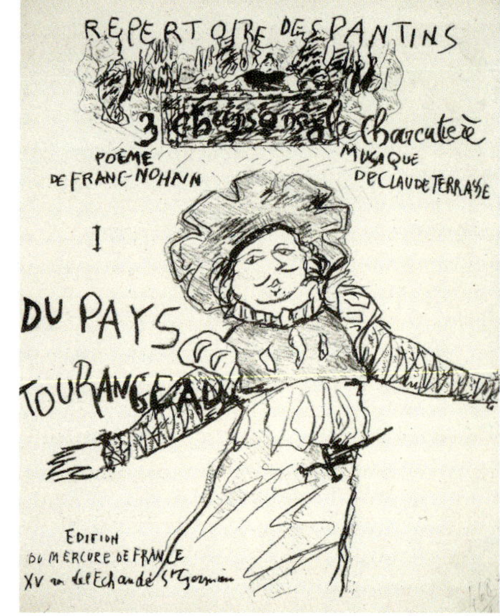

essence of a scene or motif with just a few eloquent lines. Bonnard, especially, was likely to have taken a keen interest in the exaggerated poses of caricature and to have found inspiration in the levity and casual ease with which this "low art" addressed the themes of everyday modern life. Yet however great the similarity may seem at first glance, on closer inspection we find that Bonnard actually goes considerably further than the illustrations in the popular press, leaving aside the anecdotal aspect that tended, for the most part, to prevail in popular prints.[14] What distinguishes Bonnard's distortions and exaggerations from the art of caricature—including the work of Honoré Daumier—is the fact that they are not rooted in conventional European tradition but based instead on the entirely different and therefore unfamiliar rhythms of movement in East Asian art. Bonnard's figure in motion reflects a shift in perception that corresponds to the speed of urban life and captures a sense of the modern world in a fresh way.

Just how well this fitted in with the spirit of the times is evident when one considers the forms of entertainment that were popular in Paris at that time. Shadow theater, *pantomime anglaise*, and puppet theater all tended to feature similar distortions, reflecting a new feeling for life and a new physical awareness. According to William Rubin, "These distortions are the consequence of a whole new attitude towards the human body characteristic of the last decades of the [nineteenth] century," beginning with the art of Edgar Degas. The concept of physical integrity that had held sway since the Renaissance was seriously undermined. Now the human body was twisted into unnatural and exaggerated poses, in ungainly and animal-like movements.[15]

The Nabis were interested not only in shadow theater and pantomime but

also, most notably, in puppet theater. At the studio of Paul Ranson, the famous
"temple" where the Nabis met each week, there was a little theater that could be
used at any time for an impromptu puppet show. Ranson had invented a number of figures for it, including the avaricious Abbé Prout. Bonnard was also
involved when his brother-in-law, the musician Claude Terrasse, founded the
Théâtre des Pantins together with Alfred Jarry and Franc-Nohain in 1898, in which
the actors were marionettes. Jarry and Bonnard made the marionettes and designed
the programs. For the lithographed cover pages of the *Répertoire des Pantins* album
featuring poems by Franc-Nohain set to music by Terrasse, Bonnard captured the
jerky, fragmented movements of the marionettes, freed from gravity and directed
from above by wires or strings (figs. 101, 102, plates 39, 40). In his famous 1810 essay
Über das Marionettentheater, Heinrich von Kleist had described the weightlessness
of marionettes which, being unaware of the inertia of matter, are able to execute
movements that would be impossible for a human being.[16] Bonnard's unstable,
floating figures in motion, apparently independent of all conventional laws of proportion or movement, are ultimately forms of expression that convey a new feeling
for life, in which the sensitivities of what Schopenhauer described as the "destabilised world" of the fin de siècle became palpable. Schopenhauer spoke of a world
in which "no stability of any kind, nor any state of permanence is possible, for all is
caught in a restless whirl and change, all is rushing, flying, balancing on the rope by
means of constant strides and movement."[17]

The Fragmented Image

Many of Bonnard's pictures, especially the city scenes on which he focused
between 1894 and 1900, concentrate on portraying details excerpted from a larger whole. Degas and the impressionists, who had also been inspired by the
Japanese woodblock print, sought to capture the fleeting and arbitrary moment
by means of overlap in much the same manner as photography. Whereas Degas
was interested in the carefully chosen, unusual detail, Bonnard's compositions
are to be regarded more in the sense of the East Asian approach in which the
rendering of apparently coincidental and fragmentary aspects is indicative of the
wider context (fig. 103). His figures cropped by the edge of the picture—passersby, horses, coaches, and wheels—represent the irregular ebb and flow of city life
that cannot be rendered in its entirety. Bonnard succeeds in making this tangible by creating figures that are neither clearly outlined nor perfectly completed,
but merely sketchily unfinished forms linked to the other elements of the picture
by a shared movement (as in the enigmatic *Montmartre in the Rain* (plate 37)
and *The Square at Evening* (plate 31) in the 1899 lithographic cycle *Some Scenes
of Parisian Life).* It is this fragmentary and interwoven approach that makes so
many of Bonnard's works rather difficult to read. He sought not to achieve a
precise rendering, but to make reality tangible by suggestion rather than by

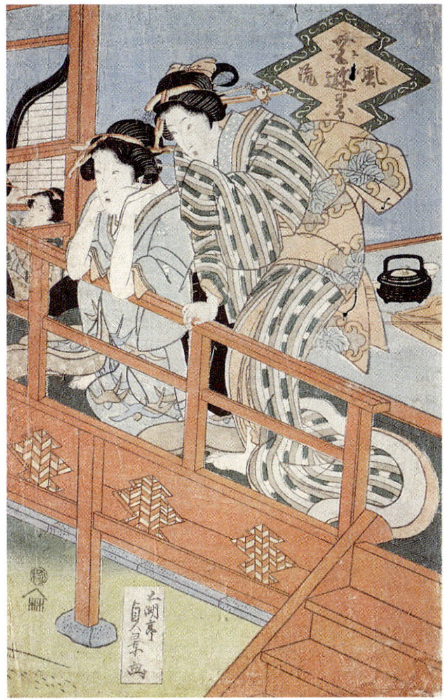

103. Sadakage
Gotokei, ca.
1820–1830, Japanese
woodblock print,
Private collection.
Former collection of
Maurice Denis.

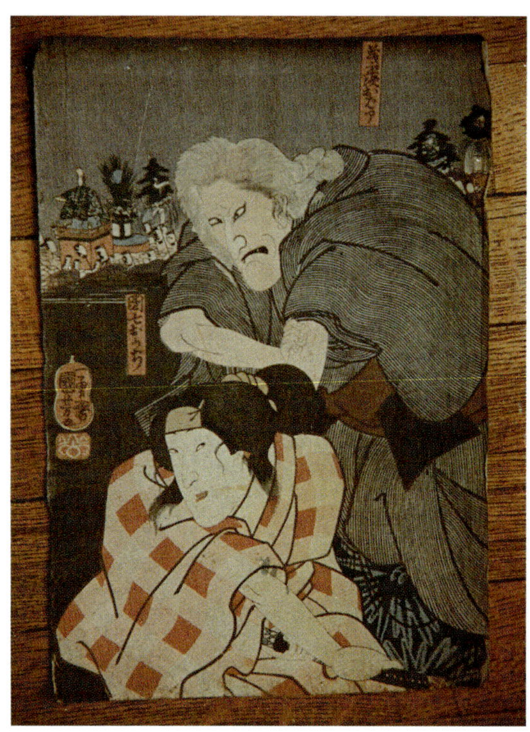

104. Utagawa
Kuniyoshi,
Theatre Scene,
ca. 1840, Japanese
woodblock print,
Private collection.
Former collection of
Maurice Denis.

explicit description, creating evocative compositions that give the viewer's imagination free rein. The excerpt-like aspect of his street scenes expresses the fact that the whole can be perceived only as a fragment. The experience of the fragmentation of reality has been described by scholars such as David Frisby as the definitive experience of modernism.[18]

A New Handling of Space

In his 1891 painting *Women with Dog* (plate 6) Bonnard achieves a handling of space that is to determine his entire later oeuvre. The main group in the foreground is shown from above and in close-up, resulting in a section so narrow that the three figures (his sister Andrée, his cousin Berthe Schaedlin, and the dog Ravageau) are cropped by the edges of the picture on every side. This view of the group from above enables Bonnard to portray their spatial relationship in the plane although the figures themselves are completely flat and the checked dress whose pattern does not follow the movement of the wearer looks like a chessboard. Yet the contour line is drawn in such a way that it takes into account the perspectival foreshortening, thereby clearly indicating the crouching position and, by extension, the spatial situation.

The view from above was employed as a means of handling space in medieval art, and the Nabis had closely studied the works of artists active in the age before the advent of one-point perspective. Yet the unusually steep angle in connection with extreme close-up and surprising cropping stems from Bonnard's interest in East Asian art. In Japanese painting, a steep view from above was common practice in scrolls as early as the twelfth century. In an art unaware of European one-point perspective, this device was applied, together with a kind of parallel perspective, as a means of portraying space while at the same time permitting a decorative compositional structuring of the picture plane. Horizontal scrolls showing lyrical courtly scenes frequently combined this angle with close-up. It is a perspective that was primarily adopted from Japanese woodcuts. The close-up was shown predominantly in the half-figures and heads. Bonnard himself had bust portrayals of actors in his own collection. There is a comparable woodblock print by Utagawa Kuniyoshi, which Bonnard must surely have known, since it belonged to his friend Denis (fig. 104). The group of figures is drawn forward in a similar way in Bonnard's work and cropped by the edge of the picture, and the close-up is also combined with a view from above, emphasizing the spatial relationship of the two protagonists. Moreover, Bonnard could build on the compositional achievements of his predecessors, especially Degas, Claude Monet, Paul Cézanne, Gauguin, and Vincent van Gogh, who had begun to call into question the perspectival rules that had prevailed since the Renaissance. Since they, too, had been inspired by Japanese woodcuts, direct and indirect influences converged in the work of Bonnard.

In the picture *Women with Dog* all suggestion of perspective is avoided. Only the stark discrepancies in size indicate the distance between the groups of figures in the foreground and background. What is surprising in Bonnard's approach is the fact that the figures in the background, who appear as onlookers, are seen from an entirely different angle, slightly from below. In other words, the picture has several points of view. As the eye leaps from one object to another there is an impression of space between the figures. The notion of showing things from an angle that does not focus on the single vanishing point cultivated by the system of one-point perspective was derived from East Asian art. Chinese and Japanese *kakemono* landscapes are intended to be read vertically rather than toward the background, and they do not possess a consistently uniform spatial construction, but instead have several focal points, with views from below, from above, and from the front, united in one and the same painting (fig. 105). They express a visual concept entirely different from the one prevailing in Europe. East Asian culture does not expect just one aspect of landscape to be shown from a specific standpoint. Instead, the picture is regarded as a fragment of a greater whole, to be perceived as part of the greater scheme of things, of which the viewer is also a part.[19] The reason why the East Asian handling of space had such an impact on the European aesthetic is because its arrival in the Western world coincided with an emergent desire to abandon the fixed standpoint of scientific perspective. According to Jean Gebser, "Seeing or thinking perspectivally means: seeing and thinking in terms of fixed space."[20] Perspective fixes the viewer as well as that which is viewed. The negative outcome of this is that it places the individual in a fragmentary sector, so that he is able to see and grasp only that sector, which is but one small piece of the greater whole, ignoring all the other 'sectors' alongside, above or even behind him.

For artists seeking to portray the essential traits of things and the emotions triggered by them rather than their outward appearance, conventional perspective with its illusionistic aspect remained a vehicle that merely reiterated the arbitrary appearance of things and distracted from their essence. The desire to see beyond things and to abandon the standpoint of the distant observer promoted a break from one-point perspective and corporeal plasticity. Bonnard and his contemporaries had every opportunity of familiarizing themselves with the potential ways of seeing and portraying contained not only in Japanese woodblock prints but also in the hanging scrolls and horizontal scrolls that had been presented to the wider public as early as 1883 by Louis Gonse. His 1883 book *L'Art japonais* and the publication of Siegfried Bing's *Le Japon artistique* series in 1888–1891, both of which contained many illustrations of works by early Japanese masters, made these art forms even more widely known.

In the 1890s Bonnard continued to develop the new perspective. This is particularly evident in such works as *Montmartre in the Rain* or *Rue Tholozé* of

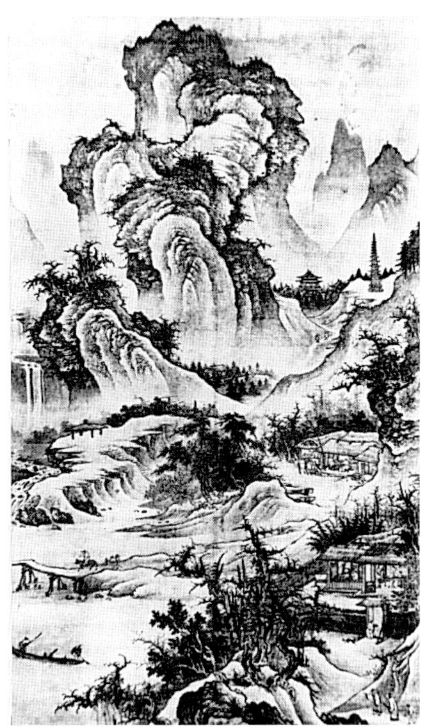

105. Style of Kuo Hsi, *Writers in their Mountain Retreats*, Possibly Ming Period, Taichung (Formosa) Palace Collection. Goepper, Roger. *Vom Wesen Chinesischer Malerei*. Munich: Prestel, 1962, cat. 39.

106. Andō Hiroshige (1797–1858), *Kazusa Kasamoru Hanatsukuri Kannon (The Temple of Kasamoru Hanatsukuri in the Kazusa Region)*, From the Series *Shokoku Meisho Hyakkei*, Japanese woodblock print, Private collection. Former collection of Pierre Bonnard.

about 1897 (plate 37), which shows the view from Bonnard's studio window, looking to the houses opposite and to the firewall, slanting downward toward the rooftops just below the window, and even more steeply down onto the rain-soaked street on the right, whose vibrant to-and-fro is set at a distance by means of the bird's-eye perspective. These shifting viewpoints of the painting create a sense of space that has little in common with conventional perspective. In some paintings, the new visual space is given a distinctive quality by blurring the position of the figures. This compositional approach can be found throughout Bonnard's entire oeuvre. In his early work, the position of the figure is rarely defined with precision. Either it is cropped by the edge of the picture as in *Jeune Femme avec son chien* (Dauberville 95), or it blends imperceptibly into the empty or unbounded background as in *Femmes au jardin* (Dauberville 01716), *Le Peignoir* (Dauberville 14), and the 1899 *Nannies' Promenade, Frieze of Carriages* screen (plate 24). The position can also be concealed by foreground bushes, as in *Partie de croquet* (Dauberville 38). In many pictures, the stance itself is unstable, creating a floating sense of space, which, for Bonnard, is another means of portraying a space independent of conventional one-point perspective. This recalls the East Asian handling of space in which figures and objects are ordered "without a point fixed precisely to the floor level or another location" and in which "all things, including the space itself, seem to glide and hover"[21] (fig. 106).

The Late Work

The compositional devices that Bonnard developed in his Nabis period to evoke spatiality in the plane take on a new significance in his works after 1900, when he combines them with visual elements aimed at opening up a sense of space, such as diagonals, light and shadow, and modeling. Even though Bonnard began to abandon the flat style of his Nabis period toward the end of the 1890s, he continued to strike a balance between perspectival depth and planarity. Right up to his very late works, he used different points of view to create a visual space. Together with his distinctive handling of color, his new visual approach created a spatial atmosphere in which things remained bound to the plane. Bonnard's profound reflections on the problems of perception are documented in his statements to his nephew Charles Terrasse in 1927. He saw the portrayal of the masses and objects within a space on a flat surface as a problem of drawing for which there were countless solutions:

> The eye perceives the most distant masses in an almost linear manner without relief, without depth. But the closer objects come toward the eye. The lines at the side flee. And these lines of flight are sometimes straight—at a distance, sometimes curved—close up. The appearance of distance is flat. It is the closer levels that convey the impression of the universe as perceived by the human eye, a universe that is either concave or convex.[22]

Moreover, as Erwin Panofsky writes, the human eye "shows forms projected on a concave plane rather than a flat surface," a fact ignored by scientific perspective and one that ignores the fact "that we do not see with a fixed eye, but with two constantly moving eyes, whereby the visual field takes on a spherical form."[23] This is clearly evident in Bonnard's later landscapes, such as *The Terrace* of 1918 (plate 86). The distant hill with the high horizon line appears entirely flat. The closer things come to the spectator, the steeper the view from above, straight down onto the table in the foreground. In the middle ground, the lines of lush vegetation in the garden form a semicircle that suggests a curved space. The eye of the painter, according to Bonnard, lends objects a human value, in contrast to photography, and reproduces things in the way they are seen by the human eye. "And this view is mobile. And this view is variable."[24]

The same is true of the many late interiors such as *The Red Checkered Tablecloth* or *The Dog's Lunch* 1910 (plate 71) and *The Table* of 1925 (plate 102). The gaze of the viewer runs across the laden table from bottom to top, falling on the closest plate, which appears as a perfect circle. The plates farther away are seen from a flattened viewpoint and are therefore presented as ovals. Then we look frontally at Marthe, who is seated at the table. Bonnard, in speaking of a "vision mobile et variable" evokes the very quintessence of the revolutionary concept of space by which he paved the way for the artistic solutions of the twentieth century.

Many Japanese-inspired compositional devices can be found throughout Bonnard's entire oeuvre. They are, however, modified by new elements. New pictorial relationships are created, for example, by the handling of color, which takes on an increasingly important role beginning in 1900 and gains increasing luminosity under the impressionism of Monet, Pierre-Auguste Renoir, and Degas. One of the compositional devices that Bonnard uses throughout his oeuvre, heightening to an extreme in his late work, is the eccentricity of his figures and their overlaps. Even before 1900, the figures in his asymmetrical compositions are frequently shifted well off-center and starkly overlapped or cropped by the edge of the picture. Even the head of the figure may be cropped by the upper edge of the picture (Dauberville 217, 496). As a rule, however, the human figure remains the dominant object in the picture. It is here that the viewer's interest is concentrated. In his later work, by contrast, the human figures are often pushed so far toward the edge of the picture that they become secondary, as in *The Breakfast Room* of about 1930–1931 (plate 118).

Occasionally, only a human torso juts into the picture, as in the 1925 *Nude in the Bath* (fig. 107). The right-hand side of the picture is occupied by a cropped bathtub in which only the legs of the nude figure can be seen at a steep angle from above. On the left-hand side of the picture, a "headless" figure is stepping into the picture. Similar torsos can be found in the "mirror" pictures that show only details of the room and figures as seen in a mirror parallel to the picture

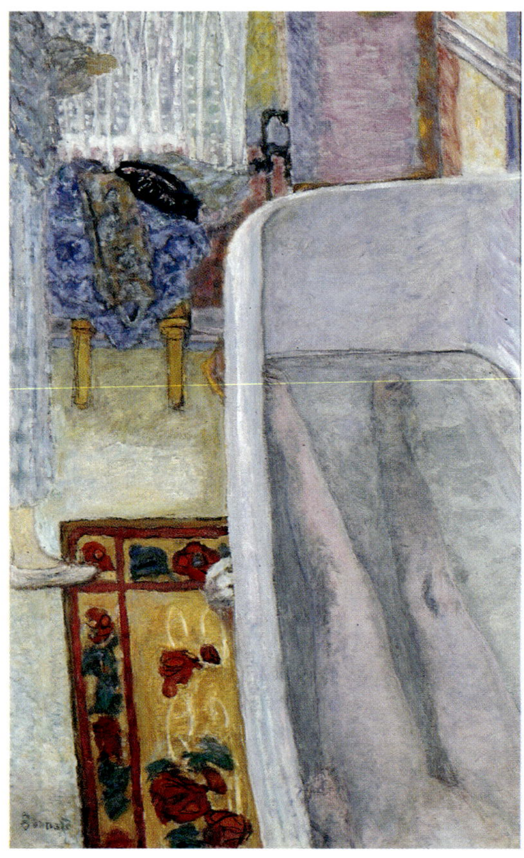

107. Pierre Bonnard,
Nude in the Bath,
1925, Oil on canvas,
40½ × 25¼ in.
(103 × 64 cm),
Private collection.

plane (see *The Dressing Table*, 1908, plate 66). The neglect of the human figure goes so far in some of his late works that only half a face or an arm appears in some corner and is recognizable only after lengthy perusal. For example, in *The Open Window* of 1921 (plate 93) only the head of the female figure on the lower right in a deck chair can be seen, while Bonnard's main interest focuses on the contrast between the clearly structured interior in warm orange tones and the landscape seen through the open window in cool shades of blue, green, and violet. The head of Marthe in *Studio with Mimosas* of 1939–1946 (plate 131) is even more starkly cropped; in the lower left-hand corner of the picture the head almost disappears against the pink wall panel, while the radiantly sunny yellow of the mimosas in the garden bursts into the studio through the broad window, imbuing it with a mysterious glow.

This compositional approach is to be considered in the light of Bonnard's gradual and increasing shift away from the mimesis of nature toward the transfiguration of reality in an ever richer and more luminous tapestry of color. His late paintings blossom into freely executed color compositions that follow no law but their own. By this time, Bonnard is no longer interested in figuration, which goes some way toward explaining the difficulty involved in reading many of his works, and the individuality of his figures becomes secondary to their function as carriers of color. In an art that has yet to make the decisive step to abstraction, the depersonalization and devaluation of the object is pushed to the utmost. The intricately woven tapestry of color with its warp and weft of figures and objects draws proximity and distance together in a vibrant fabric. This lends the space a floating aspect, which is a continuation, albeit in another form, of the floating world inspired by East Asian art in his early works. Bonnard's later work betrays something of what Hans Jantzen once described as a fin-de-siècle tendency "to substitute color for all non-color means of portrayal."[25] Bonnard's own statement on Japanese woodblock prints springs to mind: "It was through the contact with these popular images that I realized that color could express anything, as it does here, with no need for relief or modeling. It seemed to me that it was possible to translate light, forms, and character using nothing but color, without recourse to values."[26]

From the vantage point of his later work, it becomes easier to understand how the inspiration of East Asian art could have been so intense and so long-lasting. Bonnard saw in it the achievement of something that seemed to him to embody the essence of all painting. In his relatively rare statements on art, he is remarkably consistent in his insistence that the artist should never allow the appearance of the object to distract him from his original idea to the extent that he merely paints coincidences that no longer have anything in common with his initial inspiration. "The presence of the object, of the motif, is extremely distracting for the painter at the moment of painting. Since the point of departure is an idea, the presence of the object invariably subjects the artist to the risk of being so influenced by the immediate view that he loses sight of the original idea. . . . It is through seduction or the initial idea that the painter achieves the universal."[27]

East Asian artists, too, portrayed the essence of things rather than their arbitrary appearance. This is described as follows by Dietrich Seckel:

> Things are grasped from within, not from the outer standpoint of the subject, which is invariably one-sided and therefore relative. . . . This explains the lack of perspective, the floating and shifting viewpoint, the independence from any claim to truth and probability of an illusionistic realism that all too easily hinders artistic freedom, but also the absence of all claims for an unrealistic and spiritually conceived ideal. It also explains the rejection of a coolly detached objectivity and the strong inclusion of the spectator and his seeing, involved activity in the independent sphere of the work of art.[28]

Here it becomes evident that, for Bonnard, the inspirations of East Asian Art did not mean reproducing outward appearances and similarities, but drawing on a wellspring of essential affinities.[29]

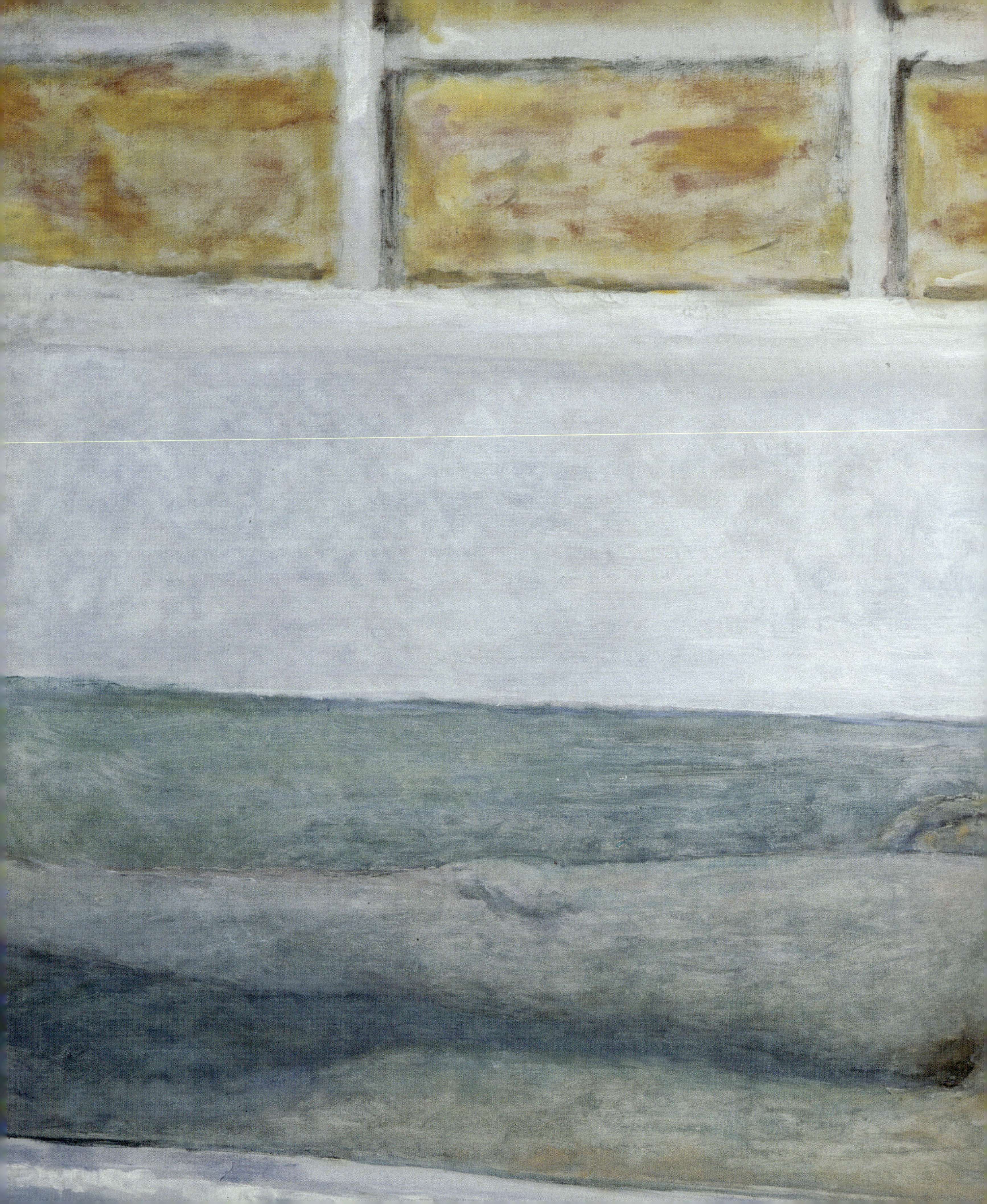

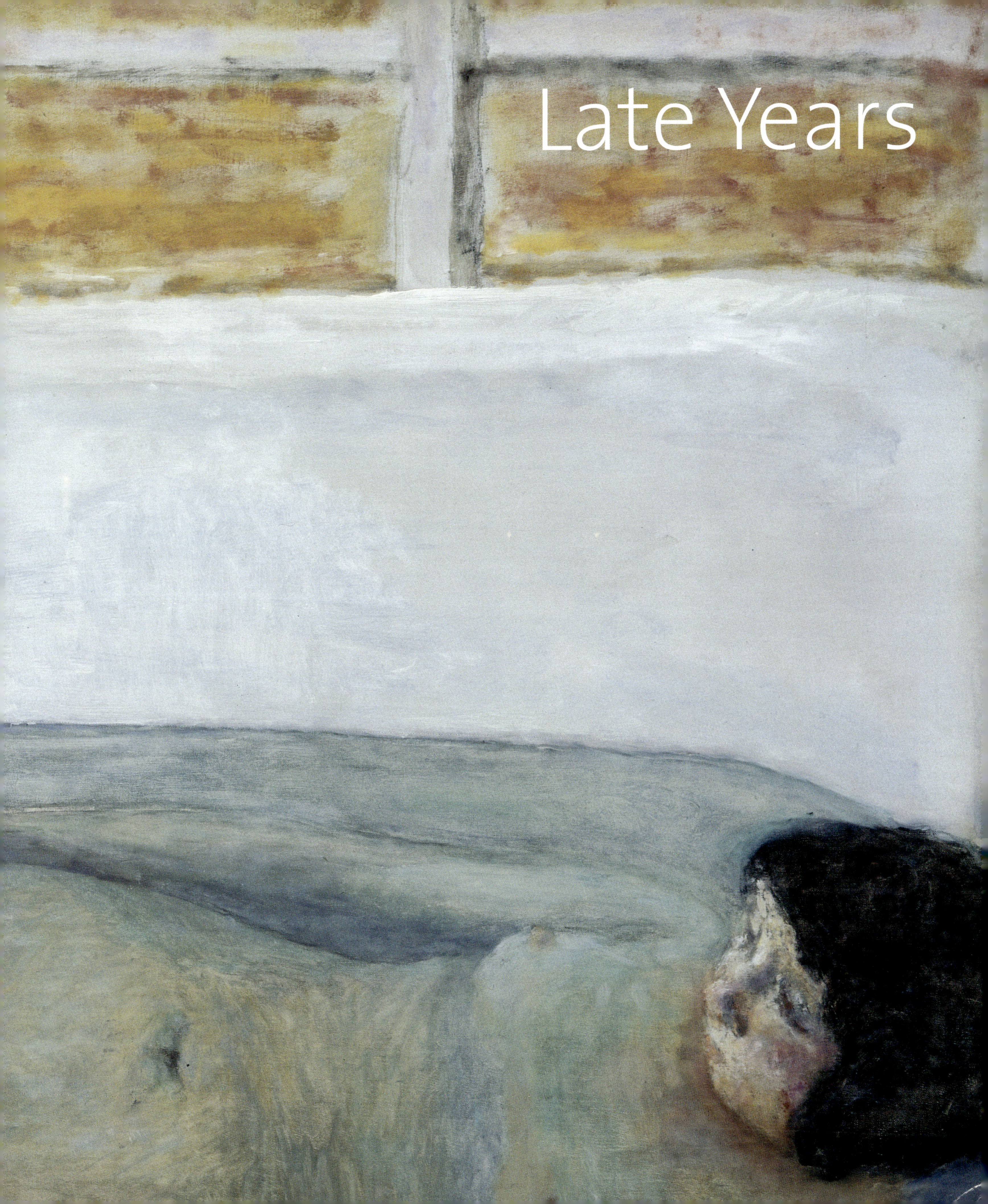
Late Years

Late Years

Previous spread:
The Bath
(detail), 1925, Oil on canvas, 33⅞ × 47¼ in.
(86 × 120.6 cm), Tate. Presented by Lord
Ivor Spencer Churchill through the
Contemporary Art Society, 1930.

Portrait of Ambroise Vollard
ca. 1924, Etching, 17⁵⁄₁₆ × 11⁷⁄₁₆ in. (44 × 29 cm),
Museum of Fine Arts, Boston. George
Peabody Gardner Fund, 1954 54.666.

The Checkered Table Cover
ca. 1925, Oil on canvas, 13¼ × 24 in.
(33.7 × 60.7 cm), Liza Phillips.

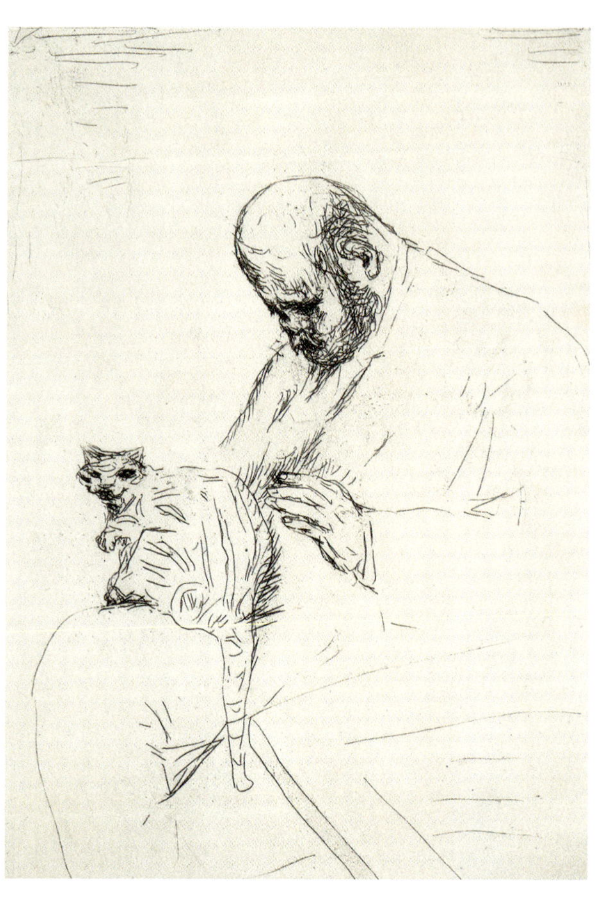

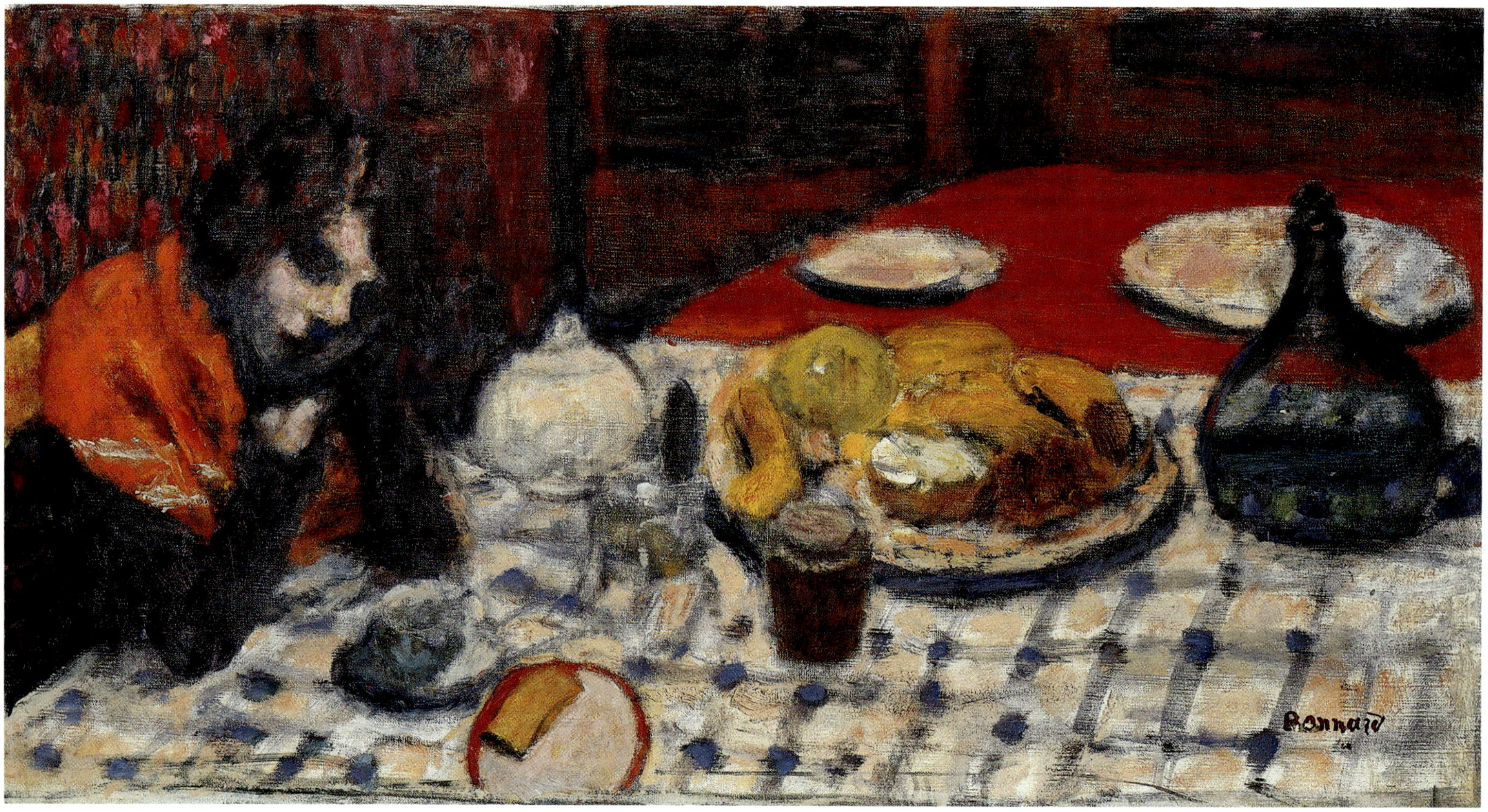

96

Woman with Dog
1922, Oil on canvas, 27¼ × 15½ in.
(69.2 × 39.3 cm), The Phillips Collection,
Washington, D.C.

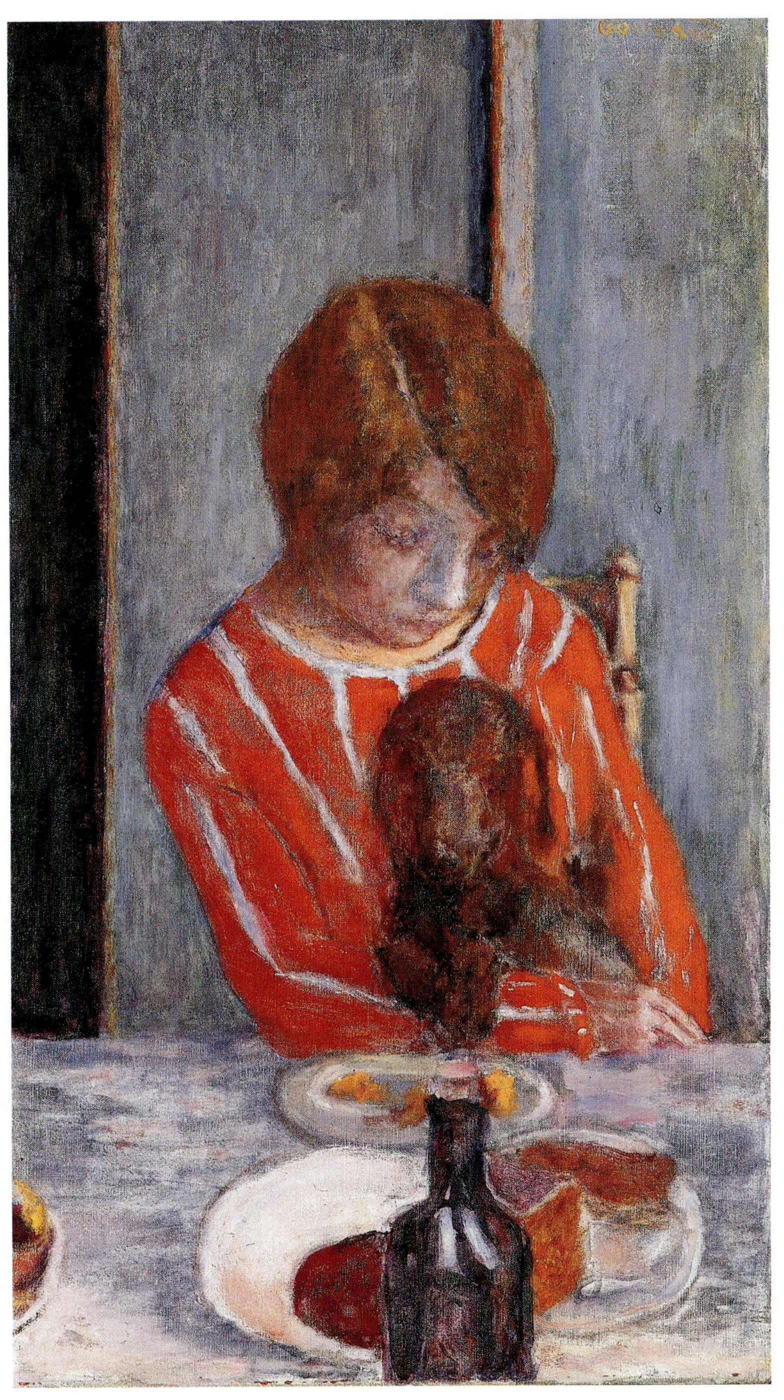

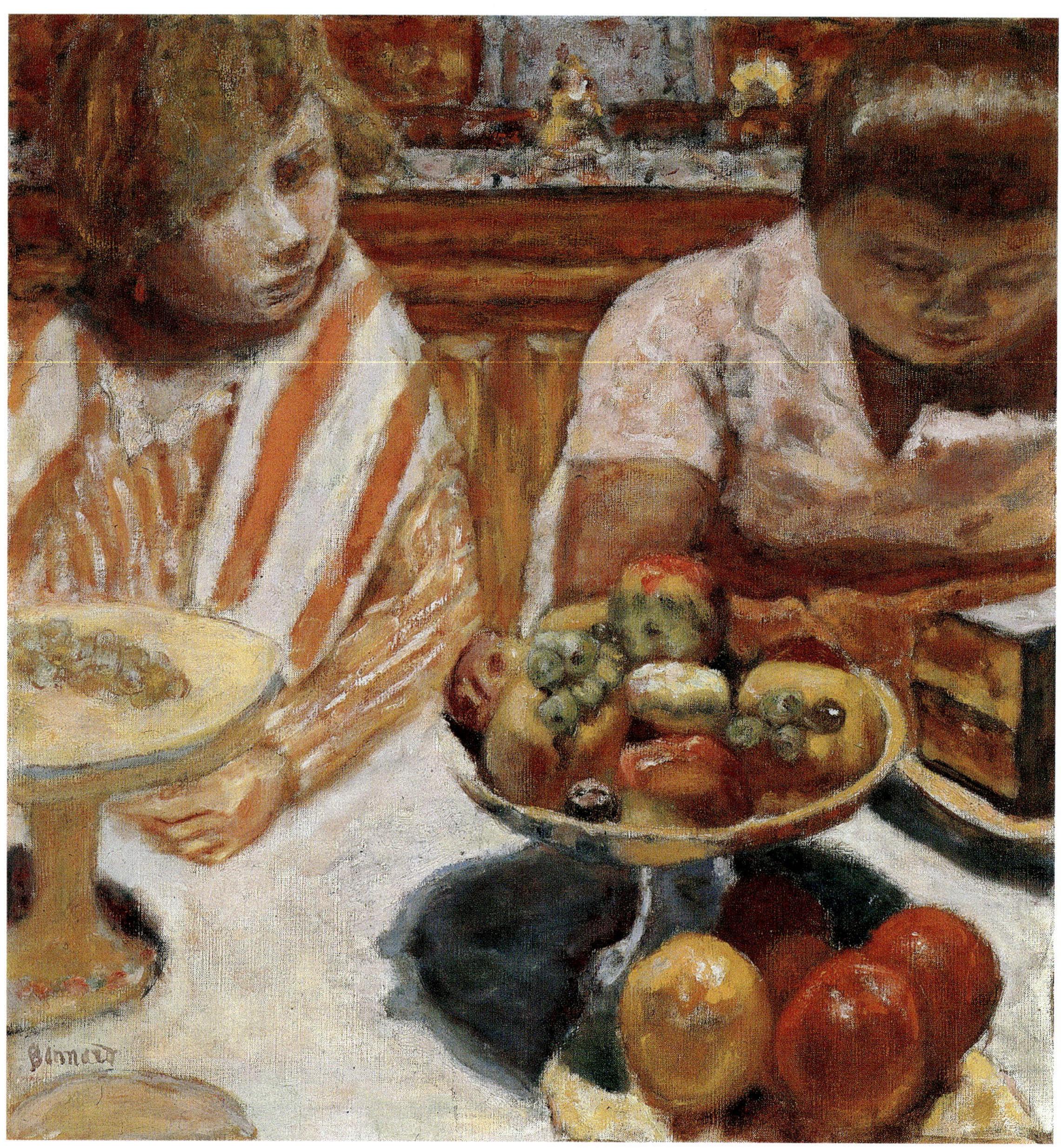

97

Reflecting on the Day
1924, Oil on canvas, 21¼ × 19¹¹⁄₁₆ in.
(54 × 50 cm), Private collection; Courtesy
Guggenheim, Asher Associates, Inc., New
York.

Opposite page: **Reflecting on the Day** (detail).

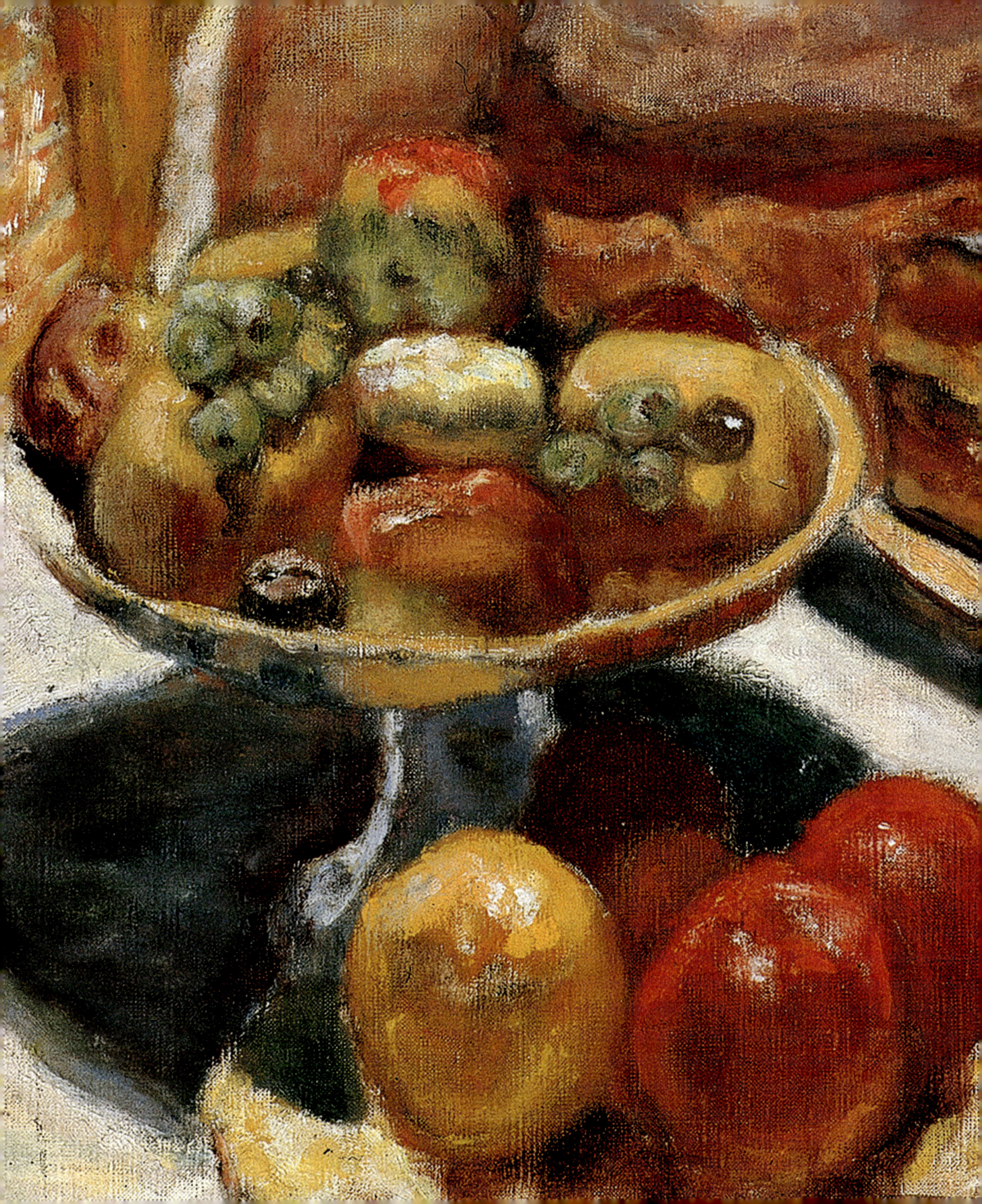

The Menu

ca. 1924–1925, Lithograph, 19½ × 12¹¹⁄₁₆ in. (49.5 × 32.2 cm), The Metropolitan Museum of Art, The Elisha Whittelsey Collection, The Elisha Whittelsey Fund, 1988 (1988.1017.2).

The Letter

ca. 1925, Lithograph, 12⅝ × 19⅜ in. (32.1 × 49.2 cm), Prints and Photographs Division, Library of Congress, Washington, D.C., Reproduction numbers: LC-USZC4-10008, LC-USZ62-130233.

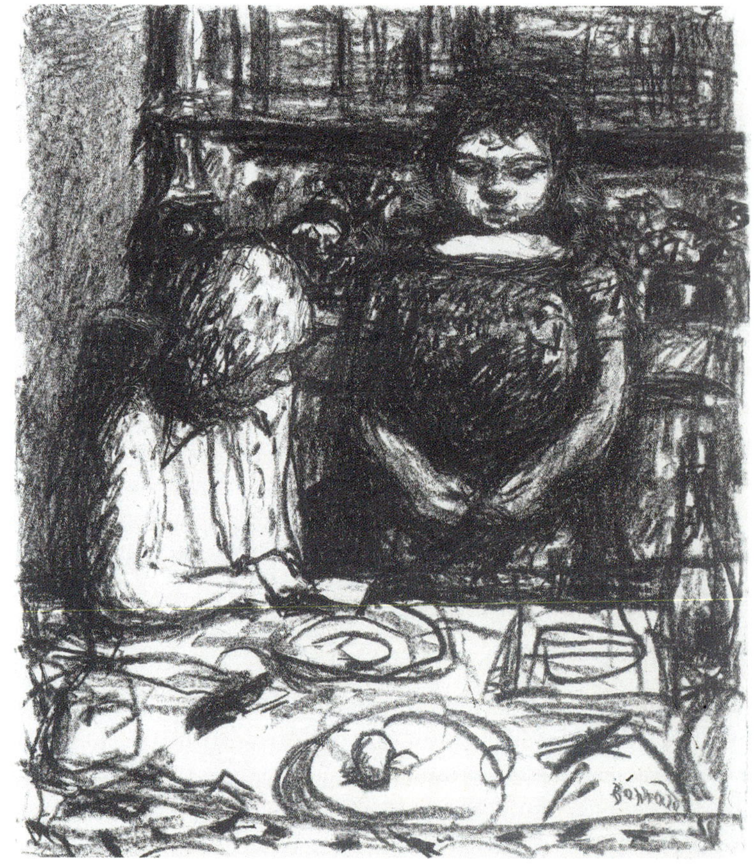

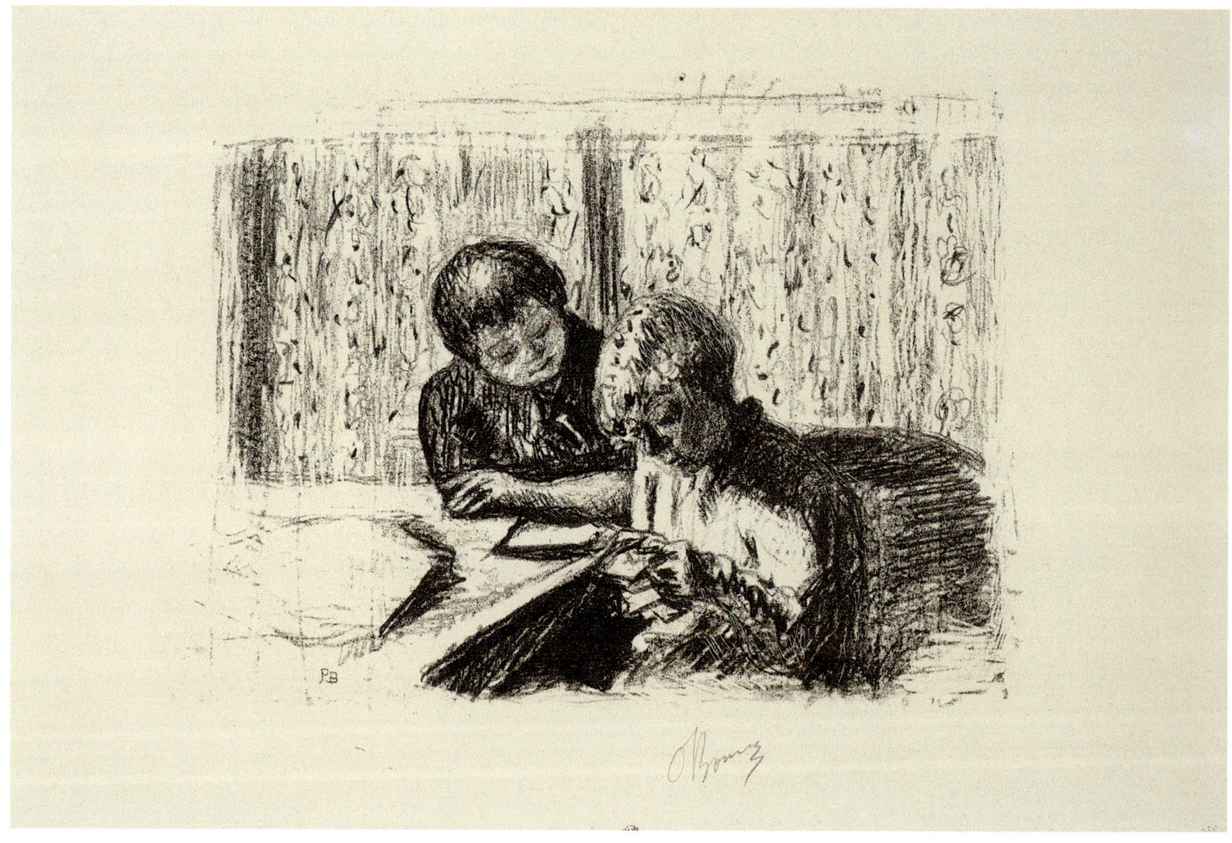

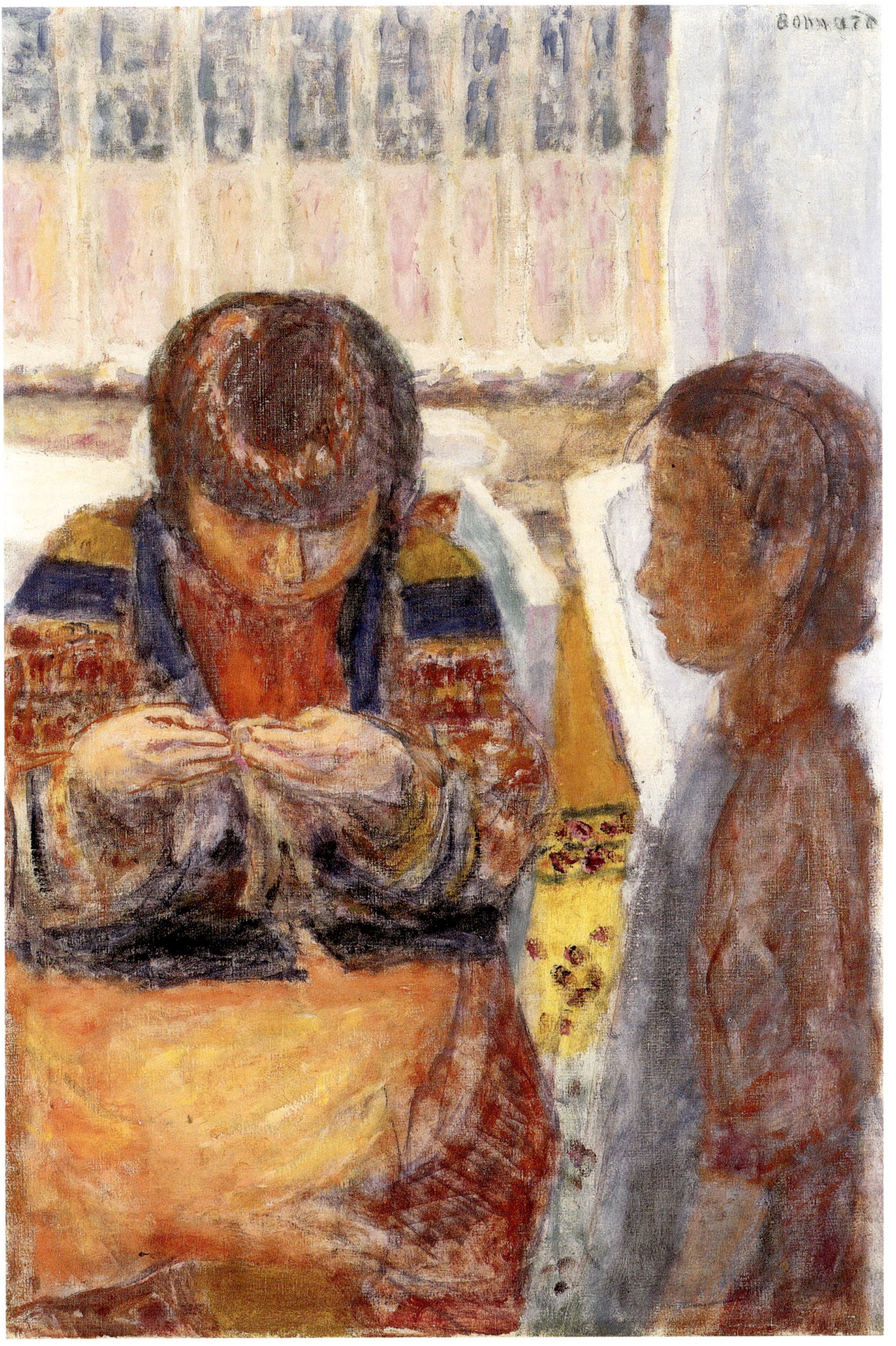

The Lesson
1926, Oil on canvas, 30 × 20 in. (76 × 51 cm),
The Phillips Collection, Washington, D.C.

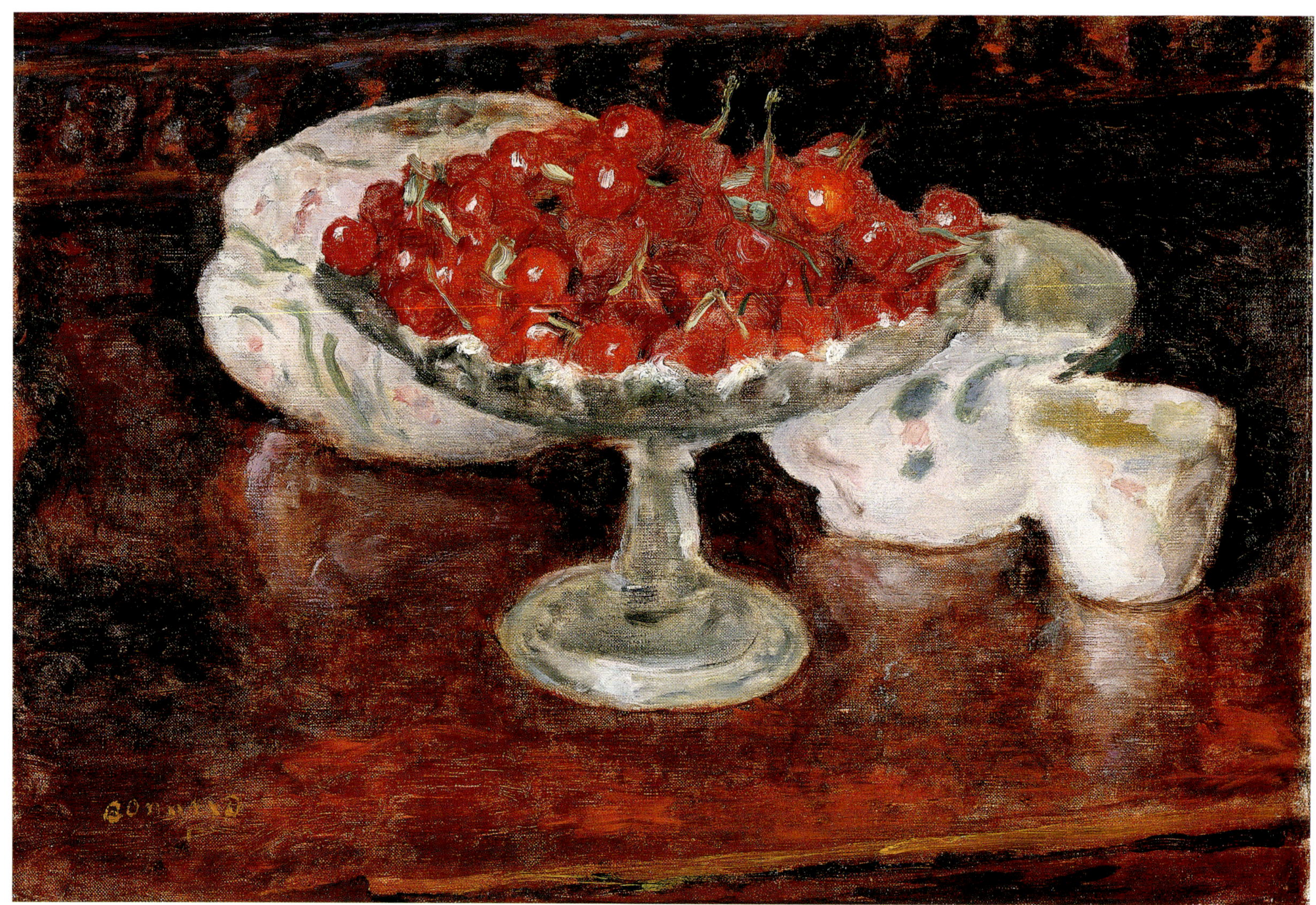

101

Bowl of Cherries
1920, Oil on canvas, 11⅞ × 16½ in.
(30.2 × 41.9 cm), The Phillips Collection,
Washington, D.C.

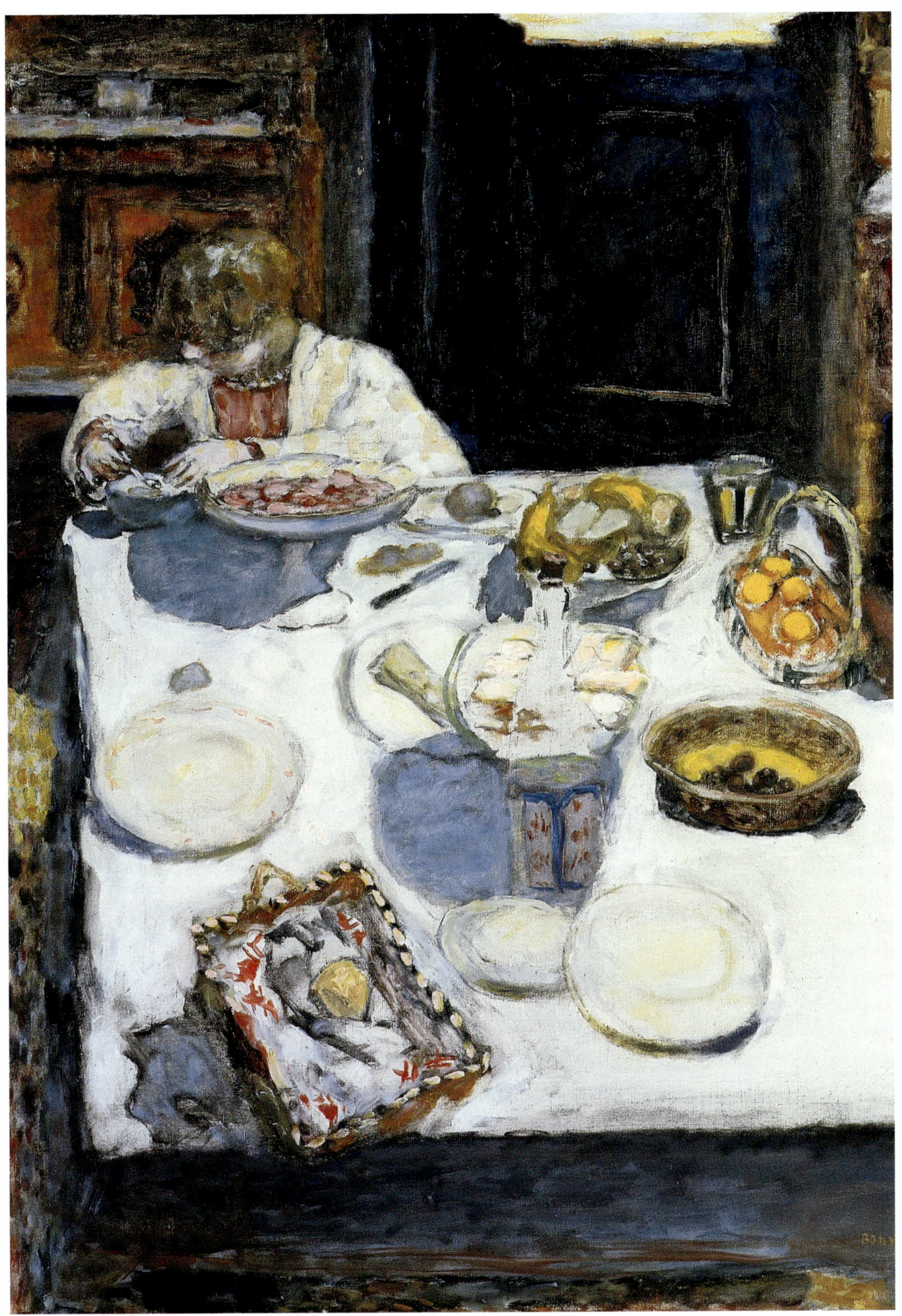

102

The Table
1925, Oil on canvas, 40⅝ × 29¼ in.
(102.9 × 74.3 cm), Tate. Presented by the
Courtauld Fund Trustees, 1926.

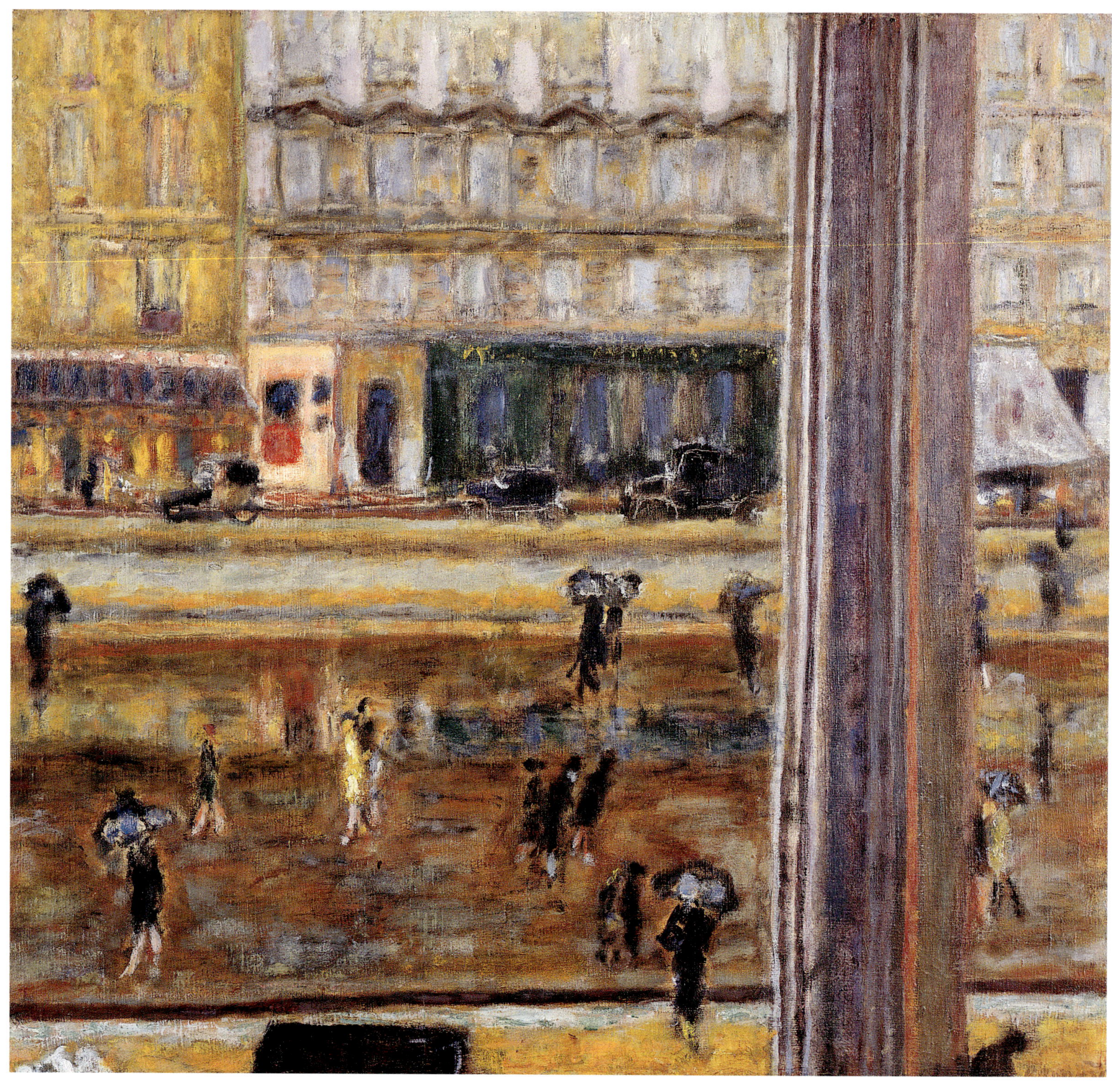

103

Boulevard des Batignolles
1926, Oil on canvas, 24¾ × 25⅝ in.
(62.9 × 65.1 cm), Private collection,
Washington, D.C.

104

Evening by the Lamp
1921, Oil on canvas, 28¾ × 35¹⁄₁₆ in. (73 × 89 cm),
Private collection; Paris, Musée d'Orsay, Gift
with Reserved Use, 2000.

105

Place Clichy
1922, Lithograph printed in five colors,
22⁷⁄₁₆ × 29½ in. (57 × 75 cm), Museum of Fine
Arts, Boston. Bequest of W. G. Russell Allen,
1960 60.70.

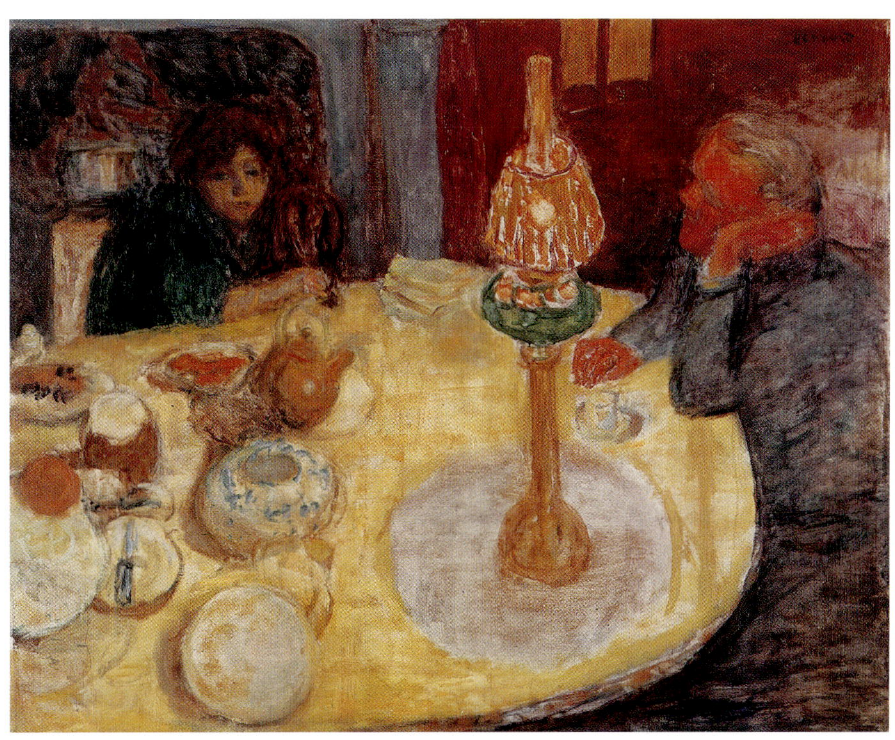

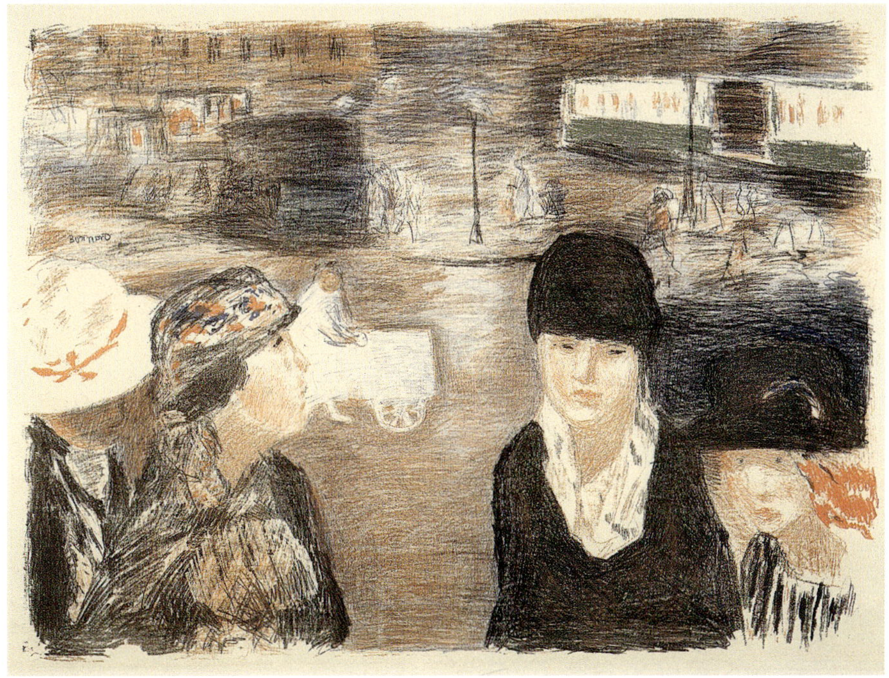

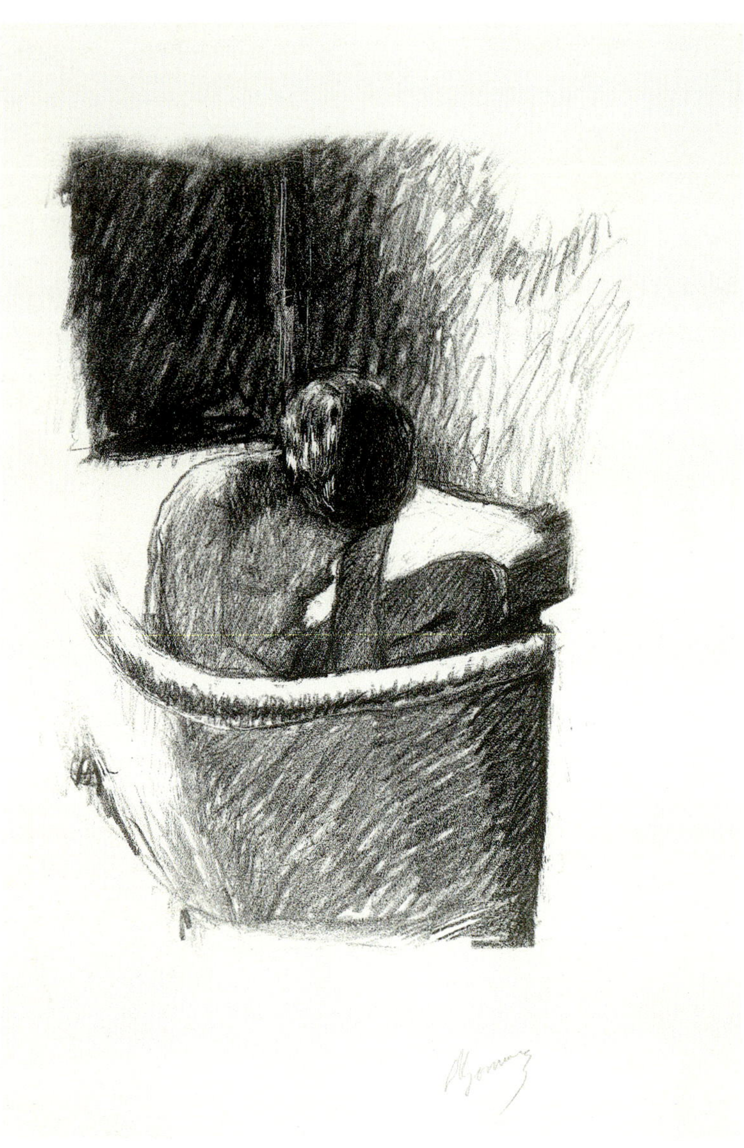 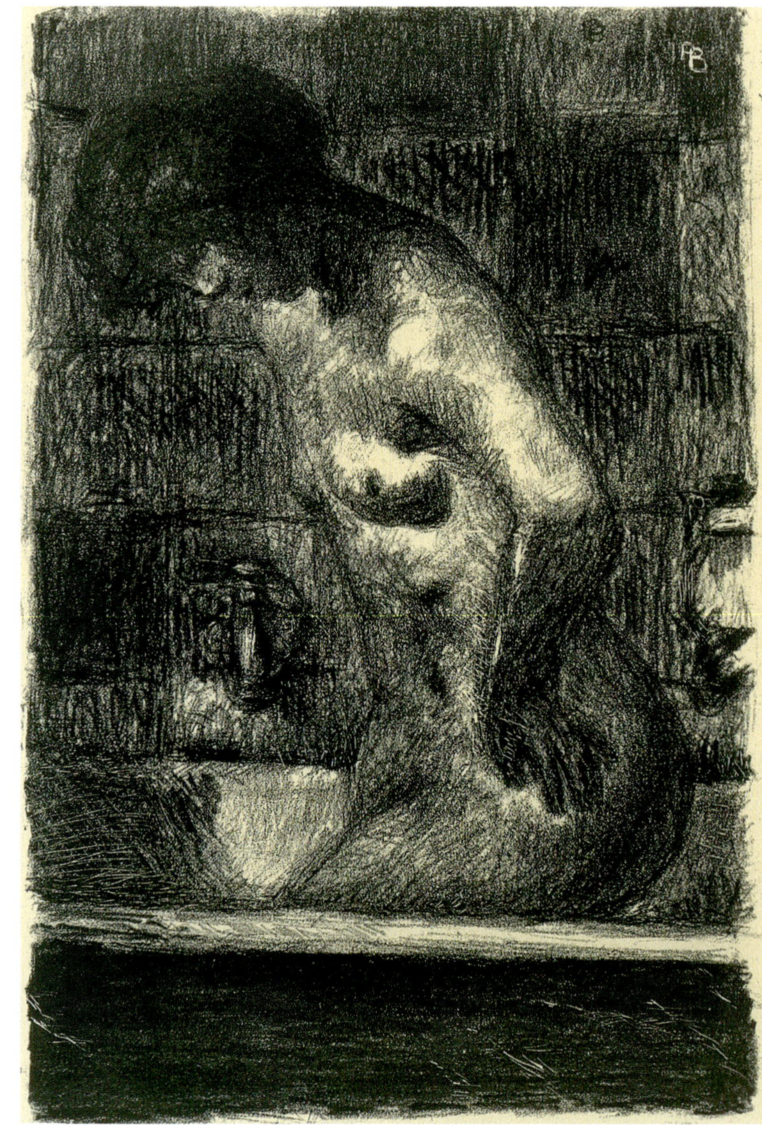

106

The Bath
ca. 1925, Lithograph, 19½ × 12¾ in.
(49.5 × 32.4 cm), Prints and Photographs
Division, Library of Congress, Washington,
D.C., Reproduction numbers: LC-USZC4-
10006, LC-USZ62-130234.

107

Woman Standing in Her Bathtub
1925, Lithograph on heavy cream wove
paper, 18⅝ × 13 in. (47.3 × 32.9 cm), The
Phillips Collection, Washington, D.C.

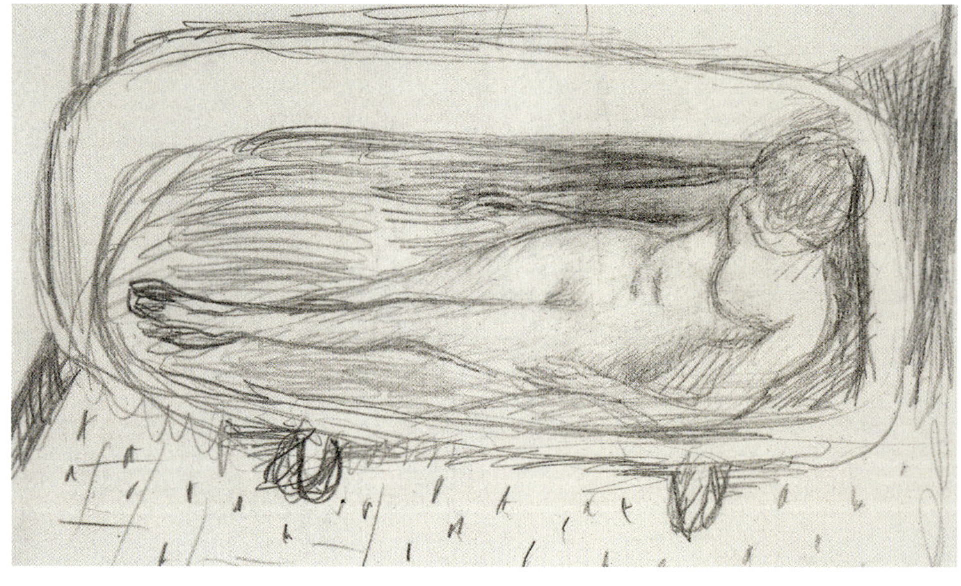

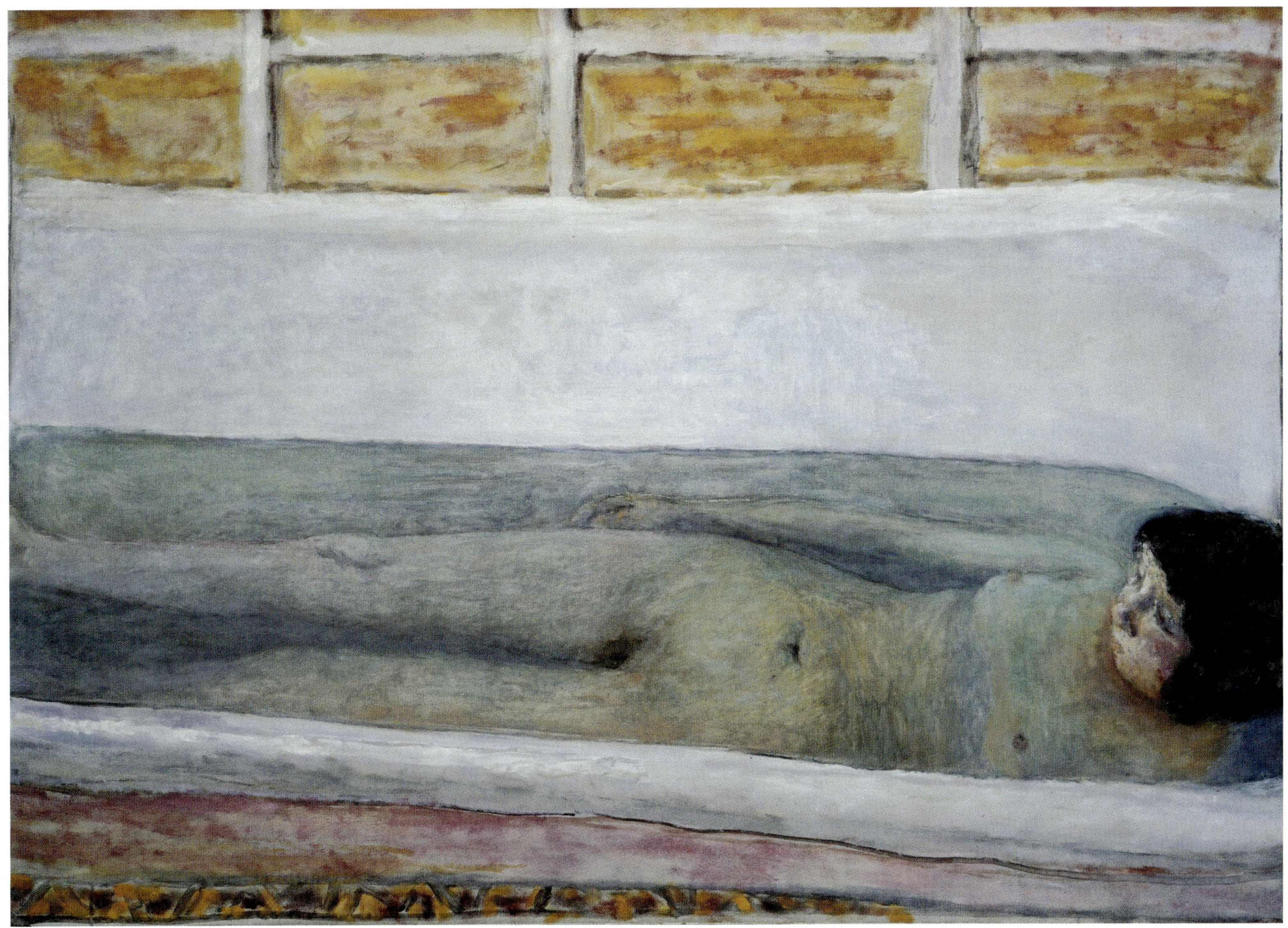

108

Study for "The Bath"
1925, Graphite on paper, Private collection.

109

The Bath
1925, Oil on canvas, 33⅞ × 47¼ in. (86 × 120.6 cm),
Tate. Presented by Lord Ivor Spencer Churchill
through the Contemporary Art Society, 1930.

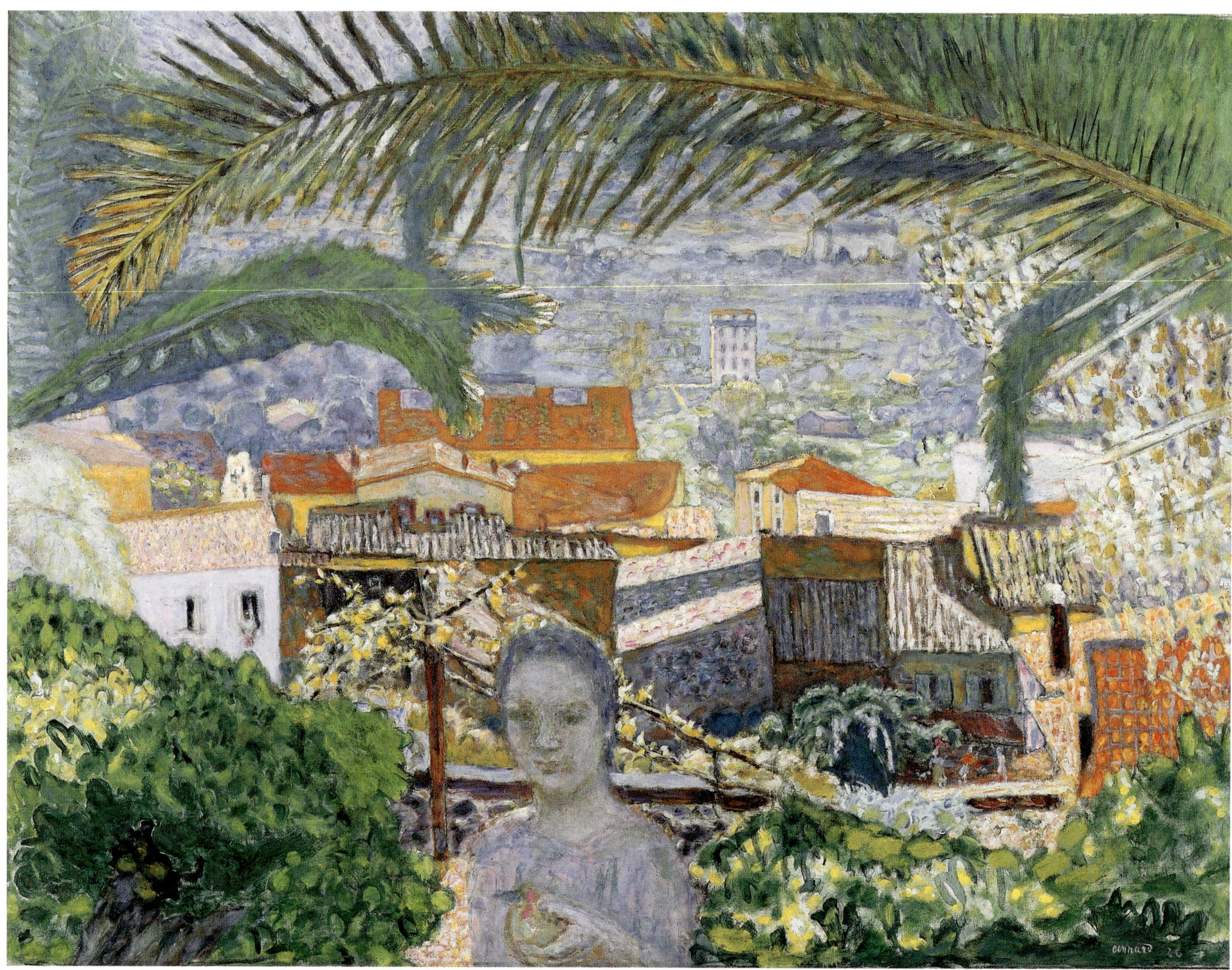

110

The Palm
1926, Oil on canvas, 45 × 57⅞ in. (114.3 × 147 cm),
The Phillips Collection, Washington, D.C.

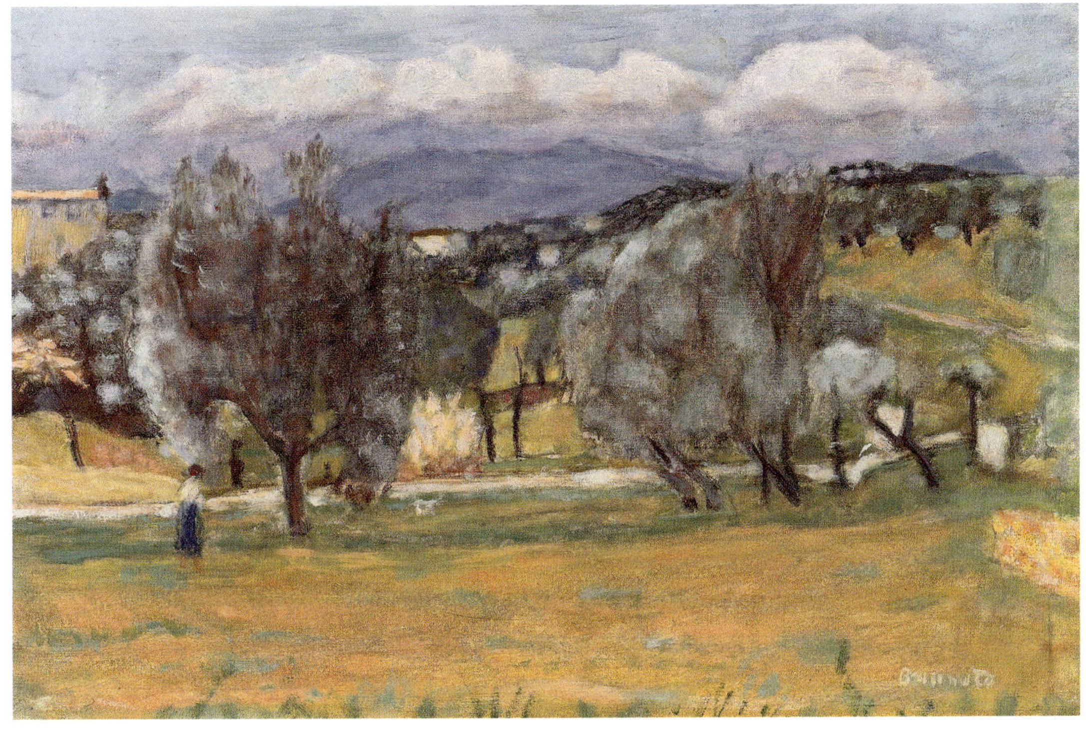

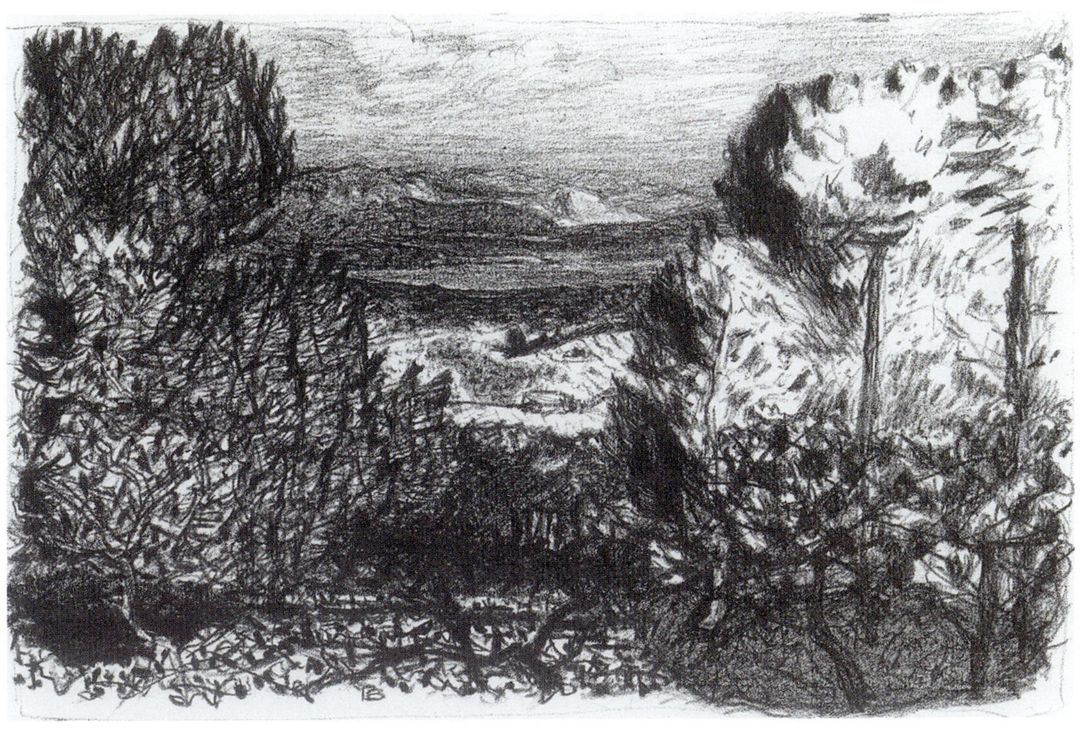

111

Landscape with Mountain
1924, Oil on canvas, 15¾ × 23¼ in. (40 × 59 cm),
The Phillips Collection, Washington, D.C.

112

Last Light
ca. 1927-1928, Lithograph, 12¹¹⁄₁₆ × 18⅛ in.
(32.2 × 46 cm), The Metropolitan Museum of
Art, The Elisha Whittelsey Collection,
The Elisha Whittelsey Fund, 1985 (1985.1096.2).

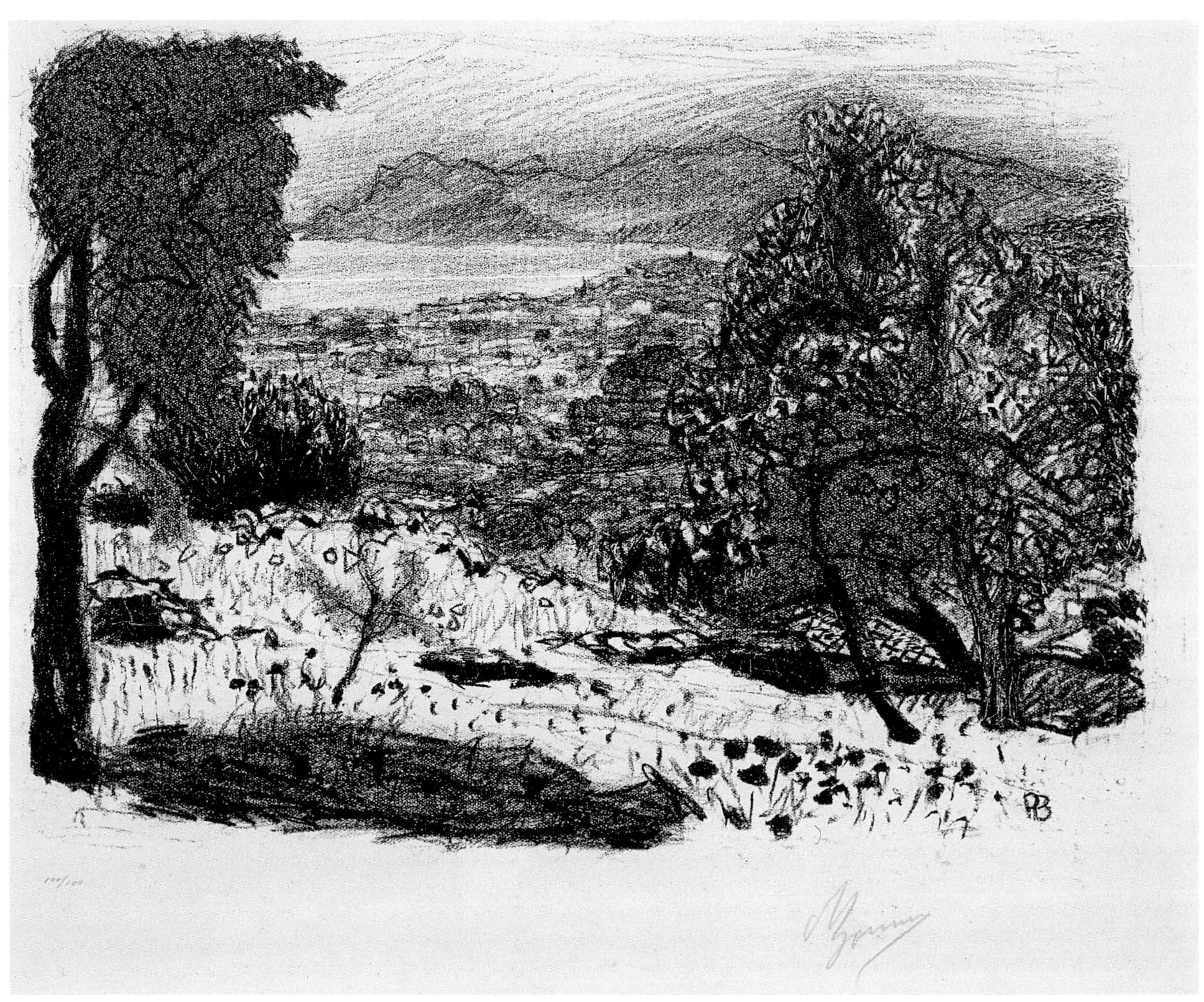

113

Landscape in the South of France
1925, Lithograph on heavy cream wove
paper, 8½ × 11½ in. (21.5 × 29.2 cm), The
Phillips Collection, Washington, D.C.

114

The Riviera
ca. 1923, Oil on canvas, 31 × 30 in. (79 × 76.2 cm),
The Phillips Collection, Washington, D.C.

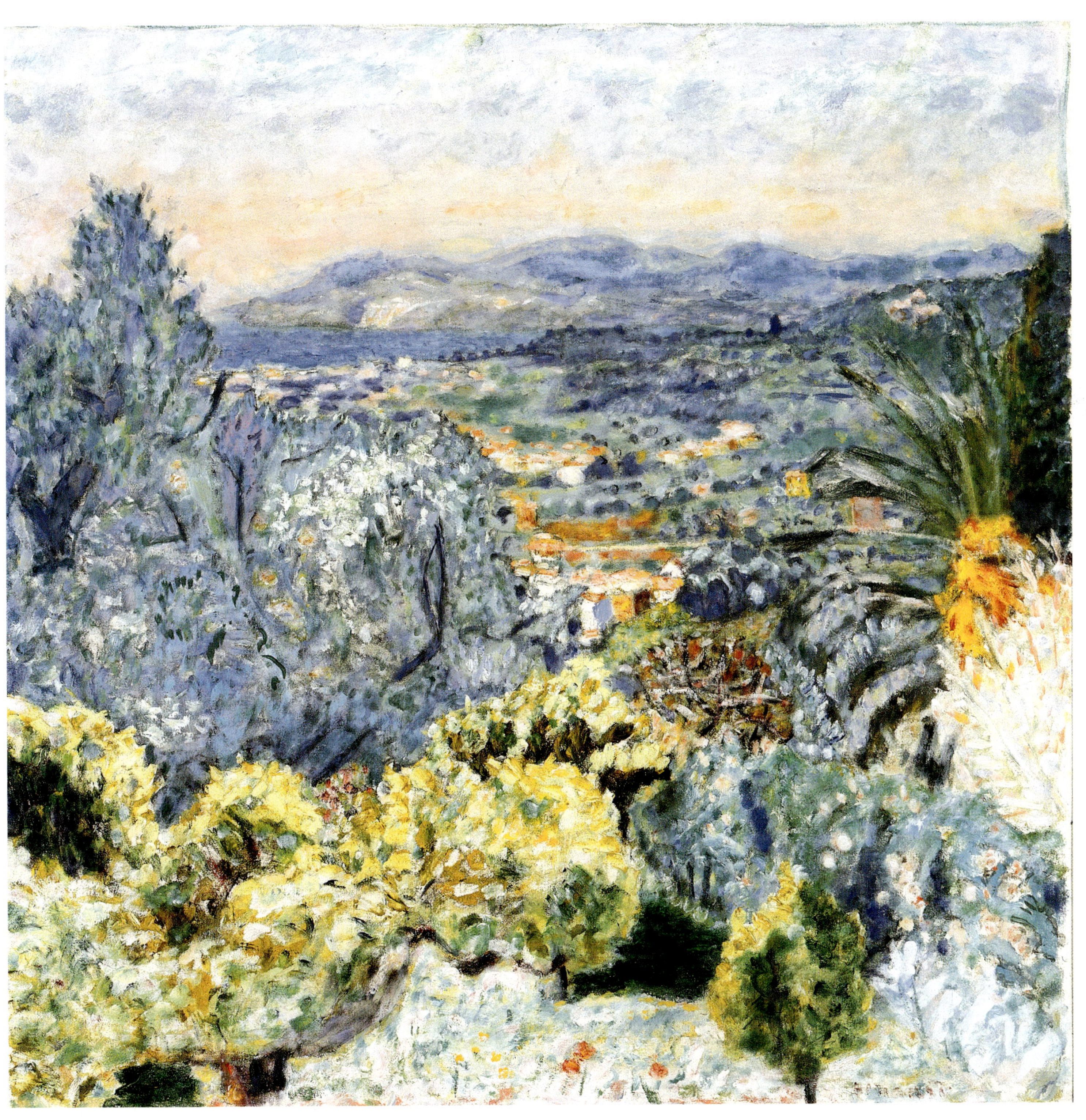

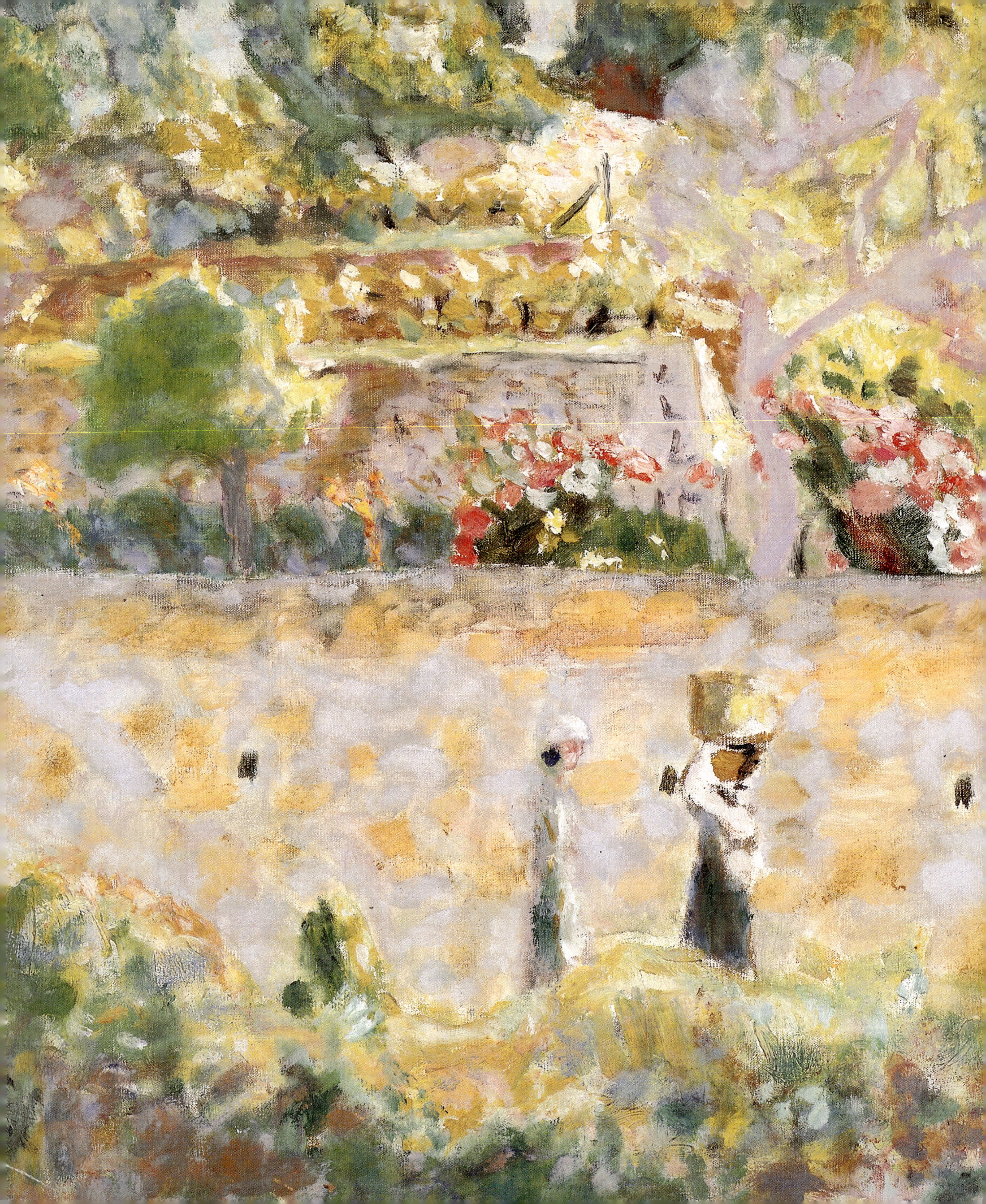

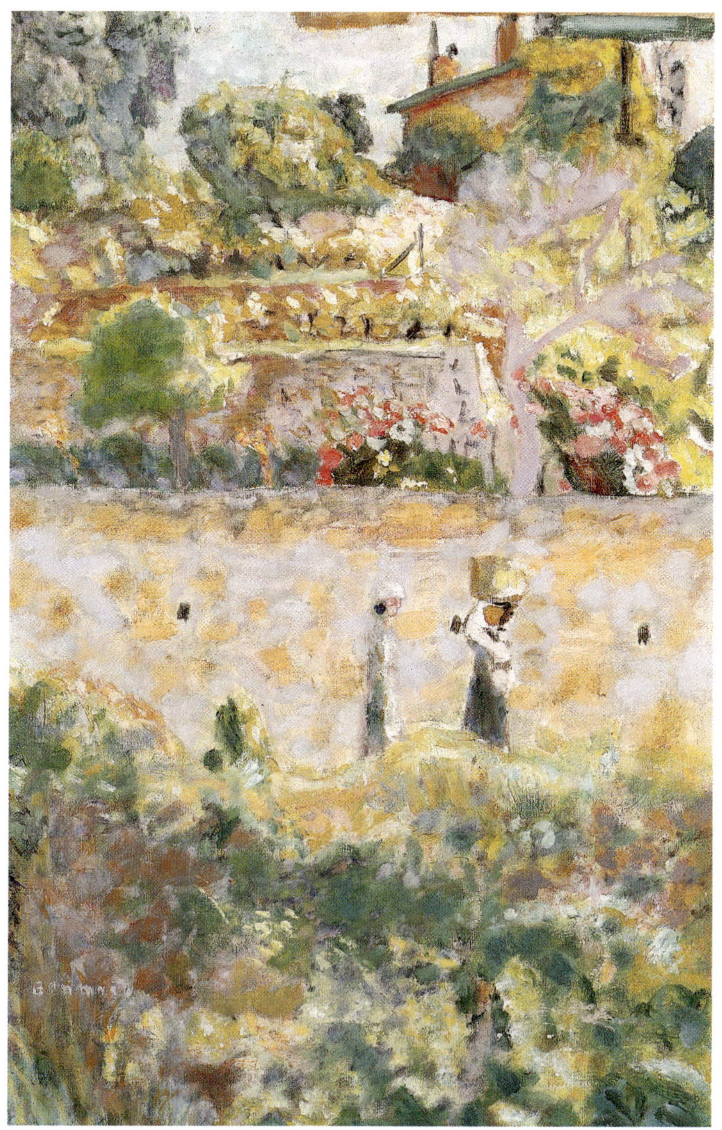

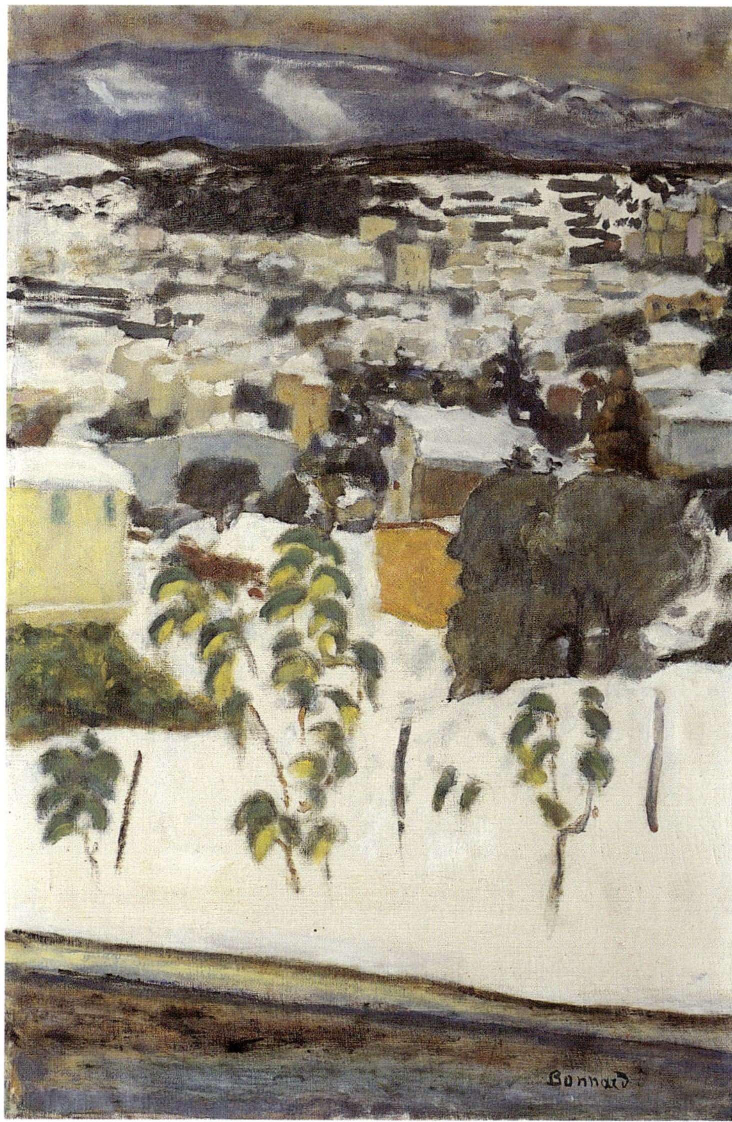

115

Grape Harvest
1926, Oil on canvas, 25 × 15¾ in. (63.5 × 40 cm),
The Phillips Collection, Washington, D.C.

Opposite page: **Grape Harvest** (detail).

116

Effect of Snow or Le Cannet under the Snow
1927, Oil on canvas, 29⅛ × 19⁵⁄₁₆ in. (74 × 49 cm),
Kunstmuseum Winterthur, inv. no. 1531. Gift of
Dr. Herbert and Charlotte Wolfer-de Armas, 1973.

117

Study for "The Breakfast Room"
1931, Graphite on paper, Private collection.

118

The Breakfast Room
ca. 1930–1931, Oil on canvas, 62⅞ × 44⅞ in.
(159.6 × 113.8 cm), The Museum of Modern
Art, New York. Given anonymously, 1941.

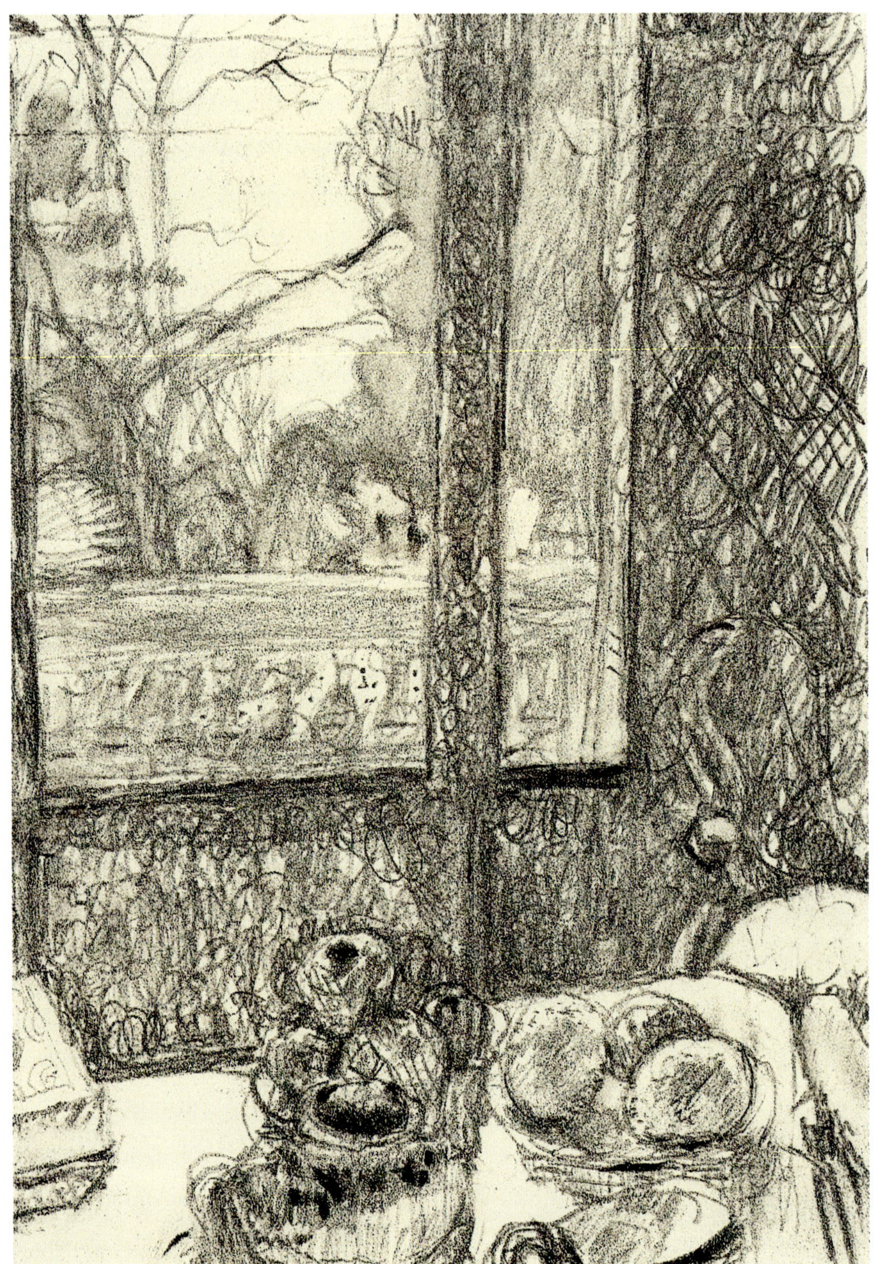

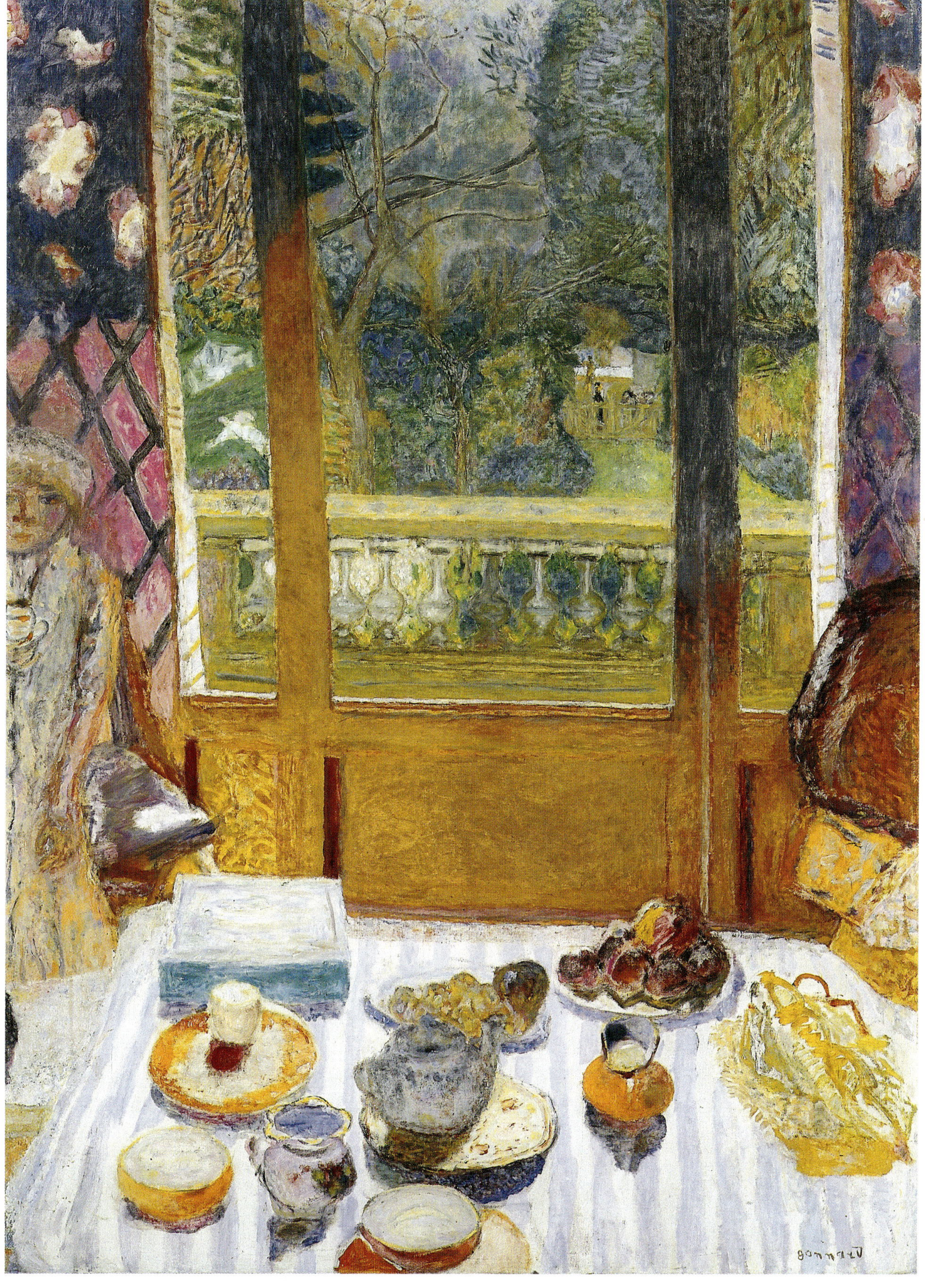

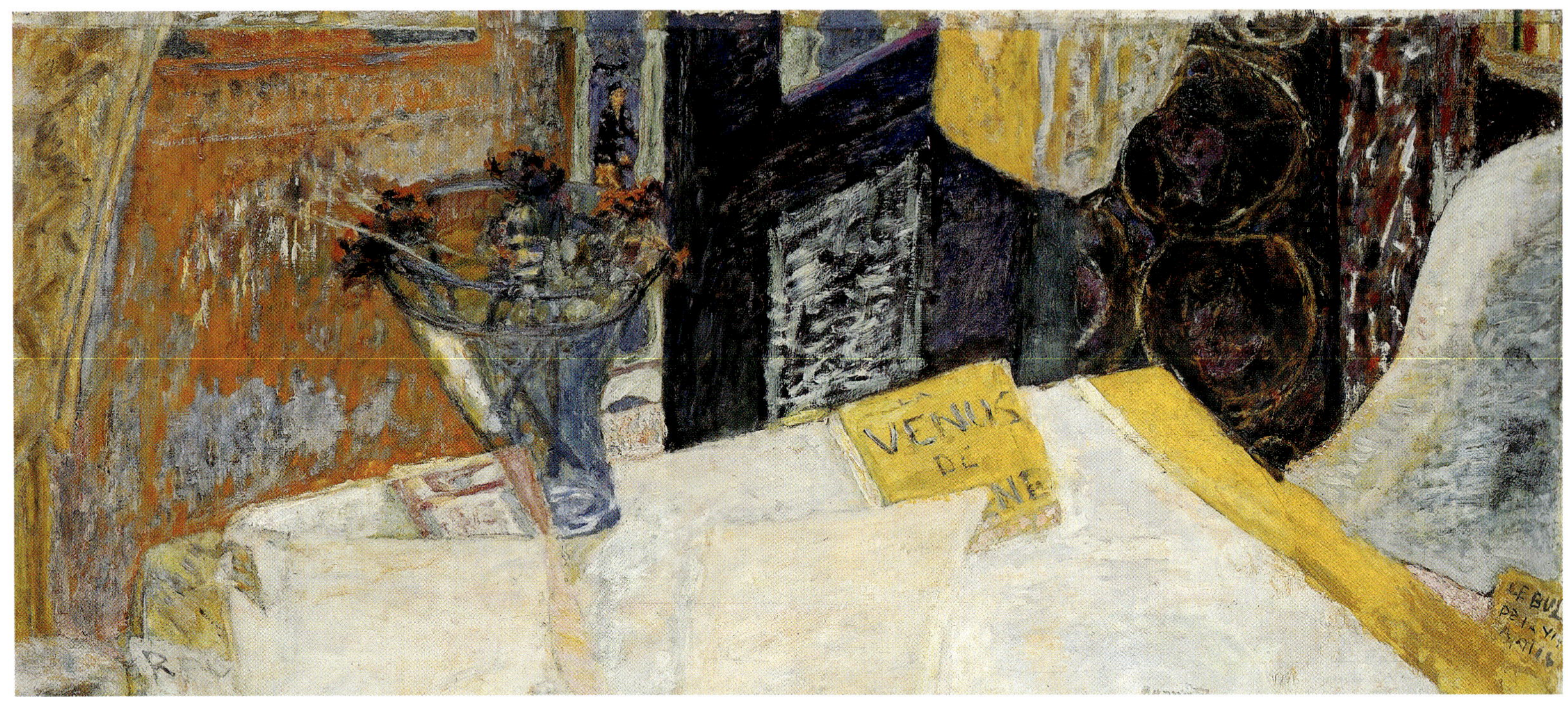

119

Still Life with Bouquet of Flowers or **Venus and Cyrene**
1930, Oil on canvas, 23⅝ × 51⅜ in. (60 × 130.5 cm),
Öffentliche Kunstsammlung Basel,
Kunstmuseum.

120

The Coffee Grinder
1930, Oil on canvas, 18⅞ × 22½ in. (48 × 57 cm),
Kunstmuseum Winterthur, inv. no. 1528. Gift of
Dr. Herbert and Charlotte Wolfer-de Armas, 1973.

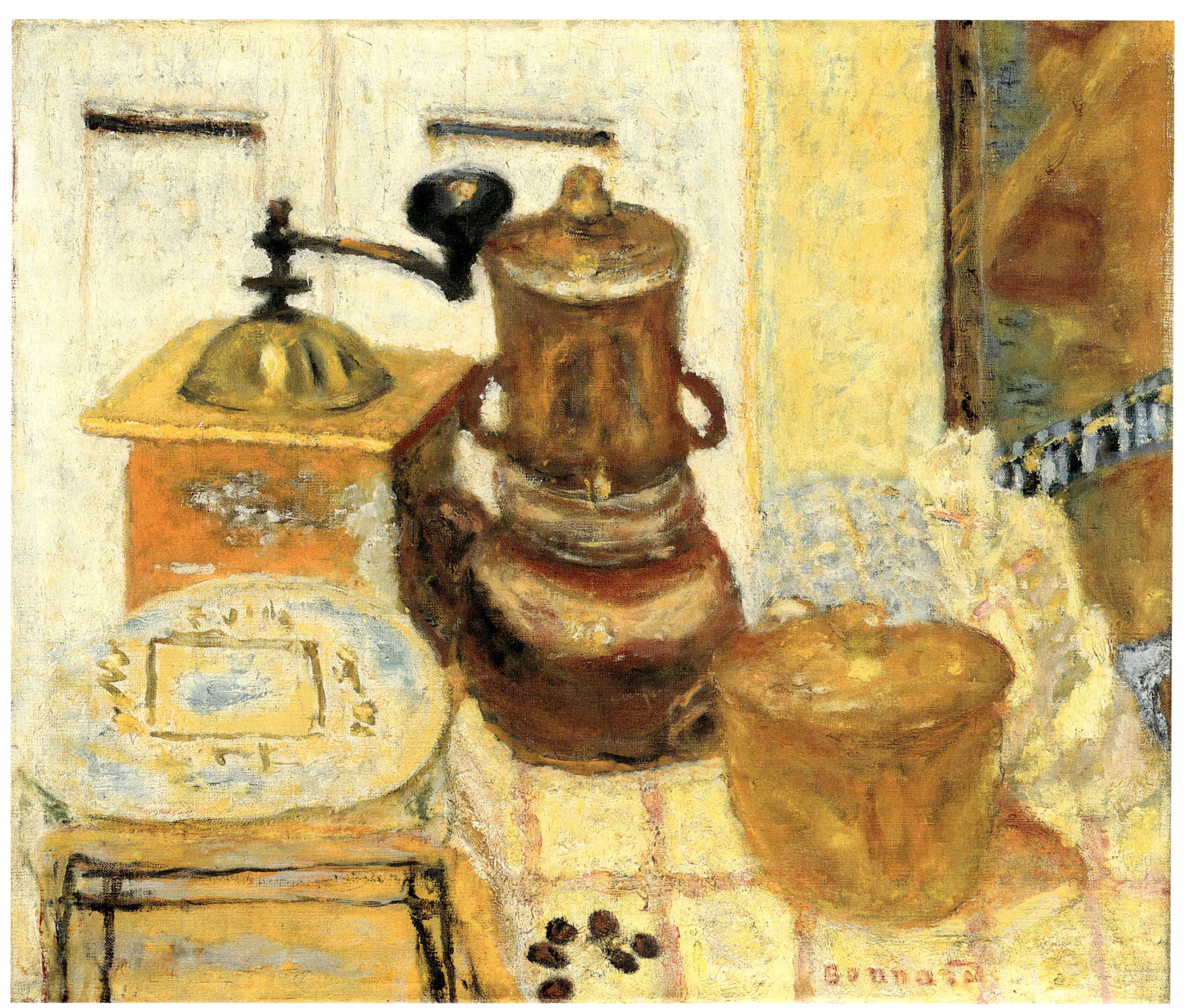

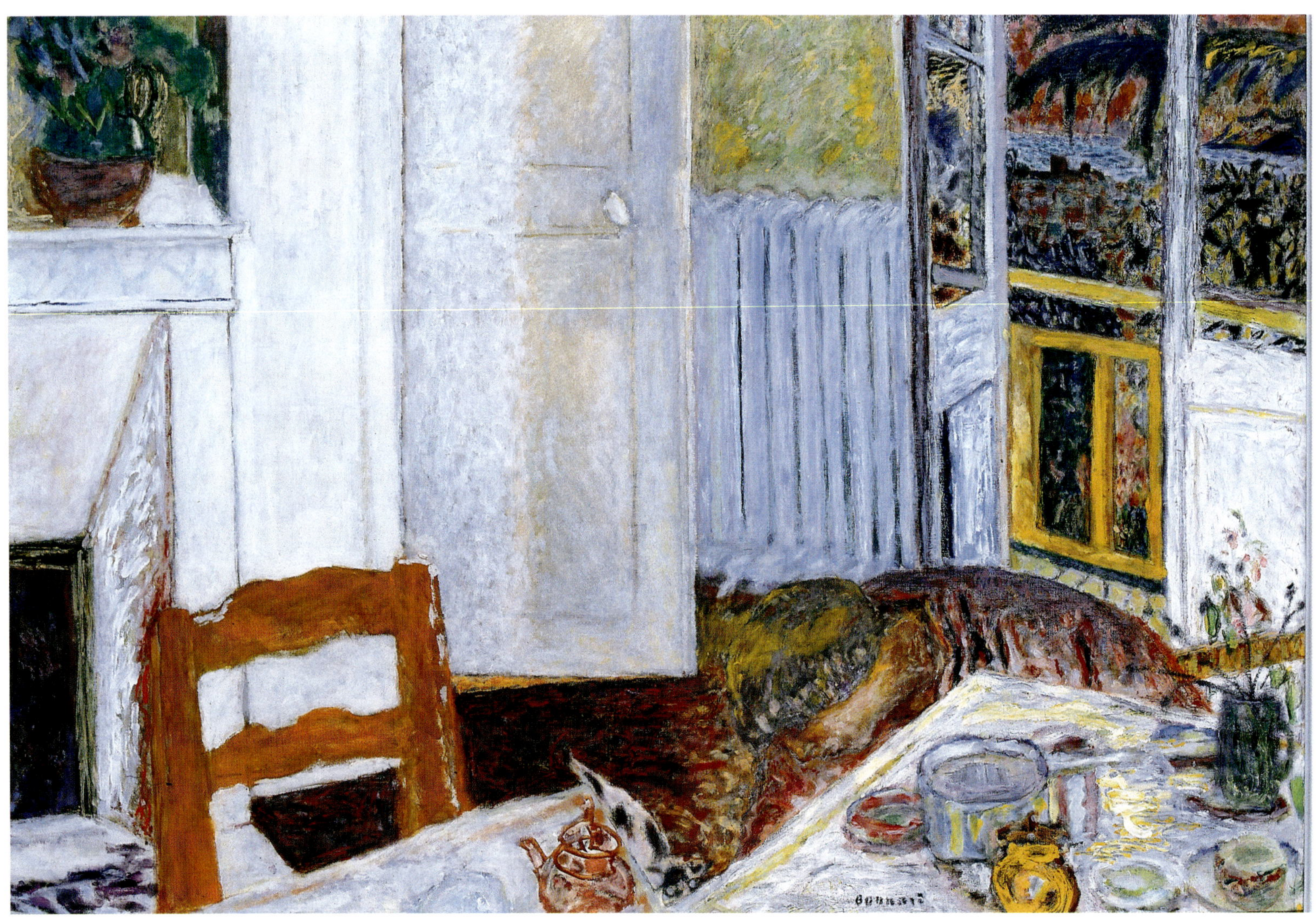

121

White Interior
1932, Oil on canvas, 43¹⁄₁₆ × 61⁵⁄₁₆ in.
(109.5 × 155.8 cm), Musée de Grenoble.

122

Still Life with a Bowl of Fruit
1933, Oil on canvas, 22¹³⁄₁₆ × 20⁷⁄₈ in.
(57.9 × 53 cm), Philadelphia Museum of Art,
Bequest of Lisa Norris Elkins, 1950.

Pages 230–231: **Still Life with a Bowl of Fruit**
(detail).

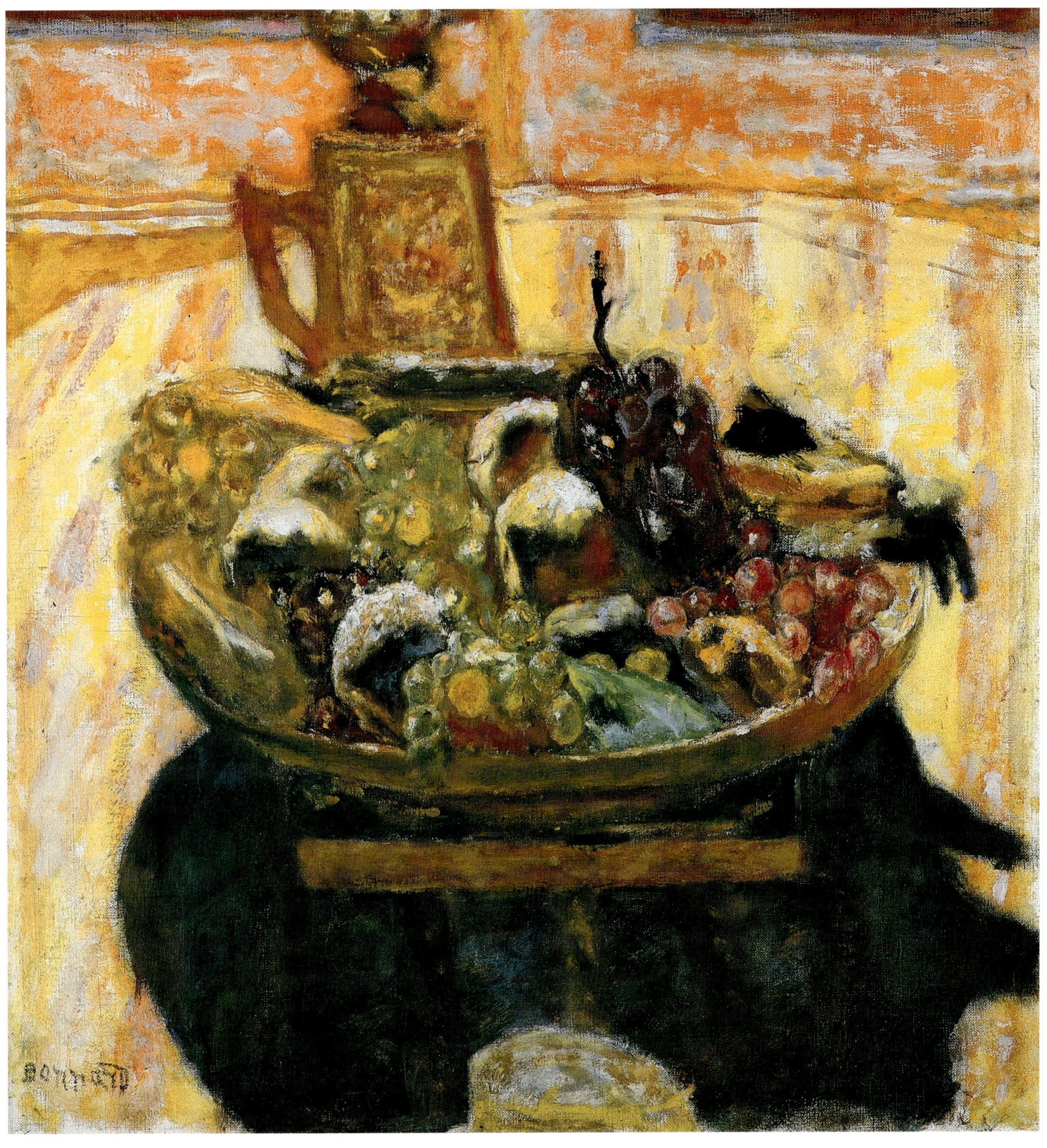

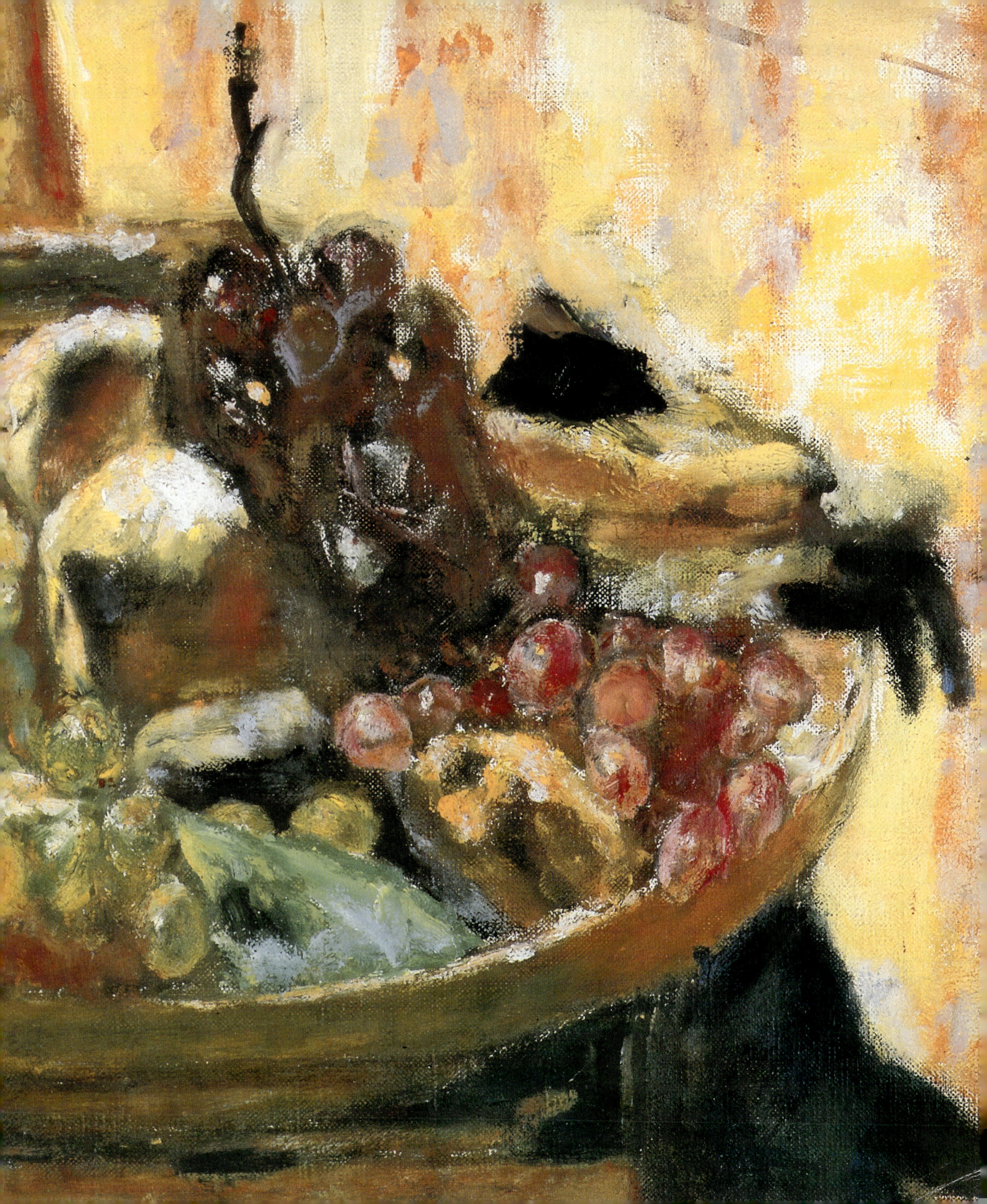

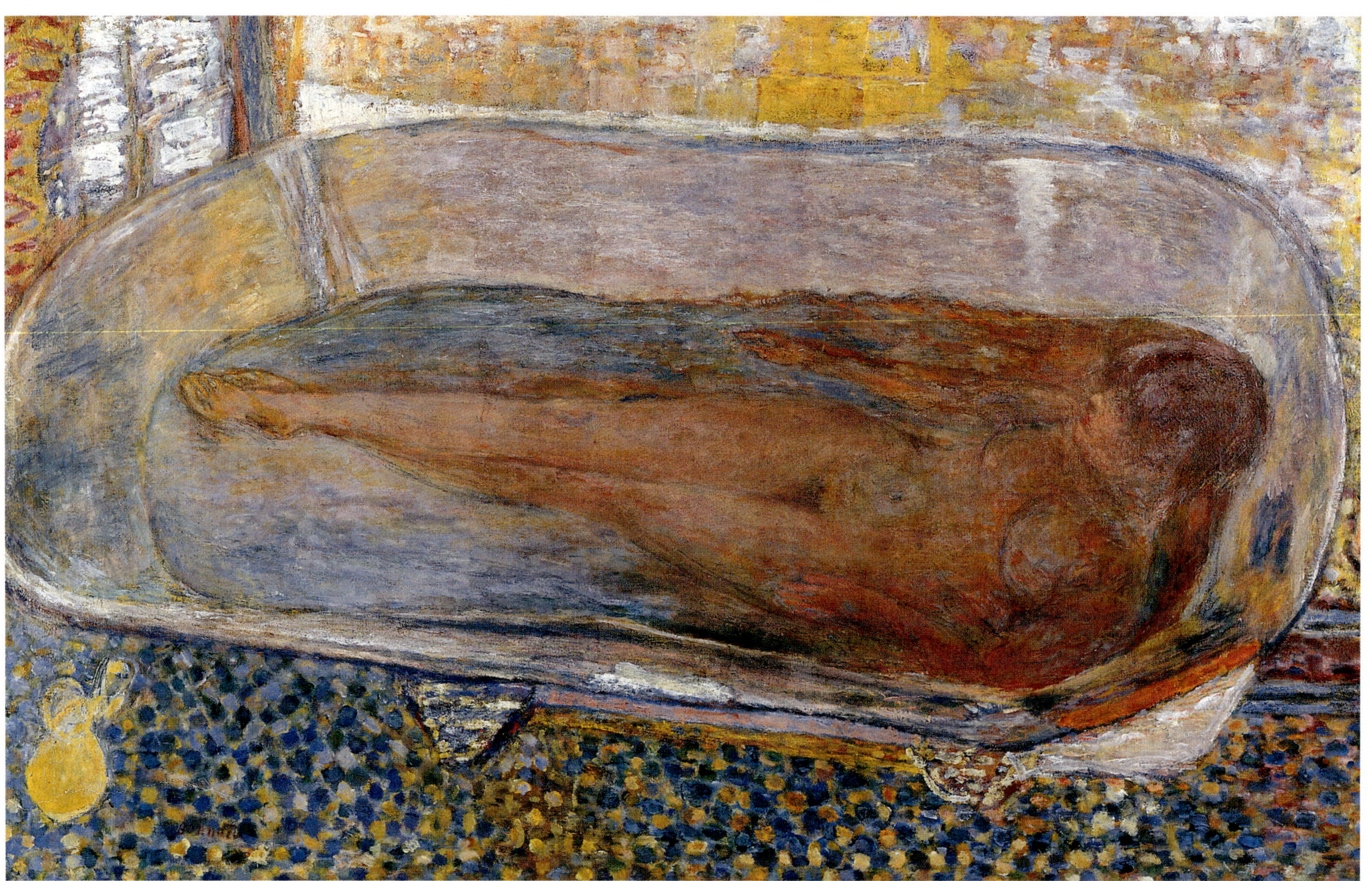

123

The Large Bath, Nude
1937–1939, Oil on canvas, 37 × 56¾ in.
(94 × 144 cm), Private collection.

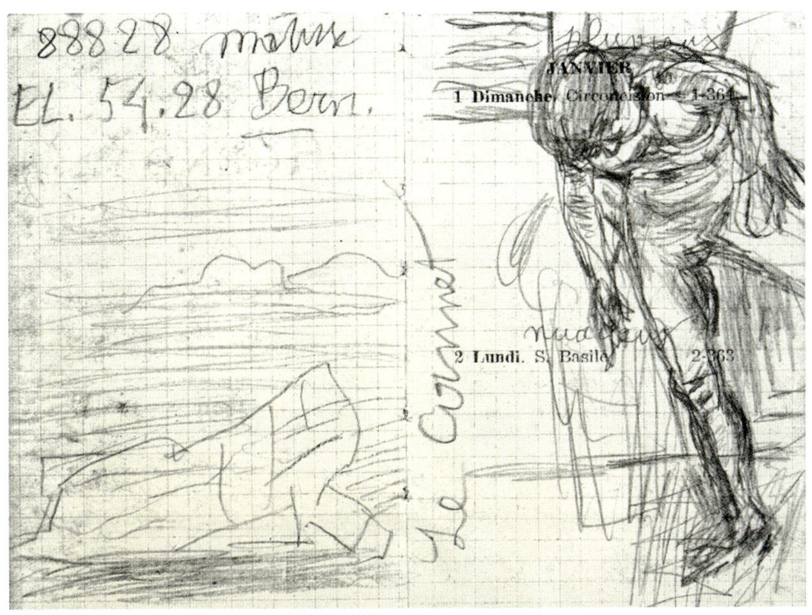

124

Daybook of 1933
1933, Pencil on paper, 5⅛ × 3⅛ × ½ in.
(13 × 8 × 1.2 cm), Bibliothèque Nationale de
France. Département des Estampes et de la
Photographie.

125

Nude in an Interior
ca. 1935, Oil on canvas, 28¾ × 19¾ in.
(73 × 50.2 cm), The Phillips Collection,
Washington, D.C.

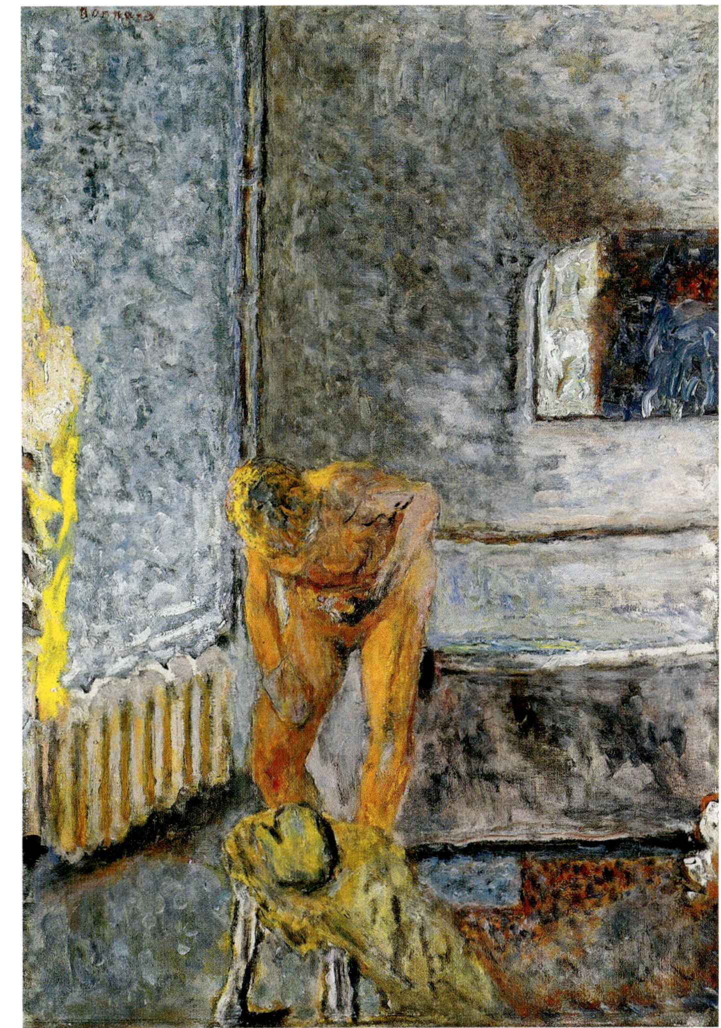

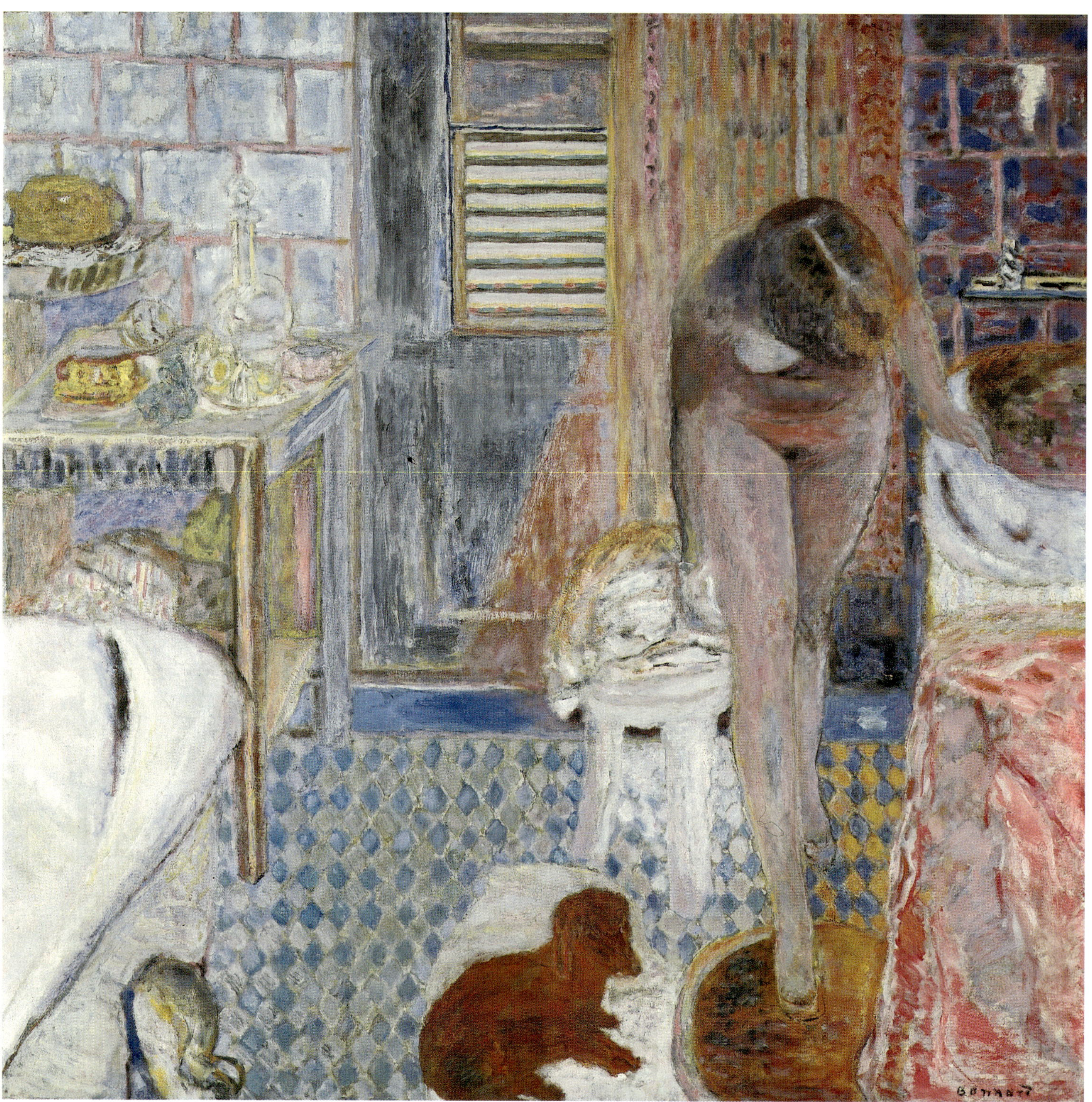

126

Nude in Bathroom
1932, Oil on canvas, 47⅝ × 46½ in. (121 × 118.1 cm),
The Museum of Modern Art, New York,
Florene May Schoenborn Bequest, 1996.

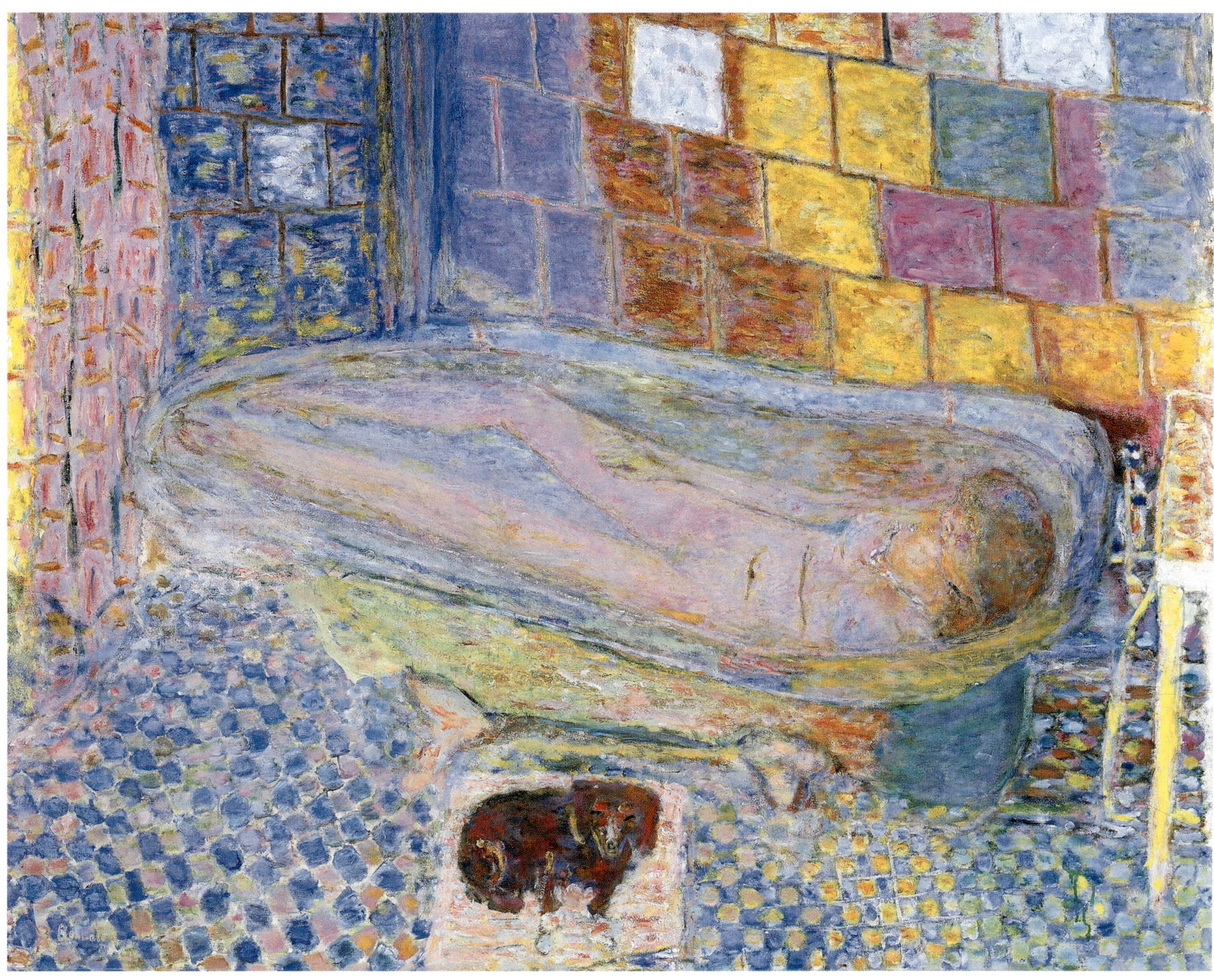

127

Nude in Bathtub
1941–1946, Oil on canvas, 48 × 59½ in.
(121.9 × 151.1 cm), Carnegie Museum of Art,
Pittsburgh. Acquired through the generosity
of the Sarah Mellon Scaife Family, 1970.

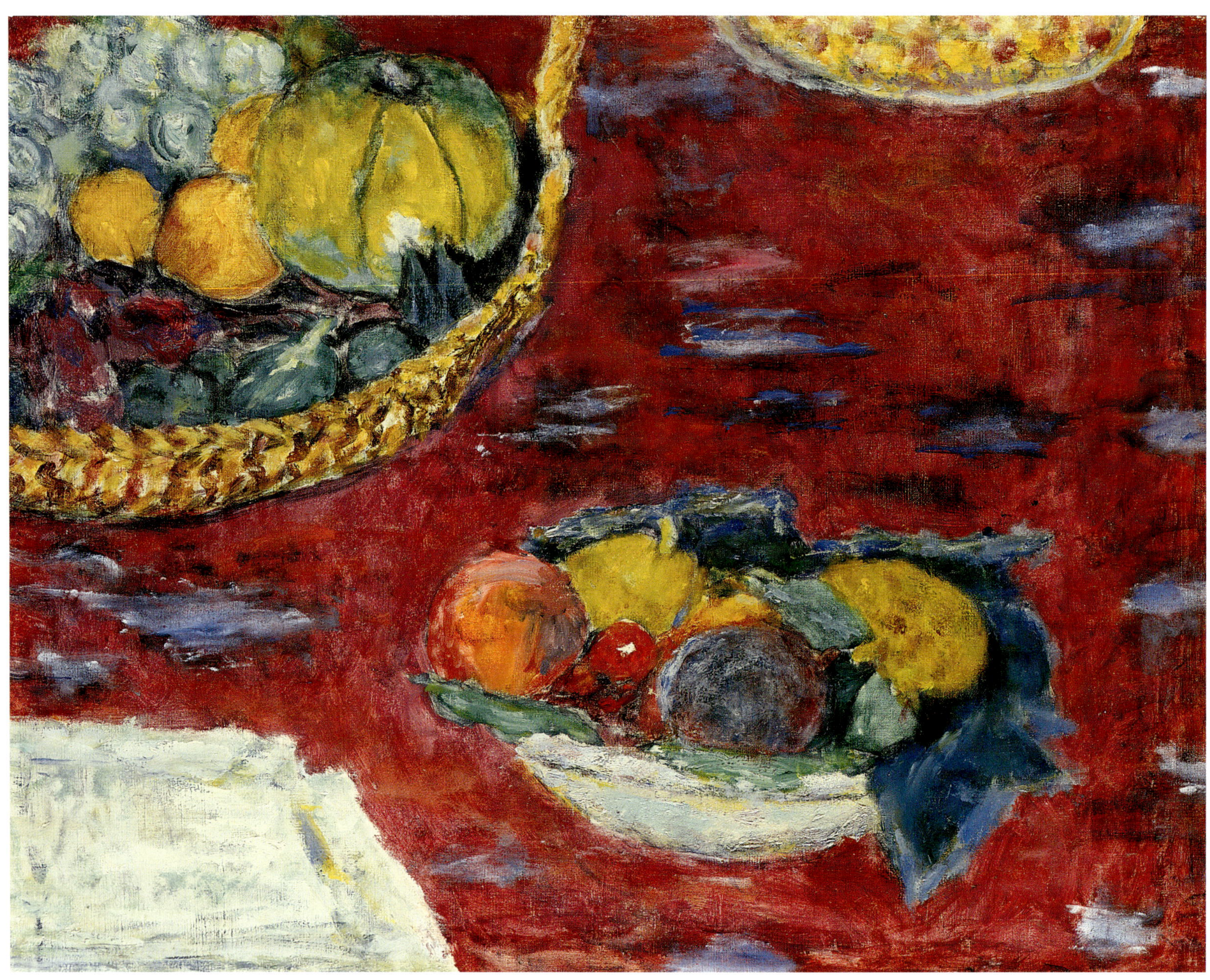

128

A Dish and a Basket of Fruit
1944, Oil on canvas, 17 × 21¹³⁄₁₆ in. (43.2 × 55.4 cm),
Private collection.

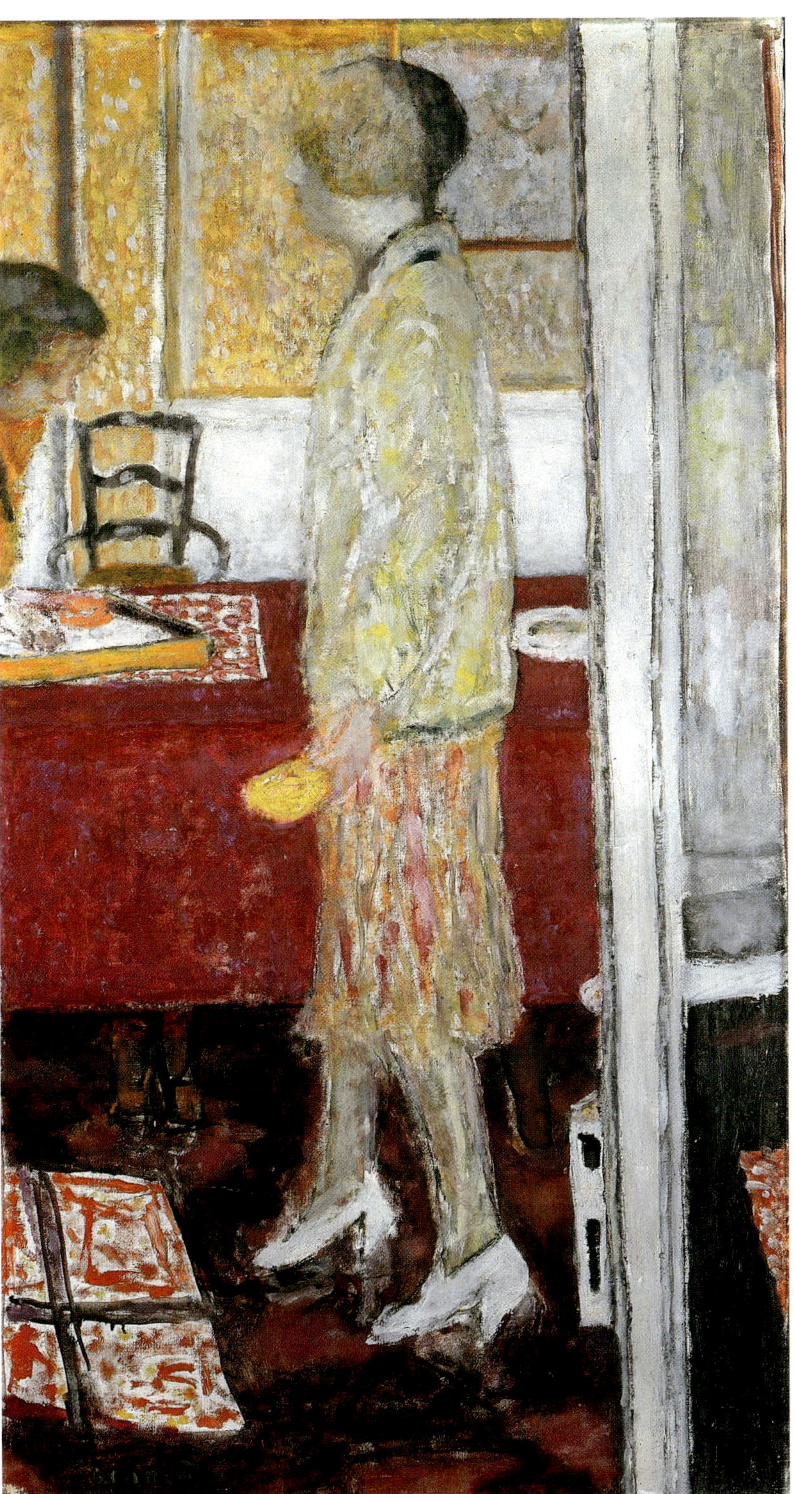

129

Marthe in the Dining Room
1933, Oil on canvas, 43⅞ × 23¼ in. (111.5 × 59 cm),
Lyon, Musée des Beaux-Arts.

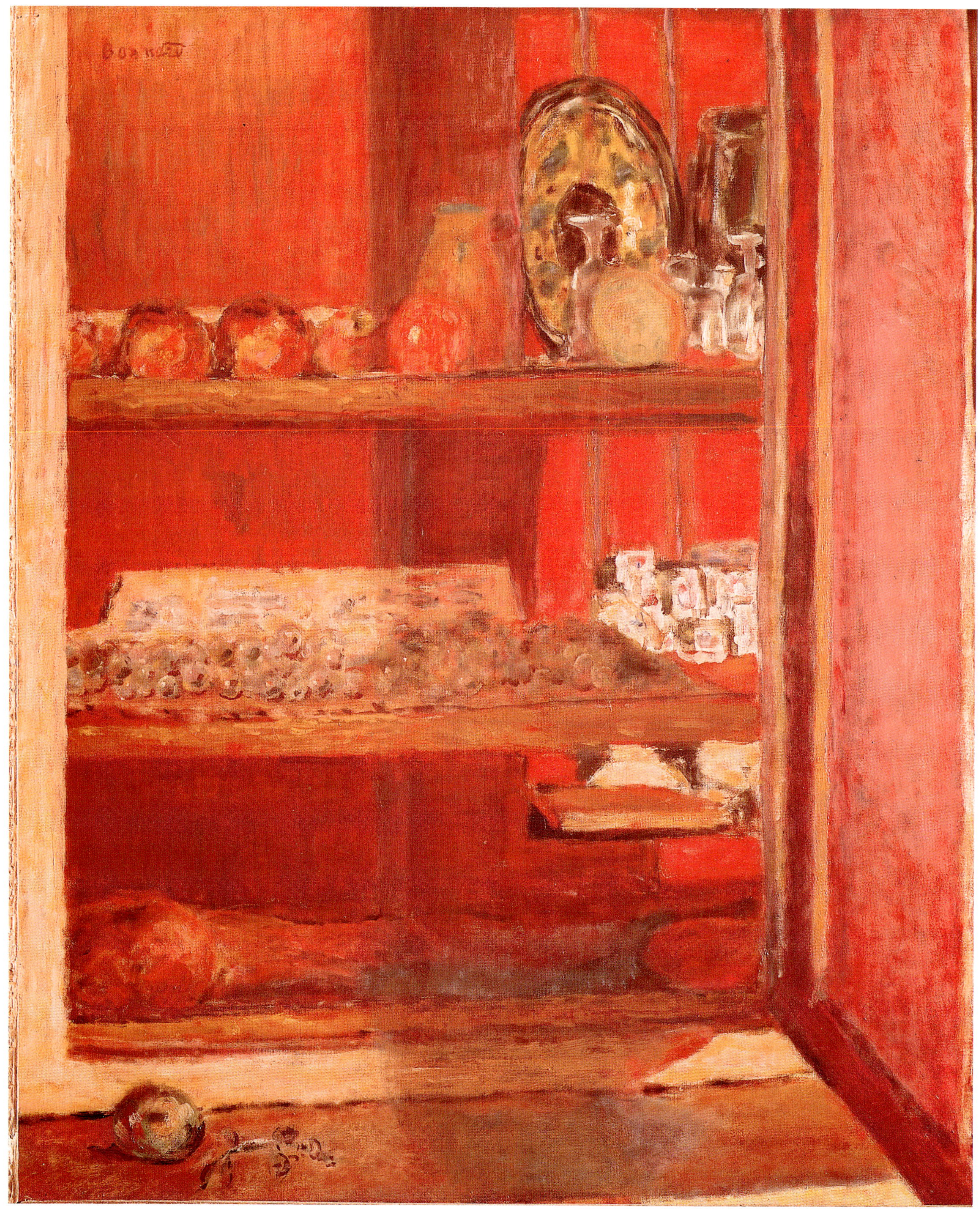

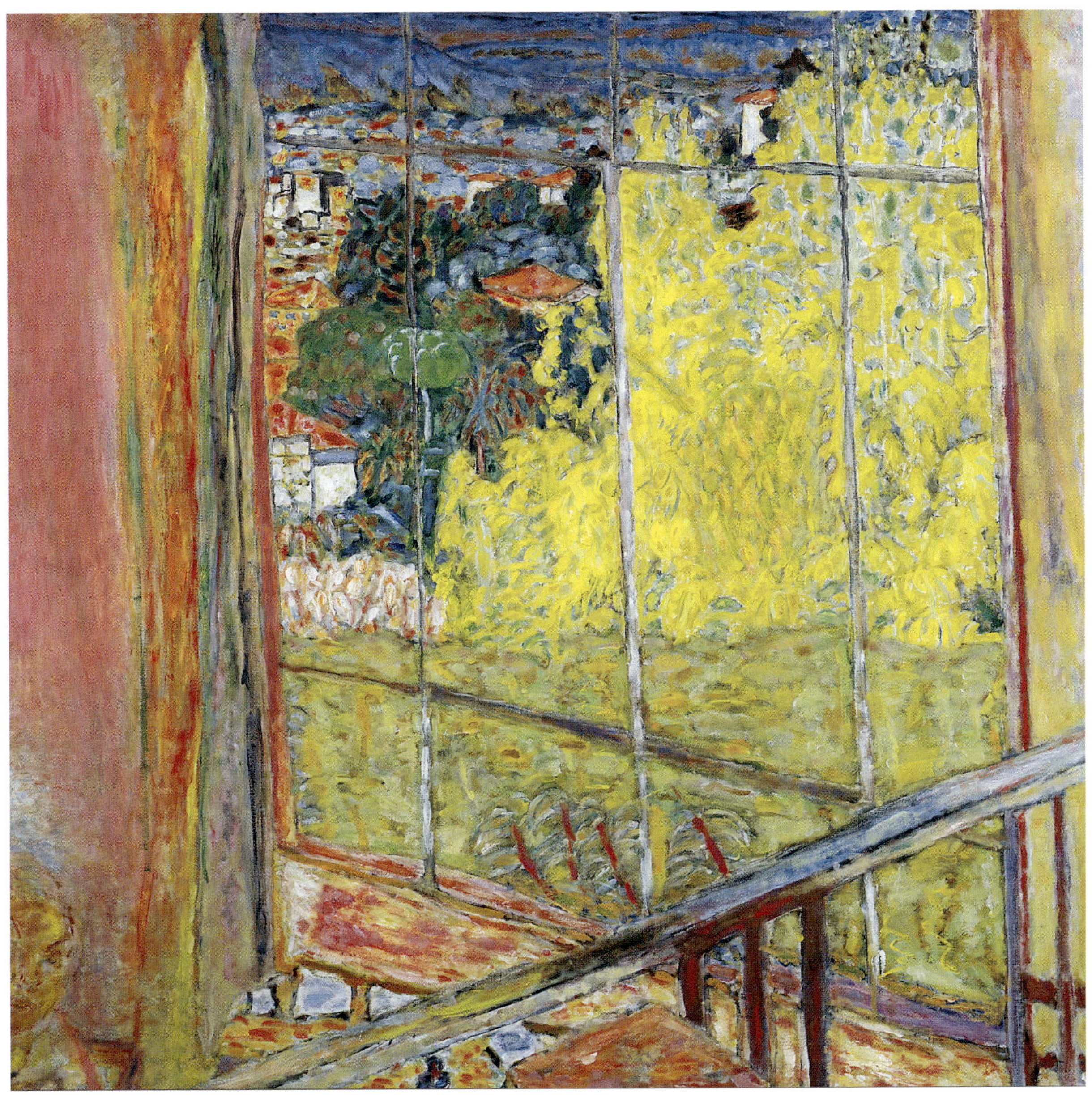

130

The Red Cupboard
ca. 1939, Oil on canvas, 32 × 25½ in.
(81.3 × 64.8 cm), Private collection.

131

Studio with Mimosas
1939–October 1946, Oil on canvas, 50 × 50 in.
(127.5 × 127.5 cm), Centre Georges
Pompidou, Paris. Musée National d'Art
Moderne/ Centre de Création Industrielle.

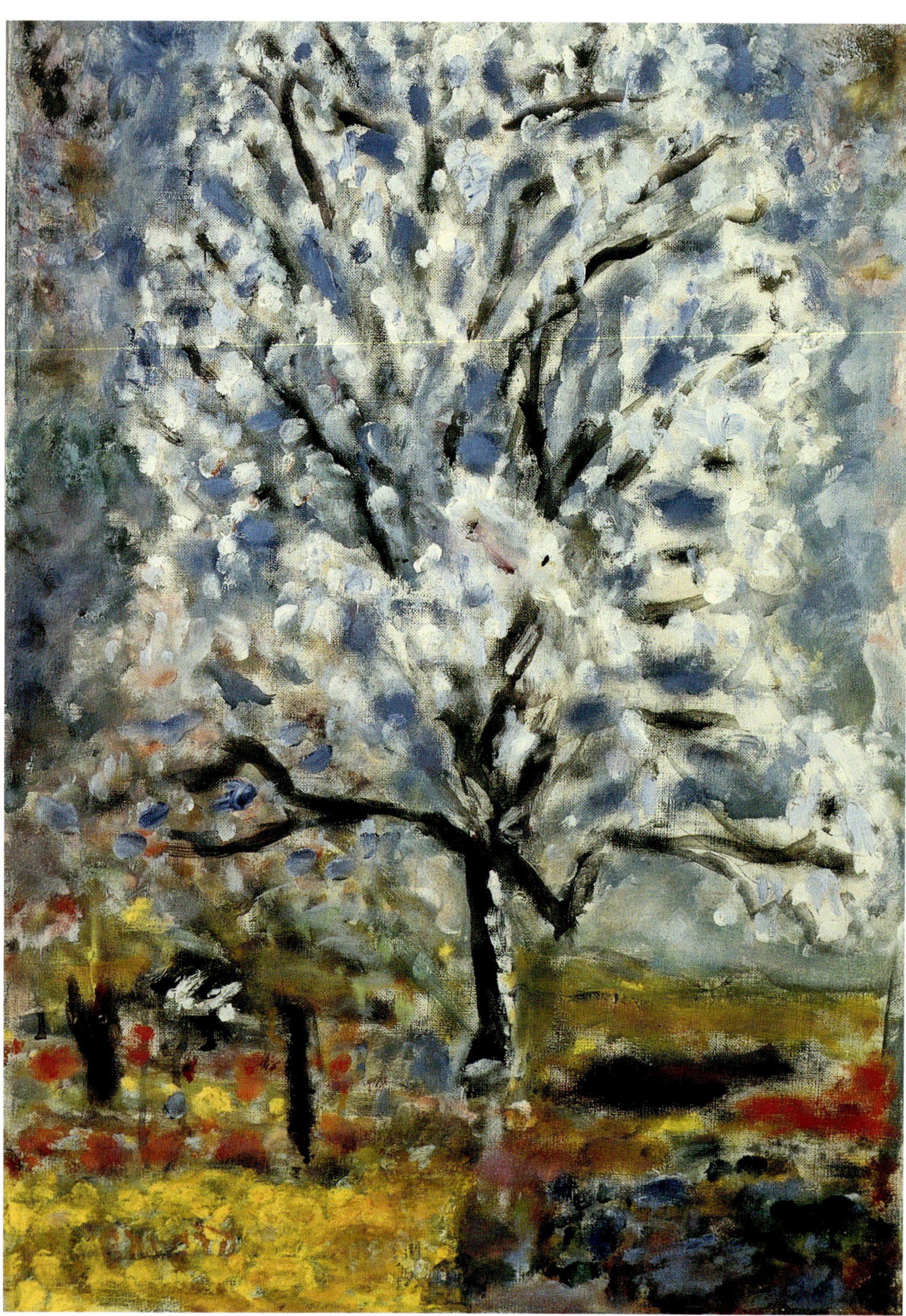

132

Blossoming Almond Tree
ca. 1946–1947, Oil on canvas, 21⅝ × 14¾ in.
(55 × 37.5 cm), Centre Georges Pompidou,
Paris. Musée National d'Art Moderne/
Centre de Création Industrielle. Gift of Mr.
and Mrs. Charles Zadok, 1964.

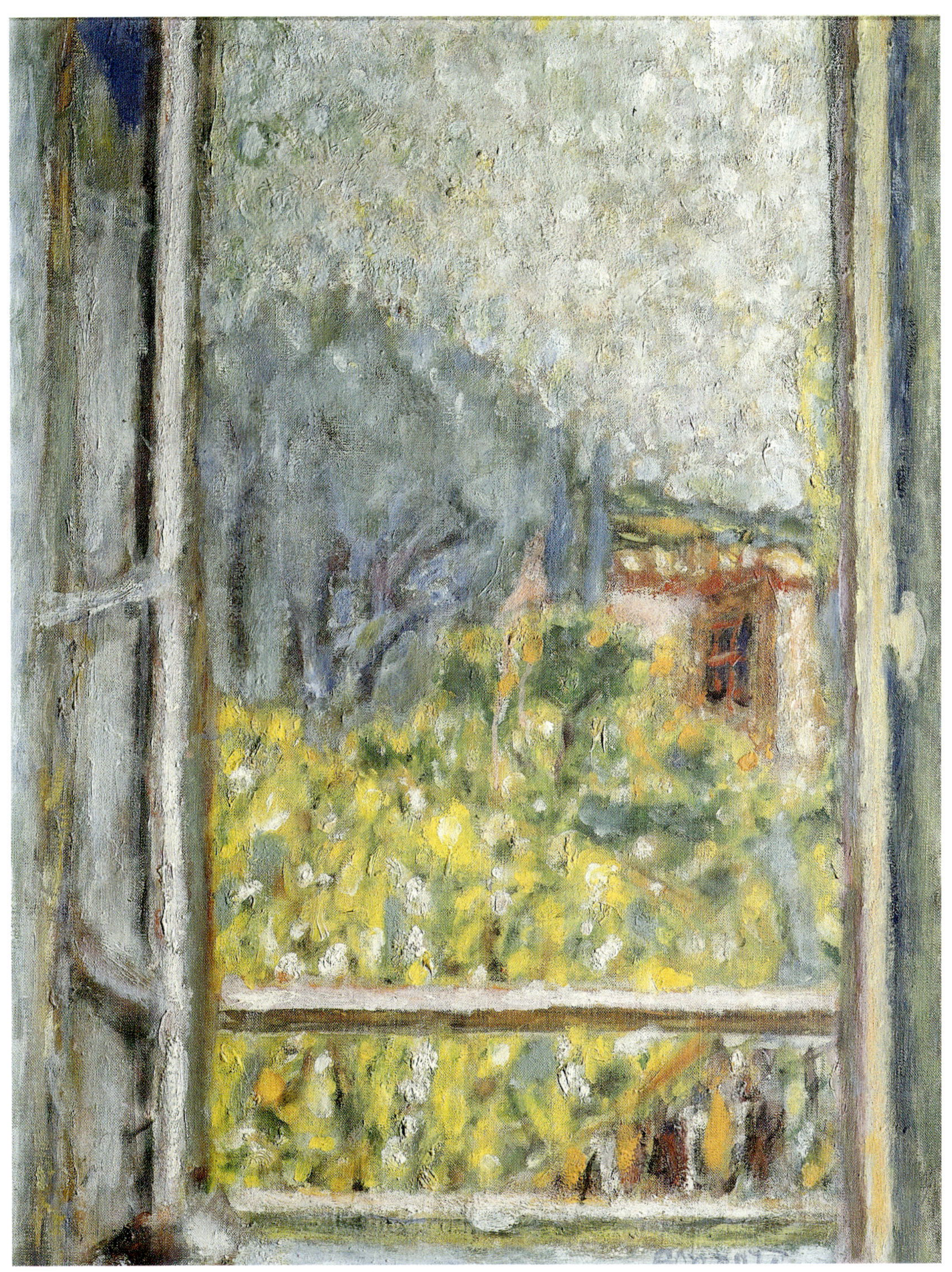

133

The Small Window
1946, Oil on canvas, 22⅞ × 17¾ in.
(58 × 45 cm), Private collection, courtesy
Galerie Schmit, Paris.

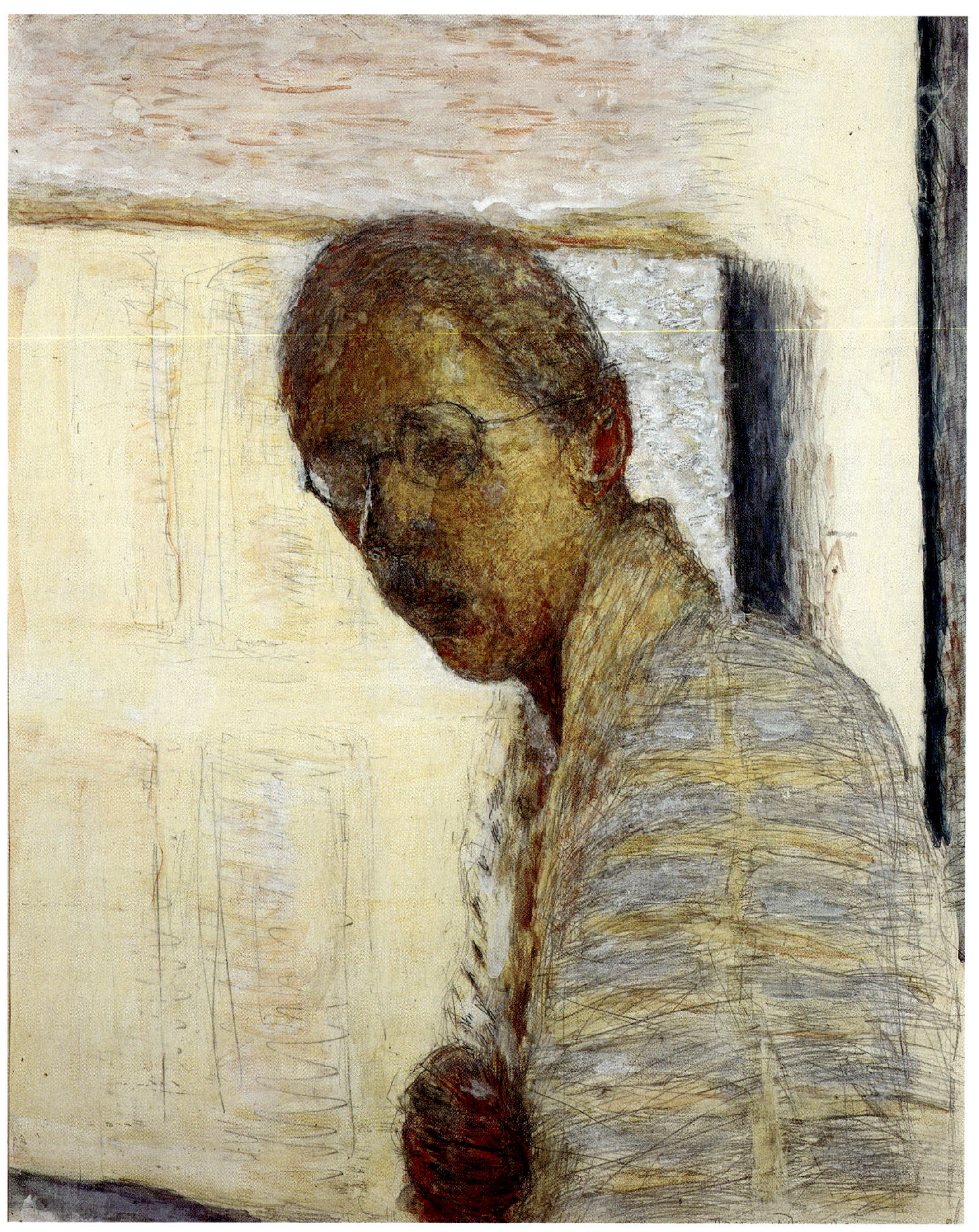

Self-Portrait
1930, Gouache and pencil, 25⅝ × 19⅝ in.
(65 × 50 cm), Private collection.

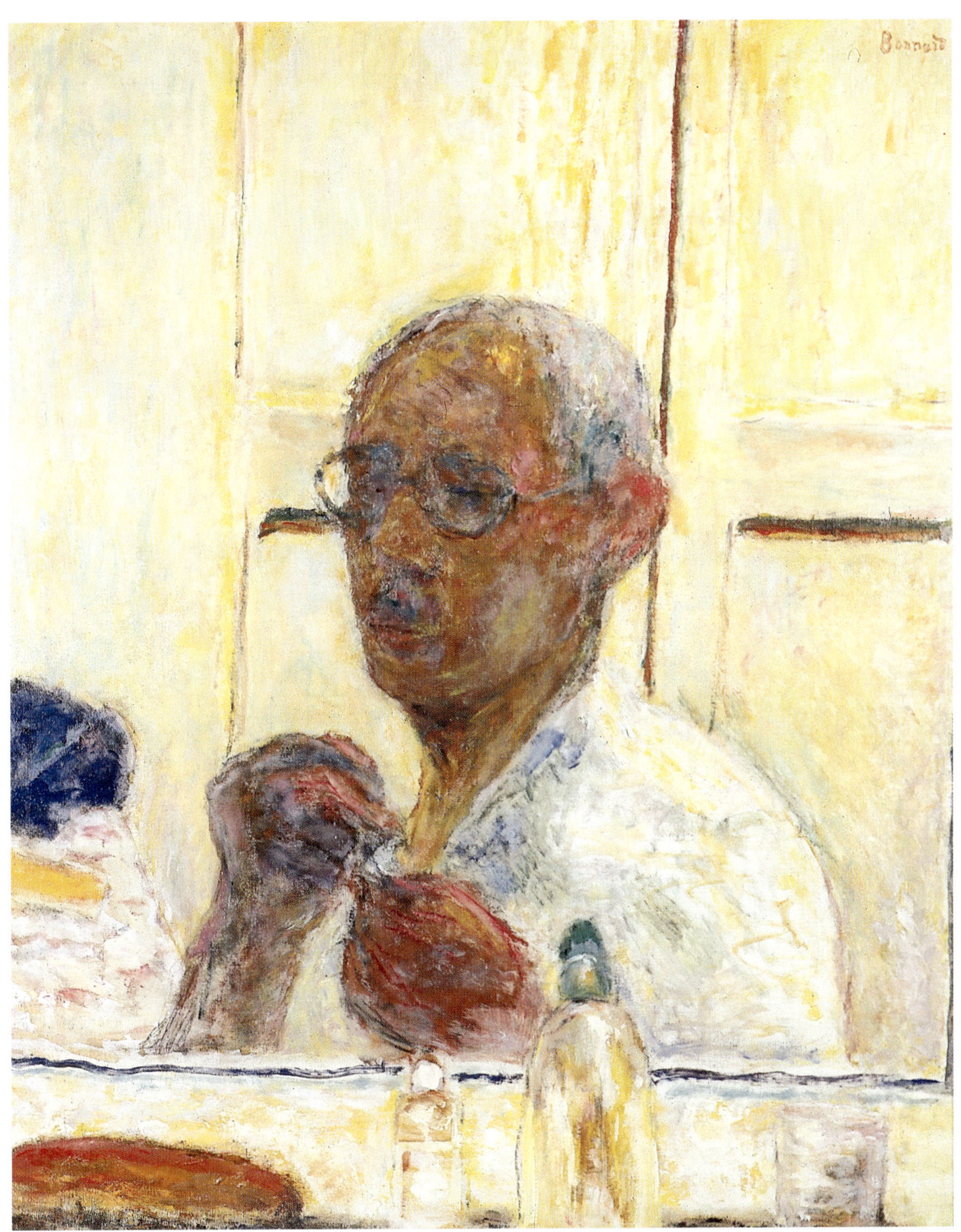

135

Self-Portrait
ca. 1938–1940, Oil on canvas, 30 × 24 in.
(76.2 × 61 cm), Art Gallery of New South
Wales, Sydney. Purchased 1972.

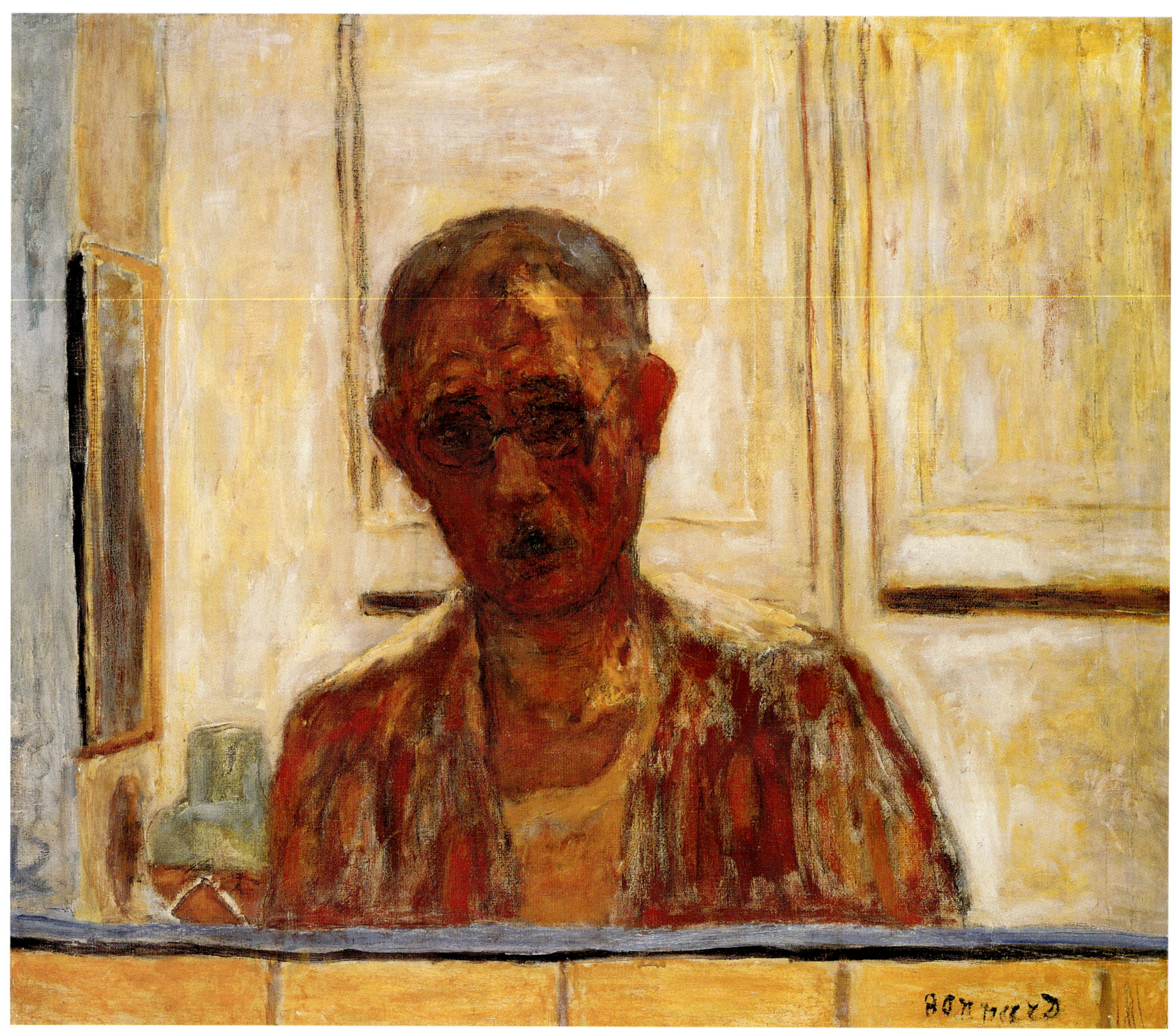

136

Self-Portrait
1938, Oil on canvas, 23 × 26⅜ in.
(58.4 × 67 cm), Private collection.

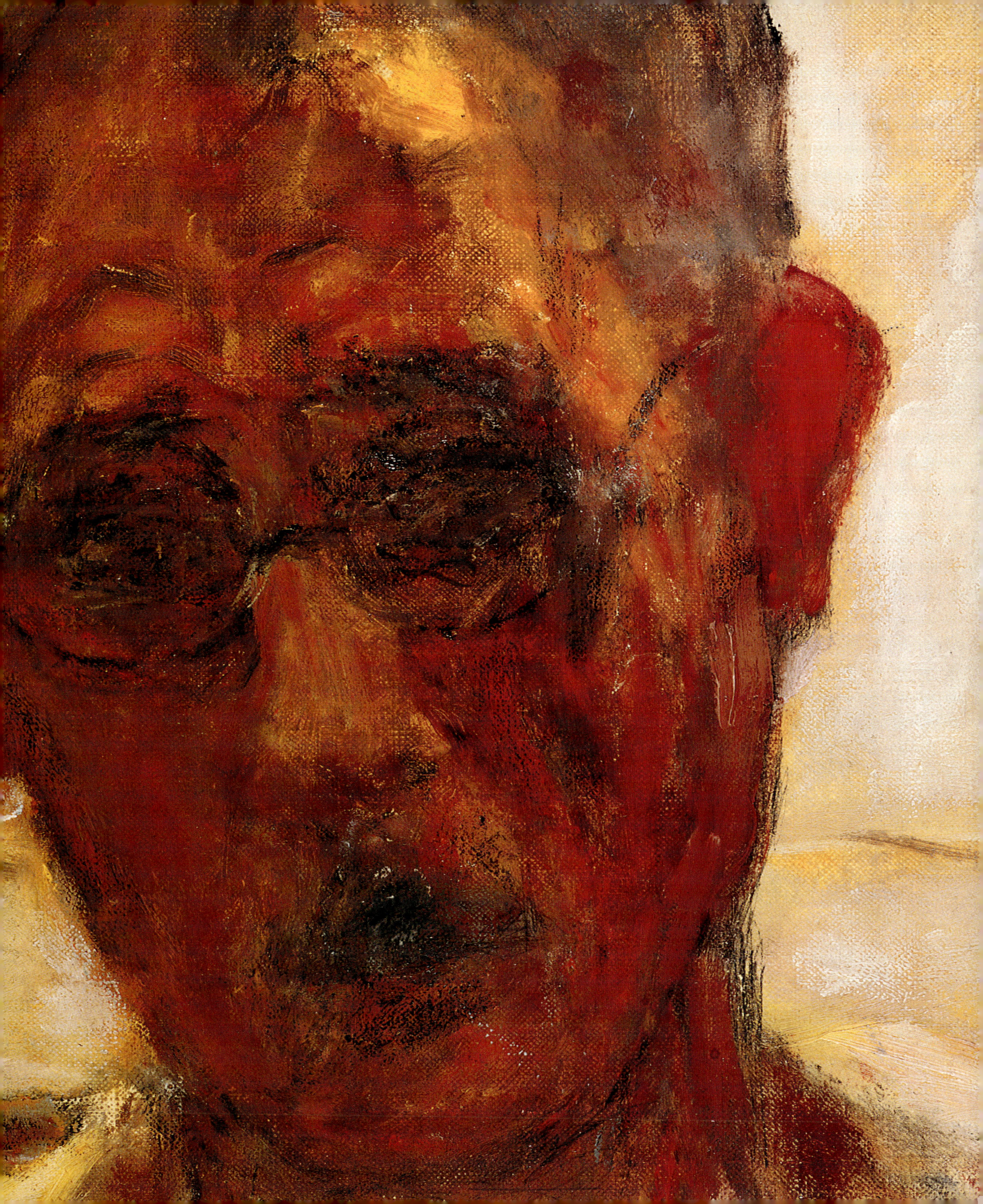

Bonnard's Notes

Antoine Terrasse

Previous page:
Self-Portrait (detail),
1938, Oil on canvas,
23 × 26⅜ in.
(58.4 × 67 cm), Private
collection.

Pierre Bonnard used the title "Observations sur la peinture" for a sequence of observations he had assembled in a school notebook. He selected them from among the thoughts he had jotted down in his pocket diaries over the years. Thoughts springing, in every case, from his experience as a painter—a situation rather like that of an artisan who chats about his work in the evenings.

Nothing simpler, at first glance, than those jottings, originally scribbled here and there in pencil, in the limited space available, among indications of the day's weather, appointments, shopping lists, and interspersed with sketches of all kinds. Bonnard had gathered them for himself before submitting a selection of them to the review *Verve*. But we must look at them under their original date, in the midst of innumerable quick sketches of figures, landscapes, nudes, or seascapes, all incredibly lively in spite of their small size. Among so many different subjects, we find a whole bestiary, in which cats appear most often. Hence his remark, inspired by his closeness to the animal kingdom, and of greater significance than we might think: "States of daydreaming like a cat. Sleep between states of exaltation like the dog."

From the surviving diaries, the majority dating mainly from the 1920s, it would also be possible to extract a history of the weather in France—at least in whichever region the artist happened to be. "Fair," "Overcast," "Rain and sunshine," "Cold"—he would make a note every day. "It reminds me of the light," he used to say, "and it's enough to remind me of all that happened on that day." And how precise he is, sometimes: "Fine but cold weather; there is some vermilion in the orange shadows and purple in the grays." As for the sketches, often multiplied over the weeks to check a detail or deepen a perspective, they often reveal the inspiration for a painting at the very moment when an idea first came to him and was imprinted on his mind. Therefore, they are very moving for the viewer, who can feel that he is a witness to the genesis of a work: he feels the spontaneous element in that genesis but, at the same time, the strain and the complexity. Strokes, volutes, dots, light or heavy hatchings—all provide, in their different ways, signs to suggest the transparency of the air, the thickness of foliage, the splashing of water; to preserve a gesture or capture a figure. Such a wealth of lines corresponds to what we know of the richness of his colors.

The "observations" on painting, scattered here and there like notes between the lines, strengthen even more our impression of being in a shrine of creation. They reveal the artist's obsessions, his untiring search for the best means of translating a visual emotion, the "seduction or first idea," to which everything must surrender. "One always talks of surrendering to nature. There is also such a thing as surrendering to the picture." "The main subject is the surface which has its color, its laws, over and above those of the objects." Which all builds up to the wonderful formula to characterize the relationship between painting and life: "It's not a matter of painting life. It's a matter of giving life to painting."

And so, one must "see things once, or see them a thousand times." Think of the succession of planes, of distances. Consider the size of the paper or canvas. "Some beauties in nature are impossible to convey without large dimensions." Establish new relationships between line and color: "Color doesn't just embellish the line; it strengthens it." And that is the entire role of color in that art which it illuminates: "Color has to be thought out more than line." The color, studied at length, applied after deep pondering, will, for him, give balance to the whole composition.

We find no didactic intention in those notes; no attempt to generalize a rule valid only for himself. Nothing purely "intellectual." Nonetheless, with all his love for life, and all the intelligence of his painting, Bonnard is a painter, a natural painter, and nothing but a painter. It is precisely because of his culture, which is considerable, that he knows how much one must avoid introducing culture into a work. "In our memory, we find what we ourselves have felt, and also what we have acquired through images transmitted by previous artists. We must beware." "One must feel that the painter was there, that he was aware of things in their own light, conceived from the beginning."

Just so. In that thought we find the embodiment of conscientiousness and utter sincerity. And more and more a single preoccupation: how to translate light.

Certainly, Bonnard looked all around him. He looked for and discovered himself—like all great artists—among other creative minds among the old masters, Titian, Poussin, and Corot: among his contemporaries, Matisse perhaps, or even Munch at a certain point. But those whose work will have gone along with him most often would include Renoir, Monet, Degas, Cézanne, and Redon—however different they may have been one from another and from himself. He actually made this note in his diaries, "Ingres, Boucher—the first modern craftsmen." As intercessors between them and him were to be found, respectively, Degas and Renoir. And to these names should also be added—on account of a certain outburst of color—that of Van Gogh, "a great artist, whom I admire," as he wrote in 1935, in a letter to Charles Terrasse. However, it has to be emphasized in this regard that everything that struck him was translated into his own language—something so personal and uncompromisingly *different*. Take his drawing: it represents the sensation he experienced, in its first flight.

Allow yourself to become imbued with his color; it, too, has its own immediacy, but it is considered, thought out. "Drawing represents feeling: color, judgment"—a paradox, perhaps, but Bonnard, like Cézanne, used color to build up his composition.

And that global vision, "mobile and changing," to the point of being disconcerting; this world, constructed like some woven web, which is gradually revealed to the onlooker. All this is peculiar to Bonnard.

A painter, nothing but a painter; true. Overwhelmed and, as it were, surrounded by his art, he was seeking only to project onto our world the vision that obsessed him. Take the late self-portraits, in which a melancholy and sadness are clearly seen (and he himself could secretly vouchsafe that "the man who sings is not always happy"); these convey perhaps even more the anguish of a creator always making but so rarely fulfilling demands of himself. "I am only beginning to understand. I should start all over again." Light in his paintings is not the same as that of the solar spectrum. The greatest minds, trying to discover his secret, have recognized that it remains a mystery. Then again, there exists a sort of nostalgia, despite the feeling of insufficiency in the face of the goal to be attained. "There is always color, [but] it has yet to become light."

For us today, dazzled as we are by these paintings, we are nonetheless aware of the fact that it is a rare thing for a painter to have managed to convey through his art such a love of life, such an understanding of painting.

The pages that follow include a selection, both in pictures and in words, of Bonnard's thoughts and sketches derived from his diaries and letters, direct and spontaneous evidence of the artist's feelings and of his creative process.

Pages 249–252:
Pierre Bonnard, *Daybook of 1933*, 1933, Pencil on paper, 5⅛ × 3⅛ in. (13 × 8 cm), Bibliothèque Nationale de France. Département des Estampes et de la Photographie.

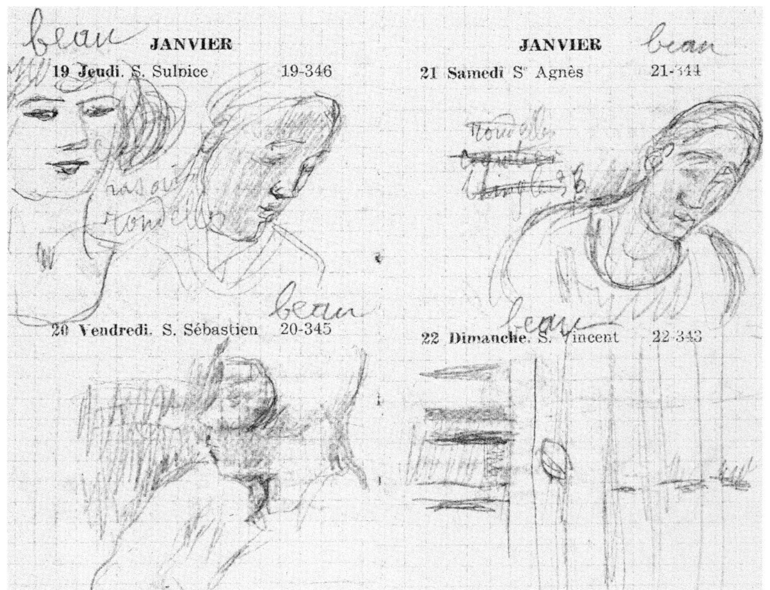

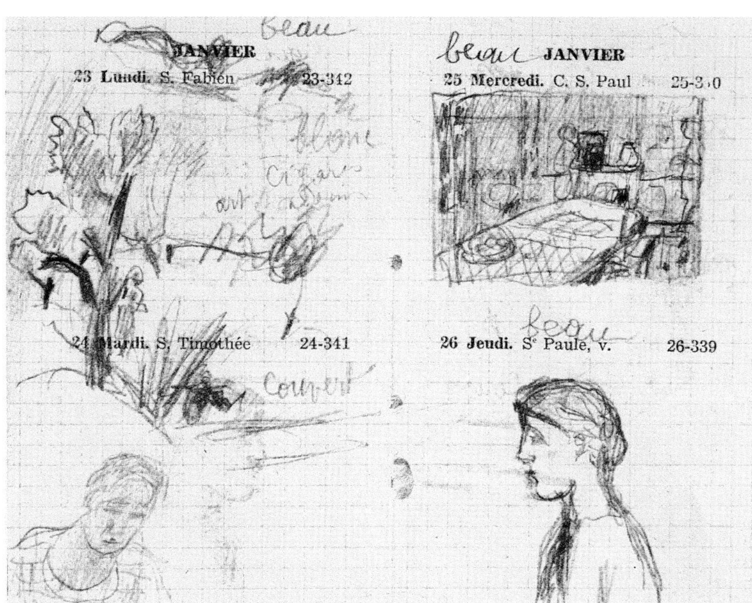

1927

February 7
Purple in the grays.
Vermilion in the orange shadows, on a cold, fine day.
April 4
Beautiful conventional coloring on a line drawing with two adjoining colors.
April 16
Proximity of white, lending a luminosity to some bright colored spots.
May 4
Make possible strong colors in the light through the proximity of black and white.

1929

February 15
Large shapes, even in small formats.
February 23
Beauty of drawing.
Harmony of lines for the directions and proportions of large spaces.

April 24
Rhetoric in the realization of the work. Calling up one's mental reserves of beautiful shapes and colors, the outcome of personal observation, and of observations of the masters, conjured up before one's eyes at each brushstroke.
June 1
Pascal's thought, "What vanity in painting." The originals do not interest us; on the contrary, they delight us.

1930

January 14
Understanding of nature, sincerity: means to the end of expression.
January 18
A guideline other than an analytical likeness of objects.
June 13
The demands and the pleasures of seeing, and its rewards. Crude seeing and intelligent seeing.

November 9
Drawing with a light touch shapes: out of shadows.

1931

April 22
In the act of seeing, the mind has a reduced capacity to feel a large number of plastic elements in groups, or near each other. One can increase that capacity.
October 25
The whole pictorial effect must be given by line equivalents. Before you add color, you must see things once, or see them a thousand times.

1932

February 16
Show nature when it's beautiful.
Everything has its moment of beauty.
Beauty is the fulfillment of seeing. Seeing is fulfilled by simplicity and order. Simplicity

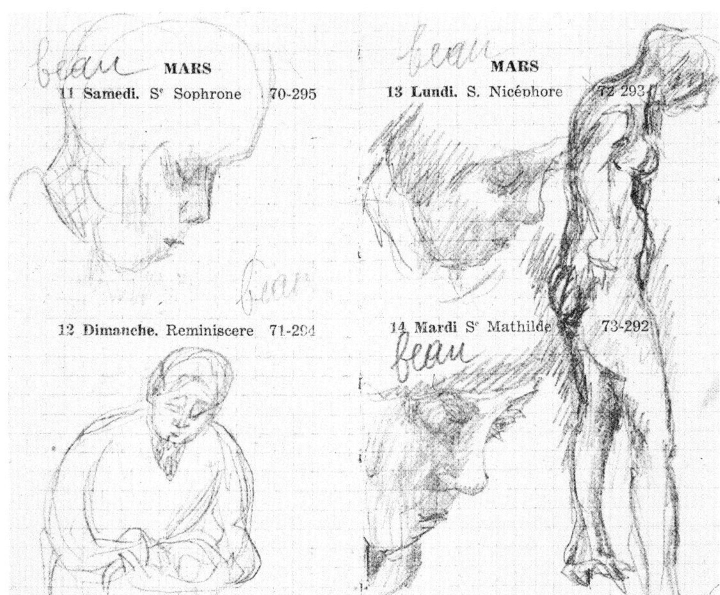

and order are produced by dividing legible surfaces, grouping compatible colors, etc.

March 14
Activity and understanding under the sign of success.

March 15
. . . under the sign of apathy.

March 16
. . . under the sign of energy.

March 17
. . . under the sign of uncertainty

March 19
 . . . under the sign of restraint.

March 28
Linking with black chalk. Or by connecting tones.

May 13
What is beautiful in nature is not always beautiful in painting. For instance: evening or night effects.

1934

January 1
Expressing feelings through painting and drawing. Distortion for visibility's sake. Any object, any effect can be interpreted visually in several ways. Feeling is one.

January 4
A sentimental vision which holds the wall together. (A feeling which holds the wall together.)

January 13
To judge oneself, change places: the wall— the open air. Distortion of differences. Distortion of the drawing for visibility's sake.

January 14
First image means. While working, find those which will be bound to occur.

January 15
One can take all possible liberties of line, form, proportions, colors, to make feeling intelligible and clearly visible. Intentions count for nothing.

January 16
When one distorts nature, it still remains underneath, unlike purely imaginative works.

January 22
Untruth is cutting out a piece of nature and copying it.

February 1
Painting or the transcription of the adventures of the optic nerve.

February 10
The very first convention is limitation, and the effect at a distance.

February 15
The child has an ideal of solitude (Robinson Crusoe) which is sufficiently fulfilled by his relationship with nature.

1935

January 2
Planes through color. Rough out with color contrasts.

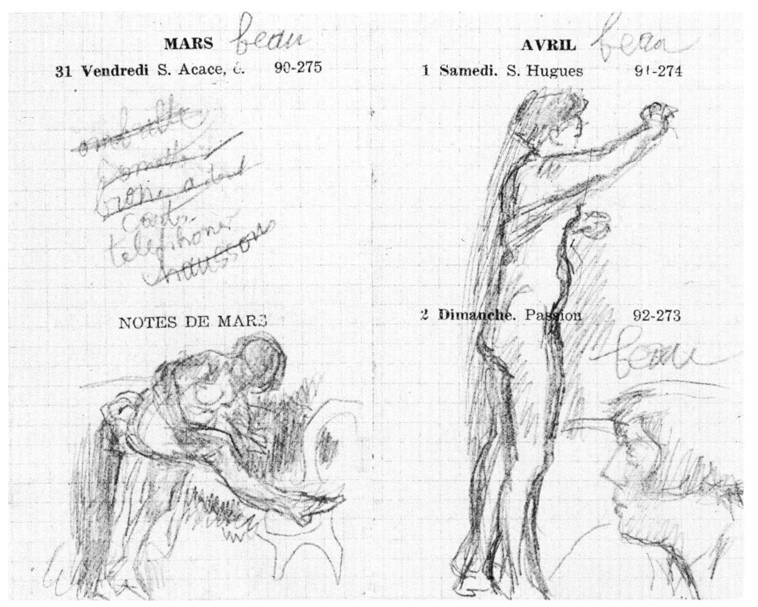

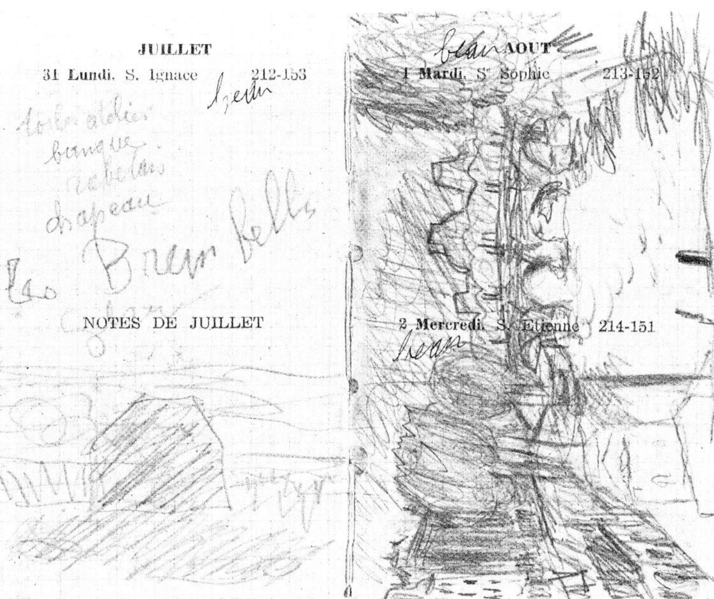

January 14
Coherence.
July 3
The model you have before your eyes, and the model you have in your hand.
July 19
Draw your pleasure—paint your pleasure—express your pleasure strongly.
October 3
The aesthetic rendering of objects or acceptance of raw seeing.
October 12
A strict compartmentalizing of one's vision nearly always produces something false. The second stage of composition involves integrating certain elements which are outside that rectangle.
October 27
In painting too, truth is next to falsehood.
November 7
For the sake of hygiene, avoid the amusing, picturesque, trite motif.

December 2
The main subject is the surface, which has its color, its laws, over and above those of the objects.
December 4
Aesthetic rendering of movement and gestures. There must be a stop, a support. Or if the gesture is emphatic, accompany it by other emphatic forms.

1936

January 1
Painting and the public, latest manifestation: the Grand Salon. The life of color. The life of black, the life of lines.
January 2
2 operations:
1. Imagine the means.
2. Recognize and use the unexpected quirks of matter during the execution.
The means: dark or light paint, group of colors, standard or general values.

February 29
Sunday painters: their naïve love of objects leads them to discoveries. Techniques correspond to necessary artifice, the requirements of nature causing a limitation.
April 23
The reason for transposition: nature is infinite, the work is finite, limited, legible, surrounded by hostile neighboring objects.
May 2
A group of coherent relationships produce something true. The choice of that group is a matter of convenience. One can swim in chocolate or in a blue sky.
May 8
Identity of the individual character, sensations of hearing and smelling. Consciousness, the shock of feeling and memory.
May 10
Attraction of action. One envies the man who devotes himself to creating something but if one does it oneself, one soon becomes tired of it.

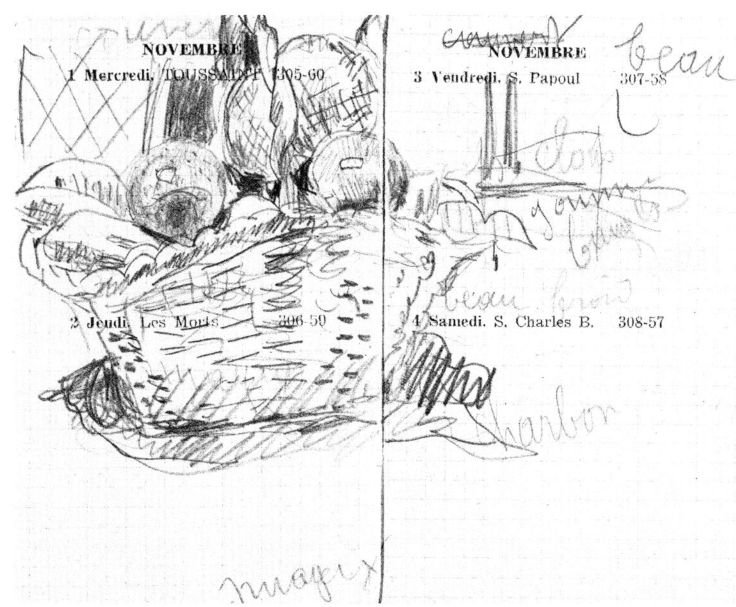

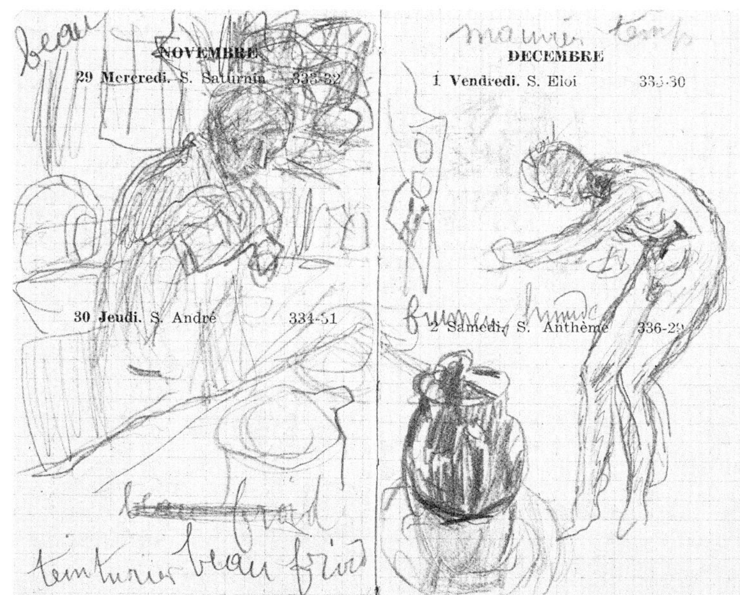

November 16
The work of art: a moment in time.

1937

April 27
Sensation leads you to color tones. Tones, in return, bring about a revelation of sensation.

1938

March 5
Use the idea of likeness in order to work, not to judge oneself. In his modeling, Cézanne replaced the black chalk of the old masters by variations in color.

March 7
Conception or preparation and execution; the true painter finds something new even while realizing the elements planned in the conception.

October 6
Keep watch: the moment when color takes on a value.

October 19
In the most servile imitation, there is a margin. Execution: the inner model combines with imitation of the material model: one is warned by the first lines and the first applications of paint to a given surface.

1939

January 2
Drawing a movement and static drawing. Rubens's drawing: the movement of figures is accompanied by animated lines in the landscape of draperies.

January 15
Likeness is a means and not an end. Values appear after a period of looking.

January 18
That an inner feeling of beauty coincides with nature, *that's* the point.

February 6
Squaring the circle: one can never make a surface covered with countless dots identical with a color.

February 8
One always talks of surrendering to nature. There is also such a thing as surrendering to the picture.

February 12
The minute one says one is happy, one isn't anymore.

February 14
Observe nature, and work on the canvas, indicating the colors: the climate of the work transcends all else.

February 20
The vision of details is wrong; as for light, it's only a question of understanding.

October 15
Simple relationships rarely simple in nature; the difference between noise and music: simple relationships.

1940

September 1
Mallarmé. Searching for the absolute.
November 4
Reason while working. Judge without
reasoning.

1944

January 17
The man who sings is not always happy.
March 3-4
States of daydreaming like the cat. Sleep
between states of exaltation like the dog.

1945

There is a formula which fits painting perfectly: many little lies to create a great truth.

Since all painters undertake the same
things, struggle with the same difficulties,
use the same means, it is from within that
differences arise. In this subtle balance
between lies and truth, everything is relative,
a question of more or less. Extreme sincerity
runs an equal risk of seeming either ridicu-
lous or untenable.

If one forgets everything, all that remains
is one's self, and that is not enough. It is always
necessary to have a subject, however minimal,
in order to keep one foot on the ground.

When one covers a surface with colors,
one should always be able to try any number
of new approaches, find a never-ending
supply of new combinations of forms and
colors which satisfy emotional needs.

1946

In art, it is only reactions that count.

It's not a matter of painting life. It's a
matter of giving life to painting.

I have a palette. But assessments allow
me to separate colors, whereas the palette
has a drawback: it proposes, it imposes them,
which is a danger. Those are things one
learns only very late. It would only be too
easy to place oneself in front of a landscape,
to observe it, and simply to transpose it onto
the canvas. One must also think of the place
where the canvas will be seen afterwards.

As Delacroix wrote in his diary: "one
never paints violently enough." In the light
experienced in the South of France, everything sparkles and the whole painting
vibrates. Take your picture to Paris: the
blues turn to gray. Seen from afar, those
blues also turn to gray. Therefore one thing
is necessary in painting: heightening the
tone. Primitive painters had understood
this, clearly, for they derived their brightest
reds and blues from precious colorings:
lapis lazuli, gold, and cochineal. Nature sets
traps for us with its themes, which intelligence and above all craftsmanship manage
to avoid. It's the only advantage of getting
old: learning from personal experience.

I hope that my painting will endure without craquelure. I should like to present
myself to the young painters of the year
2000 with the wings of a butterfly.

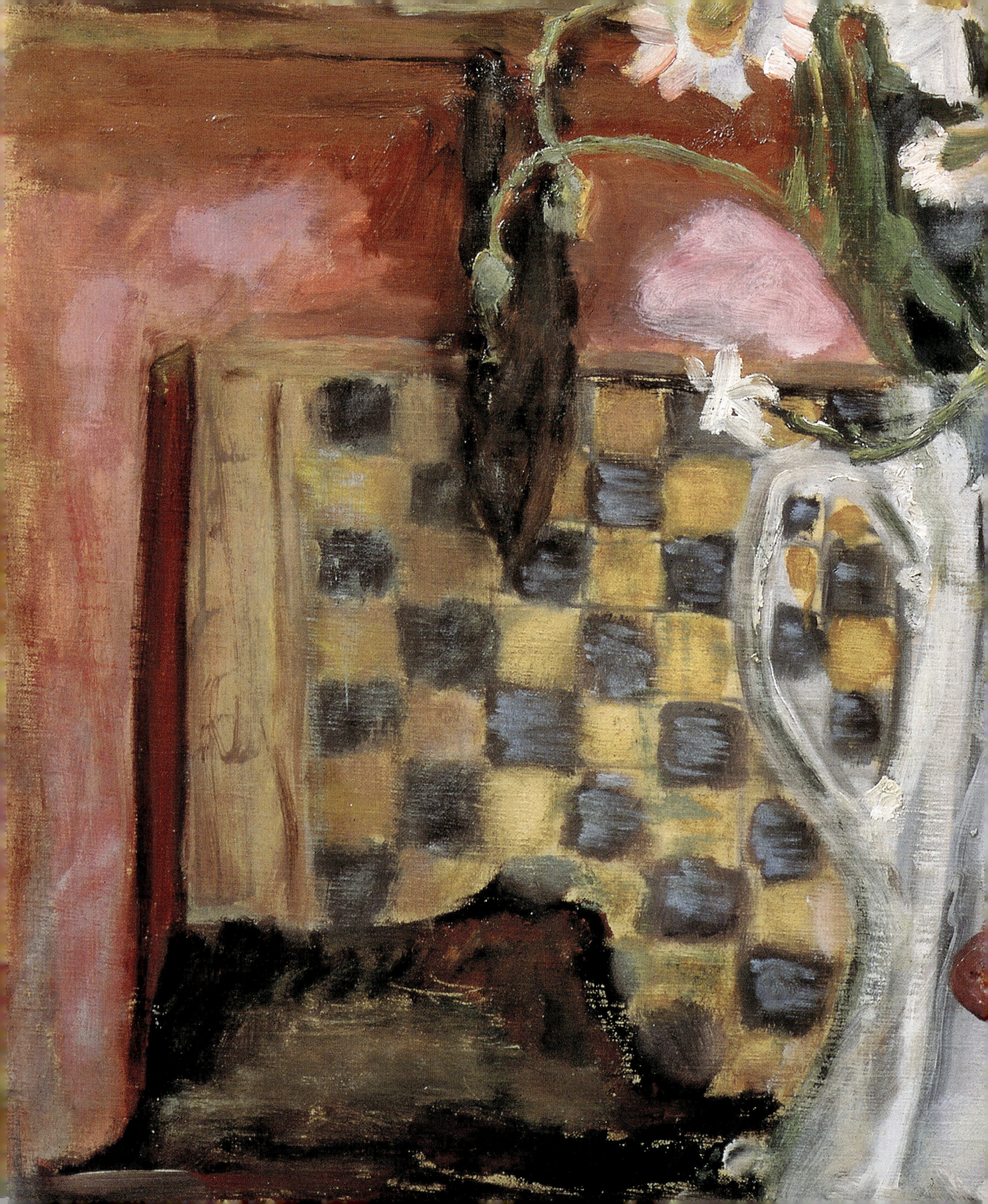

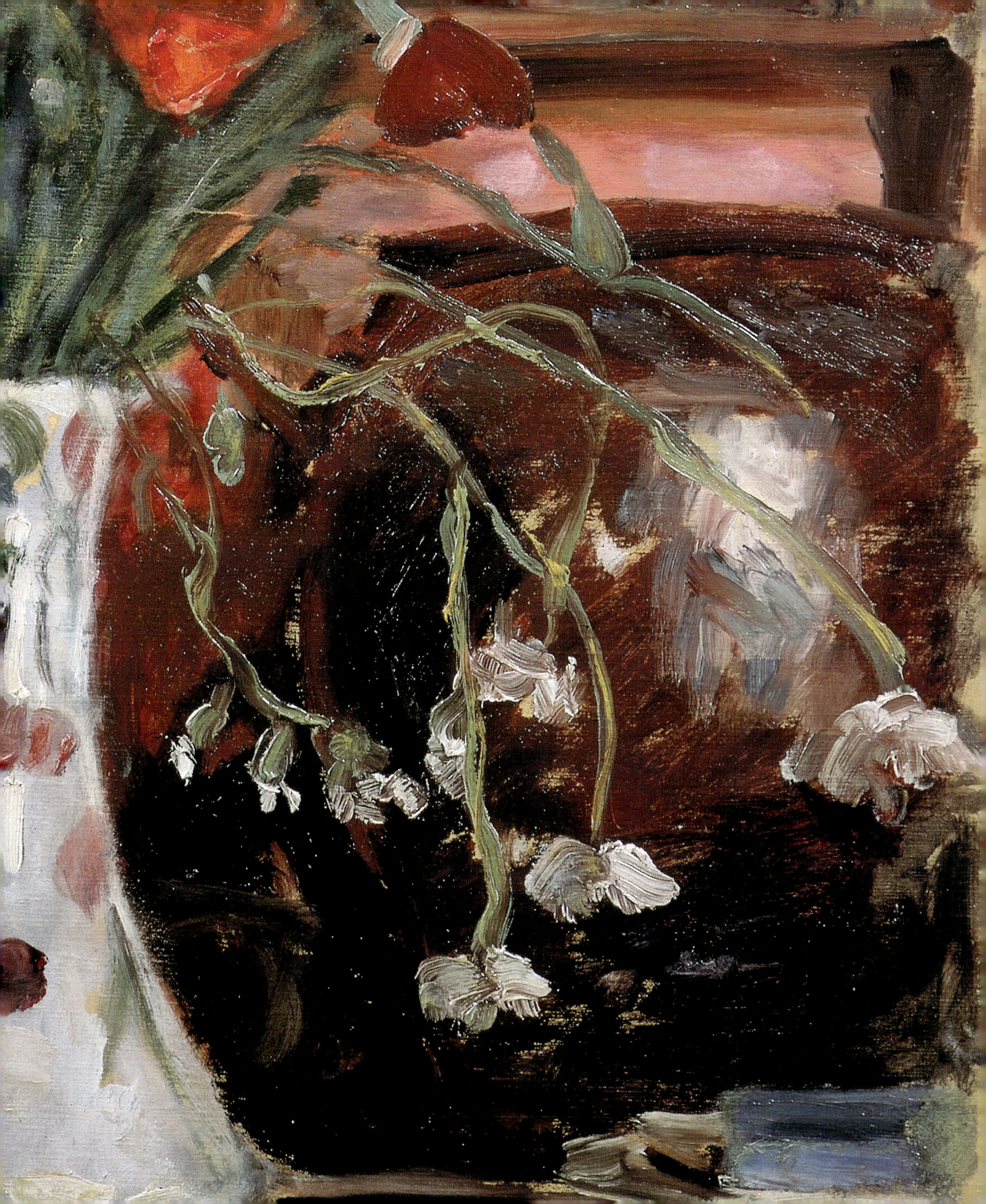

Unless otherwise noted, dimensions are unframed, support size, height preceding width.

Self-Portrait (Portrait de l'artiste par lui-même)
1889
Oil on board, 7⅞ × 6⅛ in. (20 × 15.5 cm)
Private collection
[plate 1]
Provenance
Family of the artist; private collection
Exhibitions
Pierre Bonnard, Kunsthaus Zurich, 14 December 1984–10 March 1985, Städtische Galerie im Städelschen Kunstinstitut, Frankfurt, 3 May–14 July 1985, no. 1; *Pierre Bonnard*, Palazzo Reale, Milan, 28 October 1988–8 January 1989, no. 2; *Pierre Bonnard*, Fondation de l'Hermitage, Lausanne, 7 June–6 October 1991, no. 1; *Pierre Bonnard*, Aichi Prefectural Museum of Art, Nagoya, 28 March–18 May 1997, Bunkamura Museum of Art, Tokyo, 24 May–21 July 1997, no. 2; *Bonnard*, Tate Gallery, London, 12 February–17 May 1998, The Museum of Modern Art, New York, 17 June–13 October 1998, no. 2; *Bonnard*, Fondation Pierre Gianadda, Martigny, Switzerland, 11 June–14 November 1999, no. 2; Musée Maillol, Paris, 2000; Fondation Vieira De Silva, Lisbon, 2001.

Marabout (Stork) and Four Frogs (Le Marabout et les quatre grenouilles)
ca. 1889
Distemper on fine canvas (three-paneled screen), each panel, 62¾ × 21½ in. (159.5 × 54.5 cm)
Private collection
Washington only
[plate 2]
Provenance
Madame Claude Terrasse, Paris; Madame Vivette Floury (by descent), Paris; private collection, Paris; Galerie Hopkins-Thomas-Custot, Paris; private collection.

Studies for "France-Champagne"
ca. 1889
Pencil and ink on wove paper, 12³⁄₁₆ × 7¹³⁄₁₆ in. (30.9 × 19.9 cm) (recto)
Pencil and ink on wove paper, 7¹³⁄₁₆ × 12³⁄₁₆ in. (19.9 × 30.9 cm) (verso)
Virginia and Ira Jackson Collection. Partial and Promised Gift to the National Gallery of Art, Washington.
[plate 4a–b]
Provenance
Collection Cass Canfield; Virginia and Ira Jackson Collection.
Exhibitions
Pierre Bonnard: The Graphic Art, The Metropolitan Museum of Art, New York, 2 December 1989–4 February 1990, The Museum of Fine Arts, Houston, 25 February–29 April 1990, Museum of Fine Arts, Boston, 25 May–29 July 1990, no. 2; *Prints Abound: Paris in the 1890s*, National Gallery of Art, Washington, D.C., 22 October 2000–25 February 2001, nos. 6a–b.

Poster for "France-Champagne"
1891
Color lithograph, 31⁷⁄₁₆ × 23¾ in. (79.8 × 60.3 cm)
Virginia and Ira Jackson Collection. Partial and Promised Gift to the National Gallery of Art, Washington.
[plate 5]
Provenance
Virginia and Ira Jackson Collection
Exhibitions
Prints Abound: Paris in the 1890s, National Gallery of Art, Washington, D.C., 22 October 2000–25 February 2001, no. 5.

Afternoon in the Garden
(L'Après-midi au jardin or Goûter au jardin)
1891
Oil and pen and black ink over pencil on canvas, 14¾ × 17¾ in. (37.5 × 45.1 cm)
Private collection
Washington only
[plate 9]
Provenance
Mrs. Caroline Hary, Paris, gift from the artist; private collection by descent (until 1998); private collection, Switzerland; private collection.

Two Poodles (Deux Chiens)
1891
Oil on canvas, 14⁹⁄₁₆ × 15⅝ in. (37 × 39.7 cm)
Southampton City Art Gallery
[plate 7]
Provenance
O. Bateman Brown, London; sold, Sotheby's, London, 23 November 1960, no. 81, to Arthur Jeffress, London; bequeathed to Southampton City Art Gallery, 1963.
Exhibitions
8ème Salon de la Société des artistes indépendants, 19 March–27 April 1892, no. 171; *Exposition de peinture de "La Dépêche de Toulouse,"* Toulouse, 15 May–end June 1894; Royal Academy of Arts, London, 1966, no. 6; *Pierre Bonnard*, Haus der Kunst, Munich, 8 October 1966–1 January 1967, Musée du Louvre, Paris, 13 January–15 April 1967, no. 6; Nottingham Castle Museum, 1984, no. 115; *Pierre Bonnard*, Kunsthaus Zurich, 14 December 1984–10 March 1985, Städtische Galerie im Städelschen Kunstinstitut, Frankfurt, 3 May–14 July 1985, no. 7; *Pierre Bonnard*, Isetan Museum of Art, Tokyo, 4–30 July 1991, Nara Sogo Museum of Art, 7 August–1 September 1991, Sogo Museum of Art, Yokohama, 7 September–10 October 1991, Fukuoka Art Museum, 17 October–10 November, 1991, no. 2; *Die Nabis: Propheten der Moderne*, Kunsthaus Zurich, 28 May–15 August 1993, traveled as *Nabis 1888–1900*, Galeries Nationales du Grand Palais, Paris, 21 September 1993–3 January 1994, no. 7; *Bonnard*, Kunsthalle der Hypo–Kulturstiftung, Munich, 28 January–24 April 1994, no. 5; *Pierre Bonnard*, Aichi Prefectural Museum of Art, Nagoya, 28 March–18 May 1997, Bunkamura Museum of Art, Tokyo, 24 May–21 July 1997, no. 6; *Beyond the Easel: Decorative Painting by Bonnard, Vuillard, Denis and Roussel, 1890–1930*, The Art Institute of Chicago, 25 February–16 May 2001, The Metropolitan Museum of Art, New York, 26 June–9 September 2001, no. 4.

Women with Dog (Femmes au chien)
1891
Oil on canvas, 16 × 12¾ in. (40.6 × 32.4 cm)
Sterling and Francine Clark Art Institute, Williamstown, Massachusetts
Washington only
[plate 6]
Provenance
Saincère collection; Palais Galléria, Paris, 19 June 1963; Philippe Durand-Ruel, Paris, 1963–1965; Hirschl and Adler Galleries, New York, 1965; Mr. and Mrs. Lowell S. Dillingham, 1965–1973; Hirschl and Adler Galleries, New York; sold to the Sterling and Francine Clark Art Institute.
Exhibitions
Bonnard, Bernheim-Jeune, Paris, 1950, no. 7; *Hommage à Bonnard*, Bernheim-Jeune, Paris, 1956, no. 2; *Die Nabis und ihre Freunde*, Städtische Kunsthalle, Mannheim, 1964, no. 39; *Retrospective of a Gallery: Twenty Years*, Hirschl and Adler Galleries, New York, 1973, no. 8; *Twenty Years of Post-Impressionism, 1880–1900*, Hirschl and Adler Galleries, New York, 1974, no. 5; *Twenty-five Selections from the European Collection of Hirschl and Adler Galleries*, Hirschl and Adler Galleries, New York, 1977, no. 2; *Post-Impressionism: Cross-Currents in European Paintings*, Royal Academy of Arts, London, 1980, no. 28; *The Inquiring Eye of Pierre Bonnard: A Loan Exhibition for the Benefit of The Memorial Sloan-Kettering Cancer Center*, Wildenstein and Co., New York, 1981, no. 1; *A la mode: Women's Fashions in French Art, 1850–1900*, Sterling and Francine Clark Art Institute, Williamstown, Mass., 1982, no. 3; *Recent Acquisitions and Long-Term Loans 1977–1982*, Sterling and Francine Clark Art Institute, Williamstown, Mass., 1983; *Pierre Bonnard*, Kunsthaus Zurich, 14 December 1984–10 March 1985, Städtische Galerie im Städelschen Kunstinstitut, Frankfurt, 3 May–14 July 1985, no. 6; *A Magic Mirror: The Portrait in France, 1700–1900*, The Museum of Fine Arts, Houston, 1986–1987, no. 43; *Pierre Bonnard: The Graphic Art*, The Metropolitan Museum of Art, New York, 2 December 1989–4 February 1990, The Museum of Fine Arts, Houston, 25 February–29 April 1990, Museum of Fine Arts, Boston, 25 May–29 July 1990, no. 97; *Pierre Bonnard*, Isetan Museum of Art, Tokyo, 4–30 July 1991, Nara Sogo Museum of Art, 7 August–1 September 1991, Sogo Museum of Art, Yokohama, 7 September–10 October 1991, Fukuoka Art Museum, 17 October–10 November 1991, no. 1; *Die Nabis: Propheten der Moderne*, Kunsthaus Zurich, 28 May–15 August 1993, traveled as *Nabis 1888–1900*, Galeries Nationales du Grand Palais, Paris, 21 September 1993–3 January 1994, no. 6; *Bonnard*, Kunsthalle der Hypo-Kulturstiftung, Munich, 28 January–24 April 1994, no. 4.

Checked Blouse; Portrait of Mme Claude Terrasse, the Artist's Sister (Le Corsage à carreaux; Portrait de Mme Claude Terrasse, soeur de l'artiste)
1892
Oil on canvas, 23⅝ × 13 in. (60 × 33 cm)
Private collection, courtesy Galerie Cazeau-Béraudière, Paris
[plate 3]
Provenance
Madame Claude Terrasse; Madame Floury; private collection, Zurich.

Previous spread:
Vase of Flowers and Checkers
(detail) 1912, Oil on canvas,
31⅛ × 22 ½ in. (79.5 × 57 cm),
Mr. and Mrs. Joe L. Allbritton.

Exhibitions
Bonnard, Fondation Pierre Gianadda, Martigny, Switzerland,
11 June–14 November 1999, no. 4.

Dogs (Les Chiens)
1893
Lithograph on cream wove paper, 15 × 11 in. (38.1 × 27.8 cm)
The Phillips Collection, Washington, D.C.
[plate 17]
Provenance
The Phillips Collection, Gift of Marjorie Phillips, 1984.
Exhibitions
Pont-Aven to Nabis, Isetan Museum of Art, Tokyo, 2–14 April
1987, Niigata City Art Museum, 18 April–17 May 1987,
Daimaru Museum, Osaka, 20 May–9 June 1987, Shizuoka
Prefectural Museum, 13 June–19 July 1987, Himeji City
Museum of Art, 25 July–23 August 1987, Yamanashi
Prefectural Museum, 27 August–27 September 1987, no. 17.

**In Private; Young Woman in Black Stockings
(Dans l'Intimité; Jeune Femme aux bas noirs)**
1893
Lithograph on cream wove paper, 11¼ × 5 in.
(28.6 × 12.7 cm)
The Phillips Collection, Washington, D.C.
[plate 19]
Provenance
The Phillips Collection, acquired from Peter Deitsch in 1954.
Exhibitions
Works on Paper: Pierre Bonnard, The Phillips Collection,
Washington, D.C., 30 June–25 October 1992.

**"Leçon sur les mesures composées" in Claude Terrasse's
"Petit Solfège illustré"**
1893
Lithograph in book, 8⅜ × 11¼ in. (21.3 × 28.3 cm)
Heineman Foundation Collection in Honor of Edward
N. Waters, Music Division, Library of Congress,
Washington, D.C.
[plate 14b]
Provenance
Library of Congress.

**Municipal Guard (Garde municipal or L'Amusement des
enfants. La Tranquilité des parents)**
1893
Lithograph on cream wove paper, 15 × 11⅛ in.
(38.1 × 28.2 cm)
The Phillips Collection, Washington, D.C.
[plate 16]
Provenance
The Phillips Collection, acquired from Peter Deitsch in 1954.
Exhibitions
Drawings and Prints from the Collection, The Phillips Gallery,
Washington, D.C., July–9 November 1956; *Drawings from the
Collection*, The Phillips Gallery, Washington, D.C., 15 July–1
November 1957; *Six Prints and Drawings from the Collection*,
The Phillips Gallery, Washington, D.C., 1–15 October 1958;
*Paintings and Drawings by Pierre Bonnard: An Exhibition
from The Phillips Collection and the Collections of Mrs.*

Phillips and Mr. and Mrs. Laughlin Phillips, The Phillips
Collection, Washington, D.C., 7 January–28 February 1967;
Works on Paper: Pierre Bonnard, The Phillips Collection,
Washington, D.C., 30 June–25 October 1992.

"Rêverie" in Claude Terrasse's "Petites Scènes familières"
1893
Lithograph, 13⅞ × 10¾ in. (35.2 × 27 cm)
Museum of Fine Arts, Boston. Bequest of W. G. Russell
Allen, 1963 63.723
[plate 15]
Provenance
W. G. Russell Allen (1882–1955), Boston; Museum of Fine
Arts, Boston, acquired by bequest 1963.

The Parisians (Les Parisiennes)
1893
Lithograph, 8⅜ × 5 in. (21.3 × 12.7 cm)
Prints and Photographs Division, Library of Congress,
Washington, D.C. Reproduction numbers: LC-USZC4-
10009, LC-USZ62-130235
[plate 18]
Provenance
Library of Congress

Woman Pulling on Her Stockings (Femme enfilant ses bas)
1893
Oil on board, 13⅞ × 10⅝ in. (35.2 × 27 cm)
Private collection. Courtesy The Fine Art Society plc.
[plate 21]
Provenance
Galerie Paul Petrides, Paris; private collection, New York;
JPL Fine Arts, London; private collection, England.
Exhibitions
L'Europe des Peintres, 1893, no. 42; *Bonnard*, Galerie Salis,
Salzburg, 27 July–15 September 1991, JPL Fine Arts, London,
3 October–6 December 1991, no. 2; Musée d'Orsay, Paris,
1993; The Fine Art Society, London, 1997, no. 39; *Bonnard*,
Tate Gallery, London, 12 February–17 May 1998, The
Museum of Modern Art, New York, 17 June–13 October
1998, no. 6.

Circus Rider (Cirque)
1894
Oil on cardboard, 10⅝ × 13¾ in. (27 × 34.9 cm)
The Phillips Collection, Washington, D.C.
[plate 22]
Provenance
Thadée Natanson, Paris; sale Natanson, Hôtel Drouot, Paris,
June 1908; Bernheim-Jeune, Paris, 1908; Aurélien
Lugné-Poë, 1909; Dr. Soubies, Paris; Félix Fénéon, Paris,
1928; sale Collection Fénéon, Deuxième Vente, Tableaux
Modernes. . . au Profit de l'Université de Paris, Hôtel
Drouot, Paris, 30 May 1947; The Phillips Collection, acquired
December 1947 from Theodore Schempf.
Exhibitions
Chez Vollard, rue Laffitte, 1894 or 1895; *Bonnard*, Galeries
Durand-Ruel, Paris, 1896, no. 6; *Tableaux de Pierre Bonnard
de 1891 à 1922*, Galerie Druet, Paris, 7–18 April 1924, no. 3; *Les
Peintres de la Revue Blanche entre 1891 et 1903*, Galerie

Bolette Natanson, Paris, June 1936, no. 1; *Parijsche Schilders*,
Stedelijk Museum, Amsterdam, February–April 1939, no. 1;
Paintings in the Collection by Bonnard, The Phillips Gallery,
Washington, D.C., 3 February–31 March 1952; *Horse and
Rider*, Fort Worth Art Center, 7 January–3 March 1957, no.
87; *Paintings and Drawings from the Collection*, The Phillips
Gallery, Washington, D.C., after 8 January–1 April 1958;
Paintings by Pierre Bonnard from the Collection, The Phillips
Gallery, Washington, D.C., 15 March–30 June 1959; *Paintings
and Drawings by Pierre Bonnard: An Exhibition from The
Phillips Collection and the Collections of Mrs. Phillips and Mr.
and Mrs. Laughlin Phillips,* The Phillips Collection,
Washington, D.C., 7 January–28 February 1967; *Bonnard and
Vuillard: An Exhibition for the Benefit of The Phillips
Collection*, Adams Davidson Galleries, Washington, D.C., 17
May–17 June 1978, no. 1; *Duncan Phillips: Centennial
Exhibition*, The Phillips Collection, Washington, D.C., 14
June–31 August 1986; *Pont-Aven to Nabis*, Isetan Museum of
Art, Tokyo, 2–14 April 1987, Niigata City Art Museum, 18
April–17 May 1987, Daimaru Museum, Osaka, 20 May–9
June 1987, Shizuoka Prefectural Museum, 13 June–19 July
1987, Himeji City Museum of Art, 25 July–23 August 1987,
Yamanashi Prefectural Museum, 27 August–27 September
1987, no. 14; *Renoir to Rothko: The Eye of Duncan Phillips*,
The Phillips Collection, Washington, D.C., 25 September
1999–23 January 2000.

Poster for "La Revue blanche"
1894
Lithograph printed in four colors, 31⁵⁄₁₆ × 24⁷⁄₁₆ in. (79.5 × 62
cm)
Museum of Fine Arts, Boston. Bequest of W. G. Russell
Allen, 1960 60.65
[plate 23]
Provenance
W. G. Russell Allen (1882–1955), Boston; Museum of Fine
Arts, Boston, acquired by bequest, 1960.

Three Panels of a Screen (Ensemble champêtre)
1894–1895
Oil on brown twill lined with canvas, each panel,
65¾ × 20 in. (167 × 50.8 cm)
The Museum of Modern Art, New York; Gift of Mr. and
Mrs. Allan D. Emil 1955
[plate 10]
Provenance
Collections artist, Madame Jeanne Bucher, Pierre Loeb,
Bernheim-Jeune & Cie, Gimpel Fils, 1951, and Mr. and Mrs.
Allan D. Emil; Purchased by the donor from Gimpel Fils,
London.
Exhibitions
Bonnard, Bernheim-Jeune, Paris, 1950, no. 2; *XIXth and
XXth Century French Paintings*, The Lefevre Gallery, London,
February–March 1960, no. 8; *Van Gogh, Gauguin and Their
Circle*, Christie's, New York, 13–30 November 1968; *Die Nabis:
Propheten der Moderne*, Kunsthaus Zurich, 28 May–15
August 1993, traveled as *Nabis 1888–1900*, Galeries Nationales
du Grand Palais, 22 September 1993–3 January 1994.

Cover for the album "Some Scenes of Parisian Life"
(Cover for the album "Quelques aspects de la vie de Paris")
1895
Lithograph printed in two colors, 21¹⁄₁₆ × 15⅞ in.
(53.5 × 40.4 cm)
Museum of Fine Arts, Boston. Bequest of W. G. Russell
Allen, 1960 60.52
[plate 30]
Provenance
W. G. Russell Allen (1882–1955), Boston; Museum of Fine
Arts, Boston, acquired by bequest, 1960.

The Omnibus (L'Omnibus)
1895
Oil on canvas, 23¼ × 16⅛ in. (59 × 41 cm)
Courtesy Galerie Félix Vercel
[plate 26]
Provenance
Vicomtesse de Maublanc, Paris; Galerie Félix Vercel; private
collection.
Exhibitions
*Chefs d'œuvre de collections françaises (Dix-neuvième-
vingtième siècle)*, Galerie Charpentier, Paris, 1962, no. 4;
Bonnard dans sa lumière, Fondation Maeght, Saint-Paul-de-
Vence, 12 July–28 September 1975; 25ᵉ Salon de Montrouge
Bonnard, 1980; *Eclatement de l'impressionnisme*, Tokyo, 1981;
Musée du Prieuré, Saint-Germaine-en-Laye, September
1982–March 1983; *Bonnard, Vuillard, Roussel*, Salon des
Artistes français, Grand Palais, Paris, 1983; *Bonnard*,
Kunsthaus Zurich, 14 December 1984–10 March 1985;
Bonnard, Städtische Galerie im Städelschen Kunstinstitut,
Frankfurt, 3 May–14 July 1985, no. 20; *Hommage à Bonnard*,
Galerie des Beaux–Arts, Bordeaux, 10 May–25 August 1986,
no. 13; *L'Europe des Grands Maîtres,* Musée Jacquemart
André, Paris, 1989, Tokyo, Kyoto, Haraki, Osaka,
May–September 1991; *Premiers chefs d'œuvre des
Grands Maîtres Européens*, Madrid, Barcelona, Bilbao, 15
October 1991–15 January 1992; Dong A. Museum, Seoul,
1 March–15 April 1992; *Die Nabis: Propheten der Moderne*,
Kunsthaus Zurich, 28 May–15 August 1993, traveled as
Nabis 1888–1900 to Galeries Nationales du Grand Palais,
Paris, 21 September 1993–3 January 1994, no. 21; *Les
Nabis au Musée d'Orsay*, 11 January–13 February 1994;
Bonnard, Kunsthalle der Hypo–Kulturstiftung, Munich,
27 January–24 April 1994, no. 5; *Bonnard*, Fondation Pierre
Gianadda, Martigny, Switzerland, 11 June–14 November
1999, no. 6.

Nannies Promenade, Frieze of Carriages
(La Promenade des nourrices, frise des fiacres)
1895; published 1899
Lithograph printed in five colors, mounted on four-fold
screen, each panel approximately 59⅞ × 19⅞ in.
(151.8 × 50.5 cm)
Museum of Fine Arts, Boston. Ernest W. Longfellow Fund,
1976 1976.605
Denver only
[plate 24]
Provenance
Mrs. Ivor Leclerc; Mrs. Ralph J. Hines; purchased by

Museum of Fine Arts, Boston, from Angus Whyte
Gallery, Boston.

Nannies' Promenade, Frieze of Carriages
(La Promenade des nourrices, frise des fiacres)
1895; published 1899
Lithograph printed in five colors, mounted on four-fold
screen, panel one: 58¹³⁄₁₆ × 20⁵⁄₁₆ in. (149.1 × 51.5 cm), panel
two: 59⁵⁄₁₆ × 19¹⁄₁₆ in. (150.4 × 48.4 cm), panel three: 58⅞
× 20⁷⁄₁₆ in. (149.3 × 51.8 cm), panel four: 60¹⁄₁₆ × 18¾ in.
(152.1 × 47.6 cm),
Property of Mr. and Mrs. Donald B. Marron
Washington only
[plate 24]
Provenance
Property from estate of private collection and partial interest
of Philadelphia Museum of Art.

The Cab Horse (Le Cheval de fiacre)
ca. 1895
Oil on wood, 11¾ × 15¾ in. (29.7 × 40 cm)
National Gallery of Art, Washington, Ailsa Mellon Bruce
Collection 1970.17.4
[plate 25]
Provenance
Shchukin, Moscow; sold 1899 to Bernheim-Jeune, Paris.
Anonymous collection, New York. Capt. Edward H.
Molyneux (1894–1974), Paris, by 1947; sold 15 August 1955 to
Ailsa Mellon Bruce [1901–1969], New York; gift 1970 to
National Gallery of Art, Washington. *Exhibitions*
Bonnard, Musée de l'Orangerie, Paris, 1947, no. 10; *Pierre
Bonnard*, The Museum of Modern Art, New York, 1948, no.
6; *French Paintings from the Molyneux Collection*, National
Gallery of Art, Washington, D.C., The Museum of Modern
Art, New York, 1952 (as *Boulevard des Batignolles*); Hampton
National Historic Site, Towson, Md., May–October 1956 (as
Boulevard des Batignolles); *Bonnard*, Society of the Four Arts,
Palm Beach, Fla., 4–27 January 1957, no. 25; *Paintings from
the Collection of Mrs. Mellon Bruce*, Society of the Four Arts,
Palm Beach, Fla., 1958, no. 25 (as *Boulevard des Batignolles*);
*French Paintings of the Nineteenth Century from the
Collection of Mrs. Mellon Bruce*, California Palace of the
Legion of Honor, San Francisco, 1961, no. 4; *Bonnard and
His Environment*, The Museum of Modern Art, New York, 7
October–29 November 1964, The Art Institute of Chicago, 8
January–28 February 1965, Los Angeles County Museum of
Art, 31 March–31 May 1965; *French Paintings from the
Collections of Mr. and Mrs. Paul Mellon and Mrs. Mellon
Bruce*, National Gallery of Art, Washington, D.C., 1966, no.
155; *Van Gogh, Gauguin and Their Circle*, Christie's, New
York, 1968, no. 37; *Small French Paintings from the Bequest of
Ailsa Mellon Bruce*, National Gallery of Art, Washington,
D.C., 1978; *Pierre Bonnard*, Kunsthaus Zurich, 1985, no. 18
(as *Batignolles avec la devanture fleurie*); *Impressionisti della
National Gallery of Art di Washington*, Ala Napoleonica e
Museo Correr, Venice, Palazzo Reale, Milan, 1989;
*Französische Impressionisten und ihre Wegbereiter aus dem
National Gallery of Art, Washington und dem Cincinnati Art
Museum*, Neue Pinakothek, Munich, 1990, no. 74; *Die Nabis:
Propheten der Moderne*, Kunsthaus Zurich, 28 May–15

August 1993, traveled as *Nabis 1888–1900* to Galeries
Nationales du Grand Palais, Paris, 21 September 1993–3
January 1994, no. 20.

Houses in the Courtyard (Maisons dans la cour)
1895–1896
Pastel on wove paper, 15⅝ × 12¼ in. (39.7 × 31.1 cm)
Museum of Fine Arts, Boston. Gift of Jessie H. Wilkinson,
Jessie H. Wilkinson Fund, 1979.2
[plate 35]
Provenance
Maurice Loncle; purchased by Museum of Fine Arts, Boston,
from R. M. Light & Co., Santa Barbara, Calif., January 1979.
Exhibitions
Pierre Bonnard: The Graphic Art, The Metropolitan Museum
of Art, New York, 2 December 1989–4 February 1990, The
Museum of Fine Arts, Houston, 25 February–29 April 1990,
Museum of Fine Arts, Boston, 25 May–29 July 1990, no. 61.

Houses in the Courtyard (Maisons dans la cour)
1895–1896; published 1899
Lithograph printed in four colors, 21¹⁄₁₆ × 16 in.
(53.5 × 40.7 cm)
Museum of Fine Arts, Boston. Bequest of W. G. Russell
Allen, 1960 60.55
[plate 34]
Provenance
W. G. Russell Allen (1882–1955), Boston; Museum of Fine
Arts, Boston, acquired by bequest, 1960.

The Little Laundry Girl (La Petite blanchisseuse)
1896
Color lithograph, 21⅛ × 15⅜ in. (53.7 × 39.5 cm)
Prints and Photographs Division, Library of Congress,
Washington, D.C. Reproduction numbers: LC-USZC4-
10048, LC-USZ62-72223
[plate 27]
Provenance
Library of Congress, Pennell Fund acquisition, selected by
the Pennell Committee established by Joseph Pennell.
Exhibitions
The Pennell Legacy: Two Centuries of Printmaking, Library of
Congress, Washington, D.C., December 1983–May 1984.

Street Corner Seen from Above (Coin de rue, vu d'en haut)
1896–1897; published 1899
Lithograph printed in four colors, 20⅞ × 16⅛ in.
(53 × 41 cm)
Museum of Fine Arts, Boston. Bequest of W. G. Russell
Allen, 1960 60.64
[plate 36]
Provenance
W. G. Russell Allen (1882–1955), Boston; Museum of Fine
Arts, Boston, acquired by bequest, 1960.

Cover for the Second "Album d'estampes originales"
1897
Lithograph printed in four colors, 27¹⁵⁄₁₆ × 36⁷⁄₁₆ in.
(71 × 92.5 cm)
Museum of Fine Arts, Boston. Frederick Brown Fund, 1955

55.943
[plate 29]
Provenance
Museum of Fine Arts, Boston, purchased from Ferdinand Roten, Baltimore dealer, 1955.

Child with Lamp (L'Enfant à la lampe)
ca. 1897
Lithograph printed in five colors, 17⅛ × 22¹¹⁄₁₆ in.
(43.5 × 57.7 cm)
Museum of Fine Arts, Boston. Bequest of W. G. Russell Allen, 1960 60.67
[plate 28]
Provenance
W. G. Russell Allen (1882–1955), Boston; Museum of Fine Arts, Boston, acquired by bequest, 1960.

Montmartre in the Rain or **Rue Tholozé**
(Montmartre dans la pluie or **Rue Tholozé)**
ca. 1897
Oil on paper, laid down on panel, 27⁹⁄₁₆ × 37⅜ in.
(70 × 95 cm)
Galerie Jan Krugier, Diteshein & Cie, Geneva
Washington only
[plate 37]
Provenance
Adams Gallery, London, 1935; private collection, London; Galerie de l'Elysée, Paris; Mrs. Sylvie Nathanson, New York; Galerie Jan Krugier, New York.
Exhibitions
20th Century French Paintings, Lefevre Gallery, London, 1943, no. 3; *Bonnard and His French Contemporaries*, Lefevre Gallery, London, 1947, no. 5; Adams Gallery, London, June 1948; *Exhibition of Paintings by Pierre Bonnard and Edouard Vuillard*, Royal Scottish Academy, Edinburgh, 1948, no. 5; *Pierre Bonnard*, Kunsthaus Zurich, 6 June–24 July 1949, no. 6; *Bonnard*, Roland, Browse and Delbanco, London, 1950, no. 11; *Bonnard*, Museum Boymans, Rotterdam, 1953, no. 8; Albert Loeb & Krugier Gallery, New York, 1969, no. 29b; *Paris sous le ciel de la peinture*, Hôtel de Ville de Paris, Salle Saint-Jean, 14 September–17 December 2000; *Die Nabis und das moderne Paris aus der Sammlung Arthur und Hedy Hahnloser-Bühler und aus Schweizer Museums und Privatbesitz*, Villa Flora, Winterthur, 4 May–1 September 2001, no. 16.

Narrow Street in Paris (Rue étroite de Paris or **Rue Tholozé)**
ca. 1897
Oil on cardboard set into wood panel, 14⅝ × 7¾ in.
(37.1 × 19.6 cm)
The Phillips Collection, Washington, D.C.
[plate 33]
Provenance
Bought then sold by Josse Hessel, Paris; Phillips Memorial Gallery, purchased from Carroll Carstairs Gallery, New York, 1937.
Exhibitions
Paintings and Drawings from the Collection, The Phillips Gallery, Washington, D.C., after 8 January–1 April 1958; *Paintings by Pierre Bonnard from the Collection*, The Phillips Gallery, Washington, D.C., 15 March–30 June 1959; *Paintings*

and Drawings by Pierre Bonnard: An Exhibition from The Phillips Collection and the Collections of Mrs. Phillips and Mr. and Mrs. Laughlin Phillips, The Phillips Collection, Washington, D.C., 7 January–28 February 1967 (as ca. 1904); *Bonnard and Vuillard: An Exhibition for the Benefit of The Phillips Collection*, Adams Davidson Galleries, Washington, D.C., 17 May–22 June 1978, no. 4; *Duncan Phillips: Centennial Exhibition*, The Phillips Collection, Washington, D.C., 14 June–31 August 1986; *Pont-Aven to Nabis*, Isetan Museum of Art, Tokyo, 2–14 April 1987, Niigata City Art Museum, 18 April–17 May 1987, Daimaru Museum, Osaka, 20 May–9 June 1987, Shizuoka Prefectural Museum, 13 June–19 July 1987, Himeji City Museum of Art, 25 July–23 August 1987, Yamanashi Prefectural Museum, 27 August–27 September 1987, no. 15; *Pierre Bonnard: The Graphic Art*, The Metropolitan Museum of Art, New York, 2 December 1989–4 February 1990, The Museum of Fine Arts, Houston, 25 February–29 April 1990, Museum of Fine Arts, Boston, 25 May–29 July 1990, no. 67; *Bonnard*, Tate Gallery, London, 12 February–17 May 1998, The Museum of Modern Art, New York, 17 June–13 October 1998, no. 98; *Renoir to Rothko: The Eye of Duncan Phillips*, The Phillips Collection, Washington, D.C., 25 September 1999–23 January 2000.

Cover for "From the Land of Touraine" from "Répertoire des Pantins" (Cover for "Du pays tourangeau" from "Répertoire des Pantins")
1898
Lithograph, 12¹³⁄₁₆ × 9¹³⁄₁₆ in. (32.6 × 24.9 cm)
Virginia and Ira Jackson Collection. Partial and Promised Gift to the National Gallery of Art, Washington.
[plate 40]
Provenance
Virginia and Ira Jackson Collection.

Cover for "Unfortunate Adèle" from "Répertoire des Pantins" (Cover for "Malheureuse Adèle" from "Répertoire des Pantins")
1898
Lithograph, 12¹³⁄₁₆ × 9¹³⁄₁₆ in. (32.6 × 24.9 cm)
Virginia and Ira Jackson Collection. Partial and Promised Gift to the National Gallery of Art, Washington.
[plate 39]
Provenance
Virginia and Ira Jackson Collection.

"Marie Putting on Her Stockings" in Peter Nansen's "Marie" ("Marie enfilant ses bas" in Peter Nansen's "Marie")
1898
Process print, 7⅜ × 4⅝ in. (18.7 × 11.7 cm)
The Metropolitan Museum of Art, The Elisha Whittelsey Collection, The Elisha Whittelsey Fund, 1969 (69.636)
[plate 20]
Provenance
The Metropolitan Museum of Art, Purchased from Deighton, Bell and Co., 13 Trinity Street, Cambridge, England.
Exhibitions
Bonnard, Musée des Ponchettes, Nice, August–September 1955, no. 68; *Pierre Bonnard: The Graphic Art*, The

Metropolitan Museum of Art, New York, 2 December 1989–4 February 1990, The Museum of Fine Arts, Houston, 25 February–29 April 1990, Museum of Fine Arts, Boston, 25 May–29 July 1990, no. 58.

Boulevard
1899
Color lithograph on cream wove paper, 16⅛ × 20¾ in.
(40.9 × 52.7 cm)
The Phillips Collection, Washington, D.C.
[plate 32]
Provenance
The Phillips Collection, acquired from Peter Deitsch in 1954.
Exhibitions
Drawings and Prints from the Collection, The Phillips Gallery, Washington, D.C., July–9 November 1956; *Drawings from the Collection*, The Phillips Gallery, Washington, D.C., 15 July–1 November 1957; *Prints and Drawings from the Collection*, The Phillips Gallery, Washington, D.C., 1–15 October 1958; *Paintings and Drawings by Pierre Bonnard: An Exhibition from The Phillips Collection and the Collections of Mrs. Phillips and Mr. and Mrs. Laughlin Phillips*, The Phillips Collection, Washington, D.C., 7 January–28 February 1967; *Bonnard and Vuillard: An Exhibition for the Benefit of The Phillips Collection*, Adams Davidson Galleries, Washington, D.C., 17 May–17 June 1978, no. 3; *Pont-Aven to Nabis*, Isetan Museum of Art, Tokyo, 2–14 April 1987, Niigata City Art Museum, 18 April–17 May 1987, Daimaru Museum, Osaka, 20 May–9 June 1987, Shizuoka Prefectural Museum, 13 June–19 July 1987, Himeji City Museum of Art, 25 July–23 August 1987, Yamanashi Prefectural Museum, 27 August–27 September 1987, no. 18; *The Aftermath of Impressionism: Selected Works from The Phillips Collection*, Michael C. Carlos Museum, Emory University, Atlanta, 13 November 1991–9 February 1992, no. 3; *Works on Paper: Pierre Bonnard*, The Phillips Collection, Washington, D.C., 30 June–25 October 1992; *French Works on Paper from Van Gogh to Matisse*, The Phillips Collection, Washington, D.C., 2 March–5 July 1993.

The Orchard (Le Verger)
1899
Color lithograph on China paper, 15¼ × 19½ in.
(38.7 × 49.5 cm)
The Phillips Collection, Washington, D.C.
[plate 11]
Provenance
The Phillips Collection, acquisition date unknown.
Exhibitions
Drawings and Prints from the Collection, The Phillips Gallery, Washington, D.C., July–9 November 1956; *Drawings from the Collection*, The Phillips Gallery, Washington, D.C., 15 July–1 November 1957; *Paintings and Drawings by Pierre Bonnard: An Exhibition from The Phillips Collection and the Collections of Mrs. Phillips and Mr. and Mrs. Laughlin Phillips*, The Phillips Collection, Washington, D.C., 7 January–28 February 1967; *Bonnard and Vuillard: An Exhibition for the Benefit of The Phillips Collection*, Adams Davidson Galleries, Washington, D.C., 17 May–22 June 1978,

no. 7; *Works on Paper: Pierre Bonnard*, The Phillips
Collection, Washington, D.C., 30 June–25 October 1992.

The Square at Evening (Place le soir)
1899
Color lithograph on cream wove paper, 16 × 21 in.
(40.6 × 53.3 cm)
The Phillips Collection, Washington, D.C.
[plate 31]
Provenance
The Phillips Collection, acquired from Peter Deitsch, 1954.
Exhibitions
Drawings and Prints from the Collection, The Phillips
Collection, Washington, D.C., July 1972; *Bonnard and
Vuillard: An Exhibition for the Benefit of The Phillips
Collection*, Adams Davidson Galleries, Washington, D.C.,
17 May–22 June 1978, no. 2; *Works on Paper: Pierre Bonnard*,
The Phillips Collection, Washington, D.C., 30 June–25
October 1992; *French Works on Paper from Van Gogh to
Matisse*, The Phillips Collection, Washington, D.C.,
2 March–5 July 1993.

The Lamp (La Lampe)
ca. 1899
Oil on academy board mounted on panel, 22¼ × 27½ in.
(56.5 × 69.9 cm)
Collection of the Flint Institute of Arts, Gift of The Whiting
Foundation and Mr. and Mrs. Donald E. Johnson, 1977.25
[plate 38]
Provenance
Ex-collection A.J.L. McDonnell, London; Wildenstein, 1939;
Hirschl and Adler Galleries, New York; Flint Institute of
Arts, 1977.
Exhibitions
Pierre Bonnard, Tate Gallery, London, 12 February–17 May
1998, The Museum of Modern Art, New York, 17 June–13
October 1998.

**Le Grand-Lemps. The Gathering of Fruit, Andrée Terrasse
and Renée (Le Grand-Lemps. La Cueillette des fruits, Andrée
Terrasse et Renée)**
1899–1900
Contemporary print from original film negative,
11¹³⁄₁₆ × 15⅜ in. (30 × 39 cm)
Paris, Musée d'Orsay, donation with a life interest from
Charles Terrasse's children, 1987, inv: PHO 1987 30 26
[plate 12]

**Le Grand-Lemps. The Gathering of Fruit, Andrée Terrasse,
an Unknown Child and in the Background, Renée (Le Grand-
Lemps. La Cueillette de fruits, Andrée Terrasse avec un
enfant inconnu et, en arrière-plan, Renée)**
1899–1900
Contemporary print from original film negative,
11¹³⁄₁₆ × 15⅜ in. (30 × 39 cm)
Paris, Musée d'Orsay, donation with a life interest from
Charles Terrasse's children, 1987, inv: PHO 1987 30 25
[plate 13]

**Edouard Vuillard Holding His Kodak and Madame
Mertzdorff, Renée, and Ker-Xavier Roussel (Edouard
Vuillard tenant son appareil Kodak et Madame Mertzdorff,
Renée, et Ker-Xavier Roussel)**
1900
Original contact print on gelatin paper, 1½ × 2³⁄₁₆ in. and
1½ × 2 in. (3.8 × 5.5 cm and 3.8 × 5.1 cm)
Paris, Musée d'Orsay, donation with a life interest from
Charles Terrasse's children, 1987, inv: PHO 1987 31 18 and
PHO 1987 31 19
Washington only
[plate 44]

**Marthe Bending to Touch the Ground in the Garden at
Montval (Marthe se baissant, la main droite au sol, dans le
jardin de Montval)**
1900–1901
Contemporary print from original film negative,
9⁹⁄₁₆ × 12³⁄₁₆ in. (23 × 31 cm)
Paris, Musée d'Orsay, donation with a life interest from
Charles Terrasse's children, 1987, inv: PHO 1987 30 35
[plate 55]

**Marthe Crouching down in the Garden at Montval
(Marthe accroupie dans le jardin de Montval)**
1900–1901
Contemporary print from original film negative,
9⁹⁄₁₆ × 12³⁄₁₆ in. (23 × 31 cm)
Paris, Musée d'Orsay, donation with a life interest from
Charles Terrasse's children, 1987, inv: PHO 1987 30 36
[plate 54]

**Marthe Crouching down in the Garden at Montval and
Marthe Standing in the Sunlight in the Garden at Montval
(Marthe accroupie dans le jardin de Montval and Marthe
debout au soleil dans le jardin de Montval)**
1900–1901
Original contact print on gelatin paper, 1⁷⁄₁₆ × 2¹⁄₁₆ in. and
1½ × 1¹⁵⁄₁₆ in. (3.7 × 5.2 cm and 3.8 × 5 cm)
Paris, Musée d'Orsay, donation with a life interest from
Charles Terrasse's children, 1987, inv: PHO 1987 31 36 and
PHO 1987 31 34
Washington only
[plate 45]

**Marthe Holding Her Nightdress in the Garden at Montval
(Marthe tenant sa chemise de nuit dans le jardin de Montval)**
1900–1901
Contemporary print from original film negative,
9⁹⁄₁₆ × 12³⁄₁₆ in. (23 × 31 cm)
Paris, Musée d'Orsay, donation with a life interest from
Charles Terrasse's children, 1987, inv: PHO 1987 30 38
[plate 50]

**Marthe Removing Her Nigthdress in the Garden at Montval
(Marthe enlevant sa chemise de nuit dans le jardin de
Montval)**
1900–1901
Contemporary print from original film negative,
9⁹⁄₁₆ × 12³⁄₁₆ in. (23 × 31 cm)

Paris, Musée d'Orsay, donation with a life interest from
Charles Terrasse's children, 1987, inv: PHO 1987 27 23
[plate 48]

**Marthe Seated in Her Nightdress in the Garden at Montval
(Marthe assise en chemise de nuit dans le jardin de Montval)**
1900–1901
Contemporary print from original film negative,
9⁹⁄₁₆ × 12³⁄₁₆ in. (23 × 31 cm)
Paris, Musée d'Orsay, donation with a life interest from
Charles Terrasse's children, 1987, inv: PHO 1987 27 21
[plate 47]

**Marthe Seated with Her Hand on Her Right Breast in the
Garden at Montval (Marthe assise, la main gauche sur le sein
droit dans le jardin de Montval)**
1900–1901
Contemporary print from original film negative,
9⁹⁄₁₆ × 12³⁄₁₆ in. (23 × 31 cm)
Paris, Musée d'Orsay, donation with a life interest from
Charles Terrasse's children, 1987, inv: PHO 1987 30 40
[plate 53]

**Marthe Seated with Her Left Hand behind Her Neck in the
Garden at Montval (Marthe assise, la main gauche à la nuque
dans le jardin de Montval)**
1900–1901
Contemporary print from original film negative,
9⁹⁄₁₆ × 12³⁄₁₆ in. (23 × 31 cm)
Paris, Musée d'Orsay, donation with a life interest from
Charles Terrasse's children, 1987, inv: PHO 1987 30 39
[plate 51]

**Marthe Standing in the Sunlight in the Garden at Montval
(Marthe debout au soleil dans le jardin de Montval)**
1900–1901
Contemporary print from original film negative,
9⁹⁄₁₆ × 12³⁄₁₆ in. (23 × 31 cm)
Paris, Musée d'Orsay, donation with a life interest from
Charles Terrasse's children, 1987, inv: PHO 1987 27 29
[plate 55a]

**Marthe Standing next to a Chair in the Garden at Montval
(Marthe debout près d'une chaise dans le jardin de Montval)**
1900–1901
Contemporary print from original film negative,
9⁹⁄₁₆ × 12³⁄₁₆ in. (23 × 31 cm)
Paris, Musée d'Orsay, donation with a life interest from
Charles Terrasse's children, 1987, inv: PHO 1987 30 37
[plate 52]

**Marthe with Her Back to the Camera in the Garden at
Montval (Marthe de dos dans le jardin de Montval)**
1900–1901
Contemporary print from original film negative,
9⁹⁄₁₆ × 12³⁄₁₆ in. (23 × 31 cm)
Paris, Musée d'Orsay, donation with a life interest from
Charles Terrasse's children, 1987, inv: PHO 1987 27 25
[plate 49]

"Séguidille" in Paul Verlaine's "Parallèlement"
1900
Lithograph in book, 12 × 9⅞ in. (30.5 × 25 cm)
Lessing J. Rosenwald Collection, Library of Congress,
Washington, D.C.
[plate 43]
Provenance
Library of Congress

Woman Bathing (Baigneuse)
ca. 1900–1906
Bronze, 10¾ × 5 × 4¼ in. (27.3 × 12.7 × 10.8 cm)
Hirshhorn Museum and Sculpture Garden, Smithsonian
Institution. Gift of Joseph H. Hirshhorn, 1966
[plate 57]
Provenance
[Ambroise Vollard, Paris], Félix Fénéon, Paris, 1923–1944,
[Fénéon estate, Paris, 1944–1955?]; Peridot Gallery, New
York, late 1955–9 November 1957, Joseph H. Hirshhorn, New
York, 9 November 1957–17 May 1966; Gift of Joseph H.
Hirshhorn, 1966.
Exhibitions
Sculpture in Our Time: Collected by Joseph H. Hirshhorn, The
Detroit Institute of Arts, 5 May–23 August 1959, Milwaukee
Art Center, 10 September–11 October 1959, Walker Art
Center, Minneapolis, 25 October–6 December 1959, William
Rockhill Nelson Gallery of Art, Kansas City, 20 December–31
January 1960, The Museum of Fine Arts, Houston, 1–27
March 1960, Los Angeles County Museum of History,
Science, and Art, 11 April–15 May 1960, M. H. de Young
Memorial Museum, San Francisco, 29 May–10 July 1960,
Colorado Springs Fine Arts Center, 24 July–4 September
1960, Art Gallery of Toronto, 30 September–31 October 1960,
no. 57; *Modern Sculpture from the Joseph H. Hirshhorn
Collection,* Solomon R. Guggenheim Museum, New York,
3 October 1962–6 January 1963, no. 34; *Inaugural Exhibition,*
Hirshhorn Museum and Sculpture Garden, Smithsonian
Institution, Washington, D.C., 1 October 1974–15 September
1975; *Pierre Bonnard,* Fondation de l'Hermitage, Lausanne,
7 June–6 October 1991, no. 103.

**"Alphabet du Père Ubu" in Alfred Jarry's "Almanach illustré
du Père Ubu"**
1901
Lithograph, each image, 11⁵⁄₁₆ × 8 in. (28.7 × 20.3 cm)
Virginia and Ira Jackson Collection. Partial and Promised
Gift to the National Gallery of Art, Washington.
[plate 42]
Provenance
Virginia and Ira Jackson Collection.
Exhibitions
Prints Abound: Paris in the 1890s, National Gallery of Art,
Washington, D.C., 22 October 2000–25 February 2001,
no. 88.

**"Ubu à Paris" in Alfred Jarry's "Almanach illustré du
Père Ubu"**
1901
Lithograph, 11⁵⁄₁₆ × 16 in. (28.7 × 40.6 cm)
Virginia and Ira Jackson Collection. Partial and Promised

Gift to the National Gallery of Art, Washington
[plate 41]
Provenance
Virginia and Ira Jackson Collection
Exhibitions
Prints Abound: Paris in the 1890s, National Gallery of Art,
Washington, D.C., 22 October 2000–25 February 2001, no. 87.

**Illustration for Longus's "Les Pastorales" or
"Daphnis et Chloé"**
1902
Lithograph in book, 12 × 9⅞ in. (30.5 × 25 cm)
Lessing J. Rosenwald Collection, Library of Congress,
Washington, D.C.
[plate 56]
Provenance
Library of Congress

Screen with Rabbits (Paravent aux lapins)
ca. 1902–1906
Oil on paper mounted on canvas, each panel,
63⅜ × 17¾ in. (161 × 45 cm)
Musée Départemental Maurice Denis,
Saint-Germain-en-Laye
[plate 59]
Provenance
Estate of the artist; Musée Départemental Maurice Denis
"Le Prieuré," Saint-Germain-en-Laye, from 1983.
Exhibitions
Hommage à Bonnard, Galerie des Beaux-Arts, Bordeaux, 10
May–25 August 1986, no. 19; *Beyond the Easel: Decorative
Painting by Bonnard, Vuillard, Denis and Roussel, 1890–1930,*
The Art Institute of Chicago, 25 February–16 May 2001, The
Metropolitan Museum of Art, New York, 26 June–9
September 2001, no. 44.

Ants (Fourmis)
1904
Ink on *chine collé,* 2¾ × 7¾ in. (7 × 19.7 cm)
The Phillips Collection, Washington, D.C.
[plate 64]
Provenance
The artist to The Weyhe Gallery, New York, as of 20 March
1937; Phillips Memorial Gallery purchase from The Weyhe
Gallery, 1937.
Exhibitions
*An Exhibition of Drawings by Pierre Bonnard for "Histoires
Naturelles" by Jules Renard,* Phillips Memorial Gallery,
Washington, D.C., 15–30 April 1937; *Great Modern Drawings,*
Phillips Memorial Gallery, Washington, D.C., 7 April–1 May
1940, no. 4; *Prints and Drawings from the Collection,* Phillips
Memorial Gallery, Washington, D.C., 26 October–10
November 1941, no. 18; *20th Century Drawings: A Loan
Exhibition,* Phillips Memorial Gallery, Washington, D.C.,
4–30 April 1943, no. 15; *European Drawings,* Phillips
Memorial Gallery, Washington, D.C., 25 June–5 November
1944; *Drawings, Prints and Small Paintings from the
Collection,* Phillips Memorial Gallery, Washington, D.C.,
1 June–22 September 1947; *Prints and Drawings from the
Permanent Collection,* The Phillips Gallery, Washington,

D.C., 2 December 1951–3 January 1952; *Drawings and Prints
from the Collection,* The Phillips Gallery, Washington, D.C.,
July–9 November 1956; *Drawings from the Collection,* The
Phillips Gallery, Washington, D.C., 15 July–1 November 1957;
Drawings from the Collection, The Phillips Collection,
Washington, D.C., summer 1962; *Drawings from the
Collection, Including "Birds in Flight" by Nicolas de Staël,* The
Phillips Collection, Washington, D.C., 14 June–summer
1964; *Drawings from the Collection,* The Phillips Collection,
Washington, D.C., 1 August–September 1965; *Drawings from
the Collection,* The Phillips Collection, Washington, D.C., 9
July–6 September 1966; *Paintings and Drawings by Pierre
Bonnard: An Exhibition from The Phillips Collection and the
Collections of Mrs. Phillips and Mr. and Mrs. Laughlin Phillips,*
The Phillips Collection, Washington, D.C., 7 January–28
February 1967; *Prints and Drawings from the Collection,* The
Phillips Collection, Washington, D.C., 15 July–31 August
1967; *Impressionism and the Modern Vision: Master Paintings
from The Phillips Collection,* The Nihonbashi Takashimaya
Art Galleries, Tokyo, 25 August–4 October 1983, Nara
Prefectural Museum of Art, 9 October–13 November 1983,
no. 51; *Paintings and Drawings from The Phillips Collection,*
IBM Gallery of Science and Art, New York, 9 December
1983–21 January 1984, no. 3; *French Drawings from The
Phillips Collection,* The Phillips Collection, Washington,
D.C., 23 November–12 January 1986, no. 1; *Le Japonisme,*
Grand Palais, Paris, 17 May–15 August 1988, National
Museum of Western Art, Tokyo, 23 September–11 December
1988, no. 330; *Pierre Bonnard,* Isetan Museum of Art, Tokyo,
4–30 July 1991, Nara Sogo Museum of Art, 7 August–1
September 1991, Sogo Museum of Art, Yokohama, 7
September–10 October 1991, Fukuoka Art Museum, 17
October–10 November 1991, no. 66; *Works on Paper: Pierre
Bonnard,* The Phillips Collection, Washington, D.C., 30
June–25 October 1992.

Canaries (Serins)
1904
Ink on *chine collé,* 11⅞ × 7½ in. (30.3 × 19 cm)
The Phillips Collection, Washington, D.C.
[plate 62]
Provenance
The Phillips Collection, acquired from E. Weyhe (?),
York, 1937.
Exhibitions
*An Exhibition of Drawings by Pierre Bonnard for "Histoires
Naturelles" by Jules Renard,* Phillips Memorial Gallery,
Washington, D.C., 15–30 April 1937; *Great Modern Drawings,*
Phillips Memorial Gallery, Washington, D.C., 7 April–1 May
1940, no. 6; *20th Century Drawings,* Phillips Memorial
Gallery, Washington, D.C., 4–30 April 1943, no. 13 (as *Birds
in Cage*); *European Drawings,* Phillips Memorial Gallery,
Washington, D.C., 25 June–5 November 1944, no. 4;
Drawings, Prints and Small Paintings from the Collection,
Phillips Memorial Gallery, Washington, D.C., 1 June–22
September 1947; *Prints and Drawings from the Permanent
Collection,* The Phillips Gallery, Washington, D.C., 2
December 1951–3 January 1952; *Twentieth Century Drawings,*
Yale University Art Gallery, New Haven, 16 February–20
March 1955; *Drawings and Prints from the Collection,* The

Phillips Gallery, Washington, D.C., July–9 November 1956; *Drawings from the Collection, Including "Birds in Flight" by Nicolas de Staël*, The Phillips Collection, Washington, D.C., 14 June–summer 1964; *Birds in Contemporary Art: A Loan Exhibition*, The Phillips Collection, Washington, D.C., 12 February–31 March 1966, no. 22 (as *Birds in Cage*); *Drawings from the Collection*, The Phillips Collection, Washington, D.C., 9 July–6 September 1966; *Paintings and Drawings by Pierre Bonnard: An Exhibition from The Phillips Collection and the Collections of Mrs. Phillips and Mr. and Mrs. Laughlin Phillips*, The Phillips Collection, Washington, D.C., 7 January–28 February 1967; *Prints and Drawings from the Collection*, The Phillips Collection, Washington, D.C., 15 July–31 August 1967, no. 52; *Impressionism and the Modern Vision: Master Paintings from The Phillips Collection*, The Nihonbashi Takashimaya Art Galleries, Tokyo, 25 August–4 October 1983, Nara Prefectural Museum of Art, 9 October–13 November 1983; *Paintings and Drawings from The Phillips Collection*, IBM Gallery of Science and Art, New York, 9 December 1983–21 January 1984, no. 4; *French Drawings from The Phillips Collection*, The Phillips Collection, Washington, D.C., 23 November 1985–12 January 1986, no. 2; *Works on Paper: Pierre Bonnard*, The Phillips Collection, Washington, D.C., 30 June–25 October 1992; *Pierre Bonnard: Stealing the Image: Works on Paper*, New York Studio School of Drawing, Painting, and Sculpture, 16 October–15 November 1997.

Grasshoppers (Sauterelles)
1904
Ink on *chine collé*, 7½ × 6⅛ in. (19.1 × 15.6 cm)
The Phillips Collection, Washington, D.C.
[plate 63]
Provenance
The Phillips Collection, acquired 1937.
Exhibitions
20th Century Drawings: A Loan Exhibition, Phillips Memorial Gallery, Washington, D.C., 4–30 April 1943, no. 17; *Drawings, Prints and Small Paintings from the Collection*, Phillips Memorial Gallery, Washington, D.C., 1 June–22 September 1947; *Drawings from the Collection*, The Phillips Gallery, Washington, D.C., 15 July–1 November 1957; *Prints and Drawings from the Collection*, The Phillips Gallery, Washington, D.C., 1–15 October 1958; *Drawings from the Collection, Including "Birds in Flight" by Nicolas de Staël*, The Phillips Collection, Washington, D.C., 14 June–summer 1964; *Drawings from the Collection*, The Phillips Collection, Washington, D.C., 9 July–6 September 1966; *Paintings and Drawings by Pierre Bonnard: An Exhibition from The Phillips Collection and the Collections of Mrs. Phillips and Mr. and Mrs. Laughlin Phillips*, The Phillips Collection, Washington, D.C., 7 January–28 February 1967; *Prints and Drawings from the Collection*, The Phillips Collection, Washington, D.C., 15 July–31 August 1967; *Impressionism and the Modern Vision: Master Paintings from The Phillips Collection*, The Nihonbashi Takashimaya Art Galleries, Tokyo, 25 August–4 October 1983, Nara Prefectural Museum of Art, 9 October–13 November 1983, no. 50; *Paintings and Drawings from The Phillips Collection*, IBM Gallery of Science and Art, New York, 9 December 1983–21 January 1984, no. 5; *French Drawings from The Phillips Collection*, The Phillips

Collection, Washington, D.C., 23 November 1985–12 January 1986, no. 4; *Le Japonisme*, Grand Palais, Paris, 17 May–15 August 1988, National Museum of Western Art, Tokyo, 23 September–11 December 1988, no. 329; *Works on Paper: Pierre Bonnard*, The Phillips Collection, Washington, D.C., 30 June–25 October 1992.

"The Flea" in Jules Renard's "Histoires naturelles" ("La Puce" in Jules Renard's "Histoires naturelle")
1904
Lithograph in book, 7¹¹⁄₁₆ × 4¹⁵⁄₁₆ in. (19.5 × 12.5 cm)
Lessing J. Rosenwald Collection, Library of Congress, Washington, D.C.
[plate 60b]
Provenance
Library of Congress.

Daphnis and Chloe (Daphnis et Chloé, surtout de table)
1904–1905
Bronze and glass, 5¹⁵⁄₁₆ × 32¹¹⁄₁₆ × 19¹¹⁄₁₆ in. (15 × 83 × 50 cm)
Paris, Musée d'Orsay
[plate 58]
Provenance
Acquired by the Musées Nationaux, 1953; Musée National d'Art Moderne, 1953–1977; granted to the Musée du Louvre, 1977; assumed by Musée d'Orsay, 1978.
Exhibitions
Bonnard, Musée de Lyon, 1954, no. 106; *Pierre Bonnard*, Kunsthalle Basel, 28 May–17 July 1955, no. 172; *Pierre Bonnard*, Milan, Basel, Nice, 16 March–11 August 1955; *Yverdon*, 1956; *Stichting Sonsbeek*, Arnhem, 15 June–15 September; Bonnard, New York, 1961; *Pierre Bonnard*, Milan, Basel, Nice, 16 March–11 August 1955; Yverdon, 1956; *Stichting Sonsbeek*, Arnhem, 15 June–15 September; *Bonnard*, New York, 1961; *Ambroise Vollard Editeur: Prints, Books, Bronzes*, The Museum of Modern Art, New York, 1977, no. 215; *19th and 20th Century Paintings and Sculpture*, London, 1989, no. 13; *Pierre Bonnard*, Fondation de l'Hermitage, Lausanne, 7 June–6 October 1991, no. 109; *Bonnard*, Fondation Pierre Gianadda, Martigny Switzerland, 11 June–14 November 1999, no. 150.

Decorated Plate (Assiette décorée)
ca. 1905
Glazed ceramic, diam. 9¼ in. (23.5 cm)
Private collection
[plate 61]
Provenance
Family of the artist; private collection.
Exhibitions
Musée Maillol, Paris, 2000.

Interior with Screen (Intérieur au paravent)
ca. 1906
Oil on paper laid down on canvas, 18¾ × 24¾ in. (47.8 × 62.9 cm)
Private collection
Washington only
[plate 65]

Provenance
Estate of the artist; private collection (by descent); private collection.
Exhibitions
Pierre Bonnard 1867–1947, Arthur Tooth & Sons, London, 17 June–17 July 1969, no. 31.

Portrait of Ambroise Vollard (Portrait d'Ambroise Vollard)
ca. 1906
Oil on canvas, 29⅛ × 36⅜ in. (74 × 92.5 cm)
Kunsthaus Zurich
[plate 67]
Provenance
Ambroise Vollard; Dufresne, Paris; acquired from Dufresne by the Kunsthaus Zurich, 1950.
Exhibitions
Portraits d'aujourd'hui, Galerie Bernier, Paris, 1928; *L'Art Vivant*, Théâtre Pigalle, Paris 16–31 May 1930, no. 6; *European Art 13th–20th Centuries*, Kunsthaus Zurich, 1950; *Bonnard*, Museum Boymans, Rotterdam, 1953, no. 37; *Alte Zürcher Meister*, Stadthaus Zurich, 1953; *Bonnard*, Musée de Lyon, 1954, no. 27; *Pierre Bonnard*, Palazzo della Permanente, Milan, April–May 1955; *Pierre Bonnard*, Kunsthalle Basel, 28 May–17 July 1955, no. 25; *Bonnard*, Kunstverein Braunschweig, 1955; *Pierre Bonnard*, Haus Salve Hospes, Braunschweig, 11 November–16 December 1956, Kunsthalle Bremen, 30 December 1956–3 February 1957, Kunsthaus Lempertz, Cologne, 10 February–10 March 1957, no. 10; *Jugend hat Geist*, Jelmoli, Zurich, 1962; *Pierre Bonnard*, Haus der Kunst, Munich, 8 October 1966–1 January 1967, no. 47, Musée du Louvre, Paris, 13 January–15 April 1967, no. 52; *Bonnard*, Louisiana Museum of Modern Art, Humlebaek, Denmark, 16 September–20 October 1967; *Suites No. 23: Bonnard*, Galerie Krugier & Co., Geneva, June–July 1969, no. 3; *Pierre Bonnard, Gemälde, Aquarelle, Zeichnungen und Druckgraphik*, Kunstverein Hamburg, 6 February–5 April 1970, no. 22; *Der Einzelne und die Masse*, Städtische Kunsthalle Recklinghausen, 1975; *Masterpieces of Modern Portraiture*, National Portrait Gallery, London, 1978; *Pierre Bonnard*, Kunsthaus Zurich, 14 December 1984–10 March 1985, Städtische Galerie im Städelschen Kunstinstitut, Frankfurt, 3 May–14 July 1985, no. 36; *Pierre Bonnard*, Palazzo Reale, Milan, 28 October 1988–8 January 1989, no. 15; *Pierre Bonnard*, Musée de Saint-Tropez, 1998, Stiftung Langmatt, Baden, Switzerland, 2000.

The Dressing Table (La Table de toilette)
1908
Oil on canvas, 20½ × 17¹¹⁄₁₆ in. (52 × 45 cm)
Paris, Musée d'Orsay; Bequest of Mr. and Mrs. Frédéric I. Ling, 1961
Washington only
[plate 66]
Provenance
Acquired by Bernheim-Jeune from the artist, 6 March 1908; sold to E. Druet, Hôtel Drouot, Paris, 8 December 1908; Eugène Blot; sale Eugène Blot, 2 June 1933, no. 32; bought by Monsieur and Madame Frédéric Ling, 1961; given to the Musées Nationaux by Monsieur and Madame Frédéric Ling; Musée National d'Art Moderne, Paris, 1961–1977; granted to

the Musée du Louvre by the Musée National d'Art Moderne, 1977; assumed by the Musée d'Orsay, 1977.
Exhibitions
Le Parisien chez lui au 19e siècle, 1814–1914, Archives Nationales, Paris, 1977, no. 661; *La Nature morte et l'objet de Delacroix à Picasso*, Palais de Tokyo, Paris, 1983, no. 2; *La Peinture française 1870–1920*, Peking, 1985, no. 29; *Hommage à Bonnard*, Galerie des Beaux-Arts, Bordeaux, 10 May–25 August 1986, no. 32; *Correspondances, Französische Malerei aus dem Musée d'Orsay*, Städtische Galerie im Städelschen Kunstinstitut, Frankfurt, 5 October–7 January, 1990; *Paris belle époque*, Kulturstiftung Ruhr, Villa Hugel, Essen, 11 June–13 November 1994; *La modernité*, Musée Municipal, Tokyo, 14 January–13 March 1996, Musée Municipal, Kobé, 13 April–23 June 1996; *Pierre Bonnard*, Musée de Saint-Tropez, 1998, no. 33; *L'Impressionisme et l'art moderne*, Seoul, 2000–2001.

Reclining Nude (Nue couché, fond carreaux blancs et bleus)
ca. 1909
Oil on canvas, 23⅝ × 25⁹⁄₁₆ in. (60 × 65 cm)
Städelscher Museums-Verein e.V., Frankfurt am Main
[plate 72]
Provenance
Estate of the artist; Galerie Beyeler, Basel; Dr. Karl and Sophie Binding-Stiftung, gift to Städelsches Kunstinstitut Frankfurt am Main, 1988.

Early Spring (Premier Printemps)
1910
Oil on canvas, 34¼ × 52 in. (86.9 × 132 cm)
The Phillips Collection, Washington, D.C.
[plate 68]
Provenance
Purchased from the artist by Bernheim-Jeune, Paris, 20 February 1909; intermediate owner by at least 1923; Phillips Memorial Gallery purchase, 1925.
Exhibitions
Exposition Bonnard, Oeuvres Récentes, Bernheim-Jeune, Paris, 1–20 February 1909, no. 9 (as *Les Pensées*); *Twenty-third Annual International Exhibition of Paintings*, Carnegie Institute, Pittsburgh, 24 April–15 June 1924, no. 125 (as *Premier Printemps*); *Intimate Impressionists: Berthe Morisot, Alfred Sisley, Pierre Bonnard, Albert André, Maurice Prendergast, Marjorie Phillips, Paul Dougherty, Samuel Halpert*, Phillips Memorial Gallery, Washington, D.C., 8–30 May 1926, no. 5; *Sensibility and Simplification in Ancient Sculpture and Contemporary Painting*, Phillips Memorial Gallery, Washington, D.C., 5 February–April 1927; *Bonnard*, De Hauke & Co., New York, 6–28 April 1928, no. 2; Untitled Exhibition, Phillips Memorial Gallery, Washington, D.C., February–June 1929; Phillips Memorial Gallery, Washington, D.C., September 1930; *Pierre Bonnard*, Phillips Memorial Gallery, Washington, D.C., 5 October 1930–25 January 1931, no. 90; *French Painting from Manet to Derain*, Phillips Memorial Gallery, Washington, D.C., 2 February–June 1931, no. 89; *A Century of Progress: Exhibition of Paintings and Sculpture*, The Art Institute of Chicago, 1 June–1 November 1933, no. 675; *Freshness of Vision: Classic and Romantic*, Phillips Memorial Gallery, Washington, D.C., 5 November

1933–15 February 1934; *Loan Exhibition of Paintings and Prints by Pierre Bonnard and Edouard Vuillard*, The Art Institute of Chicago, 15 December 1938–15 January 1939, no. 15; *The Function of Color in Painting: An Educational Loan Exhibition*, Phillips Memorial Gallery, Washington, D.C., 16 February–23 March 1941, no. 137; *Paintings by Pierre Bonnard*, Phillips Memorial Gallery, Washington, D.C., 18 March–30 September 1945; *Paintings by the Impressionists and Post-Impressionists*, Virginia Museum of Fine Arts, Richmond, 21 October–19 November 1950; *Modern French and American Paintings from the Collection*, The Phillips Gallery, Washington, D.C., summer 1951; *Paintings in the Collection by Bonnard*, The Phillips Gallery, Washington, D.C., 3 February–31 March 1952; *Loan Exhibition of Paintings by Pierre Bonnard*, Paul Rosenberg & Co., New York, 12 March–7 April 1956, no. 4; *Paintings by Bonnard from the Collection*, The Phillips Gallery, Washington, D.C., 15 March–30 June 1959; *Paintings and Drawings by Pierre Bonnard: An Exhibition from The Phillips Collection and the Collection of Mrs. Duncan Phillips and Mr. and Mrs. Laughlin Phillips*, The Phillips Collection, Washington, D.C., 7 January–28 February 1967; *The Paintings by Pierre Bonnard in the Collection*, The Phillips Collection, Washington, D.C., 17 July–31 August 1971; *Impressionism and the Modern Vision: Master Paintings from The Phillips Collection*, The Nihonbashi Takashimaya Galleries, Tokyo, 25 August–4 October 1983, Nara Prefectural Museum of Art, 9 October–13 November 1983, no. 46; *Paintings and Drawings from The Phillips Collection*, IBM Gallery of Science and Art, New York, 9 December 1983–21 January 1984, no. 6; *Pierre Bonnard*, Kunsthaus Zurich, 14 December 1984–10 March 1985, no. 50 (as *Les Pensées* or *Premier Printemps*), Städtische Galerie im Städelschen Kunstinstitut, Frankfurt, 3 May–14 July 1985, no. 50; *Duncan Phillips Centennial Exhibition*, The Phillips Collection, Washington, D.C., 14 June–31 August 1986; *Pierre Bonnard*, Isetan Museum of Art, Tokyo, 4–30 July 1991, Nara Sogo Museum of Art, 7 August–1 September 1991, Sogo Museum of Art, Yokohama, 7 September–10 October 1991, Fukuoka Art Museum, 17 October–10 November, 1991, no. 22; *Pierre Bonnard*, Aichi Prefectural Museum of Art, Nagoya, 28 March–18 May 1997, Bunkamura Museum of Art, Tokyo, 24 May–21 July 1997, no. 24; *Renoir to Rothko: The Eye of Duncan Phillips*, The Phillips Collection, Washington, D.C., 25 September 1999–23 January 2000.

Interior with Boy (Intérieur à l'enfant)
1910
Oil on canvas, 16 × 25 in. (41 × 63.5 cm)
The Phillips Collection, Washington, D.C.
Washington only
[plate 69]
Provenance
The Phillips Memorial Gallery, acquired from Valentine Gallery, 1927.
Exhibitions
Sensibility and Simplification in Ancient Sculpture and Contemporary Painting, Phillips Memorial Gallery, Washington, D.C., 5 February–April 1927 (as *Interior*); *An Exhibition of Paintings Lent by Phillips Memorial Gallery,*

Washington: French Paintings from Daumier to Derain and Contemporary American Paintings, Grange Park, The Art Gallery of Toronto, November 1928, no. 1; *An Exhibition of the School of Paris, 1910–1928*, The Harvard Society for Contemporary Art, Boston, 20 March–12 April 1929, no. 2; *The First Tri-Unit Exhibition of the Season of 1929–1930: Modern French and American Paintings including Daumier's "Strong Man," Manet's "Ballet Espagnol," and a Group of Water Colors by John Marin*, Phillips Memorial Gallery, Washington, D.C., 19 October 1929–February 1930, no. 9; *Painting in Paris from American Collections*, The Museum of Modern Art, New York, 19 January–16 February 1930, no. 2; *An Exhibition of a Selected Group of Paintings from The Phillips Memorial Gallery*, Century Club, New York, 16–31 March 1930, Carnegie Institute, Pittsburgh, 8 April–18 May 1930, The Rochester Memorial Art Gallery, N.Y., 4 June–5 September 1930, no. 22; Untitled Exhibition, Phillips Memorial Gallery, Washington, D.C., September 1930; *Pierre Bonnard*, Phillips Memorial Gallery, Washington, D.C., 5 October 1930–25 January 1931, no. 94; *Pierre Bonnard*, Phillips Memorial Gallery, Washington, D.C., 2 February–June 1931, no. 99; Untitled Exhibition, Phillips Memorial Gallery, Washington, D.C., February–June 1932, no. 24; [*Painting by Pierre Bonnard*], Phillips Memorial Gallery, Washington, D.C., 5 November 1933–15 February 1934; *Bonnard-Vuillard*, The Art Institute of Chicago, 28 November 1938–21 January 1939, no. 17; *For the Benefit of American Relief for France, "La Vie Française": An Exhibition of Paintings Chiefly by Pierre Bonnard and Edouard Vuillard*, The Institute of Modern Art, Boston, 3 October 1944–11 November 1944; *Paintings by Bonnard. The Collection's Unit of Seventeen Paintings on View in the Main Gallery*, Phillips Memorial Gallery, Washington, D.C., 18 March–30 September 1945; *Loan Exhibition of Paintings by Pierre Bonnard*, Paul Rosenberg & Co., New York, 12 March–12 April 1956, no. 8; *Paintings and Drawings from the Collection*, The Phillips Gallery, Washington, D.C., after 8 January–1 April 1958; *Paintings by Pierre Bonnard from the Collection*, The Phillips Gallery, Washington, D.C., 15 March–30 June 1959; *Paintings and Drawings by Pierre Bonnard: An Exhibition from The Phillips Collection and the Collections of Mrs. Phillips and Mr. and Mrs. Laughlin Phillips*, The Phillips Collection, Washington, D.C., 7 January–28 February 1967; *The Paintings by Pierre Bonnard in the Collection*, The Phillips Collection, Washington, D.C., 17 July–31 August 1971 (as *Boy in an Interior*); *Pont-Aven to Nabis*, Isetan Museum of Art, Tokyo, 2–14 April 1987, Niigata City Art Museum, 18 April–17 May 1987, Daimaru Museum, Osaka, 20 May–9 June 1987, Shizuoka Prefectural Museum, 13 June–19 July 1987, Himeji City Museum of Art, 25 July–23 August 1987, Yamanashi Prefectural Museum, 27 August–27 September 1987, no. 47; *Pierre Bonnard*, Aichi Prefectural Museum of Art, Nagoya, 28 March–18 May 1997, Bunkamura Museum of Art, Tokyo, 24 May–21 July 1997, no. 61.

The Red Checkered Tablecloth or **The Dog's Lunch (La Nappe à carreaux rouges** or **Le Déjeuner du chien)**
1910
Oil on canvas, 32¹¹⁄₁₆ × 33½ in. (83 × 85 cm)
Private collection

[plate 71]
Provenance
Acquired by Bernheim-Jeune from the artist; sold to Dr.
Hahnloser; Professor Hans R. Hahnloser; private collection.
Exhibitions
Exposition de peinture française, Winterthur,
October–November 1916, no. 19; *Bonnard et Vuillard*,
Kunsthaus Zurich, May–July 1932, no. 39; *Die Hauptwerke
der Sammlung Hahnloser, Winterthur*, Kunstmuseum
Lucerne, 1940, no. 11; *Europäische Kunst aus Berner Privat-
Besitz*, Kunsthalle Bern, 1953, no. 8; *De Géricault à Matisse,
Chefs-d'œuvre des collections suisses*, Musée du Petit Palais,
Paris, March–May 1959, no. 6; *Pierre Bonnard*, Haus der
Kunst, Munich, 8 October 1966–1 January 1967, Musée du
Louvre, Paris, 13 January–15 April 1967, no. 58; *Künstler
Freunde um Arthur und Hedy Hahnloser-Bühler*,
Kunstmuseum Winterthur, 23 September–11 November 1973,
no. 29; *Bonnard*, Musée National d'Art Moderne, Centre
Georges Pompidou, Paris, 23 February–21 May 1984, no. 7,
traveled as *Bonnard: The Late Paintings* to The Phillips
Collection, Washington, D.C., 9 June–25 August 1984, Dallas
Museum of Art, 13 September–11 November 1984, no. 6, trav-
eled as *Pierre Bonnard* to Kunsthaus Zurich, 14 December
1984–10 March 1985, Städtische Galerie im Städelschen
Kunstinstitut, Frankfurt, 3 May–14 July 1985, no. 62;
Bonnard, Kunsthalle der Hypo-Kulturstiftung, Munich, 28
January–24 April 1994, no. 46; *Intime Welten: Das Interieur
bei den Nabis: Bonnard, Vuillard, Vallotton aus der Sammlung
Arthur und Hedy Hahnloser-Bühler*, Villa Flora Winterthur,
Bern, 1999, no. 9.

Vase of Flowers and Checkers (Vase de fleurs et jeu de dames)
1912
Oil on canvas, 31⅛ × 22½ in. (79.5 × 57 cm)
Mr. and Mrs. Joe L. Allbritton
[plate 70]
Provenance
Acquired by Bernheim-Jeune from the artist, Paris, 1912;
sold to Paul Vallotton; private collection, Paris, 1950;
private collection.
Exhibitions
Pierre Bonnard 1867–1947, Galerie Schmit, Paris, 3 May–12
July 1995, no. 26.

Woman Bathing (La Femme au tub or Nu accroupi au tub)
1912
Oil on canvas, 26 × 17¾ in. (66 × 45.1 cm)
Private collection courtesy Sotheby's New York
Washington only
[plate 73]
Provenance
Private collection, Paris; sold by Sotheby and Co., London,
27 March 1957; Vallotton and Co., London; H. Belien,
Brussels; Galerie Beyeler, Basel; Galerie Knoedler, New York;
Henry Ford II, 1965; private collection.
Exhibitions
Bonnard, Kunsthaus Zurich, 1949, no. 49; *XIXth and XXth
Century French Masters*, Marborough Fine Arts, London,
November–December 1955, no. 2; *L'Ecole de Paris dans les
collections belges*, Musée d'Art Moderne, Paris, 9 July–18

October 1959, no. 13; *Bonnard*, Royal Academy of Arts,
London, 6 January–6 March 1966, no. 102; *Bonnard*,
Kunsthalle der Hypo-Kulturstiftung, Munich, 28 January–24
April 1994, no. 58; *Pierre Bonnard*, Aichi Prefectural Museum
of Art, Nagoya, 28 March–18 May 1997, Bunkamura Museum
of Art, Tokyo, 24 May–21 July 1997, no. 49; *Pierre Bonnard.
Das Glück zu malen*, Kunstsammlung Nordrhein-Westfalen,
Düsseldorf, 23 January–12 April 1993, no. 15.

**Study for "The Dining Room in the Country"
(Study for "La Salle à manger à la campagne")**
1913
Graphite on paper, 4¹⁵⁄₁₆ × 8¼ in. (12.5 × 21 cm)
Private collection
Denver only
[plate 75]
Provenance
Family of the artist; private collection.

**Study for "The Dining Room in the Country"
(Study for "La Salle à manger à la campagne")**
1913
Graphite on paper, 4¹⁵⁄₁₆ × 8¼ in. (12.5 × 21 cm)
Private collection
Denver only
[plate 76]
Provenance
Family of the artist; private collection.

**Study for "The Dining Room in the Country"
(Study for "La Salle à manger à la campagne")**
1913
Graphite on paper, 4¹⁵⁄₁₆ × 8¼ in. (12.5 × 21 cm)
Private collection
Denver only
[plate 77]
Provenance
Family of the artist; private collection.

**The Dining Room in the Country
("La Salle à manger à la campagne")**
1913
Oil on canvas, 64¾ × 81 in. (164.5 × 205.7 cm)
The Minneapolis Institute of Arts, The John R. Van Derlip
Fund 54.15
Denver only
[plate 78]
Provenance
Bought from the artist by Bernheim-Jeune, 1913; Gaston
Bernheim de Villers, Paris; bought from Sam Salz, New
York, 1954; The Minneapolis Institute of Arts.
Exhibitions
Salon d'Automne, Paris, 1913–1914, no. 217; *Panama-Pacific
International Exhibition*, section *Fine Arts, French*, San
Francisco, 1915, no. 259; *Exhibition of French and Belgian Art
Selected from the Panama-Pacific International Exhibition*,
Albright Art Gallery, Buffalo, 1916, The Minneapolis Institute
of Arts, 1916–1917, no. 38; *Contemporary Art, Golden Gate
International Exhibition*, San Francisco, 1939, no. 4; *Paintings*

and Sculpture from The Minneapolis Institute of Arts,
Knoedler Galleries, New York, The Society of the Four Arts,
Palm Beach, Fla, 1957; *A Loan Exhibition: Six Paintings by
Bonnard*, The Phillips Gallery, Washington, D.C., 12
January–12 February 1958, no. 1; *The Nabis and Their Circle*,
The Minneapolis Institute of Arts, 1962, p. 140; *Bonnard and
His Environment*, The Museum of Modern Art, New York, 7
October–29 November 1964, The Art Institute of Chicago, 8
January–28 February 1965, Los Angeles County Museum of
Art, 31 March–31 May 1965, no. 21; *People to People*,
Winnipeg, 16 August–12 September 1974; *Vuillard/Bonnard*,
The Minneapolis Institute of Arts, 29 January–9 March 1975;
Bonnard, Musée National d'Art Moderne, Centre Georges
Pompidou, Paris, 23 February–21 May 1984, no. 8, traveled as
Bonnard: The Late Paintings to The Phillips Collection,
Washington, D.C., 9 June–20 August, Dallas Museum of Art,
16 September–20 November, 1984, no. 8; *Impressionism:
Selections from Five American Museums*, Carnegie Museum
of Art, 4 November–31 December 1989, The Minneapolis
Institute of Arts, 27 January–25 March 1990, The Nelson-
Atkins Museum of Art, Kansas City, 21 April–17 June 1990,
The Saint Louis Art Museum, 14 July–9 September 1990,
Toledo Museum of Art, 30 September–25 November 1990,
no. 2; *Bonnard*, Tate Gallery, London, 12 February–17 May
1998, The Museum of Modern Art, New York, 17 June–13
October 1998, no. 26.

Woman with Basket of Fruit (Femme au panier de fruits)
1915–1918
Oil on canvas, 27¼ × 15¾ in. (69.2 × 40 cm)
The Baltimore Museum of Art: The Cone Collection, formed
by Dr. Claribel Cone and Miss Etta Cone of Baltimore,
Maryland, BMA 1950.190
[plate 74]
Provenance
Bought by L'Art Moderne, Lausanne, 1928; sold to M.
Degryse; sold to Frederic W. Cone, 1933; bequeathed to the
Baltimore Museum of Art, 1950.
Exhibitions
Bonnard, The Museum of Modern Art, New York, 1948; *The
Cone Collection*, Virginia Museum of Fine Arts, Richmond,
1953; *Bonnard and His Environment*, The Museum of Modern
Art, New York, 7 October–29 November 1964, The Art
Institute of Chicago, 8 January–28 February 1965, Los
Angeles County Museum of Art, 31 March–31 May 1965, no.
24; *Pierre Bonnard Exhibition*, Royal Academy of Arts,
London, 8 January–6 March 1966, no. 124; *Painting
Naturally: Fairfield Porter and His Influences*, Parrish Art
Museum, Southampton, N.Y., 15 April–3 June 1984; *Van
Gogh to Matisse: Impressionist and Modern Masters from the
Cone Collection, The Baltimore Museum of Art*, The Museum
of Fine Arts, Houston, 21 November 1993–30 January 1994;
Pierre Bonnard, Aichi Prefectural Museum of Art, Nagoya,
28 March–18 May 1997, Bunkamura Museum of Art, Tokyo,
24 May–21 July 1997, no. 62; *Matisse and Modern Masters
from the Cone Collection of the Baltimore Museum of Art*,
Isetan Museum of Art, Tokyo, 3 October–28 December 1996,
Osaka Municipal Museum of Art, Osaka, 8 January–11
February 1997; *The Triumph of French Painting*, The
Baltimore Museum of Art and The Walters Art Gallery,

Baltimore, 12 March–16 July 2000, The Philbrook Museum of Art, Tulsa, 13 August–26 November 2000, The Norton Museum of Art, West Palm Beach, Fla., 6 January 18 March 2001, Dayton Art Institute, 7 April–3 June 2001, Royal Academy of Arts, London, 30 June–23 September 2001, Albright-Knox Art Gallery, Buffalo, 3 November–6 January 2002.

Portrait of Renoir (Portrait de Renoir)
ca. 1916
Etching, 12¼ × 9⅞ in. (31.1 × 25.1 cm)
Prints and Photographs Division, Library of Congress, Washington, D.C. Reproduction numbers: LC-USZC4-10007, LC-USZ62-130236
Washington only
[plate 84a]
Provenance
Library of Congress, Pennell Fund acquisition, selected by the Pennell Committee established by Joseph Pennell.

Earthly Paradise (Le Paradis terrestre)
1916–1920
Oil on canvas, 51½ × 63 in. (130 × 160 cm)
The Art Institute of Chicago, Estate of Joanne Toor Cummings; Bette and Neison Harris and Searle Family Trust endowments; through prior gifts of Mrs. Henry C. Woods
[plate 80]
Provenance
Gaston Bernheim de Villers and Josse Bernheim, Paris, by 1920; Gaston Bernheim de Villers; Madame Gaston Bernheim de Villers, by 1955; private collection, Paris; The Art Institute of Chicago, 1996.
Exhibitions
Exposition Bonnard, Galerie Bernheim-Jeune, Paris, 24 May–11 June 1921, no. 4; *Cinquante ans de peinture française*, Musée des Arts Décoratifs, Paris, 28 May–12 July 1925; *Bonnard, exposition rétrospective*, Galerie Bernheim-Jeune, Paris, May–June 1950, no. 25; *Bonnard*, Musée des Ponchettes, Nice, August–September 1955, no. 23; *Coup de chapeau à Bonnard*, Galerie Bernheim-Jeune, Paris, 2 March–8 April 1967; *Bonnard*, Kunsthalle der Hypo–Kulturstiftung, Munich, summer 1994, no. 72; *Bonnard*, Tate Gallery, London, 12 February–17 May 1998, The Museum of Modern Art, New York, 17 June–13 October 1998, no. 36; *Beyond the Easel: Decorative Painting by Bonnard, Vuillard, Denis, and Roussel, 1890–1930*, The Art Institute of Chicago, 25 February–16 May 2001, The Metropolitan Museum of Art, 26 June–9 September 2001, no. 52.

Hommage to Maillol (Hommage à Maillol)
1917
Oil on canvas, 48 × 18½ in. (121.9 × 47 cm)
Philadelphia Museum of Art, Louis E. Stern Collection, 1963
[plate 81]
Provenance
Bernheim-Jeune, Paris; Sam Salz, New York; Louis E. Stern, New York; Philadelphia Museum of Art.
Exhibitions
Bonnard, Bernheim-Jeune, Paris, 1926; *XXXIV peintures de Pierre Bonnard*, Galerie Bernheim-Jeune, Paris, 15 June–13

July 1946; *Hommage à Bonnard*, Grand Palais, Paris, 1947; *The Louis E. Stern Collection*, Museum of Art, Brooklyn, 1962–1963, no. 2; *Pierre Bonnard,* Royal Academy of Arts, London, 6 January–13 March 1966, no. 132; *European Painting and Sculpture from the Philadelphia Museum of Art: Towards the Twentieth-Century*, Hokkaido Museum of Art, Sapporo, 18 July–23 August 1992, Yamanashi Prefectural Museum of Art, Kofu, 5 September–4 October 1992, Matsuzakaya Art Museum, Nagoya, 10 October–23 November 1992, no. 48; *Bonnard, Decorator*, The Montreal Museum of Art, 9 July–8 November 1998.

The Terrace (Le Jardin sauvage or **La Grande Terrasse)**
1918
Oil on canvas, 62¾ × 98¼ in. (159.4 × 249.5 cm)
The Phillips Collection, Washington, D.C.
[plate 86]
Provenance
Galerie Bernheim-Jeune, Paris, from 1919; Phillips Memorial Gallery purchase 1935.
Exhibitions
Salon d'Automne, Grand Palais des Champs-Elysees, Paris, 1 November–10 December 1919, no. 183 (as *Le Jardin sauvage*); Untitled Exhibition, Phillips Memorial Gallery, Washington, D.C., by 6 October 1935; Untitled Exhibition, Phillips Memorial Gallery, Washington, D.C., by 12 January 1936; Untitled Exhibition, Phillips Memorial Gallery, Washington, D.C., by 15 May 1937; *Loan Exhibition of Paintings and Prints by Bonnard and Vuillard,* The Art Institute of Chicago, 15 December 1938–15 January 1939, no. 21 (as 1911); Untitled Exhibition, Phillips Memorial Gallery, Washington, D.C., by 12 May–June 1940; *Prints and Drawings from the Collection*, Phillips Memorial Gallery, Washington, D.C., 26 October–10 November 1941; *Paintings by Bonnard. The Collection's Unit of Seventeen Paintings on View in the Main Gallery*, Phillips Memorial Gallery, Washington, D.C., 18 March–30 September 1945; *Paintings in the Collection by Bonnard*, The Phillips Gallery, Washington, D.C., 3 February–31 March 1952; *Paintings by Pierre Bonnard from the Collection*, The Phillips Gallery, Washington, D.C., 15 March–30 June 1959; *Paintings and Drawings by Pierre Bonnard: An Exhibition from The Phillips Collection and the Collections of Mrs. Phillips and Mr. and Mrs. Laughlin Phillips,* The Phillips Collection, Washington, D.C., 7 January–28 February 1967; *The Paintings by Pierre Bonnard in the Collection*, The Phillips Collection, Washington, D.C., 17 July–August 1971 (extended until at least June 1975); *Bonnard*, Musée National d'Art Moderne, Centre Georges Pompidou, Paris, 23 February–21 May 1984, no. 13, traveled as *Bonnard: The Late Paintings* to The Phillips Collection, Washington, D.C., 9 June–25 August 1984, Dallas Museum of Art, 13 September–11 November 1984, no. 15, traveled as *Pierre Bonnard* to Kunsthaus Zurich, 14 December 1984–10 March 1985, Städtische Galerie im Städelschen Kunstinstitut, Frankfurt, 3 May–14 July 1985, no. 87; *Duncan Phillips: Centennial Exhibition*, The Phillips Collection, Washington, D.C., 14 June–31 August 1986; *Renoir to Rothko: The Eye of Duncan Phillips*, The Phillips Collection, Washington, D.C., 25 September 1999–23 January 2000; *Beyond the Easel: Decorative Painting by Bonnard, Vuillard, Denis and Roussel,*

1890–1930, The Art Institute of Chicago, 25 February–16 May 2001, The Metropolitan Museum of Art, New York, 26 June–9 September 2001, no. 55.

Young Women in the Garden (Jeunes Femmes au jardin)
1918
Oil on canvas, 36¼ × 40½ in. (92 × 103 cm)
Galerie Jan Krugier, Ditesheim & Cie, Geneva
Washington only
[plate 85]
Provenance
Estate of the artist; private collection, New York.
Exhibitions
Un Siècle de peinture française, 1850–1950, Lisbon, 1965; *Bonnard*, Louisiana Museum of Modern Art, Humlebaek, Denmark, 16 September–20 October 1967, no. 47; *Pierre Bonnard. Das Glück zu malen*, Kunstsammlung Nordrhein-Westfalen, Düsseldorf, 23 January–12 April 1993, no. 21; *Bonnard*, Kunsthalle der Hypo-Kulturstiftung, Munich, 28 January–24 April 1994, no. 77.

Interior with Flowers (Intérieur avec des fleurs)
1919
Oil on canvas, 45¾ × 35⅛ in. (116.2 × 89.2 cm)
Riggs National Corporation
[plate 87]
Provenance
Paul Rosenberg & Co., New York; Mr. and Mrs. Walter Bareiss, Greenwich, Conneticut; private collection.
Exhibitions
Collector's Choice, Paul Rosenberg & Co., New York, 17 March–18 April 1953; *Loan Exhibition of Paintings by Pierre Bonnard*, Paul Rosenberg and Co., New York, 12 March–7 April 1956, no. 9; *Bonnard and His Environment*, The Museum of Modern Art, New York, 7 October–29 November 1964, The Art Institute of Chicago, 8 January–28 February 1965, Los Angeles County Museum of Art, 31 March–31 May 1965, no. 32 (as 1924); *Bonnard dans sa lumière*, Fondation Maeght, Saint-Paul-de-Vence, 12 July–28 September 1975, no. 25? (as *Fleurs dans un intérieur*); *Bonnard: The Late Paintings*, The Phillips Collection, Washington, D.C., 9 June–25 August 1984, Dallas Museum of Art, 13 September–11 November 1984, no. 16, traveled as *Pierre Bonnard* to Kunsthaus Zurich, 14 December 1984–10 March 1985, Städtische Galerie im Städelschen Kunstinstitut, Frankfurt, 3 May–14 July 1985, no. 89.

The Abduction of Europa (L'Enlèvement d'Europe)
1919
Oil on canvas, 46¼ × 60¼ in. (117.5 × 153 cm)
Toledo Museum of Art; Purchased with funds from the Libbey Endowment, Gift of Edward Drummond Libbey
[plate 79]
Provenance
Galerie Druet, Paris; Ethel Hughes, Versailles; René Gimpel, Paris; Toledo Museum of Art, 1930.
Exhibitions
Accession of the Year 1930, Toledo Museum of Art, 14 January–22 February 1931; *French Painting*, California Palace of the Legion of Honor, San Francisco, 8 June–8 July 1934,

no. 61; *La Vie française*, The Institute of Modern Art, Boston, 6 October–11 November 1944, no. 12; *Pierre Bonnard Memorial Exhibition*, The Cleveland Museum of Art, 3 March–11 April 1948, traveled as *Pierre Bonnard* to The Museum of Modern Art, New York, 10 May–6 September 1948, no. 37; *L'Œuvre du XXe siècle*, Musée National d'Art Moderne, Paris, May–June 1952, no. 4; *Bonnard*, Musée de Lyon, 1954, no. 42; *Bonnard*, Society of the Four Arts, Palm Beach, Fla., 4–27 January 1957, no. 12; *What is Modern Art*, Toledo Museum of Art, 1960; *Pierre Bonnard*, Royal Academy of Arts, London, 6 January–13 March 1966, no. 138; *Pierre Bonnard*, Kunsthaus Zurich, 14 December 1984–10 March 1985, Städtische Galerie im Städelschen Kunstinstitut, Frankfurt, 3 May–14 July 1985, no. 90; *Impressionism: Selections from Five American Museums*, Carnegie Museum of Art, Pittsburgh, 4 November–31 December 1989, The Minneapolis Institute of Arts, 27 January–25 March 1990, The Nelson-Atkins Museum of Art, Kansas City, 21 April–17 June 1990, The Saint Louis Art Museum, 14 July–9 September 1990, Toledo Museum of Art, 30 September–25 November 1990; no. 3; *Beyond the Easel: Decorative Painting by Bonnard, Vuillard, Denis and Roussel, 1890–1930*, The Art Institute of Chicago, 25 February–16 May 2001, The Metropolitan Museum of Art, New York, 26 June–9 September 2001, no. 56.

Bowl of Cherries (Compotier de cerises)
1920
Oil on canvas, 11⅞ × 16½ in. (30.2 × 41.9 cm)
The Phillips Collection, Washington, D.C.
[plate 101]
Provenance
Acquired by Bernheim-Jeune from the artist, 1920; sold to Dr. Soubies; sold "collection d'un amateur, tableaux modernes," Hôtel Drouot, Paris, 17 December 1927, no. 2; purchased by Georges Renand; private collection, Paris; Robert Sinclair; Paul Rosenberg, New York, purchase from Robert Sinclair, 1952; Rosenberg sale to Gustave Ring, 1953; Gift of Marion Ring Estate to The Phillips Collection, 1987.
Exhibitions
Les Maîtres de l'art indépendant, 1895–1937, Musée du Petit Palais, Paris, June–October 1937, no. 9; *Bonnard*, Bernheim-Jeune, Paris, 1950, no. 43; *20th Century French Paintings*, Paul Rosenberg Galleries, New York, 5–31 January 1953, no. 1; *Selections from the Collection of Marion and Gustave Ring*, Hirshhorn Museum and Sculpture Garden, Washington, D.C., 17 October–12 January, 1986, no. 4; *The Aftermath of Impressionism: Selected Works from The Phillips Collection*, Michael C. Carlos Museum, Emory University, Atlanta, 13 November 1991–9 February 1992, no. 2.

Normandy Landscape (Paysage Normand)
1920
Oil on canvas, 41⅜ × 22⅜ in. (105 × 57.9 cm)
Musée d'Unterlinden, Colmar
Washington only
[plate 82]
Provenance
Acquired by Bernheim-Jeune from the artist, 1920; given in exchange to J. Rodier; private collection, Paris; Musée d'Unterlinden, Colmar.
Exhibitions
Exposition Retrospective Bonnard, Bernheim-Jeune, Paris, May–June 1950, no. 36; *A propos de Bonnard*, Musée d'Unterlinden, Colmar, 19 June–26 September 1982, no. 24; *Bonnard*, Kunsthaus Zurich, 14 December–10 March 1985, no. 120; *Pierre Bonnard*, Palazzo Reale, Milan, 28 October 1988–8 January 1989, no. 28; *Pierre Bonnard*, Isetan Museum of Art, Tokyo, 4–30 July 1991, Nara Sogo Museum of Art, 7 August–1 September 1991, Sogo Museum of Art, Yokohama, 7 September–10 October 1991, Fukuoka Art Museum, 17 October–10 November 1991, no. 39; *Pierre Bonnard*, Aichi Prefectural Museum of Art, Nagoya, 28 March–18 May 1997, Bunkamura Museum of Art, Tokyo, 24 May–21 July 1997, no. 30; *Bonnard*, Tate Gallery, London, 12 February–17 May 1998, The Museum of Modern Art, New York, 17 June–13 October 1998, no. 38.

Strawberries (Fraises)
1920
Oil on canvas, 10⅝ × 9⅞ in. (27 × 25.1 cm)
Private collection on loan to The Phillips Collection, Washington, D.C.
[plate 83]
Provenance
Bought from Rodrigues by Bernheim-Jeune, 1928; sold to Turner; Mrs. Duncan Phillips, 1948; private collection.
Exhibitions
The Second Tri-Unit Exhibition of the Season 1929–1930: An Exhibition of Lyric Painters, Phillips Memorial Gallery, Washington, D.C., March–June 1930, no. 53; Untitled Exhibition, Phillips Memorial Gallery, Washington, D.C., September 1930; *Pierre Bonnard*, Phillips Memorial Gallery, Washington, D.C., 5 October 1930–25 January 1931, no. 102; *A Classic Cézanne with Pictures of More Personal Approach*, Phillips Memorial Gallery, Washington, D.C., 27 September 1931–January 1932, no. 12; Untitled Exhibition, Phillips Memorial Gallery, Washington, D.C., February–June 1932, no. 13; *Pierre Bonnard: Twelve Paintings*, Smith College Museum of Art, Northampton, Mass., 19 November–14 December 1932, no. 11; *Bonnard/Vuillard*, The Art Institute of Chicago, 15 December 1938–15 January 1939, no. 20; *Paintings by Bonnard: The Collection's Unit of Seventeen Paintings on View in the Main Gallery*, Phillips Memorial Gallery, Washington, D.C., 18 March–30 September 1945; *Pierre Bonnard Memorial Exhibition*, The Cleveland Museum of Art, 3 March–11 April 1948, traveled as *Pierre Bonnard* to The Museum of Modern Art, New York, 10 May–6 September 1948, no. 56; *Paintings in the Collection by Bonnard*, The Phillips Gallery, Washington, D.C., 3 February–31 March 1952; *Paintings by Pierre Bonnard from the Collection*, The Phillips Gallery, Washington, D.C., 15 March–30 June 1959; *Paintings and Drawings by Pierre Bonnard: An Exhibition from The Phillips Collection and the Collections of Mrs. Phillips and Mr. and Mrs. Laughlin Phillips*, The Phillips Collection, Washington, D.C., 7 January–28 February 1967.

The Terrace at Vernonnet (Décor à Vernonnet)
1920/1939
Oil on canvas, 58¼ × 76¾ in. (148 × 194.9 cm)

The Metropolitan Museum of Art, Gift of Mrs. Frank Jay Gould 1968 (68.1)
Washington only
[plate 88]
Provenance
Estate of the artist; Mrs. Frank Jay Gould, Cannes, France, ca. 1947–1968; The Metropolitan Museum of Art, New York, Gift of Mrs. Frank Gould, 1968. 68.1
Exhibitions
Bonnard and His Environment, The Museum of Modern Art, New York, 7 October–29 November 1964, The Art Institute of Chicago, 8 January–28 February 1965, Los Angeles County Museum of Art, 31 March–31 May 1965, no. 53; *Bonnard*, National Museum of Western Art, Tokyo, 20 March–5 May 1968, National Museum of Modern Art, Kyoto, 11 May–16 June 1968, no. 43; *Masterpieces of Fifty Centuries*, The Metropolitan Museum of Art, New York, 14 November 1970–1 June 1971, no. 388; *Treasured Masterpieces of The Metropolitan Museum of Art*, Tokyo National Museum, 9 August–1 October 1972, The Kyoto Municipal Museum, 8 October–26 November 1972, no. 106; *100 Paintings from The Metropolitan Museum of Art*, The Hermitage, Leningrad, The Pushkin Museum, Moscow, August–September 1975; *Bonnard: The Late Paintings*, The Phillips Collection, Washington, D.C., 9 June–25 August 1984, Dallas Museum of Art, 13 September–11 November 1984, no. 18, traveled as *Pierre Bonnard* to Kunsthaus Zurich, 14 December 1984–10 March 1985, Städtische Galerie im Städelschen Kunstinstitut, Frankfurt, 3 May–14 July 1985, no. 96; *20th-Century Masters from The Metropolitan Museum of Art*, Australian National Gallery, Canberra, 1 March–27 April 1986, Queensland Art Gallery, 7 May–1 July 1986, p. 31; Kunstsammlung Nordrhein Westfalen, Düsseldorf, 23 January–12 April 1993, no. 71; *Beyond the Easel: Decorative Painting by Bonnard, Vuillard, Denis and Roussel, 1890–1930*, The Art Institute of Chicago, 25 February–16 May 2001, The Metropolitan Museum of Art, New York, 26 June–9 September 2001, no. 57.

Self-Portrait with Beard
(Autoportrait à la barbe or Portrait de l'artiste)
ca. 1920
Oil on canvas mounted on panel, 11⅝ × 18 in. (29.5 × 45.7 cm)
Private collection
[plate 89]
Provenance
Estate of the artist (inv. no. 854); private collection, U.S.A.
Exhibitions
Pierre Bonnard, Royal Academy of Arts, London, 1966, no. 156; *Pierre Bonnard*, Kunstnerforbundet, Oslo, 1966, no. 23; *Bonnard*, National Museum of Western Art, Tokyo, 20 March–5 May 1968, National Museum of Modern Art, Kyoto, 11 May–16 June 1968, no. 45; *Bonnard, Vuillard, Roussel*, Musées Royaux des Beaux-Arts de Belgique, Brussels, 26 September–30 November 1975, no. 11; *Exposition Pierre Bonnard*, The Nihonbashi Takashimaya Art Galleries, Tokyo, 10 October–11 November 1980, Aichi Prefectural Museum of Modern Art, Kobe, 16 November–21 December 1980, Aichi Prefectural Museum of Art, Nagoya, 6 January–18 January 1981, Fukuoka Museum of Art, 28

January–22 February, 1981, no. 47; *Pierre Bonnard*, Musée Rath, Geneva, 9 April–8 June 1981, no. 45; *The Inquiring Eye of Pierre Bonnard*, Wildenstein and Co., New York, 6 November–11 December, 1981, no. 26; *Bonnard*, Fundación Juan March, Madrid, 29 September–27 November 1983, Sala de exposiciones Caixa de Barcelona, 6 December 1983–24 January 1984, no. 27; *Bonnard*, Musée National d'Art Moderne, Centre Georges Pompidou, Paris, 23 February–21 May 1984, no. 15, traveled as *Bonnard: The Late Paintings* to The Phillips Collection, Washington, D.C., 9 June–25 August 1984, Dallas Museum of Art, 13 September–11 November 1984, no. 17, Kunsthaus Zurich, 14 December 1984–10 March 1985, Städtische Galerie im Städelschen Kunstinstitut, Frankfurt, 3 May–14 July 1985, no. 95; *Pierre Bonnnard et son monde enchanté,* Fondation de L'Hermitage, Lausanne, 7 June–6 October 1991, no. 44; *Bonnard*, Kunsthalle der Hypo–Kulturstiftung, Munich, 28 January–24 April 1994, no. 88; *1918–1958, La Côte d'Azur et la modernité,* Musée Picasso, Antibes, 28 June–30 September 1997, no. 2; *Bonnard*, Tate Gallery, London, 12 February–17 May 1998, The Museum of Modern Art, New York, 17 June–13 October 1998, no. 37; *The Artist and the Camera: Degas to Picasso*, San Francisco Museum of Modern Art, 2 October 1999–4 January 2000, Dallas Museum of Art, 1 February–7 May 2000, no. 396.

Study for "The Open Window"
(Study for "La Fenêtre ouverte")
ca. 1920–1921
Graphite on paper, 4¾ × 8¹/₁₆ in. (12 × 20.5 cm)
Private collection
[plate 91]
Provenance
Family of the artist; private collection.

Study for "The Open Window"
(Study for "La Fenêtre ouverte")
ca. 1920–1921
Graphite on paper, 4¾ × 8¹/₁₆ in. (12 × 20.5 cm)
Private collection
[plate 92]
Provenance
Family of the artist; private collection.

The Open Window (La Fenêtre ouverte)
1921
Oil on canvas, 46½ × 37¾ in. (118 × 96 cm)
The Phillips Collection, Washington, D.C.
[platc 93]
Provenance
Acquired by Bernheim-Jeune from the artist, 1922; sold to Georges Bésnard, Paris, by at least 1924; Jacques Seligmann and Co., New York, 1930; purchase, Phillips Memorial Gallery, 1930.
Exhibitions
Première Exposition de collectionneurs organisée au Profit de la Société des Amis du Luxembourg, Chambre Syndicale de l'Antiquité et des Beaux-Arts, Paris, March–April 1924, no. 46 (as *Soleil d'avril*); *Pierre Bonnard*, Phillips Memorial Gallery, Washington, D.C., 5 October 1930–25 January 1931, no. 125; *Exhibition of Paintings by Bonnard, Vuillard, Roussel,*

Jacques Seligmann & Co., New York, 6–25 October 1930, no. 14; *A Survey of Modern Painting*, Phillips Memorial Gallery, Washington, D.C., 27 September 1931–January 1932, no. 125; Untitled Exhibition, Phillips Memorial Gallery, Washington, D.C., February–June 1932, no. 11; *Summer Exhibition: Painting and Sculpture*, The Museum of Modern Art, New York, 10 July–30 September 1933; *Modern European Art*, The Museum of Modern Art, New York, 4–25 October 1933; [*Painting by Pierre Bonnard*], Phillips Memorial Gallery, Washington, D.C., 5 November 1933–15 February 1934; Untitled Exhibition, Phillips Memorial Gallery, Washington, D.C., by 12 January 1936; *Loan Exhibition of Paintings and Prints by Bonnard and Vuillard,* The Art Institute of Chicago, 15 December 1938–15 January 1939, no. 3; *The Functions of Color in Painting: An Educational Loan Exhibition*, Phillips Memorial Gallery, Washington, D.C., 16 February–23 March 1941, no. 3; *French Painting of the XIX and XX Centuries*, Fogg Art Museum, Cambridge, Mass., July–August 1941; *French Paintings from The Phillips Memorial Gallery*, William Rockhill Nelson Gallery, Kansas City, 16 February–1 March 1942; *Paintings by Bonnard. The Collection's Unit of Seventeen Paintings on View in the Main Gallery*, Phillips Memorial Gallery, Washington, D.C., 18 March–30 September 1945; *Exhibition of Paintings by Pierre Bonnard*, Bignon Gallery, New York, December 1946–January 1947, no. 14; *Pierre Bonnard Memorial Exhibition*, The Cleveland Museum of Art, 3 March–11 April 1948, traveled as *Pierre Bonnard* to The Museum of Modern Art, New York, 10 May–6 September 1948, no. 42; *Paintings in the Collection by Bonnard*, The Phillips Gallery, Washington, D.C., 3 February–31 March 1952; *European Masters of Our Time*, Museum of Fine Arts, Boston, 10 October–17 November 1957, no. 14; *Paintings by Pierre Bonnard from the Collection*, The Phillips Gallery, Washington, D.C., 15 March–30 June 1959; *Masterpieces of Art*, Fine Arts Pavilion, Seattle World's Fair, 21 April–4 September 1962, no. 57 (as ca. 1921); *Paintings and Drawings by Pierre Bonnard: An Exhibition from The Phillips Collection and the Collections of Mrs. Phillips and Mr. and Mrs. Laughlin Phillips,* The Phillips Collection, Washington, D.C., 7 January–28 February 1967; *The Paintings by Pierre Bonnard in the Collection*, The Phillips Collection, Washington, D.C., 17 July–31 August 1971; *Bonnard dans sa lumière*, Fondation Maeght, Saint-Paul-de-Vence, 12 July–28 September 1975, no. 28; *Impressionism and the Modern Vision: Master Paintings from The Phillips Collection*, The Fine Arts Museums of San Francisco, 4 July–1 November 1981, Dallas Museum of Fine Arts, 22 November 1981–16 February 1982, The Minneapolis Institute of Arts, 14 March–30 May 1982, High Museum of Art, Atlanta, 24 June–5 September 1982, The Oklahoma Art Center, 17 October 1982–9 January 1983, no. 2; The Nihonbashi Takashimaya Art Galleries, Tokyo, 25 August–4 October 1983, Nara Prefectural Museum of Art, 9 October–13 November 1983, no. 47; *Paintings and Drawings from The Phillips Collection*, IBM Gallery of Science and Art, New York, 9 December 1983–21 January 1984, no. 7; *Bonnard*, Musée National d'Art Moderne, Centre Georges Pompidou, Paris, 23 February–21 May 1984, no. 17, traveled as *Bonnard: The Late Paintings* to The Phillips Collection, Washington, D.C., 9 June–25 August 1984, Dallas Museum of Art, 13 September–11 November 1984, no. 20, traveled as

Pierre Bonnard to Kunsthaus Zurich, 14 December 1984–10 March 1985, Städtische Galerie im Städelschen Kunstinstitut, Frankfurt, 3 May–14 July 1985, no. 97; *Duncan Phillips: Centennial Exhibition*, The Phillips Collection, Washington, D.C., 14 June–31 August 1986; *Masterpieces from The Phillips Collection*, Palm Springs Desert Museum, Palm Springs, Calif., 21 March–17 May 1987, traveled as *Selections from The Phillips Collection* to Center for the Fine Arts, Miami, 13 June–30 August 1987; *Old Masters—New Visions: El Greco to Rothko from The Phillips Collection, Washington, D.C.,* Australian National Gallery, Canberra, October 3–December 6, 1987, Art Gallery of Western Australia, Perth, 22 December 1987–21 February 1988; Art Gallery of South Australia, Adelaide, 4 March–1 May 1988, no. 42; *Master Paintings from The Phillips Collection*, Hayward Gallery, London, 19 May–14 August 1988, no. 49; *Master Paintings from The Phillips Collection, Washington*, Schirn Kunsthalle, Frankfurt, 27 August–6 November 1988, no. 49; Centro de Arte Reina Sofia, Madrid, 30 November 1988–16 February 1989; *The Return of the Master Paintings*, The Phillips Collection, Washington, D.C., 22 April–27 August 1989; *Duncan Phillips Collects: Paris between the Wars*, The Phillips Collection, Washington, D.C., 14 September 1990–12 January 1991; *Pierre Bonnard*, Louisiana Museum of Modern Art, Humlebaek, Denmark, 12 September 1992–10 January 1993, no. 60; *Pierre Bonnard: Das Glück zu malen,* Kunstsammlung Nordrhein-Westfalen, Düsseldorf, 23 January–12 April 1993, no. 27; *Bonnard at the Villa Le Bosquet*, Hayward Gallery, London, 23 June–29 August 1994, Laing Art Gallery, Newcastle, 9 September–30 October 1994; *Bonnard*, Tate Gallery, London, 12 February–17 May 1998, The Museum of Modern Art, New York, 17 June–13 October 1998, no. 42; *Renoir to Rothko: The Eye of Duncan Phillips*, The Phillips Collection, Washington, D.C., 25 September 1999–23 January 2000; *Masterworks from The Phillips Collection*, The Bellagio Gallery of Fine Arts, Las Vegas, 1 September 2000–4 March 2001.

Evening by the Lamp (La Soirée sous la lampe or Intimité)
1921
Oil on canvas, 28¾ × 35¹/₁₆ in. (73 × 89 cm)
Private collection; Paris, Musée d'Orsay, Gift with Reserved Use, 2000
Washington only
[plate 104]
Provenance
Pierre Bonnard, Paris; Galerie Bernheim-Jeune, Paris, until 1921; M. Jacques Canonne, Paris; sold Hôtel Drouot, Paris, 5 June 1942; Gustav Zumsteg, Zurich; Sylvan Kocher, Soleure; private collection.
Exhibitions
Bonnard, Galerie Bernheim-Jeune, Paris, 24 May–11 June 1921, no. 17; *Bonnard*, De Hauke and Co., New York, 6–28 April 1928; *Bonnard*, Stedelijk Museum, Amsterdam, 1947, no. 18; *Pierre Bonnard Memorial Exhibition*, The Cleveland Museum of Art, 3 March–11 April 1948, traveled as *Pierre Bonnard* to The Museum of Modern Art, New York, 10 May–6 September 1948, no. 41; *Bonnard*, Kunsthaus Zurich, 1949, no. 60; *Bonnard*, Museum Boymans, Rotterdam, 1953, no. 74; *Pierre Bonnard*, Kunsthalle Basel, 28 May–17 July

1955, no. 74; *Pierre Bonnard*, Musée des Ponchettes, Nice, August–September 1955; *Exposition Pierre Bonnard*, The Nihonbashi Takashimaya Art Galleries, Tokyo, 10 October–11 November 1980, Aichi Prefectural Museum of Modern Art, Kobe, 16 November–21 December 1980, Aichi Prefectural Museum of Art, Nagoya, 6 January–18 January 1981, Fukuoka Art Museum, 28 January–22 February, 1981, no. 43; *Pierre Bonnard*, Musée Rath, Geneva, 9 April–8 June 1981, no. 46; *Bonnard*, Fondation Juan March, Madrid, October–November 1983, no. 28; *Pierre Bonnard*, Louisiana, Museum of Modern Art, Humleback, Denmark; 12 September 1992–10 January 1993; *Pierre Bonnard. Das Glück zu malen*, Kunstsammlung Nordrhein-Westfalen, Düsseldorf, 23 January–12 April 1993; *Bonnard*, Fondation Pierre Gianadda, Martigny, 11 June–14 November 1999, no. 39; *Cézanne à Giacometti*, Musée d'Orsay, Paris, 2000; *Bonnard*, Musée Granet, Aix-en-Provence, 2001.

Young Women in the Garden (Renée Monchaty and Marthe Bonnard) (Jeunes Femmes au jardin)
ca. 1921–1923, 1945–1946
Oil on canvas, 23¹³⁄₁₆ × 30⁵⁄₁₆ in. (60.5 × 77 cm)
Private collection
Washington only
[plate 90]
Provenance
Estate of the artist (inv. no. 5155); Charles Terrasse, Paris; private collection, New York.
Exhibitions
Pierre Bonnard, Royal Academy of Arts, London, 6 January–13 March 1966, no. 172; *Pierre Bonnard*, Kunstnerforbundet, Oslo, 24 March–26 April 1966, no. 26; *Pierre Bonnard*, Haus der Kunst, Munich, 8 October 1966–1 January 1967, Paris, no. 94; *Pierre Bonnard: Centenaire de sa naissance*, Musée du Louvre, Paris, 13 January–15 April 1967, no. 102; *Bonnard*, Louisiana Museum of Modern Art, Humlebaek, Denmark, 16 September–29 October 1967, no. 47; *Suites No. 23: Bonnard*, Galerie Krugier & Co., Geneva, June–July 1969, no. 17; *Bonnard (1867–1947)*, Accademia di Francia, Villa Medici, Rome, 18 November 1971–23 January 1972, Museo d'Art Contemporanea, Turin, 1–28 February 1972, no. 11; *Bonnard dans sa lumière*, Fondation Maeght, Saint-Paul-de-Vence, 12 July–28 September 1975, no. 31; *A propos de Bonnard*, Musée d'Unterlinden, Colmar, 19 June–26 September 1982, no. 27; *Bonnard*, Musée National d'Art Moderne, Centre Georges Pompidou, Paris, 23 February–21 May 1984, no. 20, traveled as *Bonnard: The Late Paintings* to The Phillips Collection, Washington, D.C., 9 June–25 August 1984, Dallas Museum of Art, 13 September–11 November 1984, no. 21, traveled as *Pierre Bonnard* to Kunsthaus Zurich, 14 December 1984–10 March 1985, Städtische Galerie im Städelschen Kunstinstitut, Frankfurt, 3 May–14 July 1985, no. 98; *Hommage à Bonnard*, Galerie des Beaux-Arts, Bordeaux, 10 May–25 August 1986, no. 53; *Bonnard*, Kunsthalle der Hypo-Kulturstiftung, Munich, 1991, no. 93; *Pierre Bonnard. Das Glück zu malen*, Kunstsammlung Nordrhein-Westfalen, Düsseldorf, 23 January–12 April 1993, no. 29; *Pierre Bonnard*, Galerie Schmit, Paris, 3 May–12 July 1995, no. 33; *Bonnard*, Tate

Gallery, London, 12 February–17 May 1998, The Museum of Modern Art, New York, 17 June–13 October 1998, no. 43.

Claude Anet's "Notes sur l'amour"
1922
Lithograph on cover of book, 8¹¹⁄₁₆ × 11 in. (22 × 28 cm)
Lessing J. Rosenwald Collection, Library of Congress, Washington, D.C.
Provenance
Library of Congress

Place Clichy (Place Clichy or Dans la Rue de Paris)
1922
Lithograph printed in five colors, 22⁷⁄₁₆ × 29½ in. (57 × 75 cm)
Museum of Fine Arts, Boston. Bequest of W. G. Russell Allen, 1960 60.70
[plate 105]
Provenance
W. G. Russell Allen (1882–1955), Boston; Museum of Fine Arts, Boston, acquired by bequest, 1960.

Woman with Dog (Femme au chien)
1922
Oil on canvas, 27¼ × 15½ in. (69.2 × 39.3 cm)
The Phillips Collection, Washington, D.C.
Denver only
[plate 96]
Provenance
The artist to Bernheim-Jeune, Paris, November 1923; Phillips Memorial Gallery purchase from *Twenty-fourth Annual International Exhibition of Paintings*, Carnegie Institute, 1925.
Exhibitions
Peinture, Sculpture, Dessin, Gravure, Architecture et Art Décoratif, Salon d'Automne, Grand Palais, Paris, 1 November–16 December 1923, no. 192 (as *Jeune femme et chien*); *Twenty-fourth Annual International Exhibition of Paintings*, Carnegie Institute, Pittsburgh, 15 October–6 December 1925, Arts Club, Philadelphia, January–February 1926, Grand Central Galleries, New York, until 20 April 1926 (removed from tour), no. 56; *Intimate Impressionists: Berthe Morisot, Pierre Bonnard, Maurice Prendergast, Paul Dougherty, Alfred Sisley, Albert André, Marjorie Phillips, Samuel Halpert*, Phillips Memorial Gallery, Washington, D.C., 8–30 May 1926 (as *Girl and Dog*); *Sensibility and Simplification in Ancient Sculpture and Contemporary Painting*, Phillips Memorial Gallery, Washington, D.C., 5 February–April 1927; *Leaders of French Art To-Day: Exhibition of Characteristic Works by Matisse, Picasso, Braque, Segonzac, Bonnard, Vuillard, Derain, André, Maillol*, Phillips Memorial Gallery, Washington, D.C., December 1927–January 1928; *Bonnard*, De Hauke and Co., New York, 6–28 April 1928, no. 3; *Painting in Paris from American Collections*, The Museum of Modern Art, New York, 19 January–16 February 1930, no. 1 (as *Woman and Dog*, 1923); Untitled Exhibition, Phillips Memorial Gallery, Washington, D.C., September 1930; *Pierre Bonnard*, Phillips Memorial Gallery, Washington, D.C., 5 October 1930–25 January 1931, no. 93; *French Paintings from Manet to Derain*, Phillips Memorial Gallery, Washington, D.C., February–June 1931,

no. 82; Untitled Exhibition, Phillips Memorial Gallery, Washington, D.C., February–June 1932, no. 23; *Pierre Bonnard: Twelve Paintings*, Smith College Museum of Art, Northampton, Mass., 19 November–14 December 1932, no. 6 (as 1918); [*Painting by Pierre Bonnard*], Phillips Memorial Gallery, Washington, D.C., 5 November 1933–15 February 1934; *Loan Exhibition of Paintings and Prints by Pierre Bonnard and Edouard Vuillard*, The Art Institute of Chicago, 15 December 1938–15 January 1939, no. 16; *The Functions of Color in Painting: An Educational Loan Exhibition*, Phillips Memorial Gallery, Washington, D.C., 16 February–23 March 1941, no. 93; *Paintings by Bonnard: The Collection's Unit of Seventeen Paintings on View in the Main Gallery*, Phillips Memorial Gallery, Washington, D.C., 18 March–30 September 1945; *Pierre Bonnard Memorial Exhibition*, The Cleveland Museum of Art, 3 March–11 April 1948, traveled as *Pierre Bonnard* to The Museum of Modern Art, New York, 10 May–6 September 1948, no. 43; *A Selection of 20th Century European Paintings from The Phillips Collection*, University of North Carolina, Chapel Hill, 1 June–31 August 1951; *Paintings in the Collection by Bonnard*, The Phillips Gallery, Washington, D.C., 3 February–31 March 1952; *Modern European and American Paintings from the Collection Including Cross Section of Contemporary Trends*, The Phillips Gallery, Washington, D.C., 16 June–21 October 1953; *Retrospective Exhibition of Paintings from Previous Internationals*, Department of Fine Arts, Carnegie Institute, Pittsburgh, 5 December 1958–8 February 1959, no. 40; *Paintings by Pierre Bonnard from the Collection*, The Phillips Gallery, Washington, D.C., 15 March–30 June 1959; *Paintings and Drawings by Pierre Bonnard: An Exhibition from The Phillips Collection and the Collections of Mrs. Phillips and Mr. and Mrs. Laughlin Phillips*, The Phillips Collection, Washington, D.C., 7 January–28 February 1967; *Bonnard*, National Museum of Western Art, Tokyo, 20 March–5 May 1968, National Museum of Modern Art, Kyoto, 11 May–16 June 1968, no. 57 (as *Femme au chien*); *The Paintings by Pierre Bonnard in the Collection*, The Phillips Collection, Washington, D.C., 17 July–31 August 1971 (as *Girl and Dog*); *Small Paintings from Famous Collections*, The Taft Museum, Cincinnati, 4 April–7 June 1981; *Impressionism and the Modern Vision: Master Paintings from The Phillips Collection*, The Fine Arts Museums of San Francisco, 4 July–1 November 1981, Dallas Museum of Fine Arts, 22 November 1981–16 February 1982, The Minneapolis Institute of Arts, 14 March–30 May 1982, High Museum of Art, Atlanta, 24 June–5 September 1982, The Oklahoma Art Center, Oklahoma City, 17 October 1982–9 January 1983, no. 3; *Bonnard*, Musée National d'Art Moderne, Centre Georges Pompidou, Paris, 23 February–21 May 1984, no. 19, traveled as *Bonnard: The Late Paintings* to The Phillips Collection, Washington, D.C., 9 June–25 August 1984, Dallas Museum of Art, 13 September–11 November 1984, no. 23, traveled as *Pierre Bonnard* to Kunsthaus Zurich, 14 December 1984–10 March 1985, Städtische Galerie im Städelschen Kunstinstitut, Frankfurt, 3 May–14 July 1985, no. 101; *Duncan Phillips: Centennial Exhibition*, The Phillips Collection, Washington, D.C., 14 June–31 August 1986; *Old Masters—New Visions: El Greco to Rothko from The Phillips Collection, Washington, D.C.*, Australian National Gallery, Canberra, 3 October–6

December 1987, Art Gallery of Western Australia, Perth, 22 December 1987–21 February 1988; Art Gallery of South Australia, Adelaide, 4 March–1 May 1988, no. 43; *Master Paintings from The Phillips Collection, Washington*, The Hayward Gallery, London, 19 May–14 August 1988, no. 50; *Master Paintings from The Phillips Collection, Washington*, Schirn Kunsthalle, Frankfurt, 27 August–6 November 1988; *Master Paintings from The Phillips Collection, Washington*, Centro de Arte Reina Sofia, Madrid, 30 November 1988–16 February 1989; *The Return of the Master Paintings*, The Phillips Collection, Washington, D.C., 22 April–27 August 1989; *Duncan Phillips Collects: Paris between the Wars*, The Phillips Collection, Washington, D.C., 14 September 1990–12 January 1991; *Renoir to Rothko: The Eye of Duncan Phillips*, The Phillips Collection, Washington, D.C., 25 September 1999–23 January 2000.

The Riviera (La Côte d'Azur)
ca. 1923
Oil on canvas, 31 × 30 in. (79 × 76.2 cm)
The Phillips Collection, Washington, D.C.
[plate 114]
Provenance
Claude Anet, Paris; De Hauke and Co., Paris and New York, 1928; Phillips Memorial Gallery purchase 1928.
Exhibitions
Bonnard, De Hauke and Co., New York, 6–28 April 1928, no. 13 (as *Grand paysage du midi*); *Tri-Unit Exhibition of Paintings and Sculpture: An International Group*, Phillips Memorial Gallery, Washington, D.C., October 1928–January 1929 (as *Southern France*); Untitled Exhibition, Phillips Memorial Gallery, Washington, D.C., February–June 1929, no. 10 (as *The Midi*); *The First Tri-Unit Exhibition of the Season of 1929-30 of the Phillips Memorial Gallery*, Phillips Memorial Gallery, Washington, D.C., 19 October 1929–February 1930, no. 10 (as *The Midi*); *Painting in Paris from American Collections*, The Museum of Modern Art, New York, 19 January–16 February 1930, no. 3 (as *Southern France, 1927*); *Exhibition of a Selected Group of Contemporary European Paintings from The Phillips Memorial Gallery*, Syracuse Museum of Fine Arts, Syracuse, N.Y., 3–30 June 1930, no. 9 (as *Southern France*), Rochester Memorial Art Gallery, N.Y., early July–September 15 1930; *Pierre Bonnard*, Phillips Memorial Gallery, Washington, D.C., 5 October 1930–25 January 1931, no. 99; *A Survey of Modern Painting*, Phillips Memorial Gallery, Washington, D.C., 27 September 1931–January 1932, no. 124; Untitled Exhibition, Phillips Memorial Gallery, Washington, D.C., February–June 1932, no. 12; *Summer Exhibition: Painting and Sculpture*, The Museum of Modern Art, New York, 10 July–30 September 1933; *Modern European Art*, The Museum of Modern Art, New York, 3–27 October 1933; [*Painting by Pierre Bonnard*], Phillips Memorial Gallery, Washington, D.C., 5 November 1933–15 February 1934; *The Post-Impressionists*, Philadelphia Museum of Art, 2 February–13 March 1935; [*Paintings From Phillips Memorial Gallery*], Yale University Art Gallery, New Haven, 28 February–27 March 1936; *Loan Exhibition of Paintings and Prints by Bonnard and Vuillard*, The Art Institute of Chicago, 15 December 1938–15 January 1939, no. 19 (as *Riviera [Le Midi]; Midi Landscape*); *Golden Gate*

International Exposition, Palace of Fine Arts, San Francisco, 10 May–16 October 1940, no. 607; *Corot to Picasso*, The American British Art Center, New York, 1–23 June 1934, no. 1; *Paintings by Bonnard. The Collection's Unit of Seventeen Paintings on View in the Main Gallery*, Phillips Memorial Gallery, Washington, D.C., 18 March–30 September 1945; *Pierre Bonnard Memorial Exhibition*, The Cleveland Museum of Art, 3 March–11 April 1948, traveled as *Pierre Bonnard* to The Museum of Modern Art, New York, 10 May–6 September 1948, no. 44 (as *The Riviera–Large Midi Landscape*); *Paintings in the Collection by Bonnard*, The Phillips Gallery, Washington, D.C., 3 February–31 March 1952; *Paintings by Pierre Bonnard from the Collection*, The Phillips Gallery, Washington, D.C., 15 March–30 June 1959; *Paintings and Drawings by Pierre Bonnard: An Exhibition from The Phillips Collection and the Collections of Mrs. Phillips and Mr. and Mrs. Laughlin Phillips*, The Phillips Collection, Washington, D.C., 7 January–28 February 1967; *The Paintings by Bonnard in the Collection*, The Phillips Collection, Washington, D.C., 17 July–31 August 1971; *Bonnard dans sa lumière*, Fondation Maeght, Saint-Paul-de-Vence, 12 July–28 September 1975, no. 34; *Bonnard and Vuillard: An Exhibition for the Benefit of The Phillips Collection*, Adams Davidson Galleries, Washington, D.C., 17 May–22 June 1978, no. 8 (as 1923–1925); *Paris-Moscou: 1900-1930*, Musée National d'Art Moderne Centre Georges Pompidou, Paris, 16 May–15 October 1979 (removed from USSR tour); *The Enchantment of Art: Highlights from The Phillips Collection*, Garfinckel's, Washington, D.C., 17 June–24 December 1983, no. 3; *Bonnard*, Musée National d'Art Moderne, Centre Georges Pompidou, Paris, 23 February–21 May 1984, no. 21, traveled as *Bonnard: The Late Paintings* to The Phillips Collection, Washington, D.C., 9 June–25 August 1984, Dallas Museum of Art, 13 September–11 November 1984, no. 24, Kunsthaus Zurich, 14 December 1984–10 March 1985, no. 102, Städtische Galerie im Städelschen Kunstinstitut, Frankfurt, 3 May–14 July 1985, no. 102; *Duncan Phillips: Centennial Exhibition*, The Phillips Collection, Washington, D.C., 14 June–31 August 1986; *Pont-Aven to Nabis*, Isetan Museum of Art, Tokyo, 2–14 April 1987, Niigata City Art Museum, 18 April–17 May 1987, Daimaru Museum, Osaka, 20 May–9 June 1987, Shizuoka Prefectural Museum, 13 June–19 July 1987, Himeji City Museum of Art, 25 July–23 August 1987, Yamanashi Prefectural Museum, 27 August–27 September 1987, no. 17; *The Return of the Master Paintings*, The Phillips Collection, Washington, D.C., 22 April–27 August 1989; *Bonnard at Le Bosquet*, Hayward Gallery, London, 23 June–29 August 1994, Laing Art Gallery, Newcastle, 9 September–30 October 1994, no. 1; *Renoir to Rothko: The Eye of Duncan Phillips*, The Phillips Collection, Washington, D.C., 25 September 1999–23 January 2000; *Méditerranée: de Courbet à Matisse*, Galeries Nationales du Grand Palais, Paris, 19 September 2000–15 January 2001, no. 5.

Landscape with Mountain (Paysage avec montagne)
1924
Oil on canvas, 15¾ × 23¼ in. (40 × 59 cm)
The Phillips Collection, Washington, D.C.
Denver only

[plate 111]
Provenance
Purchased from the artist by Galerie Bernheim-Jeune, Paris; sold to Theodore Schempp & Co., New York, 1935; purchased by Mrs. George Warrington, Cincinnati, 1935; inherited by son, John Warrington, Cincinnati, and sold to Theodore Schempp & Co., New York, 1951; Phillips Memorial Gallery, 1951.
Exhibitions
Paintings in the Collection by Bonnard, The Phillips Gallery, Washington, D.C., 3 February–31 March 1952; *Paintings by Pierre Bonnard from the Collection*, The Phillips Gallery, Washington, D.C., 15 March–30 June 1959; *Paintings and Drawings by Pierre Bonnard: An Exhibition from The Phillips Collection and the Collections of Mrs. Phillips and Mr. and Mrs. Laughlin Phillips*, The Phillips Collection, Washington, D.C., 7 January–28 February 1967; *The Paintings by Pierre Bonnard in the Collection*, The Phillips Collection, Washington, D.C., 17 July–31 August 1971, extended through at least June 1975 (removed from exhibition on 8 September 1971); *Pierre Bonnard*, Isetan Museum of Art, Tokyo, 4–30 July 1991, Nara Sogo Museum of Art, 7 August–1 September 1991, Sogo Museum of Art, Yokohama, 7 September–10 October 1991, Fukuoka Art Museum, 17 October–10 November 1991, no. 45; *Pierre Bonnard*, Aichi Prefectural Museum of Art, Nagoya, 28 March–18 May 1997, Bunkamura Museum of Art, Tokyo, 24 May–21 July 1997, no. 32.

Reflecting on the Day (Les Comptes de la journée)
1924
Oil on canvas, 21¼ × 19¹¹/₁₆ in. (54 × 50 cm)
Private collection; Courtesy Guggenheim, Asher Associates, Inc., New York
Washington only
[plate 97]
Provenance
Félix Fénéon, Paris, acquired directly from the artist; sold, Hôtel Drouot, Paris, 4 December 1941, no. 31; private collection, 1999.
Exhibitions
Bonnard, Galerie Bernheim-Jeune, Paris, 1924; *Exposition du Cercle Manes*, Prague, 1926, no. 3; *IVème Salon du Sud-Est*, Lyon, 1928, no. 4; *Exposition d'art français moderne*, Palais des Beaux-Arts, Brussels, 1929, no. 430; *Parisje Schilder*, Stedelijk Museum, Amsterdam, 1939, no. 9; *Cinquante ans de peinture française dans les collection parisiennes, de Cézanne à Matisse*, Musée des Arts Décoratifs, Paris, 1952, no. 12; *1850-1950. Tableaux des collections parisiennes*, Galerie des Beaux-Arts, Paris, 13 January–15 April 1967, no. 4; *Depuis Bonnard*, Musée d'Art Moderne, Paris, 1957, no. 40; *Von Bonnard bis heute, Meisterwerke aus französischen Privatbesitz*, Haus der Kunst, Munich, 1961, no. 6; *Pierre Bonnard*, Musée du Louvre, 13 January–15 April, 1967, continuation of exhibition at Haus der Kunst, Munich, 8 October 1966–1 January 1967; *French Paintings since 1900 from Private Collections in France*, Royal Academy of Arts, London, 1969, no. 19; *Portraits français, XIXe et XXe siècles*, Galerie Schmit, Paris, 1974, no. 1.

Portrait of Ambroise Vollard (Portrait d'Ambroise Vollard)
ca. 1924
Etching, 17⁵⁄₁₆ × 11⁷⁄₁₆ in. (44 × 29 cm)
Museum of Fine Arts, Boston. George Peabody Gardner
Fund, 1954 54.666
[plate 94]
Provenance
Museum of Fine Arts, Boston, purchased from Peter
Deitsch, New York dealer, 1954.

The Menu (Le Menu)
ca. 1924–1925
Lithograph, 19½ × 12¹¹⁄₁₆ in. (49.5 × 32.2 cm)
The Metropolitan Museum of Art, The Elisha Whittelsey
Collection, The Elisha Whittelsey Fund, 1988 (1988.1017.2)
[plate 98]
Provenance
The Metropolitan Museum of Art, New York, purchased
from Libby Howie, London, 1988.
Exhibitions
Pierre Bonnard: The Graphic Art, The Metropolitan Museum
of Art, New York, 2 December 1989–4 February 1990, The
Museum of Fine Arts, Houston, 25 February–29 April 1990,
Museum of Fine Arts, Boston, 25 May–29 July 1990, no. 107;
Bonnard Stealing the Image: Works on Paper, New York
Studio School Gallery of Drawing, Painting, and Sculpture,
16 October–15 November 1997.

Landscape in the South of France (Paysage du midi)
1925
Lithograph on heavy cream wove paper, 8½ × 11½ in.
(21.5 × 29.2 cm)
The Phillips Collection, Washington, D.C.
[plate 113]
Provenance
The Phillips Collection, purchased from E. Weyhe, New
York, 1938.

The Bath (Le Bain)
1925
Oil on canvas, 33⅞ × 47¼ in. (86 × 120.6 cm)
Tate. Presented by Lord Ivor Spencer Churchill through the
Contemporary Art Society, 1930
[plate 109]
Provenance
Bernheim-Jeune, Paris, purchased from the artist, 7
December 1925; Tate Gallery, London, 1930.
Exhibitions
Salon d'Automne, Paris, September–November 1925, no. 140;
The CAS: Second Loan Exhibition of Foreign Paintings, M.
Knoedler, London, February 1928, no. 52; *Acquisitions of the
Contemporary Art Society*, Tate Gallery, London,
September–October 1946, no. 7; *Exhibition of Paintings by
Pierre Bonnard and Edouard Vuillard*, Royal Scottish
Academy, Edinburgh, 17 August–18 September 1948, no. 27;
Bonnard, Roland, Browse and Delbanco, London, June 1950,
no. 5; *Pierre Bonnard*, Royal Academy of Arts, London,
January–March 1966, no. 177; *Bonnard*, Kunsthaus Zurich, 14
December 1984–10 March 1985, no. 112, Städtische Galerie im
Städelschen Kunstinstitut, Frankfurt, 3 May–14 July 1985, no.

112; *Pierre Bonnard*, Louisiana Museum of Modern Art,
Humlebaek, Denmark, 12 September 1992–10 January 1993;
Art Gallery of New South Wales, Sydney, August–December
1997; *Bonnard*, Tate Gallery, London, 12 January–17 May
1998, The Museum of Modern Art, New York, 17 June–13
October 1998, no. 48.

The Table (La Table)
1925
Oil on canvas, 40⅝ × 29¼ in. (102.9 × 74.3 cm)
Tate. Presented by the Courtauld Fund Trustees, 1926.
[plate 102]
Provenance
Bernheim-Jeune, Paris, purchased from the artist;
Independent Gallery, London; the Trustees of the Courtauld
Fund, by whom presented to the Tate Gallery, London, 1926.
Exhibitions
Royal Scottish Academy, Edinburgh, April–August 1932, no.
211; Royal Scottish Academy, Edinburgh, April–August 1946,
no. 104; *Samuel Courtauld Memorial Exhibition*, Tate
Gallery, London, May–September 1948, no. 1; *La Collection
Courtauld*, Musée de l'Orangerie, Paris, November
1955–January 1956, no. 2; *Bonnard and His Environment,* The
Museum of Modern Art, New York, 7 October–29
November 1964, The Art Institute of Chicago, 8 January–28
February 1965, Los Angeles County Museum of Art, 31
March–31 May 1965, no. 34; *Pierre Bonnard*, Royal Academy
of Arts, London, January–March 1966, no. 179; *Bonnard*,
Musée National d'Art Moderne, Paris, Centre Georges
Pompidou, 23 February–21 May 1984, no. 27, traveled as
Bonnard: The Late Paintings to The Phillips Collection,
Washington, D.C., 9 June–25 August 1984, Dallas Museum of
Art, 13 September–11 November 1984, no. 31, Kunsthaus,
Zurich, 14 December 1984–10 March 1985, no. 111, Städtische Galerie
im Städelschen Kunstinstitut, Frankfurt, 3 May–14 July 1985,
no. 111; National Gallery, London, January 1993–January
1994; *Bonnard*, Tate Gallery, London, 12 February–17 May
1998, The Museum of Modern Art, New York, 17 June–13
October, 1998, no. 50.

**Woman Standing in Her Bathtub
(Femme debout dans sa baignoire)**
1925
Lithograph on heavy cream wove paper, 18⅝ × 13 in.
(47.3 × 32.9 cm)
The Phillips Collection, Washington, D.C.
[plate 107]
Provenance
The Phillips Collection, Gift of Marjorie Phillips, 1984.
Exhibitions
Duncan Phillips Collects: Paris between the Wars, The Phillips
Collection, Washington, D.C., 14 September 1990–12 January
1991; *Works on Paper: Pierre Bonnard*, The Phillips
Collection, Washington, D.C., 30 June–25 October 1992.

The Bath (Le Bain)
ca. 1925
Lithograph, 19½ × 12¾ in. (49.5 × 32.4 cm)
Prints and Photographs Division, Library of Congress,
Washington, D.C. Reproduction numbers: LC-USZC4-

10006, LC-USZ62-130234
[plate 106]
Provenance
Library of Congress, Pennell Fund acquisition, selected by
the Pennell Committee established by Joseph Pennell.

The Checkered Table Cover (La Nappe)
ca. 1925
Oil on canvas, 13¼ × 24 in. (33.7 × 60.7 cm)
Liza Phillips
[plate 95]
Provenance
Henri Canonne, Paris; Marjorie Phillips, Washington, D.C.;
Liza Phillips.
Exhibitions
Contemporary European Masters, Phillips Memorial Gallery,
Washington, D.C., 16 January–9 February 1944, no. 1 (as *The
Tablecloth*); *Paintings by Bonnard. The Collection's Unit of
Seventeen Paintings on View in the Main Gallery*, Phillips
Memorial Gallery, Washington, D.C., 18 March–30
September 1945, (as *The Tablecloth*); *Pierre Bonnard
Memorial Exhibition*, The Cleveland Museum of Art, 3
March–11 April 1948, traveled as *Pierre Bonnard* to The
Museum of Modern Art, New York, 10 May–6 September
1948, no. 46; *Paintings by Pierre Bonnard from the Collection*,
The Phillips Gallery, Washington, D.C., 15 March–30 June
1959; *Paintings and Drawings by Pierre Bonnard: An
Exhibition from The Phillips Collection and the Collections of
Mrs. Phillips and Mr. and Mrs. Laughlin Phillips,* The Phillips
Collection, Washington, D.C., 7 January–28 February 1967;
Pierre Bonnard. Das Glück zu malen, Kunstsammlung
Nordrhein-Westfalen, Düsseldorf, 23 January–12 April 1993,
no. 36.

The Letter (La Lettre)
ca. 1925
Lithograph, 12⅝ × 19⅜ in. (32.1 × 49.2 cm)
Prints and Photographs Division, Library of Congress,
Washington, D.C. Reproduction numbers: LC-USZC4-
10008, LC-USZ62-13023.
[plate 99]
Provenance
Library of Congress, Pennell Fund acquisition, selected by
the Pennell Committee established by Joseph Pennell.

Boulevard des Batignolles
1926
Oil on canvas, 24¾ × 25⅝ in. (62.9 × 65.1 cm)
Private collection, Washington, D.C.
[plate 103]
Provenance
Acquired from the artist by Bernheim-Jeune, June 1931; sold
to Katia Granoff; Sir Kenneth Clark, K.C.B., London;
Roland, Browse and Delbanco, London; The Lefevre Gallery,
London; Mrs. John Armstrong, London; Fritz and Peter
Nathan, Zurich; Jacques Koerfer, Bolligen, Bern.
Exhibitions
Bonnard, Roland, Browse and Delbanco, London, 1950, no.
31; *Roussel, Bonnard, Vuillard*, Marlborough Fine Arts,
London, 1954, no. 39; *De Géricault à Matisse. Chefs-d'œuvre*

français des collections suisses, Musée du Petit Palais, Paris, March–May 1959, no. 5.

Grape Harvest (Terrasses *or* Vendages)
1926
Oil on canvas, 25 × 15¾ in. (63.5 × 40 cm)
The Phillips Collection, Washington, D.C.
[plate 115]
Provenance
Acquired from the artist by Bernheim-Jeune in 1927; sold to Turner; The Phillips Collection, acquired in 1928 from Cesar De Hauke.
Exhibitions
Untitled Exhibition, Phillips Memorial Gallery, Washington, D.C., September 1930; *Pierre Bonnard*, Phillips Memorial Gallery, Washington, D.C., 5 October 1930–25 January 1931; *French Painting from Manet to Derain*, Phillips Memorial Gallery, Washington, D.C., 2 February–June 1931; Untitled Exhibition, Phillips Memorial Gallery, Washington, D.C., February–June 1932, no. 10; *Pierre Bonnard: Twelve Paintings*, Smith College Museum of Art, Northampton, Mass., 19 November–14 December 1932, no. 8; *Summer Exhibition: Painting and Sculpture*, The Museum of Modern Art, New York, 10 July–30 September 1933; *Freshness of Vision: Classic and Romantic*, Phillips Memorial Gallery, Washington, D.C., 5 November 1933–15 February 1934; *Gardens in Paintings, Drawings, Prints, and Other Arts*, Lyman Allyn Museum, New London, Conn., 2 March–15 April 1935, no. 4; Buffalo Fine Arts Academy, December 1935–February 1936; *Paintings of Springtime by American and European Artists From the Permanent Collection*, Phillips Memorial Gallery, Washington, D.C., by 15 May–30 June 1938; *The Functions of Color in Painting: An Educational Loan Exhibition*, Phillips Memorial Gallery, Washington, D.C., 16 February–23 March 1941, no. 28; *Paintings by Bonnard. The Collection's Unit of Seventeen Paintings on View in the Main Gallery*, Phillips Memorial Gallery, Washington, D.C., 18 March–30 September 1945; *Paintings in the Collection by Bonnard*, The Phillips Gallery, Washington, D.C., 3 February–31 March 1952; *Paintings by Pierre Bonnard from the Collection*, The Phillips Gallery, Washington, D.C., 15 March –30 June 1959; *Paintings and Drawings by Pierre Bonnard*, The Phillips Collection, Washington, D.C., 7–28 February 1967; *Retrospective for a Critic: Duncan Phillips*, University of Maryland Art Department and Art Gallery, J. Millard Tawes Fine Arts Center, College Park, 12 February–16 March 1969; *Duncan Phillips Collects: Paris between the Wars*, The Phillips Collection, Washington, D.C., 14 September 1990–12 January 1991; *Renoir to Rothko: The Eye of Duncan Phillips*, The Phillips Collection, Washington, D.C., 25 September 1999–23 January 2000.

The Lesson (La Leçon de couture)
1926
Oil on canvas, 30 × 20 in. (76 × 51 cm)
The Phillips Collection, Washington, D.C.
[plate 100]
Provenance
Acquired from the artist by Bernheim-Jeune, 1927; sold to Valentine Dudensing; The Phillips Collection, acquired in

1927 from Valentine Dudensing.
Exhibitions
Exposition Bonnard, œuvres récentes, Bernheim-Jeune, Paris, 24 November–17 December 1926, no. 3; *Tri-Unit Exhibition of Paintings and Sculpture: Art Is International*, Phillips Memorial Gallery, Washington, D.C., October 1928–January 1929; Untitled Exhibition, Phillips Memorial Gallery, Washington, D.C., February–June 1929; Untitled Exhibition, Phillips Memorial Gallery, Washington, D.C., September 1930; *Pierre Bonnard*, Phillips Memorial Gallery, Washington, D.C., 5 October 1930–25 January 1931, no. 96; *Pierre Bonnard*, Phillips Memorial Gallery, Washington, D.C., 2 February–June 1931, no. 98; *A Survey of Modern Painting*, Phillips Memorial Gallery, Washington, D.C., 27 September 1931–January 1932, no. 126; Untitled Exhibition, Phillips Memorial Gallery, Washington, D.C., February–June 1932, no. 22; *Pierre Bonnard: Twelve Paintings*, Smith College Museum of Art, Northampton, Mass., 19 November–14 December 1932, no. 9; [*Painting by Pierre Bonnard*], Phillips Memorial Gallery, Washington, D.C., 5 November 1933–15 February 1934; *The Functions of Color in Painting: An Educational Loan Exhibition*, Phillips Memorial Gallery, Washington, D.C., 16 February–23 March 1941, no. 92 (as *The Sewing Lesson*); *Paintings by Bonnard: The Collection's Unit of Seventeen Paintings on View in the Main Gallery*, Phillips Memorial Gallery, Washington, D.C., 18 March–30 September 1945; *Paintings in the Collection by Bonnard*, The Phillips Gallery, Washington, D.C., 3 February–31 March 1952; *Modern European and American Paintings From the Collection Including Cross Section of Contemporary Trends*, The Phillips Gallery, Washington, D.C., 16 June–21 October 1953; *Paintings by Pierre Bonnard From the Collection*, The Phillips Gallery, Washington, D.C., 15 March–30 June 1959; *Paintings and Drawings by Pierre Bonnard: An Exhibition from The Phillips Collection and the Collections of Mrs. Phillips and Mr. and Mrs. Laughlin Phillips*, The Phillips Collection, Washington, D.C., 7 January–28 February 1967; *The Paintings by Pierre Bonnard in the Collection*, The Phillips Collection, Washington, D.C., 17 July–31 August 1971; *Duncan Phillips: Centennial Exhibition*, The Phillips Collection, Washington, D.C., 14 June–31 August 1986; *Bonnard*, Tate Gallery, London, 19 February–10 May 1998, The Museum of Modern Art, New York, 24 June–1 September 1998, no. 52 (as *The Sewing Lesson*); *Renoir to Rothko: The Eye of Duncan Phillips*, The Phillips Collection, Washington, D.C., 25 September 1999–23 January 2000.

The Palm (La Palme)
1926
Oil on canvas, 45 × 57⅞ in. (114.3 × 147 cm)
The Phillips Collection, Washington, D.C.
[plate 110]
Provenance
The artist to Felix Fénéon, Paris; De Hauke and Co., New York; Phillips Memorial Gallery purchase from De Hauke and Co. exhibition, 1928.
Exhibitions
Bonnard, De Hauke and Co., New York, 6–28 April 1928, no. 14; *Tri-Unit Exhibition of Paintings and Sculpture: Art Is International*, Phillips Memorial Gallery, Washington, D.C.,

October 1928–January 1929; Untitled Exhibition, Phillips Memorial Gallery, Washington, D.C., February–June 1929; *Exhibition of French Art since Eighteen Hundred*, The Cleveland Museum of Art, 7 November–10 December 1929; *Painting in Paris from American Collections*, The Museum of Modern Art, New York, 19 January–16 February 1930, no. 4 (as 1927); Untitled Exhibition, Phillips Memorial Gallery, Washington, D.C., September 1930; *Pierre Bonnard*, Phillips Memorial Gallery, Washington, D.C., 5 October 1930–25 January 1931, no. 98; *Pierre Bonnard*, Phillips Memorial Gallery, Washington, D.C., 2 February–June 1931, no. 97; Untitled Exhibition, Phillips Memorial Gallery, Washington, D.C., February–June 1932, no. 9; *Pierre Bonnard: Twelve Paintings*, Smith College Museum of Art, Northampton, Mass., 19 November–14 December 1932, no. 10; *A Century of Progress: Exhibition of Paintings and Sculpture Lent from American Collections*, The Art Institute of Chicago, 1 June–1 November 1933, no. 676; *Loan Exhibition of Paintings and Prints by Bonnard and Vuillard*, The Art Institute of Chicago, 15 December 1938–15 January 1939, no. 18; *The Functions of Color in Painting: An Educational Loan Exhibition*, Phillips Memorial Gallery, Washington, D.C., 16 February–23 March 1941, no. 29; *Paintings by Bonnard: The Collection's Unit of Seventeen Paintings on View in the Main Gallery*, Phillips Memorial Gallery, Washington, D.C., 18 March–30 September 1945; *Pierre Bonnard Memorial Exhibition*, The Cleveland Museum of Art, 3 March–11 April 1948, traveled as *Pierre Bonnard* to The Museum of Modern Art, New York, 10 May–6 September 1948, no. 52; *Paintings in the Collection by Bonnard*, The Phillips Gallery, Washington, D.C., 3 February–31 March 1952; *Paintings by Pierre Bonnard From the Collection*, The Phillips Gallery, Washington, D.C., 15 March–4 May 1959 (extended through 30 June); *Bonnard and His Environment*, The Museum of Modern Art, New York, 7 October–29 November 1964, The Art Institute of Chicago, 8 January–28 February 1965, Los Angeles County Museum of Art, 31 March–30 May 1965, no. 37; *Pierre Bonnard's "The Palm,"* The Phillips Collection, Washington, D.C., 15 September–11 October 1965; *Pierre Bonnard*, Musée du Louvre, Paris, 13 January–15 April 1967, no. 113 (painting did not travel to Munich); *The Paintings by Pierre Bonnard in the Collection*, The Phillips Collection, Washington, D.C., 17 July–31 August 1971; extended through at least June 1975 (removed from exhibition 8 September 1971); *Impressionism and the Modern Vision: Master Paintings from The Phillips Collection*, The Fine Arts Museums of San Francisco, 4 July–1 November 1981, Dallas Museum of Fine Arts, 22 November 1981–16 February 1982, The Minneapolis Institute of Arts, 14 March–30 May 1982, High Museum of Art, Atlanta, 24 June–5 September 1982, The Oklahoma Art Center, Oklahoma City, 17 October 1982–9 January 1983, no. 4; *Impressionism and the Modern Vision: Master Paintings from The Phillips Collection*, Nihonbashi Takashimaya Art Galleries, Tokyo, 25 August–4 October 1983, Nara Prefectural Museum of Art, 9 October–13 November 1983, no. 48; *Paintings and Drawings from The Phillips Collection*, IBM Gallery of Science and Art, New York, 9 December 1983–21 January 1984, no. 8; *Bonnard*, Musée National d'Art Moderne, Centre Georges Pompidou, Paris, 23 February–21 May 1984, no. 28, traveled as *Bonnard: The Late Paintings*,

The Phillips Collection, Washington, D.C., 9 June–25 August 1984, Dallas Museum of Art, 13 September–11 November 1984, no. 32, traveled as *Pierre Bonnard*, Kunsthaus Zurich, 14 December 1984–10 March 1985, Städtische Galerie im Städelschen Kunstinstitut, Frankfurt, 3 May–14 July 1985, no. 113; *Duncan Phillips: Centennial Exhibition*, The Phillips Collection, Washington, D.C., 14 June–31 August 1986; *Old Masters—New Visions: El Greco to Rothko from The Phillips Collection, Washington, D.C.*, Australian National Gallery, Canberra, 3 October–6 December 1987, Art Gallery of Western Australia, Perth, December 22, 1987–February 21, 1988; Art Gallery of South Australia, Adelaide, 4 March–1 May 1988, no. 44; *Master Paintings from The Phillips Collection, Washington,* The Hayward Gallery, London, 19 May–14 August, 1988, no. 55; *Master Paintings from The Phillips Collection, Washington*, Centro de Arte Reina Sofia, Madrid, 30 November 1988–16 February 1989; *The Return of the Master Paintings*, The Phillips Collection, Washington, D.C, 22 April–27 August 1989; *Duncan Phillips Collects: Paris between the Wars*, The Phillips Collection, Washington, D.C, 14 September 1990–12 January 1991; *Renoir to Rothko: The Eye of Duncan Phillips*, The Phillips Collection, Washington, D.C., 25 September 1999–23 January 2000; *Méditerranée: de Courbet à Matisse*, Galeries Nationales du Grand Palais, 19 September 2000–15 January 2001, no. 7.

Effect of Snow or **Le Cannet under the Snow**
(**Effet de neige** or **Le Cannet sous la neige**)
1927
Oil on canvas, 29⅛ × 19⁵⁄₁₆ in. (74 × 49 cm)
Kunstmuseum Winterthur, inv. no. 1531. Gift of Dr. Herbert and Charlotte Wolfer-de Armas, 1973
[plate 116]
Provenance
Galerie L'Art Moderne, Lucerne; Collection Heinri⅞ch Wolfer; Kunstmuseum Winterthur, Gift of Dr. Herbert and Charlotte Wolfer-de Armas, 1973.
Washington only
Exhibitions
Winterthur, 1949, no. 67; Basel, 1955, no. 68; *Hommage à Bonnard*, Galerie des Beaux-Arts, Bordeaux, 10 May–25 August 1986, no. 63; *Pierre Bonnard, Gemälde, Aquarelle, Zeichnungen und Druckgraphik*, Kunstverein in Hamburg, 6 February–5 April 1970, no. 48; *Bonnard*, Kunsthaus Zurich, 14 December 1984–10 March 1985, no. 117; *Pierre Bonnard*, Kunsthalle der Hypo-Kulturstiftung, Munich, 28 January–24 April 1994.

Last Light (Dernier reflet)
ca. 1927–1928
Lithograph, 12¹¹⁄₁₆ × 18⅛ in. (32.2 × 46 cm)
The Metropolitan Museum of Art, The Elisha Whittelsey Collection, The Elisha Whittelsey Fund, 1985 (1985.1096.2)
[plate 112]
Provenance
The Metropolitan Museum of Art, New York, Purchased from David Tunick in 1985.
Exhibitions
Pierre Bonnard: The Graphic Art, The Metropolitan Museum of Art, New York, 2 December 1989–4 February 1990, The Museum of Fine Arts, Houston, 25 February–29 April 1990,

Museum of Fine Arts, Boston, 25 May–29 July 1990, no. 112; *Bonnard Stealing the Image: Works on Paper*, New York Studio School of Drawing, Paintings, and Sculpture, 16 October–15 November 1997.

Still Life with Bouquet of Flowers or **Venus and Cyrene**
(**Nature morte au bouquet de fleurs** or **La Vénus de Cyrène**)
1930
Oil on canvas, 23⅝ × 51⅜ in. (60 × 130.5 cm)
Öffentliche Kunstsammlung Basel, Kunstmuseum
[plate 119]
Provenance
Acquired by Bernheim-Jeune from the artist; painting disappeared during the Occupation; Galerie Beyeler, Basel; given by the Foundation Esther Mengold in 1956 to the Kunstmuseum Basel.
Exhibitions
Maîtres de l'art moderne, Galerie Beyeler, Basel, 1955, no. 4; *Bonnard*, Kunsthaus Zurich, 14 December 1984–10 March 1985, Städtische Galerie im Städelschen Kunstinstitut, Frankfurt, 3 May–14 July 1985, no. 126; *Pierre Bonnard. Das Glück zu malen*, Kunstsammlung Nordrhein-Westfalen, Düsseldorf, 23 January–12 April 1993, no. 43.

The Coffee Grinder (Le Moulin à café)
1930
Oil on canvas, 18⅞ × 22½ in. (48 × 57 cm)
Kunstmuseum Winterthur, inv. no. 1528. Gift of Dr. Herbert and Charlotte Wolfer-de Armas, 1973
[plate 120]
Provenance
Acquired by Bernheim-Jeune from the artist, September 1930; sold to Alphonse Kahn; private collection, Winterthur; Kunstmuseum Winterthur, Gift of Dr. Herbert and Charlotte Wolfer-de Armas, 1973.
Washington only
Exhibitions
Salon d'Automne, Paris, 1 November–14 December 1930, no. 288; *Pierre Bonnard*, Kunsthalle, Basel, 28 May–17 July 1955, no. 91; *Bonnard*, Musée National d'Art Moderne, Centre Georges Pompidou, Paris, 23 February–21 May 1984, no. 36, traveled as *Pierre Bonnard* to Kunsthaus Zurich, 14 December 1984–10 March 1985, Städtische Galerie im Städelschen Kunstinstitut, Frankfurt, 3 May–14 July 1985, no. 129; *Pierre Bonnard*, Palazzo Reale, Milan, 28 October 1988–8 January 1989, no. 33; *Pierre Bonnard*, Kunsthalle der Hypo-Kulturstiftung, Munich, January 28–24 April 1994.

The Breakfast Room (Salle à manger sur le jardin)
ca. 1930–1931
Oil on canvas, 62⅞ × 44⅞ in. (159.6 × 113.8 cm)
The Museum of Modern Art, New York. Given anonymously, 1941
Washington only
[plate 118]
Provenance
Jacques Seligmann Galleries, New York (Cesar M. de Hauke); Stephen C. Clark, New York, purchased from Jacques Seligmann, 1931; The Museum of Modern Art, 1941.
Exhibitions

Modern Works of Art: 5th Anniversary Exhibition, The Museum of Modern Art, New York, November 1934–January 1935; *Art in Our Time: 10th Anniversary Exhibition*, The Museum of Modern Art, New York, 1939, *Art in Progress: 15th Anniversary Exhibition*, Museum of Modern Art, New York, 1944; *Exposition Bonnard*, Musée de l'Orangerie, Paris, 1 October–9 December 1947, no. 65; *Pierre Bonnard Memorial Exhibition*, The Cleveland Museum of Art, 3 March–11 April 1948, traveled as *Pierre Bonnard* to The Museum of Modern Art, New York, 10 May–6 September 1948, no. 64; *25th Anniversary Exhibition*, The Museum of Modern Art, New York, 1954; *Great French Paintings: An Exhibition in Memory of Chauncey McCormick*, The Art Institute of Chicago, 20 January–20 February 1955, no. 1; *Bonnard*, The Phillips Gallery, Washington, D.C., 12 January–12 February 1958, no. 4; *Paintings from The Museum of Modern Art, New York*, National Gallery of Art, Washington, D.C., 16 December 1963–1 March 1964 (extended to 22 March); *Bonnard and His Environment*, The Museum of Modern Art, New York, 7 October–29 November 1964, The Art Institute of Chicago, 8 January–28 February 1965, Los Angeles County Museum of Art, 31 March–30 May 1965, no. 52; *Bonnard*, Musée National d'Art Moderne, Centre Georges Pompidou, Paris, 23 February–21 May 1984, no. 42, traveled as *Bonnard: The Late Paintings* to The Phillips Collection, Washington, D.C., 9 June–25 August 1984, Dallas Museum of Art, 13 September–11 November 1984, no. 46; *Jubilee Exhibition*, The Hermitage Museum, Leningrad, 17 October–28 November 1989; *Pierre Bonnard*, Kunstsammlung Nordrhein-Westfalen, Dusseldorf, 22 January–12 April 1993; *Bonnard/Rothko, Color and Light*, PaceWildenstein, New York, 19 February–22 March 1997; *Bonnard*, Tate Gallery, London, 12 February–17 May 1998, The Museum of Modern Art, New York, 17 June–13 October 1998, no. 62; *Masterworks from The Museum of Modern Art 1900–1950*, Ueno Museum, Tokyo, 6 October 2001–2003 February 2002.

Nude in Bathroom (Le Cabinet de toilette)
1932
Oil on canvas, 47⅝ × 46½ in. (121 × 118.1 cm)
The Museum of Modern Art, New York, Florene May Schoenborn Bequest, 1996
Washington only
[plate 126]
Provenance
Acquired by Bernheim-Jeune from the artist, 1932; Samuel A. Marx, Chicago; Florence May Schoenborn (Mrs. Wolfgang Schoenborn); The Museum of Modern Art, New York, Florene May Schoenborn Bequest, 1996.
Exhibitions
Œuvres récentes de Bonnard, Bernheim-Jeune, Paris, 15 June–23 July 1933, no. 17; *Exhibition of Paintings by Bonnard*, Wildenstein and Co., New York, 26 February–17 March 1934, no. 44; *Exposition de la peinture française de Manet à nos jours*, Musée National, Warsaw, February–March 1937, no. 43; *XXXIV Peintures de Pierre Bonnard*, Bernheim-Jeune, Paris, 15 June–13 July 1946, no. 31; *Pierre Bonnard Memorial Exhibition*, The Cleveland Museum of Art, 3 March–11 April 1948, The Museum of Modern Art, New York, 10 May–6 September

1948, no. 66; *A Loan Exhibition: Six Paintings by Bonnard*,
The Phillips Gallery, Washington, D.C., 12 January–12
February 1958, no. 5; *Bonnard and His Environment*, The
Museum of Modern Art, New York, 7 October–29
November 1964, The Art Institute of Chicago, 8 January–28
February 1965, Los Angeles County Museum of Art, 31
March–30 May 1965, no. 54; *Pierre Bonnard*, Tate Gallery,
London, 12 February–17 May 1998, The Museum of Modern
Art, New York, 24 June 1998–29 September 1998, no. 66.

White Interior (Intérieur blanc)
1932
Oil on canvas, 43¹⁄₁₆ × 61⁵⁄₁₆ in. (109.5 × 155.8 cm)
Musée de Grenoble
[plate 121]
Provenance
Acquired by Bernheim-Jeune from the artist; purchased by
the Musée de Peinture et de Sculpture de Grenoble from
Bernheim-Jeune after the June 1933 exhibition.
Exhibitions
Œuvres récentes de Bonnard, Bernheim-Jeune, Paris, 15
June–23 July 1933, no. 18; *Exposition du Musée de Grenoble*,
Musée du Petit Palais, Paris, 1935; *Aus Museum und
Bibliothek der Stadt Grenoble*, Kunsthaus Zurich,
July–August 1946; *Bonnard, Udstilling i anledning of
Glyptotekets 50-aars Jubilaeum*, Ny Carlsberg Glyptotek,
Copenhagen, May 1947, no. 33; *Pierre Bonnard*, Stedelijk
Museum, Amsterdam, June–July 1947, no. 43; *Exposition
Bonnard*, Musée de l'Orangerie, Paris, October–November
1947, no. 74; *Pierre Bonnard Memorial Exhibition*, The
Cleveland Museum of Art, 3 March–11 April 1948, The
Museum of Modern Art, New York, 10 May–6 September
1948, no. 66; *Pierre Bonnard, 1867–1947*, Kunsthaus Zurich, 6
June–24 July 1949, no. 111; *Pierre Bonnard*, Haus der Kunst,
Munich, 8 October 1966–1 January 1967, Musée du Louvre,
Paris, 13 January–15 April 1967, no. 130; *Twentieth Century
Masterpieces from the Musée de Grenoble*, University of
Maryland Art Gallery, College Park, 7 November–21
December 1973, J. B. Speed Art Museum, Louisville, Ky., 7
January–3 February 1974, University Art Museum, Austin,
Tex., 17 February–24 March 1974; *Figurations*, Musée de
Grenoble, July 1978; *Andry-Farcy, un conservateur novateur.
Le Musée de Grenoble de 1919 à 1949*, Musée de Peinture
Grenoble, 1982; *Bonnard*, Musée National d'Art Moderne,
Centre Georges Pompidou, Paris, 23 February–21 May 1984,
traveled as *Bonnard: The Late Paintings* to The Phillips
Collection, Washington, D.C., 9 June–25 August 1984, Dallas
Museum of Art, 13 September–11 November 1984, no. 43;
Pierre Bonnard, Palazzo Reale, Milan, 27 October 1988–8
January 1989; *Pierre Bonnard. Das Glück zu malen*,
Kunstsammlung Nordrhein–Westfalen, Düsseldorf, 23
January–12 April 1993, no. 49; Louisiana Museum of Modern
Art, Humlebaek, Denmark, 12 September 1992–10 January
1993, no. 91; *Pierre Bonnard*, Aichi Prefectural Museum of
Art, Nagoya, 28 March–18 May 1997, Bunkamura Museum of
Art, Tokyo, 24 May–21 July 1997, no. 79; *Pierre Bonnard*,
Tate Gallery, London, 12 February–17 May 1998; *Pierre
Bonnard*, Musée de l'Annonciade, St.-Tropez, 4 July–5
October 1998; *Bonnard*, Fondation Pierre Gianadda,
Martigny, Switzerland, 11 June–14 November 1999, no. 52.

Daybook of 1933 (Agenda de 1933)
1933
Pencil on paper, 5⅛ × 3⅛ × ½ in. (13 × 8 × 1.2 cm)
Bibliothèque nationale de France. Département des
Estampes et de la Photographie
[plate 124]
Provenance
Bibliothèque Nationale de France, acquired from the
Terrasse family.

Marthe in the Dining Room (Marthe dans la salle à manger)
1933
Oil on canvas, 43⅞ × 23¼ in. (111.5 × 59 cm)
Lyon, Musée des Beaux-Arts
[plate 129]
Provenance
Musée des Beaux-Arts, Lyon, Gift of Mesdames Bremond
and Lignel, 1967.
Exhibitions
Bonnard, Bernheim-Jeune, Paris, 15–23 June 1933, no. 12;
Chefs-d'œuvre du musée de Lyon, Fondation de l'Hermitage,
Lausanne, 9 June–21 September 1989, no. 87; *Chefs-d'œuvre
du musée des Beaux-Arts de Lyon*, Metropolitan Art
Museum, Tokyo, 7 October–1 December 1989, Municipal
Museum of Art, Kitakyushu, 9 December–21 January 1990,
no. 91; *Bonnard at Le Bosquet*, Hayward Gallery, London, 23
June–29 August 1994, Laing Art Gallery, Newcastle, 9
September–30 October 1994, no. 20.

Still Life with a Bowl of Fruit (Coupe de fruits)
1933
Oil on canvas, 22¹³⁄₁₆ × 20⅞ in. (57.9 × 53 cm)
Philadelphia Museum of Art: Bequest of Lisa Norris Elkins,
1950
[plate 122]
Provenance
Purchased by Bernheim-Jeune from the artist; Gaston
Bernheim de Villers; Gallery Knoedler, New York; W.
Elkins, Philadelphia; Bequest of Lisa Norris Elkins to
Philadelphia Museum of Art, 1950.
Exhibitions
Bonnard, Bernheim-Jeune, Paris, 15–23 June 1933; *Chefs-
d'œuvre de l'art français*, Belgrade, 1937; *XXXIV Peintures de
Pierre Bonnard*, Bernheim-Jeune, Paris, 15 June–13 July 1946,
no. 32; *Masterpieces*, Philadelphia Museum of Art, 31 May–28
September 1947; *Pierre Bonnard Memorial Exhibition*, The
Cleveland Museum of Art, 3 March–11 April 1948, The
Museum of Modern Art, New York, 10 May–6 September
1948, no. 67; *Exposition rétrospective Bonnard*,
Bernheim-Jeune, Paris, May–July 1950, no. 58; *Pierre
Bonnard*, Paul Rosenberg and Co., New York, 12 March–7
April 1956, no. 15; *Still Lifes of Fruit and Flowers*, Rosenberg
Gallery, New York, 1956; *Bonnard*, Society of the Four Arts,
Palm Beach, Fla., 4–27 January 1957, no. 24; *Bonnard and His
Environment*, The Museum of Modern Art, New York, 7
October–29 November 1964, The Art Institute of Chicago, 8
January–28 February 1965, Los Angeles County Museum of
Art, 31 March–31 May 1965, no. 56; *Pierre Bonnard*, Haus der
Kunst, Munich, 8 October 1966–1 January 1967, Musée du
Louvre, Paris, 13 January–15 April 1967, no. 116; *Bonnard*,

Kunsthaus Zurich, 14 December 1984–10 March 1985, no. 143,
Städtische Galerie im Städelschen Kunstinstitut, Frankfurt, 3
May–14 July 1985, no. 143; *Bonnard*, Kunsthalle der Hypo-
Kulturstiftung, Munich, 28 January–24 April 1994, no. 120;
Pierre Bonnard, Aichi Prefectural Museum of Art, Nagoya,
28 March–18 May 1997, Bunkamura Museum of Art, Tokyo,
24 May–21 July 1997, no. 72.

**Nude in an Interior (Nu debout près d'une baignoire or Nu
dans un intérieur)**
ca. 1935
Oil on canvas, 28¾ × 19¾ in. (73 × 50.2 cm)
The Phillips Collection, Washington, D.C.
[plate 125]
Provenance
Dr. and Mrs. Frederick B. Deknatel, Cambridge, Mass.;
Knoedler & Co., New York, December 1951; M. Knoedler to
Sidney Janis Gallery, New York, 1952; The Phillips
Collection, acquired from Sidney Janis, April 1952.
Exhibitions
*Paintings and Drawings by Pierre Bonnard: An Exhibition
from The Phillips Collection and the Collections of Mrs.
Phillips and Mr. and Mrs. Laughlin Phillips*, The Phillips
Collection, Washington, D.C., 7 January–28 February 1967
(as *After the Bath*); *Bonnard and Vuillard: An Exhibition for
the Benefit of The Phillips Collection*, Adams Davidson
Galleries, Washington, D.C., 17 May–17 June 1978, no. 9;
*Impressionism and the Modern Vision: Master Paintings from
The Phillips Collection*, The Fine Arts Museums of San
Francisco, 4 July–1 November 1981, Dallas Museum of Fine
Arts, 22 November 1981–16 February 1982, The Minneapolis
Institute of Arts, 14 March–30 May 1982, High Museum of
Art, Atlanta, 24 June–5 September 1982, The Oklahoma Art
Center, Oklahoma City, 17 October 1982–9 January 1983, no.
5; The Nihonbashi Takashimaya Art Galleries, Tokyo, 25
August–4 October 1983, Nara Prefectural Museum of Art, 9
October–13 November 1983, no. 49; *Paintings and Drawings
from The Phillips Collection*, IBM Gallery of Science and Art,
New York, 9 December 1983–21 January 1984, no. 9; *French
Masterpieces from The Phillips Collection: Impressionism and
Post-Impressionism*, J. B. Speed Art Museum, Louisville, Ky.,
19 February–8 April 1984; *Duncan Phillips: Centennial
Exhibition*, The Phillips Collection, Washington, D.C., 14
June–31 August 1986; *Old Masters—New Visions: El Greco to
Rothko from The Phillips Collection, Washington, D.C.*,
Australian National Gallery, Canberra, 3 October–6
December 1987, Art Gallery of Western Australia, Perth, 22
December 1987–21 February 1988, Art Gallery of South
Australia, Adelaide, 4 March–1 May 1988, no. 45; *Master
Paintings from The Phillips Collection*, Hayward Gallery,
London, 19 May–14 August 1988, no. 65; *Master Paintings
from The Phillips Collection, Washington*, Centro de Arte
Reina Sofia, Madrid, 30 November 1988–16 February 1989,
no. 65; *Duncan Phillips Collects: Paris between the Wars*, The
Phillips Collection, Washington, D.C., 14 September 1990–12
January 1991; *Renoir to Rothko: The Eye of Duncan Phillips*,
The Phillips Collection, Washington, D.C., 25 September
1999–23 January 2000.

The Large Bath, Nude (La Grande baignoire, nu)
1937–1939
Oil on canvas, 37 × 56¾ in. (94 × 144 cm)
Private collection
Washington only
[plate 123]
Provenance
Estate of the artist (Inv. no. 702); Galerie Beyeler, Basel;
private collection.
Exhibitions
Bonnard, Kunsthaus Zurich, 14 December 1984–10 March
1985, Städtische Galerie im Städelschen Kunstinstitut,
Frankfurt, 3 May–14 July 1985, no. 142; *Bonnard*, Kunsthalle
der Hypo-Kulturstiftung, Munich, 28 January–24 April 1994;
Bonnard, Tate Gallery, London, 12 February–17 May 1998,
The Museum of Modern Art, New York, 17 June–13 October
1998, no. 80.

Self-Portrait (Autoportrait dans la glace)
1938
Oil on canvas, 23 × 26⅜ in. (58.4 × 67 cm)
Private collection
[plate 136]
Provenance
Acquired by Georges Wildenstein from the artist; private
collection.
Exhibitions
Pierre Bonnard Memorial Exhibition, The Cleveland Museum
of Art, 3 March–11 April 1948, The Museum of Modern Art,
New York, 10 May–6 September 1948, no. 74; *L'œuvre du
XXe Siècle*, Musée National d'Art Moderne, Paris, May–June
1952, no. 6; *Masterpieces of French Paintings through Five
Centuries, 1400–1900*, Isaac Delgado Museum of Art, New
Orleans, 17 October 1953–10 January 1954, no. 82; *Pierre
Bonnard*, Palazzo della Permanente, Milan, 1955, no. 66;
Pierre Bonnard, Kunsthalle Basel, 1955, no. 92; *Bonnard*, The
Society of the Four Arts, Palm Beach, Fla., 4–27 January
1957, no. 25; *A Loan Exhibition: Six Paintings by Bonnard*,
The Phillips Gallery, Washington, D.C., 12 January–12
February 1958, no. 6; *A Treasury of French Art from the
Renaissance to Modern Times*, Wildenstein and Co., New
York, summer 1964, no. 4; *Bonnard and His Environment*,
The Museum of Modern Art, New York, 7 October–29
November 1964, The Art Institute of Chicago, 8 January–28
February 1965, Los Angeles County Museum of Art, 31
March–31 May 1965, no. 66; *Bonnard*, Wildenstein and Co.,
Buenos Aires, July–September 1965, no. 1; *Pierre Bonnard*,
Haus der Kunst, Munich, 8 October 1966–1 January 1967,
Musée du Louvre, Paris, 13 January–15 April 1967, no. 153;
Bonnard, National Museum of Western Art, Tokyo, 20
March–5 May 1968, National Museum of Modern Art,
Kyoto, 11 May–16 June 1968, no. 69; *From El Greco to Pollock:
Early and Late Works by European and American Artists*,
Baltimore Museum of Art, 22 October–8 December 1968, no.
96; *Pierre Bonnard*, National Gallery of Victoria, Melbourne,
Art Gallery of New South Wales, Sydney, Art Gallery of
South Australia, Adelaide, Art Gallery of Western Australia,
Perth, 1971, no. 36; *Faces from the World of Impressionism and
Post-Impressionism*, Wildenstein and Co., New York, 2
November–9 December 1972, no. 5; *Spiegel Bilder*,

Kunstverein, Hannover, 9 May–30 June 1982, Wilhelm-
Lehmbruck-Museum der Stadt, Duisburg, 11 July–25 August
1982, Haus am Waldsee, Berlin, 10 September–24 October
1982; *Bonnard*, Fundación Juan March, Madrid, 29
September–27 November 1983, Sala de Exposiciones Caixa
de Barcelona, 6 December 1983–24 January 1984, no. 53;
Bonnard, Musée National d'Art Moderne, Centre Georges
Pompidou, Paris, 23 February–21 May 1984, no. 52, traveled
as *Bonnard: The Late Paintings*, The Phillips Collection,
Washington, D.C., 9 June–25 August 1984, Dallas Museum of
Art, 13 September–11 November 1984, no. 56; *Pierre Bonnard,
1867–1947*, Fondation de l'Hermitage, Lausanne, 7 June–6
October 1991, no. 70; *Bonnard*, Kunsthalle der Hypo-
Kulturstiftung, Munich, 28 January–24 April 1994, no. 126;
Bonnard at Le Bosquet, Hayward Gallery, London, 23
June–29 August 1994, Laing Art Gallery, Newcastle, 9
September–30 October 1994, no. 31; *La Biennale di Venezia,
46. Esposizione Internazionale d'Arte: Identity and Alterity,
Figures of the Body 1895/1995*, Palazzo Grassi and Museo
Correr, Venice, 7 June–15 October 1995; *1918–1958, La Côte
d'Azur et la modernité*, Musée Picasso, Antibes, 28 June–30
September 1997, no. 4; *Bonnard*, Tate Gallery, London, 12
February–17 May 1998, The Museum of Modern Art, New
York, 17 June–13 October 1998, no. 77; *Bonnard*, Fondation
Pierre Gianadda, Martigny, 11 June–14 November 1999, no.
58; *Pierre Bonnard*, Fondation Dina Vierny-Musée Maillol,
Paris, 31 May–9 October 2000, no. 45; *Bonnard*, Tel Aviv
Museum of Art, 8 November 2000–10 February 2001, no. 52.

Self-Portrait (Autoportrait)
ca. 1938–1940
Oil on canvas, 30 × 24 in. (76.2 × 61 cm)
Art Gallery of New South Wales, Sydney. Purchased 1972
[plate 135]
Provenance
Bonnard-Terrasse; Wildenstein and Co., U.S.A., Art Gallery
of New South Wales, Sydney, 1972.
Exhibitions
Accessions and Proposals, The Museum of Fine Arts,
Houston, 30 April–24 May 1964; *Bonnard and His
Environment*, The Museum of Modern Art, New York, 7
October–29 November 1964, The Art Institute of Chicago, 8
January–28 February 1965, Los Angeles County Museum of
Art, 31 March–31 May 1965, no. 74; *Pierre Bonnard*, Royal
Academy of Arts, London, 6 January–6 March 1966, no. 246;
Pierre Bonnard, National Gallery of Victoria, May–mid June
1971, Art Gallery of South Australia, Adelaide, 24 June–25
July 1971, Art Gallery of Western Australia, Perth, 6
August–12 September 1971, Australian Museum, 15
October–10 November 1971, no. 36; *Bonnard*, Kunsthaus
Zurich, 14 December 1984–10 March 1985, Städtische Galerie
im Städelschen Kunstinstitut, 3 May–14 July 1985, no. 145;
The Last Gaze: Late Self-Portraits (from Bonnard to Bacon),
Museu d'Art Contemporani, Barcelona, 16 October 1997–6
January 1998; *Bonnard*, Tate Gallery, London, 12 February–17
May 1998, The Museum of Modern Art, New York, 17
June–13 October 1998, no. 78.

The Red Cupboard (Nature morte rouge)
ca. 1939
Oil on canvas, 32 × 25½ in. (81.3 × 64.8 cm)
Private collection
[plate 130]
Provenance
Roger Hauert, Paris; private collection.
Exhibitions
Bonnard, Musée de Lyon, 1954, no. 33; *Depuis Bonnard*,
Musée d'Art Moderne, Paris, March 1957, no. 45; Los
Angeles County Museum of Art, 1965, no. 12; *Pierre Bonnard*,
Haus der Kunst, Munich, 8 October 1966–1 January 1967, no.
114; Musée du Louvre, Paris, 13 January–15 April 1967, no.
131; Seibu Department Store, Tokyo, 1973, no. 28; *Bonnard:
The Late Paintings*, The Phillips Collection, Washington,
D.C., 9 June–25 August 1984, Dallas Museum of Art, 13
September–11 November 1984, no. 55; traveled as *Pierre
Bonnard* to Kunsthaus Zurich, 14 December 1984–10 March
1985, Städtische Galerie im Städelschen Kunstinstitut,
Frankfurt, 3 May–14 July 1985, no. 144; *Bonnard at Le
Bosquet*, Hayward Gallery, London, 23 June–29 August 1994,
Laing Art Gallery, Newcastle, 9 September–30 October 1994.

Studio with Mimosas (L'Atelier au mimosa)
1939–October 1946
Oil on canvas, 50 × 50 in. (127.5 × 127.5 cm)
Centre Georges Pompidou, Paris. Musée National d'Art
Moderne/ Centre de Création Industrielle
Washington only
[plate 131]
Provenance
Collection of the artist; Charles Terrasse, Paris; Centre
Georges Pompidou, Paris, Musée National d'Art Moderne/
Centre de Création Industrielle, purchase from Charles
Terrasse, 1979.
Exhibitions
Peintures contemporaines, Château de Fontainebleau,
April–September 1945, no. 3; *Exhibition of Paintings by Pierre
Bonnard and Edouard Vuillard*, Royal Scottish Academy,
Edinburgh, 17 August–18 September 1948, no. 48; *Pierre
Bonnard, 1867–1947*, Kunsthaus Zurich, 6 June–24 July 1949,
no. 118; *Bonnard and His Environment*, The Museum of
Modern Art, New York, 7 October–29 November 1964, The
Art Institute of Chicago, 8 January–28 February 1965, Los
Angeles County Museum of Art, 31 March–31 May 1965, no.
72; *Pierre Bonnard 1867–1947*, Royal Academy of Arts,
London, 6 January–13 March 1966, no. 242; *Pierre Bonnard*,
Haus der Kunst, Munich, 8 October 1966–1 January 1967,
Musée du Louvre, 13 January–15 April 1967, Paris, 13
January–15 April 1967, no. 138; *Bonnard*, Musée Cantini,
Marseille, 1 May–11 June 1967, no. 36; *Pierre Bonnard:
centenaire de sa naissance*, Musée du Louvre, Paris, 13
January–15 April 1967; *Chefs-d'œuvre des collections suisses
de Manet à Picasso*, Musée du Louvre, Paris, 10 May–30
September 1967, no. 158; *Bonnard*, Louisiana Museum of
Modern Art, Humlebaek, Denmark, 16 September–20
October 1967, no. 82; *Bonnard*, National Museum of Western
Art, Tokyo, 20 March–5 May 1968, National Museum of
Modern Art, Kyoto, 11 May–16 June 1968, no. 77; *Dessins et
tableaux de Pierre Bonnard*, Galerie de l'Oeil, Paris,

November 1968, no. 13; *Suites no. 23: Bonnard*, Galerie Krugier et Cie, Geneva, June–July 1969, no. 26; *Bonnard (1867–1947)*, Accademia de Francia, Villa Medici, Rome, 18 November 1971–23 January 1972, Galleria Civica d'Arte Moderna, Turin, 1–28 February 1972, no. 22; *Bonnard dans sa lumière*, Fondation Maeght, Saint-Paul-de-Vence, 12 July–28 September 1975, no. 75; *Manet, Degas, Monet, Cézanne, Bonnard: œuvres tardives*, June–September 1977; *Aftermath: France 1945–54*, Barbican Art Gallery, London, March–June 1982; *Bonnard*, Musée National d'Art Moderne, Centre Georges Pompidou, Paris, 23 February–21 May 1984, no. 61, traveled as *Bonnard: The Late Paintings* to The Phillips Collection, Washington, D.C., 9 June–25 August 1984, Dallas Museum of Art, 13 September–11 November 1984, no. 65; *La Grande Parade*, Stedelijk Museum, Amsterdam, 18 December–15 April 1985; *L'Art en Europe: les années décisives 1945–1955*, Musée d'Art Moderne, Saint-Etienne, 1 December 1987–28 February 1988; *L'Art en France, un siècle d'inventions (du Fauvisme aux années quatre vingt)*, The Pushkin Museum, Moscow, 27 March–9 May 1989, The State Hermitage Museum, Leningrad, 1 June–1 September 1989; *La Côte d'Azur et la modernité, 1918–1958*, Musée Picasso, Antibes, 27 June–19 October 1997; *La Collection du Centre Georges Pompidou*, Musée d'Art Moderne de la Ville de Paris, 18 June–19 September 1999.

Nude in Bathtub (Nu dans le bain)
1941–1946
Oil on canvas, 48 × 59½ in. (121.9 × 151.1 cm)
Carnegie Museum of Art, Pittsburgh. Acquired through the generosity of the Sarah Mellon Scaife Family, 1970
Washington only
[plate 127]
Provenance
Estate of the artist; private collection, Paris, 1948; Mrs. Genia Zadok, New York; acquired in 1970 from the family of Sarah Mellon Scaife by the Carnegie Institute, Museum of Art, Pittsburgh, Pennsylvania.
Exhibitions
Bonnard, Musée de l'Orangerie, Paris, October–November 1947, no. 85; *Pierre Bonnard Memorial Exhibition*, The Cleveland Museum of Art, 3 March–11 April 1948, The Museum of Modern Art, New York, 10 May–6 September 1948, no. 75; *Bonnard and His Environment*, The Museum of Modern Art, New York, 7 October–29 November 1964, The Art Institute of Chicago, 8 January–28 February 1965, Los Angeles County Museum of Art, 31 March–31 May 1965, no. 71; *Pierre Bonnard 1867–1947*, Royal Academy of Arts, London, 6 January–13 March 1966, no. 237; *Twelve Years of Collecting*, Wildenstein and Co., New York, 7 November–15 December 1973, High Museum of Art, Atlanta, 4–27 January 1974; *Bonnard: The Late Paintings*, The Phillips Collection, Washington, D.C., 9 June–25 August 1984, Dallas Museum of Art, 13 September–11 November 1984, no. 66; *Paris— Créations en France, 1937–1957*, Musée National d'Art Moderne, Centre Georges Pompidou, Paris, 26 May–2 November 1981, no. 85; *Impressionism: Selections from Five American Museums*, The Carnegie Museum of Art, 4 November–31 December 1989, The Minneapolis Institute of Arts, 27 January–25 March 1990, The Nelson-Atkins

Museum of Art, Kansas City, 21 April–17 June 1990, The Saint Louis Art Museum, 14 July–9 September 1990, Toledo Museum of Art, 30 September–25 November 1990; *Bonnard at Le Bosquet*, Hayward Gallery, London, 23 June–29 August 1994, Laing Art Gallery, Newcastle, 9 September–30 October 1994, no. 56; *Pierre Bonnard*, Tate Gallery, London, 12 February–10 May 1998, The Museum of Modern Art, New York, 17 June–13 October 1998, no. 94.

A Dish and a Basket of Fruit (Coupe et corbeille de fruits)
1944
Oil on canvas, 17 × 21¹³⁄₁₆ in. (43.2 × 55.4 cm)
Private collection
[plate 128]
Provenance
Private collection
Exhibitions
Bonnard, Fondation Anne et Albert Prouvost, Marcq-en-Baroeul, France, 15 April–9 July 1978, no. 40; *Bonnard*, Musée National d'Art Moderne, Centres Georges Pompidou, Paris, 23 February–21 May 1984, no. 56, traveled as *Bonnard: The Late Paintings* to The Phillips Collection, Washington, D.C., 9 June–25 August 1984, Dallas Museum of Art, 13 September–11 November 1984, no. 59.

The Small Window (La Petite Fenêtre)
1946
Oil on canvas, 22⅞ × 17¾ in. (58 × 45 cm)
Private collection, courtesy Galerie Schmit, Paris
[plate 133]
Provenance
Private collection
Exhibitions
Bonnard, Musée de Lyon, 1954, no. 43; *Pierre Bonnard*, Kunsthalle Basel, 28 May–17 July 1955, no. 97; *Bonnard*, Musée des Ponchettes, Nice, August–September 1955, no. 43; *Pierre Bonnard*, Haus der Kunst, Munich, 8 October 1966–1 January 1967, Musée du Louvre, Paris, 13 January–15 April 1967, no. 136; *Bonnard*, Fondation Anne et Albert Prouvost, Marcq-en-Baroeul, France, 15 April–9 July 1978, no. 44; *A propos de Bonnard*, Musée d'Unterlinden, Colmar, 19 June–26 September 1982, no. 35; *Pierre Bonnard*, Galerie Schmit, Paris, 3 May–12 July 1995, no. 50.

Blossoming Almond Tree (L'Amandier en fleur)
ca. 1946–1947
Oil on canvas, 21⅝ × 14¾ in. (55 × 37.5 cm)
Centre Georges Pompidou, Paris. Musée National d'Art Moderne/Centre de Création Industrielle. Gift of Mr. and Mrs. Charles Zadok, 1964
Washington only
[plate 132]
Provenance
Estate of the artist; Zadok, New York, 1964; given by M. Zadok, in 1965, to the Centre Georges Pompidou, Paris, Musée National d'Art Moderne/Centre de Création Industrielle.
Exhibitions
Bonnard, Ny Carlsberg Glyptotek, Copenhagen, May 1947, no. 58; *Bonnard*, Stedelijk Museum, Amsterdam, June–July

1947, no. 71; *Exposition Bonnard*, Musée de l'Orangerie, Paris, October–November 1947, no. 95; *Pierre Bonnard Memorial Exhibition*, The Cleveland Museum of Art, 3 March–11 April 1948, The Museum of Modern Art, New York, 10 May–6 September 1948, no. 82; *Bonnard, exposition rétrospective*, Bernheim-Jeune, Paris, May–July 1950; *Bonnard*, Museum Boymans, Rotterdam, March–April 1953, no. 97; *Bonnard and His Environment*, The Museum of Modern Art, New York, 7 October–29 November 1964, The Art Institute of Chicago, 8 January–28 February 1965, Los Angeles County Museum of Art, 31 March–31 May 1965, no. 102; *Dix ans d'art vivant 1945–1955*, Fondation M. and A. Maeght, Saint-Paul-de-Vence, 9 April–31 May 1966; *Pierre Bonnard*, Haus der Kunst, Munich, 8 October 1966–1 January 1967, Musée du Louvre, Paris, 13 January–15 April 1967, no. 141; *Pierre Bonnard: centenaire de sa naissance*, Musée du Louvre, Paris, 13 January–15 April 1967; *Chefs-d'oeuvre des collections Suisses de Manet à Picasso*, Musée du Louvre, Paris, 10 May–30 September 1967, no. 159; *Bonnard*, National Museum of Western Art, Tokyo, 20 March–5 May 1968, National Museum of Modern Art, Kyoto, 11 May–16 June 1968, no. 79; *Bonnard (1867–1947)*, Accademia de Francia, Villa Medici, Rome, 18 November 1971–23 January 1972, Galleria Civica d'Arte Moderna, Turin, 1–28 February 1972, no. 25; *Bonnard*, Fondation Anne et Albert Prouvost, Marcq-en-Baroeul, France, 15 April–9 July 1978, no. 46; *Bonnard*, Musée National d'Art Moderne, Centre Georges Pompidou, Paris, 23 February–21 May 1984, no. 63, traveled as *Bonnard: The Late Paintings* to The Phillips Collection, Washington, D.C., 9 June–25 August 1984, Dallas Museum of Art, 13 September–11 November 1984, no. 67, Kunsthaus Zurich, 14 December 1984–10 March 1985, Städtische Galerie im Städelschen Kunstinstitut, Frankfurt, 3 May–14 July 1985, no. 160; *Bonnard*, Kunsthalle der Hypo-Kulturstiftung, Munich, 28 January–24 April 1994, no. 138; *Bonnard at Le Bosquet*, Hayward Gallery, London, 23 June–29 August 1994, Laing Art Gallery, Newcastle, 9 September–30 October 1994, no. 64; *Jean Cassou 1897–1986: un musée imaginé*, Bibliothèque Nationale de France, Paris, 15 March–18 June 1995; *Hommage à Jean Cassou*, Réfectoire des Jacobins, Toulouse, 1 March–31 May 1996; *Pierre Bonnard*, Tate Gallery, London, 12 February–17 May 1998, The Museum of Modern Art, New York, 21 June–13 October 1998, no. 97; *La Magie des arbres*, Fondation Beyeler, Basel, 22 November 1998–5 April 1999.

Maria Boursin
Pierre Bonnard Seated in Profile and Pierre Bonnard Viewed from the Back
(Pierre Bonnard de profil and Pierre Bonnard de dos)
1900–1901
Original contact print on gelatin paper, 1⁷⁄₁₆ × 2³⁄₁₆ in. and 1 ⁷⁄₁₆ × 2¹⁄₁₆ in. (3.6 × 5.5 cm and 3.6 × 5.3 cm)
Paris, Musée d'Orsay, donation with a life interest from Charles Terrasse's children, 1987, inv. PHO 1987 31 42 and PHO 1987 31 43
Washington only
[plate 46]

SELECTED BIBLIOGRAPHY

Listed here are the writings that have been of use in the making of this exhibition catalogue. This bibliography is by no means a comprehensive or complete record of all the works and sources related to Bonnard that have been consulted. It includes the general monographic studies, substantive essays, critical reviews, interviews, and published first-hand accounts of Bonnard's artistic life and process.

Books

Barr, Alfred H., Jr. *Painting and Sculpture in the Museum of Modern Art*. New York: The Museum of Modern Art, 1958.

Basler, Adolf, and C. Kunstler. *La Peinture indépendante en France*. Vol. 1, *De Monet à Bonnard*. Paris: G. Crès, 1929.

Beer, François-Joachim. *Pierre Bonnard*. Marseille: Editions Françaises d'Art, 1947.

Bell, Julian. *Bonnard*. London: Phaidon Press Limited, 1994.

Bonnard/Matisse: Letters between Friends. Preface by Jean Clair. Introduction by Antoine Terrasse. Translated by Richard Howard. New York: Harry N. Abrams, 1992.

Bouret, Jean. *Bonnard: The Magic Ring*. Translated by Diana Imber. New York: French and European Publications, 1967. French ed., *Bonnard: Séductions*. Lausanne: International Art Book, 1967.

Bouvet, Francis. *Bonnard: The Complete Graphic Work*. Translated by Jane Brenton. Introduction by Antoine Terrasse. New York: Rizzoli; London: Thames and Hudson, 1981. French ed., *Bonnard. L'Œuvre gravé*. Paris: Flammarion, 1981.

Cogeval, Guy. *Bonnard*. Paris: Hazan, 1993.

Cogniat, Raymond. *Bonnard*. Paris: Flammarion, 1989.

Coquiot, Gustave. *Bonnard*. Paris: Bernheim-Jeune, 1922.

Courthion, Pierre. *Bonnard: Peintre du merveilleux*. Lausanne: Marguerat, 1945.

Dauberville, Jean, and Henry Dauberville. *Bonnard: Catalogue raisonné de l'œuvre peint.* Paris: Editions J. H. Bernheim-Jeune. Vol. 1, *1888–1905* (1965, rev. ed. 1992); vol. 2 *1906–1919* (1968); vol. 3, *1920–1939* (1973); vol. 4, *1940–1947* and supplement *1887–1939* (1974).

Dunstan, Bernard. *Painting Methods of the Impressionists*. New York: Watson-Guptil, 1976.

Fermigier, André. *Pierre Bonnard*. New York: Harry N. Abrams, 1969.

Fosca, François [pseud. Georges de Traz]. *Bonnard*. Geneva: Kundig, 1919.

Fossier, François. *La Nébuleuse Nabie: Les Nabis et l'art graphique*. Paris: Réunion des Musées Nationaux, 1993.

Frèches-Thory, Claire, and Antoine Terrasse. *The Nabis: Bonnard, Vuillard, and Their Circle*. Translated by Mary Pardoe. New York: Harry N. Abrams, 1991. French ed., *Les Nabis*. Paris: Flammarion, 1990.

Giambruni, Helen Emery. "Early Bonnard, 1885–1900." Ph.D. diss., University of California, Berkeley, 1983.

Heilbrun, Françoise, and Philippe Néagu. *Pierre Bonnard: Photographs and Paintings*. New York: Aperture, 1988. French ed., *Bonnard Photographe*. Paris: Philippe Sers, Réunion des Musées Nationaux, 1987.

Hobhouse, Janet. *The Bride Stripped Bare: The Artist and the Female Nude in the Twentieth Century*. New York: Weidenfeld & Nicolson, 1988.

Hyman, Timothy. *Bonnard*. New York and London: Thames and Hudson, 1998.

Ives, Colta Feller. *The Great Wave: The Influence of Japanese Woodcuts on French Prints*. New York: The Metropolitan Museum of Art, 1974.

Jedlicka, G. *Pierre Bonnard, ein Besuch*. Erlenbach and Zurich: E. Rentsch, 1949.

Laprade, Jacques de. *Bonnard*. Lyon: Amplepuis-Rhône, 1944.

Liberman, Alexander. *The Artist in His Studio*. Rev. ed. New York: Random House, 1988.

Mauner, George L. *The Nabis: Their History and Their Art, 1888–1896*. New York and London: Garland Publishing, 1978.

Natanson, Thadée. *Le Bonnard que je propose*. Geneva: Pierre Cailler, 1951. ———Peints à leur tour. Paris: A. Michel, 1948.

Perucchi-Petri, Ursula. *Die Nabis und Japan: Das Frühwerk von Bonnard, Vuillard und Denis*. Studien zur Kunst des neunzehnten Jahrhunderts 37. Munich: Prestel-Verlag, 1976.

Pissarro, Camille. *Camille Pissarro: Letters to His Son Lucien*. Edited with the assistance of Lucien Pissarro by John Rewald. Translated from the French manuscript by Lionel Able. New York: Pantheon Books, 1943.

Roger-Marx, Claude. *Bonnard lithographe*. Monte Carlo: André Sauret, 1952. ———*French Original Engravings from Manet to the Present Time*. London and New York: Hyperion Press, 1939. ——— *Pierre Bonnard*. Paris: Henry Babou, 1931.

Terrasse, Antoine. *Bonnard: Shimmering Color*. New York: Harry N. Abrams, 2000. French ed., *Bonnard 'La Couleur agit'*. Paris: Editions Gallimard, 1999. ——— *Pierre Bonnard, Illustrator: A Catalogue Raisonné*. Translated by Jean-Marie Clarke. New York: Harry N. Abrams, 1989. French ed., *Bonnard illustrateur: catalogue raisonné*. Paris: Editions Adam Biro, 1988. ——— *Bonnard*. Paris: Editions Gallimard, 1967. ——— *Bonnard*. Geneva: Skira, 1964. ———, ed. *Bonnard/Vuillard Correspondance*. Paris: Editions Gallimard, 2001.

Terrasse, Charles. *Bonnard*. Paris: Floury, 1927.

Terrasse, Michel. *Bonnard at Le Cannet*. Preface by Jean Leymarie. Translated by Sebastian Wormell. New York: Pantheon Books, 1988. French ed., *Bonnard et Le Cannet*. Paris: Editions Herscher, 1987. ———*Bonnard: From the Drawings to the Paintings*. Translated by Cynthia Hope Liebow. Paris: Imprimerie Nationale Editions, 1998. French ed., *Bonnard du dessin au tableau*, Paris: Imprimerie Nationale Editions, 1996.

Vaillant, Annette. *Bonnard*. Greenwich, Conn.: New York Graphic Society, 1965.

Watkins, Nicholas. *Bonnard*. London: Phaidon Press Ltd., 1994. ———*Bonnard: Colour and Light*. London: Tate Gallery Publishing, 1998.

Werth, Léon. *Bonnard*. Paris: Cahiers d'aujourd'hui, 1919. Rev. ed. 1923.

Wolsk, Nancy Coleman. "The Lycee and the Nabis Formation and Realization." Ph.D. diss., University of Kentucky, Lexington, 1998.

Articles

A.-D., M. "L'Actualité et la curiosité: les expositions: deux expositions de Pierre Bonnard." *L'Art et les artistes* 26, no. 139 (July 1933): 351.

Aurier, G. Albert. "Les Symbolistes." *La Revue encyclopédique* 2, no. 32 (1 April 1892): 475–486.

Bell, Clive. "The Art of Pierre Bonnard." *The Listener* 37, no. 946 (13 March 1947): 379–380. ———"Fine Arts, Bonnard." *The Athenaeum* 4690 (March 1920): 374-375.

Benedikt, Michael. "The Continuity of Pierre Bonnard." *Art News* 63 (October 1964): 20–23, 55–56.

Besson, George. "Signalements: Pierre Bonnard." *Arts de France* 4 (March 1946): 7–12.

Bonnard, Pierre. "Couleur de Bonnard." *Verve* 5, nos. 17–18 (August 1947).

Bouvier, Marguette. "Bonnard at the Royal Academy." *The Burlington Magazine* 108 (February 1966): 105–107. ———"Pierre Bonnard revient à la litho." *Comœdia*, no. 82 (23 January 1943).

Clément-Janin, Noël. [Review of 'Parallèlement'] "Les Editions de bibliophiles." *Almanach du bibliophile*, 1901, 245–246.

Courthion, Pierre. "Impromptus—Pierre Bonnard." *Les Nouvelles littéraires*, 24 June 1933.

Cousturier, Lucien. "Pierre Bonnard." *L'Art décoratif* 14, no. 186 (20 December 1912): 361–376.

Diehl, Gaston. "Pierre Bonnard dans son univers enchanté." *Comœdia*, no. 106 (10 July 1943).

Dorival, Bernard. "Le Corsage à carreaux." *Revue du Louvre et des musées de France* 19, no. 1 (1969): 21-24.

Estienne, Charles. "Les Grandes Expositions de Paris. Musée de l'Orangerie: Pierre Bonnard." *Arts* 1, no. 136 (17 October 1947): 8.

Fénéon, Félix. "Sur les murs." *Le Chat noir* 10 (6 June 1891): 1760.

Fosca, François. "Pierre Bonnard." *Art et décoration* 38 (September 1920): 65–74.

Frèches-Thory, Claire. "Pierre Bonnard: tableaux récemment acquis par le musée d'Orsay." *Revue du Louvre et des musées de France* 36, no. 6 (1986): 417–431.

Gauthier, E. Paul. "Lithographs of the 'Revue Blanche' 1893–1895." *Magazine of Art* 45 (October 1952): 273–278.

George, Waldemar. "Pierre Bonnard et l'antique." *L'Art et les artistes* 31 (December 1935): 88. ———"Le Salon d'Automne: I: La peinture et la sculpture." *L'Amour de l'art* 4 (October 1923): 707–711.

Hassey, Edmund. "Bonnard-The Last Impressionist." *Queen's Quarterly* 54 (1947): 352–358.

Heilbut, Emil. "Lithographien von P. Bonnard." *Kunst und Künstler* 4 (1906): 210–224.

Hoefliger, Alfred. "Bonnard und Maillol als Illustratoren von 'Daphnis und Chloe.'" *Werk* 34, no. 6 (June 1947): 193–197.

Jarry, Alfred. "Paul Verlaine: 'Parallèlement', illustré par Pierre Bonnard." *La Revue blanche* 24 (1901): 317.

Johnson, Lincoln F., Jr. "Pierre Bonnard and Impressionism." *Baltimore Museum of Art News* 17, no. 2 (December 1953): 1–6.

Kozloff, Max. "A Vertigo of the Senses." *Art in America* (July 1998): 54–61.

Laprade, Jacques de. "Gravures, illustrations, dessins de Pierre Bonnard." *Formes et couleurs* 2 (1944): 50–62.

Lhote, André. "Bonnard." *Formes et couleurs* 2 (1944): 3–10. ——— "Les Arts: Visite à J. M. Sert. - Expositions J. E. Blanche, Bonnard, Picasso, Kisling, Lurçat, O. des Garets, Yves Alix." *La Nouvelle Revue Française* 22 (1924): 645–650.

Meier-Graefe, Julius. "Bonnard." *The Art News* 37 (31 December 1938): 8–9.

Miller, Donald. "Pierre Bonnard's Paintings Bloom with Psychology of Color." *Pittsburgh Post-Gazette* (18 August 1984): 4.

Morsell, Mary. "Art of Bonnard Finely Surveyed at Wildenstein's." *The Art News* 32 (3 March 1934): 3, 5.

Natanson, Thadée. "Des peintres intelligents." *La Revue blanche* 22 (1 May 1900): 53–56. ———"IXe de la Société des Artistes Indépendants." *La Revue blanche* 4, no. 18 (April 1893): 275–276.

Newman, Sasha. "Pierre Bonnard in London and New York." *Apollo* 148, no. 450 (October 1998): 50–51.

Nochlin, Linda. "Bonnard's Bathers." *Art in America* (July 1998): 63–67, 105.

Perucchi-Petri, Ursula. "Les Nabis et le Japon." In *Japonisme in Art: An International Symposium*. Tokyo: Kodansha International, 1980, 261–277.

"Pierre Bonnard." *L'Art d'aujourd'hui* 4 (1927): 21–27.

Polaillon-Kerven, G. "Le Compotier dans la peinture moderne." *Le Jardin des arts*, no. 13 (November 1955): 8.

Pradel-de Grandry, Marie Noëlle. "Musée National d'Art Moderne: don d'une peinture et de dessins de Bonnard." *La Revue du Louvre et des musées de France* 16, nos. 4–5 (1966): 249–256.

Roger-Marx, Claude. "Bonnard, illustrateur et lithogaphe." *Art et décoration* 43 (April 1923): 115–120.

Rouir, E. "Quelques remarques sur les litho-graphies de Pierre Bonnard." *Le Livre et l'estampe*, nos. 53–54 (1968): 27–35.

Schindler, Herbert. "Bonnard oder der Traum: 'La vie est belle.'" *Epoca*, no. 1 (January 1967): 40–48.

Seurière, Michelle. "Hommage à Bonnard." *Arts*, 16 May 1956, 11.

Sutton, Denys. "The Inquiring Eye of Pierre Bonnard." *Apollo* 125, no. 300 (February 1987): 132–137.

Sylvester, David. "Bonnard's 'The Table.'" *The Listener* 67 (15 March 1962): 478–479.

Terrasse, Charles. "Recollections of Bonnard." *Apollo* 83 (January 1966): 62–67. ———"La Vie des musées: nouvelles acquisitions du Musée national d'art moderne. 'L'Amandier en Fleur,' de Bonnard." *La Revue du Louvre et des musées de France* 14, no. 3 (1964): 144. ———"Bonnard. An Intimate Memoir of the Man and the Artist Revealed by His Nephew." Translated by Shannon Eames. *Art News Annual* 28 (1959): 84–107. ———"Pierre Bonnard." *Le Point Revue artistique et littéraire*, no. 9 (July 1937): 93–95.

Thibault, Bernard. "Essai de bibliographie des ouvrages illustrés par Pierre Bonnard." *Le Portique* 7 (1950): 19–20.

Thomé, J. R. "Pierre Bonnard." *Le Livre et ses amis* 17 (March 1947): 9–17.

Towndrow, Kenneth Romney. "French Painters II—Bonnard." *Apollo* 55, no. 325 (March 1952): 79–83.

Waldfogel, Melvin. "Bonnard and Vuillard as Lithographers." *The Minneapolis Institute of Arts Bulletin* 52, no. 3 (September 1963): 67–80.

Exhibition Catalogues

Bordeaux, Galerie des Beaux-Arts. *Hommage à Bonnard*. Essays by Philippe Le Leyzour, and Claire Frèches-Thory, 1986.

Boyer, Eckert Patricia, ed. *The Nabis and the Parisian Avant-Garde*. New Brunswick, and London: Rutgers University Press for the Jane Voorhees Zimmerli Art Museum, 1988.

Groom, Gloria. *Beyond the Easel: Decorative Paintings by Bonnard, Vuillard, Denis, and Roussel, 1890–1930*. New Haven and London: Yale University Press, 2001.

Ives, Colta. *Pierre Bonnard: The Graphic Art*. New York: Harry N. Abrams, 1989.

Johnson, Una E. *Ambroise Vollard, Editeur: Prints, Books, Bronzes*. New York: The Museum of Modern Art, 1977.

Komanecky, Michael. *The Folding Image: Screens by Western Artists of the Nineteenth and Twentieth Centuries*. New Haven: Yale University Art Gallery, 1984.

Lawrence, University of Kansas, Spencer Museum of Art. *Ubu's Almanac: Alfred Jarry and the Graphic Arts*. Essays by Stephen H. Goddard, and Brian Parshall, 1998.

London: Hayward Gallery. *Bonnard at Le Bosquet*. Essays by Belinda Thomson, and Sargy Mann, 1994.

Melbourne, National Gallery of Victoria. *Pierre Bonnard, 1867–1947*. Essays by Raymond Cogniat, and Charles Kunstler, 1971.

Nagoya, Aichi Prefectural Museum of Art. *Bonnard*. Essays by Hineori Kurita, and Ursula Perucchi-Petri, 1997.

Newman, Sasha M., ed. *Bonnard: The Late Paintings*. London: Thames and Hudson, 1984.

Nickson, Graham. *Pierre Bonnard: Stealing the Image*. New York: New York Studio School of Drawing, Painting and Sculpture, 1997.

Paris, Galeries nationals du Grand Palais. *Nabis 1888–1900*. Essays by Ursula Perucchi-Petri, and Claire Frèches-Thory. Paris: Editions de la Réunion des musées nationaux, 1993.

Rewald, John. *Pierre Bonnard*. New York: The Museum of Modern Art, 1948.

Soby, James Thrall. *Bonnard and His Environment*. New York: The Museum of Modern Art, 1965.

Sutton, Denys. *Pierre Bonnard, 1867–1947. Royal Academy of Arts Winter Exhibition, 1966*. London: Royal Academy of Arts, 1966. ———*Bonnard (1867–1947)*. London: Royal Academy of Arts and The Faber Gallery, 1957.

Tokyo, Art Life Ltd. *Pierre Bonnard*. Essays by Gabriel P. Weisberg, Nicholas Watkins, and Vincent Pomarède, 1991.

Waller, Bret, and Grace Seiberling. *Artists of La Revue blanche: Bonnard, Toulouse-Lautrec, Vallotton, Vuillard*. Rochester: Memorial Art Gallery of the University of Rochester, 1984.

Whitfield, Sarah, and John Elderfield. *Bonnard*. London: Tate Gallery Publishing, 1998.

Notes

Chronology

1 Quoted in Raymond Cogniat, "Les Nouvelles artistiques," *Les Nouvelles littéraires*, 29 July 1933, translated in Antoine Terrasse, *Bonnard: Shimmering Color*, trans. Laurel Hirsh (New York: Harry N. Abrams, 2000), 126–127.

2 The town of Le Grand-Lemps lies between Lyon and Grenoble, twenty miles east of La Côte-Saint-André.

3 Terrasse, *Bonnard: Shimmering Color*, 14, 15.

4 See Helen Emery Giambruni, "Early Bonnard, 1885–1900," Ph.D. diss., University of California, Berkeley, 1983, 7–8.

5 Nancy Wolsk, *The Lycée and the Nabis Formation and Realization* (Ann Arbor, Mich.: University Microfilms International, 1998), 114.

6 See Giambruni, "Early Bonnard," 12, 258 n. 27; and Wolsk, *The Lycée*, 114.

7 Giambruni, "Early Bonnard," 285.

8 Charles Terrasse, "Recollections of Bonnard," *Apollo* 83 (January 1966): 65.

9 See Colta Ives, Helen Giambruni, and Sasha M. Newman, *Pierre Bonnard: The Graphic Art*, exh. cat. (New York: Harry N. Abrams, 1989), 75, 199 n. 68, 239. They cite Claude Roger-Marx, "Bonnard, illustrateur de La Fontaine," Le Portique 5 (1947): 42–50, for knowledge of this illustration project, but disagree with him on the date of its completion.

10 Giambruni, "Early Bonnard," 11.

11 Quoted in Terrasse, *Bonnard: Shimmering Color*, 16.

12 "peignait gris et copiait scrupuleusement le modèle." Maurice Denis, "Pierre Bonnard," *Le Point* 4, no. 24 (January 1943): 4.

13 Terrasse, *Bonnard: Shimmering Color*, 15.

14 Quoted in Terrasse, *Bonnard: Shimmering Color*, 16.

15 Terrasse, *Bonnard: Shimmering Color*, 132, says that while Bonnard was living in Paris he visited Le Grand-Lemps each autumn and perhaps also in the winter if he had not seen his mother for some time. For the date of his last visit, see Sarah Whitfield and John Elderfield, *Bonnard*, exh. cat. (New York: Harry N. Abrams., 1998), 256. The sale date of the property has been variously given as either 1928 by Whitfield and Elderfield, *Bonnard*, 256, or 1929 by Timothy Hyman, *Bonnard* (London: Thames and Hudson., 1998), 70.

16 See Françoise Heilbrun and Philippe Néagu, *Pierre Bonnard: Photographs and Paintings* (New York: Aperture Foundation, 1988), 8, 117. They indicate Bonnard's friendship with the Lumière brothers was through

his future brother-in-law and suggest they were "frequent guests" to Le Grand-Lemps.

17 Giambruni, "Early Bonnard," 26.

18 Quoted in Terrasse, *Bonnard: Shimmering Color*, 25.

19 Terrasse, *Bonnard: Shimmering Color*, 25.

20 Quoted in Cogniat, "Les Nouvelles artistiques," in Terrasse, *Bonnard: Shimmering Color*, 126.

21 [Bonnard and Vuillard] étudièrent les maîtres, parcoururent les musées, et finirent par être particulièrement intéressés par l'art de la Chine et par l'art du Japon. Les Orientaux amenèrent chez eux la 'libération.'" Charles Terrasse, *Bonnard* (Paris: Henri Floury, 1927), 20.

22 Terrasse, *Bonnard: Shimmering Color*, 19.

23 Quoted in Terrasse, *Bonnard: Shimmering Color*, 19.

24 Terrasse, *Bonnard: Shimmering Color*, 19.

25 "le fantaisiste de la recherche, de la ligne et de la colour." Quoted in Aurelien François Lugné-Poë, *Le Sot de Tremplin: Souvenirs et impressions de théâtre* (Paris: Gallimard, Editions de la Nouvelle revue française, 1931), 195.

26 "Il peignait avec cette lenteur, cette indif-férence apparente mais secrètement fiévreuse que nous lui avons toujours connue." Quoted in Terrasse, *Pierre Bonnard* (Paris: Gallimard, 1967), 20.

27 "C'est là que je trouvais pour un ou deux sous des crépons ou des papiers de riz frois-sés aux couleurs étonnantes. Je remplis les murs de ma chambre de cette imagerie naïve et criarde. Gauguin, Sérusier se référèrent en fait au passé. Mais là ce que j'avais devant moi, c'était quelque chose de bien vivant, d'extrêmement savant. . . . J'avais compris au contact de ces frustes images populaires que la couleur pouvait comme ici exprimer toutes choses sans besoin de relief ou de modelé. Il m'apparut qu'il était possible de traduire lumière, formes et caractère rien qu'avec la couleur sans faire appel aux valeurs." Quoted in Gaston Diehl, "Pierre Bonnard dans son univers enchanté," *Comœdia*, no. 106 (10 July 1943). On the influence of Japanese art on Bonnard, see Ursula Perruchi-Petri, "Pierre Bonnard and Japonisme," in *Pierre Bonnard*, exh. cat. (Nagoya, Japan: Aichi Prefectural Museum of Art, 1997); Gabriel Weisberg, "Bonnard and Japan," in *Pierre Bonnard*, exh. cat. (Tokyo, Japan: Isetan Museum of Art, 1991); Claire Frèches-Thory and Antoine Terrasse, *The Nabis: Bonnard, Vuillard and Their Circle* (Paris: Flammarion, 1990), 79–91.

28 Letter to Vuillard, quoted in Antoine Terrasse, *Bonnard-Vuillard Correspondance*

(Paris: Gallimard, 2001), 17.

29 Félix Fénéon, "Sur les murs," *Chat noir* 10 (June 1891): 1760.

30 Signac journal, 29 September 1894, quoted in Colta Ives, *The Influence of Japanese Woodcuts on French Prints*, exh. cat. (New York: The Metropolitan Museum of Art, 1974), 57.

31 Whether the furniture design preceded the painting is unclear. Terrasse, *Bonnard: Shimmering Color*, 26–27, suggests it did. However, Gloria Groom believes that the painting came after the design, based on the exhibition of the painting in March 1892. See Gloria Groom, *Beyond the Easel: Decorative Painting by Bonnard, Vuillard, Denis, and Roussel, 1890–1930* (New Haven and London: Yale University Press, 2001), 65, 258.

32 "Bonnard", excerpt from interview in Jacques Daurelle, "Chez les jeunes peintres," *L'Echo de Paris*, 28 December 1891, 2, quoted in Giambruni, "Early Bonnard," 75.

33 "Se rappeler qu'un tableau—avant d'être un cheval de bataille, une femme nue, ou une quelconque anecdote—est essentiellement une surface plane recouverte de couleurs en un certain ordre assemblées." Maurice Denis, "Définition du néo-traditionnisme," *Art et critique*, no. 65 and 66 (23 and 30 August 1890): 540–542; 556–558, reprinted in Denis, *Théories, 1890–1910, du symbolisme et de Gauguin vers un nouvel ordre classique*, 4th ed. (Paris: L. Rouart et J. Watelin, 1920), 1 and in Denis, *Le Ciel et l'arcadie*, ed. Jean-Paul Bouillon, Collection Savoir sur l'Art (Paris: Hermann, 1993), 5.

34 Quoted in Terrasse, *Bonnard: Shimmering Color*, 32.

35 Félix Fénéon, "Au pavillon de la ville de Paris," *Chat noir* 11 (2 April 1892).

36 "un délicieux ornemaniste, habile et ingénieux comme un Japonais . . ." G. Albert Aurier, "Les Symbolistes," *Revue ency-clopédique* 2, no. 32 (1 April 1892), 485.

37 Bonnard to Vuillard, September 1892, in Terrasse, *Bonnard-Vuillard Correspondance*, 23.

38 "L'œil ne peut trouver qu'à se réjouir en constatant ces filiations chez deux de ces artistes, MM. Pierre Bonnard et Edouard Vuillard, qui sont certainement en posses-sion du don de la nuance et d'un jeu de lignes symétriques et contrariées." Gustave Geffroy, "Chez le Barc de Boutteville," *Le Journal*, 28 November 1892, 381.

39 Bonnard to Vuillard, 15 October 1893, in Terrasse, *Bonnard-Vuillard Correspondance*, 30.

40 "Il nous a bien aidés. Les éditions qu'il a faites resteront et peu d'hommes auront le

courage de faire de tels chefs d'oeuvre." Quoted in transcript of André Giverny, "Bonnard," *La France libre* (London) 6, no. 31 (15 May 1943).

41 Bonnard to his mother, 11 February 1893, quoted in Antoine Terrasse, *Bonnard illustra-teur* (Paris: Editions Adam Biro, 1988), 312.

42 Claude Roger-Marx, "Les Indépendants," Le Voltaire, 28 March 1893, quoted in Elderfield, "Seeing Bonnard," in *Bonnard*, 33, n. 3.

43 Hyman, *Bonnard*, 24.

44 Quoted in Terrasse, *Bonnard: Shimmering Color*, 68.

45 Quoted in Raymond Cogniat, "Les Nouvelles artistiques," translated in Terrasse, *Bonnard: Shimmering Color*, 126–127.

46 For more on the stained-glass window commission, see Groom, *Beyond the Easel*, 96, 114–117; 262, n. 3, 265, nn. 3, 5.

47 Arthur Gold and Robert Fizdale, Misia: *The Life of Misia Sert* (New York: Morrow Quill Paperbacks, 1981), 56. Hyman, *Bonnard*, 40, refers to it as a kind of "utopian community."

48 "Quand on doit étudier le rapport des tons, en jouant de 4 ou 5 couleurs seulement qu'on superpose ou qu'on rapproche, on découvre beaucoup de choses." Bonnard to André Suarès, quoted in Giverny, "Bonnard," transcript.

49 Pissarro to son Lucien, 6 February 1896, in Janine Bailly-Herzberg, *Correspondance de Camille Pissarro*, vol. 4, 1895–98 (Paris: Editions du Valhermeil, 1980), 159.

50 "Mais on trouve, chez lui . . . . l'erreur de mêler les principes de la décoration à ceux du tableau, qui en sont totalement dif-férents." Camille Mauclair, "Choses d'art," *Mercure de France* 42, no. 75 (March 1896): 418.

51 Hyman, *Bonnard*, 40–41.

52 "Je confie cette lettre à Vollard pour vous dire que je trouve vos dessins de la Revue blanche tout ce qu'il y a de plus exquis. C'est bien à vous, gardez cette art." Renoir to Bonnard, 1897, quoted in *La Revue blanche: Paris in the Days of Post-Impressionism and Symbolism*, exh. cat. (New York: Wildenstein, 1983), n.p.

53 Arsène Alexandre, *Le Figaro*, 27 March 1899, translated in Antoine Terrasse, "Chronology," in *Bonnard: The Late Paintings* (New York and London: Thames and Hudson, 1984), 247.

54 "Tout autour, il y avait des toiles, des chevalets, et dans un angle une petite table où l'on déjeunait. Le balcon était un endroit particulièrement séduisant. De là on voyait tant de choses! Tout un monde. La rue, en

bas, était grouillante . . . agitée comme une mer." Charles Terrasse, *Bonnard*, 74–75.

55 Heilbrun and Néagu, *Bonnard: Photographs and Paintings*, 10–11.

56 Terrasse, *Bonnard: Shimmering Color*, 133.

57 Heilbrun and Néagu, *Bonnard: Photographs and Paintings*, 127–128.

58 "Son système étant de n'en pas avoir, il échappe aisément à l'analyse. . . . C'est aux circonstances d'époque et à son esprit malicieux qu'il doit d'avoir été un peintre de la vie moderne." Denis, "Bonnard," *Le Point*, 4.

59 "M. Bonnard ne se plaît plus guère aux déformations capricieuses où sa verve sarcastique se dépensait jadis si finement. Il est revenu à de l'observation plus calme et plus réfléchi, et son oeuvre gagne en profondeur et en solidité ce qu'elle a peut-être perdu en vivacité." André Fontainas, "Art moderne," *Mercure de France* 34 (May 1900), 544.

60 Translated in Francis Bouvet, *Bonnard: The Complete Graphic Work* (New York: Rizzoli; London: Thames and Hudson, 1981), 106.

61 Gordon N. Ray, *The Art of the French Illustrated Book, 1900–1914* (1982; reprint, New York: Dover, 1986), 504.

62 "ses dons de compositeur." Thadée Natanson, "Des peintres intelligents," *La Revue blanche* 22, no. 166 (1 May 1900): 55.

63 Hyman, *Bonnard*, 24.

64 "Avec une légèreté admirable, il a mollement culbuté sur les draps candides des pages." Alfred Jarry, "Parallèlement," *La Revue blanche* 24 (1901), 317.

65 "M. Bonnard a peint d'une touche légère, d'un dessin un peu paradoxal, et dans une jolie teinte grise." Henry Cochin, "Quelques Réflexions sur les Salons," *Gazette des Beaux-Arts*, 3e pér., 29 (1 June 1903): 454.

66 "Plus d'esprit, d'espièglerie même, que de raison fait de la composition de chacune quelque chose de bizarrement neuf et d'excitant. . . . Qu'il peigne un omnibus, un chien, un chat, une escabelle, sa touche même est polissonne, tout indépendamment du sujet." André Gide, "Promenade au Salon d'Automne," *Gazette des Beaux-Arts* 34 (1 December 1905): 481.

67 Letter to his mother, December 1905, quoted in Terrasse "Chronology," 249.

68 Ambroise Vollard, Memories of a Picture Dealer, quoted in Terrasse, "Chronology," 250.

69 Terrasse, *Bonnard: Shimmering Color*, 45.

70 George Besson, "Lettre à Pierre Betz," *Le Point* 4, no. 24 (January 1943), translated in Terrasse, *Bonnard: Shimmering Color*, 125.

71 Bouvier, "Bonnard revient à la litho."

72 Octave Mirbeau, 1908, quoted in *Exhibition of Paintings by Bonnard*, exh. cat.

(New York: Wildenstein & Co., 1934), 5.

73 Quoted in Annette Vaillant, *Bonnard: With a Dialogue between Jean Cassou and Raymond Cogniat* (Greenwich, Conn: New York Graphic Society, 1966), 115.

74 Charles Terrasse, "Bonnard: An Intimate Memoir of the Man and Artist Revealed by His Nephew," *Artnews Annual* 28 (1959), 97.

75 Terrasse, "Bonnard: An Intimate Memoir," 105.

76 Terrasse, *Bonnard: Shimmering Color*, 68, 103.

77 "Il sait ce qu'il fait et il s'arrange pour le faire du premier coups. Tandis que moi, je pars, je retouche, et je ne sais jamais où celà m'emmènere." Quoted in Giverny, "Bonnard," transcript.

78 Charles Terrasse, *Formes et couleurs* 2 (1944), quoted in Terrasse, *Bonnard: Shimmering Color*, 133.

79 "Je me suis remis à l'école. . . . J'ai voulu oublier tout ce que je savais, je cherche à apprendre ce que je ne sais pas. Je refais mes études, depuis les principes, depuis l'a b c . . . et je me défie de moi-même, de tout ce qui m'avait tant passionné, de cette couleur qui vous affole. . . . Certes, la couleur m'avait entraîné. Je lui sacrifiais, et presque inconsciemment, la forme. Mais il est bien vrai que la forme existe, que l'on ne peut arbitrairement et indéfiniment la réduire ou la transposer; c'est donc le dessin qu'il me faut étudier." Quoted in Charles Terrasse, *Bonnard*, 128.

80 "Je crois que Bonnard, dans la peinture moderne, a une place unique." Terrasse, *Pierre Bonnard: Illustrator*, trans. Jean-Marie Clarke (New York: Harry N. Abrams, 1989), 176.

81 See Heilbrun and Néagu, *Bonnard: Photographs and Paintings*, 143, who suggest that the attribution of two photographs of Renoir, which seem to have informed Bonnard's etching, remains inconclusive.

82 Terrasse, *Bonnard: Shimmering Color*, 80.

83 Quoted in *Bonnard: The Late Paintings*, 132.

84 Heilbrun and Néagu, *Bonnard: Photographs and Paintings*, 12.

85 "Une obéissance aussi scrupuleuse à la nature est plus neuve qu'on ne le pense. Les impressionnistes, eux-mêmes, à part Degas, n'avaient point osé aller jusqu-là." François Fosca, "Pierre Bonnard," *Art et décoration* 38 (September 1920), 10–11.

86 Terrasse, *Bonnard: Shimmering Color*, 76; *Dictionary of Artists' Models*, ed. Jill Berk Jiminez (Chicago: Fitzroy Dearborn Publishers, 2001), 378–379.

87 "Tandis que les impressionnistes—dont il n'est guère débiteur, même à ses débuts—ne

voient partout qu'apparences, à ses yeux, au contraire, tout est réalité, tout vit et s'affirme à titre égal, tout respire et participe du désordre charmant que l'être humain crée autour de lui. . . . Rarement une toile est achevée d'emblée; il la reprend, à plusieurs semaines, parfois à plusieurs années d'intervalle, menant de front trois ou quatre ouvrages, attendant qu'une analogie imprévue lui permette de donner enfin à tel problème, qui demeurait irrésolu, une réponse sincère. . . . Bonnard travaille avec lenteur et produit peu." Claude Roger-Marx, "Bonnard et son oeuvre," *Les Peintres français nouveaux*, no. 19 (1924): 6, 7.

88 "incomparable à l'analyse aigně, presque cruelle d'un Toulouse-Lautrec." "un spirituel dédain des formules académiques (fussent-elles de l'Académie Julian) . . . et la fantaisie la plus personnelle." Jacques Trapenard, "Exposition Bonnard," *Combat* April 1924.

89 "Pour moi qu n'ai jamais été un fanatique du cubisme 'conceptual', je me réjouis, devant un tableaux de Bonnard, de voir la surface de la toile divisée de si ingénieuse façon." André Lhote, "Les Arts. Visite À J. M. Sert—Expositions J. E. Blanche, Bonnard, Picasso, Kisling, Lurçat, O. Des Garets, Yves Alix," *La Nouvelle Revue française* 22 (1924): 648.

90 Phillips, to Charles Wheeler, president, Royal Academy of Arts, London, ca. 1964, draft, The Phillips Collection Archives.

91 Terrasse, *Bonnard: Shimmering Color*, 94–95.

92 "notre vision est avant tout empirique et conventionnelle. . . . Ce reflet conventionnel du monde extérieur que nous donne le dessin, est incomparablement plus vrai que le procédé sec de la photographie. . . . L'oeil du peintre donne aux objects une valeur humaine…Et cette vision est mobile. Et cette vision est variable." Quoted in Charles Terrasse, *Bonnard*, 163.

93 "Il n' y a pas de première ou de seconde manière de Bonnard. Il n'y en a qu'une, qui fut et qui est perpétuellement changeante et diverse. Son art évoluc constamment, [et?] est un incessant devenir." Charles Terrasse, *Bonnard*, 38.

94 Duncan Phillips, "Pierre Bonnard," in Tri-Unit Exhibition of Paintings and Sculpture (Washington, D.C.: Phillips Memorial Gallery, 1927), 15–16.

95 Michel Terrasse, *Bonnard at Le Cannet*, preface by Jean Leymarie, trans. Sebastian Wormell (London: Thames and Hudson, 1988), 14.

96 Roger Fry, "Pierre Bonnard," *Nation and the Athenaeum* 42, no. 231 (25 February 1928):

778–779.

97 Claude Anet, introduction to *Bonnard* (New York: De Hauke and Co., 1928), n.p.

98 Margaret Breuning, "Exhibition by Pierre Bonnard on View at De Hauke's—Work by Artist Members of American Woman's Assocation Shown—Other Notes of Current Activity," *New York Evening Post*, 14 April 1928, 7.

99 "On pouvait mesurer ainsi l'étendue de sa conquête, aussi bien dans le domaine de la composition que dans celui de la couleur. Dédaignant de plus en plus le morcellement impressionniste des objets, Bonnard s'efforce de les rendre solidaires des formes architecturales qui leur font un cadre quotidien." André Lhote, "A propos du Jubilé du Salon d'Automne.—Bonnard (chez Bernheim-Jeune)," *La Nouvelle Revue française* 16, no. 184 (1 January 1929): 133.

100 Terrasse, *Bonnard: Shimmering Color*, 152–153.

101 Waldemar George, "Bonnard and the Charm of Life," *Formes*, 1933, 381.

102 Bonnard to Phillips, postmarked 7 August 1931, trans. in *The Eye of Duncan Phillips: A Collection in the Making*, ed. Erica Passantino with consulting ed. David W. Scott (Washington, D.C.: The Phillips Collection, 1999), 190.

103 Phillips, "Modern Art, 1930," *Art and Understanding* 1, no. 2 (March 1930): 143.

104 Adolphe Basler and Charles Kunstler, *Modern French Painting: The Modernists from Matisse to De Segonzac* (New York: William Farquhar Payson, 1931), 10, 56.

105 Quoted in Cogniat, "Les Nouvelles artistiques," translated in Terrasse, *Bonnard: Shimmering Color*, 127.

106 Bonnard to Charles Terrasse, Le Cannet, quoted in Terrasse, "Chronology," 259.

107 "Je ne passe guère à Paris que deux mois de l'année. Je viens y reprendre du ton, comparer mes peintures à d'autres peintures; à Paris, je suis un critique, je ne peux pas y travailler: trop de bruit, trop de distractions. . . . Je passe habituellement six mois dans le Midi et quatre en Normandie, dans ma maison de Vernon, où je vais retourner." Quoted in Pierre Courthion, "Impromptus—Pierre Bonnard," *Les Nouvelles littéraires*, 24 June 1933, n.p.

108 Je crois que lorsqu'on est jeune, c'est l'objet, le monde extérieur qui vous enthousiasme: on est emballé. Plus tard, c'est intérieur, le besoin d'exprimer une émotion pousse le peintre à choisir tel ou tel point de départ, telle ou telle forme." Quoted in Courthion, "Impromptus—Pierre Bonnard," n.p.

109 Signac to Bonnard, quoted in Terrasse, "Chronology," 260.
110 "Bonnard, sans y penser, est devenu le peintre le plus abstraite de notre temps." André Lhote, "Irréalisme et surréalisme: Bonnard, Dali," *La Nouvelle Revue française* 4 (1933): 307.
111 Claude Roger-Marx, *L'Europe nouvelle*, June 1933, trans. Terrasse, "Chronology," 260.
112 "Bonnard a traversé l'art de notre temps comme un solitaire. . . . ce grand peintre a eu longtemps une position une peu écartée. Aujourd'hui un grand mouvement d'opinion se dessine en faveur de Bonnard et il semble, à bien des symptômes, que beaucoup soient près de le considérer comme le plus grand maître de notre temps. A retardement il exerce même actuellement sur les jeunes une influence dont on constate maintes fois les effets dans des expositions." Germain Bazin, "Les Expositions," *L'Amour de l'art* 14 no. 7 (July 1933): 2.
113 Terrasse, *Bonnard: Shimmering Color*, 101.
114 Margaret Breuning, "Art World Events. Bonnard's Paintings at Wildenstein's Show: Strong Gallic Influences," *New York Evening Post*, 2 March 1934, 11.
115 Mary Morsell, "Art of Bonnard Finely Surveyed at Wildenstein's," *The Art News*, 32, no. 22 (3 March 1934).
116 Henry McBride, "Bonnard's One-Man Show," *New York Sun*, 3 March 1934, 11.
117 "l'exemple d'un peintre demeuré fidèle à l'esthétique de ses débuts. . . . On vante la jeunesse persistante de ses oeuvres les plus récentes." Maurice Denis, "L'Epoque du symbolisme," *Gazette des Beaux-Arts* 76 (March 1934): 178.
118 Bonnard to Ingrid Rydbeck, quoted in "Hos Bonnard I Deauville," *Konstrevy* (Stockholm), 1937, translated in Terrasse, *Bonnard: Shimmering Color*, 123.
119 The two had begun exchanging letters and postcards in 1925. Their correspondence continues through 1946. Bonnard to Matisse, 1 February 1935, in *Bonnard/Matisse: Letters between Friends*, preface by Jean Clair, intro. and notes by Antoine Terrasse, trans. Richard Howard (New York: Harry N. Abrams, 1991), 50.
120 "Bonnard et Vuillard sont donc les derniers survivants d'un paradis qu'il faut reconquérir. Ils sont à nos yeux comme les témoins suprêmes d'un âge d'or." Waldemar George, "Exposition des peintres de la Revue blanche," *L'Amour de l'art* 17, no. 7 (July 1936): 268.
121 Bonnard to Ingrid Rydbeck, quoted in "Hos Bonnard I Deauville," *Konstrevy*, translated in Terrasse, *Bonnard: Shimmering Color*, 122.

122 Terrasse, *Bonnard: Shimmering Color*, 124, 105.
123 Julius Meier-Graefe, "Bonnard," *The Art News* 37 (31 December 1938): 9.
124 "l'impressionniste cent pour cent: le peintre de l'instant qui passe, du reflet sur une soucoupe, de l'atmosphère qu'une lampe répand dans une salle à manger, de l'attitude gauche souvent puérile d'une femme rousse qui tient une tasse de thé au-dessus d'une nappe blanche à carreaux roses." Albert Charpentier, "Trois Peintres à la Galerie Durand-Ruel: Bonnard, Laprade, et Bouche," Prométhée: *L'Amour de l'art* 20 no. 5 (June 1939): 2.
125 Matisse to Bonnard, 8 January 1940; Bonnard to Matisse, 1940, in *Bonnard/Matisse: Letters between Friends*, 55, 57.
126 Bonnard to Matisse, 9 February 1940, in *Bonnard/Matisse: Letters between Friends*, 60.
127 Quoted in Antoine Terrasse, "Bonnard's Notes," in *Bonnard: The Late Paintings*, 70.
128 Whitfield and Elderfield, *Bonnard*, 262.
129 Bonnard to Matisse, end February 1941, in *Bonnard/Matisse: Letters between Friends*, 80.
130 Bouvet, Bonnard: *The Complete Graphic Work*, 292.
131 André Girard, "Pierre Bonnard," *Vogue*, June 1948, 151, quoted in Rebecca A. Rabinow, "The Creation of Bonnard's 'Correspondances,'" *Print Quarterly* 15 (1998): 176.
132 Bonnard to Matisse, early February 1942, in *Bonnard/Matisse: Letters between Friends*, 101.
133 Bonnard to Tériade, 6 January 1943, quoted in Rabinow, "Bonnard's 'Correspondances,'" 177.
134 "sa peinture est restée jeune, et fidèle à l'esprit juvénile de ses premiers débuts. . . . Il est le plus moderne, le plus avancé des peintres d'aujourd'hui." Denis goes on to say "il a sa place à l'aile marchanate de l'art contemporain. Cette situation de maître admireé des générations nouvelles lui plaît sans doute davantage que celle du membre de l'Institute où Vuillard aurait voulu qu'il posât sa candidature." Denis, "Bonnard," 4.
135 George Besson, "Lettre à Pierre Betz," *Le Point* 4, no. 24 (January 1943): 44, translated in Terrasse, *Bonnard: Shimmering Color*, 125–126.
136 "Il est à l'âge des chefs-d'oeuvre chez les peintres, à l'âge ou Renoir et Cézanne ont gagné leurs plus belles victoires." "Il porte aliègrement ses soixante-quinze ans avec sa minceur, sa peau ivoirine, son petit crane bombé, Bonnard fait penser à un Japonais, dont il a d'ailleurs les gestes mesures et

précautionneux." Bouvier, "Bonnard revient à la litho."
137 "il y a seulement au mur deux grandes lithos de Renoir. . . . Dans cet espace très limité, de grandes toiles punaisées au mur sont en cours d'achèvement. . . . Je me promène très tôt le matin, je vais derrière le Cannet . . . et je réfléchis, puis vers 10h. je reviens et je travaille" Giverny, "Bonnard."
138 "Tout l'art est composition, c'est la clé de tout. Le pouvoir d'invention réside davantage dans la mise en place et dans le sens des proportions." Quoted in Gaston Diehl, "Pierre Bonnard dans son univers enchanté," *Comœdia*, no. 106 (10 July 1943).
139 Bonnard to Tériade, quoted in Rabinow, "Bonnard's 'Correspondances,'" 184.
140 "Il s'évade par une porte négligée: celle des affiches, des illustrations, des lithographes. Il paraît s'en tenir à l'art décoratif et c'est ainsi qu'il s'instruit. . . . "L'illustrateur l'emporte si bien . . . sur le peintre. . . . Je crois bien que la pratique de la lithographie a enseigné à Bonnard la science de choisir des tons rares et d'en réduire à l'extreme le nombre." Pierre Laprade, "Bonnard," *Formes et couleurs* 2 (1944): 50.
141 "ses oeuvres s'orientent vers l'abstraction, c'est-à-dire vers la mise en évidence . . . des valeurs les plus pures de la peinture." André Lhote, "Bonnard," *Formes et couleurs* 2 (1944): 4.
142 Louis Parrot, "Pierre Bonnard et le livre," *Les Lettres françaises* 4, no. 34 (16 December 1944): 3.
143 Terrasse, *Bonnard: Shimmering Color*, 109.
144 Charles Terrasse, "La Vie des musées: nouvelles acquisitions du Musée national d'art moderne. L'Amandier en Fleur, de Bonnard," *La Revue du Louvre et des musées de France* 14, no. 3 (1964), 144, quoted in *Bonnard: The Late Paintings*, 241.
145 Terrasse, *Bonnard: Shimmering Color*, 109.
146 Charles Terrasse, "La vie des musées." *La Revue du Louvre et des musées de France*, Quoted in *Bonnard: The Late Paintings*, 241.

Elizabeth Hutton Turner
I deeply thank Roger Shattuck, Marjorie Balge-Crozier, and Merry Foresta for their careful reading of my manuscript.
1 Jacques Daurelle, "Chez les jeunes peintres," *L'Echo de Paris*, 28 December 1891, quoted in Helen Emery Giambruni, "Early Bonnard, 1885–1900," Ph.D. diss., University of California, Berkeley, 1983, 75.
2 For a review of the criticism pertaining to Bonnard and the physiology of vision, see John Elderfield, "Seeing Bonnard," in Bonnard,

exh. cat. (New York: Harry N. Abrams, 1998), 33.
3 Charles Terrasse, *Bonnard* (Paris: Floury, 1927), 162, quoted in Hidenori Kurita, "Bonnard's Assimilation of Impressionism and the Beginnings of a New Development in His Art as Seen in Animated Landscape," *Pierre Bonnard*, exh. cat. (Nagoya: Aichi Prefectural Museum of Art; Tokyo: The Bunkamura Museum of Art, 1997), 227.
4 "Couleur de Bonnard," *Verve* 5, nos. 17–18 (1947): n.p., trans. in Michel Anthonioz, ed., *Verve: The Ultimate Review on Art and Literature (1937–1960)* (New York: Harry N. Abrams, 1987), 174.
5 Jean-François Chevrier, "Bonnard and Photography," in *Bonnard: The Late Paintings*, exh. cat. (London: Thames and Hudson, 1984), 103.
6 Angèle Lamotte, "Le Bouquet de Roses: propos de Pierre Bonnard recueillis en 1943," special issue "Couleur de Bonnard," *Verve* 5, nos. 17–18, (August 1947), typescript, Phillips Collection Archives, n.p.
7 Jacques Daurelle, "Chez les jeunes peintres," *L'Echo de Paris*, 28 December 1891, quoted in Giambruni, "Early Bonnard, 75.
8 Maurice Denis, "L'Influence de Paul Gauguin," *L'Occident*, October 1903, quoted in Nicholas Watkins, *Bonnard: Colour and Light* (London: Tate Gallery Publishing, 1998), 32.
9 Ernest Fenollosa, *Epochs of Chinese and Japanese Art: An Outline History of East Asiatic Design*, ed. Mary Fenollosa, vol. 2 (New York: Frederick A. Stokes Company; London: William Heinemann, 1921), 5.
10 Signac journal, 29 September 1894, quoted in Colta Feller Ives, *The Great Wave: The Influence of Japanese Woodcuts on French Prints*, exh. cat. (New York: The Metropolitan Museum of Art, 1974), 57.
11 Bonnard's own direct quotations of Japan are laden with contemporary comment. Consider his cautionary tale told in the guise of a Japanese folding screen complete with the vocabulary of the pine, bamboo, and peonies in flat, unmodulated colors. The screen, made for his sister Andrée, was entitled *Marabout and Four Frogs*, which the Bonnard family recognized as a fable from La Fontaine. (See Jean de la Fontaine, "The Frogs Who Demanded a King," *The Fables of Jean de La Fontaine*, trans. Joseph Auslander and Jacques le Clercq (New York: The Limited Editions Club, 1930), 102–103. The fable tells of a colony of frogs that demand a king. Jupiter sends first a log. The dissatisfied frogs ask again. Jupiter sends a crane that starts to eat the frogs. If they ask for yet

another, Jupiter exclaims, the next king will be worse. Color alone structures and unites both image and narrative. Standing tall in the upper register of the crimson red screen, the exotic marabout with its elaborate feathers steps forward from among the reeds and flanking flourishes of flowers. Below him dart five green frogs. In keeping with the story a vibration, a visual jump associated with the fleeing frogs, is caused by the shared intensities of the green and red. Did Bonnard's red painting recall another? Looking ahead, one may think of the jump of red against the blue of Matisse's *Dance*? Quite contemporary with Bonnard's screen and on view at the Café Volpini on the grounds of the 1889 international exposition was Gauguin's *Vision after the Sermon*. Is there a message here for Bonnard's studiomates? In turning to Gauguin were they exchanging one master for another? My understanding of *Marabout and Four Frogs* within the context of Bonnard's decorative painting is indebted to *Gloria Groom, Beyond the Easel: Decorative Painting by Bonnard, Vuillard, Denis, and Roussel, 1890–1930*, exh. cat. (New Haven and London: Yale University Press, 2001), 59–60.

12 Gaston Diehl, "Bonnard dans son univers enchanté," *Comoedia*, no. 106 (10 July 1943), n.p.

13 The idea of capturing the sudden intuition triggered by the coincidence of vision and emotion had a certain currency among his colleagues who read Henri Bergson's "Essai sur les données immédiates de la conscience," published in 1889, and who attended Bergson's public lectures in Paris in 1891. See Giambruni, "Early Bonnard," 162.

14 Ives, *The Great Wave*, 37.

15 Phillip Dennis Cate, "Japonisme and the Revival of Printmaking," *Japonisme in Art: An International Symposium*, ed. The Society for the Study of Japonisme (Tokyo: Kodansha International, 1980), 286.

16 Clive Bell, "Review of Bonnard by Léon Werth," *The Athenaeum* (19 March 1920): 374–375.

17 Max Kozloff, "Pierre Bonnard: From Impressionism to Abstraction," M.A. thesis, University of Chicago, 1956, 50.

18 Félix Fénéon, *Le Chat noir*, 6 June 1891, quoted in Antoine Terrasse, "Chronology," in *Bonnard: The Late Paintings*, 243.

19 Pierre Bonnard and others, "Hommage à Maurice Denis," *L'Art sacré*, 3, no. 25 (December, 1937): 160, quoted in Giambruni, "Early Bonnard," 22.

20 Kozloff, "From Impressionism to Abstraction," 50.

21 For further discussion of the importance of the gaze in symbolist art, see Dorothy Kozinski, "The Gaze of Fernand Khnopff," in *The Artist and the Camera: Degas to Picasso*, exh. cat. (New Haven and London: Yale University Press, 1999), 145.

22 Thadée Natanson, Le Bonnard que je propose (Geneva: Pierre Cailler, 1951), 17, quoted in Kozloff, "From Impressionism to Abstraction," 46.

23 Bonnard to his mother, 21 May 1891, quoted in Giambruni, "Early Bonnard," 85.

24 Antoine Terrasse, *Bonnard: Shimmering Color*, trans. Laurel Hirsh (New York: Harry N. Abrams, 2000), 33.

25 Phillip Dennis Cate, "Prints Abound: Paris in the 1890s," in *Prints Abound: Paris in the 1890s from the Collections of Virginia and Ira Jackson and the National Gallery of Art*, exh. cat. (Washington, D.C.: National Gallery of Art, 2000), 16, 22, 24, 26.

26 Terrasse, *Bonnard: Shimmering Color*, 34.

27 Félix Fénéon, "Quelques Peintres idéistes," *Le Chat noir*, 10, no. 505 (19 September 1891): 1822, reprinted in Fènéon, *Oeuvres plus que complètes: Chroniques d'Art*, vol. 1, ed. Joan U. Halperin, (Genev: Librairie Droz, 1970), 201.

28 As an avant-garde periodical dedicated to supporting (in some cases providing entertainment and shelter for) both writers and artists including Bonnard, Vuillard, André Gide, Bernard, Marcel Proust, and Stéphane Mallarmé, *La Revue blanche* carried the motto: "we respectfully solicit our master and gladly welcome the young." See: Thadée Natanson, *La Revue blanche* 1, no. 1 (15 October 1891): 1, quoted in Grace Seiberling, "The Artists of the Revue Blanche and the 1890's," *Artists of the Revue Blanche*, exh. cat. (Rochester, N.Y.: Memorial Art Gallery, 1984), 28–29.

29 For a discussion of Bonnard and Fernand Khnopff, see Chevrier, "Bonnard and Photography," 90.

30 Hans Hahnloser believed that this story is close to life, that it recapitulated the day Bonnard followed Marthe, a young shop girl, along the street, and brought her to his studio. See "The Identification of Pierre Bonnard's Sitters," *Times of London*, 15 February 1966, 13.

31 Bonnard to his parents, 1894, quoted in Antoine Terrasse, *Bonnard* (Paris: Editions Gallimard, 1988), 44–45.

32 Nicholas Watkins writes that Bonnard's breakthrough as a colorist came when he realized the power of paint to generate light. See Nicholas Watkins, "The Alchemy of Light," in *Bonnard: Colour and Light*, 53–72.

33 Raymond Cogniat, "Les Nouvelles artistiques," Les Nouvelles litteraires, 19 July 1933, quoted in Terrasse, *Bonnard: Shimmering Color*, 127.

34 Françoise Heilbrun and Philippe Néagu, introduction to *Pierre Bonnard: Photographs and Paintings*, exh. cat. (New York: Aperture Foundation, 1988), 8.

35 Institute Lumière website, http://www.institutlumiere.org/English/lumiere/scinematographe.html, p. 2.

36 Among the earliest published reviews from the summer of 1895 include Louis Rossingnol, "Le Nouvel Appareil chronophotographique de MM. Auguste et Louis Lumière," *La Photographie française* 6 (June 1895): 3, quoted in Raymond Andrew Foery, "Images that Move: The Pioneering Work of Louis Lumière," Ph.D. diss., Columbia University, 1997, 74–75.

37 *Le Journal*, 8 January 1896 quoted in Kozloff, "From Impressionism to Abstraction," 57.

38 "Chronology of Bonnard's Graphic Work," in *Pierre Bonnard: The Graphic Art*, 238.

39 Camille Pissarro to Lucien Pissarro, 31 January 1896, *Correspondance de Camille Pissarro*, vol. 4, 1895–1898, ed. Janine Bailly-Herzberg (Paris: Editions de Valhermeil, 1980), 158.

40 Guillaume Apollinaire, *Le Flâneur des deux rives* (1918; reprinted, Paris: Gallimard, 1993), quoted in Phillips Dennis Cate, "The Spirit of Montmartre," in *The Spirit of Montmartre: Cabarets, Humor and the Avant-Garde, 1875–1905*, exh. cat. (Rutgers: Jane Voorhees Zimmerli Art Museum, The State University of New Jersey, 1996), 82.

41 A firsthand account is given in *L'Echo de Paris*, 1 April 1898, quoted in Francis Bouvet, *Bonnard: The Complete Graphic Work* (New York: Rizzoli, 1981), 59.

42 Introduction to *Selected Works of Alfred Jarry*, ed. Roger Shattuck and Simon Watson Taylor (New York: Grove Press, 1965), 13.

43 Gale B. Murray, "Music Illustration in the Circle of Bonnard," in *Prints Abound*, 77–78.

44 Cate, "Prints Abound," 34.

45 *Selected Works of Alfred Jarry*, 103–105.

46 Cate, "Prints Abound," 34.

47 *Selected Works of Alfred Jarry*, 234–236. While Ubu's illogic takes the world apart, Dr. Faustroll's pataphysics with its science of exceptions creates a new world where anything seems possible. For a description of the action of Dr. Faustroll's painting machine, see: "Clinamen," in *Selected Works of Alfred Jarry*, 238.

48 Bonnard's photographs were not discussed until the 1970s. Bonnard did little to preserve or date them. There now exist 155 prints and 106 negatives. All agree that Bonnard's earliest known photograph is of his cousin Berthe Schaedlin taken in 1892. Two possibly date from 1897. From 1898 until 1903 Bonnard took family snapshots at Le Clos and Noisy-le-Grand, at the home of his sister Andrée outside Pairs. Bonnard's nude photographs of Marthe have been dated ca. 1900 since they correspond with the book illustrations for *Daphnis and Chloë*. Bonnard continued to make photographs sporadically up to World War I. See Heilbrun and Néagu, *Pierre Bonnard: Photographs and Paintings*, 8, 11. Sasha Newman stresses the relationship between Bonnard's photography and the development of his approach to the nude in "Nudes and Landscapes," in *Pierre Bonnard: The Graphic Art*, 145–191.

49 See Hans Hahnloser's account in "The Identification of Pierre Bonnard's Sitters," *Times of London*, 15 February 1966, 13.

50 Michel Terrasse told me simply, "He needed her in order to paint." Interview with author, Paris, 15 February 1998.

51 Heilbrun and Néagu, *Pierre Bonnard: Photographs and Paintings*, 9.

52 "Interview with Emile Zola," *Photo-miniature*, no. 21 (December 1900): 396.

53 Annie Perez, "Entretiens avec Dina Vierny," *Hommage à Bonnard*, exh. cat. (Bordeaux: Galerie des Beaux-Arts, 1986), 136, quoted in Sarah Whitfield, "Fragments of an Identical World," in *Bonnard*, 20.

54 Charles Terrasse, *Bonnard*, 162.

55 For further discussion regarding the ironic rapport between illegal pornographic photographs and academic études during this period, see Cate, "Prints Abound," 41–44, and Elizabeth Hutton Turner, "Who Is in the Brothel of Avignon? A Case for Context," *Artibus et Historiae*, no. 9 (1984): 139ff.

56 Ingrid Rydbeck, "Hos Bonnard I Deauville," *Konstrevy* 13, no. 4 (1937): typescript translation by Henrik von Schenck, The Phillips Collection Archives, n.p.

57 Hidenori Kurita, "Bonnard's Assimilation of Impressionism and the Beginnings of a New Development in His Art, as Seen in Animated Landscape," in *Pierre Bonnard*, 226.

58 Henri Matisse, "Notes d'un peintre," *La Grande Revue* 52, no. 24 (25 December 1908): 731–745, quoted in Jack Flam, *Matisse on Art* (London: Phaidon, 1973), 37.

59 Roger Shattuck, *The Banquet Years* (New York: Vintage, 1968) 241.

60 Rydbeck, "Hos Bonnard I Deauville."

61 Charles Terrasse, *Bonnard* (Paris, 1927) quoted in Hyman, Bonnard (London:

Thames and Hudson, 1998), 97.

62 L. Gimpel, "La Photographie des couleurs à *L'Illustration*," *L'Illustration*, 15 June 1907, 387, quoted in *Les Autochromes Lumière*, n.p.

63 L. Pellerano, "L'Autochromie et ses application artistiques," *La Fotografia Artistica*, no. 7 (1909): 104, quoted in *Les Autochromes Lumière*, n.p.

64 G. Salle, "Chronique," *Revue Photographique de l'Ouest*, no. 10 (1910): 151, quoted in *Les Autochromes Lumière*, n.p.

65 Quoted in Aaron Scharf, *Art and Photography* (Baltimore: Penguin, 1974), 252.

66 Maurice Denis, "L'Epoque du symbolisme," *Gazette des Beaux-Arts* 11, (March 1934): 178.

67 Rydbeck, "Hos Bonnard I Deauville."

68 *Les Autochromes Lumière*, n.p.

69 Lucie Cousturier, "Bonnard," *L'Art décoratif*, 20 December 1912, 366.

70 Félix Fénéon, quoted by A. Charpentier, in introduction to *Bonnard, Laprade, Bouche*, exh. cat. (Paris: Durand-Ruel Galleries, 1939), n.p, quoted in John Rewald, *Pierre Bonnard*, exh. cat. (New York: Simon & Schuster, 1948), 51.

71 Max Kozloff, "From Impressionism to Abstraction," 5.

72 Bonnard to Matisse, 1 February 1935, quoted in Terrasse, *Bonnard: Shimmering Color*, 119.

73 Bonnard, "Notes," 1946, quoted in Antoine Terrasse, "Bonnard's Notes," in *Bonnard: The Late Paintings*, 70. Bonnard's judging of color in painting compares to searching for color in photography, as was stated in 1849: "to look for a sensitive preparation, which under the influence of a suitably refined solar spectrum at each point adopts colorations identical to those which the rays of light striking it produces on our organs, thus obtaining an image of the spectrum that is as similar as possible to the one directly perceived by our eyes." "Rapport sur un mémoire de M. Edmond Becquerel, ayant pour Titre: 'De L'Image Photochromatique de Spectre Solaire,' Commissaires MM. Biot, Chevreul, Regnault Rapporteur," Comptes Rendus Hebdomadaires des Séances de L'Académie des Sciences 28 (1849): 203, quoted in *Les Autochromes Lumière*, n.p.

74 A. Stieglitz, "The Colour Problem for Practical Work Solved," *Photography* 13 (August 1907): 136, quoted in *Les Autochromes Lumière*, n.p.

75 Charles Terrasse, *Bonnard*, quoted in Hyman, Bonnard, 97.

76 Ibid.

77 Timothy Hyman believes that by 1916 this kind of automatic drawing is coincident with Bonnard's waning use of photography. See ibid., 100–101.

78 Terrasse, "Bonnard's Notes," in *Bonnard: The Late Paintings*, 52.

79 Michel Terrasse, *Bonnard: From the Drawings to the Paintings*, trans. Cynthia Hope Liebow (Paris: Imprimerie Nationale, 1998), 169.

80 Margrit Hahnloser-Ingold, "Promenade en mer—image and portrait," in *Bonnard: The Late Paintings*, 82. Marjorie Phillips also recollected drawing on photographs of his paintings. See: *Marjorie Phillips, Duncan Phillips and His Collection* (New York and London: W. W. Norton & Company, 1982), 84.

81 Bonnard, "Notes," 23 February 1929, quoted in Antoine Terrasse, "Bonnard's Notes," in *Bonnard: The Late Paintings*, 69.

82 Bengt Häger, *Ballet Suédois*, trans. Ruth Sharman (New York: Harry N. Abrams, 1996), 74.

83 Hyman, Bonnard, 118.

84 S. McCormick, "Renee Monchaty," *Dictionary of Artists' Models*, ed. Jill Berk Jiminez (Chicago: Fitzroy Dearborn, 2001), 379.

85 "The Identification of Pierre Bonnard's Sitters," *Times of London*, 15 February 1966, 13.

86 Nicholas Watkins, "The Death of Renée Monchaty, Bonnard's Model and Lover," *The Burlington Magazine* 160, no. 1142 (May 1998): 327.

87 John Berger, "Bonnard," in *The Moment of Cubism* (New York: Pantheon Books, 1969), 121.

88 Ibid., 120.

89 Georges Rodenbach, *Bruges-la-Morte*, trans. Philip Mosley (Paisley, Scotland: Wilfion Books, Publishers, 1991), 14. E. Neurdein's heliogravures for the 1892 edition of Rodenbach's Bruges-la-Morte are discussed in relation to Fernand Khnopff's exploration of reality and representation in Kosinski, "The Gaze of Fernand Khnopff," 152.

90 Newman asserts that the nude in the tub is a suppressed memory of the dead Renée Monchaty. See Newman, "Nudes and Landscapes," 190.

91 Max Kozloff, "A Vertigo of the Senses," *Art in America* 86, no. 7 (July 1998): 56.

92 Charles Terrasse, *Bonnard*, quoted in Hyman, *Bonnard*, 162.

93 Rydbeck, "Hos Bonnard I Deauville."

94 John Berger, "Bonnard," 121.

95 Marjorie Phillips, *Duncan Phillips and His Collection*, 178. In the eyes of his friends, Bonnard was the defender of painting. In 1933, André Lhote said, "Without trying, Bonnard has become the most abstract painter of our time. Picasso, by comparison, seems haunted by depths, shadow, material details."See André Lhote,"Irréalisme et surréalisme: Bonnard, Dali," *La Nouvelle Revue française* 4 (1933): 307.

96 Pierre Bonnard to Duncan Phillips, August 1931, quoted in Marjorie Phillips, *Duncan Phillips and His Collection*, 82.

97 Ingrid Rydbeck, "Hos Bonnard I Deauville," quoted in Terrasse, *Bonnard: Shimmering Color*, 123–124.

98 Christian Zervos, "Pierre Bonnard: Est-il un grand peintre?" Cahier d'art 22 (1947): 5, quoted in Terrasse, *Bonnard: Shimmering Color*, 135.

Nancy Coleman Wolsk

1 According to the Lycée Charlemagne's "Registre des entrées et sorties des élèves. Octobre 1887 à 1881," deposited at the Annexe of the Archives of Paris in Ville Moisson-sur-Onge, Pierre Bonnard entered the school in the fall of 1881. The subsequent "Registres" for 1882–1883 and 1883–1884 confirm his presence at this *lycée*. The note on his withdrawal appears in the "Registre" for 1883–1884, entry number 159; the registers for 1884–1885 no longer list him as a student.

2 Certificates for all the *baccalauréat* examinations are housed in the Archives Nationales in Paris (hereafter AN) under the call number AJ_{16}. According to these records, Bonnard took the first series *bac*, $AJ_{16}3253$ on 5 August 1884 and the second series recorded in $AJ_{16}3334$ on 9 July 1885. The documents give the questions asked on both the written and oral sections of the exam, the examiner's rating for each response, and a summary grade.

3 Octave Gréard, *Le Baccalauréat et l'enseignement secondaire. Mémoire présenté au conseil académique de Paris, le 7 juillet 1885* (Paris: Imprimérie Nationale, 1885), 105.

4 AN, $AJ_{16}3334$.

5 Short discussions of Bonnard's history in this period appear in a number of accessible texts. For the latest of these, see Antoine Terrasse, *Bonnard: Shimmering Color*, trans. Laurel Hirsh (New York: Harry N. Abrams, 2000), 15–20, and Nicolas Watkins, *Bonnard* (London: Phaidon Press, 1994), 10–18. Still the best summary of the period is Helen Emery Giambruni, "Early Bonnard, 1885–1900," Ph.D. diss., University of California, Berkeley, 1983, 15–23. Records of Bonnard's enrollment at the Ecole des Beaux-Arts are listed in the "Registres matri-coles des élèves des sections de peinture et de sculpture, 1807–1894" microfilm, AN, AJ_{52}; Bonnard's registration is listed in $AJ_{52}253$. In confirming Bonnard's entry into the Ecole des Beaux-Arts, see "Elèves: Inscriptions des élèves dans les ateliers 1863 à 1887," microfilm, AN, $AJ_{52}464$, 136v, no. 5208. The latter listing states that Bonnard was sponsored on 15 March 1887 by Gustave Boulanger and Jules-Joseph Lefèbvre, both academic artists and teachers at Julian's and at the Ecole des Beaux-Arts.

6 Henri-Gabriel Ibels, one of the group's *lycée*-educated friends at the Académie Julian, wrote in an unpublished memoir that he and his friends were intellectually superior to the other students. See "Promenades," a copy of which is at the St. Germain-en-Laye Bibliothèque, Musée Prieuré. Maurice Denis spoke well for the group when he railed against the *bêtises* (absurdities) of naturalism; he declared that the crime of academic instruction was to "fix in the brain the idea that Art is the imitation of something." See Denis's "Préface de la IX Exposition des peintres impressionistes et symbolistes," in *Théories, 1890–1910*, 3d ed. (Paris: L'Occident, 1913), 28.

7 The dates of Bonnard's exit from the Académie Julian and the Ecole des Beaux-Arts are not clear. For a recent chronology of this period, see Sarah Whitfield and John Elderfield, *Bonnard*, exh. cat. (New York: Harry N. Abrams, 1998), 256.

8 For an excellent discussion of the encounter between Sérusier and Gauguin, see Carolyn Boyle-Turner, "Sérusier's Talisman," *Gazette des Beaux-Arts* 105 (May–June 1985): 191–196.

9 See Maurice Denis, "L'Influence de Paul Gauguin," in *Théories* and for an account of Sérusier's disaffection with Gauguin, see his letter to Denis in *ABC de la peinture suivie d'une correspondance inédité*, 3d ed. (Paris: Floury, 1950), 39–41.

10 G. Albert Aurier, "Les Symbolistes," *La Revue encyclopédique* 2, no. 32 (1 April 1892): 485.

11 Maurice Denis, "De Gauguin et de van Gogh au classicisme," *L'Occident*, (May 1909), reprinted in *Théories*, 259 n. 2.

12 Philippe Lejeune, who studied with Denis in 1944, confirmed in an interview in July 2001 that the artist and his friends always regarded their work as layered. Reality for the artists was not really a metaphor, as Aurier suggested; rather, the connected "layers" all had equal value and one was meant to "read" the paintings in a rich variety of ways that included reality.

13 For a discussion of the influence of Japanese prints on this painting, see the catalogue entry by Claire Frèches-Thory in *Les Nabis, 1888–1900*, exh. cat. (Munich: Prestel, 1993), 120.

14 See Sasha Newman in *Bonnard: The Late Paintings*, exh. cat. (London: Thames and Hudson, 1984), 152.

15 Several art historians have remarked on the connection between the *lycée* curriculum and the Nabis. See, for example, Charles Chassé, "The Lycée Concorcet, Cradle of the Nabis," *The Nabis and Their Period*, trans. Michael Bullock, 2d ed. (New York and Washington, D.C.: Praeger, 1969), 9–14. Most scholars who deal with the Nabis, or any of its members, simply note the fact that the artists were similarly educated. Though brief, the most useful connection between the Nabis and their schooling—because she actually cites textbooks as a source for later ideas—is made by Feliz Eda Burhan, "Visions and Visionaries, Nineteenth-Century Psychological Theory: The Occult Sciences and the Formation of the Symbolist Aesthetic in France," Ph.D. diss., Princeton University, 1979, 42–45.

16 Tying Bonnard's images to the *lycée* curriculum depends on the premise that profoundly held ways of thinking rarely, if ever, grow from a single experience. Instead, as the French sociologist Pierre Bourdieu has shown, an intellectual and artistic disposition—the *habitus*—proceeds from carefully structured, consistent, and repeated exposure to information and ideas. For more than a quarter century, Bourdieu has developed a multivalent methodology for examining the effects of education on patterns of thought. Among the studies that show how education inculcates habits of thought are *Les Héritiers: Les Etudiants et la culture* (Paris: Les Editions de Minuit, 1964), translated as *The Inheritors: French Students and Their Relation to Culture*, trans. Richard Nice (Chicago: University of Chicago Press, 1979). Also, see *Esquisse d'une théorie de la pratique* (Geneva: Droz, 1972) translated as *The Outline of a Theory of Practice*, trans. Richard Nice (Cambridge: Cambridge University Press, 1977); "Systems of Education and Systems of Thought," *International Social Science Journal* 19 (1967): 338–358; and, especially, *La Distinction: Critique social du jugement* (Paris: Les Editions de Minuit, 1979), translated as *Distinction: A Social Critique of the Judgment of Taste*, trans. Richard Nice (Cambridge, Mass.: Harvard University Press, 1984).

17 The educational historian Fritz Ringer in *Fields of Knowledge: French Academic Culture in Comparative Perspective, 1890–1920* (Cambridge and New York: Cambridge University Press, 1992), 5–12, emphasizes the need to examine a variety of sources—curriculum, texts, and educational debates, for example—as the means of analyzing *habitus*.

18 In her doctoral dissertation on Bonnard, Helen Giambruni discusses the pressures on Bonnard from school and family; in particular, the elder Bonnard was said to have been a severe, demanding paterfamilias; see her "Early Bonnard," 3–15. For a firsthand account, though written long after the fact, of Bonnard's relationships with his fellow Nabis, see Thadée Natanson, *Le Bonnard que je propose* (Geneva: Pierre Cailler, 1951), 32, 51, 99–100. Bonnard met Maria Boursin—she called herself Marthe de Méligny—in 1893.

19 Emile Durkheim, *L'Evolution pédagogique en France de la Revolution à nos jours*, vol. 2, ed. Maurice Halbwachs (Paris: Alcan, 1938), 272, laments that the *lycée* curriculum was fragmented in the nineteenth century; though he was mistaken about literature, history, and philosophy, he was right about science, which lay outside the core of the curriculum.

20 For a detailed discussion of the debates on Latin versus French in the curriculum, see Clément Falcucci, "L'Humanisme dans l'enseignement secondaire en France au XIX siècle," Ph.D. diss., Université de Strasbourg, 1939. The debate raged in the high-brow public press as well; as an example, see Emile Beaussire, "Les Questions de l'enseignement secondaire sous le troisième république," *Revue des deux mondes* 52, special issue, 1 August 1882): 607–633.

21 Ferry actually declared that the program was founded on the idea that objects lay at the foundation of everything ("Les choses sont à la base de tout"). For a good review of the legislation here, see Falcucci, "L'Humanisme," 335–369, especially 351–355.

22 All the legislation, administrative acts, and official texts on education were published contemporaneously in two bound sets: the *Bulletin administratif de l'instruction publique* and the *Receuil des lois et des actes de l'instruction publique*. Official programs of study also appeared in specialized educational journals like the *Revue philosophique* and in the official *Revue de l'enseignement secondaire et de l'enseigne-*

ment supérieur. Every professor was required to follow the official programs or *plans d'études*, and because the minister's advisory council was made up of professors from Paris's *lycées*, the reformed curriculum was immediately practiced in the schools of the nation's capital. For the reforms of 1872 and 1873, see *Receuil des lois* 18 (1874): 292–299; 19 (1874): 324–354; and 20 (1874): 364–365. For 1880, see the Bulletin administratif 456 (1880): 890–973. André Chervel, *Les Auteurs français, latins et grecs au programme de l'enseignement secondaire de 1800 à nos jours* (Paris: INRP, 1986), 8–9, gives a clear, short summary of this integration.

23 Jules Simon, *La Réforme de l'enseignement* (Paris: Hachette, 1894), 308.

24 Simon, *La Réforme*, 305.

25 Gustav Dupont-Ferrier, *La Vie quotidienne d'un collège parisien pendant plus de trois cent cinquante ans du Collège de Clermont à Louis-le-Grand* (Paris: E. de Boccard, 1922), 2: 162.

26 Simon, *La Réforme*, 202–203, particularly emphasized that his administration had not changed the actual programs of study; instead, he said that his administration engaged children in their own reality as the basis for abstraction. For the new teaching methods see Simon, *La Réforme*, 329ff.

27 For the programs of study that specified La Fontaine, see *Receuil des lois* (1880): 894, 902.

28 Bonnard's friend and colleague Aurélien Lugné-Poë, a graduate of the Lycée Condorcet and founder and director of the symbolist Théâtre de l'Oeuvre in Paris, wrote that he found Faguet "the best of professors." See his *Le Sot de tremplin, souvenirs et impressions de théâtre*, vol. 1, *La Parade* (Paris: Gallimard, 1930), 30–31. Edouard de Colonne, *Receuil des compositions françaises en vue du baccalauréat des lettres* (Paris: Paul Dupont, 1884), 4–7.

29 Désiré Blanchet, "Discours," *Revue de l'enseignement secondaire et de l'enseignement supérieur*, 1888, 62.

30 Gustave Jalliffier, "Discours," *Revue de l'enseignement secondaire et de l'enseignement supérieure*, 1884, 657.

31 Victor Duruy, *Histoire de l'Europe et particulièrement de la France de 1610 à 1789 redigée conformément aux programmes de 1879* (Paris: Librairie Hachette, 1879 and 1880), 130.

32 Duruy, 1880, 277.

33 James-Jean-Pierre Condamin, *La Composition française du baccalauréat, conseils et places synoptiques pour traiter les*

principaux sujets proposés depuis 1881 (Paris: Croville-Morant, 1884), 455–456.

34 See Falcucci, "L'Humanisme," 297, and Robert David Anderson, *Education in France, 1848–1870* (Oxford: Clarendon Press, 1975), 178.

35 Of course, one could not freely publish a text that was overtly at odds with the curriculum. Janet actually produced an innovative work in terms of its new emphasis on physiology and expanded emphasis on psychology. Certainly the fact that he was a senior, respected member of the minister of education's executive council ensured approval of the text. Instead of the first edition of 1879, I cite here the virtually identical text *Traité élémentaire de philosophie*, 4th ed. (Paris: Delagrave, 1884), the edition available to Bonnard in his philosophy year, 1884–1885. For reviews of other texts approved by the ministry of education—by the early 1880s, they all looked to physiology as the basis of psychology and to psychology as the path to understanding the self—see successive issues of the journal *Le Lycéen en philosophie*, first published in 1890. For a good review of Janet's text see *L'Instruction publique* 14 (3 January 1885): 8–9.

36 Janet, *Traité*, 77–87.

37 See the opening section of this chapter, Janet, *Traité*, 20–21. The organization of the psychology section of the text moves in ascending, interlocking stages from physiology beginning on page 13 to intelligence on pages 344–346.

38 Roques's notes, "Henri Bergson: Cours de Philosophie, Lycée Henri Quatre, 1891–92," bound in two volumes, are housed in the library of the Institut National de Recherche Pédagogique, rue d'Ulm, Paris, 138.636. A selection of Jarry's notes are reproduced in Catherine Stehlin, "Jarry, le cours Bergson et la philosophie," *Europe* 59 (March–April 1991): 34–51.

39 Until 1880, *explication* was practiced in Latin and followed formulas that were based on rhetorical models.

40 A variety of texts illustrate this emphasis; see, for example, Eugène Geruzez, *Cours de la literature* (Paris: Delalain, 1879).

41 These changes were laid out in the programs of study published in the *Bulletins administratifs*, 1880, 899–908. For a good discussion of the disappearance of rhetoric from modern language and literature, see John Bender and David Wellbury, "Rhetoricality: On the Modernist Return to Rhetoric," in *The Ends of Rhetoric: History, Theory, Practice* (Stanford, Calif.: Stanford

University Press, 1990), 4–6.

42 Auguste Gazier, *Traité d'explication française ou méthode pour expliquer littéralement les auteurs français*, 8th ed. (Paris: Belin Frères, 1908). Though I cite here a later edition of the text than the one Bonnard would have used, the contents are the same as that of the versions published in the 1880s.

43 Gazier, *Traité*, 1–48.

44 Gazier, *Traité*, 59. In a letter to his friend and fellow art student Maurice Denis, Paul Sérusier cast aesthetic theory in terms of literary language when he wrote that like the writer, the artist must have "a system of signs"; this system for the writer was "*écriture*" (the equivalent of painting), which embraced writing itself and the system of writing. See Denis, in *ABC de la peinture*, 43–45.

45 Denis, in *ABC de la peinture*, 78.

46 Janet, *Traité*, 68–72.

47 Janet, *Traité*, 73.

48 Janet, *Traité*, 219–220.

49 Emile Faguet, *Etudes littéraires, Dix-septième siècle* (Paris: Bonvin, n.d.), 248–249.

50 Faguet, *La Fontaine, fables et epîtres* (Paris: Nelson, n.d.), vii.

51 Bonnard's twenty little pocket diaries, measuring 13.4 × 6.7 cm, are housed in the Bibliothèque nationale de France, Paris. See "Carnet de Bonnard," *Verve, Revue artistique et littéraire*, numéro special Bonnard 5 (1947): 17–18. The "Observations" are reprinted with a short introduction by Antoine Terrasse in *Bonnard, The Late Paintings*, 69–70.

52 The first quotation is given in the entirety from 16 January 1934; the second, from 1945, is an excerpt.

53 19 October 1938.

54 1 January 1934 and 4 January 1934.

55 27 April 1937 and 2 January 1935.

56 15 January 1934, 14 January 1935, and 4 November 1940.

57 24 April 1929.

Ursula Perucchi-Petri

1 "C'est là que je trouvais pour un ou deux sous des crêpons ou des papiers de riz froissés aux couleurs étonnantes. Je remplis les murs de ma chambre de cette imagerie naive et criarde." Quoted in Antoine Terrasse, *Pierre Bonnard* (Paris: Gallimard, 1967), 24.

2 "Beaucoup plus tard j'ai compris la beauté des grands graveurs japonais tellement plus sobres mais moins révélateurs des rapports de couleur pure." Quoted in Annette Vaillant, *Bonnard ou le bonheur de voir* (Neuchâtel: Ides et Calendes, 1965), 182.

3 "Gauguin, Sérusier se réfèrent en fait au passé. Mais là ce que j'avais devant moi, c'était quelque chose de bien vivant, d'extrêmement savant." Quoted in Terrasse, *Pierre Bonnard*, 24.

4 Walter Benjamin, *Gesammelte Schriften V (Das Passagenwerk)*, ed. Rolf Tiedemann, 2nd ed. (Frankfurt am Main: Suhrkamp, 1982), 436. For a detailed discussion of the *Poster for France-Champagne*, see Ursula Perucchi-Petri, Die Nabis und Japan: *Das Frühwerk von Bonnard, Vuillard und Denis* (Munich: Prestel, 1976), 31–37.

5 Ary Renan, in *Le Japon artistique*, no. 8 (December 1888): 91.

6 Ary Renan in *Le Japon artistique*, no. 9 (January 1889): 108.

7 Charles Baudelaire, *The Painter of Modern Life*, trans. and ed. Jonathan Mayne (London, 1964), excerpted in Charles Harrison, Paul Wood, and Jason Gaiger, eds., *Art in Theory, 1815–1900: An Anthology of Changing Ideas* (Oxford: Blackwell, 1998), 495.

8 Quoted in Annette Kreutziger-Herr, "Die Kindheit als Paradies," *Neue Zürcher Zeitung* 8–9 (February 1997): 68.

9 Bonnard to Hedy Hahnloser-Bühler, 4 January 1946, quoted in Vaillant, *Bonnard ou le bonheur de voir*, 182.

10 Maurice Denis, "Pierre Bonnard," *Le Point* 4, no. 24 (January 1943): 4.

11 Maurice Denis, "De Gauguin et de van Gogh au classicisme," *L'Occident*, May 1909, reprinted in Maurice Denis, *Théories, 1890–1910*, 3rd ed. (Paris: *L'Occident*, 1913), 255.

12 Denis, *Théories*, 255.

13 See also *The Nabis and the Parisian Avant-Garde*, ed. Patricia Eckert-Boyer and Elizabeth Prelinger (New Brunswick, N.J., and London: Rutgers University Press for The Jane Voorhees Zimmerli Art Museum, 1988).

14 In any discussion of this subject it should be borne in mind that, since the caricaturists of Montmartre and the artists of the shadow theater were also inspired by Japanese woodblock prints, any similarities in their work may well have been due to this shared source of inspiration.

15 William Rubin, "Shadows, Pantomimes and the Art of the 'Fin de Siècle,'" *Magazine of Art* 46, no. 3 (March 1953): 114–122.

16 Heinrich von Kleist, "Ueber das Marionettentheater" (1810), in *Sämtliche Werke* (Munich and Zurich, 1963).

17 Arthur Schopenhauer, *Parerga und Paralipomena*, chap. 2, para. 144, quoted by Tobia Bezzola in *Equilibre. Gleichgewicht,*

Aequivalenz und Harmonie in der Kunst des 20. Jahrhunderts, exh. cat. (Aarau: Aargauer Kunsthaus, 1993), 10.

18 David Frisby, *Fragments of Modernity: Theories of Modernity in the Work of Simmel, Kracauer and Benjamin* (Cambridge, Mass., 1986), quoted in Bernd Kiefer, *Rettende Kritik der Moderne. Studien zum Gesamtwerk Walter Benjamins* (Frankfurt am Main: Peter Lang, 1994), 322 n. 13.

19 Dietrich Seckel, *Einführung in die Kunst Ostasiens* (Munich: Piper, 1960), 375.

20 Jean Gebser, Ursprung und Gegenwart, Bd. 1, *Die Fundamente der aperspektivischen Welt* (Stuttgart: Deutsche Verlags-Anstalte, 1949), 38.

21 Dietrich Seckel, *Buddhistische Kunst Ostasiens* (Stuttgart: Kohlauser, 1957), 144f.

22 Quoted in Charles Terrasse, *Pierre Bonnard* (Paris: Floury, 1927), 162ff.

23 Erwin Panofsky, *Aufsaetze zu Grundfragen der Kunstwissenschaft* (Berlin: Bruno Hessling, 1964), 101f.

24 Quoted in Charles Terrasse, *Pierre Bonnard*, 162ff.

25 Hans Jantzen, *Ueber den gotischen Kirchenraum und andere Aufsaetze* (Berlin: Mann, 1951), 66.

26 "J'avais compris au contact de ces frustes images populaires que la couleur pouvait comme ici exprimer toutes choses sans besoin de relief ou de modelé. Il m'apparut qu'il était possible de traduire lumière, formes et caractère rien qu'avec la couleur, sans faire appel aux valeurs." Quoted in Antoine Terrasse, *Pierre Bonnard*, 10.

27 Pierre Bonnard, "Le Bouquet de roses," statements to Angèle Lamotte, 1943, printed in *Verve, Revue artistique et littéraire*, numéro special Bonnard 5, nos. 17 and 18 (1947).

28 Seckel, *Einführung in die Kunst Ostasiens*, 357f.

29 For a detailed discussion of Japonisme in the work of Pierre Bonnard, see Perucchi-Petri, Die Nabis und Japan; Ursula Perucchi-Petri, "Les Nabis et le Japon," in *Japonism in Art: An International Symposium*, ed. The Society for the Study of Japonisme (Tokyo: Kodansha, 1980) 261–277; Perucchi-Petri, "Les Nabis et le japonisme," in Nabis, 1888–1900, ed. Claire Frèches-Thory and Perucchi-Petri, exh. cat. (Zurich: Kunsthaus; Paris: Galeries Nationales du Grand Palais, 1993), Ursula Perucchi Petri, "Pierre Bonnard and Japonisme," in *Pierre Bonnard*, exh. cat. (Nagoya: Aichi Prefectural Museum of Art; Tokyo: The Bunkamura Museum of Art, 1997).

Photographic Credits

Unless otherwise noted, photographs were supplied by the owners of the works of art listed in the captions. All rights reserved.

Figures

Pages 6–7 © Henri Cartier-Bresson; Pages 8–9 © Henri Cartier-Bresson; Page 10 ©Henri Cartier-Bresson; Fig. 3 © Réunion des Musées Nationaux/ Art Resource, NY. Photograph by Herve Lewandowski; Fig. 5 © Sterling and Francine Clark Art Institute, Williamstown, Massachusetts; Fig. 7 © Réunion des Musées Nationaux/ Art Resource, NY; Fig. 9 © Réunion des Musées Nationaux/ Art Resource, NY; Fig. 10 © Réunion des Musées Nationaux/ Art Resource, NY. Photograph by Herve Lewandowski; Fig. 11 © Réunion des Musées Nationaux/ Art Resource, NY; Fig. 12 © Réunion des Musées Nationaux/ Art Resource, NY; Fig. 13 © Réunion des Musées Nationaux/ Art Resource, NY; Fig. 14 © Réunion des Musées Nationaux/Art Resource, NY. Photograph by Herve Lewandowski; Fig. 16 © P. Léger and Gallimard; Fig. 17 © Réunion des Musées Nationaux/Art Resource, NY. Photograph by Herve Lewandowski; Fig. 18 © Réunion des Musées Nationaux/ Art Resource, NY; Fig. 21 © Réunion des Musées Nationaux/ Art Resource, NY. Photograph by Jean Schormans; Fig. 23 © P Léger and Gallimard; Fig. 24 © P. Léger and Gallimard; Fig. 28 © 2001, The Art Institute of Chicago, All Rights Reserved. Photograph by Greg Williams; Fig. 31 © 2002, The Museum of Modern Art, New York; Fig. 38 © Giraudon/Art Resource, NY; Fig. 40 © Henri Cartier-Bresson; Fig. 41 © Henri Cartier-Bresson; Fig. 42 © Henri Cartier-Bresson; Fig. 43 © Gilbert Brassaï; Fig. 44 © The National Gallery of Scotland; Fig. 45 Courtesy, Museum of Fine Arts, Boston. Reproduced with permission. © 2000 Museum of Fine Arts, Boston. All Rights Reserved; Fig. 46 Courtesy, Museum of Fine Arts, Boston. Reproduced with permission. © 2000 Museum of Fine Arts, Boston. All Rights Reserved; Fig. 52 © 2001 Board of Trustees, National Gallery of Art, Washington; Fig. 53 Photograph © 2002 The Metropolitan Museum of Art; Fig. 54 © Réunion des Musées Nationaux/ Art Resource, NY. Photograph by B. Hatala; Fig. 55 © Réunion des Musées Nationaux/ Art Resource, NY; Fig. 56 © Réunion des Musées Nationaux/ Art Resource, NY. Photograph by P. Schmidt; Fig. 57 © Réunion des Musées Nationaux/ Art Resource, NY. Photograph by Herve Lewandowski; Fig. 58 © Réunion des Musées Nationaux/ Art Resource, NY; Fig. 59 © Réunion des Musées Nationaux/ Art Resource, NY; Fig. 60 © Réunion des Musées Nationaux/ Art Resource, NY; Fig. 61 © Réunion des Musées Nationaux/ Art Resource, NY. Photograph by J. G. Berizzi; Fig. 62 © Réunion des Musées Nationaux/ Art Resource, NY. Photograph by J. G. Berizzi; Fig. 63 © Réunion des Musées Nationaux/ Art Resource, NY. Photograph by J. G. Berizzi; Fig. 64 © Réunion des Musées Nationaux/ Art Resource, NY. Photograph by Herve Lewandowski; Fig. 67 Le Musée Départemental du Prieuré, Symbolistes et Nabis, Maurice Denis et son temps. Saint-Germain-en-Laye (France); Fig. 68 © Erich Lessing/ Art Resource, NY; Fig. 71 Courtesy of Sotheby's; Fig. 78a © Musée Autochrome Lumière; Fig. 78b © Musée Autochrome Lumière; Fig. 83 Photograph © 1980 The Metropolitan Museum of Art; Fig. 87 © 2001 Artists Rights Society (ARS), New York/ ADAGP, Paris. Photo: AGNSW; Fig. 88 © Henri Cartier-Bresson; Fig. 99 © 2002 Board of Trustees, National Gallery of Art, Washington; Fig. 101 © 2001 Board of Trustees, National Gallery of Art, Washington; Fig. 102 © 2001 Board of Trustees, National Gallery of Art, Washington.

Plates

Plate 1 Photo Josse; Plate 4a–b © 2001 Board of Trustees, National Gallery of Art, Washington; Plate 5 © 2001 Board of Trustees, National Gallery of Art, Washington; Plate 6 © Sterling and Francine Clark Art Institute, Williamstown, Massachusetts; Plate 7 Southampton City Art Gallery, Hampshire, UK/Bridgeman Art Library; Plate 8 © Réunion des Musées Nationaux/Art Resource, NY. Photograph by Gerard Blot; Plate 10 Digital Image © 2001 The Museum of Modern Art, New York; Plate 12 © Réunion des Musées Nationaux/Art Resource, NY; Plate 13 © Réunion des Musées Nationaux/ Art Resource, NY; Plate 15 Courtesy Museum of Fine Arts, Boston. Reproduced with permission. © 2000 Museum of Fine Arts, Boston. All Rights Reserved; Plate 20 Photograph © 2002 The Metropolitan Museum of Art; Plate 23 Courtesy Museum of Fine Arts, Boston. Reproduced with permission. Plate 24 Courtesy Museum of Fine Arts, Boston. Reproduced with permission. © 2000 Museum of Fine Arts, Boston. All Rights Reserved; Plate 25 © 2001 Board of Trustees, National Gallery of Art, Washington; Plate 28 Courtesy Museum of Fine Arts, Boston. Reproduced with permission. © 2000 Museum of Fine Arts, Boston. All Rights Reserved; Plate 29 Courtesy Museum of Fine Arts, Boston. Reproduced with permission. © 2000 Museum of Fine Arts, Boston. All Rights Reserved; Plate 30 Courtesy Museum of Fine Arts, Boston. Reproduced with permission. © 2000 Museum of Fine Arts, Boston. All Rights Reserved; Plate 33 Courtesy Museum of Fine Arts, Boston. Reproduced with permission. © 2000 Museum of Fine Arts, Boston. All Rights Reserved; Plate 34 Courtesy Museum of Fine Arts, Boston. Reproduced with permission. © 2000 Museum of Fine Arts, Boston. All Rights Reserved; Plate 35 Courtesy Museum of Fine Arts, Boston. Reproduced with Permission. © 2000 Museum of Fine Arts, Boston. All Rights Reserved; Plate 36 Courtesy Museum of Fine Arts, Boston. Reproduced with permission. © 2000 Museum of Fine Arts, Boston. All Rights Reserved; Plate 39 © 2001 Board of Trustees, National Gallery of Art, Washington; Plate 40 © 2001 Board of Trustees, National Gallery of Art, Washington; Plate 41 © 2001 Board of Trustees, National Gallery of Art, Washington; Plate 42 © 2001 Board of Trustees, National Gallery of Art, Washington; Plate 44 © Réunion des Musées Nationaux/ Art Resource, NY. Photograph by Herre Lewandowski; Plate 45 © Réunion des Musées Nationaux/ Art Resource, NY; Plate 46 © Réunion des Musées Nationaux/ Art Resource, NY. Photograph by Herve Lewandowski; Plate 47 © Réunion des Musées Nationaux/ Art Resource, NY. Photograph by Herve Lewandowski; Plate 48 © Réunion des Musées Nationaux/ Art Resource, NY. Photograph by P. Schmidt; Plate 49 © Réunion des Musées Nationaux/ Art Resource, NY; Plate 50 © Réunion des Musées Nationaux/ Art Resource, NY; Plate 51 © Réunion des Musées Nationaux/Art Resource, NY; Plate 52 © Réunion des Musées Nationaux/ Art Resource, NY; Plate 53 © Réunion des Musées Nationaux/ Art Resource, NY; 54 © Réunion des Musées Nationaux/ Art Resource, NY; Plate 55 © Réunion des Musées Nationaux/Art Resource, NY; Plate 55a © Réunion des Musées Nationaux/Art Resource, NY; Plate Plate 57 Photograph by Lee Stalsworth; Plate 58 © Erich Lessing/ Art Resource, NY; Plate 59 Le Musée Départemental du Prieuré, Symbolistes et Nabis, Maurice Denis et son temps. Saint-Germain-en-Laye (France); Plate 66 © Giraudon/ Art Resource, NY; Plate 67 © Kunsthaus Zurich; Plate 72 © Photograph by Ursula Edelmann, Frankfurt a.M.; Plate 80 © 2001, The Art Institute of Chicago. All Rights Reserved. Photograph by Greg Williams; Plate 81 Photograph by Eric Mitchell, 1992; Plate 82 © Musée d'Unterlinden Colmar. Photograph by O. Zimmermann; Plate 84 © Réunion des Musées Nationaux/ Art Resource, NY. Photograph by Herve Lewandowski; Plate 88 Photograph © 1980 The Metropolitan Museum of Art; Plate 94 Courtesy Museum of Fine Arts, Boston. Reproduced with permission. © 2000 Museum of Fine Arts, Boston. All Rights Reserved; Plate 97 Private collection; Courtesy Guggenheim, Asher Assoc.; Plate 98 Photograph © 2002 The Metropolitan Museum of Art; Plate 102 © Tate, London 2001; Plate 104 © Réunion des Musées Nationaux/ Art Resource, NY. Photograph by Michele Bellot; Plate 105 Courtesy Museum of Fine Arts, Boston. Reproduced with permission. © 2000 Museum of Fine Arts, Boston. All Rights Reserved; Plate 109 © Tate, London 2001; Plate 112 Photograph © 2002 The Metropolitan Museum of Art; Plate 118 © 2002 The Museum of Modern Art, New York; Plate 119 Öffentliche Kunstsammlung Basel, Martin Bühler; Plate 121 © Musée de Grenoble; Plate 126 © 2001 The Museum of Modern Art, New York; Plate 129 © Réunion des Musées Nationaux/Art Resource, NY. Photograph by R. G. Ojeda; Plate 131 Giraudon/ Art Resource, NY; Plate 132 CNAC/ MNAM/Dist. Réunion des Musées Nationaux/ Art Resource, NY; Plate 135 © 2001 Artists Rights Society (ARS), New York/ ADAGP, Paris. Photo: AGNSW.

Index